OpenCL
Programming Guide

OpenCL
Programming Guide

Aaftab Munshi
Benedict R. Gaster
Timothy G. Mattson
James Fung
Dan Ginsburg

✦ Addison-Wesley

Upper Saddle River, NJ • Boston • Indianapolis • San Francisco
New York • Toronto • Montreal • London • Munich • Paris • Madrid
Capetown • Sydney • Tokyo • Singapore • Mexico City

Many of the designations used by manufacturers and sellers to distinguish their products are claimed as trademarks. Where those designations appear in this book, and the publisher was aware of a trademark claim, the designations have been printed with initial capital letters or in all capitals.

The authors and publisher have taken care in the preparation of this book, but make no expressed or implied warranty of any kind and assume no responsibility for errors or omissions. No liability is assumed for incidental or consequential damages in connection with or arising out of the use of the information or programs contained herein.

The publisher offers excellent discounts on this book when ordered in quantity for bulk purchases or special sales, which may include electronic versions and/or custom covers and content particular to your business, training goals, marketing focus, and branding interests. For more information, please contact:

U.S. Corporate and Government Sales
(800) 382-3419
corpsales@pearsontechgroup.com

For sales outside the United States please contact:

International Sales
international@pearson.com

Visit us on the Web: informit.com/aw

Cataloging-in-publication data is on file with the Library of Congress.

Copyright © 2012 Pearson Education, Inc.

All rights reserved. Printed in the United States of America. This publication is protected by copyright, and permission must be obtained from the publisher prior to any prohibited reproduction, storage in a retrieval system, or transmission in any form or by any means, electronic, mechanical, photocopying, recording, or likewise. For information regarding permissions, write to:

Pearson Education, Inc.
Rights and Contracts Department
501 Boylston Street, Suite 900
Boston, MA 02116
Fax: (617) 671-3447

ISBN-13: 978-0-321-74964-2
ISBN-10:   0-321-74964-2
Text printed in the United States on recycled paper at Edwards Brothers in Ann Arbor, Michigan.
First printing, July 2011

Editor-in-Chief
Mark Taub

Acquisitions Editor
Debra Williams Cauley

Development Editor
Michael Thurston

Managing Editor
John Fuller

Project Editor
Anna Popick

Copy Editor
Barbara Wood

Indexer
Jack Lewis

Proofreader
Lori Newhouse

Technical Reviewers
Andrew Brownsword
Yahya H. Mizra
Dave Shreiner

Publishing Coordinator
Kim Boedigheimer

Cover Designer
Alan Clements

Compositor
The CIP Group

Contents

Figures xv

Tables xxi

Listings xxv

Foreword. xxix

Preface xxxiii

Acknowledgments. xli

About the Authors xliii

Part I   The OpenCL 1.1 Language and API 1

1.   An Introduction to OpenCL 3

What Is OpenCL, or . . . Why You Need This Book 3
Our Many-Core Future: Heterogeneous Platforms 4
Software in a Many-Core World 7
Conceptual Foundations of OpenCL 11
    Platform Model 12
    Execution Model 13
    Memory Model 21
    Programming Models 24
OpenCL and Graphics. 29
The Contents of OpenCL 30
    Platform API 31
    Runtime API 31
    Kernel Programming Language 32
    OpenCL Summary. 34
The Embedded Profile 35
Learning OpenCL 36

2.   HelloWorld: An OpenCL Example **39**

Building the Examples. 40
    Prerequisites. 40
    Mac OS X and Code::Blocks 41
    Microsoft Windows and Visual Studio 42
    Linux and Eclipse 44
HelloWorld Example 45
    Choosing an OpenCL Platform and Creating a Context 49
    Choosing a Device and Creating a Command-Queue 50
    Creating and Building a Program Object 52
    Creating Kernel and Memory Objects 54
    Executing a Kernel 55
Checking for Errors in OpenCL 57

3.   Platforms, Contexts, and Devices **63**

OpenCL Platforms 63
OpenCL Devices 68
OpenCL Contexts 83

4.   Programming with OpenCL C **97**

Writing a Data-Parallel Kernel Using OpenCL C 97
Scalar Data Types. 99
    The `half` Data Type 101
Vector Data Types 102
    Vector Literals 104
    Vector Components. 106
Other Data Types. 108
Derived Types 109
Implicit Type Conversions. 110
    Usual Arithmetic Conversions 114
Explicit Casts. 116
Explicit Conversions 117
Reinterpreting Data as Another Type 121
Vector Operators 123
    Arithmetic Operators 124
    Relational and Equality Operators 127

Bitwise Operators 127

Logical Operators 128

Conditional Operator 129

Shift Operators 129

Unary Operators 131

Assignment Operator 132

Qualifiers 133

Function Qualifiers 133

Kernel Attribute Qualifiers 134

Address Space Qualifiers 135

Access Qualifiers 140

Type Qualifiers 141

Keywords 141

Preprocessor Directives and Macros 141

Pragma Directives 143

Macros 145

Restrictions 146

5. OpenCL C Built-In Functions 149

Work-Item Functions 150

Math Functions 153

Floating-Point Pragmas 162

Floating-Point Constants 162

Relative Error as `ulps` 163

Integer Functions 168

Common Functions 172

Geometric Functions 175

Relational Functions 175

Vector Data Load and Store Functions 181

Synchronization Functions 190

Async Copy and Prefetch Functions 191

Atomic Functions 195

Miscellaneous Vector Functions 199

Image Read and Write Functions 201

Reading from an Image 201

Samplers 206

Determining the Border Color 209

Writing to an Image 210
Querying Image Information 214

6. **Programs and Kernels** **217**

Program and Kernel Object Overview 217
Program Objects 218
Creating and Building Programs 218
Program Build Options 222
Creating Programs from Binaries 227
Managing and Querying Programs 236
Kernel Objects 237
Creating Kernel Objects and Setting Kernel Arguments 237
Thread Safety. 241
Managing and Querying Kernels 242

7. **Buffers and Sub-Buffers**. **247**

Memory Objects, Buffers, and Sub-Buffers Overview. 247
Creating Buffers and Sub-Buffers 249
Querying Buffers and Sub-Buffers. 257
Reading, Writing, and Copying Buffers and Sub-Buffers. 259
Mapping Buffers and Sub-Buffers 276

8. **Images and Samplers** **281**

Image and Sampler Object Overview 281
Creating Image Objects 283
Image Formats. 287
Querying for Image Support 291
Creating Sampler Objects 292
OpenCL C Functions for Working with Images 295
Transferring Image Objects 299

9. **Events** **309**

Commands, Queues, and Events Overview 309
Events and Command-Queues 311
Event Objects. 317

Generating Events on the Host 321
Events Impacting Execution on the Host 322
Using Events for Profiling 327
Events Inside Kernels. 332
Events from Outside OpenCL 333

10. Interoperability with OpenGL **335**

OpenCL/OpenGL Sharing Overview 335
Querying for the OpenGL Sharing Extension 336
Initializing an OpenCL Context for OpenGL Interoperability 338
Creating OpenCL Buffers from OpenGL Buffers 339
Creating OpenCL Image Objects from OpenGL Textures 344
Querying Information about OpenGL Objects. 347
Synchronization between OpenGL and OpenCL. 348

11. Interoperability with Direct3D **353**

Direct3D/OpenCL Sharing Overview 353
Initializing an OpenCL Context for Direct3D Interoperability 354
Creating OpenCL Memory Objects from Direct3D Buffers
   and Textures. 357
Acquiring and Releasing Direct3D Objects in OpenCL 361
Processing a Direct3D Texture in OpenCL 363
Processing D3D Vertex Data in OpenCL. 366

12. C++ Wrapper API **369**

C++ Wrapper API Overview 369
C++ Wrapper API Exceptions 371
Vector Add Example Using the C++ Wrapper API 374
   Choosing an OpenCL Platform and Creating a Context 375
   Choosing a Device and Creating a Command-Queue 376
   Creating and Building a Program Object 377
   Creating Kernel and Memory Objects 377
   Executing the Vector Add Kernel 378

13. OpenCL Embedded Profile **383**

OpenCL Profile Overview 383
64-Bit Integers 385
Images 386
Built-In Atomic Functions................................. 387
Mandated Minimum Single-Precision Floating-Point
Capabilities.. 387
Determining the Profile Supported by a Device in an
OpenCL C Program 390

Part II   OpenCL 1.1 Case Studies **391**

14. Image Histogram **393**

Computing an Image Histogram 393
Parallelizing the Image Histogram 395
Additional Optimizations to the Parallel Image Histogram....... 400
Computing Histograms with Half-Float or Float Values for
Each Channel 403

15. Sobel Edge Detection Filter **407**

What Is a Sobel Edge Detection Filter? 407
Implementing the Sobel Filter as an OpenCL Kernel........... 407

**16. Parallelizing Dijkstra's Single-Source Shortest-Path
Graph Algorithm** **411**

Graph Data Structures 412
Kernels.. 414
Leveraging Multiple Compute Devices 417

17. Cloth Simulation in the Bullet Physics SDK **425**

An Introduction to Cloth Simulation 425
Simulating the Soft Body 429
Executing the Simulation on the CPU 431
Changes Necessary for Basic GPU Execution 432
Two-Layered Batching.................................... 438

Optimizing for SIMD Computation and Local Memory 441

Adding OpenGL Interoperation 446

18. Simulating the Ocean with Fast Fourier Transform 449

An Overview of the Ocean Application 450

Phillips Spectrum Generation 453

An OpenCL Discrete Fourier Transform 457

Determining 2D Decomposition 457

Using Local Memory 459

Determining the Sub-Transform Size 459

Determining the Work-Group Size 460

Obtaining the Twiddle Factors 461

Determining How Much Local Memory Is Needed 462

Avoiding Local Memory Bank Conflicts 463

Using Images 463

A Closer Look at the FFT Kernel 463

A Closer Look at the Transpose Kernel 467

19. Optical Flow 469

Optical Flow Problem Overview 469

Sub-Pixel Accuracy with Hardware Linear Interpolation 480

Application of the Texture Cache 480

Using Local Memory 481

Early Exit and Hardware Scheduling 483

Efficient Visualization with OpenGL Interop 483

Performance 484

20. Using OpenCL with PyOpenCL 487

Introducing PyOpenCL 487

Running the PyImageFilter2D Example 488

PyImageFilter2D Code 488

Context and Command-Queue Creation 492

Loading to an Image Object 493

Creating and Building a Program 494

Setting Kernel Arguments and Executing a Kernel 495

Reading the Results 496

21. Matrix Multiplication with OpenCL. **499**

The Basic Matrix Multiplication Algorithm 499
A Direct Translation into OpenCL 501
Increasing the Amount of Work per Kernel 506
Optimizing Memory Movement: Local Memory 509
Performance Results and Optimizing the Original CPU Code 511

22. Sparse Matrix-Vector Multiplication. **515**

Sparse Matrix-Vector Multiplication (SpMV) Algorithm 515
Description of This Implementation. 518
Tiled and Packetized Sparse Matrix Representation 519
Header Structure 522
Tiled and Packetized Sparse Matrix Design Considerations. 523
Optional Team Information 524
Tested Hardware Devices and Results 524
Additional Areas of Optimization. 538

A. Summary of OpenCL 1.1 . . . . **541**

The OpenCL Platform Layer 541
Contexts 541
Querying Platform Information and Devices. 542
The OpenCL Runtime. 543
Command-Queues 543
Buffer Objects 544
Create Buffer Objects. 544
Read, Write, and Copy Buffer Objects 544
Map Buffer Objects 545
Manage Buffer Objects 545
Query Buffer Objects. 545
Program Objects 546
Create Program Objects. 546
Build Program Executable. 546
Build Options 546
Query Program Objects. 547
Unload the OpenCL Compiler 547

Kernel and Event Objects 547
   Create Kernel Objects 547
   Kernel Arguments and Object Queries 548
   Execute Kernels 548
   Event Objects 549
   Out-of-Order Execution of Kernels and Memory
     Object Commands 549
   Profiling Operations 549
   Flush and Finish 550
Supported Data Types 550
   Built-In Scalar Data Types 550
   Built-In Vector Data Types 551
   Other Built-In Data Types 551
   Reserved Data Types 551
Vector Component Addressing 552
   Vector Components 552
   Vector Addressing Equivalencies 553
   Conversions and Type Casting Examples 554
   Operators 554
   Address Space Qualifiers 554
   Function Qualifiers 554
Preprocessor Directives and Macros 555
Specify Type Attributes 555
Math Constants 556
Work-Item Built-In Functions 557
Integer Built-In Functions 557
Common Built-In Functions 559
Math Built-In Functions 560
Geometric Built-In Functions 563
Relational Built-In Functions 564
Vector Data Load/Store Functions 567
Atomic Functions 568
Async Copies and Prefetch Functions 570
Synchronization, Explicit Memory Fence 570
Miscellaneous Vector Built-In Functions 571
Image Read and Write Built-In Functions 572

Image Objects 573
    Create Image Objects. 573
    Query List of Supported Image Formats 574
    Copy between Image, Buffer Objects 574
    Map and Unmap Image Objects 574
    Read, Write, Copy Image Objects 575
    Query Image Objects. 575
Image Formats 576
Access Qualifiers 576
Sampler Objects. 576
Sampler Declaration Fields 577
OpenCL Device Architecture Diagram 577
OpenCL/OpenGL Sharing APIs. 577
    CL Buffer Objects > GL Buffer Objects 578
    CL Image Objects > GL Textures. 578
    CL Image Objects > GL Renderbuffers 578
    Query Information 578
    Share Objects. 579
    CL Event Objects > GL Sync Objects. 579
    CL Context > GL Context, Sharegroup. 579
OpenCL/Direct3D 10 Sharing APIs. 579

Index **581**

Figures

Figure 1.1   The rate at which instructions are retired is the same in these two cases, but the power is much less with two cores running at half the frequency of a single core. 5

Figure 1.2   A plot of peak performance versus power at the thermal design point for three processors produced on a 65nm process technology. Note: This is not to say that one processor is better or worse than the others. The point is that the more specialized the core, the more power-efficient it is. 6

Figure 1.3   Block diagram of a modern desktop PC with multiple CPUs (potentially different) and a GPU, demonstrating that systems today are frequently heterogeneous 7

Figure 1.4   A simple example of data parallelism where a single task is applied concurrently to each element of a vector to produce a new vector. 9

Figure 1.5   Task parallelism showing two ways of mapping six independent tasks onto three PEs. A computation is not done until every task is complete, so the goal should be a well-balanced load, that is, to have the time spent computing by each PE be the same. 10

Figure 1.6   The OpenCL platform model with one host and one or more OpenCL devices. Each OpenCL device has one or more compute units, each of which has one or more processing elements. .12

Figure 1.7   An example of how the global IDs, local IDs, and work-group indices are related for a two-dimensional NDRange. Other parameters of the index space are defined in the figure. The shaded block has a global ID of $(g_x, g_y) = (6, 5)$ and a work-group plus local ID of $(w_x, w_y) = (1, 1)$ and $(l_x, l_y) = (2, 1)$ 16

Figure 1.8   A summary of the memory model in OpenCL and how the different memory regions interact with the platform model 23

Figure 1.9   This block diagram summarizes the components of OpenCL and the actions that occur on the host during an OpenCL application.. 35

Figure 2.1   CodeBlocks `CL_Book` project. 42

Figure 2.2   Using cmake-gui to generate Visual Studio projects 43

Figure 2.3   Microsoft Visual Studio 2008 Project 44

Figure 2.4   Eclipse `CL_Book` project 45

Figure 3.1   Platform, devices, and contexts. 84

Figure 3.2   Convolution of an 8×8 signal with a 3×3 filter, resulting in a 6×6 signal 90

Figure 4.1   Mapping `get_global_id` to a work-item 98

Figure 4.2   Converting a `float4` to a `ushort4` with round-to-nearest rounding and saturation. 120

Figure 4.3   Adding two vectors 125

Figure 4.4   Multiplying a vector and a scalar with widening 126

Figure 4.5   Multiplying a vector and a scalar with conversion and widening. 126

Figure 5.1   Example of the work-item functions. 150

Figure 7.1   (a) 2D array represented as an OpenCL buffer; (b) 2D slice into the same buffer. 269

Figure 9.1   A failed attempt to use the `clEnqueueBarrier()` command to establish a barrier between two command-queues. This doesn't work because the barrier command in OpenCL applies only to the queue within which it is placed. .316

Figure 9.2   Creating a barrier between queues using `clEnqueueMarker()` to post the barrier in one queue with its exported event to connect to a `clEnqueueWaitForEvent()` function in the other queue. Because `clEnqueueWaitForEvents()` does not imply a barrier, it must be preceded by an explicit `clEnqueueBarrier()`. .317

Figure 10.1   A program demonstrating OpenCL/OpenGL interop. The positions of the vertices in the sine wave and the background texture color values are computed by kernels in OpenCL and displayed using Direct3D. 344

Figure 11.1   A program demonstrating OpenCL/D3D interop. The sine positions of the vertices in the sine wave and the texture color values are programmatically set by kernels in OpenCL and displayed using Direct3D. 368

Figure 12.1   C++ Wrapper API class hierarchy 370

Figure 15.1   OpenCL Sobel kernel: input image and output image after applying the Sobel filter 409

Figure 16.1   Summary of data in Table 16.1: NV GTX 295 (1 GPU, 2 GPU) and Intel Core i7 performance 419

Figure 16.2   Using one GPU versus two GPUs: NV GTX 295 (1 GPU, 2 GPU) and Intel Core i7 performance 420

Figure 16.3   Summary of data in Table 16.2: NV GTX 295 (1 GPU, 2 GPU) and Intel Core i7 performance—10 edges per vertex 421

Figure 16.4   Summary of data in Table 16.3: comparison of dual GPU, dual GPU + multicore CPU, multicore CPU, and CPU at vertex degree 1 423

Figure 17.1   AMD's Samari demo, courtesy of Jason Yang 426

Figure 17.2   Masses and connecting links, similar to a
mass/spring model for soft bodies. 426

Figure 17.3   Creating a simulation structure from a cloth mesh 427

Figure 17.4   Cloth link structure. 428

Figure 17.5   Cloth mesh with both structural links that stop
stretching and bend links that resist folding of the
material 428

Figure 17.6   Solving the mesh of a rope. Note how the motion
applied between (a) and (b) propagates during
solver iterations (c) and (d) until, eventually, the
entire rope has been affected. 429

Figure 17.7   The stages of Gauss-Seidel iteration on a set of
soft-body links and vertices. In (a) we see the mesh
at the start of the solver iteration. In (b) we apply
the effects of the first link on its vertices. In (c) we
apply those of another link, noting that we work
from the positions computed in (b). 432

Figure 17.8   The same mesh as in Figure 17.7 is shown in (a). In
(b) the update shown in Figure 17.7(c) has occurred
as well as a second update represented by the dark
mass and dotted lines. 433

Figure 17.9   A mesh with structural links taken from the
input triangle mesh and bend links created across
triangle boundaries with one possible coloring into
independent batches 434

Figure 17.10   Dividing the mesh into larger chunks and applying
a coloring to those. Note that fewer colors are
needed than in the direct link coloring approach.
This pattern can repeat infinitely with the same
four colors. 439

Figure 18.1   A single frame from the Ocean demonstration. 450

Figure 19.1   A pair of test images of a car trunk being closed. The first (a) and fifth (b) images of the test sequence are shown. 470

Figure 19.2   Optical flow vectors recovered from the test images of a car trunk being closed. The fourth and fifth images in the sequence were used to generate this result. 471

Figure 19.3   Pyramidal Lucas-Kanade optical flow algorithm 473

Figure 21.1   A matrix multiplication operation to compute a single element of the product matrix, C. This corresponds to summing into each element $C_{i,j}$ the dot product from the ith row of A with the jth column of B. 500

Figure 21.2   Matrix multiplication where each work-item computes an entire row of the C matrix. This requires a change from a 2D NDRange of size 1000×1000 to a 1D NDRange of size 1000. We set the work-group size to 250, resulting in four work-groups (one for each compute unit in our GPU). 506

Figure 21.3   Matrix multiplication where each work-item computes an entire row of the C matrix. The same row of A is used for elements in the row of C so memory movement overhead can be dramatically reduced by copying a row of A into private memory. 508

Figure 21.4   Matrix multiplication where each work-item computes an entire row of the C matrix. Memory traffic to global memory is minimized by copying a row of A into each work-item's private memory and copying rows of B into local memory for each work-group. 510

Figure 22.1   Sparse matrix example. 516

Figure 22.2   A tile in a matrix and its relationship with input and output vectors. 520

Figure 22.3   Format of a single-precision 128-byte packet 521

Figure 22.4   Format of a double-precision 192-byte packet 522

Figure 22.5   Format of the header block of a tiled and
packetized sparse matrix 523

Figure 22.6   Single-precision SpMV performance across
22 matrices on seven platforms. .528

Figure 22.7   Double-precision SpMV performance across
22 matrices on five platforms 528

Tables

Table 2.1   OpenCL Error Codes 58

Table 3.1   OpenCL Platform Queries 65

Table 3.2   OpenCL Devices 68

Table 3.3   OpenCL Device Queries. 71

Table 3.4   Properties Supported by `clCreateContext` 85

Table 3.5   Context Information Queries 87

Table 4.1   Built-In Scalar Data Types 100

Table 4.2   Built-In Vector Data Types. 103

Table 4.3   Application Data Types 103

Table 4.4   Accessing Vector Components. 106

Table 4.5   Numeric Indices for Built-In Vector Data Types 107

Table 4.6   Other Built-In Data Types 108

Table 4.7   Rounding Modes for Conversions. 119

Table 4.8   Operators That Can Be Used with Vector Data Types. . . .123

Table 4.9   Optional Extension Behavior Description 144

Table 5.1   Built-In Work-Item Functions 151

Table 5.2   Built-In Math Functions 154

Table 5.3   Built-In *half_* and *native_* Math Functions 160

Table 5.4   Single- and Double-Precision Floating-Point Constants . . 162

Table 5.5   `ulp` Values for Basic Operations and Built-In Math
Functions 164

Table 5.6   Built-In Integer Functions 169

Table 5.7   Built-In Common Functions 173

Table 5.8   Built-In Geometric Functions 176

Table 5.9   Built-In Relational Functions 178

Table 5.10   Additional Built-In Relational Functions 180

Table 5.11   Built-In Vector Data Load and Store Functions 181

Table 5.12   Built-In Synchronization Functions 190

Table 5.13   Built-In Async Copy and Prefetch Functions 192

Table 5.14   Built-In Atomic Functions 195

Table 5.15   Built-In Miscellaneous Vector Functions 200

Table 5.16   Built-In Image 2D Read Functions 202

Table 5.17   Built-In Image 3D Read Functions 204

Table 5.18   Image Channel Order and Values for Missing
Components 206

Table 5.19   Sampler Addressing Mode 207

Table 5.20   Image Channel Order and Corresponding Bolor
Color Value 209

Table 5.21   Built-In Image 2D Write Functions 211

Table 5.22   Built-In Image 3D Write Functions 212

Table 5.23   Built-In Image Query Functions 214

Table 6.1   Preprocessor Build Options 223

Table 6.2   Floating-Point Options (Math Intrinsics) 224

Table 6.3   Optimization Options 225

Table 6.4   Miscellaneous Options 226

Table 7.1   Supported Values for `cl_mem_flags` 249

Table 7.2   Supported Names and Values for
`clCreateSubBuffer` 254

Table 7.3   OpenCL Buffer and Sub-Buffer Queries 257

Table 7.4   Supported Values for `cl_map_flags` 277

Table 8.1   Image Channel Order 287

Table 8.2   Image Channel Data Type 289

Table 8.3   Mandatory Supported Image Formats 290

Table 9.1   Queries on Events Supported in `clGetEventInfo()` . . .319

Table 9.2   Profiling Information and Return Types 329

Table 10.1   OpenGL Texture Format Mappings to OpenCL
Image Formats 346

Table 10.2   Supported `param_name` Types and Information
Returned 348

Table 11.1   Direct3D Texture Format Mappings to OpenCL
Image Formats 360

Table 12.1   Preprocessor Error Macros and Their Defaults 372

Table 13.1   Required Image Formats for Embedded Profile 387

Table 13.2   Accuracy of Math Functions for Embedded Profile
versus Full Profile 388

Table 13.3   Device Properties: Minimum Maximum Values for
Full Profile versus Embedded Profile 389

Table 16.1   Comparison of Data at Vertex Degree 5 418

Table 16.2   Comparison of Data at Vertex Degree 10 420

Table 16.3   Comparison of Dual GPU, Dual GPU + Multicore
CPU, Multicore CPU, and CPU at Vertex Degree 10 422

Table 18.1   Kernel Elapsed Times for Varying Work-Group Sizes 458

Table 18.2   Load and Store Bank Calculations. 465

Table 19.1   GPU Optical Flow Performance. .485

Table 21.1   Matrix Multiplication (Order-1000 Matrices)
Results Reported as MFLOPS and as Speedup
Relative to the Unoptimized Sequential C Program
(i.e., the Speedups Are "Unfair") .512

Table 22.1   Hardware Device Information. 525

Table 22.2   Sparse Matrix Description 526

Table 22.3   Optimal Performance Histogram for Various
Matrix Sizes 529

Listings

Listing 2.1   HelloWorld OpenCL Kernel and Main Function 46

Listing 2.2   Choosing a Platform and Creating a Context. 49

Listing 2.3   Choosing the First Available Device and Creating a
Command-Queue. 51

Listing 2.4   Loading a Kernel Source File from Disk and
Creating and Building a Program Object 53

Listing 2.5   Creating a Kernel. 54

Listing 2.6   Creating Memory Objects 55

Listing 2.7   Setting the Kernel Arguments, Executing the
Kernel, and Reading Back the Results 56

Listing 3.1   Enumerating the List of Platforms 66

Listing 3.2   Querying and Displaying Platform-Specific
Information 67

Listing 3.3   Example of Querying and Displaying Platform-
Specific Information 79

Listing 3.4   Using Platform, Devices, and Contexts—Simple
Convolution Kernel 90

Listing 3.5   Example of Using Platform, Devices, and
Contexts—Simple Convolution 91

Listing 6.1   Creating and Building a Program Object 221

Listing 6.2   Caching the Program Binary on First Run 229

Listing 6.3   Querying for and Storing the Program Binary 230

Listing 6.4   Example Program Binary for `HelloWorld.cl` (NVIDIA) 233

Listing 6.5   Creating a Program from Binary .235

Listing 7.1   Creating, Writing, and Reading Buffers and Sub-Buffers Example Kernel Code 262

Listing 7.2   Creating, Writing, and Reading Buffers and Sub-Buffers Example Host Code 262

Listing 8.1   Creating a 2D Image Object from a File 284

Listing 8.2   Creating a 2D Image Object for Output 285

Listing 8.3   Query for Device Image Support 291

Listing 8.4   Creating a Sampler Object 293

Listing 8.5   Gaussian Filter Kernel 295

Listing 8.6   Queue Gaussian Kernel for Execution 297

Listing 8.7   Read Image Back to Host Memory 300

Listing 8.8   Mapping Image Results to a Host Memory Pointer 307

Listing 12.1   Vector Add Example Program Using the C++ Wrapper API 379

Listing 13.1   Querying Platform and Device Profiles 384

Listing 14.1   Sequential Implementation of RGB Histogram 393

Listing 14.2   A Parallel Version of the RGB Histogram—Compute Partial Histograms 395

Listing 14.3   A Parallel Version of the RGB Histogram—Sum Partial Histograms 397

Listing 14.4   Host Code of CL API Calls to Enqueue Histogram Kernels 398

Listing 14.5   A Parallel Version of the RGB Histogram—Optimized Version 400

Listing 14.6   A Parallel Version of the RGB Histogram for Half-Float and Float Channels 403

Listing 15.1   An OpenCL Sobel Filter 408

Listing 15.2   An OpenCL Sobel Filter Producing a Grayscale Image 410

Listing 16.1   Data Structure and Interface for Dijkstra's Algorithm 413

Listing 16.2   Pseudo Code for High-Level Loop That Executes Dijkstra's Algorithm 414

Listing 16.3   Kernel to Initialize Buffers before Each Run of Dijkstra's Algorithm 415

Listing 16.4   Two Kernel Phases That Compute Dijkstra's Algorithm 416

Listing 20.1   `ImageFilter2D.py` 489

Listing 20.2   Creating a Context 492

Listing 20.3   Loading an Image 494

Listing 20.4   Creating and Building a Program 495

Listing 20.5   Executing the Kernel 496

Listing 20.6   Reading the Image into a Numpy Array 496

Listing 21.1   A C Function Implementing Sequential Matrix Multiplication 500

Listing 21.2   A kernel to compute the matrix product of *A* and *B* summing the result into a third matrix, *C*. Each work-item is responsible for a single element of the *C* matrix. The matrices are stored in global memory 501

Listing 21.3   The Host Program for the Matrix Multiplication Program 503

Listing 21.4   Each work-item updates a full row of *C*. The kernel code is shown as well as changes to the host code from the base host program in Listing 21.3. The only change required in the host code was to the dimensions of the NDRange...........................507

Listing 21.5   Each work-item manages the update to a full row of *C*, but before doing so the relevant row of the *A* matrix is copied into private memory from global memory...................................508

Listing 21.6   Each work-item manages the update to a full row of *C*. Private memory is used for the row of *A* and local memory (Bwrk) is used by all work-items in a work-group to hold a column of *B*. The host code is the same as before other than the addition of a new argument for the *B*-column local memory.........510

Listing 21.7   Different Versions of the Matrix Multiplication Functions Showing the Permutations of the Loop Orderings 513

Listing 22.1   Sparse Matrix-Vector Multiplication OpenCL Kernels 530

Foreword

During the past few years, heterogeneous computers composed of CPUs and GPUs have revolutionized computing. By matching different parts of a workload to the most suitable processor, tremendous performance gains have been achieved.

Much of this revolution has been driven by the emergence of many-core processors such as GPUs. For example, it is now possible to buy a graphics card that can execute more than a trillion floating point operations per second (teraflops). These GPUs were designed to render beautiful images, but for the right workloads, they can also be used as high-performance computing engines for applications from scientific computing to augmented reality.

A natural question is why these many-core processors are so fast compared to traditional single core CPUs. The fundamental driving force is innovative parallel hardware. Parallel computing is more efficient than sequential computing because chips are fundamentally parallel. Modern chips contain billions of transistors. Many-core processors organize these transistors into many parallel processors consisting of hundreds of floating point units. Another important reason for their speed advantage is new parallel software. Utilizing all these computing resources requires that we develop parallel programs. The efficiency gains due to software and hardware allow us to get more FLOPs per Watt or per dollar than a single-core CPU.

Computing systems are a symbiotic combination of hardware and software. Hardware is not useful without a good programming model. The success of CPUs has been tied to the success of their programming models, as exemplified by the C language and its successors. C nicely abstracts a sequential computer. To fully exploit heterogeneous computers, we need new programming models that nicely abstract a modern *parallel* computer. And we can look to techniques established in graphics as a guide to the new programming models we need for heterogeneous computing.

I have been interested in programming models for graphics for many years. It started in 1988 when I was a software engineer at PIXAR, where I developed the RenderMan shading language. A decade later graphics systems became fast enough that we could consider developing shading languages for GPUs. With Kekoa Proudfoot and Bill Mark, we developed a real-time shading language, RTSL. RTSL ran on graphics hardware by compiling shading language programs into pixel shader programs, the assembly language for graphics hardware of the day. Bill Mark subsequently went to work at NVIDIA, where he developed Cg. More recently, I have been working with Tim Foley at Intel, who has developed a new shading language called Spark. Spark takes shading languages to the next level by abstracting complex graphics pipelines with new capabilities such as tesselation.

While developing these languages, I always knew that GPUs could be used for much more than graphics. Several other groups had demonstrated that graphics hardware could be used for applications beyond graphics. This led to the GPGPU (General-Purpose GPU) movement. The demonstrations were hacked together using the graphics library. For GPUs to be used more widely, they needed a more general programming environment that was not tied to graphics. To meet this need, we started the Brook for GPU Project at Stanford. The basic idea behind Brook was to treat the GPU as a data-parallel processor. Data-parallel programming has been extremely successful for parallel computing, and with Brook we were able to show that data-parallel programming primitives could be implemented on a GPU. Brook made it possible for a developer to write an application in a widely used parallel programming model.

Brook was built as a proof of concept. Ian Buck, a graduate student at Stanford, went on to NVIDIA to develop CUDA. CUDA extended Brook in important ways. It introduced the concept of cooperating thread arrays, or thread blocks. A cooperating thread array captured the locality in a GPU core, where a block of threads executing the same program could also communicate through local memory and synchronize through barriers. More importantly, CUDA created an environment for GPU Computing that has enabled a rich ecosystem of application developers, middleware providers, and vendors.

OpenCL (Open Computing Language) provides a logical extension of the core ideas from GPU Computing—the era of ubiquitous heterogeneous parallel computing. OpenCL has been carefully designed by the Khronos Group with input from many vendors and software experts. OpenCL benefits from the experience gained using CUDA in creating a software standard that can be implemented by many vendors. OpenCL implementations run now on widely used hardware, including CPUs and GPUs from NVIDIA, AMD, and Intel, as well as platforms based on DSPs and FPGAs.

By standardizing the programming model, developers can count on more software tools and hardware platforms.

What is most exciting about OpenCL is that it doesn't only standardize what has been done, but represents the efforts of an active community that is pushing the frontier of parallel computing. For example, OpenCL provides innovative capabilities for scheduling tasks on the GPU. The developers of OpenCL have have combined the best features of task-parallel and data-parallel computing. I expect future versions of OpenCL to be equally innovative. Like its father, OpenGL, OpenCL will likely grow over time with new versions with more and more capability.

This book describes the complete OpenCL Programming Model. One of the coauthors, Aaftab, was the key mind behind the system. He has joined forces with other key designers of OpenCL to write an accessible authoritative guide. Welcome to the new world of heterogeneous computing.

—*Pat Hanrahan*
  Stanford University

Preface

Industry pundits love drama. New products don't build on the status quo to make things better. They "revolutionize" or, better yet, define a "new paradigm." And, of course, given the way technology evolves, the results rarely are as dramatic as the pundits make it seem.

Over the past decade, however, something revolutionary has happened. The drama is real. CPUs with multiple cores have made parallel hardware ubiquitous. GPUs are no longer *just* specialized graphics processors; they are heavyweight compute engines. And their combination, the so-called heterogeneous platform, truly is redefining the standard building blocks of computing.

We appear to be midway through a revolution in computing on a par with that seen with the birth of the PC. Or more precisely, we have the *potential* for a revolution because the high levels of parallelism provided by heterogeneous hardware are meaningless without parallel software; and the fact of the matter is that outside of specific niches, parallel software is rare.

To create a parallel software revolution that keeps pace with the ongoing (parallel) heterogeneous computing revolution, we need a parallel software industry. That industry, however, can flourish only if software can move between platforms, both cross-vendor and cross-generational. The solution is an industry standard for heterogeneous computing.

OpenCL is that industry standard. Created within the Khronos Group (known for OpenGL and other standards), OpenCL emerged from a collaboration among software vendors, computer system designers (including designers of mobile platforms), and microprocessor (embedded, accelerator, CPU, and GPU) manufacturers. It is an answer to the question "How can a person program a heterogeneous platform with the confidence that software created today will be relevant tomorrow?"

Born in 2008, OpenCL is now available from multiple sources on a wide range of platforms. It is evolving steadily to remain aligned with the latest microprocessor developments. In this book we focus on OpenCL 1.1. We describe the full scope of the standard with copious examples to explain how OpenCL is used in practice. Join us. *Vive la révolution.*

Intended Audience

This book is written by programmers for programmers. It is a pragmatic guide for people interested in writing code. We assume the reader is comfortable with C and, for parts of the book, C++. Finally, we assume the reader is familiar with the basic concepts of parallel programming. We assume our readers have a computer nearby so they can write software and explore ideas as they read. Hence, this book is overflowing with programs and fragments of code.

We cover the entire OpenCL 1.1 specification and explain how it can be used to express a wide range of parallel algorithms. After finishing this book, you will be able to write complex parallel programs that decompose a workload across multiple devices in a heterogeneous platform. You will understand the basics of performance optimization in OpenCL and how to write software that probes the hardware and adapts to maximize performance.

Organization of the Book

The OpenCL specification is almost 400 pages. It's a dense and complex document full of tediously specific details. Explaining this specification is not easy, but we think that we've pulled it off nicely.

The book is divided into two parts. The first describes the OpenCL specification. It begins with two chapters to introduce the core ideas behind OpenCL and the basics of writing an OpenCL program. We then launch into a systematic exploration of the OpenCL 1.1 specification. The tone of the book changes as we incorporate reference material with explanatory discourse. The second part of the book provides a sequence of case studies. These range from simple pedagogical examples that provide insights into how aspects of OpenCL work to complex applications showing how OpenCL is used in serious application projects. The following provides more detail to help you navigate through the book:

Part I: The OpenCL 1.1 Language and API

- **Chapter 1, "An Introduction to OpenCL":** This chapter provides a high-level overview of OpenCL. It begins by carefully explaining why heterogeneous parallel platforms are destined to dominate computing into the foreseeable future. Then the core models and concepts behind OpenCL are described. Along the way, the terminology used in OpenCL is presented, making this chapter an important one to read even if your goal is to skim through the book and use it as a reference guide to OpenCL.

- **Chapter 2, "HelloWorld: An OpenCL Example"**: Real programmers learn by writing code. Therefore, we complete our introduction to OpenCL with a chapter that explores a working OpenCL program. It has become standard to introduce a programming language by printing "hello world" to the screen. This makes no sense in OpenCL (which doesn't include a print statement). In the data-parallel programming world, the analog to "hello world" is a program to complete the element-wise addition of two arrays. That program is the core of this chapter. By the end of the chapter, you will understand OpenCL well enough to start writing your own simple programs. And we urge you to do exactly that. You can't learn a programming language by reading a book alone. Write code.

- **Chapter 3, "Platforms, Contexts, and Devices"**: With this chapter, we begin our systematic exploration of the OpenCL specification. Before an OpenCL program can do anything "interesting," it needs to discover available resources and then prepare them to do useful work. In other words, a program must discover the platform, define the context for the OpenCL program, and decide how to work with the devices at its disposal. These important topics are explored in this chapter, where the OpenCL Platform API is described in detail.

- **Chapter 4, "Programming with OpenCL C"**: Code that runs on an OpenCL device is in most cases written using the OpenCL C programming language. Based on a subset of C99, the OpenCL C programming language provides what a kernel needs to effectively exploit an OpenCL device, including a rich set of vector instructions. This chapter explains this programming language in detail.

- **Chapter 5, "OpenCL C Built-In Functions"**: The OpenCL C programming language API defines a large and complex set of built-in functions. These are described in this chapter.

- **Chapter 6, "Programs and Kernels"**: Once we have covered the languages used to write kernels, we move on to the runtime API defined by OpenCL. We start with the process of creating programs and kernels. Remember, the word *program* is overloaded by OpenCL. In OpenCL, the word *program* refers specifically to the "dynamic library" from which the functions are pulled for the kernels.

- **Chapter 7, "Buffers and Sub-Buffers"**: In the next chapter we move to the buffer memory objects, one-dimensional arrays, including a careful discussion of sub-buffers. The latter is a new feature in

OpenCL 1.1, so programmers experienced with OpenCL 1.0 will find this chapter particularly useful.

- **Chapter 8, "Images and Samplers":** Next we move to the very important topic of our other memory object, images. Given the close relationship between graphics and OpenCL, these memory objects are important for a large fraction of OpenCL programmers.

- **Chapter 9, "Events":** This chapter presents a detailed discussion of the event model in OpenCL. These objects are used to enforce ordering constraints in OpenCL. At a basic level, events let you write concurrent code that generates correct answers regardless of how work is scheduled by the runtime. At a more algorithmically profound level, however, events support the construction of programs as directed acyclic graphs spanning multiple devices.

- **Chapter 10, "Interoperability with OpenGL":** Many applications may seek to use graphics APIs to display the results of OpenCL processing, or even use OpenCL to postprocess scenes generated by graphics. The OpenCL specification allows interoperation with the OpenGL graphics API. This chapter will discuss how to set up OpenGL/OpenCL sharing and how data can be shared and synchronized.

- **Chapter 11, "Interoperability with Direct3D":** The Microsoft family of platforms is a common target for OpenCL applications. When applications include graphics, they may need to connect to Microsoft's native graphics API. In OpenCL 1.1, we define how to connect an OpenCL application to the DirectX 10 API. This chapter will demonstrate how to set up OpenCL/Direct3D sharing and how data can be shared and synchronized.

- **Chapter 12, "C++ Wrapper API":** We then discuss the OpenCL C++ API Wrapper. This greatly simplifies the host programs written in C++, addressing automatic reference counting and a unified interface for querying OpenCL object information. Once the C++ interface is mastered, it's hard to go back to the regular C interface.

- **Chapter 13, "OpenCL Embedded Profile":** OpenCL was created for an unusually wide range of devices, with a reach extending from cell phones to the nodes in a massively parallel supercomputer. Most of the OpenCL specification applies without modification to each of these devices. There are a small number of changes to OpenCL, however, needed to fit the reduced capabilities of low-power processors used in embedded devices. This chapter describes these changes, referred to in the OpenCL specification as the OpenCL embedded profile.

Part II: OpenCL 1.1 Case Studies

- **Chapter 14, "Image Histogram":** A histogram reports the frequency of occurrence of values within a data set. For example, in this chapter, we compute the histogram for R, G, and B channel values of a color image. To generate a histogram in parallel, you compute values over local regions of a data set and then sum these local values to generate the final result. The goal of this chapter is twofold: (1) we demonstrate how to manipulate images in OpenCL, and (2) we explore techniques to efficiently carry out a histogram's global summation within an OpenCL program.

- **Chapter 15, "Sobel Edge Detection Filter":** The Sobel edge filter is a directional edge detector filter that computes image gradients along the x- and y-axes. In this chapter, we use a kernel to apply the Sobel edge filter as a simple example of how kernels work with images in OpenCL.

- **Chapter 16, "Parallelizing Dijkstra's Single-Source Shortest-Path Graph Algorithm":** In this chapter, we present an implementation of Dijkstra's Single-Source Shortest-Path graph algorithm implemented in OpenCL capable of utilizing both CPU and multiple GPU devices. Graph data structures find their way into many problems, from artificial intelligence to neuroimaging. This particular implementation was developed as part of FreeSurfer, a neuroimaging application, in order to improve the performance of an algorithm that measures the curvature of a triangle mesh structural reconstruction of the cortical surface of the brain. This example is illustrative of how to work with multiple OpenCL devices and split workloads across CPUs, multiple GPUs, or all devices at once.

- **Chapter 17, "Cloth Simulation in the Bullet Physics SDK":** Physics simulation is a growing addition to modern video games, and in this chapter we present an approach to simulating cloth, such as a warrior's clothing, using OpenCL that is part of the Bullet Physics SDK. There are many ways of simulating soft bodies; the simulation method used in Bullet is similar to a mass/spring model and is optimized for execution on modern GPUs while integrating smoothly with other Bullet SDK components that are not written in OpenCL. We show an important technique, called batching, that transforms the particle meshes for performant execution on wide SIMD architectures, such as the GPU, while preserving dependences within the mass/spring model.

- **Chapter 18, "Simulating the Ocean with Fast Fourier Transform":** In this chapter we present the details of AMD's Ocean simulation. Ocean is an OpenCL demonstration that uses an inverse discrete Fourier transform to simulate, in real time, the sea. The fast Fourier transform is applied to random noise, generated over time as a frequency-dependent phase shift. We describe an implementation based on the approach originally developed by Jerry Tessendorf that has appeared in a number of feature films, including *Waterworld*, *Titanic*, and *Fifth Element*. We show the development of an optimized 2D DFFT, including a number of important optimizations useful when programming with OpenCL, and the integration of this algorithm into the application itself and using interoperability between OpenCL and OpenGL.

- **Chapter 19, "Optical Flow":** In this chapter, we present an implementation of optical flow in OpenCL, which is a fundamental concept in computer vision that describes motion in images. Optical flow has uses in image stabilization, temporal upsampling, and as an input to higher-level algorithms such as object tracking and gesture recognition. This chapter presents the pyramidal Lucas-Kanade optical flow algorithm in OpenCL. The implementation demonstrates how image objects can be used to access texture features of GPU hardware. We will show how the texture-filtering hardware on the GPU can be used to perform linear interpolation of data, achieve the required sub-pixel accuracy, and thereby provide significant speedups. Additionally, we will discuss how shared memory can be used to cache data that is repeatedly accessed and how early kernel exit techniques provide additional efficiency.

- **Chapter 20, "Using OpenCL with PyOpenCL":** The purpose of this chapter is to introduce you to the basics of working with OpenCL in Python. The majority of the book focuses on using OpenCL from C/C++, but bindings are available for other languages including Python. In this chapter, PyOpenCL is introduced by walking through the steps required to port the Gaussian image-filtering example from Chapter 8 to Python. In addition to covering the changes required to port from C++ to Python, the chapter discusses some of the advantages of using OpenCL in a dynamically typed language such as Python.

- **Chapter 21, "Matrix Multiplication with OpenCL":** In this chapter, we discuss a program that multiplies two square matrices. The program is very simple, so it is easy to follow the changes made to the program as we optimize its performance. These optimizations focus on the OpenCL memory model and how we can work with the model to minimize the cost of data movement in an OpenCL program.

- **Chapter 22, "Sparse Matrix-Vector Multiplication":** In this chapter, we describe an optimized implementation of the Sparse Matrix-Vector Multiplication algorithm using OpenCL. Sparse matrices are defined as large, two-dimensional matrices in which the vast majority of the elements of the matrix are equal to zero. They are used to characterize and solve problems in a wide variety of domains such as computational fluid dynamics, computer graphics/vision, robotics/kinematics, financial modeling, acoustics, and quantum chemistry. The implementation demonstrates OpenCL's ability to bridge the gap between hardware-specific code (fast, but not portable) and single-source code (very portable, but slow), yielding a high-performance, efficient implementation on a variety of hardware that is almost as fast as a hardware-specific implementation. These results are accomplished with kernels written in OpenCL C that can be compiled and run on any conforming OpenCL platform.

Appendix

- **Appendix A, "Summary of OpenCL 1.1":** The OpenCL specification defines an overwhelming collection of functions, named constants, and types. Even expert OpenCL programmers need to look up these details when writing code. To aid in this process, we've included an appendix where we pull together all these details in one place.

Example Code

This book is filled with example programs. You can download many of the examples from the book's Web site at www.openclprogrammingguide.com.

Errata

If you find something in the book that you believe is in error, please send us a note at errors@opencl-book.com. The list of errata for the book can be found on the book's Web site at www.openclprogrammingguide.com.

Acknowledgments

From Aaftab Munshi

It has been a great privilege working with Ben, Dan, Tim, and James on this book. I want to thank our reviewers, Andrew Brownsword, Yahya H. Mizra, Dave Shreiner, and Michael Thurston, who took the time to review this book and provided valuable feedback that has improved the book tremendously. I want to thank our editor at Pearson, Debra Williams Cauley, for all her help in making this book happen.

I also want to thank my daughters, Hannah and Ellie, and the love of my life, Karen, without whom this book would not be possible.

From Benedict R. Gaster

I would like to thank AMD for supporting my work on OpenCL. There are four people in particular who have guided my understanding of the GPGPU revolution: Mike Houston, Justin Hensley, Lee Howes, and Laurent Morichetti.

This book would not have been possible without the continued enjoyment of life in Santa Cruz and going to the beach with Miranda, Maude, Polly, and Meg. Thanks!

From Timothy G. Mattson

I would like to thank Intel for giving me the freedom to pursue work on OpenCL. In particular, I want to thank Aaron Lefohn of Intel for bringing me into this project in the early days as it was just getting started. Most of all, however, I want to thank the amazing people in the OpenCL working group. I have learned a huge amount from this dedicated team of professionals.

From James Fung

It's been a privilege to work alongside my coauthors and contribute to this book. I would also like to thank NVIDIA for all its support during writing as well as family and friends for their support and encouragement.

From Dan Ginsburg

I would like to thank Dr. Rudolph Pienaar and Dr. Ellen Grant at Children's Hospital Boston for supporting me in writing this book and for their valuable contributions and insights. It has been an honor and a great privilege to work on this book with Affie, Ben, Tim, and James, who represent some of the sharpest minds in the parallel computing business. I also want to thank our editor, Debra Williams Cauley, for her unending patience and dedication, which were critical to the success of this project.

About the Authors

Aaftab Munshi is the spec editor for the OpenGL ES 1.1, OpenGL ES 2.0, and OpenCL specifications and coauthor of the book *OpenGL ES 2.0 Programming Guide* (with Dan Ginsburg and Dave Shreiner, published by Addison-Wesley, 2008). He currently works at Apple.

Benedict R. Gaster is a software architect working on programming models for next-generation heterogeneous processors, in particular looking at high-level abstractions for parallel programming on the emerging class of processors that contain both CPUs and accelerators such as GPUs. Benedict has contributed extensively to the OpenCL's design and has represented AMD at the Khronos Group open standard consortium. Benedict has a Ph.D. in computer science for his work on type systems for extensible records and variants. He has been working at AMD since 2008.

Timothy G. Mattson is an old-fashioned parallel programmer, having started in the mid-eighties with the Caltech Cosmic Cube and continuing to the present. Along the way, he has worked with most classes of parallel computers (vector supercomputers, SMP, VLIW, NUMA, MPP, clusters, and many-core processors). Tim has published extensively, including the books *Patterns for Parallel Programming* (with Beverly Sanders and Berna Massingill, published by Addison-Wesley, 2004) and *An Introduction to Concurrency in Programming Languages* (with Matthew J. Sottile and Craig E Rasmussen, published by CRC Press, 2009). Tim has a Ph.D. in chemistry for his work on molecular scattering theory. He has been working at Intel since 1993.

James Fung has been developing computer vision on the GPU as it progressed from graphics to general-purpose computation. James has a Ph.D. in electrical and computer engineering from the University of Toronto and numerous IEEE and ACM publications in the areas of parallel GPU Computer Vision and Mediated Reality. He is currently a Developer Technology Engineer at NVIDIA, where he examines computer vision and image processing on graphics hardware.

Dan Ginsburg currently works at Children's Hospital Boston as a Principal Software Architect in the Fetal-Neonatal Neuroimaging and Development Science Center, where he uses OpenCL for accelerating neuroimaging algorithms. Previously, he worked for Still River Systems developing GPU-accelerated image registration software for the Monarch 250 proton beam radiotherapy system. Dan was also Senior Member of Technical Staff at AMD, where he worked for over eight years in a variety of roles, including developing OpenGL drivers, creating desktop and hand-held 3D demos, and leading the development of handheld GPU developer tools. Dan holds a B.S. in computer science from Worcester Polytechnic Institute and an M.B.A. from Bentley University.

Part I

The OpenCL 1.1 Language and API

## Chapter 1

An Introduction to OpenCL

When learning a new programming model, it is easy to become lost in a sea of details. APIs and strange new terminology seemingly appear from nowhere, creating needless complexity and sowing confusion. The key is to begin with a clear high-level understanding, to provide a map to fall back on when the going gets tough.

The purpose of this chapter is to help you construct that map. We begin with a brief overview of the OpenCL 1.1 specification and the heterogeneous computing trends that make it such an important programming standard. We then describe the conceptual models behind OpenCL and use them to explain how OpenCL works. At this point, the theoretical foundation of OpenCL is established, and we move on to consider the components of OpenCL. A key part of this is how OpenCL works with graphics standards. We complete our map of the OpenCL landscape by briefly looking at how the OpenCL standard works with embedded processors.

What Is OpenCL, or . . . Why You Need This Book

OpenCL is an industry standard framework for programming computers composed of a combination of CPUs, GPUs, and other processors. These so-called heterogeneous systems have become an important class of platforms, and OpenCL is the first industry standard that directly addresses their needs. First released in December of 2008 with early products available in the fall of 2009, OpenCL is a relatively new technology.

With OpenCL, you can write a single program that can run on a wide range of systems, from cell phones, to laptops, to nodes in massive supercomputers. No other parallel programming standard has such a wide reach. This is one of the reasons why OpenCL is so important and has the potential to transform the software industry. It's also the source of much of the criticism launched at OpenCL.

OpenCL delivers high levels of portability by exposing the hardware, not by hiding it behind elegant abstractions. This means that the OpenCL programmer must explicitly define the platform, its context, and how work is scheduled onto different devices. Not all programmers need or even want the detailed control OpenCL provides. And that's OK; when available, a high-level programming model is often a better approach. Even high-level programming models, however, need a solid (and portable) foundation to build on, and OpenCL can be that foundation.

This book is a detailed introduction to OpenCL. While anyone can download the specification (www.khronos.org/opencl) and learn the spelling of all the constructs within OpenCL, the specification doesn't describe how to use OpenCL to solve problems. That is the point of this book: solving problems with the OpenCL framework.

Our Many-Core Future: Heterogeneous Platforms

Computers over the past decade have fundamentally changed. Raw performance used to drive innovation. Starting several years ago, however, the focus shifted to performance delivered per watt expended. Semiconductor companies will continue to squeeze more and more transistors onto a single die, but these vendors will compete on power efficiency instead of raw performance.

This shift has radically changed the computers the industry builds. First, the microprocessors inside our computers are built from multiple low-power cores. The multicore imperative was first laid out by A. P. Chandrakasan et al. in the article "Optimizing Power Using Transformations."[1] The gist of their argument can be found in Figure 1.1. The energy expended in switching the gates in a CPU is the capacitance (C) times the voltage (V) squared. These gates switch over the course of a second a number of times equal to the frequency. Hence the power of a microprocessor scales as $P = CV^2f$. If we compare a single-core processor running at a frequency of f and a voltage of V to a similar processor with two cores each running at $f/2$, we have increased the number of circuits in the chip. Following the models described in "Optimizing Power Using Transformations," this nominally increases the capacitance by a factor of 2.2. But the voltage drops substantially to $0.6V$. So the number of instructions retired

---

[1] A. P. Chandrakasan, M. Potkonjak, R. Mehra, J. Rabaey, and R. W. Brodersen, "Optimizing Power Using Transformations," *IEEE Transactions on Computer-Aided Design of Integrated Circuits and Systems* 14, no. 1 (January 1995): 12–31.

per second is the same in both cases, but the power in the dual-core case is 0.396 of the power for the single-core. This fundamental relationship is what is driving the transition to many-core chips. Many cores running at lower frequencies are fundamentally more power-efficient.

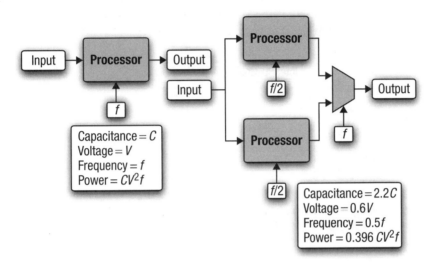

Figure 1.1   The rate at which instructions are retired is the same in these two cases, but the power is much less with two cores running at half the frequency of a single core.

The next question is "Will these cores be the same (homogeneous) or will they be different?" To understand this trend, consider the power efficiency of specialized versus general-purpose logic. A general-purpose processor by its nature must include a wide range of functional units to respond to any computational demand. This is precisely what makes the chip a general-purpose processor. Processors specialized to a specific function, however, have fewer wasted transistors because they include only those functional units required by their special function. The result can be seen in Figure 1.2, where we compare a general-purpose CPU (Intel Core 2 Quad processor model Q6700),[2] a GPU (NVIDIA GTX 280),[3] and

---

[2]   *Intel 64 and IA-32 Architectures Software Developer's Manual, Volume 1: Basic Architecture* (April 2008).

[3]   Technical Brief, *NVIDIA GeForce GTX 200 GPU Architectural Overview,* TB-04044-001_v01 (May 2008).

a highly specialized research processor (Intel 80-core Tera-scale research processor, the cores of which are just a simple pair of floating-point multiply-accumulate arithmetic units).[4] To make the comparisons as fair as possible, each of the chips was manufactured with a 65nm process technology, and we used the vendor-published peak performance versus thermal design point power. As plainly shown in the figure, as long as the tasks are well matched to the processor, the more specialized the silicon the better the power efficiency.

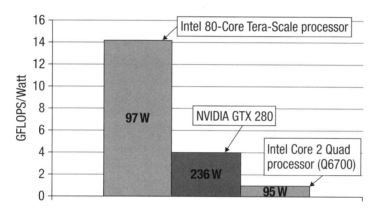

Figure 1.2   A plot of peak performance versus power at the thermal design point for three processors produced on a 65nm process technology. Note: This is not to say that one processor is better or worse than the others. The point is that the more specialized the core, the more power-efficient it is.

Hence, there is good reason to believe that in a world where maximizing performance per watt is essential, we can expect systems to increasingly depend on many cores with specialized silicon wherever practical. This is especially important for mobile devices in which conservation of battery power is critical. This heterogeneous future, however, is already upon us. Consider the schematic representation of a modern PC in Figure 1.3. There are two sockets, each potentially holding a different multicore CPU; a graphics/memory controller (GMCH) that connects to system memory (DRAM); and a graphics processing unit (GPU). This is a heterogeneous platform with multiple instruction sets and multiple levels of parallelism that must be exploited in order to utilize the full potential of the system.

---

[4]   T. G. Mattson, R. van der Wijngaart, and M. Frumkin, "Programming Intel's 80 Core Terascale Processor," *Proceedings of SC08*, Austin, TX (November 2008).

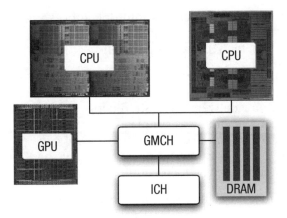

Figure 1.3   Block diagram of a modern desktop PC with multiple CPUs (potentially different) and a GPU, demonstrating that systems today are frequently heterogeneous

The basic platform, both today and in the future, at a high level is clear. A host of details and innovations will assuredly surprise us, but the hardware trends are clear. The future belongs to heterogeneous many-core platforms. The question facing us is how our software should adapt to these platforms.

Software in a Many-Core World

Parallel hardware delivers performance by running multiple operations at the same time. To be useful, parallel hardware needs software that executes as multiple streams of operations running at the same time; in other words, you need parallel software.

To understand parallel software, we must begin with the more general concept of **concurrency**. Concurrency is an old and familiar concept in computer science. A software system is concurrent when it consists of more than one stream of operations that are active and can make progress at one time. Concurrency is fundamental in any modern operating system. It maximizes resource utilization by letting other streams of operations (threads) make progress while others are stalled waiting on some resource. It gives a user interacting with the system the illusion of continuous and near-instantaneous interaction with the system.

When concurrent software runs on a computer with multiple processing elements so that threads actually run simultaneously, we have parallel computation. Concurrency enabled by hardware is parallelism.

The challenge for programmers is to find the concurrency in their problem, express that concurrency in their software, and then run the resulting program so that the concurrency delivers the desired performance. Finding the concurrency in a problem can be as simple as executing an independent stream of operations for each pixel in an image. Or it can be incredibly complicated with multiple streams of operations that share information and must tightly orchestrate their execution.

Once the concurrency is found in a problem, programmers must express this concurrency in their source code. In particular, the streams of operations that will execute concurrently must be defined, the data they operate on associated with them, and the dependencies between them managed so that the correct answer is produced when they run concurrently. This is the crux of the parallel programming problem.

Manipulating the low-level details of a parallel computer is beyond the ability of most people. Even expert parallel programmers would be overwhelmed by the burden of managing every memory conflict or scheduling individual threads. Hence, the key to parallel programming is a high-level abstraction or **model** to make the parallel programming problem more manageable.

There are way too many programming models divided into overlapping categories with confusing and often ambiguous names. For our purposes, we will worry about two parallel programming models: **task parallelism** and **data parallelism**. At a high level, the ideas behind these two models are straightforward.

In a data-parallel programming model, programmers think of their problems in terms of collections of data elements that can be updated concurrently. The parallelism is expressed by concurrently applying the same stream of instructions (a task) to each data element. The parallelism is in the data. We provide a simple example of data parallelism in Figure 1.4. Consider a simple task that just returns the square of an input value and a vector of numbers (A_vector). Using the data-parallel programming model, we update the vector in parallel by stipulating that the task be applied to each element to produce a new result vector. Of course, this example is extremely simple. In practice the number of operations in the task must be large in order to amortize the overheads of data movement and manage the parallel computation. But the simple example in the figure captures the key idea behind this programming mode.

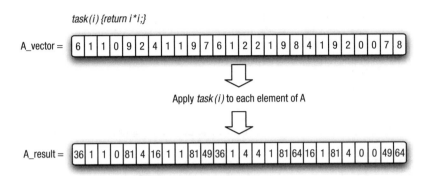

Figure 1.4   A simple example of data parallelism where a single task is applied concurrently to each element of a vector to produce a new vector

In a task-parallel programming model, programmers directly define and manipulate concurrent tasks. Problems are decomposed into tasks that can run concurrently, which are then mapped onto processing elements (PEs) of a parallel computer for execution. This is easiest when the tasks are completely independent, but this programming model is also used with tasks that share data. The computation with a set of tasks is completed when the last task is done. Because tasks vary widely in their computational demands, distributing them so that they all finish at about the same time can be difficult. This is the problem of load balancing. Consider the example in Figure 1.5, where we have six independent tasks to execute concurrently on three PEs. In one case the first PE has extra work to do and runs significantly longer than the other PEs. The second case with a different distribution of tasks shows a more ideal case where each PE finishes at about the same time. This is an example of a key ideal in parallel computing called **load balancing**.

The choice between data parallelism and task parallelism is driven by the needs of the problem being solved. Problems organized around updates over points on a grid, for example, map immediately onto data-parallel models. Problems expressed as traversals over graphs, on the other hand, are naturally expressed in terms of task parallelism. Hence, a well-rounded parallel programmer needs to be comfortable with both programming models. And a general programming framework (such as OpenCL) must support both.

Regardless of the programming model, the next step in the parallel programming process is to map the program onto real hardware. This is where heterogeneous computers present unique problems. The

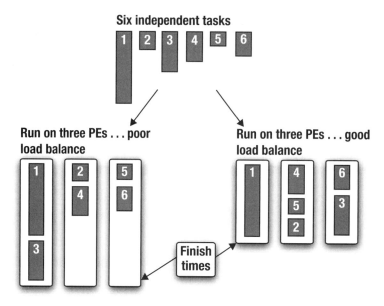

Six independent tasks

Run on three PEs . . . poor load balance

Run on three PEs . . . good load balance

Finish times

Figure 1.5   Task parallelism showing two ways of mapping six independent tasks onto three PEs. A computation is not done until every task is complete, so the goal should be a well-balanced load, that is, to have the time spent computing by each PE be the same.

computational elements in the system may have different instruction sets and different memory architectures and may run at different speeds. An effective program must understand these differences and appropriately map the parallel software onto the most suitable OpenCL devices.

Traditionally, programmers have dealt with this problem by thinking of their software as a set of modules implementing distinct portions of their problem. The modules are explicitly tied to the components in the heterogeneous platform. For example, graphics software runs on the GPU. Other software runs on the CPU.

General-purpose GPU (GPGPU) programming broke this model. Algorithms outside of graphics were modified to fit onto the GPU. The CPU sets up the computation and manages I/O, but all the "interesting" computation is offloaded to the GPU. In essence, the heterogeneous platform is ignored and the focus is placed on one component in the system: the GPU.

OpenCL discourages this approach. In essence, a user "pays for all the OpenCL devices" in a system, so an effective program should use them all. This is exactly what OpenCL encourages a programmer to do and what you would expect from a programming environment designed for heterogeneous platforms.

Hardware heterogeneity is complicated. Programmers have come to depend on high-level abstractions that hide the complexity of the hardware. A heterogeneous programming language exposes heterogeneity and is counter to the trend toward increasing abstraction.

And this is OK. One language doesn't have to address the needs of every community of programmers. High-level frameworks that simplify the programming problem map onto high-level languages, which in turn map to a low-level hardware abstraction layer for portability. OpenCL is that hardware abstraction layer.

Conceptual Foundations of OpenCL

As we will see later in this book, OpenCL supports a wide range of applications. Making sweeping generalizations about these applications is difficult. In every case, however, an application for a heterogeneous platform must carry out the following steps:

1. Discover the components that make up the heterogeneous system.

2. Probe the characteristics of these components so that the software can adapt to the specific features of different hardware elements.

3. Create the blocks of instructions (kernels) that will run on the platform.

4. Set up and manipulate memory objects involved in the computation.

5. Execute the kernels in the right order and on the right components of the system.

6. Collect the final results.

These steps are accomplished through a series of APIs inside OpenCL plus a programming environment for the kernels. We will explain how all this works with a "divide and conquer" strategy. We will break the problem down into the following models:

- **Platform model:** a high-level description of the heterogeneous system

- **Execution model:** an abstract representation of how streams of instructions execute on the heterogeneous platform

- **Memory model:** the collection of memory regions within OpenCL and how they interact during an OpenCL computation

- **Programming models:** the high-level abstractions a programmer uses when designing algorithms to implement an application

Platform Model

The OpenCL platform model defines a high-level representation of any heterogeneous platform used with OpenCL. This model is shown in Figure 1.6. An OpenCL platform always includes a single **host**. The host interacts with the environment external to the OpenCL program, including I/O or interaction with a program's user.

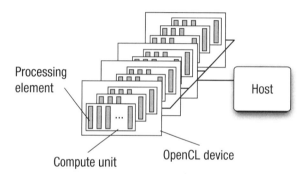

Figure 1.6   The OpenCL platform model with one host and one or more OpenCL devices. Each OpenCL device has one or more compute units, each of which has one or more processing elements.

The host is connected to one or more **OpenCL devices**. The device is where the streams of instructions (or kernels) execute; thus an OpenCL device is often referred to as a **compute device**. A device can be a CPU, a GPU, a DSP, or any other processor provided by the hardware and supported by the OpenCL vendor.

The OpenCL devices are further divided into **compute units** which are further divided into one or more **processing elements** (PEs). Computations on a device occur within the PEs. Later, when we talk about workgroups and the OpenCL memory model, the reason for dividing an OpenCL device into processing elements and compute units will be clear.

Execution Model

An OpenCL application consists of two distinct parts: the **host program** and a collection of one or more **kernels**. The host program runs on the host. OpenCL does not define the details of how the host program works, only how it interacts with objects defined within OpenCL.

The kernels execute on the OpenCL devices. They do the real work of an OpenCL application. Kernels are typically simple functions that transform input memory objects into output memory objects. OpenCL defines two types of kernels:

- **OpenCL kernels**: functions written with the OpenCL C programming language and compiled with the OpenCL compiler. All OpenCL implementations must support OpenCL kernels.

- **Native kernels**: functions created outside of OpenCL and accessed within OpenCL through a function pointer. These functions could be, for example, functions defined in the host source code or exported from a specialized library. Note that the ability to execute native kernels is an optional functionality within OpenCL and the semantics of native kernels are implementation-defined.

The OpenCL execution model defines how the kernels execute. To explain this in detail, we break the discussion down into several parts. First we explain how an individual kernel runs on an OpenCL device. Because the whole point of writing an OpenCL application is to execute kernels, this concept is the cornerstone of understanding OpenCL. Then we describe how the host defines the context for kernel execution and how the kernels are enqueued for execution.

How a Kernel Executes on an OpenCL Device

A kernel is defined on the host. The host program issues a command that submits the kernel for execution on an OpenCL device. When this command is issued by the host, the OpenCL runtime system creates an integer index space. An instance of the kernel executes for each point in this index space. We call each instance of an executing kernel a **work-item**, which is identified by its coordinates in the index space. These coordinates are the global ID for the work-item.

The command that submits a kernel for execution, therefore, creates a collection of work-items, each of which uses the same sequence of instructions defined by a single kernel. While the sequence of instructions is the same, the behavior of each work-item can vary because of branch statements within the code or data selected through the global ID.

Work-items are organized into **work-groups**. The work-groups provide a more coarse-grained decomposition of the index space and exactly span the global index space. In other words, work-groups are the same size in corresponding dimensions, and this size evenly divides the global size in each dimension. Work-groups are assigned a unique ID with the same dimensionality as the index space used for the work-items. Work-items are assigned a unique local ID within a work-group so that a single work-item can be uniquely identified by its global ID or by a combination of its local ID and work-group ID.

The work-items in a given work-group execute concurrently on the processing elements of a single compute unit. This is a critical point in understanding the concurrency in OpenCL. An implementation may serialize the execution of kernels. It may even serialize the execution of work-groups in a single kernel invocation. OpenCL only assures that the work-items within a work-group execute concurrently (and share processor resources on the device). Hence, you can never assume that work-groups or kernel invocations execute concurrently. They indeed often do execute concurrently, but the algorithm designer cannot depend on this.

The index space spans an N-dimensioned range of values and thus is called an **NDRange**. Currently, N in this N-dimensional index space can be 1, 2, or 3. Inside an OpenCL program, an NDRange is defined by an integer array of length N specifying the size of the index space in each dimension. Each work-item's global and local ID is an N-dimensional tuple. In the simplest case, the global ID components are values in the range from zero to the number of elements in that dimension minus one.

Work-groups are assigned IDs using a similar approach to that used for work-items. An array of length N defines the number of work-groups in each dimension. Work-items are assigned to a work-group and given a local ID with components in the range from zero to the size of the work-group in that dimension minus one. Hence, the combination of a work-group ID and the local ID within a work-group uniquely defines a work-item.

Let's carefully work through the different indices implied by this model and explore how they are all related. Consider a 2D NDRange. We use the lowercase letter g for the global ID of a work-item in each dimension given by a subscript x or y. An uppercase letter G indicates the size of the index space in each dimension. Hence, each work-item has a coordinate (g_x, g_y) in a global NDRange index space of size (G_x, G_y) and takes on the values $[0 .. (G_x - 1), 0 .. (G_y - 1)]$.

We divide the NDRange index space into work-groups. Following the conventions just described, we'll use a lowercase w for the work-group ID and an uppercase W for the number of work-groups in each dimension. The dimensions are once again labeled by subscripts x and y.

OpenCL requires that the number of work-groups in each dimension evenly divide the size of the NDRange index space in each dimension. This way all work-groups are full and the same size. This size in each direction (x and y in our 2D example) is used to define a local index space for each work-item. We will refer to this index space inside a work-group as the **local index space**. Following our conventions on the use of upper-case and lowercase letters, the size of our local index space in each dimension (x and y) is indicated with an uppercase L and the local ID inside a work-group uses a lowercase l.

Hence, our NDRange index space of size G_x by G_y is divided into work-groups indexed over a W_x-by-W_y space with indices (w_x, w_y). Each work-group is of size L_x by L_y where we get the following:

$$L_x = G_x/W_x$$

$$L_y = G_y/W_y$$

We can define a work-item by its global ID (g_x, g_y) or by the combination of its local ID (l_x, l_y) and work-group ID (w_x, w_y):

$$g_x = w_x * L_x + l_x$$

$$g_y = w_y * L_y + l_y$$

Alternatively we can work backward from g_x and g_y to recover the local ID and work-group ID as follows:

$$w_x = g_x/L_x$$

$$w_y = g_y/L_y$$

$$l_x = g_x \% L_x$$

$$l_y = g_y \% L_y$$

In these equations we used integer division (division with truncation) and the modulus or "integer remainder" operation (%).

In all of these equations, we have assumed that the index space starts with a zero in each dimension. Indices, however, are often selected to match those that are natural for the original problem. Hence, in OpenCL 1.1 an option was added to define an offset for the starting point of the global index space. The offset is defined for each dimension (x, y in our example), and because it modifies a global index we'll use a lowercase o for the offset. So for non-zero offset (o_x, o_y) our final equation connecting global and local indices is

$$g_x = w_x * L_x + l_x + o_x$$

$$g_y = w_y * L_y + l_y + o_y$$

In Figure 1.7 we provide a concrete example where each small square is a work-item. For this example, we use the default offset of zero in each dimension. Study this figure and make sure that you understand that the shaded square with global index (6, 5) falls in the work-group with ID (1, 1) and local index (2, 1).

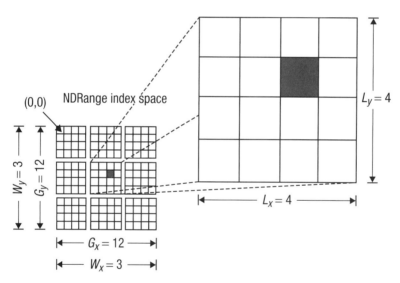

Figure 1.7   An example of how the global IDs, local IDs, and work-group indices are related for a two-dimensional NDRange. Other parameters of the index space are defined in the figure. The shaded block has a global ID of (g_x, g_y) = (6, 5) and a work-group plus local ID of (w_x, w_y) = (1, 1) and (l_x, l_y) =(2, 1).

If all of these index manipulations seem confusing, don't worry. In many cases OpenCL programmers just work in the global index space. Over time, as you work with OpenCL and gain experience working with the different types of indices, these sorts of manipulations will become second nature to you.

The OpenCL execution model is quite flexible. This model supports a wide range of programming models. In designing OpenCL, however, only two models were explicitly considered: data parallelism and task parallelism. We will return to these models and their implications for OpenCL later. But first, we need to complete our tour of the OpenCL execution model.

Context

The computational work of an OpenCL application takes place on the OpenCL devices. The host, however, plays a very important role in the OpenCL application. It is on the host where the kernels are defined. The host establishes the context for the kernels. The host defines the NDRange and the queues that control the details of how and when the kernels execute. All of these important functions are contained in the APIs within OpenCL's definition.

The first task for the host is to define the context for the OpenCL application. As the name implies, the context defines the environment within which the kernels are defined and execute. To be more precise, we define the context in terms of the following resources:

- **Devices:** the collection of OpenCL devices to be used by the host
- **Kernels:** the OpenCL functions that run on OpenCL devices
- **Program objects:** the program source code and executables that implement the kernels
- **Memory objects:** a set of objects in memory that are visible to OpenCL devices and contain values that can be operated on by instances of a kernel

The context is created and manipulated by the host using functions from the OpenCL API. For example, consider the heterogeneous platform from Figure 1.3. This system has two multicore CPUs and a GPU. The host program is running on one of the CPUs. The host program will query the system to discover these resources and then decide which devices to use in the OpenCL application. Depending on the problem and the kernels to be run, the host may choose the GPU, the other CPU, other cores on the same CPU, or any combination of these. Once made, this choice defines the OpenCL devices within the current context.

Also included in the context are one or more **program objects** that contain the code for the kernels. The choice of the name *program object* is a bit confusing. It is better to think of these as a dynamic library from which the functions used by the kernels are pulled. The program object is built at runtime within the host program. This might seem strange to programmers from outside the graphics community. Consider for a moment the challenge faced by an OpenCL programmer. He or she writes the OpenCL application and passes it to the end user, but that user could choose to run the application anywhere. The application programmer has no control over which GPUs or CPUs or other chips the end user may run the application on. All the OpenCL programmer knows is that the target platform will be conformant to the OpenCL specification.

The solution to this problem is for the program object to be built from source at runtime. The host program defines the devices within the context. Only at that point is it possible to know how to compile the program source code to create the code for the kernels. As for the source code itself, OpenCL is quite flexible about the form. In many cases, it is a regular string either statically defined in the host program, loaded from a file at runtime, or dynamically generated inside the host program.

Our context now includes OpenCL devices and a program object from which the kernels are pulled for execution. Next we consider how the kernels interact with memory. The detailed memory model used by OpenCL will be described later. For the sake of our discussion of the context, we need to understand how the OpenCL memory works only at a high level. The crux of the matter is that on a heterogeneous platform, there are often multiple address spaces to manage. The host has the familiar address space expected on a CPU platform, but the devices may have a range of different memory architectures. To deal with this situation, OpenCL introduces the idea of memory objects. These are explicitly defined on the host and explicitly moved between the host and the OpenCL devices. This does put an extra burden on the programmer, but it lets us support a much wider range of platforms.

We now understand the context within an OpenCL application. The context is the OpenCL devices, program objects, kernels, and memory objects that a kernel uses when it executes. Now we can move on to how the host program issues commands to the OpenCL devices.

Command-Queues

The interaction between the host and the OpenCL devices occurs through commands posted by the host to the **command-queue**. These commands wait in the command-queue until they execute on the OpenCL device. A command-queue is created by the host and attached to a single OpenCL device after the context has been defined. The host places commands into the command-queue, and the commands are then scheduled for execution on the associated device. OpenCL supports three types of commands:

- **Kernel execution commands** execute a kernel on the processing elements of an OpenCL device.

- **Memory commands** transfer data between the host and different memory objects, move data between memory objects, or map and unmap memory objects from the host address space.

- **Synchronization commands** put constraints on the order in which commands execute.

In a typical host program, the programmer defines the context and the command-queues, defines memory and program objects, and builds any data structures needed on the host to support the application. Then the focus shifts to the command-queue. Memory objects are moved from the host onto the devices; kernel arguments are attached to memory objects and then submitted to the command-queue for execution. When the kernel has completed its work, memory objects produced in the computation may be copied back onto the host.

When multiple kernels are submitted to the queue, they may need to interact. For example, one set of kernels may generate memory objects that a following set of kernels needs to manipulate. In this case, synchronization commands can be used to force the first set of kernels to complete before the following set begins.

There are many additional subtleties associated with how the commands work in OpenCL. We will leave those details for later in the book. Our goal now is just to understand the command-queues and hence gain a high-level understanding of OpenCL commands.

So far, we have said very little about the order in which commands execute or how their execution relates to the execution of the host program. The commands always execute asynchronously to the host program. The host program submits commands to the command-queue and then continues without waiting for commands to finish. If it is necessary for the host to wait on a command, this can be explicitly established with a synchronization command.

Commands within a single queue execute relative to each other in one of two modes:

- **In-order execution**: Commands are launched in the order in which they appear in the command-queue and complete in order. In other words, a prior command on the queue completes before the following command begins. This serializes the execution order of commands in a queue.

- **Out-of-order execution**: Commands are issued in order but do not wait to complete before the following commands execute. Any order constraints are enforced by the programmer through explicit synchronization mechanisms.

All OpenCL platforms support the in-order mode, but the out-of-order mode is optional. Why would you want to use the out-of-order mode? Consider Figure 1.5, where we introduced the concept of load balancing. An application is not done until all of the kernels complete. Hence, for an efficient program that minimizes the runtime, you want all compute units to be fully engaged and to run for approximately the same amount of time. You can often do this by carefully thinking about the order in which you submit commands to the queues so that the in-order execution achieves a well-balanced load. But when you have a set of commands that take different amounts of time to execute, balancing the load so that all compute units stay fully engaged and finish at the same time can be difficult. An out-of-order queue can take care of this for you. Commands can execute in any order, so if a compute unit finishes its work early, it can immediately fetch a new command from the command-queue and start executing a new kernel. This is called **automatic load balancing**, and it is a well-known technique used in the design of parallel algorithms driven by command-queues (see the Master-Worker pattern in T. G. Mattson et al., *Patterns for Parallel Programming*[5]).

Anytime you have multiple executions occurring inside an application, the potential for disaster exists. Data may be accidentally used before it has been written, or kernels may execute in an order that leads to wrong answers. The programmer needs some way to manage any constraints on the commands. We've hinted at one, a synchronization command to tell a set of kernels to wait until an earlier set finishes. This is often quite effective, but there are times when more sophisticated synchronization protocols are needed.

To support custom synchronization protocols, commands submitted to the command-queue generate event objects. A command can be told to wait until certain conditions on the event objects exist. These events can also be used to coordinate execution between the host and the OpenCL devices. We'll say more about these events later.

---

[5] T. G. Mattson, B. A. Sanders, and B. L. Massingill, *Patterns for Parallel Programming*, Design Patterns series (Addison-Wesley, 2004).

Finally, it is possible to associate multiple queues with a single context for any of the OpenCL devices within that context. These two queues run concurrently and independently with no explicit mechanisms within OpenCL to synchronize between them.

Memory Model

The execution model tells us how the kernels execute, how they interact with the host, and how they interact with other kernels. To describe this model and the associated command-queue, we made a brief mention of memory objects. We did not, however, define the details of these objects, neither the types of memory objects nor the rules for how to safely use them. These issues are covered by the OpenCL memory model.

OpenCL defines two types of memory objects: **buffer objects** and **image objects**. A buffer object, as the name implies, is just a contiguous block of memory made available to the kernels. A programmer can map data structures onto this buffer and access the buffer through pointers. This provides flexibility to define just about any data structure the programmer wishes (subject to limitations of the OpenCL kernel programming language).

Image objects, on the other hand, are restricted to holding images. An image storage format may be optimized to the needs of a specific OpenCL device. Therefore, it is important that OpenCL give an implementation the freedom to customize the image format. The image memory object, therefore, is an opaque object. The OpenCL framework provides functions to manipulate images, but other than these specific functions, the contents of an image object are hidden from the kernel program.

OpenCL also allows a programmer to specify subregions of memory objects as distinct memory objects (added with the OpenCL 1.1 specification). This makes a subregion of a large memory object a first-class object in OpenCL that can be manipulated and coordinated through the command-queue.

Understanding the memory objects themselves is just a first step. We also need to understand the specific abstractions that govern their use in an OpenCL program. The OpenCL memory model defines five distinct memory regions:

- **Host memory**: This memory region is visible only to the host. As with most details concerning the host, OpenCL defines only how the host memory interacts with OpenCL objects and constructs.

- **Global memory**: This memory region permits read/write access to all work-items in all work-groups. Work-items can read from or write to any element of a memory object in global memory. Reads and writes to global memory may be cached depending on the capabilities of the device.

- **Constant memory**: This memory region of global memory remains constant during the execution of a kernel. The host allocates and initializes memory objects placed into constant memory. Work-items have read-only access to these objects.

- **Local memory**: This memory region is local to a work-group. This memory region can be used to allocate variables that are shared by all work-items in that work-group. It may be implemented as dedicated regions of memory on the OpenCL device. Alternatively, the local memory region may be mapped onto sections of the global memory.

- **Private memory**: This region of memory is private to a work-item. Variables defined in one work-item's private memory are not visible to other work-items.

The memory regions and how they relate to the platform and execution models are described in Figure 1.8. The work-items run on PEs and have their own private memory. A work-group runs on a compute unit and shares a local memory region with the work-items in the group. The OpenCL device memory works with the host to support global memory.

The host and OpenCL device memory models are, for the most part, independent of each other. This is by necessity, given that the host is defined outside of OpenCL. They do, however, at times need to interact. This interaction occurs in one of two ways: by explicitly **copying** data or by **mapping** and **unmapping** regions of a memory object.

To copy data explicitly, the host enqueues commands to transfer data between the memory object and host memory. These memory transfer commands may be blocking or non-blocking. The OpenCL function call for a blocking memory transfer returns once the associated memory resources on the host can be safely reused. For a non-blocking memory transfer, the OpenCL function call returns as soon as the command is enqueued regardless of whether host memory is safe to use.

The mapping/unmapping method of interaction between the host and OpenCL memory objects allows the host to map a region from the memory object into its own address space. The memory map command (which is enqueued on the command-queue like any other OpenCL command)

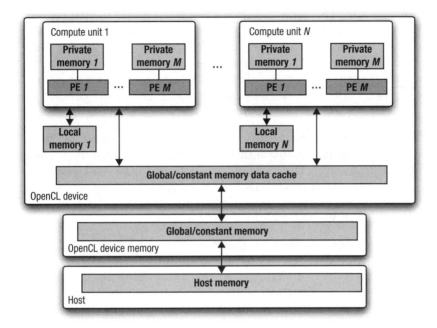

Figure 1.8   A summary of the memory model in OpenCL and how the different memory regions interact with the platform model

may be blocking or non-blocking. Once a region from the memory object has been mapped, the host can read or write to this region. The host unmaps the region when accesses (reads and/or writes) to this mapped region by the host are complete.

When concurrent execution is involved, however, the memory model needs to carefully define how memory objects interact in time with the kernel and host. This is the problem of **memory consistency**. It is not enough to say where the memory values will go. You also must define when these values are visible across the platform.

Once again, OpenCL doesn't stipulate the memory consistency model on the host. Let's start with the memory farthest from the host (private memory region) and work toward the host. Private memory is not visible to the host. It is visible only to an individual work-item. This memory follows the load/store memory model familiar to sequential programming. In other words, the loads and stores into private memory cannot be reordered to appear in any order other than that defined in the program text.

For the local memory, the values seen by a set of work-items within a work-group are guaranteed to be consistent at work-group synchronization points. For example, a work-group barrier requires that all loads and stores defined before the barrier complete before any work-items in the group proceed past the barrier. In other words, the barrier marks a point in the execution of the set of work-items where the memory is guaranteed to be in a consistent and known state before the execution continues.

Because local memory is shared only within a work-group, this is sufficient to define the memory consistency for local memory regions. For the work-items within a group, the global memory is also made consistent at a work-group barrier. Even though this memory is shared between work-groups, however, there is no way to enforce consistency of global memory between the different work-groups executing a kernel.

For the memory objects, OpenCL defines a relaxed consistency model. In other words, the values seen in memory by an individual work-item are not guaranteed to be consistent across the full set of work-items at all times. At any given moment, the loads and stores into OpenCL memory objects may appear to occur in a different order for different work-items. This is called a **relaxed consistency** model because it is less strict than the load/store model one would expect if the concurrent execution were to exactly match the order from a serial execution.

The last step is to define the consistency of memory objects relative to the commands on the command-queue. In this case, we use a modified version of release consistency. When all the work-items associated with a kernel complete, loads and stores for the memory objects released by this kernel are completed before the kernel command is signaled as finished. For the in-order queue, this is sufficient to define the memory consistency between kernels. For an out-of-order queue there are two options (called **synchronization points**). The first is for consistency to be forced at specific synchronization points such as a command-queue barrier. The other option is for consistency to be explicitly managed through the event mechanisms we'll describe later. These same options are used to enforce consistency between the host and the OpenCL devices; that is, memory is consistent only at synchronization points on the command-queue.

Programming Models

The OpenCL execution model defines how an OpenCL application maps onto processing elements, memory regions, and the host. It is a "hardware-centric" model. We now shift gears and describe how we map parallel algorithms onto OpenCL using a programming model. Programming models are intimately connected to how programmers reason about their algorithms. Hence, the nature of these models is more flexible than that of the precisely defined execution model.

OpenCL was defined with two different programming models in mind: task parallelism and data parallelism. As you will see, you can even think in terms of a hybrid model: tasks that contain data parallelism. Programmers are very creative, and we can expect over time that additional programming models will be created that will map onto OpenCL's basic execution model.

Data-Parallel Programming Model

We described the basic idea of a data-parallel programming model earlier (see Figure 1.4). Problems well suited to the data-parallel programming model are organized around data structures, the elements of which can be updated concurrently. In essence, a single logical sequence of instructions is applied concurrently to the elements of the data structure. The structure of the parallel algorithm is designed as a sequence of concurrent updates to the data structures within a problem.

This programming model is a natural fit with OpenCL's execution model. The key is the NDRange defined when a kernel is launched. The algorithm designer aligns the data structures in his or her problem with the NDRange index space and maps them onto OpenCL memory objects. The kernel defines the sequence of instructions to be applied concurrently as the work-items in an OpenCL computation.

In more complicated data-parallel problems, the work-items in a single work-group may need to share data. This is supported through data stored in the local memory region. Anytime dependencies are introduced between work-items, care must be taken that regardless of the order in which the work-items complete, the same results are produced. In other words, the work-items may need to synchronize their execution. Work-items in a single work-group can participate in a **work-group barrier**. As we stated earlier, all the work-items within a work-group must execute the barrier before any are allowed to continue execution beyond the barrier. Note that the work-group barrier must be encountered by all work-items of a work-group executing the kernel or by none at all.

OpenCL 1.1 doesn't provide any mechanism for synchronization between work-items from different work-groups while executing a kernel. This is an important limitation for programmers to keep in mind when designing parallel algorithms.

As an example of when work-items need to share information, consider a set of work-items participating in some sort of reduction. A reduction is when a collection of data elements is reduced to a single element by some type of associative operation. The most common examples are summation or finding extreme values (max or min) of a set of data elements. In a reduction, the work-items carry out a computation to produce the data elements that will be reduced. This must complete on all work-items before a subset of the work-items (often a subset of size one) does the accumulation for all the work-items.

OpenCL provides hierarchical data parallelism: data parallelism from work-items within a work-group plus data parallelism at the level of work-groups. The OpenCL specification discusses two variants of this form of data parallelism. In the **explicit model**, the programmer takes responsibility for explicitly defining the sizes of the work-groups. With the second model, the **implicit model**, the programmer just defines the NDRange space and leaves it to the system to choose the work-groups.

If the kernel doesn't contain any branch statements, each work-item will execute identical operations but on a subset of data items selected by its global ID. This case defines an important subset of the data-parallel model known as **Single Instruction Multiple Data** or SIMD. Branch statements within a kernel, however, can lead each work-item to execute very different operations. While each work-item is using the same "program" (i.e., the kernel), the actual work it accomplishes can be quite different. This is often known as a **Single Program Multiple Data** or SPMD model (see the SPMD pattern in Mattson's *Patterns for Parallel Programming*).

OpenCL supports both SIMD and SPMD models. On platforms with restricted bandwidth to instruction memory or if the processing elements map onto a vector unit, the SIMD model can be dramatically more efficient. Hence, it is valuable for a programmer to understand both models and know when to use one or the other.

There is one case when an OpenCL program is strictly SIMD: the vector instructions defined in Chapter 4, "Programming with OpenCL C." These instructions let you explicitly issue instructions for vector units attached to a processing element. For example, the following instructions come from a numerical integration program (the integrand is $4.0/(1 + x^2)$). In this program, we unroll the integration loop eightfold and compute eight steps in the integration at once using the native vector instructions on the target platform.

```
float8 x, psum_vec;
float8 ramp= (float8)(0.5, 1.5, 2.5, 3.5,
                      4.5, 5.5, 6.5, 7.5};
float8 four= (float8)(4.0);  // fill with 8 4's
float8 one = (float8)(1.0);  // fill with 8 1's
float  step_number; // step number from loop index
float  step_size;   // Input integration step size

. . . and later inside a loop body . . .

   x = ((float8)step_number +ramp)*step_size;
   psum_vec+=four/(one + x*x);
```

Given the wide range of vector instruction sets on the market, having a portable notation for explicit vector instructions is an extremely convenient feature within OpenCL.

In closing, data parallelism is a natural fit to the OpenCL execution model items. The model is hierarchical because a data-parallel computation (the work-items) may include vector instructions (SIMD) and be part of larger block-level data parallelism (work-groups). All of these work together to create a rich environment for expressing data-parallel algorithms.

Task-Parallel Programming Model

The OpenCL execution model was clearly designed with data parallelism as a primary target. But the model also supports a rich array of task-parallel algorithms.

OpenCL defines a task as a kernel that executes as a single work-item regardless of the NDRange used by other kernels in the OpenCL application. This is used when the concurrency a programmer wishes to exploit is internal to the task. For example, the parallelism may be expressed solely in terms of vector operations over vector types. Or perhaps the task uses a kernel defined with the native kernel interface and the parallelism is expressed using a programming environment outside of OpenCL.

A second version of task parallelism appears when kernels are submitted as tasks that execute at the same time with an out-of-order queue. For example, consider the collection of independent tasks represented schematically in Figure 1.5. On a quad-core CPU, one core could be the host and the other three cores configured as compute units within an OpenCL device. The OpenCL application could enqueue all six tasks and leave it to the compute units to dynamically schedule the work. When the number of tasks is much greater than the number of compute units, this strategy can be a very effective way to produce a well-balanced load. This style of task parallelism, however, will not work on all OpenCL platforms because the out-of-order mode for a command-queue is an optional feature in OpenCL 1.1.

A third version of task parallelism occurs when the tasks are connected into a task graph using OpenCL's event model. Commands submitted to an event queue may optionally generate events. Subsequent commands can wait for these events before executing. When combined with a command-queue that supports the out-of-order execution model, this lets the OpenCL programmer define static task graphs in OpenCL, with the nodes in the graph being tasks and the edges dependencies between the nodes (managed by events). We will discuss this topic in great detail in Chapter 9, "Events."

Parallel Algorithm Limitations

The OpenCL framework defines a powerful foundation for data-parallel and task-parallel programming models. A wide range of parallel algorithms can map onto these models, but there are restrictions. Because of the wide range of devices that OpenCL supports, there are limitations to the OpenCL execution model. In other words, the extreme portability of OpenCL comes at a cost of generality in the algorithms we can support.

The crux of the matter comes down to the assumptions made in the execution model. When we submit a command to execute a kernel, we can only assume that the work-items in a group will execute concurrently. The implementation is free to run individual work-groups in any order—including serially (i.e., one after the other). This is also the case for kernel executions. Even when the out-of-order queue mode is enabled, a conforming implementation is free to serialize the execution of the kernels.

These constraints on how concurrency is expressed in OpenCL limit the way data can be shared between work-groups and between kernels. There are two cases you need to understand. First, consider the collection of work-groups associated with a single kernel execution. A conforming implementation of OpenCL can order these any way it chooses. Hence, we cannot safely construct algorithms that depend on the details of how data is shared between the work-groups servicing a single kernel execution.

Second, consider the order of execution for multiple kernels. They are submitted for execution in the order in which they are enqueued, but they execute serially (in-order command-queue mode) or concurrently (out-of-order command-queue mode). However, even with the out-of-order queue an implementation is free to execute kernels in serial order. Hence, early kernels waiting on events from later kernels can deadlock. Furthermore, the task graphs associated with an algorithm can only have edges that are unidirectional and point from nodes enqueued earlier in the command-queue to kernels enqueued later in the command-queue.

These are serious limitations. They mean that there are parallel design patterns that just can't be expressed in OpenCL. Over time, however, as hardware evolves and, in particular, GPUs continue to add features to support more general-purpose computing, we will fix these limitations in future releases of OpenCL. For now, we just have to live with them.

Other Programming Models

A programmer is free to combine OpenCL's programming models to create a range of hybrid programming models. We've already mentioned the case where the work-items in a data-parallel algorithm contain SIMD parallelism through the vector instructions.

As OpenCL implementations mature, however, and the out-of-order mode on command-queues becomes the norm, we can imagine static task graphs where each node is a data-parallel algorithm (multiple work-items) that includes SIMD vector instructions.

OpenCL exposes the hardware through a portable platform model and a powerful execution model. These work together to define a flexible hardware abstraction layer. Computer scientists are free to layer other programming models on top of the OpenCL hardware abstraction layer. OpenCL is young and we can't cite any concrete examples of programming models from outside OpenCL's specification running on OpenCL platforms. But stay tuned and watch the literature. It's only a matter of time until this happens.

OpenCL and Graphics

OpenCL was created as a response to GPGPU programming. People had GPUs for graphics and started using them for the non-graphics parts of their workloads. And with that trend, heterogeneous computing (which has been around for a very long time) collided with graphics, and the need for an industry standard emerged.

OpenCL has stayed close to its graphics roots. OpenCL is part of the Khronos family of standards, which includes the graphics standards OpenGL (www.khronos.org/opengl/) and OpenGL ES (www.khronos.org/opengles/). Given the importance of the operating systems from Microsoft, OpenCL also closely tracks developments in DirectX (www.gamesforwindows.com/en-US/directx/).

To start our discussion of OpenCL and graphics we return to the image memory objects we mentioned earlier. Image memory objects are one-, two-, or three-dimensional objects that hold textures, frame buffers, or images. An implementation is free to support a range of image formats, but at a minimum, it must support the standard RGBA format. The image objects are manipulated using a set of functions defined within OpenCL. OpenCL also defines sampler objects so that programmers can sample and filter images. These features are integrated into the core set of image manipulation functions in the OpenCL APIs.

Once images have been created, they must pass to the graphics pipeline to be rendered. Hence including an interface to the standard graphics APIs would be useful within OpenCL. Not every vendor working on OpenCL, however, is interested in these graphics standards. Therefore, rather than include this in the core OpenCL specification, we define these as a number of optional extensions in the appendices to the OpenCL standard. These extensions include the following functionalities:

- Creating an OpenCL context from an OpenGL context

- Sharing memory objects between OpenCL, OpenGL, and OpenGL ES

- Creating OpenCL event objects from OpenGL sync objects

- Sharing memory objects with Direct3D version 10

These will be discussed later in the book.

The Contents of OpenCL

So far we have focused on the ideas behind OpenCL. Now we shift gears and talk about how these ideas are supported within the OpenCL framework. The OpenCL framework is divided into the following components:

- **OpenCL platform API**: The platform API defines functions used by the host program to discover OpenCL devices and their capabilities as well as to create the context for the OpenCL application.

- **OpenCL runtime API**: This API manipulates the context to create command-queues and other operations that occur at runtime. For example, the functions to submit commands to the command-queue come from the OpenCL runtime API.

- **The OpenCL programming language**: This is the programming language used to write the code for kernels. It is based on an extended subset of the ISO C99 standard and hence is often referred to as the OpenCL C programming language.

In the next few subsections we will provide a high-level overview of each of these components. Details will be left for later in the book, but it will be helpful as you start working with OpenCL to understand what's happening at a high level.

Platform API

The term *platform* has a very specific meaning in OpenCL. It refers to a particular combination of the host, the OpenCL devices, and the OpenCL framework. Multiple OpenCL platforms can exist on a single heterogeneous computer at one time. For example, the CPU vendor and the GPU vendor may define their own OpenCL frameworks on a single system. Programmers need a way to query the system about the available OpenCL frameworks. They need to find out which OpenCL devices are available and what their characteristics are. And they need to control which subset of these frameworks and devices will constitute the platform used in any given OpenCL application.

This functionality is addressed by the functions within OpenCL's platform API. As you will see in later chapters when we focus on the code OpenCL programmers write for the host program, every OpenCL application opens in a similar way, calling functions from the platform API to ultimately define the context for the OpenCL computation.

Runtime API

The functions in the platform API ultimately define the context for an OpenCL application. The runtime API focuses on functions that use this context to service the needs of an application. This is a large and admittedly complex collection of functions.

The first job of the runtime API is to set up the command-queues. You can attach a command-queue to a single device, but multiple command-queues can be active at one time within a single context.

With the command-queues in place, the runtime API is used to define memory objects and any objects required to manipulate them (such as sampler objects for image objects). Managing memory objects is an important task. To support garbage collection, OpenCL keeps track of how many instances of kernels use these objects (i.e., retain a memory object) and when kernels are finished with a memory object (i.e., release a memory object).

Another task managed by the runtime API is to create the program objects used to build the dynamic libraries from which kernels are defined. The program objects, the compiler to compile them, and the definition of the kernels are all handled in the runtime layer.

Finally, the commands that interact with the command-queue are all issued by functions from the runtime layer. Synchronization points for managing data sharing and to enforce constraints on the execution of kernels are also handled by the runtime API.

As you can see, functions from the runtime API do most of the heavy lifting for the host program. To attempt to master the runtime API in one stretch, starting from the beginning and working through all the functions, is overwhelming. We have found that it is much better to use a pragmatic approach. Master the functions you actually use. Over time you will cover and hence master them all, but you will learn them in blocks driven by the specific needs of an OpenCL application.

Kernel Programming Language

The host program is very important, but it is the kernels that do the real work in OpenCL. Some OpenCL implementations let you interface to native kernels written outside of OpenCL, but in most cases you will need to write kernels to carry out the specific work in your application.

The kernel programming language in OpenCL is called the OpenCL C programming language because we anticipate over time that we may choose to define other languages within the specification. It is derived from the ISO C99 language.

In OpenCL, we take great care to support portability. This forces us to standardize around the least common dominator between classes of OpenCL devices. Because there are features in C99 that only CPUs can support, we had to leave out some of the language features in C99 when we defined the OpenCL C programming language. The major language features we *deleted* include

- Recursive functions

- Pointers to functions

- Bit fields

In addition, we cannot support the full set of standard libraries. The list of standard headers not allowed in the OpenCL programming language is long, but the ones programmers will probably miss the most are `stdio.h` and `stdlib.h`. Once again, these libraries are hard to support once you move away from a general-purpose processor as the OpenCL device.

Other restrictions arise from the need to maintain fidelity to OpenCL's core abstractions. For example, OpenCL defines a range of memory address spaces. A union or structure cannot mix these types. Also, there are types defined in OpenCL that are opaque, for example, the memory objects that support images. The OpenCL C programming language prevents one from doing anything with these types other than passing them as arguments to functions.

We restricted the OpenCL C programming language to match the needs of the key OpenCL devices used with OpenCL. This same motivation led us to extend the languages as well as

- Vector types and operations on instances of those types

- Address space qualifiers to support control over the multiple address spaces in OpenCL

- A large set of built-in functions to support functionality commonly needed in OpenCL applications

- Atomic functions for unsigned integer and single-precision scalar variables in global and local memory

Most programming languages ignore the specifics of the floating-point arithmetic system. They import the arithmetic system from the hardware and avoid the topic altogether. Because all major CPUs support the IEEE 754 and 854 standards, this strategy has worked. In essence, by converging around these floating-point standards, the hardware vendors took care of the floating-point definition for the language vendors.

In the heterogeneous world, however, as you move away from the CPU, the support for floating-point arithmetic is more selective. Working closely with the hardware vendors, we wanted to create momentum that would move them over time to complete support for the IEEE floating-point standards. At the same time, we didn't want to be too hard on these vendors, so we gave them flexibility to avoid some of the less used but challenging-to-implement features of the IEEE standards. We will discuss the details later, but at a high level OpenCL requires the following:

- Full support for the IEEE 754 formats. Double precision is optional, but if it is provided, it must follow the IEEE 754 formats as well.

- The default IEEE 754 rounding mode of "round to nearest." The other rounding modes, while highly encouraged (because numerical analysts need them), are optional.

- Rounding modes in OpenCL are set statically, even though the IEEE specifications require dynamic variation of rounding modes.

- The special values of INF (infinity) and NaN (Not a Number) must be supported. The signaling NaN (always a problem in concurrent systems) is not required.

- Denormalized numbers (numbers smaller than one times the largest supported negative exponent) can be flushed to zero. If you don't understand why this is significant, you are in good company. This is another feature that numerical analysts depend on but few programmers understand.

There are a few additional rules pertaining to floating-point exceptions, but they are too detailed for most people and too obscure to bother with at this time. The point is that we tried very hard to require the bulk of IEEE 754 while leaving off some of the features that are more rarely used and difficult to support (on a heterogeneous platform with vector units).

The OpenCL specification didn't stop with the IEEE standards. In the OpenCL specification, there are tables that carefully define the allowed relative errors in math functions. Getting all of these right was an ambitious undertaking, but for the programmers who write detailed numerical code, having these defined is essential.

When you put these floating-point requirements, restrictions, and extensions together, you have a programming language well suited to the capabilities of current heterogeneous platforms. And as the processors used in these platforms evolve and become more general, the OpenCL C programming language will evolve as well.

OpenCL Summary

We have now covered the basic components of the core OpenCL framework. It is important to understand them in isolation (as we have largely presented them). To pull this together to create a complete picture of OpenCL, we provide a summary of the basic workflow of an application as it works through the OpenCL framework, shown in Figure 1.9.

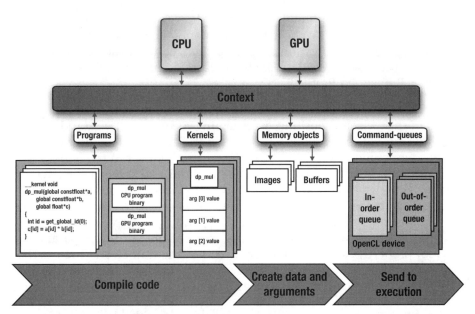

Figure 1.9   This block diagram summarizes the components of OpenCL and the actions that occur on the host during an OpenCL application.

You start with a host program that defines the context. The context in Figure 1.9 contains two OpenCL devices, a CPU and a GPU. Next we define the command-queues. In this case we have two queues, an in-order command-queue for the GPU and an out-of-order command-queue for the CPU. The host program then defines a program object that is compiled to generate kernels for both OpenCL devices (the CPU and the GPU). Next the host program defines any memory objects required by the program and maps them onto the arguments of the kernels. Finally, the host program enqueues commands to the command-queues to execute the kernels.

The Embedded Profile

OpenCL programs address the needs of a tremendous range of hardware platforms. From HPC Servers to laptops to cell phones, OpenCL has a tremendous reach. For most of the standard, this range is not a problem.

For a few features, however, the embedded processors just can't match the requirements in the standard.

We had two choices: take the easy route and leave it to each vendor to decide how to relax the OpenCL specification to meet their needs, or do the hard work ourselves and define exactly how to change OpenCL for embedded processors. We chose the harder approach; that is, we defined how the OpenCL specification should be changed to fit the needs of embedded processors. We describe the embedded profile in Chapter 13, "OpenCL Embedded Profile."

We did not want to create a whole new standard, however. To do so would put us in the awkward position of struggling to keep the two standards from diverging. Hence, the final section of the OpenCL specification defines the "embedded profile," which we describe later in the book. Basically, we relaxed the floating-point standards and some of the larger data types because these are not often required in the embedded market. Some of the image requirements (such as the 3D image format) were also relaxed. Atomic functions are not required, and the relative errors of built-in math functions were relaxed. Finally, some of the minimum parameters for properties of different components of the framework (such as the minimum required size of the private memory region) were reduced to match the tighter memory size constraints used in the embedded market.

As you can see, for the most part, OpenCL for embedded processors is very close to the full OpenCL definition. Most programmers will not even notice these differences.

Learning OpenCL

OpenCL is an industry standard for writing parallel programs to execute on heterogeneous platforms. These platforms are here today and, as we hope we have shown you, will be the dominant architecture for computing into the foreseeable future. Hence, programmers need to understand heterogeneous platforms and become comfortable programming for them.

In this chapter we have provided a conceptual framework to help you understand OpenCL. The platform model defines an abstraction that applies to the full diversity of heterogeneous systems. The execution model within OpenCL describes whole classes of computations and how they map onto the platform model. The framework concludes with programming models and a memory model, which together give the programmer the tools required to reason about how software elements in an OpenCL program interact to produce correct results.

Equipped with this largely theoretical knowledge, you can now start to learn how to use the contents of OpenCL. We begin with the following chapter, where we will write our first OpenCL program.

## Chapter 2

HelloWorld: An OpenCL Example

In order to introduce you to OpenCL, we begin with a simple example program. This chapter demonstrates the code required to set up and execute a kernel on an OpenCL device. The example executes a simple kernel that adds the values stored in two arrays and saves the result in another. This chapter introduces the following concepts:

- Choosing an OpenCL platform and creating a context

- Enumerating devices and creating a command-queue

- Creating and building a program object

- Creating a kernel object and memory objects for kernel arguments

- Executing a kernel and reading its result

- Checking for errors in OpenCL

This chapter will go over the basics of each of these steps. Later in the book, we will fill in the details of each of these steps and further document OpenCL. In addition to these topics, we will also introduce the CMake-based build system used for the sample code in the book. Our purpose here is to get you running your first simple example so that you get an idea of what goes into creating an application with OpenCL.

Downloading the Sample Code

Many chapters in the book include sample code. The sample code can be downloaded from the book's Web site: www.openclprogrammingguide.com/.

Because OpenCL is designed to run on multiple platforms, the sample code was designed with the same goal. The code has been tested on Mac OS X, Linux, and Windows using various implementations of OpenCL. You are free to use the platform and OpenCL implementation that work for you.

Building the Examples

All of the sample code was set up to build using CMake (www.cmake.org), a cross-platform build tool. CMake has the ability to generate build projects for many platforms and development tools including Eclipse, Code::Blocks, Microsoft Visual Studio, Xcode, KDevelop, and plain old UNIX makefiles. Some of these development tools are cross-platform (e.g., Eclipse, Code::Blocks), and some are specific to a particular OS such as Xcode for Mac OS X and Visual Studio for Windows. You are free to use whichever development tool and platform work for you. The only requirement is that you have some implementation of OpenCL on your platform to build and run against. For the purposes of explanation, this section will review how to set up your build environment for a few select platforms and tools. If your platform is not among the ones covered here, you should be able to use these sections as a guide for building in your desired environment.

Prerequisites

Regardless of your platform, you are going to need a copy of CMake. An installable package for Windows, Mac OS X, and various flavors of Linux/UNIX is available on the CMake Web site (www.cmake.org). On Ubuntu Linux, for example, you can also install CMake directly from the package manager using `sudo apt-get install cmake`.

In addition to CMake, you will also need an implementation of OpenCL. As of this writing, we are aware of at least the following implementations:

- **Mac OS X 10.6+:** Starting in Snow Leopard, Mac OS X has shipped with an OpenCL implementation. If you download and install the Xcode development tool, you will have access to the OpenCL headers and libraries.

- **Microsoft Windows:** AMD provides access to OpenCL on Windows through the ATI Stream SDK available from AMD's developer Web site. The ATI Stream SDK contains various OpenCL sample programs along with the required headers and libraries. The OpenCL implementation itself works with the standard ATI Catalyst drivers on supported GPUs. The ATI Stream SDK also provides support for multicore CPUs (from either AMD or Intel). NVIDIA also provides its own OpenCL implementation as part of its GPU Computing SDK, which also contains OpenCL headers and libraries. As of this writing, the NVIDIA implementation provides acceleration only for NVIDIA GPUs (no CPU devices). Intel provides an implementation of OpenCL as well, but currently only for CPUs that support AUX or SSE4.1 (or higher).

- **Linux:** Both AMD and NVIDIA provide their development SDKs on many flavors of Linux, including Ubuntu, RedHat, and openSUSE. Intel's Linux SDK supports SUSE Enterprise Server and Red Hat. These SDKs are similar to their Windows counterparts in that they contain the OpenCL libraries and headers along with various sample programs.

After installing CMake and OpenCL—assuming the necessary compiler tools are present—you should be able to build the sample code from the book. The sample code relies on `FindOpenCL.cmake` to find your OpenCL implementation. For details on this project, visit the `findopencl` page on http://gitorious.org/findopencl. This file is included in the sample source download from the book's Web site.

The sample code for the book is structured into the following directories:

- `/CMakeLists.txt`: the primary CMake input file for a project

- `/cmake/`: contains the `FindOpenCL.cmake` file required for finding an OpenCL implementation

- `/src/Chapter_X`: contains the example programs for each chapter along with the `CMakeLists.txt` files required for building the sample

Mac OS X and Code::Blocks

If you are developing on Mac OS X, you have many choices for development tools including Eclipse, Xcode, and Code::Blocks. Here we show you how to build and execute the code using the Code::Blocks tool.

First, to generate the Code::Blocks project files, in the root directory of the sample code (assuming you unzipped the code to the directory `/CL_Book`):

```
CL_Book$ mkdir build
CL_Book$ cd build
CL_Book/build$ cmake ../ -G "CodeBlocks - Unix Makefiles"
```

If CMake is successful, it will generate Code::Blocks project files for each of the samples. Note that if you wish to just build from the command line rather than an IDE on the Mac, omitting the (-G) argument to `cmake` will generate makefiles that can be built by just typing `make`.

The main project file will be named `CL_Book.cbp`, located at the root of the created build folder. If you open this file in Code::Blocks, you should see a project in your workspace like the one in Figure 2.1. All of the samples can now be built simply by clicking Build from the Code::Blocks build menu.

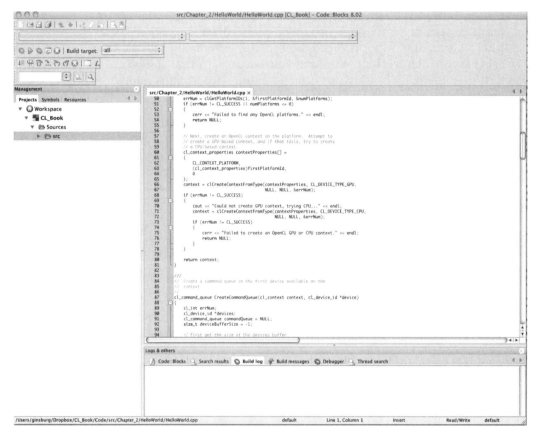

Figure 2.1   CodeBlocks `CL_Book` project

Microsoft Windows and Visual Studio

If you are developing on Microsoft Windows, you can use CMake to generate projects for any version of Microsoft Visual Studio. On Windows, the CMake installer will install the cmake-gui, which is the most straightforward way to generate a project. In addition to installing CMake, you will need to install an implementation of OpenCL such as the ATI Stream SDK or NVIDIA GPU Computing SDK. In the case of the example in this section, the ATI Stream SDK v2.1 was installed using the downloadable installer.

After installing CMake, simply open the cmake-gui and point the GUI to the location where you have unzipped the source code, as shown in Figure 2.2. Create a folder to build the binaries underneath that base directory and set that as the location to build the binaries in the GUI. You can then click Configure and choose the version of Microsoft Visual Studio you are using. Assuming you installed OpenCL, CMake should automatically find its location. If it is not found, manually adjust the directories in the GUI. Finally, click Configure again and then Generate, and the Visual Studio projects will be generated.

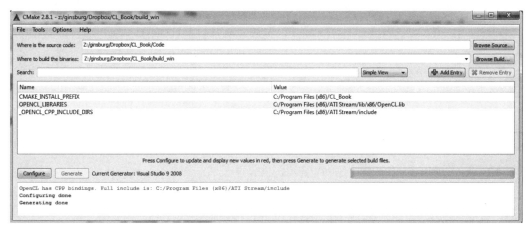

Figure 2.2　　Using cmake-gui to generate Visual Studio projects

After generating the project in cmake-gui, open the ALL_BUILD project from within Visual Studio, as shown in Figure 2.3. Building this project will build all of the example programs for the book. Each of the individual examples will also have its own Visual Studio project, and you can build and run the examples directly from within Visual Studio. This also allows you to use OpenCL-based profiling/debugging tools for Visual Studio such as the ATI Stream Profiler when running the example code.

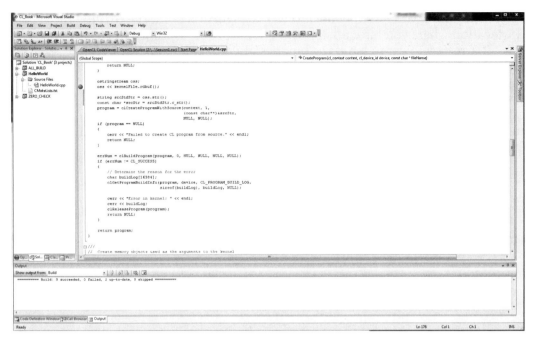

Figure 2.3   Microsoft Visual Studio 2008 Project

Linux and Eclipse

Finally, if you are developing on Linux, there are a large number of choices for a development environment. Many users will prefer to just use command-line make, but for those who wish to use an integrated development environment (IDE), CMake can generate projects for Eclipse, KDevelop, and Code::Blocks. After installing CMake and Eclipse CDT on Linux, the process of generating a project using CMake is much the same as on the other platforms. You will need to install an implementation of OpenCL. As of now, the three choices are the ATI Stream SDK, the NVIDIA GPU Computing SDK, or the Intel CPU SDK.

After installing an OpenCL implementation from one of the SDKs, you can generate the Eclipse project file using cmake. In order to have access to the source code in the generated Eclipse project, it is important that you create your CMake build directory outside of the source tree (at a level above the highest-level CMakeLists.txt). For example, if you have unzipped the code to the directory /devel/CL_Book, you would create the project as follows:

```
/devel$ mkdir build
/devel$ cd build
/devel/build$ cmake ../CL_Book -G "Eclipse CDT4 - Unix Makefiles"
```

This will generate an Eclipse-compatible project in your build/ folder. In order to use this project in Eclipse, select File, Import to import that project as a General, Existing project. Provide the full directory path to your build/ folder, and Eclipse should automatically detect a CL_Book project that can be imported into your workspace. After importing the project, you should have a full project in your workspace with the sample code as shown in Figure 2.4.

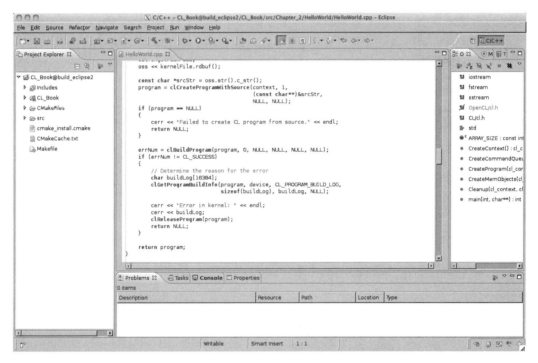

Figure 2.4 Eclipse CL_Book project

HelloWorld Example

The remainder of this chapter will cover the HelloWorld sample located in src/Chapter_2/HelloWorld. In Listing 2.1 the main() function from the example program is reproduced along with the source code to the kernel. The `main()` function either implements or calls functions that perform the following operations:

- Create an OpenCL context on the first available platform.

- Create a command-queue on the first available device.

- Load a kernel file (`HelloWorld.cl`) and build it into a program object.

- Create a kernel object for the kernel function `hello_kernel()`.

- Create memory objects for the arguments to the kernel (`result, a, b`).

- Queue the kernel for execution.

- Read the results of the kernel back into the result buffer.

Each of the steps that this program performs will be covered in detail in the rest of this section.

Listing 2.1   HelloWorld OpenCL Kernel and Main Function

```
HelloWorld.cl:

__kernel void hello_kernel(__global const float *a,
                           __global const float *b,
                           __global float *result)
{
    int gid = get_global_id(0);

    result[gid] = a[gid] + b[gid];
}

HelloWorld.cpp:

int main(int argc, char** argv)
{
    cl_context context = 0;
    cl_command_queue commandQueue = 0;
    cl_program program = 0;
    cl_device_id device = 0;
    cl_kernel kernel = 0;
    cl_mem memObjects[3] = { 0, 0, 0 };
    cl_int errNum;

    // Create an OpenCL context on first available platform
    context = CreateContext();
    if (context == NULL)
    {
```

```
        cerr << "Failed to create OpenCL context." << endl;
        return 1;
    }

    // Create a command-queue on the first device available
    // on the created context
    commandQueue = CreateCommandQueue(context, &device);
    if (commandQueue == NULL)
    {
        Cleanup(context, commandQueue, program, kernel, memObjects);
        return 1;
    }

    // Create OpenCL program from HelloWorld.cl kernel source
    program = CreateProgram(context, device, "HelloWorld.cl");
    if (program == NULL)
    {
        Cleanup(context, commandQueue, program, kernel, memObjects);
        return 1;
    }

    // Create OpenCL kernel
    kernel = clCreateKernel(program, "hello_kernel", NULL);
    if (kernel == NULL)
    {
        cerr << "Failed to create kernel" << endl;
        Cleanup(context, commandQueue, program, kernel, memObjects);
        return 1;
    }

    // Create memory objects that will be used as arguments to
    // kernel. First create host memory arrays that will be
    // used to store the arguments to the kernel
    float result[ARRAY_SIZE];
    float a[ARRAY_SIZE];
    float b[ARRAY_SIZE];
    for (int i = 0; i < ARRAY_SIZE; i++)
    {
        a[i] = i;
        b[i] = i * 2;
    }

    if (!CreateMemObjects(context, memObjects, a, b))
    {
        Cleanup(context, commandQueue, program, kernel, memObjects);
        return 1;
    }
```

```
    // Set the kernel arguments (result, a, b)
    errNum = clSetKernelArg(kernel, 0,
                            sizeof(cl_mem), &memObjects[0]);
    errNum |= clSetKernelArg(kernel, 1, sizeof(cl_mem),
                            &memObjects[1]);
    errNum |= clSetKernelArg(kernel, 2, sizeof(cl_mem),
                            &memObjects[2]);
    if (errNum != CL_SUCCESS)
    {
        cerr << "Error setting kernel arguments." << endl;
        Cleanup(context, commandQueue, program, kernel, memObjects);
        return 1;
    }

    size_t globalWorkSize[1] = { ARRAY_SIZE };
    size_t localWorkSize[1] = { 1 };

    // Queue the kernel up for execution across the array
    errNum = clEnqueueNDRangeKernel(commandQueue, kernel, 1, NULL,
                                    globalWorkSize, localWorkSize,
                                    0, NULL, NULL);
    if (errNum != CL_SUCCESS)
    {
        cerr << "Error queuing kernel for execution." << endl;
        Cleanup(context, commandQueue, program, kernel, memObjects);
        return 1;
    }

    // Read the output buffer back to the Host
    errNum = clEnqueueReadBuffer(commandQueue, memObjects[2],
                            CL_TRUE, 0, ARRAY_SIZE * sizeof(float),
                            result, 0, NULL, NULL);
    if (errNum != CL_SUCCESS)
    {
        cerr << "Error reading result buffer." << endl;
        Cleanup(context, commandQueue, program, kernel, memObjects);
        return 1;
    }

    // Output the result buffer
    for (int i = 0; i < ARRAY_SIZE; i++)
    {
        cout << result[i] << " ";
    }
    cout << endl;
    cout << "Executed program successfully." << endl;
    Cleanup(context, commandQueue, program, kernel, memObjects);

    return 0;
}
```

Choosing an OpenCL Platform and Creating a Context

The first step required to set up OpenCL is to choose a platform. OpenCL uses an installable client driver (ICD) model where multiple implementations of OpenCL can coexist on a single system. For example, in a system with an NVIDIA GPU and an AMD CPU, you might have one implementation on your system for the CPU and another for the GPU. It is also common for a single implementation to support multiple devices such as the Mac OS X OpenCL implementation or the ATI Stream SDK (which supports ATI GPUs and Intel or AMD CPUs). It is up to the application to choose the platform that is most appropriate for it.

The HelloWorld example demonstrates the simplest approach to choosing an OpenCL platform: it selects the first available platform. In the next chapter, we will discuss in more detail how to query an OpenCL platform for information and choose among the available platforms. In Listing 2.2 the code from the `CreateContext()` function of the HelloWorld example is provided. First, `clGetPlatformIDs()` is invoked to retrieve the first available platform. After getting the `cl_platform_id` of the first available platform, the example then creates a context by calling `clCreate-ContextFromType()`. This call to `clCreateContextFromType()` attempts to create a context for a GPU device. If this attempt fails, then the program makes another attempt, this time at creating a CPU device as a fallback.

Listing 2.2 Choosing a Platform and Creating a Context

```
cl_context CreateContext()
{
    cl_int errNum;
    cl_uint numPlatforms;
    cl_platform_id firstPlatformId;
    cl_context context = NULL;

    // First, select an OpenCL platform to run on.
    // For this example, we simply choose the first available
    // platform. Normally, you would query for all available
    // platforms and select the most appropriate one.
    errNum = clGetPlatformIDs(1, &firstPlatformId, &numPlatforms);
    if (errNum != CL_SUCCESS || numPlatforms <= 0)
    {
        cerr << "Failed to find any OpenCL platforms." << endl;
        return NULL;
    }
```

```
    // Next, create an OpenCL context on the platform. Attempt to
    // create a GPU-based context, and if that fails, try to create
    // a CPU-based context.
    cl_context_properties contextProperties[] =
    {
        CL_CONTEXT_PLATFORM,
        (cl_context_properties)firstPlatformId,
        0
    };
    context = clCreateContextFromType(contextProperties,
                                      CL_DEVICE_TYPE_GPU,
                                      NULL, NULL, &errNum);
    if (errNum != CL_SUCCESS)
    {
        cout << "Could not create GPU context, trying CPU..."
            << endl;
        context = clCreateContextFromType(contextProperties,
                                          CL_DEVICE_TYPE_CPU,
                                          NULL, NULL, &errNum);
        if (errNum != CL_SUCCESS)
        {
            cerr <<
                "Failed to create an OpenCL GPU or CPU context.";
            return NULL;
        }
    }

    return context;
}
```

Choosing a Device and Creating a Command-Queue

After choosing a platform and creating a context, the next step for the
HelloWorld application is to select a device and create a command-
queue. The device is the underlying compute hardware, such as a single
GPU or CPU. In order to communicate with the device, the application
must create a command-queue for it. The command-queue is used to
queue operations to be performed on the device. Listing 2.3 contains the
CreateCommandQueue() function that chooses the device and creates
the command-queue for the HelloWorld application.

The first call to clGetContextInfo() queries the context for the size of
the buffer required to store all of the device IDs available on the context.
This size is used to allocate a buffer to store the device IDs, and another
call is made to clGetContextInfo() that retrieves all of the devices

available on the context. Normally, a program would iterate over these devices querying for information to choose the best (or multiple) of the devices. In the HelloWorld sample, the first device is selected. In Chapter 3, we cover how to query devices for information so that you can select the most appropriate device for your application. After selecting the device to use, the application calls `clCreateCommandQueue()` to create a command-queue on the selected device. The command-queue will be used later in the program to queue the kernel for execution and read back its results.

Listing 2.3   Choosing the First Available Device and Creating a Command-Queue

```
cl_command_queue CreateCommandQueue(cl_context context,
                                    cl_device_id *device)
{
    cl_int errNum;
    cl_device_id *devices;
    cl_command_queue commandQueue = NULL;
    size_t deviceBufferSize = -1;

    // First get the size of the devices buffer
    errNum = clGetContextInfo(context, CL_CONTEXT_DEVICES, 0, NULL,
                              &deviceBufferSize);
    if (errNum != CL_SUCCESS)
    {
        cerr << "Failed call to
                clGetContextInfo(...,GL_CONTEXT_DEVICES,...)";
        return NULL;
    }

    if (deviceBufferSize <= 0)
    {
        cerr << "No devices available.";
        return NULL;
    }

    // Allocate memory for the devices buffer
    devices = new cl_device_id[deviceBufferSize /
                               sizeof(cl_device_id)];
    errNum = clGetContextInfo(context, CL_CONTEXT_DEVICES,
                              deviceBufferSize, devices, NULL);
    if (errNum != CL_SUCCESS)
    {
        cerr << "Failed to get device IDs";
        return NULL;
    }
```

```
    // In this example, we just choose the first available device.
    // In a real program, you would likely use all available
    // devices or choose the highest performance device based on
    // OpenCL device queries.

    commandQueue = clCreateCommandQueue(context,
                                        devices[0], 0, NULL);
    if (commandQueue == NULL)
    {
        cerr << "Failed to create commandQueue for device 0";
        return NULL;
    }

    *device = devices[0];
    delete [] devices;
    return commandQueue;
}
```

Creating and Building a Program Object

The next step in the HelloWorld example is to load the OpenCL C kernel source from the file `HelloWorld.cl` and create a program object from it. The program object is loaded with the kernel source code, and then the code is compiled for execution on the device attached to the context. In general, a program object in OpenCL stores the compiled executable code for all of the devices that are attached to the context. In the case of HelloWorld, only a single device is created on a context, but it is possible to have multiple devices, in which case the program object will hold the compiled code for each.

In Listing 2.4, the `HelloWorld.cl` file is loaded from disk and stored in a string. The program object is then created by calling `clCreateProgram-WithSource()`, which creates the program object from the kernel source code. After creating the program object, the kernel source code is compiled by calling `clBuildProgram()`. This function compiles the kernel for the attached devices and, if successful, stores the compiled code in the program object. If there is any failure during compilation, the build log is retrieved using `clGetProgramBuildInfo()`. The build log will contain a string with any compiler errors that were produced by the OpenCL kernel compilation.

Listing 2.4 Loading a Kernel Source File from Disk and Creating and Building a Program Object

```
cl_program CreateProgram(cl_context context, cl_device_id device,
                         const char* fileName)
{
    cl_int errNum;
    cl_program program;

    ifstream kernelFile(fileName, ios::in);
    if (!kernelFile.is_open())
    {
        cerr << "Failed to open file for reading: " << fileName <<
                endl;
        return NULL;
    }

    ostringstream oss;
    oss << kernelFile.rdbuf();

    string srcStdStr = oss.str();
    const char *srcStr = srcStdStr.c_str();
    program = clCreateProgramWithSource(context, 1,
                                        (const char**)&srcStr,
                                        NULL, NULL);
    if (program == NULL)
    {
        cerr << "Failed to create CL program from source." << endl;
        return NULL;
    }

    errNum = clBuildProgram(program, 0, NULL, NULL, NULL, NULL);
    if (errNum != CL_SUCCESS)
    {
        // Determine the reason for the error
        char buildLog[16384];
        clGetProgramBuildInfo(program, device, CL_PROGRAM_BUILD_LOG,
                              sizeof(buildLog), buildLog, NULL);

        cerr << "Error in kernel: " << endl;
        cerr << buildLog;
        clReleaseProgram(program);
        return NULL;
    }

    return program;
}
```

Creating Kernel and Memory Objects

In order to execute the OpenCL compute kernel, the arguments to the kernel function need to be allocated in memory that is accessible to it on the OpenCL device. The kernel for the HelloWorld example was provided in Listing 2.1. The kernel in this example is a simple function that computes the sum of the values at each element in two arrays (a and b) and stores it in another array (result). In Listing 2.5, a kernel object is created for the "hello_kernel" that was compiled into the program object. The arrays (a, b, and result) are allocated and filled with data. After these arrays are created in host memory, CreateMemObjects() is called, which copies the arrays into memory objects that will be passed to the kernel.

Listing 2.5   Creating a Kernel

```
// Create OpenCL kernel
kernel = clCreateKernel(program, "hello_kernel", NULL);
if (kernel == NULL)
{
    cerr << "Failed to create kernel" << endl;
    Cleanup(context, commandQueue, program, kernel, memObjects);
    return 1;
}

// Create memory objects that will be used as arguments to
// kernel. First create host memory arrays that will be
// used to store the arguments to the kernel
float result[ARRAY_SIZE];
float a[ARRAY_SIZE];
float b[ARRAY_SIZE];
for (int i = 0; i < ARRAY_SIZE; i++)
{
    a[i] = (float)i;
    b[i] = (float)(i * 2);
}

if (!CreateMemObjects(context, memObjects, a, b))
{
    Cleanup(context, commandQueue, program, kernel, memObjects);
    return 1;
}
```

The code for the CreateMemObjects() function is provided in Listing 2.6. For each array, the function calls clCreateBuffer() to create a memory object. The memory object is allocated in device memory and can be accessed directly by the kernel function. For the input arrays (a

and b) the buffer is created with memory type CL_MEM_READ_ONLY |
CL_MEM_COPY_HOST_PTR, which means that the array will be read-only
by the kernel and copied from host memory to device memory. The arrays
themselves are passed as an argument to clCreateBuffer(), which
causes the contents of the arrays to be copied into the storage space allocated for the memory object on the device. The result array is created
with type CL_MEM_READ_WRITE, which means that the kernel can both
read and write to the array.

Listing 2.6   Creating Memory Objects

```
bool CreateMemObjects(cl_context context, cl_mem memObjects[3],
                      float *a, float *b)
{
    memObjects[0] = clCreateBuffer(context, CL_MEM_READ_ONLY |
                                   CL_MEM_COPY_HOST_PTR,
                                   sizeof(float) * ARRAY_SIZE, a,
                                   NULL);
    memObjects[1] = clCreateBuffer(context, CL_MEM_READ_ONLY |
                                   CL_MEM_COPY_HOST_PTR,
                                   sizeof(float) * ARRAY_SIZE, b,
                                   NULL);
    memObjects[2] = clCreateBuffer(context, CL_MEM_READ_WRITE,
                                   sizeof(float) * ARRAY_SIZE,
                                   NULL, NULL);

    if (memObjects[0] == NULL || memObjects[1] == NULL ||
        memObjects[2] == NULL)
    {
        cerr << "Error creating memory objects." << endl;
        return false;
    }

    return true;
}
```

Executing a Kernel

Now that the kernel and memory objects have been created, the Hello-
World program can finally queue up the kernel for execution. All of the
arguments to the kernel function need to be set using clSetKernel-
Arg(). The first argument to this function is the index of the argument.
The hello_kernel() takes three arguments (a, b, and result), which
correspond to indices 0, 1, and 2. The memory objects that were created
in CreateMemObjects() are passed to the kernel object in Listing 2.7.

After setting the kernel arguments, the HelloWorld example finally queues the kernel for execution on the device using the command-queue. This is done by calling `clEnqueueNDRangeKernel()`. The `globalWorkSize` and `localWorkSize` determine how the kernel is distributed across processing units on the device. The HelloWorld example takes a very simple approach of having a global work size equal to the size of the array and the local work size equal to 1. Determining how to distribute your kernel efficiently over a data set is one of the most challenging aspects of using OpenCL. This will be discussed in many examples throughout the book.

Queuing the kernel for execution does not mean that the kernel executes immediately. The kernel execution is put into the command-queue for later consumption by the device. In other words, after the call is made to `clEnqueueNDRangeKernel()`, the kernel may not yet have executed on the device. It is possible to make a kernel wait for execution until previous events are finished. This will be discussed in detail in Chapter 9, "Events." In order to read the results back from the kernel, the HelloWorld example calls `clEnqueueReadBuffer()` to read back the `result` array (`memObjects[2]`).

The third argument to `clEnqueueReadBuffer()` is a Boolean `blocking_read` that determines whether the call should wait until the results are ready before returning. In this example, `blocking_read` is set to `CL_TRUE`, which means that it will not return until the kernel read is done. It is guaranteed that operations that are put into the command-queue are executed in order (unless the command-queue is created with `CL_QUEUE_OUT_OF_ORDER_EXEC_MODE_ENABLE`, which was not done in the HelloWorld example). As such, the read will not occur until execution of the kernel is finished, and the read will not return until it is able to read the results back from the device. Therefore, once the program returns from `clEnqueueReadBuffer()`, the `result` array has been read back from the device to the host and is ready for reading or writing. Finally, at the end of Listing 2.7, the values in the results array are output to the standard output.

Listing 2.7   Setting the Kernel Arguments, Executing the Kernel, and Reading Back the Results

```
// Set the kernel arguments (result, a, b)
errNum = clSetKernelArg(kernel, 0, sizeof(cl_mem),
                                   &memObjects[0]);
errNum |= clSetKernelArg(kernel, 1, sizeof(cl_mem),
                            &memObjects[1]);
errNum |= clSetKernelArg(kernel, 2, sizeof(cl_mem),
                            &memObjects[2]);
```

```
if (errNum != CL_SUCCESS)
{
    cerr << "Error setting kernel arguments." << endl;
    Cleanup(context, commandQueue, program, kernel, memObjects);
    return 1;
}

size_t globalWorkSize[1] = { ARRAY_SIZE };
size_t localWorkSize[1] = { 1 };

// Queue the kernel up for execution across the array
errNum = clEnqueueNDRangeKernel(commandQueue, kernel, 1, NULL,
                                globalWorkSize, localWorkSize,
                                0, NULL, NULL);
if (errNum != CL_SUCCESS)
{
    cerr << "Error queuing kernel for execution." << endl;
    Cleanup(context, commandQueue, program, kernel, memObjects);
    return 1;
}

// Read the output buffer back to the Host
errNum = clEnqueueReadBuffer(commandQueue, memObjects[2],
                             CL_TRUE,0,
                             ARRAY_SIZE * sizeof(float), result,
                             0, NULL, NULL);
if (errNum != CL_SUCCESS)
{
    cerr << "Error reading result buffer." << endl;
    Cleanup(context, commandQueue, program, kernel, memObjects);
    return 1;
}

// Output the result buffer
for (int i = 0; i < ARRAY_SIZE; i++)
{
    cout << result[i] << " ";
}
```

Checking for Errors in OpenCL

In the HelloWorld example and throughout the book, the example code demonstrates checking for error codes returned by OpenCL functions. At this point, we want to mention the mechanism by which OpenCL reports errors. In terms of error reporting, there are two types of functions in OpenCL: those that return OpenCL objects and those that don't.

For example, in this chapter we saw that `clCreateContextFromType()` returns a `cl_context` object. However, the function `clSetKernelArg()` does not return a new object. `clSetKernelArg()` returns an error code to the caller, and `clCreateContextFromType()` takes a parameter as its last argument that is a pointer to the error code generated by the function.

These two functions illustrate the simple rule in OpenCL in terms of reporting errors:

- OpenCL functions that return `cl_xxx` objects take a last argument that is a pointer to a returned error code.

- OpenCL functions that do not return objects will return an error code.

There are a large number of potential errors in OpenCL. Each API call can return a subset of these errors. The list of possible error codes in OpenCL is provided in Table 2.1.

Table 2.1   OpenCL Error Codes

Error	Description
CL_SUCCESS	Command executed successfully without error.
CL_DEVICE_NOT_FOUND	No OpenCL devices found matching criteria.
CL_DEVICE_NOT_AVAILABLE	OpenCL device is not currently available.
CL_COMPILER_NOT_AVAILABLE	Program created with source, but no OpenCL C compiler is available.
CL_MEM_OBJECT_ALLOCATION_FAILURE	Failure to allocate memory for a memory or image object.
CL_OUT_OF_RESOURCES	Insufficient resources to execute command.
CL_OUT_OF_HOST_MEMORY	Insufficient memory available on the host to execute command.
CL_PROFILING_INFO_NOT_AVAILABLE	Profiling information is not available for the event or the command-queue does not have profiling enabled.
CL_MEM_COPY_OVERLAP	Two buffers overlap the same region of memory.

Table 2.1 OpenCL Error Codes (*Continued*)

Error	Description
CL_IMAGE_FORMAT_MISMATCH	Images do not share the same image format.
CL_IMAGE_FORMAT_NOT_SUPPORTED	Specified image format is not supported.
CL_BUILD_PROGRAM_FAILURE	Unable to build executable for program.
CL_MAP_FAILURE	Memory region could not be mapped into host memory.
CL_INVALID_VALUE	An invalid value was specified for one or more arguments to the command.
CL_INVALID_DEVICE_TYPE	The passed-in device type is not a valid value.
CL_INVALID_PLATFORM	The passed-in platform is not a valid value.
CL_INVALID_DEVICE	The passed-in device is not a valid value.
CL_INVALID_CONTEXT	The passed-in context is not a valid value.
CL_INVALID_QUEUE_PROPERTIES	The device does not support command-queue properties.
CL_INVALID_COMMAND_QUEUE	The passed-in command-queue is not a valid value.
CL_INVALID_HOST_PTR	The host pointer is not valid.
CL_INVALID_MEM_OBJECT	The passed-in memory object is not a valid value.
CL_INVALID_IMAGE_FORMAT_DESCRIPTOR	The passed-in image format descriptor is not valid.
CL_INVALID_IMAGE_SIZE	The device does not support the image dimensions.
CL_INVALID_SAMPLER	The passed-in sampler is not a valid value.
CL_INVALID_BINARY	An invalid program binary was passed in.
CL_INVALID_BUILD_OPTIONS	One or more build options are not valid.
CL_INVALID_PROGRAM	The passed-in program is not a valid value.

continues

Table 2.1 OpenCL Error Codes (*Continued*)

Error	Description
CL_INVALID_PROGRAM_EXECUTABLE	The program was not successfully built into an executable for the devices associated with the command-queue.
CL_INVALID_KERNEL_NAME	The named kernel does not exist in the program.
CL_INVALID_KERNEL_DEFINITION	The kernel defined in the program source is not valid.
CL_INVALID_KERNEL	The passed-in kernel is not a valid value.
CL_INVALID_ARG_INDEX	The argument referred to by the argument index is not valid for the kernel.
CL_INVALID_ARG_VALUE	The kernel argument value is NULL for a nonlocal argument or non-NULL for a local argument.
CL_INVALID_ARG_SIZE	The argument size does not match the kernel argument.
CL_INVALID_KERNEL_ARGS	One or more kernel arguments have not been assigned values.
CL_INVALID_WORK_DIMENSION	The value of the work dimension is not a value between 1 and 3.
CL_INVALID_WORK_GROUP_SIZE	The local or global work size is not valid.
CL_INVALID_WORK_ITEM_SIZE	One or more work-item sizes exceed the maximum size supported by the device.
CL_INVALID_GLOBAL_OFFSET	The global offset exceeds supported bounds.
CL_INVALID_EVENT_WAIT_LIST	The wait list provided is either an invalid size or contains nonevents in it.
CL_INVALID_EVENT	The passed-in event is not a valid value.
CL_INVALID_OPERATION	Executing the command caused an invalid operation to occur.
CL_INVALID_GL_OBJECT	There was a problem with the OpenGL-referenced object.
CL_INVALID_BUFFER_SIZE	The buffer size specified was out of bounds.

Table 2.1   OpenCL Error Codes (*Continued*)

Error	Description
`CL_INVALID_MIP_LEVEL`	The mipmap level specified for an OpenGL texture is not valid for the OpenGL object.
`CL_INVALID_GLOBAL_WORK_SIZE`	The global work size passed in is not valid because it is either 0 or exceeds the dimensions supported by the device.

## Chapter 3

Platforms, Contexts, and Devices

Chapter 2 described an OpenCL program that included the basic API calls to create a context, device, program, kernel, and memory buffers; write and read the buffers; and finally execute the kernel on the chosen device. This chapter looks, in more detail, at OpenCL contexts (i.e., environments) and devices and covers the following concepts:

- Enumerating and querying OpenCL platforms

- Enumerating and querying OpenCL devices

- Creating contexts, associating devices, and the corresponding synchronization and memory management defined by this implied environment

OpenCL Platforms

As discussed in Chapter 2, the first step of an OpenCL application is to query the set of OpenCL platforms and choose one or more of them to use in the application. Associated with a platform is a profile, which describes the capabilities of the particular OpenCL version supported. A profile can be either the full profile, which covers functionality defined as part of the core specification, or the embedded profile, defined as a subset of the full profile which in particular drops some of the requirements of floating conformance to the IEEE 754 standard. For the most part this book covers the full profile, and Chapter 13 covers the differences with the embedded profile in detail.

The set of platforms can be queried with the command

```
cl_int clGetPlatformIDs (cl_uint num_entries,
                         cl_platform_id * platforms,
                         cl_uint * num_platforms)
```

This command obtains the list of available OpenCL platforms. In the case that the argument `platforms` is `NULL`, then `clGetPlatformIDs` returns the number of available platforms. The number of platforms returned can be limited with `num_entries`, which can be greater than 0 and less than or equal to the number of available platforms.

You can query the number of available platforms by setting the arguments `num_entries` and `platforms` to `0` and `NULL`, respectively. In the case of Apple's implementation this step is not necessary, and rather than passing a queried platform to other API calls, such as `clGetDeviceIds()`, the value `NULL` is passed instead.

As a simple example of how you might query and select a platform, we use `clGetPlatformIDs()` to obtain a list of platform IDs:

```
cl_int errNum;
cl_uint numPlatforms;
cl_platform_id * platformIds;
cl_context context = NULL;

errNum = clGetPlatformIDs(0, NULL, &numPlatforms);

platformIds = (cl_platform_id *)alloca(
    sizeof(cl_platform_id) * numPlatforms);

errNum = clGetPlatformIDs(numPlatforms, platformIds, NULL);
```

Given a platform, you can query a variety of properties with the command

```
cl_int clGetPlatformInfo (cl_platform_id platform,
                          cl_platform_info param_name,
                          size_t param_value_size,
                          void * param_value,
                          size_t * param_value_size_ret)
```

This command returns specific information about the OpenCL platform. The allowable values for `param_name` are described in Table 3.1.

The set of valid queries is given in Table 3.1, and you can query the size of a returned value by setting the values of `param_value_size` and `param_value` to `0` and `NULL`, respectively.

Table 3.1 OpenCL Platform Queries

cl_platform_info	Return Type	Description
CL_PLATFORM_PROFILE	char[]	OpenCL profile string. The profile can be one of these two strings:
		FULL_PROFILE: OpenCL implementation supports all functionality defined as part of the core specification.
		EMBEDDED_PROFILE: OpenCL implementation supports a subset of functionality defined as part of the core specification.
CL_PLATFORM_VERSION	char[]	OpenCL version string.
CL_PLATFORM_NAME	char[]	Platform name string.
CL_PLATFORM_VENDOR	char[]	Platform vendor string.
CL_PLATFORM_EXTENSIONS	char[]	OpenCL version string.

As a simple example of how you might query and select a platform, we use clGetPlatformInfo() to obtain the associated platform name and vendor strings:

```
cl_int err;
size_t size;

err = clGetPlatformInfo(id, CL_PLATFORM_NAME, 0, NULL, &size);
char * name = (char *)alloca(sizeof(char) * size);
err = clGetPlatformInfo(id, CL_PLATFORM_NAME, size, info, NULL);

err = clGetPlatformInfo(id, CL_PLATFORM_VENDOR, 0, NULL, &size);
char * vname = (char *)alloca(sizeof(char) * size);
err = clGetPlatformInfo(id, CL_PLATFORM_VENDOR, size, info, NULL);

std::cout << "Platform name: " << name  << std::endl
          << "Vendor name  : " << vname << std::endl;
```

On ATI Stream SDK this code displays

```
Platform name: ATI Stream
Vendor name  : Advanced Micro Devices, Inc.
```

Putting this all together, Listing 3.1 enumerates the set of available platforms, and Listing 3.2 queries and outputs the information associated with a particular platform.

Listing 3.1   Enumerating the List of Platforms

```
void displayInfo(void)
{
  cl_int errNum;
  cl_uint numPlatforms;
  cl_platform_id * platformIds;
  cl_context context = NULL;

  // First, query the total number of platforms
  errNum = clGetPlatformIDs(0, NULL, &numPlatforms);
  if (errNum != CL_SUCCESS || numPlatforms <= 0)
  {
    std::cerr << "Failed to find any OpenCL platform." << std::endl;
    return;
  }

  // Next, allocate memory for the installed platforms, and query
  // to get the list.
  platformIds = (cl_platform_id *)alloca(
      sizeof(cl_platform_id) * numPlatforms);

  // First, query the total number of platforms
  errNum = clGetPlatformIDs(numPlatforms, platformIds, NULL);
  if (errNum != CL_SUCCESS)
  {
    std::cerr << "Failed to find any OpenCL platforms."
              << std::endl;
    return;
  }

  std::cout << "Number of platforms: \t"
            << numPlatforms
            << std::endl;
  // Iterate through the list of platforms displaying associated
  // information
  for (cl_uint i = 0; i < numPlatforms; i++) {
    // First we display information associated with the platform
    DisplayPlatformInfo(
      platformIds[i], CL_PLATFORM_PROFILE, "CL_PLATFORM_PROFILE");
    DisplayPlatformInfo(
      platformIds[i], CL_PLATFORM_VERSION, "CL_PLATFORM_VERSION");
    DisplayPlatformInfo(
      platformIds[i], CL_PLATFORM_VENDOR, "CL_PLATFORM_VENDOR");
```

```
    DisplayPlatformInfo(
      platformIds[i],
      CL_PLATFORM_EXTENSIONS,
      "CL_PLATFORM_EXTENSIONS");
  }
}
```

Listing 3.2 Querying and Displaying Platform-Specific Information

```
void DisplayPlatformInfo(
  cl_platform_id id,
  cl_platform_info name,
  std::string str)
{
  cl_int errNum;
  std::size_t paramValueSize;

  errNum = clGetPlatformInfo(
    id,
    name,
    0,
    NULL,
    &paramValueSize);
  if (errNum != CL_SUCCESS)
  {
    std::cerr << "Failed to find OpenCL platform "
              << str << "." << std::endl;
    return;
  }

  char * info = (char *)alloca(sizeof(char) * paramValueSize);
  errNum = clGetPlatformInfo(
    id,
    name,
    paramValueSize,
    info,
    NULL);
  if (errNum != CL_SUCCESS)
  {
    std::cerr << "Failed to find OpenCL platform "
              << str << "." << std::endl;
    return;
  }

  std::cout << "\t" << str << ":\t" << info << std::endl;
}
```

OpenCL Devices

Associated with each platform is a set of compute devices that an application uses to execute code. Given a platform, a list of supported devices can be queried with the command

```
cl_int clGetDeviceIDs (cl_platform_id platform,
                       cl_device_type device_type,
                       cl_uint num_entries,
                       cl_device_id *devices,
                       cl_uint *num_devices)
```

This command obtains the list of available OpenCL devices associated with `platform`. In the case that the argument `devices` is `NULL`, then `clGetDeviceIDs` returns the number of devices. The number of devices returned can be limited with `num_entries`, where 0 < `num_entries` <= number of devices.

The type of compute device is specified by the argument `device_type` and can be one of the values given in Table 3.2. Each device shares the same execution and memory model as described in Chapter 1 and captured in Figures 1.6, 1.7, and 1.8.

The CPU device is a single homogeneous device that maps across the set of available cores or some subset thereof. They are often optimized, using large caches, for latency hiding; examples include AMD's Opteron series and Intel's Core i7 family.

Table 3.2 OpenCL Devices

`cl_device_type`	Description
CL_DEVICE_TYPE_CPU	OpenCL device that is the host processor.
CL_DEVICE_TYPE_GPU	OpenCL device that is a GPU.
CL_DEVICE_TYPE_ACCELERATOR	OpenCL accelerator (e.g., IBM Cell Broadband).
CL_DEVICE_TYPE_DEFAULT	Default device.
CL_DEVICE_TYPE_ALL	All OpenCL devices associated with the corresponding platform.

The GPU device corresponds to the class of throughput-optimized devices marketed toward both graphics and general-purpose computing. Well-known examples include ATI's Radeon family and NVIDIA's GTX series.

The accelerator device is intended to cover a broad range of devices ranging from IBM's Cell Broadband architecture to less well-known DSP-style devices.

The default device and all device options allow the OpenCL runtime to assign a "preferred" device and all the available devices, respectively.

For the CPU, GPU, and accelerator devices there is no limit on the number that are exposed by a particular platform, and the application is responsible for querying to determine the actual number. The following example shows how you can query and select a single GPU device given a platform, using clGetDeviceIDs and first checking that there is at least one such device available:

```
cl_int errNum;
cl_uint numDevices;
cl_device_id deviceIds[1];
errNum = clGetDeviceIDs(
  platform,
  CL_DEVICE_TYPE_GPU,
  0,
  NULL,
  &numDevices);


if (numDevices < 1)
{
  std::cout << "No GPU device found for platform "
          << platform << std::endl;
  exit(1);
}
errNum = clGetDeviceIDs(
  platform,
  CL_DEVICE_TYPE_GPU,
  1,
  &deviceIds[0],
  NULL);
```

Given a device, you can query a variety of properties with the command

```
cl_int clGetDeviceInfo (cl_device_id device,
                        cl_device_info param_name,
                        size_t param_value_size,
                        void * param_value,
                        size_t * param_value_size_ret)
```

This command returns specific information about the OpenCL platform. The allowable values for param_name are described in Table 3.3. The size of a returned value can be queried by setting the values of param_value_ size and param_value to 0 and NULL, respectively.[1]

Following is a simple example of how you can query a device, using clGetDeviceInfo(), to obtain the maximum number of compute units:

```
cl_int err;
size_t size;

err = clGetDeviceInfo(
   deviceID,
   CL_DEVICE_MAX_COMPUTE_UNITS,
   sizeof(cl_uint),
   &maxComputeUnits,
   &size);

std::cout << "Device has max compute units: "
          << maxComputeUnits << std::endl;
```

On ATI Stream SDK this code displays the following for an Intel i7 CPU device:

```
Device 4098 has max compute units: 8
```

---

[1] The pattern for querying device information, using clGetDeviceInfo(), is the same as that used for platforms and in fact matches that for all OpenCL clGetXXInfo() functions. The remainder of this book will not repeat the details of how to query the size of a value returned from the clGetXXInfo() operation.

Table 3.3 OpenCL Device Queries

cl_device_info	Return Type	Description
CL_DEVICE_TYPE	cl_device_type	The OpenCL device type; see Table 3.2 for the set of valid types.
CL_DEVICE_VENDOR_ID	cl_uint	A unique device vendor identifier.
CL_DEVICE_MAX_COMPUTE_UNITS	cl_uint	The number of parallel compute cores on the OpenCL device.
CL_DEVICE_MAX_WORK_ITEM_DIMENSIONS	cl_uint	Maximum dimensions that specify the global and local work-item IDs used by the data-parallel execution model.
CL_DEVICE_MAX_WORK_ITEM_SIZES	size_t []	Maximum number of work-items that can be specified in each dimension of the work-group to clEnqueueNDRangeKernel. Returns *n* size_t entries, where *n* is the value returned by the query for CL_DEVICE_MAX_WORK_ITEM_DIMENSIONS. The minimum value is (1, 1, 1).
CL_DEVICE_MAX_WORK_GROUP_SIZE	size_t	Maximum number of work-items in a work-group executing a kernel using the data-parallel execution model.

continues

Table 3.3 OpenCL Device Queries (*Continued*)

cl_device_info	Return Type	Description
CL_DEVICE_PREFERRED_VECTOR_WIDTH_CHAR CL_DEVICE_PREFERRED_VECTOR_WIDTH_SHORT CL_DEVICE_PREFERRED_VECTOR_WIDTH_INT CL_DEVICE_PREFERRED_VECTOR_WIDTH_LONG CL_DEVICE_PREFERRED_VECTOR_WIDTH_FLOAT CL_DEVICE_PREFERRED_VECTOR_WIDTH_DOUBLE CL_DEVICE_PREFERRED_VECTOR_WIDTH_HALF	cl_uint	Preferred native vector width size for built-in scalar types that can be put into vectors, defined as the number of scalar elements that can be stored in the vector.
CL_DEVICE_NATIVE_VECTOR_WIDTH_CHAR CL_DEVICE_NATIVE_VECTOR_WIDTH_SHORT CL_DEVICE_NATIVE_VECTOR_WIDTH_INT CL_DEVICE_NATIVE_VECTOR_WIDTH_LONG CL_DEVICE_NATIVE_VECTOR_WIDTH_FLOAT CL_DEVICE_NATIVE_VECTOR_WIDTH_DOUBLE CL_DEVICE_NATIVE_VECTOR_WIDTH_HALF	cl_uint	Returns the native instruction set architecture (ISA) vector width, where the vector width is defined as the number of scalar elements that can be stored in the vector.
CL_DEVICE_MAX_CLOCK_FREQUENCY	cl_uint	Maximum configured clock frequency of the device in megahertz.
CL_DEVICE_ADDRESS_BITS	cl_uint	The default compute device address space size specified as an unsigned integer value in bits.
CL_DEVICE_MAX_MEM_ALLOC_SIZE	cl_ulong	Maximum size of memory object allocation in bytes.
CL_DEVICE_IMAGE_SUPPORT	cl_bool	Is CL_TRUE if images are supported by the OpenCL device and CL_FALSE otherwise.
CL_DEVICE_MAX_READ_IMAGE_ARGS	cl_uint	Maximum number of simultaneous image objects that can be read by a kernel. The minimum value is 128 if CL_DEVICE_IMAGE_SUPPORT is CL_TRUE.

cl_device_info	Return Type	Description
CL_DEVICE_MAX_WRITE_IMAGE_ARGS	cl_uint	Maximum number of simultaneous image objects that can be written to by a kernel. The minimum value is 8 if CL_DEVICE_ IMAGE_SUPPORT is CL_TRUE.
CL_DEVICE_IMAGE2D_MAX_WIDTH	size_t	Maximum width of a 2D image in pixels.
CL_DEVICE_IMAGE2D_MAX_HEIGHT	size_t	Maximum height of a 2D image in pixels.
CL_DEVICE_IMAGE3D_MAX_WIDTH	size_t	Maximum width of a 3D image in pixels.
CL_DEVICE_IMAGE3D_MAX_HEIGHT	size_t	Maximum height of a 3D image in pixels.
CL_DEVICE_IMAGE3D_MAX_DEPTH	size_t	Maximum depth of a 3D image in pixels.
CL_DEVICE_MAX_SAMPLERS	cl_uint	Maximum number of samplers that can be used in a kernel.
CL_DEVICE_MAX_PARAMETER_SIZE	size_t	Maximum size in bytes of the arguments that can be passed to a kernel.
CL_DEVICE_MEM_BASE_ADDR_ALIGN	cl_uint	Describes the alignment in bits of the base address of any allocated memory object.
CL_DEVICE_MIN_DATA_TYPE_ALIGN_SIZE	cl_uint	The smallest alignment in bytes that can be used for any data type.

continues

Table 3.3 OpenCL Device Queries (*Continued*)

cl_device_info	Return Type	Description
CL_DEVICE_SINGLE_FP_CONFIG	cl_device_fp_config	Describes the single-precision floating-point capability of the device. This is a bit field that describes one or more of the following values: CL_FP_DENORM: Denorms are supported. CL_FP_INF_NAN: INF and quiet NaNs are supported. CL_FP_ROUND_TO_NEAREST: Round-to-nearest-even rounding mode is supported. CL_FP_ROUND_TO_ZERO: Round-to-zero rounding mode is supported. CL_FP_ROUND_TO_INF: Round-to-+ve and -ve infinity rounding modes are supported. CL_FP_FMA: IEEE 754-2008 fused multiply-add is supported. CL_FP_SOFT_FLOAT: Basic floating-point operations (such as addition, subtraction, multiplication) are implemented in software. The mandated minimum floating-point capability is CL_FP_ROUND_TO_NEAREST | CL_FP_INF_NAN.
CL_DEVICE_GLOBAL_MEM_CACHE_TYPE	cl_device_mem_cache_type	Type of global memory cache supported. Valid values are CL_NONE, CL_READ_ONLY_CACHE, and CL_READ_WRITE_CACHE.
CL_DEVICE_GLOBAL_MEM_CACHELINE_SIZE	cl_uint	Size of global memory cache line in bytes.
CL_DEVICE_GLOBAL_MEM_CACHE_SIZE	cl_ulong	Size of global memory cache in bytes.

cl_device_info	Return Type	Description
CL_DEVICE_GLOBAL_MEM_SIZE	cl_ulong	Size of global device memory in bytes.
CL_DEVICE_MAX_CONSTANT_BUFFER_SIZE	cl_ulong	Maximum size in bytes of a constant buffer allocation.
CL_DEVICE_MAX_CONSTANT_ARGS	cl_uint	Maximum number of arguments declared with the __constant qualifier in a kernel.
CL_DEVICE_LOCAL_MEM_TYPE	cl_device_local_mem_type	Type of local memory supported. This can be set to CL_LOCAL, implying dedicated local memory storage such as SRAM, or CL_GLOBAL.
CL_DEVICE_LOCAL_MEM_SIZE	cl_ulong	Size of local memory area in bytes.
CL_DEVICE_ERROR_CORRECTION_SUPPORT	cl_bool	Is CL_TRUE if the device implements error correction for the memories, caches, registers, etc., in the device. Is CL_FALSE if the device does not implement error correction. This can be a requirement for certain clients of OpenCL.
CL_DEVICE_HOST_UNIFIED_MEMORY	cl_bool	Is CL_TRUE if the device and the host have a unified memory subsystem and is CL_FALSE otherwise.
CL_DEVICE_PROFILING_TIMER_RESOLUTION	size_t	Describes the resolution of the device timer measured in nanoseconds.
CL_DEVICE_ENDIAN_LITTLE	cl_bool	Is CL_TRUE if the OpenCL device is a little endian device and CL_FALSE otherwise.
CL_DEVICE_AVAILABLE	cl_bool	Is CL_TRUE if the device is available and CL_FALSE if the device is not available.

continues

Table 3.3 OpenCL Device Queries (*Continued*)

cl_device_info	Return Type	Description
CL_DEVICE_COMPILER_AVAILABLE	cl_bool	Is CL_FALSE if the implementation does not have a compiler available to compile the program source. Is CL_TRUE if the compiler is available.
CL_DEVICE_EXECUTION_CAPABILITIES	cl_device_exec_capabilities	Describes the execution capabilities of the device. This is a bit field that describes one or more of the following values: CL_EXEC_KERNEL: The OpenCL device can execute OpenCL kernels. CL_EXEC_NATIVE_KERNEL: The OpenCL device can execute native kernels. The mandated minimum capability is CL_EXEC_KERNEL.
CL_DEVICE_QUEUE_PROPERTIES	cl_command_queue_properties	Describes the command-queue properties supported by the device. This is a bit field that describes one or more of the following values: CL_QUEUE_OUT_OF_ORDER_EXEC_MODE_ENABLE CL_QUEUE_PROFILING_ENABLE The mandated minimum capability is CL_QUEUE_PROFILING_ENABLE.
CL_DEVICE_PLATFORM	cl_platform_id	The platform associated with this device.

cl_device_info	Return Type	Description
CL_DEVICE_NAME	char[]	Device name string.
CL_DEVICE_VENDOR	char[]	Vendor name string.
CL_DRIVER_VERSION	char[]	OpenCL software driver version string in the form *major_number.minor_number.*
CL_DEVICE_PROFILE1	char[]	OpenCL profile string. Returns the profile name supported by the device. The profile name returned can be one of the following strings: FULL_PROFILE if the device supports the OpenCL specification (functionality defined as part of the core specification and does not require any extensions to be supported). EMBEDDED_PROFILE if the device supports the OpenCL embedded profile.
CL_DEVICE_VERSION	char[]	OpenCL version string. Returns the OpenCL version supported by the device. This version string has the following format: *OpenCL<space><major_version.minor_version><space><vendor-specific information>.*

continues

Table 3.3 OpenCL Device Queries (*Continued*)

cl_device_info	Return Type	Description
CL_DEVICE_EXTENSIONS	char[]	Returns a space-separated list of extension names (the extension names themselves do not contain any spaces) supported by the device. The list of extension names returned can be vendor-supported extension names and one or more of the following Khronos-approved extension names: cl_khr_fp64 cl_khr_int64_base_atomics cl_khr_int64_extended_atomics cl_khr_fp16 cl_khr_gl_sharing

Putting this all together, Listing 3.3 demonstrates a method for wrapping the query capabilities of a device in a straightforward, single call interface.[2]

Listing 3.3 Example of Querying and Displaying Platform-Specific Information

```
template<typename T>
void appendBitfield(
  T info, T value, std::string name, std::string & str)
{
   if (info & value)
   {
      if (str.length() > 0)
      {
         str.append(" | ");
      }
      str.append(name);
   }
}

template <typename T>
class InfoDevice
{
public:
  static void display(
    cl_device_id id, cl_device_info name, std::string str)
    {
      cl_int errNum;
      std::size_t paramValueSize;

      errNum = clGetDeviceInfo(id, name, 0, NULL, &paramValueSize);
      if (errNum != CL_SUCCESS)
      {
         std::cerr << "Failed to find OpenCL device info "
                   << str << "." << std::endl;
         return;
      }

      T * info = (T *)alloca(sizeof(T) * paramValueSize);
      errNum = clGetDeviceInfo(id,name,paramValueSize,info,NULL);
      if (errNum != CL_SUCCESS)
      {
```

---

[2] For simplicity, the example in Listing 3.3 admits the handling of the case when `clDeviceInfo()` returns an array of values. This is easily handled by providing a small array template and specializing the template `InfoDevice`; the complete implementation is provided as a source with the book's accompanying examples.

```
        std::cerr << "Failed to find OpenCL device info "
                  << str << "." << std::endl;
        return;
    }

    switch (name)
    {
    case CL_DEVICE_TYPE:
    {
        std::string deviceType;

        appendBitfield<cl_device_type>(

        *(reinterpret_cast<cl_device_type*>(info)),
           CL_DEVICE_TYPE_CPU, "CL_DEVICE_TYPE_CPU", deviceType);

        appendBitfield<cl_device_type>(

        *(reinterpret_cast<cl_device_type*>(info)),
           CL_DEVICE_TYPE_GPU, "CL_DEVICE_TYPE_GPU", deviceType);

        appendBitfield<cl_device_type>(
           *(reinterpret_cast<cl_device_type*>(info)),
           CL_DEVICE_TYPE_ACCELERATOR,
           "CL_DEVICE_TYPE_ACCELERATOR",
           deviceType);

        appendBitfield<cl_device_type>(
           *(reinterpret_cast<cl_device_type*>(info)),
           CL_DEVICE_TYPE_DEFAULT,
           "CL_DEVICE_TYPE_DEFAULT",
           deviceType);

            std::cout << "\t\t" << str << ":\t"
                      << deviceType << std::endl;
    }
    break;
    case CL_DEVICE_SINGLE_FP_CONFIG:
    {
        std::string fpType;

        appendBitfield<cl_device_fp_config>(
           *(reinterpret_cast<cl_device_fp_config*>(info)),
           CL_FP_DENORM, "CL_FP_DENORM", fpType);

          appendBitfield<cl_device_fp_config>(
             *(reinterpret_cast<cl_device_fp_config*>(info)),
             CL_FP_INF_NAN, "CL_FP_INF_NAN", fpType);
```

```cpp
            appendBitfield<cl_device_fp_config>(
                *(reinterpret_cast<cl_device_fp_config*>(info)),
                CL_FP_ROUND_TO_NEAREST,
                "CL_FP_ROUND_TO_NEAREST",
                fpType);

            appendBitfield<cl_device_fp_config>(
                *(reinterpret_cast<cl_device_fp_config*>(info)),
                CL_FP_ROUND_TO_ZERO, "CL_FP_ROUND_TO_ZERO", fpType);

            appendBitfield<cl_device_fp_config>(
                *(reinterpret_cast<cl_device_fp_config*>(info)),
                CL_FP_ROUND_TO_INF, "CL_FP_ROUND_TO_INF", fpType);

            appendBitfield<cl_device_fp_config>(
                *(reinterpret_cast<cl_device_fp_config*>(info)),
                CL_FP_FMA, "CL_FP_FMA", fpType);

            appendBitfield<cl_device_fp_config>(
                *(reinterpret_cast<cl_device_fp_config*>(info)),
                CL_FP_SOFT_FLOAT, "CL_FP_SOFT_FLOAT", fpType);

            std::cout << "\t\t" << str << ":\t" << fpType << std::endl;
        }
        break;
        case CL_DEVICE_GLOBAL_MEM_CACHE_TYPE:
        {
            std::string memType;

            appendBitfield<cl_device_mem_cache_type>(
                *(reinterpret_cast<cl_device_mem_cache_type*>(info)),
                CL_NONE, "CL_NONE", memType);

            appendBitfield<cl_device_mem_cache_type>(
                *(reinterpret_cast<cl_device_mem_cache_type*>(info)),
                CL_READ_ONLY_CACHE, "CL_READ_ONLY_CACHE", memType);

            appendBitfield<cl_device_mem_cache_type>(
                *(reinterpret_cast<cl_device_mem_cache_type*>(info)),
                CL_READ_WRITE_CACHE, "CL_READ_WRITE_CACHE", memType);

            std::cout << "\t\t" << str << ":\t" << memType << std::endl;
        }
        break;
        case CL_DEVICE_LOCAL_MEM_TYPE:
        {
            std::string memType;
```

```
            appendBitfield<cl_device_local_mem_type>(
                *(reinterpret_cast<cl_device_local_mem_type*>(info)),
                CL_GLOBAL, "CL_LOCAL", memType);

            appendBitfield<cl_device_local_mem_type>(
                *(reinterpret_cast<cl_device_local_mem_type*>(info)),
                CL_GLOBAL, "CL_GLOBAL", memType);

            std::cout << "\t\t" << str << ":\t" << memType << std::endl;
        }
        break;
        case CL_DEVICE_EXECUTION_CAPABILITIES:
        {
            std::string memType;

            appendBitfield<cl_device_exec_capabilities>(
                *(reinterpret_cast<cl_device_exec_capabilities*>(info)),
                CL_EXEC_KERNEL, "CL_EXEC_KERNEL", memType);

            appendBitfield<cl_device_exec_capabilities>(
                *(reinterpret_cast<cl_device_exec_capabilities*>(info)),
                CL_EXEC_NATIVE_KERNEL, "CL_EXEC_NATIVE_KERNEL", memType);

            std::cout << "\t\t" << str << ":\t" << memType << std::endl;
        }
        break;
        case CL_DEVICE_QUEUE_PROPERTIES:
        {
            std::string memType;

            appendBitfield<cl_device_exec_capabilities>(
                *(reinterpret_cast<cl_device_exec_capabilities*>(info)),
                CL_QUEUE_OUT_OF_ORDER_EXEC_MODE_ENABLE,
                "CL_QUEUE_OUT_OF_ORDER_EXEC_MODE_ENABLE", memType);

            appendBitfield<cl_device_exec_capabilities>(
                *(reinterpret_cast<cl_device_exec_capabilities*>(info)),
                CL_QUEUE_PROFILING_ENABLE, "CL_QUEUE_PROFILING_ENABLE",
                memType);

            std::cout << "\t\t" << str << ":\t" << memType << std::endl;
        }
        break;
        default:
            std::cout << "\t\t" << str << ":\t" << *info << std::endl;
            break;
        }
    }
};
```

The template class `InfoDevice` does the hard work, proving the single public method, `display()`, to retrieve and display the requested information. The earlier example, querying a device's maximum compute units, can be recast as follows:

```
InfoDevice<cl_uint>::display(
    deviceID,
    CL_DEVICE_MAX_COMPUTE_UNITS,
    "DEVICE has max compute units");
```

OpenCL Contexts

Contexts are the heart of any OpenCL application. Contexts provide a container for associated devices, memory objects (e.g., buffers and images), and command-queues (providing an interface between the context and an individual device). It is the context that drives communication with, and between, specific devices, and OpenCL defines its memory model in terms of these. For example, a memory object is allocated with a context but can be updated by a particular device, and OpenCL's memory guarantees that all devices, within the same context, will see these updates at well-defined synchronization points.

It is important to realize that while these stages often form the foundation of any OpenCL program, there is no reason not to use multiple contexts, each created from a different platform, and distribute work across the contexts and associated devices. The difference is that OpenCL's memory model is not lifted across devices, and this means that corresponding memory objects cannot be shared by different contexts, created either from the same or from different platforms. The implication of this is that any data that is to be shared across contexts must be manually moved between contexts. This concept is captured in Figure 3.1.

Unlike platforms and devices, often queried at the beginning of the program or library, a context is something you may want to update as the program progresses, allocating or deleting memory objects and so on. In general, an application's OpenCL usage looks similar to this:

1. Query which platforms are present.

2. Query the set of devices supported by each platform:

    a. Choose to select devices, using `clGetDeviceInfo()`, on specific capabilities.

3. Create contexts from a selection of devices (each context must be created with devices from a single platform); then with a context you can

   a. Create one or more command-queues

   b. Create programs to run on one or more associated devices

   c. Create a kernel from those programs

   d. Allocate memory buffers and images, either on the host or on the device(s)

   e. Write or copy data to and from a particular device

   f. Submit kernels (setting the appropriate arguments) to a command-queue for execution

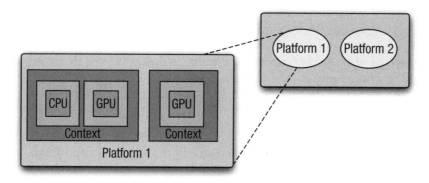

Figure 3.1   Platform, devices, and contexts

Given a platform and a list of associated devices, an OpenCL context is created with the command clCreateContext(), and with a platform and device type, clCreateContextFromType() can be used. These two functions are declared as

```
cl_context clCreateContext (
    const cl_context_properties *properties,
    cl_uint num_devices,
    const cl_device_id *devices,
    void (CL_CALLBACK *pfn_notify)
        (const char *errinfo,

        const void *private_info,
```

```
      size_t cb,

      void *user_data),
   void *user_data,
   cl_int *errcode_ret)


cl_context
clCreateContextFromType (
   const cl_context_properties *properties,
   cl_device_type device_type,
   void (CL_CALLBACK *pfn_notify)
      (const char *errinfo,

      const void *private_info,

      size_t cb,

      void *user_data),
   void *user_data,
   cl_int *errcode_ret)
```

This creates an OpenCL context. The allowable values for the argument `properties` are described in Table 3.4.

The list of properties is limited to the platform with which the context is associated. Other context properties are defined with certain OpenCL extensions. See Chapters 10 and 11 on sharing with graphics APIs, for examples. The arguments `devices` and `device_type` allow the set of devices to be specified explicitly or restricted to a certain type of device, respectively. The arguments `pfn_notify` and `user_data` are used together to define a callback that is called to report information on errors that occur during the lifetime of the context, with `user_data` being passed as the last argument to the callback.

The following example shows that given a platform, you can query for the set of GPU devices and create a context, if one or more devices are available:

Table 3.4 Properties Supported by `clCreateContext`

`cl_context_properties`	Property Value	Description
CL_CONTEXT_PLATFORM	cl_platform_id	Specifies the platform to use

```
cl_platform pform;
size_t num;
cl_device_id * devices;
cl_context context;
size_t size;

clGetDeviceIDs(platform, CL_DEVICE_TYPE_GPU, 0, NULL, &num);

if (num > 0)
{
  devices = (cl_device_id *)alloca(num);
  clGetDeviceIDs(
    platform,
    CL_DEVICE_TYPE_GPU,
    num,
    &devices[0],
    NULL);
}

cl_context_properties properties [] =
{
  CL_CONTEXT_PLATFORM, (cl_context_properties)platform, 0
};

context = clCreateContext(
  properties,
  size / sizeof(cl_device_id),
  devices,
  NULL,
  NULL,
  NULL);
```

Given a context, you can query a variety of properties with the command

```
cl_int clGetContextInfo (cl_context context,
                         cl_context_info param_name,
                         size_t param_value_size,
                         void * param_value,
                         size_t * param_value_size_ret)
```

This command returns specific information about the OpenCL context. The allowable values for param_name, defining the set of valid queries, are described in Table 3.5.

Table 3.5 Context Information Queries

cl_context_info	Return Type	Description
CL_CONTEXT_REFERENCE_COUNT	cl_uint	Returns the *context* reference count.
CL_CONTEXT_NUM_DEVICES	cl_uint	Returns the number of devices in *context*.
CL_CONTEXT_DEVICES	cl_device_id[]	Returns the list of devices in *context*.
CL_CONTEXT_PROPERTIES	cl_context_properties[]	Returns the *properties* argument specified in clCreateContext or clCreateContextFromType. If the *properties* argument specified in clCreateContext or clCreateContextFromType used to create *context* is not NULL, the implementation must return the values specified in the *properties* argument. If the *properties* argument specified in clCreateContext or clCreateContextFromType used to create *context* is NULL, the implementation may return either a param_value_size_ret of 0 (that is, there is no context property value to be returned) or a context property value of 0 (where 0 is used to terminate the context properties list) in the memory that param_value points to.

Following is an example of how you can query a context, using
clGetContextInfo(), to obtain the list of associated devices:

```
cl_uint numPlatforms;
cl_platform_id * platformIDs;
cl_context context = NULL;
size_t size;

clGetPlatformIDs(0, NULL, &numPlatforms);
platformIDs = (cl_platform_id *)alloca(
sizeof(cl_platform_id) * numPlatforms);

clGetPlatformIDs(numPlatforms, platformIDs, NULL);

cl_context_properties properties[] =
{
  CL_CONTEXT_PLATFORM, (cl_context_properties)platformIDs[0], 0
};

context = clCreateContextFromType(
  properties, CL_DEVICE_TYPE_ALL, NULL, NULL, NULL);

clGetContextInfo(context, CL_CONTEXT_DEVICES, 0, NULL, &size);

cl_device_id * devices = (cl_device_id*)alloca(
  sizeof(cl_device_id) * size);

clGetContextInfo(context,CL_CONTEXT_DEVICES, size, devices, NULL);

for (size_t i = 0; i < size / sizeof(cl_device_id); i++)
{
  cl_device_type type;

  clGetDeviceInfo(
    devices[i],CL_DEVICE_TYPE, sizeof(cl_device_type), &type, NULL);

  switch (type)
  {
    case CL_DEVICE_TYPE_GPU:
      std::cout << "CL_DEVICE_TYPE_GPU" << std::endl;
break;
    case CL_DEVICE_TYPE_CPU:
      std::cout << "CL_DEVICE_TYPE_CPU" << std::endl;
break;
    case CL_DEVICE_TYPE_ACCELERATOR:
      std::cout << "CL_DEVICE_TYPE_ACCELERATOR" << std::endl;
break;
  }
}
```

On ATI Stream SDK this code displays as follows for a machine with an Intel i7 CPU device and ATI Radeon 5780:

```
CL_DEVICE_TYPE_CPU
CL_DEVICE_TYPE_GPU
```

Like all OpenCL objects, contexts are reference-counted and the number of references can be incremented and decremented with the following two commands:[3]

```
cl_int clRetainContext (cl_context context)

cl_int clReleaseContext(cl_context context)
```

These increment and decrement, respectively, a context's reference count.

To conclude this chapter, we build a simple example that performs a convolution of an input signal. Convolution is a common operation that appears in many signal-processing applications and in its simplest form combines one signal (input signal) with another (mask) to produce a final output (output signal). Convolution is an excellent application for OpenCL; it shows a good amount of data parallelism for large inputs and has good data locality that enables use of OpenCL's sharing constructs.

Figure 3.2 shows the process of applying a 3×3 mask to an 8×8 input signal, resulting in a 6×6 output signal.[4] The algorithm is straightforward; each sample of the final signal is generated by

1. Placing the mask over the input signal, centered at the corresponding input location

2. Multiplying the input values by the corresponding element in the mask

3. Accumulating the results of step 2 into a single sum, which is written to the corresponding output location

---

[3] The exception to this rule is for OpenCL platforms that do not have corresponding retain/release calls.

[4] For simplicity, edge cases are not considered; a more realistic convolution example can be found in Chapter 11.

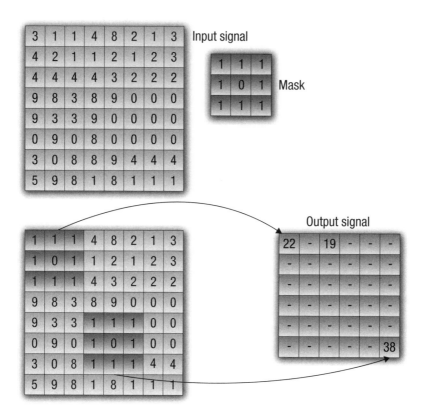

Figure 3.2 Convolution of an 8×8 signal with a 3×3 filter, resulting in a 6×6 signal

For each location in the output signal the kernel `convolve`, given in Listing 3.4, performs the preceding steps; that is, each output result can be computed in parallel.

Listing 3.4 Using Platform, Devices, and Contexts—Simple Convolution Kernel

```
Convolution.cl

__kernel void convolve(
    const __global  uint * const input,
    __constant uint * const  mask,
    __global  uint * const output,
    const int inputWidth,
    const int maskWidth)
```

```
{
    const int x = get_global_id(0);
    const int y = get_global_id(1);

    uint sum = 0;
    for (int r = 0; r < maskWidth; r++)
    {
        const int idxIntmp = (y + r) * inputWidth + x;

        for (int c = 0; c < maskWidth; c++)
        {
            sum += mask[(r * maskWidth)  + c] * input[idxIntmp + c];
        }
    }

    output[y * get_global_size(0) + x] = sum;
}
```

Listing 3.5 contains the host code for our simple example. The start of the main function queries the list of available platforms, then it iterates through the list of platforms using `clGetDeviceIDs()` to request the set of CPU device types supported by the platform, and in the case that it finds at least one, the loop is terminated. In the case that no CPU device is found, the program simply exits; otherwise a context is created with the list of devices, and then the kernel source is loaded from disk and compiled and a kernel object is created. The input/output buffers are then created, and finally the kernel arguments are set and the kernel is executed. The program completes by reading the outputted signal and outputting the result to `stdout`.

Listing 3.5 Example of Using Platform, Devices, and Contexts—Simple Convolution

```
Convolution.cpp

#include <iostream>
#include <fstream>
#include <sstream>
#include <string>

#ifdef __APPLE__
#include <OpenCL/cl.h>
#else
#include <CL/cl.h>
#endif
```

```
// Constants
const unsigned int inputSignalWidth  = 8;
const unsigned int inputSignalHeight = 8;

cl_uint inputSignal[inputSignalWidth][inputSignalHeight] =
{
    {3, 1, 1, 4, 8, 2, 1, 3},
    {4, 2, 1, 1, 2, 1, 2, 3},
    {4, 4, 4, 4, 3, 2, 2, 2},
    {9, 8, 3, 8, 9, 0, 0, 0},
    {9, 3, 3, 9, 0, 0, 0, 0},
    {0, 9, 0, 8, 0, 0, 0, 0},
    {3, 0, 8, 8, 9, 4, 4, 4},
    {5, 9, 8, 1, 8, 1, 1, 1}
};

const unsigned int outputSignalWidth  = 6;
const unsigned int outputSignalHeight = 6;

cl_uint outputSignal[outputSignalWidth][outputSignalHeight];

const unsigned int maskWidth  = 3;
const unsigned int maskHeight = 3;

cl_uint mask[maskWidth][maskHeight] =
{
    {1, 1, 1}, {1, 0, 1}, {1, 1, 1},
};

inline void checkErr(cl_int err, const char * name)
{
    if (err != CL_SUCCESS)
    {
        std::cerr << "ERROR: " << name
                  << " (" << err << ")" << std::endl;
        exit(EXIT_FAILURE);
    }
}

void CL_CALLBACK contextCallback(
    const char * errInfo,
    const void * private_info,
    size_t cb,
    void * user_data)
{
    std::cout << "Error occurred during context use: "
              << errInfo << std::endl;
    exit(EXIT_FAILURE);
}
```

```
int main(int argc, char** argv)
{
    cl_int errNum;
    cl_uint numPlatforms;
    cl_uint numDevices;
    cl_platform_id * platformIDs;
    cl_device_id * deviceIDs;
    cl_context context = NULL;
    cl_command_queue queue;
    cl_program program;
    cl_kernel kernel;
    cl_mem inputSignalBuffer;
    cl_mem outputSignalBuffer;
    cl_mem maskBuffer;

    errNum = clGetPlatformIDs(0, NULL, &numPlatforms);
    checkErr(
        (errNum != CL_SUCCESS) ? errNum :
            (numPlatforms <= 0 ? -1 : CL_SUCCESS),
                                "clGetPlatformIDs");

    platformIDs = (cl_platform_id *)alloca(
            sizeof(cl_platform_id) * numPlatforms);

    errNum = clGetPlatformIDs(numPlatforms, platformIDs, NULL);
    checkErr(
        (errNum != CL_SUCCESS) ? errNum :
        (numPlatforms <= 0 ? -1 : CL_SUCCESS), "clGetPlatformIDs");

    deviceIDs = NULL;
    cl_uint i;
    for (i = 0; i < numPlatforms; i++)
    {
        errNum = clGetDeviceIDs(
            platformIDs[i],
            CL_DEVICE_TYPE_CPU,
            0,
            NULL,
            &numDevices);
        if (errNum != CL_SUCCESS && errNum != CL_DEVICE_NOT_FOUND)
        {
            checkErr(errNum, "clGetDeviceIDs");
        }
        else if (numDevices > 0)
        {
            deviceIDs = (cl_device_id *)alloca(
                sizeof(cl_device_id) * numDevices);
```

```
            errNum = clGetDeviceIDs(
                platformIDs[i], CL_DEVICE_TYPE_CPU, numDevices,
                &deviceIDs[0], NULL);
            checkErr(errNum, "clGetDeviceIDs");
            break;
        }
    }

    if (deviceIDs == NULL) {
        std::cout << "No CPU device found" << std::endl;
        exit(-1);
    }

    cl_context_properties contextProperties[] =
    {
        CL_CONTEXT_PLATFORM,(cl_context_properties)platformIDs[i], 0
    };
    context = clCreateContext(
        contextProperties, numDevices, deviceIDs,
        &contextCallback, NULL, &errNum);
    checkErr(errNum, "clCreateContext");

    std::ifstream srcFile("Convolution.cl");
    checkErr(srcFile.is_open() ? CL_SUCCESS : -1,
            "reading Convolution.cl");

    std::string srcProg(
        std::istreambuf_iterator<char>(srcFile),
        (std::istreambuf_iterator<char>()));

    const char * src = srcProg.c_str();
    size_t length = srcProg.length();

    program = clCreateProgramWithSource(
        context, 1, &src, &length, &errNum);
    checkErr(errNum, "clCreateProgramWithSource");

    errNum = clBuildProgram(
        program, numDevices, deviceIDs, NULL, NULL, NULL);
    checkErr(errNum, "clBuildProgram");

    kernel = clCreateKernel(program, "convolve", &errNum);
    checkErr(errNum, "clCreateKernel");

    inputSignalBuffer = clCreateBuffer(
        context, CL_MEM_READ_ONLY | CL_MEM_COPY_HOST_PTR,
        sizeof(cl_uint) * inputSignalHeight * inputSignalWidth,
        static_cast<void *>(inputSignal), &errNum);
    checkErr(errNum, "clCreateBuffer(inputSignal)");
```

```
maskBuffer = clCreateBuffer(
    context, CL_MEM_READ_ONLY | CL_MEM_COPY_HOST_PTR,
    sizeof(cl_uint) * maskHeight * maskWidth,
    static_cast<void *>(mask), &errNum);
checkErr(errNum, "clCreateBuffer(mask)");

outputSignalBuffer = clCreateBuffer(
    context, CL_MEM_WRITE_ONLY,
    sizeof(cl_uint) * outputSignalHeight * outputSignalWidth,
    NULL, &errNum);
checkErr(errNum, "clCreateBuffer(outputSignal)");

queue = clCreateCommandQueue(
    context, deviceIDs[0], 0, &errNum);
checkErr(errNum, "clCreateCommandQueue");

errNum  = clSetKernelArg(
  kernel, 0, sizeof(cl_mem), &inputSignalBuffer);
errNum |= clSetKernelArg(
    kernel, 1, sizeof(cl_mem), &maskBuffer);
errNum |= clSetKernelArg(
    kernel, 2, sizeof(cl_mem), &outputSignalBuffer);
errNum |= clSetKernelArg(
    kernel, 3, sizeof(cl_uint), &inputSignalWidth);
errNum |= clSetKernelArg(
    kernel, 4, sizeof(cl_uint), &maskWidth);
checkErr(errNum, "clSetKernelArg");

const size_t globalWorkSize[1] =
    { outputSignalWidth * outputSignalHeight };
const size_t localWorkSize[1]  = { 1 };

errNum = clEnqueueNDRangeKernel(
    queue,
    kernel,
    1,
    NULL,
    globalWorkSize,
    localWorkSize,
    0,
    NULL,
    NULL);
checkErr(errNum, "clEnqueueNDRangeKernel");

errNum = clEnqueueReadBuffer(
    queue, outputSignalBuffer, CL_TRUE, 0,
    sizeof(cl_uint) * outputSignalHeight * outputSignalHeight,
    outputSignal, 0, NULL, NULL);
checkErr(errNum, "clEnqueueReadBuffer");
```

```cpp
    for (int y = 0; y < outputSignalHeight; y++)
    {
        for (int x = 0; x < outputSignalWidth; x++)
        {
            std::cout << outputSignal[x][y] << " ";
        }
        std::cout << std::endl;
    }

    return 0;
}
```

## Chapter 4

Programming with OpenCL C

The OpenCL C programming language is used to create programs that describe data-parallel kernels and tasks that can be executed on one or more heterogeneous devices such as CPUs, GPUs, and other processors referred to as accelerators such as DSPs and the Cell Broadband Engine (B.E.) processor. An OpenCL program is similar to a dynamic library, and an OpenCL kernel is similar to an exported function from the dynamic library. Applications directly call the functions exported by a dynamic library from their code. Applications, however, cannot call an OpenCL kernel directly but instead queue the execution of the kernel to a command-queue created for a device. The kernel is executed asynchronously with the application code running on the host CPU.

OpenCL C is based on the ISO/IEC 9899:1999 C language specification (referred to in short as C99) with some restrictions and specific extensions to the language for parallelism. In this chapter, we describe how to write data-parallel kernels using OpenCL C and cover the features supported by OpenCL C.

Writing a Data-Parallel Kernel Using OpenCL C

As described in Chapter 1, data parallelism in OpenCL is expressed as an N-dimensional computation domain, where $N = 1$, 2, or 3. The N-D domain defines the total number of work-items that can execute in parallel. Let's look at how a data-parallel kernel would be written in OpenCL C by taking a simple example of summing two arrays of floats. A sequential version of this code would perform the sum by summing individual elements of both arrays inside a for loop:

```
void
scalar_add (int n, const float *a, const float *b, float *result)
{
    int i;
```

```
    for (i=0; i<n; i++)
        result[i] = a[i] + b[i];
}
```

A data-parallel version of the code in OpenCL C would look like this:

```
kernel void
scalar_add (global const float *a,
            global const float *b,
            global float *result)
{
    int id = get_global_id(0);
    result[id] = a[id] + b[id];
}
```

The scalar_add function declaration uses the kernel qualifier to indicate that this is an OpenCL C kernel. Note that the scalar_add kernel includes only the code to compute the sum of each individual element, aka the inner loop. The N-D domain will be a one-dimensional domain set to n. The kernel is executed for each of the n work-items to produce the sum of arrays a and b. In order for this to work, each executing work-item needs to know which individual elements from arrays a and b need to be summed. This must be a unique value for each work-item and should be derived from the N-D domain specified when queuing the kernel for execution. The get_global_id(0) returns the one-dimensional global ID for each work-item. Ignore the global qualifiers specified in the kernel for now; they will be discussed later in this chapter.

Figure 4.1 shows how get_global_id can be used to identify a unique work-item from the list of work-items executing a kernel.

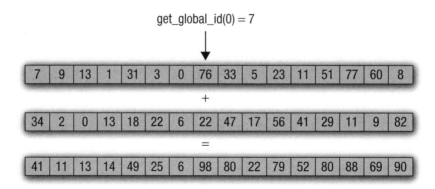

Figure 4.1   Mapping get_global_id to a work-item

The OpenCL C language with examples is described in depth in the sections that follow. The language is derived from C99 with restrictions that are described at the end of this chapter.

OpenCL C also adds the following features to C99:

- **Vector data types.** A number of OpenCL devices such as Intel SSE, AltiVec for POWER and Cell, and ARM NEON support a vector instruction set. This vector instruction set is accessed in C/C++ code through built-in functions (some of which may be device-specific) or device-specific assembly instructions. In OpenCL C, vector data types can be used in the same way scalar types are used in C. This makes it much easier for developers to write vector code because similar operators can be used for both vector and scalar data types. It also makes it easy to write portable vector code because the OpenCL compiler is now responsible for mapping the vector operations in OpenCL C to the appropriate vector ISA for a device. Vectorizing code also helps improve memory bandwidth because of regular memory accesses and better coalescing of these memory accesses.

- **Address space qualifiers.** OpenCL devices such as GPUs implement a memory hierarchy. The address space qualifiers are used to identify a specific memory region in the hierarchy.

- **Additions to the language for parallelism.** These include support for work-items, work-groups, and synchronization between work-items in a work-group.

- **Images.** OpenCL C adds image and sampler data types and built-in functions to read and write images.

- **An extensive set of built-in functions such as math, integer, geometric, and relational functions.** These are described in detail in Chapter 5.

Scalar Data Types

The C99 scalar data types supported by OpenCL C are described in Table 4.1. Unlike C, OpenCL C describes the sizes, that is, the exact number of bits for the integer and floating-point data types.

Table 4.1   Built-In Scalar Data Types

Type	Description
bool	A conditional data type that is either true or false. The value true expands to the integer constant 1, and the value false expands to the integer constant 0.
char	A signed two's complement 8-bit integer.
unsigned char, uchar	An unsigned 8-bit integer.
short	A signed two's complement 16-bit integer.
unsigned short, ushort	An unsigned 16-bit integer.
int	A signed two's complement 32-bit integer.
unsigned int, uint	An unsigned 32-bit integer.
long	A signed two's complement 64-bit integer.
unsigned long, ulong	An unsigned 64-bit integer.
float	A 32-bit floating-point. The float data type must conform to the IEEE 754 single-precision storage format.
double	A 64-bit floating-point. The double data type must conform to the IEEE 754 double-precision storage format. This is an optional format and is available only if the double-precision extension (cl_khr_fp64) is supported by the device.
half	A 16-bit floating-point. The half data type must conform to the IEEE 754-2008 half-precision storage format.
size_t	The unsigned integer type of the result of the sizeof operator. This is a 32-bit unsigned integer if the address space of the device is 32 bits and is a 64-bit unsigned integer if the address space of the device is 64 bits.
ptrdiff_t	A signed integer type that is the result of subtracting two pointers. This is a 32-bit signed integer if the address space of the device is 32 bits and is a 64-bit signed integer if the address space of the device is 64 bits.
intptr_t	A signed integer type with the property that any valid pointer to void can be converted to this type, then converted back to a pointer to void, and the result will compare equal to the original pointer.

Table 4.1 Built-In Scalar Data Types (*Continued*)

Type	Description
uintptr_t	An unsigned integer type with the property that any valid pointer to void can be converted to this type, then converted back to a pointer to void, and the result will compare equal to the original pointer.
void	The void type constitutes an empty set of values; it is an incomplete type that cannot be completed.

The half Data Type

The half data type must be IEEE 754-2008-compliant. half numbers have 1 sign bit, 5 exponent bits, and 10 mantissa bits. The interpretation of the sign, exponent, and mantissa is analogous to that of IEEE 754 floating-point numbers. The exponent bias is 15. The half data type must represent finite and normal numbers, denormalized numbers, infinities, and NaN. Denormalized numbers for the half data type, which may be generated when converting a float to a half using the built-in function vstore_half and converting a half to a float using the built-in function vload_half, cannot be flushed to zero.

Conversions from float to half correctly round the mantissa to 11 bits of precision. Conversions from half to float are lossless; all half numbers are exactly representable as float values.

The half data type can be used only to declare a pointer to a buffer that contains half values. A few valid examples are given here:

```
void
bar(global half *p)
{
    ...
}

void
foo(global half *pg, local half *pl)
{
    global half *ptr;
    int offset;

    ptr = pg + offset;
    bar(ptr);
}
```

Following is an example that is not a valid usage of the `half` type:

```
half a;
half a[100];

half *p;
a = *p;      // not allowed. must use vload_half function
```

Loads from a pointer to a `half` and stores to a pointer to a `half` can be performed using the `vload_half`, `vload_half`*n*, `vloada_half`*n* and `vstore_half`, `vstore_half`*n*, and `vstorea_half`*n* functions, respectively. The load functions read scalar or vector `half` values from memory and convert them to a scalar or vector float value. The `store` functions take a scalar or vector float value as input, convert it to a `half` scalar or vector value (with appropriate rounding mode), and write the `half` scalar or vector value to memory.

Vector Data Types

For the scalar integer and floating-point data types described in Table 4.1, OpenCL C adds support for vector data types. The vector data type is defined with the type name, that is, `char`, `uchar`, `short`, `ushort`, `int`, `uint`, `float`, `long`, or `ulong` followed by a literal value *n* that defines the number of elements in the vector. Supported values of *n* are 2, 3, 4, 8, and 16 for all vector data types. Optionally, vector data types are also defined for `double` and `half`. These are available only if the device supports the double-precision and half-precision extensions. The supported vector data types are described in Table 4.2.

Variables declared to be a scalar or vector data type are always aligned to the size of the data type used in bytes. Built-in data types must be aligned to a power of 2 bytes in size. A built-in data type that is not a power of 2 bytes in size must be aligned to the next-larger power of 2. This rule does not apply to structs or unions.

For example, a `float4` variable will be aligned to a 16-byte boundary and a `char2` variable will be aligned to a 2-byte boundary. For 3-component vector data types, the size of the data type is $4 \times$ `sizeof`(component). This means that a 3-component vector data type will be aligned to a $4 \times$ `sizeof`(component) boundary.

The OpenCL compiler is responsible for aligning data items appropriately as required by the data type. The only exception is for an argument to a

Table 4.2 Built-In Vector Data Types

Type	Description
char*n*	A vector of n 8-bit signed integer values
uchar*n*	A vector of n 8-bit unsigned integer values
short*n*	A vector of n 16-bit signed integer values
ushort*n*	A vector of n 16-bit unsigned integer values
int*n*	A vector of n 32-bit signed integer values
uint*n*	A vector of n 32-bit unsigned integer values
long*n*	A vector of n 64-bit signed integer values
ulong*n*	A vector of n 64-bit unsigned integer values
float*n*	A vector of n 32-bit floating-point values
double*n*	A vector of n 64-bit floating-point values
half*n*	A vector of n 16-bit floating-point values

kernel function that is declared to be a pointer to a data type. For such functions, the compiler can assume that the pointee is always appropriately aligned as required by the data type.

For application convenience and to ensure that the data store is appropriately aligned, the data types listed in Table 4.3 are made available to the application.

Table 4.3 Application Data Types

Type in OpenCL Language	API Type for Application
char	cl_char
uchar	cl_uchar
short	cl_short
ushort	cl_ushort
int	cl_int

continues

Table 4.3 Application Data Types (*Continued*)

Type in OpenCL Language	API Type for Application
uint	cl_uint
long	cl_long
ulong	cl_ulong
float	cl_float
double	cl_double
half	cl_half
char*n*	cl_char*n*
uchar*n*	cl_uchar*n*
short*n*	cl_short*n*
ushort*n*	cl_ushort*n*
int*n*	cl_int*n*
uint*n*	cl_uint*n*
long*n*	cl_long*n*
ulong*n*	cl_ulong*n*
float*n*	cl_float*n*
double*n*	cl_double*n*
half*n*	cl_half*n*

Vector Literals

Vector literals can be used to create vectors from a list of scalars, vectors, or a combination of scalar and vectors. A vector literal can be used either as a vector initializer or as a primary expression. A vector literal cannot be used as an l-value.

A vector literal is written as a parenthesized vector type followed by a parenthesized comma-delimited list of parameters. A vector literal operates as an overloaded function. The forms of the function that are available are the set of possible argument lists for which all arguments have the same element type as the result vector, and the total number of elements is equal to the number of elements in the result vector. In addition, a form with a single scalar of the same type as the element type of the vector is available. For example, the following forms are available for float4:

```
(float4)( float, float, float, float )
(float4)( float2, float, float )
(float4)( float, float2, float )
(float4)( float, float, float2 )
(float4)( float2, float2 )
(float4)( float3, float )
(float4)( float, float3 )
(float4)( float )
```

Operands are evaluated by standard rules for function evaluation, except that no implicit scalar widening occurs. The operands are assigned to their respective positions in the result vector as they appear in memory order. That is, the first element of the first operand is assigned to result.x, the second element of the first operand (or the first element of the second operand if the first operand was a scalar) is assigned to result.y, and so on. If the operand is a scalar, the operand is replicated across all lanes of the result vector.

The following example shows a vector float4 created from a list of scalars:

```
float4  f = (float4)(1.0f, 2.0f, 3.0f, 4.0f);
```

The following example shows a vector uint4 created from a scalar, which is replicated across the components of the vector:

```
uint4   u = (uint4)(1); // u will be (1, 1, 1, 1)
```

The following examples show more complex combinations of a vector being created using a scalar and smaller vector types:

```
float4  f = (float4)((float2)(1.0f, 2.0f), (float2)(3.0f, 4.0f));
float4  f = (float4)(1.0f, (float2)(2.0f, 3.0f), 4.0f);
```

The following examples describe how *not* to create vector literals. All of these examples should result in a compilation error.

```
float4  f = (float4)(1.0f, 2.0f);
float4  f = (float2)(1.0f, 2.0f);
float4  f = (float4)(1.0f, (float2)(2.0f, 3.0f));
```

Vector Components

The components of vector data types with 1 to 4 components (aka elements) can be addressed as `<vector>.xyzw`. Table 4.4 lists the components that can be accessed for various vector types.

Table 4.4 Accessing Vector Components

Vector Data Types	Accessible Components
`char2`, `uchar2`, `short2`, `ushort2`, `int2`, `uint2`, `long2`, `ulong2`, `float2`	`.xy`
`char3`, `uchar3`, `short3`, `ushort3`, `int3`, `uint3`, `long3`, `ulong3`, `float3`	`.xyz`
`char4`, `uchar4`, `short4`, `ushort4`, `int4`, `uint4`, `long4`, `ulong4`, `float4`	`.xyzw`
`double2`, `half2`	`.xy`
`double3`, `half3`	`.xyz`
`double4`, `half4`	`.xyzw`

Accessing components beyond those declared for the vector type is an error. The following describes legal and illegal examples of accessing vector components:

```
float2 pos;
pos.x = 1.0f; // is legal
pos.z = 1.0f; // is illegal

float3 pos;
pos.z = 1.0f; // is legal
pos.w = 1.0f; // is illegal
```

The component selection syntax allows multiple components to be selected by appending their names after the period (.). A few examples that show how to use the component selection syntax are given here:

```
float4 c;

c.xyzw = (float4)(1.0f, 2.0f, 3.0f, 4.0f);
c.z = 1.0f;
c.xy = (float2)(3.0f, 4.0f);
c.xyz = (float3)(3.0f, 4.0f, 5.0f);
```

The component selection syntax also allows components to be permuted or replicated as shown in the following examples:

```
float4 pos = (float4)(1.0f, 2.0f, 3.0f, 4.0f);
float4 swiz = pos.wzyx; // swiz = (4.0f, 3.0f, 2.0f, 1.0f)
float4 dup = pox.xxyy;  // dup = (1.0f, 1.0f, 2.0f, 2.0f)
```

Vector components can also be accessed using a numeric index to refer to the appropriate elements in the vector. The numeric indices that can be used are listed in Table 4.5.

Table 4.5 Numeric Indices for Built-In Vector Data Types

Vector Components	Usable Numeric Indices
2-component	0, 1
3-component	0, 1, 2
4-component	0, 1, 2, 3
8-component	0, 1, 2, 3, 4, 5, 6, 7
16-component	0, 1, 2, 3, 4, 5, 6 , 7, 8, 9, a, A , b, B, c, C, d, D, e, E, f, F

All numeric indices must be preceded by the letter s or S. In the following example f.s0 refers to the first element of the float8 variable f and f.s7 refers to the eighth element of the float8 variable f:

```
float8 f
```

In the following example x.sa (or x.sA) refers to the eleventh element of the float16 variable x and x.sf (or x.sF) refers to the sixteenth element of the float16 variable x:

```
float16 x
```

The numeric indices cannot be intermixed with the .xyzw notation. For example:

```
float4 f;
float4 v_A = f.xs123;  // is illegal
float4 v_B = f.s012w;  // is illegal
```

Vector data types can use the .lo (or .odd) and .hi (or .even) suffixes to get smaller vector types or to combine smaller vector types into a larger vector type. Multiple levels of .lo (or .odd) and .hi (or .even) suffixes can be used until they refer to a scalar type.

The .lo suffix refers to the lower half of a given vector. The .hi suffix refers to the upper half of a given vector. The .odd suffix refers to the odd elements of a given vector. The .even suffix refers to the even elements of a given vector. Some examples to illustrate this concept are given here:

```
float4 vf;

float2 low = vf.lo;      // returns vf.xy
float2 high = vf.hi;     // returns vf.zw
float x = low.low;       // returns low.x
float y = low.hi;        // returns low.y

float2 odd = vf.odd;     // returns vf.yw
float2 even = vf.even;   // returns vf.xz
```

For a 3-component vector, the suffixes .lo (or .odd) and .hi (or .even) operate as if the 3-component vector were a 4-component vector with the value in the w component undefined.

Other Data Types

The other data types supported by OpenCL C are described in Table 4.6.

Table 4.6 Other Built-In Data Types

Type	Description
image2d_t	A 2D image type.
image3d_t	A 3D image type.
sampler_t	An image sampler type.
event_t	An event type. These are used by built-in functions that perform async copies from global to local memory and vice versa. Each async copy operation returns an event and takes an event to wait for that identifies a previous async copy operation.

There are a few restrictions on the use of image and sampler types:

- The image and samplers types are defined only if the device supports images.

- Image and sampler types cannot be declared as arrays. Here are a couple of examples that show these illegal use cases:

```
kernel void
foo(image2d_t imgA[10]) // error. images cannot be declared
                        //        as arrays
{
    image2d_t imgB[4];  // error. images cannot be declared
                        //        as arrays
    ...
}


kernel void
foo(sampler_t smpA[10]) // error. samplers cannot be declared
                        //        as arrays
{
    sampler_t smpB[4];  // error. samplers cannot be declared
                        //        as arrays
    ...
}
```

- The `image2d_t`, `image3d_t`, and `sampler_t` data types cannot be declared in a struct.

- Variables cannot be declared to be pointers of `image2d_t`, `image3d_t`, and `sampler_t` data types.

Derived Types

The C99 derived types (arrays, structs, unions, and pointers) constructed from the built-in data types described in Tables 4.1 and 4.2 are supported. There are a few restrictions on the use of derived types:

- The struct type cannot contain any pointers if the struct or pointer to a struct is used as an argument type to a kernel function. For example, the following use case is invalid:

```
typedef struct {
    int  x;
    global float *f;
} mystruct_t;
```

```
kernel void
foo(global mystruct_t *p) // error. mystruct_t contains
                          //           a pointer
{
    ...
}
```

- The struct type can contain pointers only if the struct or pointer to a struct is used as an argument type to a non-kernel function or declared as a variable inside a kernel or non-kernel function. For example, the following use case is valid:

```
void
my_func(mystruct_t *p)
{
    ...
}


kernel void
foo(global int *p1, global float *p2)
{
    mystruct_t s;

    s.x = p1[get_global_id(0)];
    s.f = p2;
    my_func(&s);
}
```

Implicit Type Conversions

Implicit type conversion is an automatic type conversion done by the compiler whenever data from different types is intermixed. Implicit conversions of scalar built-in types defined in Table 4.1 (except void, double,[1] and half[2]) are supported. When an implicit conversion is done, it is not just a reinterpretation of the expression's value but a conversion of that value to an equivalent value in the new type.

Consider the following example:

```
float f = 3;     // implicit conversion to float value 3.0
int   i = 5.23f; // implicit conversion to integer value 5
```

---

[1] Unless the double-precision extension (cl_khr_fp64) is supported by the device.

[2] Unless the half-precision extension (cl_khr_fp16) is supported by the device.

In this example, the value 3 is converted to a `float` value `3.0f` and then assigned to `f`. The value `5.23f` is converted to an `int` value 5 and then assigned to `i`. In the second example, the fractional part of the `float` value is dropped because integers cannot support fractional values; this is an example of an unsafe type conversion.

Warning   Note that some type conversions are inherently unsafe, and if the compiler can detect that an unsafe conversion is being implicitly requested, it will issue a warning.

Implicit conversions for pointer types follow the rules described in the C99 specification. Implicit conversions between built-in vector data types are disallowed. For example:

```
float4 f;
int4   i;

f = i;  // illegal implicit conversion between vector data types
```

There are graphics shading languages such as OpenGL Shading Language (GLSL) and the DirectX Shading Language (HLSL) that do allow implicit conversions between vector types. However, prior art for vector casts in C doesn't support conversion casts. The *AltiVec Technology Programming Interface Manual* (www.freescale.com/files/32bit/doc/ref_manual/ALTIVECPIM. pdf?fsrch=1), Section 2.4.6, describes the function of casts between vector types. The casts are conversion-free. Thus, any conforming AltiVec compiler has this behavior. Examples include XL C, GCC, MrC, Metrowerks, and Green Hills. IBM's Cell SPE C language extension (*C/C++ Language Extensions for Cell Broadband Engine Architecture*; see Section 1.4.5) has the same behavior. GCC and ICC have adopted the conversion-free cast model for SSE (http://gcc.gnu.org/onlinedocs/gcc-4.2.4/gcc/Vector-Extensions.html#Vector-Extensions). The following code example shows the behavior of these compilers:

```
#include <stdio.h>

// Declare some vector types. This should work on most compilers
// that try to be GCC compatible. Alternatives are provided
// for those that don't conform to GCC behavior in vector
// type declaration.
// Here a vFloat is a vector of four floats, and
// a vInt is a vector of four 32-bit ints.
#if 1
    // This should work on most compilers that try
    // to be GCC compatible
    // cc main.c -Wall -pedantic
    typedef float vFloat __attribute__ ((__vector_size__(16)));
```

```
        typedef int   vInt   __attribute__ ((__vector_size__(16)));
        #define init_vFloat(a, b, c, d)    (const vFloat) {a, b, c, d}
#else
    //Not GCC compatible
    #if defined( __SSE2__ )
        // depending on compiler you might need to pass
        // something like -msse2 to turn on SSE2
        #include <emmintrin.h>
        typedef __m128  vFloat;
        typedef __m128i vInt;
        static inline vFloat init_vFloat(float a, float b,
                                         float c, float d);
        static inline vFloat init_vFloat(float a, float b,
                                         float c, float d)
        { union{ vFloat v; float f[4];}u;
          u.f[0] = a; u.f[1] = b;
          u.f[2] = c; u.f[3] = d;
          return u.v;
        }
    #elif defined( __VEC__ )
        // depending on compiler you might need to pass
        // something like -faltivec or -maltivec or
        // "Enable AltiVec Extensions" to turn this part on
        #include <altivec.h>
        typedef vector float vFloat;
        typedef vector int   vInt;

        #if 1
            // for compliant compilers
            #define init_vFloat(a, b, c, d) \
                    (const vFloat) (a, b, c, d)
        #else
            // for FSF GCC
            #define init_vFloat(a, b, c, d) \
                    (const vFloat) {a, b, c, d}
        #endif
    #endif
#endif

void
print_vInt(vInt v)
{
    union{ vInt v; int i[4]; }u;
    u.v = v;

    printf("vInt: 0x%8.8x 0x%8.8x 0x%8.8x 0x%8.8x\n",
                    u.i[0], u.i[1], u.i[2], u.i[3]);
}
```

```
void
print_vFloat(vFloat v)
{
    union{ vFloat v; float i[4]; }u;
    u.v = v;

    printf("vFloat: %f %f %f %f\n", u.i[0], u.i[1], u.i[2], u.i[3]);
}

int
main(void)
{
    vFloat   f = init_vFloat(1.0f, 2.0f, 3.0f, 4.0f);
    vInt     i;

    print_vFloat(f);

    printf("assign with cast:  vInt i = (vInt) f;\n" );
    i = (vInt) f;

    print_vInt(i);

    return 0;
}
```

The output of this code example demonstrates that conversions between vector data types implemented by some C compilers[3] such as GCC are cast-free.

```
vFloat: 1.000000 2.000000 3.000000 4.000000
assign with cast:  vInt i = (vInt) f;
vInt: 0x3f800000 0x40000000 0x40400000 0x40800000
```

So we have prior art in C where casts between vector data types do not perform conversions as opposed to graphics shading languages that do perform conversions. The OpenCL working group decided it was best to make implicit conversions between vector data types illegal. It turns out that this was the right thing to do for other reasons, as discussed in the section "Explicit Conversions" later in this chapter.

---

[3] Some fiddling with compiler flags to get the vector extensions turned on may be required, for example, -msse2 or -faltivec. You might need to play with the #ifs. The problem is that there is no portable way to declare a vector type. Getting rid of the sort of portability headaches at the top of the code example is one of the major value-adds of OpenCL.

Usual Arithmetic Conversions

Many operators that expect operands of arithmetic types (integer or floating-point types) cause conversions and yield result types in a similar way. The purpose is to determine a common real type for the operands and result. For the specified operands, each operand is converted, without change of type domain, to a type whose corresponding real type is the common real type. For this purpose, all vector types are considered to have a higher conversion rank than scalars. Unless explicitly stated otherwise, the common real type is also the corresponding real type of the result, whose type domain is the type domain of the operands if they are the same, and complex otherwise. This pattern is called the **usual arithmetic conversions**.

If the operands are of more than one vector type, then a compile-time error will occur. Implicit conversions between vector types are not permitted.

Otherwise, if there is only a single vector type, and all other operands are scalar types, the scalar types are *converted* to the type of the vector element, and then *widened* into a new vector containing the same number of elements as the vector, by duplication of the scalar value across the width of the new vector. A compile-time error will occur if any scalar operand has greater rank than the type of the vector element. For this purpose, the rank order is defined as follows:

1. The rank of a floating-point type is greater than the rank of another floating-point type if the floating-point type can exactly represent all numeric values in the second floating-point type. (For this purpose, the encoding of the floating-point value is used, rather than the subset of the encoding usable by the device.)

2. The rank of any floating-point type is greater than the rank of any integer type.

3. The rank of an integer type is greater than the rank of an integer type with less precision.

4. The rank of an unsigned integer type is greater than the rank of a signed integer type with the same precision.

5. `bool` has a rank less than any other type.

6. The rank of an enumerated type is equal to the rank of the compatible integer type.

7. For all types `T1`, `T2`, and `T3`, if `T1` has greater rank than `T2`, and `T2` has greater rank than `T3`, then `T1` has greater rank than `T3`.

Otherwise, if all operands are scalar, the usual arithmetic conversions apply as defined by Section 6.3.1.8 of the C99 specification.

Following are a few examples of legal usual arithmetic conversions with vectors and vector and scalar operands:

```
short a;
int4  b;
int4  c = b + a;
```

In this example, the variable a, which is of type `short`, is converted to an `int4` and the vector addition is then performed.

```
int    a;
float4 b;
float4 c = b + a;
```

In the preceding example, the variable a, which is of type `int`, is converted to a `float4` and the vector addition is then performed.

```
float4 a;
float4 b;
float4 c = b + a;
```

In this example, no conversions need to be performed because a, b, and c are all the same type.

Here are a few examples of illegal usual arithmetic conversions with vectors and vector and scalar operands:

```
int    a;
short4 b;
short4 c = b + a; // cannot convert & widen int to short4

double a;
float4 b;
float4 c = b + a; // cannot convert & widen double to float4

int4   a;
float4 b;
float4 c = b + a; // cannot cast between different vector types
```

Explicit Casts

Standard type casts for the built-in scalar data types defined in Table 4.1 will perform appropriate conversion (except void and half[4]). In the next example, f stores 0x3F800000 and i stores 0x1, which is the floating-point value 1.0f in f converted to an integer value:

```
float f = 1.0f;
int   i = (int)f;
```

Explicit casts between vector types are not legal. The following examples will generate a compilation error:

```
int4   i;
uint4  u = (uint4)i;    // compile error

float4 f;
int4   i = (int4)f;     // compile error

float4 f;
int8   i = (int8)f;     // compile error
```

Scalar to vector conversions are performed by casting the scalar to the desired vector data type. Type casting will also perform the appropriate arithmetic conversion. Conversions to built-in integer vector types are performed with the round-toward-zero rounding mode. Conversions to built-in floating-point vector types are performed with the round-to-nearest rounding mode. When casting a bool to a vector integer data type, the vector components will be set to –1 (that is, all bits are set) if the bool value is true and 0 otherwise.

Here are some examples of explicit casts:

```
float4 f = 1.0f;
float4 va = (float4)f;  // va is a float4 vector
                        // with elements ( f, f, f, f )

uchar u = 0xFF;
float4 vb = (float4)u;  // vb is a float4 vector with elements
                        // ( (float)u, (float)u,
                        //   (float)u, (float)u )

float f = 2.0f;
int2 vc = (int2)f;      // vc is an int2 vector with elements
                        // ( (int)f, (int)f )
```

---

[4] Unless the half-precision extension (cl_khr_fp16) is supported.

```
uchar4 vtrue =(uchar4)true;   // vtrue is a uchar4 vector with
                              // elements(0xFF, 0xFF, 0xFF, 0xFF)
```

Explicit Conversions

In the preceding sections we learned that implicit conversions and explicit casts do not allow conversions between vector types. However, there are many cases where we need to convert a vector type to another type. In addition, it may be necessary to specify the rounding mode that should be used to perform the conversion and whether the results of the conversion are to be saturated. This is useful for both scalar and vector data types.

Consider the following example:

```
float x;
int   i = (int)x;
```

In this example the value in x is truncated to an integer value and stored in i; that is, the cast performs round-toward-zero rounding when converting the floating-point value to an integer value.

Sometimes we need to round the floating-point value to the nearest integer. The following example shows how this is typically done:

```
float x;
int   i = (int)(x + 0.5f);
```

This works correctly for most values of x except when x is $0.5f - 1$ ulp[5] or if x is a negative number. When x is $0.5f - 1$ ulp, (int)(x + 0.5f) returns 1; that is, it rounds up instead of rounding down. When x is a negative number, (int)(x + 0.5f) rounds down instead of rounding up.

```
#include <math.h>
#include <stdio.h>
#include <stdlib.h>
#include <float.h>

int
main(void)
{
    float a = 0.5f;
    float b = a - nextafterf(a, (float)-INFINITY); // a - 1 ulp
```

---

[5] ulp(x) is the gap between two finite floating-point numbers. A detailed description of ulp(x) is given in Chapter 5 in the section "Math Functions," subsection "Relative Error as ulps."

```
    printf("a = %8x, b = %8x\n",
                    *(unsigned int *)&a, *(unsigned int *)&b);
    printf("(int)(a + 0.5f) = %d \n", (int)(a + 0.5f));
    printf("(int)(b + 0.5f) = %d \n", (int)(b + 0.5f));
}
```

The printed values are:

```
a = 3f000000, b = 3efffff  // where b = a - 1 ulp.
(int)(a + 0.5f) = 1,
(int)(b + 0.5f) = 1
```

We could fix these issues by adding appropriate checks to see what value x is and then perform the correct conversion, but there is hardware to do these conversions with rounding and saturation on most devices. It is important from a performance perspective that OpenCL C allows developers to perform these conversions using the appropriate hardware ISA as opposed to emulating in software. This is why OpenCL implements built-in functions that perform conversions from one type to another with options that select saturation and one of four rounding modes.

Explicit conversions may be performed using either of the following:

```
destType convert_destType<_sat><_roundingMode> (sourceType)
destType convert_destTypen<_sat><_roundingMode> (sourceTypen)
```

These provide a full set of type conversions for the following scalar types: char, uchar, short, ushort, int, uint, long, ulong, float, double,[6] half,[7] and the built-in vector types derived therefrom. The operand and result type must have the same number of elements. The operand and result type may be the same type, in which case the conversion has no effect on the type or value.

In the following example, convert_int4 converts a uchar4 vector u to an int4 vector c:

```
uchar4 u;
int4   c = convert_int4(u);
```

In the next example, convert_int converts a float scalar f to an int scalar i:

```
float f;
int   i = convert_int(f);
```

---

[6] Unless the double-precision extension (cl_khr_fp64) is supported.

[7] Unless the half-precision extension (cl_khr_fp16) is supported.

Table 4.7 Rounding Modes for Conversions

Rounding Mode Modifier	Rounding Mode Description
_rte	Round to nearest even.
_rtz	Round toward zero.
_rtp	Round toward positive infinity.
_rtn	Round toward negative infinity.
No modifier specified	Use the default rounding mode for this destination type: _rtz for conversion to integers or _rte for conversion to floating-point types.

The optional rounding mode modifier can be set to one of the values described in Table 4.7.

The optional saturation modifier (_sat) can be used to specify that the results of the conversion must be saturated to the result type. When the conversion operand is either greater than the greatest representable destination value or less than the least representable destination value, it is said to be out of range. When converting between integer types, the resulting value for out-of-range inputs will be equal to the set of least significant bits in the source operand element that fits in the corresponding destination element. When converting from a floating-point type to an integer type, the behavior is implementation-defined.

Conversions to integer type may opt to convert using the optional saturated mode by appending the _sat modifier to the conversion function name. When in saturated mode, values that are outside the representable range clamp to the nearest representable value in the destination format. (NaN should be converted to 0.)

Conversions to a floating-point type conform to IEEE 754 rounding rules. The _sat modifier may not be used for conversions to floating-point formats.

Following are a few examples of using explicit conversion functions.

The next example shows a conversion of a float4 to a ushort4 with round-to-nearest rounding mode and saturation. Figure 4.2 describes the values in f and the result of conversion in c.

```
float4  f = (float4)(-5.0f, 254.5f, 254.6f, 1.2e9f);

ushort4 c = convert_uchar4_sat_rte(f);
```

Figure 4.2   Converting a `float4` to a `ushort4` with round-to-nearest rounding and saturation

The next example describes the behavior of the saturation modifier when converting a signed value to an unsigned value or performing a down-conversion with integer types:

```
short4 s;

// negative values clamped to 0
ushort4 u = convert_ushort4_sat(s);

// values > CHAR_MAX converted to CHAR_MAX
// values < CHAR_MIN converted to CHAR_MIN
char4 c = convert_char4_sat(s);
```

The following example illustrates conversion from a floating-point to an integer with saturation and rounding mode modifiers:

```
float4 f;

// values implementation-defined for f > INT_MAX, f < INT_MAX, or
NaN
int4 i = convert_int4(f);

// values > INT_MAX clamp to INT_MAX,
// values < INT_MIN clamp to INT_MIN
// NaN should produce 0.
// The _rtz rounding mode is used to produce the integer values.
int4 i2 = convert_int4_sat(f);

// similar to convert_int4 except that floating-point values
// are rounded to the nearest integer instead of truncated
int4 i3 = convert_int4_rte(f);

// similar to convert_int4_sat except that floating-point values
// are rounded to the nearest integer instead of truncated
int4 i4 = convert_int4_sat_rte(f);
```

The final conversion example given here shows conversions from an integer to a floating-point value with and without the optional rounding mode modifier:

```
int4 i;

// convert ints to floats using the round-to-nearest rounding mode
float4 f = convert_float4(i);

// convert ints to floats; integer values that cannot be
// exactly represented as floats should round up to the next
// representable float
float4 f = convert_float4_rtp(i);
```

Reinterpreting Data as Another Type

Consider the case where you want to mask off the sign bit of a floating-point type. There are multiple ways to solve this in C—using pointer aliasing, unions, or memcpy. Of these, only memcpy is strictly correct in C99. Because OpenCL C does not support memcpy, we need a different method to perform this masking-off operation. The general capability we need is the ability to reinterpret bits in a data type as another data type. In the example where we want to mask off the sign bit of a floating-point type, we want to reinterpret these bits as an unsigned integer type and then mask off the sign bit. Other examples include using the result of a vector relational operator and extracting the exponent or mantissa bits of a floating-point type.

The as_type and as_typen built-in functions allow you to reinterpret bits of a data type as another data type of the same size. The as_type is used for scalar data types (except bool and void) and as_typen for vector data types. double and half are supported only if the appropriate extensions are supported by the implementation.

The following example describes how you would mask off the sign bit of a floating-point type using the as_type built-in function:

```
float f;
uint  u;

u = as_uint(f);
f = as_float(u & ~(1 << 31));
```

If the operand and result type contain the same number of elements, the bits in the operand are returned directly without modification as the new type. If the operand and result type contain a different number of elements, two cases arise:

- The operand is a 4-component vector and the result is a 3-component vector. In this case, the xyz components of the operand and the result will have the same bits. The w component of the result is considered to be undefined.

- For all other cases, the behavior is implementation-defined.

We next describe a few examples that show how to use as_type and as_typen. The following example shows how to reinterpret an int as a float:

```
uint  u = 0x3f800000;
float f = as_float(u);
```

The variable u, which is declared as an unsigned integer, contains the value 0x3f800000. This represents the single-precision floating-point value 1.0. The variable f now contains the floating-point value 1.0.

In the next example, we reinterpret a float4 as an int4:

```
float4 f = (float4)(1.0f, 2.0f, 3.0f, 4.0f);
int4 i = as_int4(f);
```

The variable i, defined to be of type int4, will have the following values in its xyzw components: 0x3f800000, 0x40000000, 0x40400000, 0x40800000.

The next example shows how we can perform the ternary selection operator (?:) for floating-point vector types using as_typen:

```
// Perform the operation f = f < g ? f : 0 for components of a
// vector
float4 f, g;
int4 is_less = f < g;

// Each component of the is_less vector will be 0 if result of <
// operation is false and will be -1 (i.e., all bits set) if
// the result of < operation is true.

f = as_float4(as_int4(f) & is_less);
// This basically selects f or 0 depending on the values in is_less.
```

The following example describes cases where the operand and result have a different number of results, in which case the behavior of as_type and as_typen is implementation-defined:

```
int i;
short2 j = as_short2(i); // Legal. Result is implementation-defined

int4 i;
short8 j = as_short8(i); // Legal. Result is implementation-defined

float4 f;
float3 g = as_float3(f); // Legal. g.xyz will have same values as
                         // f.xyz. g.w is undefined
```

This example describes reinterpreting a 4-component vector as a 3-component vector:

```
float4 f;
float3 g = as_float3(f); // Legal. g.xyz will have same values as
                         // f.xyz. g.w is undefined
```

The next example shows invalid ways of using as_type and as_type*n*, which should result in compilation errors:

```
float4 f;
double4 g = as_double4(f); // Error. Result and operand have
                           // different sizes.

float3 f;
float4 g = as_float4(f); // Error. Result and operand have
                         // different sizes
```

Vector Operators

Table 4.8 describes the list of operators that can be used with vector data types or a combination of vector and scalar data types.

Table 4.8 Operators That Can Be Used with Vector Data Types

Operator Category	Operator Symbols
Arithmetic operators	Add (+)
	Subtract (−)
	Multiply (*)
	Divide (/)
	Remainder (%)

continues

Table 4.8 Operators That Can Be Used with Vector Data Types (*Continued*)

Operator Category	Operator Symbols
Relational operators	Greater than (>)
	Less than (<)
	Greater than or equal (>=)
	Less than or equal (<=)
Equality operators	Equal (==)
	Not equal (! =)
Bitwise operators	And (&)
	Or (|)
	Exclusive or (^), not (~)
Logical operators	And (&&)
	Or (||)
Conditional operator	Ternary selection operator (? :)
Shift operators	Right shift (>>)
	Left shift (<<)
Unary operators	Arithmetic (+ or -)
	Post- and pre-increment (++)
	Post- and pre-decrement (- -)
	sizeof, not (!)
	Comma operator (,)
	Address and indirection operators (&, *)
Assignment operators	=, *= , /= , += , -= , <<= , >>= , &= , ^= , |=

The behavior of these operators for scalar data types is as described by the C99 specification. The following sections discuss how each operator works with operands that are vector data types or vector and scalar data types.

Arithmetic Operators

The arithmetic operators—add (+), subtract (-), multiply (*), and divide (/)—operate on built-in integer and floating-point scalar and vector data types. The remainder operator (%) operates on built-in integer scalar and vector data types only. The following cases arise:

- The two operands are scalars. In this case, the operation is applied according to C99 rules.

- One operand is a scalar and the other is a vector. The scalar operand may be subject to the usual arithmetic conversion to the element type used by the vector operand and is then widened to a vector that has the same number of elements as the vector operand. The operation is applied component-wise, resulting in the same size vector.

- The two operands are vectors of the same type. In this case, the operation is applied component-wise, resulting in the same size vector.

For integer types, a divide by zero or a division that results in a value that is outside the range will not cause an exception but will result in an unspecified value. Division by zero for floating-point types will result in ±infinity or NaN as prescribed by the IEEE 754 standard.

A few examples will illustrate how the arithmetic operators work when one operand is a scalar and the other a vector, or when both operands are vectors.

The first example in Figure 4.3 shows two vectors being added:

```
int4 v_iA = (int4)(7, -3, -2, 5);
int4 v_iB = (int4)(1, 2, 3, 4);
int4 v_iC = v_iA + v_iB;
```

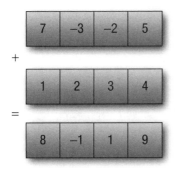

Figure 4.3   Adding two vectors

The result of the addition stored in vector v_iC is (8, -1, 1, 9).

The next example in Figure 4.4 shows a multiplication operation where operands are a vector and a scalar. In this example, the scalar is just widened to the size of the vector and the components of each vector are multiplied:

```
float4 vf = (float4)(3.0f, -1.0f, 1.0f, -2.0f);
float4 result = vf * 2.5f;
```

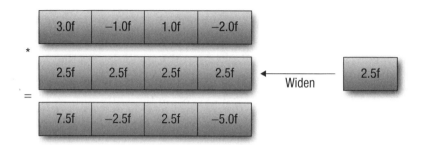

Figure 4.4   Multiplying a vector and a scalar with widening

The result of the multiplication stored in vector `result` is (`7.5f, -2.5f, 2.5f, -5.0f`).

The next example in Figure 4.5 shows how we can multiply a vector and a scalar where the scalar is implicitly converted and widened:

```
float4 vf = (float4)(3.0f, -1.0f, 1.0f, -2.0f);
float4 result = vf * 2;
```

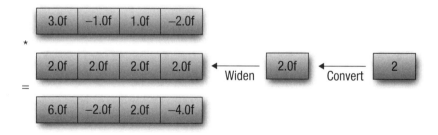

Figure 4.5   Multiplying a vector and a scalar with conversion and widening

The result of the multiplication stored in the vector `result` is (`6.0f, -2.0f, 2.0f, -4.0f`).

Relational and Equality Operators

The relational operators—greater than (>), less than (<), greater than or equal (>=), and less than or equal (<=)—and equality operators—equal (==) and not equal (!=)—operate on built-in integer and floating-point scalar and vector data types. The result is an integer scalar or vector type. The following cases arise:

- The two operands are scalars. In this case, the operation is applied according to C99 rules.

- One operand is a scalar and the other is a vector. The scalar operand may be subject to the usual arithmetic conversion to the element type used by the vector operand and is then widened to a vector that has the same number of elements as the vector operand. The operation is applied component-wise, resulting in the same size vector.

- The two operands are vectors of the same type. In this case, the operation is applied component-wise, resulting in the same size vector.

The result is a scalar signed integer of type `int` if both source operands are scalar and a vector signed integer type of the same size as the vector source operand. The result is of type `char`n if the source operands are `char`n or `uchar`n; `short`n if the source operands are `short`n, `short`n, or `half`n; `int`n if the source operands are `int`n, `uint`n, or `float`n; `long`n if the source operands are `long`n, `ulong`n, or `double`n.

For scalar types, these operators return 0 if the specified relation is false and 1 if the specified relation is true. For vector types, these operators return 0 if the specified relation is false and -1 (i.e., all bits set) if the specified relation is true. The relational operators always return 0 if one or both arguments are not a number (NaN). The equality operator equal (==) returns 0 if one or both arguments are not a number (NaN), and the equality operator not equal (!=) returns 1 (for scalar source operands) or -1 (for vector source operands) if one or both arguments are not a number (NaN).

Bitwise Operators

The bitwise operators—and (&), or (|), exclusive or (^), and not (~)—operate on built-in integer scalar and vector data types. The result is an integer scalar or vector type. The following cases arise:

- The two operands are scalars. In this case, the operation is applied according to C99 rules.

- One operand is a scalar and the other is a vector. The scalar operand may be subject to the usual arithmetic conversion to the element type used by the vector operand and is then widened to a vector that has the same number of elements as the vector operand. The operation is applied component-wise, resulting in the same size vector.

- The two operands are vectors of the same type. In this case, the operation is applied component-wise, resulting in the same size vector.

Logical Operators

The logical operators—and (&&), or (||)—operate on built-in integer scalar and vector data types. The result is an integer scalar or vector type. The following cases arise:

- The two operands are scalars. In this case, the operation is applied according to C99 rules.

- One operand is a scalar and the other is a vector. The scalar operand may be subject to the usual arithmetic conversion to the element type used by the vector operand and is then widened to a vector that has the same number of elements as the vector operand. The operation is applied component-wise, resulting in the same size vector.

- The two operands are vectors of the same type. In this case, the operation is applied component-wise, resulting in the same size vector.

If both source operands are scalar, the logical operator and (&&) will evaluate the right-hand operand only if the left-hand operand compares unequal to 0, and the logical operator or (||) will evaluate the right-hand operand only if the left-hand operand compares equal to 0. If one or both source operands are vector types, both operands are evaluated.

The result is a scalar signed integer of type int if both source operands are scalar and a vector signed integer type of the same size as the vector source operand. The result is of type char$n$ if the source operands are char$n$ or uchar$n$; short$n$ if the source operands are short$n$ or ushort$n$; int$n$ if the source operands are int$n$ or uint$n$; or long$n$ if the source operands are long$n$ or ulong$n$.

For scalar types, these operators return 0 if the specified relation is false and 1 if the specified relation is true. For vector types, these operators return 0 if the specified relation is false and -1 (i.e., all bits set) if the specified relation is true.

The logical exclusive operator (^^) is reserved for future use.

Conditional Operator

The ternary selection operator (?:) operates on three expressions (expr1 ? expr2 : expr3). This operator evaluates the first expression, expr1, which can be a scalar or vector type except the built-in floating-point types. If the result is a scalar value, the second expression, expr2, is evaluated if the result compares equal to 0; otherwise the third expression, expr3, is evaluated. If the result is a vector value, then (expr1 ? expr2 : expr3) is applied component-wise and is equivalent to calling the built-in function select(expr3, expr2, expr1). The second and third expressions can be any type as long as their types match or if an implicit conversion can be applied to one of the expressions to make their types match, or if one is a vector and the other is a scalar, in which case the usual arithmetic conversion followed by widening is applied to the scalar to match the vector operand type. This resulting matching type is the type of the entire expression.

A few examples will show how the ternary selection operator works with scalar and vector types:

```
int4    va, vb, vc, vd;
int     a, b, c, d;
float4  vf;

vc = d ? va : vb;  // vc = va if d is true, = vb if d is false

vc = vd ? va : vb; // vc.x = vd.x ? va.x : vb.x
                   // vc.y = vd.y ? va.y : vb.y
                   // vc.z = vd.z ? va.z : vb.z
                   // vc.w = vd.w ? va.w : vb.w

vc = vd ? a : vb;  // a is widened to an int4 first
                   // vc.x = vd.x ? va.x : vb.x
                   // vc.y = vd.y ? va.y : vb.y
                   // vc.z = vd.z ? va.z : vb.z
                   // vc.w = vd.w ? va.w : vb.w

vc = vd ? va : vf; // error - vector types va & vf do not match
```

Shift Operators

The shift operators—right shift (>>) and left shift (<<)—operate on built-in integer scalar and vector data types. The result is an integer scalar or vector type. The rightmost operand must be a scalar if the first operand is a scalar. For example:

```
uint   a, b, c;
uint2 r0, r1;

c = a << b;   // legal - both operands are scalars
r1 = a << r0; // illegal - first operand is a scalar and
              // therefore second operand (r0) must also be scalar.
c = b << r0;  // illegal - first operand is a scalar and
              // therefore second operand (r0) must also be scalar.
```

The rightmost operand can be a vector or scalar if the first operand is a vector. For vector types, the operators are applied component-wise.

If operands are scalar, the result of E1 << E2 is E1 left-shifted by log2(N) least significant bits in E2. The vacated bits are filled with zeros. If E2 is negative or has a value that is greater than or equal to the width of E1, the C99 specification states that the behavior is undefined. Most implementations typically return 0.

Consider the following example:

```
char x = 1;
char y = -2;
x = x << y;
```

When compiled using a C compiler such as GCC on an Intel x86 processor, (x << y) will return 0. However, with OpenCL C, (x << y) is implemented as (x << (y & 0x7)), which returns 0x40.

For vector types, N is the number of bits that can represent the type of elements in a vector type for E1 used to perform the left shift. For example:

```
char2 x = (uchar2)(1, 2);
char  y = -9;

x = x << y;
```

Because components of vector x are an unsigned char, the vector shift operation is performed as ((1 << (y & 0x7)), (2 << (y & 0x7))).

Similarly, if operands are scalar, the result of E1 >> E2 is E1 right-shifted by log2(N) least significant bits in E2. If E2 is negative or has a value that is greater than or equal to the width of E1, the C99 specification states that the behavior is undefined. For vector types, N is the number of bits that can represent the type of elements in a vector type for E1 used to perform the right shift. The vacated bits are filled with zeros if E1 is an unsigned type or is a signed type but is not a negative value. If E1 is a signed type and a negative value, the vacated bits are filled with ones.

Unary Operators

The arithmetic unary operators (+ and -) operate on built-in scalar and vector types.

The arithmetic post- and pre- increment (++) and decrement (--) operators operate on built-in scalar and vector data types except the built-in scalar and vector floating-point data types. These operators work component-wise on their operands and result in the same type they operated on.

The logical unary operator not (!) operates on built-in scalar and vector data types except the built-in scalar and vector floating-point data types. These operators work component-wise on their operands. The result is a scalar signed integer of type int if both source operands are scalar and a vector signed integer type of the same size as the vector source operand. The result is of type char$n$ if the source operands are char$n$ or uchar$n$; short$n$ if the source operands are short$n$ or ushort$n$; int$n$ if the source operands are int$n$ or uint$n$; or long$n$ if the source operands are long$n$ or ulong$n$.

For scalar types, these operators return 0 if the specified relation is false and 1 if the specified relation is true. For vector types, these operators return 0 if the specified relation is false and -1 (i.e., all bits set) if the specified relation is true.

The comma operator (,) operates on expressions by returning the type and value of the rightmost expression in a comma-separated list of expressions. All expressions are evaluated, in order, from left to right. For example:

```
// comma acts as a separator not an operator.
int a = 1, b = 2, c = 3, x;

// comma acts as an operator
x = a += 2, a + b;      // a = 3, x = 5
x = (a, b, c);          // x = 3
```

The sizeof operator yields the size (in bytes) of its operand. The result is an integer value. The result is 1 if the operand is of type char or uchar; 2 if the operand is of type short, ushort, or half; 4 if the operand is of type int, uint, or float; and 8 if the operand is of type long, ulong, or double. The result is number of components in vector * size of each scalar component if the operand is a vector type except for 3-component vectors, which return 4 * size of each scalar component. If the operand is an array type, the result is the total number of bytes in the array, and if the operand is a structure or union type, the result is the total number of bytes in such an object, including any internal or trailing padding.

The behavior of applying the `sizeof` operator to the `image2d_t`, `image3d_t`, `sampler_t`, and `event_t` types is implementation-defined. For some implementations, `sizeof(sampler_t)` = 4 and on some implementation this may result in a compile-time error. For portability across OpenCL implementations, it is recommended not to use the `sizeof` operator for these types.

The unary operator (`*`) denotes indirection. If the operand points to an object, the result is an l-value designating the object. If the operand has type "pointer to `type`," the result has type `type`. If an invalid value has been assigned to the pointer, the behavior of the indirection operator is undefined.

The unary operator (`&`) returns the address of its operand.

Assignment Operator

Assignments of values to variables names are done with the assignment operator (`=`), such as

```
lvalue = expression
```

The assignment operator stores the value of `expression` into `lvalue`. The following cases arise:

- The two operands are scalars. In this case, the operation is applied according to C99 rules.

- One operand is a scalar and the other is a vector. The scalar operand is *explicitly converted* to the element type used by the vector operand and is then widened to a vector that has the same number of elements as the vector operand. The operation is applied component-wise, resulting in the same size vector.

- The two operands are vectors of the same type. In this case, the operation is applied component-wise, resulting in the same size vector.

The following expressions are equivalent:

```
lvalue op= expression
lvalue = lvalue op expression
```

The `lvalue` and `expression` must satisfy the requirements for both operator `op` and assignment (`=`).

Qualifiers

OpenCL C supports four types of qualifiers: function qualifiers, address space qualifiers, access qualifiers, and type qualifiers.

Function Qualifiers

OpenCL C adds the `kernel` (or `__kernel`) function qualifier. This qualifier is used to specify that a function in the program source is a kernel function. The following example demonstrates the use of the kernel qualifier:

```
kernel void
parallel_add(global float *a, global float *b, global float *result)
{
    ...
}

// The following example is an example of an illegal kernel
// declaration and will result in a compile-time error.
// The kernel function has a return type of int instead of void.
kernel int
parallel_add(global float *a, global float *b, global float *result)
{
    ...
}
```

The following rules apply to kernel functions:

- The return type must be `void`. If the return type is not `void`, it will result in a compilation error.

- The function can be executed on a device by enqueuing a command to execute the kernel from the host.

- The function behaves as a regular function if it is called from a kernel function. The only restriction is that a kernel function with variables declared inside the function with the `local` qualifier cannot be called from another kernel function.

The following example shows a kernel function calling another kernel function that has variables declared with the `local` qualifier. The behavior is implementation-defined so it is not portable across implementations and should therefore be avoided.

```
kernel void
my_func_a(global float *src, global float *dst)
```

```
{
    local float l_var[32];

    ...
}

kernel void
my_func_b(global float * src, global float *dst)
{
    my_func_a(src, dst); // implementation-defined behavior
}
```

A better way to implement this example that is also portable is to pass the local variable as an argument to the kernel:

```
kernel void
my_func_a(global float *src, global float *dst, local float *l_var)
{

    ...
}

kernel void
my_func_b(global float * src, global float *dst, local float *l_var)
{
    my_func_a(src, dst, l_var);
}
```

Kernel Attribute Qualifiers

The kernel qualifier can be used with the keyword __attribute__ to declare the following additional information about the kernel:

- __attribute__((work_group_size_hint(X, Y, Z))) is a hint to the compiler and is intended to specify the work-group size that will most likely be used, that is, the value specified in the local_work_size argument to clEnqueueNDRangeKernel.

- __attribute__((reqd_work_group_size(X, Y, Z))) is intended to specify the work-group size that will be used, that is, the value specified in the local_work_size argument to clEnqueueN-DRangeKernel. This provides an opportunity for the compiler to perform specific optimizations that depend on knowing what the work-group size is.

- __attribute__((vec_type_hint(<type>))) is a hint to the compiler on the computational width of the kernel, that is, the size of the data type the kernel is operating on. This serves as a hint to an auto-vectorizing compiler. The default value of `<type>` is `int`, indicating that the kernel is scalar in nature and the auto-vectorizer can therefore vectorize the code across the SIMD lanes of the vector unit for multiple work-items.

Address Space Qualifiers

Work-items executing a kernel have access to four distinct memory regions. These memory regions can be specified as a type qualifier. The type qualifier can be `global` (or `__global`), `local` (or `__local`), constant (or `__constant`), or `private` (or `__private`).

If the type of an object is qualified by an address space name, the object is allocated in the specified address space. If the address space name is not specified, then the object is allocated in the generic address space. The generic address space name (for arguments to functions in a program, or local variables in a function) is `private`.

A few examples that describe how to specify address space names follow:

```
// declares a pointer p in the private address space that points to
// a float object in address space global
global float *p;

// declares an array of integers in the private address space
int    f[4];

// for my_func_a function we have the following arguments:
//
//    src - declares a pointer in the private address space that
//          points to a float object in address space constant
//
//    v   - allocate in the private address space
//
int
my_func_a(constant float *src, int4 v)
{
    float temp;  // temp is allocated in the private address space.
}
```

Arguments to a kernel function that are declared to be a pointer of a type must point to one of the following address spaces only: `global`, `local`, or `constant`. Not specifying an address space name for such arguments will result in a compilation error. This limitation does not apply to non-kernel functions in a program.

A few examples of legal and illegal use cases are shown here:

```
kernel void my_func(int *p) // illegal because generic address space
                            // name for p is private.

kernel void
my_func(private int *p) // illegal because memory pointed to by
                        // p is allocated in private.

void
my_func(int *p) // generic address space name for p is private.
                // legal as my_func is not a kernel function

void
my_func(private int *p) // legal as my_func is not a kernel function
```

Global Address Space

This address space name is used to refer to memory objects (buffers and images) allocated from the global memory region. This memory region allows read/write access to all work-items in all work-groups executing a kernel. This address space is identified by the `global` qualifier.

A buffer object can be declared as a pointer to a scalar, vector, or user-defined struct. Some examples are:

```
global float4 *color;     // an array of float4 elements

typedef struct {
    float3 a;
    int2   b[2];
} foo_t;
global foo_t *my_info;    // an array of foo_t elements
```

The global address qualifier should not be used for image types.

Pointers to the global address space are allowed as arguments to functions (including kernel functions) and variables declared inside functions. Variables declared inside a function *cannot* be allocated in the global address space.

A few examples of legal and illegal use cases are shown here:

```
void
my_func(global float4 *vA, global float4 *vB)
{
    global float4 *p;   // legal
    global float4 a;    // illegal
}
```

Constant Address Space

This address space name is used to describe variables allocated in global memory that are accessed inside a kernel(s) as read-only variables. This memory region allows read-only access to all work-items in all work-groups executing a kernel. This address space is identified by the `constant` qualifier.

Image types cannot be allocated in the constant address space. The following example shows `imgA` allocated in the `constant` address space, which is illegal and will result in a compilation error:

```
kernel void
my_func(constant image2d_t imgA)
{
    . . .
}
```

Pointers to the constant address space are allowed as arguments to functions (including kernel functions) and variables declared inside functions.

Variables in kernel function scope (i.e., the outermost scope of a kernel function) can be allocated in the `constant` address space. Variables in program scope (i.e., global variables in a program) can be allocated only in the `constant` address space. All such variables are required to be initialized, and the values used to initialize these variables must be compile-time constants. Writing to such a variable will result in a compile-time error.

Also, storage for all string literals declared in a program will be in the `constant` address space.

A few examples of legal and illegal use cases follow:

```
// legal - program scope variables can be allocated only
// in the constant address space
constant float wtsA[] = { 0, 1, 2, . . . };  // program scope

// illegal - program scope variables can be allocated only
// in the constant address space
global float wtsB[] = { 0, 1, 2, . . . };

kernel void
my_func(constant float4 *vA, constant float4 *vB)
{
    constant float4 *p = vA;  // legal
    constant float a;         // illegal - not initialized
    constant float b = 2.0f;  // legal - initialized with a compile-
                              //         time constant
```

```
p[0] = (float4)(1.0f);    // illegal - p cannot be modified

// the string "opencl version" is allocated in the
// constant address space
char *c = "opencl version";
```

}

Note The number of variables declared in the constant address space that can be used by a kernel is limited to `CL_DEVICE_MAX_CONSTANT_ARGS`. OpenCL 1.1 describes that the minimum value all implementations must support is eight. So up to eight variables declared in the constant address space can be used by a kernel and are guaranteed to work portably across all implementations. The size of these eight constant arguments is given by `CL_DEVICE_MAX_CONSTANT_BUFFER_SIZE` and is set to 64KB. It is therefore possible that multiple constant declarations (especially those defined in the program scope) can be merged into one constant buffer as long as their total size is less than `CL_DEVICE_MAX_CONSTANT_BUFFER_SIZE`. This aggregation of multiple variables declared to be in the constant address space is not a required behavior and so may not be implemented by all OpenCL implementations. For portable code, the developer should assume that these variables do not get aggregated into a single constant buffer.

Local Address Space

This address space name is used to describe variables that need to be allocated in local memory and are shared by all work-items of a work-group but not across work-groups executing a kernel. This memory region allows read/write access to all work-items in a work-group. This address space is identified by the `local` qualifier.

A good analogy for local memory is a user-managed cache. Local memory can significantly improve performance if a work-item or multiple work-items in a work-group are reading from the same location in global memory. For example, when applying a Gaussian filter to an image, multiple work-items read overlapping regions of the image. The overlap region size is determined by the width of the filter. Instead of reading multiple times from global memory (which is an order of magnitude slower), it is preferable to read the required data from global memory once into local memory and then have the work-items read multiple times from local memory.

Pointers to the local address space are allowed as arguments to functions (including kernel functions) and variables declared inside functions.

Variables declared inside a kernel function *can* be allocated in the local address space but with a few restrictions:

- These variable declarations must occur at kernel function scope.

- These variables cannot be initialized.

Note that variables in the local address space that are passed as pointer arguments to or declared inside a kernel function exist only for the lifetime of the work-group executing the kernel.

A few examples of legal and illegal use cases are shown here:

```
kernel void
my_func(global float4 *vA, local float4 *l)
{
    local  float4 *p;   // legal
    local  float4 a;    // legal
    a = 1;
    local  float4 b = (float4)(0); // illegal - b cannot be
                              //           initialized

    if (...)
    {
        local float c;  // illegal - must be allocated at
                        // kernel function scope
        ...
    }
}
```

Private Address Space

This address space name is used to describe variables that are private to a work-item and cannot be shared between work-items in a work-group or across work-groups. This address space is identified by the `private` qualifier.

Variables inside a kernel function not declared with an address space qualifier, all variables declared inside non-kernel functions, and all function arguments are in the `private` address space.

Casting between Address Spaces

A pointer in an address space can be assigned to another pointer only in the same address space. Casting a pointer in one address space to a pointer in a different address space is illegal. For example:

```
kernel void
my_func(global float4 *particles)
{
    // legal - particle_ptr & particles are in the
    //         same address space
    global float *particle_ptr = (global float *)particles;

    // illegal - private_ptr and particle_ptr are in different
    //           address spaces
    float *private_ptr = (float *)particle_ptr;
}
```

Access Qualifiers

The access qualifiers can be specified with arguments that are an image type. These qualifiers specify whether the image is a read-only (read_only or __read_only) or write-only (write_only or __write_only) image. This is because of a limitation of current GPUs that do not allow reading and writing to the same image in a kernel. The reason for this is that image reads are cached in a texture cache, but writes to an image do not update the texture cache.

In the following example imageA is a read-only 2D image object and imageB is a write-only 2D image object:

```
kernel void
my_func(read_only image2d_t imageA, write_only image2d_t imageB)
{
    ...
}
```

Images declared with the read_only qualifier can be used with the built-in functions that read from an image. However, these images cannot be used with built-in functions that write to an image. Similarly, images declared with the write_only qualifier can be used only to write to an image and cannot be used to read from an image. The following examples demonstrate this:

```
kernel void
my_func(read_only image2d_t imageA,
        write_only image2d_t imageB,
        sampler_t sampler)
{
    float4 clr;
    float2 coords;

    clr = read_imagef(imageA, sampler, coords); // legal
    clr = read_imagef(imageB, sampler, coords); // illegal
```

```
        write_imagef(imageA, coords, &clr);        // illegal
        write_imagef(imageB, coords, &clr);        // legal
}
```

imageA is declared to be a `read_only` image so it cannot be passed as an argument to `write_imagef`. Similarly, imageB is declared to be a `write_only` image so it cannot be passed as an argument to `read_imagef`.

The read-write qualifier (`read_write` or `__read_write`) is reserved. Using this qualifier will result in a compile-time error.

Type Qualifiers

The type qualifiers `const`, `restrict`, and `volatile` as defined by the C99 specification are supported. These qualifiers cannot be used with the `image2d_t` and `image3d_t` type. Types other than pointer types cannot use the `restrict` qualifier.

Keywords

The following names are reserved for use as keywords in OpenCL C and cannot be used otherwise:

- Names already reserved as keywords by C99

- OpenCL C data types (defined in Tables 4.1, 4.2, and 4.6)

- Address space qualifiers: `__global`, `global`, `__local`, `local`, `__constant`, `constant`, `__private`, and `private`

- Function qualifiers: `__kernel` and `kernel`

- Access qualifiers: `__read_only`, `read_only`, `__write_only`, `write_only`, `__read_write`, and `read_write`

Preprocessor Directives and Macros

The preprocessing directives defined by the C99 specification are supported. These include

```
# non-directive
#if
#ifdef
```

```
#ifndef
#elif
#else
#endif
#include
#define
#undef
#line
#error
#pragma
```

The `defined` operator is also included.

The following example demonstrates the use of `#if`, `#elif`, `#else`, and `#endif` preprocessor macros. In this example, we use the preprocessor macros to determine which arithmetic operation to apply in the kernel. The kernel source is described here:

```
#define OP_ADD          1
#define OP_SUBTRACT     2
#define OP_MULTIPLY     3
#define OP_DIVIDE       4

kernel void
foo(global float *dst, global float *srcA, global float *srcB)
{
    size_t id = get_global_id(0);
#if OP_TYPE == OP_ADD
    dst[id] = srcA[id] + srcB[id];
#elif OP_TYPE == OP_SUBTRACT
    dst[id] = srcA[id] - srcB[id];
#elif OP_TYPE == OP_MULTIPLY
    dst[id] = srcA[id] * srcB[id];
#elif OP_TYPE == OP_DIVIDE
    dst[id] = srcA[id] / srcB[id];
#else
    dst[id] = NAN;
#endif
}
```

To build the program executable with the appropriate value for `OP_TYPE`, the application calls `clBuildProgram` as follows:

```
// build program so that kernel foo does an add operation
err = clBuildProgram(program, 0, NULL,
                          "-DOP_TYPE=1", NULL, NULL);
```

Pragma Directives

The #pragma directive is described as

#pragma *pp-tokensopt new-line*

A #pragma directive where the preprocessing token OPENCL (used instead of STDC) does not immediately follow pragma in the directive (prior to any macro replacement) causes the implementation to behave in an implementation-defined manner. The behavior might cause translation to fail or cause the translator or the resulting program to behave in a nonconforming manner. Any such pragma that is not recognized by the implementation is ignored. If the preprocessing token OPENCL does immediately follow pragma in the directive (prior to any macro replacement), then no macro replacement is performed on the directive.

The following standard pragma directives are available.

Floating-Point Pragma

The FP_CONTRACT floating-point pragma can be used to allow (if the state is on) or disallow (if the state is off) the implementation to contract expressions. The FP_CONTRACT pragma definition is

```
#pragma OPENCL FP_CONTRACT on-off-switch
        on-off-switch: one of ON OFF DEFAULT
```

A detailed description of #pragma OPENCL FP_CONTRACT is found in Chapter 5 in the section "Floating-Point Pragmas."

Compiler Directives for Optional Extensions

The #pragma OPENCL EXTENSION directive controls the behavior of the OpenCL compiler with respect to language extensions. The #pragma OPENCL EXTENSION directive is defined as follows, where extension_name is the name of the extension:

```
#pragma OPENCL EXTENSION extension_name: behavior
#pragma OPENCL EXTENSION all : behavior
        behavior: enable or disable
```

The extension_name will have names of the form cl_khr_<name> for an extension (such as cl_khr_fp64) approved by the OpenCL working group and will have names of the form cl_<vendor_name>_<name> for vendor extensions. The token all means that the behavior applies to all extensions supported by the compiler. The behavior can be set to one of the values given in Table 4.9.

Table 4.9 Optional Extension Behavior Description

Behavior	Description
enable	Enable the extension `extension_name`. Report an error on the `#pragma OpenCL EXTENSION` if the `extension_name` is not supported, or if `all` is specified.
disable	Behave (including issuing errors and warnings) as if the extension `extension_name` is not part of the language definition.
	If `all` is specified, then behavior must revert back to that of the nonextended core version of the language being compiled to.
	Warn on the `#pragma OPENCL EXTENSION` if the extension `extension_name` is not supported.

The `#pragma OPENCL EXTENSION` directive is a simple, low-level mechanism to set the behavior for each language extension. It does not define policies such as which combinations are appropriate; these are defined elsewhere. The order of directives matters in setting the behavior for each extension. Directives that occur later override those seen earlier. The `all` variant sets the behavior for all extensions, overriding all previously issued extension directives, but only if the `behavior` is set to `disable`.

An extension needs to be enabled before any language feature (such as preprocessor macros, data types, or built-in functions) of this extension is used in the OpenCL program source. The following example shows how to enable the double-precision floating-point extension:

```
#pragma OPENCL EXTENSION cl_khr_fp64 : enable
double x = 2.0;
```

If this extension is not supported, then a compilation error will be reported for `double x = 2.0`. If this extension is supported, this enables the use of double-precision floating-point extensions in the program source following this directive.

Similarly, the `cl_khr_3d_image_writes` extension adds new built-in functions that support writing to a 3D image:

```
#pragma OPENCL EXTENSION cl_khr_fp64 : enable
kernel void my_func(write_only image3d_t img, ...)

{
    float4 coord, clr;
    ...
    write_imagef(img, coord, clr);
}
```

The built-in functions such as `write_imagef` with `image3d_t` in the preceding example can be called only if this extension is enabled; otherwise a compilation error will occur.

The initial state of the compiler is as if the following directive were issued, telling the compiler that all error and warning reporting must be done according to this specification, ignoring any extensions:

```
#pragma OPENCL EXTENSION all : disable
```

Every extension that affects the OpenCL language semantics or syntax or adds built-in functions to the language must also create a preprocessor `#define` that matches the extension name string. This `#define` would be available in the language if and only if the extension is supported on a given implementation. For example, an extension that adds the extension string `cl_khr_fp64` should also add a preprocessor `#define` called `cl_khr_fp64`. A kernel can now use this preprocessor `#define` to do something like this:

```
#ifdef cl_khr_fp64
    // do something using this extension
#else
    // do something else or #error
#endif
```

Macros

The following predefined macro names are available:

- `__FILE__` is the presumed name of the current source file (a character string literal).

- `__LINE__` is the presumed line number (within the current source file) of the current source line (an integer constant).

- `CL_VERSION_1_0` substitutes the integer `100`, reflecting the OpenCL 1.0 version.

- `CL_VERSION_1_1` substitutes the integer `110`, reflecting the OpenCL 1.1 version.

- `__OPENCL_VERSION__` substitutes an integer reflecting the version number of the OpenCL supported by the OpenCL device. This reflects both the language version supported and the device capabilities as given in Table 4.3 of the OpenCL 1.1 specification. The version of OpenCL described in this book will have `__OPENCL_VERSION__` substitute the integer `110`.

- `__ENDIAN_LITTLE__` is used to determine if the OpenCL device is a little endian architecture or a big endian architecture (an integer constant of 1 if the device is little endian and is undefined otherwise).

- `__kernel_exec(X, typen)` (and `kernel_exec(X, typen)`) is defined as
  `__kernel __attribute__((work_group_size_hint(X, 1, 1))) \`
  `    __attribute__((vec_type_hint(typen)))`.

- `__IMAGE_SUPPORT__` is used to determine if the OpenCL device supports images. This is an integer constant of 1 if images are supported and is undefined otherwise.

- `__FAST_RELAXED_MATH__` is used to determine if the `-cl-fast-relaxed-math` optimization option is specified in build options given to `clBuildProgram`. This is an integer constant of 1 if the `-cl-fast-relaxed-math` build option is specified and is undefined otherwise.

The macro names defined by the C99 specification but not currently supported by OpenCL are reserved for future use.

Restrictions

OpenCL C implements the following restrictions. Some of these restrictions have already been described in this chapter but are also included here to provide a single place where the language restrictions are described.

- Kernel functions have the following restrictions:

  - Arguments to kernel functions that are pointers must use the `global`, `constant`, or `local` qualifier.

  - An argument to a kernel function cannot be declared as a pointer to a pointer(s).

  - Arguments to kernel functions cannot be declared with the following built-in types: `bool`, `half`, `size_t`, `ptrdiff_t`, `intptr_t`, `uintptr_t`, or `event_t`.

  - The return type for a kernel function must be `void`.

  - Arguments to kernel functions that are declared to be a struct cannot pass OpenCL objects (such as buffers, images) as elements of the struct.

- Bit field struct members are not supported.

- Variable-length arrays and structures with flexible (or unsized) arrays are not supported.

- Variadic macros and functions are not supported.

- The `extern`, `static`, `auto`, and `register` storage class specifiers are not supported.

- Predefined identifiers such as `__func__` are not supported.

- Recursion is not supported.

- The library functions defined in the C99 standard headers— `assert.h`, `ctype.h`, `complex.h`, `errno.h`, `fenv.h`, `float.h`, `inttypes.h`, `limits.h`, `locale.h`, `setjmp.h`, `signal.h`, `stdarg.h`, `stdio.h`, `stdlib.h`, `string.h`, `tgmath.h`, `time.h`, `wchar.h`, and `wctype.h`—are not available and cannot be included by a program.

- The image types `image2d_t` and `image3d_t` can be specified only as the types of a function argument. They cannot be declared as local variables inside a function or as the return types of a function. An image function argument cannot be modified. An image type cannot be used with the `private`, `local`, and `constant` address space qualifiers. An image type cannot be used with the `read_write` access qualifier, which is reserved for future use. An image type cannot be used to declare a variable, a structure or union field, an array of images, a pointer to an image, or the return type of a function.

- The sampler type `sampler_t` can be specified only as the type of a function argument or a variable declared in the program scope or the outermost scope of a kernel function. The behavior of a sampler variable declared in a non-outermost scope of a kernel function is implementation-defined. A sampler argument or a variable cannot be modified. The sampler type cannot be used to declare a structure or union field, an array of samplers, a pointer to a sampler, or the return type of a function. The sampler type cannot be used with the `local` and `global` address space qualifiers.

- The event type `event_t` can be used as the type of a function argument except for kernel functions or a variable declared inside a function. The event type can be used to declare an array of events. The event type can be used to declare a pointer to an event, for example, `event_t *event_ptr`. An event argument or variable cannot be modified. The event type cannot be used to declare a structure or union field, or for variables declared in the program scope. The event type cannot be used with the `local`, `constant`, and `global` address space qualifiers.

- The behavior of irreducible control flow in a kernel is implementation-defined. Irreducible control flow is typically encountered in code that uses `goto`s. An example of irreducible control flow is a `goto` jumping inside a nested loop or a Duff's device.

Chapter 5

OpenCL C Built-In Functions

The OpenCL C programming language provides a rich set of built-in functions for scalar and vector argument types. These can be categorized as

- Work-item functions

- Math functions

- Integer functions

- Common functions

- Geometric functions

- Relational functions

- Synchronization functions

- Async copy and prefetch functions

- Vector data load and store functions

- Atomic functions

- Miscellaneous vector functions

- Image functions

Many of these built-in functions are similar to the functions available in common C libraries (such as the functions defined in `math.h`). The OpenCL C functions support scalar and vector argument types. It is recommended that you use these functions for your applications instead of writing your own.

In this chapter, we describe these built-in functions with examples that show how to use them. Additional information that provides special insight into these functions, wherever applicable and helpful, is also provided.

Work-Item Functions

Applications queue data-parallel and task-parallel kernels in OpenCL using the `clEnqueueNDRangeKernel` and `clEnqueueTask` APIs. For a data-parallel kernel that is queued for execution using `clEnqueue-NDRangeKernel`, an application specifies the global work size—the total number of work-items that can execute this kernel in parallel—and local work size—the number of work-items to be grouped together in a work-group. Table 5.1 describes the built-in functions that can be called by an OpenCL kernel to obtain information about work-items and work-groups such as the work-item's global and local ID or the global and local work size.

Figure 5.1 gives an example of how the global and local work sizes specified in `clEnqueueNDRangeKernel` can be accessed by a kernel executing on the device. In this example, a kernel is executed over a global work size of 16 items and a work-group size of 8 items per group.

OpenCL does not describe how the global and local IDs map to work-items and work-groups. An application, for example, cannot assume that a work-group whose group ID is 0 will contain work-items with global IDs 0 ... `get_local_size(0) - 1`. This mapping is determined by the OpenCL implementation and the device on which the kernel is executing.

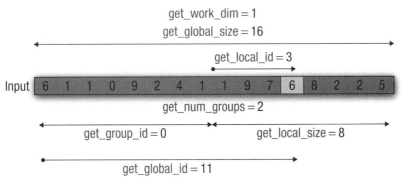

Figure 5.1   Example of the work-item functions

Table 5.1 Built-In Work-Item Functions

Function	Description
uint **get_work_dim**()	Returns the number of dimensions in use. This is the value given to the work_dim argument specified in clEnqueueNDRangeKernel. For clEnqueueTask, this function returns 1.
size_t **get_global_size**(uint *dimindx*)	Returns the number of global work-items specified for the dimension identified by *dimindx*. This value is given by the global_work_size argument to clEnqueueNDRangeKernel. Valid values of *dimindx* are 0 to get_work_dim() - 1. For other values of *dimindx*, get_global_size() returns 1. For clEnqueueTask, this function always returns 1.
size_t **get_global_id**(uint *dimindx*)	Returns the unique global work-item ID value for the dimension identified by *dimindx*. The global work-item ID specifies the work-item ID based on the number of global work-items specified to execute the kernel. Valid values of *dimindx* are 0 to get_work_dim() - 1. For other values of *dimindx*, get_global_id() returns 0. For clEnqueueTask, this function always returns 0.
size_t **get_local_size**(uint *dimindx*)	Returns the number of local work-items specified for the dimension identified by *dimindx*. This value is given by the local_work_size argument to clEnqueueNDRangeKernel if local_work_size is not NULL; otherwise the OpenCL implementation chooses an appropriate local_work_size value. Valid values of *dimindx* are 0 to get_work_dim() - 1. For other values of *dimindx*, get_local_size() returns 1. For clEnqueueTask, this function always returns 1.

continues

Table 5.1 Built-In Work-Item Functions (*Continued*)

Function	Description
size_t **get_local_id**(uint *dimindx*)	Returns the unique local work-item ID value, i.e., a work-item within a specific work-group for the dimension identified by *dimindx*. Valid values of *dimindx* are 0 to get_work_dim() − 1. For other values of *dimindx*, get_local_id() returns 0. For clEnqueueTask, this function always returns 0.
size_t **get_num_groups**(uint *dimindx*)	Returns the number of work-groups that will execute a kernel for the dimension identified by *dimindx*. Valid values of *dimindx* are 0 to get_work_dim() − 1. For other values of *dimindx*, get_num_groups() returns 1. For clEnqueueTask, this function always returns 1.
size_t **get_group_id**(uint *dimindx*)	Returns the work-group ID, which is a number from 0 to get_num_groups(*dimindx*) − 1. Valid values of *dimindx* are 0 to get_work_dim() − 1. For other values of *dimindx*, get_group_id() returns 0. For clEnqueueTask, this function always returns 0.
size_t **get_global_offset**(uint *dimindx*)	Returns the offset values specified in the global_work_offset argument to clEnqueueNDRangeKernel. Valid values of *dimindx* are 0 to get_work_dim() − 1. For other values of *dimindx*, get_global_offset() returns 0. For clEnqueueTask, this function always returns 0.

Math Functions

OpenCL C implements the math functions described in the C99 specification. Applications that want to use these math functions include the math.h header in their codes. These math functions are available as built-ins to OpenCL kernels.[1]

We use the generic type name gentype to indicate that the math functions in Tables 5.2 and 5.3 take float, float2, float3, float4, float8, float16, and, if the double-precision extension is supported, double, double2, double3, double4, double8, or double16 as the type for the arguments. The generic type name gentypei refers to the int, int2, int3, int4, int8, or int16 data types. The generic type name gentypef refers to the float, float2, float3, float4, float8, or float16 data types. The generic type name gentyped refers to the double, double2, double3, double4, double8, or double16 data types.

In addition to the math functions listed in Table 5.2, OpenCL C also implements two additional variants of the most commonly used math functions for single-precision floating-point scalar and vector data types. These additional math functions (described in Table 5.3) trade accuracy for performance and provide developers with options to make appropriate choices. These math functions can be categorized as

- A subset of functions from Table 5.2 defined with the half_ prefix. These functions are implemented with a minimum of 10 bits of accuracy, that is, a ulp value <= 8192 ulp.

- A subset of functions from Table 5.2 defined with the native_ prefix. These functions typically have the best performance compared to the corresponding functions without the native_ prefix or with the half_ prefix. The accuracy (and in some cases the input ranges) of these functions is implementation-defined.

- half_ and native_ functions for the following basic operations: divide and reciprocal.

---

[1] The math.h header does not need to be included in the OpenCL kernel.

Table 5.2 Built-In Math Functions

Function	Description
gentype **acos** (gentype *x*)	Compute the arc cosine of *x*.
gentype **acosh** (gentype *x*)	Compute the inverse hyperbolic cosine of *x*.
gentype **acospi** (gentype *x*)	Compute acos (*x*) /p.
gentype **asin** (gentype *x*)	Compute the arc sine of *x*.
gentype **asinh** (gentype *x*)	Compute the inverse hyperbolic sine of *x*.
gentype **asinpi** (gentype *x*)	Compute asin (*x*) /p.
gentype **atan** (gentype *y_over_x*)	Compute the arc tangent of *y_over_x*.
gentype **atan2** (gentype *y*, gentype *x*)	Compute the arc tangent of *y*/*x*.
gentype **atanh** (gentype *x*)	Compute the hyperbolic arc tangent of *x*.
gentype **atanpi** (gentype *x*)	Compute atan (*x*) /p.
gentype **atan2pi** (gentype *y*, gentype *x*)	Compute atan2 (*y*, *c*) /p.
gentype **cbrt** (gentype *x*)	Compute the cube root of *x*.
gentype ceil (gentype *x*)	Round to an integral value using the round-to-positive-infinity rounding mode.
gentype **copysign** (gentype *x*, gentype *y*)	Returns *x* with its sign changed to match the sign of *y*.
gentype **cos** (gentype *x*)	Compute the cosine of *x*.
gentype **cosh** (gentype *x*)	Compute the hyperbolic cosine of *x*.
gentype **cospi** (gentype *x*)	Compute cos (p*x*) .

Function	Description
gentype **erfc**(gentype x)	Compute the complementary error function $1.0 - \text{erf}(x)$.
gentype **erf**(gentype x)	Compute the error function. For argument x this is defined as $$\frac{2}{\sqrt{\pi}}\int_0^x e^{-t^2}\,dt$$
gentype **exp**(gentype x)	Compute the base-e exponential of x.
gentype **exp2**(gentype x)	Compute the base-2 exponential of x.
gentype **exp10**(gentype x)	Compute the base-10 exponential of x.
gentype **expm1**(gentype x)	Compute $e^x - 1.0$.
gentype **fabs**(gentype x)	Compute the absolute value of a floating-point number.
gentype **fdim**(gentype x, gentype y)	Returns $x - y$ if $x > y$, $+0$ if x is less than or equal to y.
gentype **floor**(gentype x)	Round to an integral value using the round-to-negative-infinity rounding mode.
gentype **fma**(gentype a, gentype b, gentype c)	Returns the correctly rounded floating-point representation of the sum of c with the infinitely precise product of a and b. Rounding of intermediate products does not occur. Edge case behavior is per the IEEE 754-2008 standard.
gentype **fmax**(gentype x, gentype y) gentypef **fmax**(gentypef x, float y) gentyped **fmax**(gentyped x, double y)	Returns y if $x < y$, otherwise it returns x. If one argument is a NaN, **fmax**() returns the other argument. If both arguments are NaNs, **fmax**() returns a NaN.

continues

Table 5.2 Built-In Math Functions (*Continued*)

Function	Description

`gentype fmin(gentype x,gentype y)`
`gentypef fmin(gentypef x, float y)`
`gentyped fmin(gentyped x, double y)`
	Returns y if $y < x$; otherwise it returns x. If one argument is a NaN, **fmin()** returns the other argument. If both arguments are NaNs, **fmin()** returns a NaN.

`gentype fmod(gentype x,gentype y)`	Returns $x - y$ * **trunc**(x/y).

`gentype fract(gentype x,`
`    global gentype *iptr)`
`gentype fract (gentype x,`
`    local gentype *iptr)`
`gentype fract (gentype x,`
`    private gentype *iptr)`
	Returns **fmin**$(x -$ **floor**(x), `0x1.fffffep-1f`).
	floor(x) is returned in *iptr*.

`gentype frexp(gentype x,`
`    global intn *exp)`
`gentype frexp (gentype x,`
`    local intn *exp)`
`gentype frexp (gentype x,`
`    private intn *exp)`
	Extract mantissa and exponent from x. For each component the mantissa returned is a float with magnitude in the interval $[1/2, 1)$ or 0. Each component of x equals mantissa returned * 2^{exp}.

`gentype hypot(gentype x, gentype y)`	Compute the value of the square root of $x^2 + y^2$ without undue overflow or underflow.
`intn ilogb(gentype x)`	Returns the exponent of x as an integer value.
`gentype ldexp gentype x, intn exp)` `gentype ldexp gentype x, int exp)`	Returns x * 2^{exp}.

`gentype lgamma(gentype x)`
`gentype lgamma_r(gentype x,`
`    global intn *signp)`
`gentype lgamma_r(gentype x,`
`    local intn *signp)`
`gentype lgamma_r(gentype x,`
`    private intn *signp)`
	Compute the log gamma function given by
	
	$$\log_e \lvert \Gamma(x) \rvert \; where \; \Gamma(x) \; is \, defined \, as \int_0^\infty e^{-t} t^{x-1} dt$$
	
	The sign of the gamma function is returned in the *signp* argument of **lgamma_r**.

Function	Description
gentype **log**(gentype x)	Compute the natural logarithm of x.
gentype **log2**(gentype x)	Compute the base-2 logarithm of x.
gentype **log10**(gentype x)	Compute the base-10 logarithm of x.
gentype **log1p**(gentype x)	Compute $\log_e(1.0 + x)$.
gentype **logb**(gentype x)	Compute the exponent of x, which is the integral part of $\log_r\lvert x \rvert$.
gentype **mad**(gentype a, gentype b, gentype c)	**mad** approximates $a * b + c$. Whether or how the product of $a * b$ is rounded and how supernormal or subnormal intermediate products are handled are not defined. **mad** is intended to be used where speed is preferred over accuracy.
gentype **maxmag**(gentype x, gentype y)	Returns x if $\lvert x \rvert > \lvert y \rvert$, y if $\lvert y \rvert > \lvert x \rvert$, otherwise $fmax(x, y)$.
gentype **minmag**(gentype x, gentype y)	Returns x if $\lvert x \rvert < \lvert y \rvert$, y if $\lvert y \rvert < \lvert x \rvert$, otherwise $fmin(x, y)$.
gentype **modf**(gentype x, global gentype *iptr) gentype **modf**(gentype x, local gentype *iptr) gentype **modf**(gentype x, private gentype *iptr)	Decompose a floating-point number. The **modf** function breaks the argument x into integral and fractional parts, each of which has the same sign as the argument. It stores the integral part in the object pointed to by iptr and returns the fractional part.
float **nan**(uint nancode); floatn **nan**(uintn nancode); double **nan**(uint nancode); doublen **nan**(uintn nancode);	Returns a quiet NaN. The nancode may be placed in the significand of the resulting NaN.
gentype **nextafter**(gentype x, gentype y);	Compute the next representable single- or double-precision floating-point value following x in the direction of y. Thus, if y is less than x, **nextafter** returns the largest representable floating-point number less than x.

continues

Table 5.2 Built-In Math Functions (*Continued*)

Function	Description
gentype **pow**(gentype x, gentype y)	Compute x to the power y.
gentype **pown**(gentype x, intn y)	Compute x to the power y, where y is an integer.
gentype **powr**(gentype x, gentype y)	Compute x to the power y, where x >= 0.
gentype **remainder**(gentype x, gentype y)	Compute the value r such that $r = x - n * y$, where n is the integer nearest the exact value of x/y. If there are two integers closest to x/y, n will be the even one. If r is zero, it is given the same sign as x.
gentype **remquo**(gentype x, gentype y, global gentypei *quo) gentype **remquo**(gentype x, gentype y, local gentypei *quo) gentype **remquo**(gentype x, gentype y, private gentypei *quo)	Compute the value r such that $r = x - n * y$, where n is the integer nearest the exact value of x/y. If there are two integers closest to x/y, n will be the even one. If r is zero, it is given the same sign as x. This is the same value that is returned by the remainder function. **remquo** also calculates the lower seven bits of the integral quotient x/y and gives that value the same sign as x/y. It stores this signed value in the object pointed to by *quo*.
gentype **rint**(gentype x)	Round to integral value (using round-to-nearest rounding mode) in floating-point format.
gentype **rootn**(gentype x, intn y)	Compute x to the power $1/y$.
gentype **round**(gentype x)	Return the integral value nearest to x, rounding halfway cases away from zero, regardless of the current rounding direction.
gentype **rsqrt**(gentype x)	Compute the inverse square root of x.
gentype **sin**(gentype x)	Compute the sine of x.

Function	Description

gentype **sincos**(gentype x,
    global gentype *cosval);
gentype **sincos**(gentype x,
    local gentype *cosval);
gentype **sincos**(gentype x,
    private gentype *cosval);
	Compute the sine and cosine of x. The computed sine is the return value and the computed cosine is returned in cosval.

gentype **sinh**(gentype x)	Compute the hyperbolic sine of x.
gentype **sinpi**(gentype x)	Compute sin(px).
gentype **sqrt**(gentype x)	Compute the square root of x.
gentype **tan**(gentype x)	Compute the tangent of x.
gentype **tanh**(gentype x)	Compute the hyperbolic tangent of x.
gentype **tanpi**(gentype x)	Compute tan(px).
gentype **tgamma**(gentype x)	Compute the gamma function.
gentype **trunc**(gentype x)	Round to integral value using the round-to-zero rounding mode.

Table 5.3 Built-In *half_* and *native_* Math Functions

Function	Description
gentypef **half_cos** (gentypef x)	Compute the cosine of x. x must be in the range -2^{16} ... $+2^{16}$.
gentypef **half_divide** (gentypef x, gentypef y)	Compute x/y.
gentypef **half_exp** (gentypef x)	Compute the base-e exponential of x.
gentypef **half_exp2** (gentypef x)	Compute the base-2 exponential of x.
gentypef **half_exp10** (gentypef x)	Compute the base-10 exponential of x.
gentypef **half_log** (gentypef x)	Compute the natural logarithm of x.
gentypef **half_log2** (gentypef x)	Compute the base-2 logarithm of x.
gentypef **half_log10** (gentypef x)	Compute the base-10 logarithm of x.
gentypef **half_powr** (gentypef x, gentypef y)	Compute x to the power y, where x >= 0.
gentypef **half_recip** (gentypef x)	Compute the reciprocal of x.
gentypef **half_rsqrt** (gentypef x)	Compute the inverse square root of x.
gentypef **half_sin** (gentypef x)	Compute the sine of x. x must be in the range -2^{16} ... $+2^{16}$.
gentypef **half_sqrt** (gentypef x)	Compute the square root of x.
gentypef **half_tan** (gentypef x)	Compute the tangent of x. x must be in the range -2^{16} ... $+2^{16}$.
gentypef **native_cos** (gentypef x)	Compute the cosine of x over an implementation-defined range. The maximum error is implementation-defined.
gentypef **native_divide** (gentypef x, gentypef y)	Compute x/y over an implementation-defined range. The maximum error is implementation-defined.

Function	Description
gentypef **native_exp** (gentypef x)	Compute the base-e exponential of x over an implementation-defined range. The maximum error is implementation-defined.
gentypef **native_exp2** (gentypef x)	Compute the base-2 exponential of x over an implementation-defined range. The maximum error is implementation-defined.
gentypef **native_exp10** (gentypef x)	Compute the base-10 exponential of x over an implementation-defined range. The maximum error is implementation-defined.
gentypef **native_log** (gentypef x)	Compute the natural logarithm of x over an implementation-defined range. The maximum error is implementation-defined.
gentypef **native_log2** (gentypef x)	Compute the base-2 logarithm of x over an implementation-defined range. The maximum error is implementation-defined.
gentypef **native_log10** (gentypef x)	Compute the base-10 logarithm of x over an implementation-defined range. The maximum error is implementation-defined.
gentypef **native_recip** (gentypef x)	Compute the reciprocal of x over an implementation-defined range. The maximum error is implementation-defined.
gentypef **native_rsqrt** (gentypef x)	Compute the inverse square root of x over an implementation-defined range. The maximum error is implementation-defined.
gentypef **native_sin** (gentypef x)	Compute the sine of x over an implementation-defined range. The maximum error is implementation-defined.
gentypef **native_sqrt** (gentypef x)	Compute the square root of x over an implementation-defined range. The maximum error is implementation-defined.
gentypef **native_tan** (gentypef x)	Compute the tangent of x over an implementation-defined range. The maximum error is implementation-defined.

Floating-Point Pragmas

The only pragma supported by OpenCL C is the `FP_CONTRACT` pragma. The `FP_CONTRACT` pragma provides a way to disallow contracted expressions and is defined to be

```
#pragma OPENCL FP_CONTRACT on-off-switch
```

`on-off-switch` is `ON`, `OFF`, or `DEFAULT`. The `DEFAULT` value is `ON`.

The `FP_CONTRACT` pragma can be used to allow (if the state is `ON`) or disallow (if the state is `OFF`) the implementation to contract expressions. If `FP_CONTRACT` is `ON`, a floating-point expression may be contracted, that is, evaluated as though it were an atomic operation. For example, the expression `a * b + c` can be replaced with an `FMA` (fused multiply-add) instruction.

Each `FP_CONTRACT` pragma can occur either outside external declarations or preceding all explicit declarations and statements inside a compound statement. When outside external declarations, the pragma takes effect from its occurrence until another `FP_CONTRACT` pragma is encountered, or until the end of the translation unit. When inside a compound statement, the pragma takes effect from its occurrence until another `FP_CONTRACT` pragma is encountered (including within a nested compound statement), or until the end of the compound statement; at the end of a compound statement the state for the pragma is restored to its condition just before the compound statement. If this pragma is used in any other context, the behavior is undefined.

Floating-Point Constants

The constants described in Table 5.4 are available. The constants with the `_F` suffix are of type `float` and are accurate within the precision of the `float` type. The constants without the `_F` suffix are of type `double`, are accurate within the precision of the `double` type, and are available only if the double-precision extension is supported by the OpenCL implementation.

Table 5.4 Single- and Double-Precision Floating-Point Constants

Constant	Description
M_E_F M_E	Value of e
M_LOG2E_F M_LOG2E	Value of $\log_2 e$

Table 5.4 Single- and Double-Precision Floating-Point Constants (*Continued*)

Constant	Description
`M_LOG10E_F` `M_LOG10E`	Value of $\log_{10}e$
`M_LN2_F` `M_LN2`	Value of $\log_{e}2$
`M_LN10_F` `M_LN10`	Value of $\log_{e}10$
`M_PI_F` `M_PI`	Value of π
`M_PI_2_F` `M_PI_2`	Value of $\pi/2$
`M_PI_4_F` `M_PI_4`	Value of $\pi/4$
`M_1_PI_F` `M_1_PI`	Value of $1/\pi$
`M_2_PI_F` `M_2_PI`	Value of $2/\pi$
`M_2_SQRTPI_F` `M_2_SQRTPI`	Value of $2/\mathrm{sqrt}(\pi)$
`M_SQRT2_F` `M_SQRT2`	Value of $\mathrm{sqrt}(\pi)$
`M_SQRT1_2_F` `M_SQRT1_2`	Value of $1/\mathrm{sqrt}(\pi)$

Relative Error as `ulps`

Table 5.5 describes the maximum relative error defined as `ulp` (units in the last place) for single-precision and double-precision floating-point basic operations and functions. The `ulp`[2] is defined thus:

> If x is a real number that lies between two finite consecutive floating-point numbers a and b, without being equal to one of them, then ulp(x) = |b – a|, otherwise ulp(x) is the distance between the two non-equal finite floating-point numbers nearest x. Moreover, ulp(NaN) is NaN.

---

[2] This definition of ulp was taken with consent from Jean-Michel Muller with slight clarification for the behavior of zero. Refer to ftp://ftp.inria.fr/INRIA/publication/publi-pdf/RR/RR-5504.pdf.

The following list provides additional clarification of ulp values and rounding mode behavior:

- The round-to-nearest rounding mode is the default rounding mode for the full profile. For the embedded profile, the default rounding mode can be either round to zero or round to nearest. If CL_FP_ROUND_TO_NEAREST is supported in CL_DEVICE_SINGLE_FP_CONFIG (refer to Table 4.3 of the OpenCL 1.1 specification), then the embedded profile supports round to nearest as the default rounding mode; otherwise the default rounding mode is round to zero.

- 0 ulp is used for math functions that do not require rounding.

- The ulp values for the built-in math functions lgamma and lgamma_r are currently undefined.

Table 5.5 ulp Values for Basic Operations and Built-In Math Functions

Function	Single-Precision Minimum Accuracy— ulp Value	Double-Precision Minimum Accuracy— ulp Value
x + y	Correctly rounded	Correctly rounded
x - y	Correctly rounded	Correctly rounded
x * y	Correctly rounded	Correctly rounded
1.0f/x	<= 2.5 ulp	Correctly rounded
x/y	<= 2.5 ulp	Correctly rounded
acos	<= 4 ulp	<= 4 ulp
acospi	<= 5 ulp	<= 5 ulp
asin	<= 4 ulp	<= 4 ulp
asinpi	<= 5 ulp	<= 5 ulp
atan	<= 5 ulp	<= 5 ulp
atan2	<= 6 ulp	<= 6 ulp
atanpi	<= 5 ulp	<= 5 ulp
atan2pi	<= 6 ulp	<= 6 ulp
acosh	<= 4 ulp	<= 4 ulp
asinh	<= 4 ulp	<= 4 ulp

Table 5.5 `ulp` Values for Basic Operations and Built-In Math Functions (*Continued*)

Function	Single-Precision Minimum Accuracy— `ulp` Value	Double-Precision Minimum Accuracy— `ulp` Value
atanh	<= 5 `ulp`	<= 5 `ulp`
cbrt	<= 2 `ulp`	<= 2 `ulp`
ceil	Correctly rounded	Correctly rounded
copysign	0 `ulp`	0 `ulp`
cos	<= 4 `ulp`	<= 4 `ulp`
cosh	<= 4 `ulp`	<= 4 `ulp`
cospi	<= 4 `ulp`	<= 4 `ulp`
erfc	<= 16 `ulp`	<= 16 `ulp`
erf	<= 16 `ulp`	<= 16 `ulp`
exp	<= 3 `ulp`	<= 3 `ulp`
exp2	<= 3 `ulp`	<= 3 `ulp`
exp10	<= 3 `ulp`	<= 3 `ulp`
expm1	<= 3 `ulp`	<= 3 `ulp`
fabs	0 ulp	0 `ulp`
fdim	Correctly rounded	Correctly rounded
floor	Correctly rounded	Correctly rounded
fma	Correctly rounded	Correctly rounded
fmax	0 `ulp`	0 `ulp`
fmin	0 `ulp`	0 `ulp`
fmod	0 `ulp`	0 `ulp`
fract	Correctly rounded	Correctly rounded
frexp	0 `ulp`	0 `ulp`
hypot	<= 4 `ulp`	<= 4 `ulp`
ilogb	0 `ulp`	0 `ulp`

continues

Table 5.5 `ulp` Values for Basic Operations and Built-In Math Functions (*Continued*)

Function	Single-Precision Minimum Accuracy— `ulp` Value	Double-Precision Minimum Accuracy— `ulp` Value
`ldexp`	Correctly rounded	Correctly rounded
`log`	<= 3 `ulp`	<= 3 `ulp`
`log2`	<= 3 `ulp`	<= 3 `ulp`
`log10`	<= 3 `ulp`	<= 3 `ulp`
`log1p`	<= 2 `ulp`	<= 2 `ulp`
`logb`	0 `ulp`	0 `ulp`
`mad`	Any value allowed (infinite `ulp`)	Any value allowed (infinite `ulp`)
`maxmag`	0 `ulp`	0 `ulp`
`minmag`	0 `ulp`	0 `ulp`
`modf`	0 `ulp`	0 `ulp`
`nan`	0 `ulp`	0 `ulp`
`nextafter`	0 `ulp`	0 `ulp`
`pow`	<= 16 `ulp`	<= 16 `ulp`
`pown`	<= 16 `ulp`	<= 16 `ulp`
`powr`	<= 16 `ulp`	<= 16 `ulp`
`remainder`	0 `ulp`	0 `ulp`
`remquo`	0 `ulp`	0 `ulp`
`rint`	Correctly rounded	Correctly rounded
`rootn`	<= 16 `ulp`	<= 16 `ulp`
`round`	Correctly rounded	Correctly rounded
`rsqrt`	<= 2 `ulp`	<= 2 `ulp`
`sin`	<= 4 `ulp`	<= 4 `ulp`
`sincos`	<= 4 `ulp` for sine and cosine values	<= 4 `ulp` for sine and cosine values

Table 5.5 ulp Values for Basic Operations and Built-In Math Functions (*Continued*)

Function	Single-Precision Minimum Accuracy— ulp Value	Double-Precision Minimum Accuracy— ulp Value
sinh	<= 4 ulp	<= 4 ulp
sinpi	<= 4 ulp	<= 4 ulp
sqrt	<= 3 ulp	Correctly rounded
tan	<= 5 ulp	<= 5 ulp
tanh	<= 5 ulp	<= 5 ulp
tanpi	<= 6 ulp	<= 6 ulp
tgamma	<= 16 ulp	<= 16 ulp
trunc	Correctly rounded	Correctly rounded
half_cos	<= 8192 ulp	N/a
half_divide	<= 8192 ulp	N/a
half_exp	<= 8192 ulp	N/a
half_exp2	<= 8192 ulp	N/a
half_exp10	<= 8192 ulp	N/a
half_log	<= 8192 ulp	N/a
half_log2	<= 8192 ulp	N/a
half_log10	<= 8192 ulp	N/a
half_power	<= 8192 ulp	N/a
half_recip	<= 8192 ulp	N/a
half_rsqrt	<= 8192 ulp	N/a
half_sin	<= 8192 ulp	N/a
half_sqrt	<= 8192 ulp	N/a
half_tan	<= 8192 ulp	N/a
native_cos	Implementation-defined	N/a
native_divide	Implementation-defined	N/a

continues

Table 5.5 `ulp` Values for Basic Operations and Built-In Math Functions (*Continued*)

Function	Single-Precision Minimum Accuracy— `ulp` Value	Double-Precision Minimum Accuracy— `ulp` Value
native_exp	Implementation-defined	N/a
native_exp2	Implementation-defined	N/a
native_exp10	Implementation-defined	N/a
native_log	Implementation-defined	N/a
native_log2	Implementation-defined	N/a
native_log10	Implementation-defined	N/a
native_powr	Implementation-defined	N/a
native_recip	Implementation-defined	N/a
native_rsqrt	Implementation-defined	N/a
native_sin	Implementation-defined	N/a
native_sqrt	Implementation-defined	N/a
native_tan	Implementation-defined	N/a

Integer Functions

Table 5.6 describes the built-in integer functions available in OpenCL C. These functions all operate component-wise. The description is per component.

We use the generic type name `gentype` to indicate that the function can take char, char2, char3, char4, char8, char16, uchar, uchar2, uchar3, uchar4, uchar8, uchar16, short, short2, short3, short4, short8, short16, ushort, ushort2, ushort3, ushort4, ushort8, ushort16, int, int2, int3, int4, int8, int16, uint, uint2, uint3, uint4, uint8, uint16, long, long2, long3, long4, long8, long16, ulong, ulong2, ulong3, ulong4, ulong8, or ulong16 as the type for the arguments.

We use the generic type name `ugentype` to refer to unsigned versions of gentype. For example, if `gentype` is char4, `ugentype` is uchar4.

Table 5.6 Built-In Integer Functions

Function	Description
ugentype **abs** (gentype x)	Returns $|x|$.
ugentype **abs_diff** (gentype x, gentype y)	Returns $|x - y|$ without modulo overflow.
gentype **add_sat** (gentype x, gentype y)	Returns $x + y$ and saturates the result.
gentype **hadd** (gentype x, gentype y)	Returns $(x + y)$ >> 1. The intermediate sum does not modulo overflow.
gentype **rhadd** (gentype x, gentype y)	Returns $(x + y + 1)$ >> 1. The intermediate sum does not modulo overflow.
gentype **clamp** (gentype x, gentype minval, gentype maxval)	Returns **min**(max(x, minval), maxval). Results are undefined if minval > maxval.
gentype **clamp** (gentype x, sgentype minval, sgentype maxval)	
gentype **clz** (gentype x)	Returns the number of leading 0 bits in x, starting at the most significant bit position.
gentype **mad_hi** (gentype a, gentype b, gentype c)	Returns **mul_hi**(a, b) + c.
gentype **mad_sat** (gentype a, gentype b, gentype c)	Returns $a * b + c$ and saturates the result.
gentype **max** (gentype x, gentype y) gentype **max** (gentype x, sgentype y)	Returns y if x < y; otherwise it returns x.
gentype **max** (gentype x, gentype y) gentype **max** (gentype x, sgentype y)	Returns y if y < x; otherwise it returns x.

continues

Table 5.6 Built-In Integer Functions (*Continued*)

Function	Description
gentype **mul_hi**(gentype x, gentype y)	Computes $x * y$ and returns the high half of the product of x and y.
gentype **rotate**(gentype v, gentype i)	For each element in v, the bits are shifted left by the number of bits given by the corresponding element in i (subject to the usual shift modulo rules described in the "Shift Operators" subsection of "Vector Operators" in Chapter 4). Bits shifted off the left side of the element are shifted back in from the right.
gentype **sub_sat**(gentype x, gentype y)	Returns $x - y$ and saturates the result.
short **upsample**(char hi, uchar lo) ushort **upsample** (uchar hi, uchar lo) shortn **upsample** (charn hi, ucharn lo) ushortn **upsample** (ucharn hi, ucharn lo) int **upsample** (short hi, ushort lo) uint **upsample** (ushort hi, ushort lo) intn **upsample** (shortn hi, ushortn lo) uintn **upsample** (ushortn hi, ushortn lo) long **upsample** (int hi, uint lo) ulong **upsample** (uint hi, uint lo) longn **upsample** (intn hi, uintn lo) ulongn **upsample** (uintn hi, uintn lo)	If hi and lo are scalar: result = ((short)hi << 8) | lo result = ((ushort) hi << 8) | lo result = ((int)hi << 16) | lo result = ((uint) hi << 16) | lo result = ((long)hi << 32) | lo result = ((ulong) hi << 32) | lo If hi and lo are scalar, then for each element of the vector: result[i] = ((short)hi[i] << 8) | lo[i] result[i] = ((ushort)hi[i] << 8) | lo[i] result[i] = ((int)hi[i] << 16) | lo[i] result[i] = ((uint)hi[i] << 16) | lo[i] result[i] = ((long)hi[i] << 32) | lo[i] result[i] = ((ulong)hi[i] << 32) | lo[i]

Function	Description
`gentype mad24 (gentype x,` `gentype y, gentype z)`	Multiply two 24-bit integer values x and y using **mul24** and add the 32-bit integer result to the 32-bit integer z.
`gentype mul24 (gentype x, gentype y)`	Multiply two 24-bit integer values x and y. x and y are 32-bit integers but only the low 24 bits are used to perform the multiplication. **mul24** should be used only when values in x and y are in the range $[-2^{23}, 2^{23} - 1]$ if x and y are signed integers and in the range $[0, 2^{24}-1]$ if x and y are unsigned integers. If x and y are not in this range, the multiplication result is implementation-defined.

We use the generic type name `sgentype` to indicate that the function can take a scalar data type, that is, `char`, `uchar`, `short`, `ushort`, `int`, `uint`, `long`, or `ulong`, as the argument type. For built-in integer functions that take `gentype` and `sgentype` arguments, the `gentype` argument must be a vector or scalar of the `sgentype` argument. For example, if `sgentype` is `uchar`, `gentype` must be `uchar`, `uchar2`, `uchar3`, `uchar4`, `uchar8`, or `uchar16`.

The following macro names are available. The values are constant expressions suitable for use in `#if` processing directives.

```
#define CHAR_BIT 8

#define CHAR_MAX SCHAR_MAX

#define CHAR_MIN SCHAR_MIN

#define INT_MAX 2147483647

#define INT_MIN (-2147483647 - 1)

#define LONG_MAX 0x7fffffffffffffffL

#define LONG_MIN (-0x7fffffffffffffffL - 1)

#define SCHAR_MAX 127

#define SCHAR_MIN (-127 - 1)

#define SHRT_MAX 32767

#define SHRT_MIN (-32767 - 1)

#define UCHAR_MAX 255

#define USHRT_MAX 65535

#define UINT_MAX 0xffffffff

#define ULONG_MAX 0xffffffffffffffffUL
```

Common Functions

Table 5.7 describes the built-in common functions available in OpenCL C. These functions all operate component-wise. The description is per component.

Table 5.7 Built-In Common Functions

Function	Description
gentype **clamp** (gentype x, gentype minval, gentype maxval) gentypef **clamp** (gentypef x, float minval, float maxval) gentyped **clamp** (gentyped x, double minval, double maxval)	Returns **fmin**(**fmax**(x, minval), maxval). Results are undefined if minval > maxval.
gentype **degrees** (gentype radians)	Converts radians to degrees; i.e., (180/p) * radians.
gentype **max** (gentype x, gentype y) gentypef **max** (gentypef x, float y) gentyped **max** (gentyped x, double y)	Returns y if x < y, otherwise it returns x. This is similar to **fmax** described in Table 5.2 except that if x or y is infinite or NaN, the return values are undefined.
gentype **min** (gentype x, gentype y) gentypef **min** (gentypef x, float y) gentyped **min** (gentyped x, double y)	Returns y if y < x, otherwise it returns x. This is similar to **fmin** described in Table 5.2 except that if x or y is infinite or NaN, the return values are undefined.
gentype **mix** (gentype x, gentype y, gentype a) gentypef **mix** (gentypef x, float y, gentype a) gentyped **mix** (gentyped x, double y, gentype a)	Returns the linear blend of x and y implemented as x + (y - x) * a a must be a value in the range 0.0 ... 1.0. If a is not in this range, the return values are undefined.
gentype **radians** (gentype degrees)	Converts degrees to radians; i.e., (p/180) * degrees.

continues

Table 5.7 Built-In Common Functions (*Continued*)

Function	Description
gentype **step**(gentype *edge*, gentype *x*) gentypef **step**(float *edge*, gentypef *x*) gentyped **step**(double *edge*, gentyped *x*)	Returns 0.0 if x < *edge*; otherwise it returns 1.0. The **step** function can be used to create a discontinuous jump at an arbitrary point.

gentype **smoothstep**(gentype *edge0*,
    gentype *edge1*,
    gentype *x*)
gentypef **smoothstep**(float *edge0*,
    float *edge1*,
    gentypef *x*)
gentyped **smoothstep**(double *edge0*,
    double *edge1*,
    gentyped *x*)
	Returns 0.0 if x <= *edge0* and 1.0 if x >= *edge1* and performs a smooth hermite interpolation between 0 and 1 when *edge0* < x < *edge1*. This is useful in cases where a threshold function with a smooth transition is needed.
	
	This is equivalent to the following where t is the same type as x:
	
	`t = clamp((x - edge0)/(edge1 - edge0), 0, 1);`
	`return t * t * (3 - 2 * t)`
	
	The results are undefined if *edge0* >= *edge1* or if x, *edge0*, or *edge1* is a NaN.

gentype **sign**(gentype *x*)	Returns 1.0 if x > 0, -0.0 if x = -0.0, +0.0 if x = +0.0, or -1.0 if x < 0. Returns 0.0 if x is a NaN.

We use the generic type name `gentype` to indicate that the function can take `float`, `float2`, `float3`, `float4`, `float8`, or `float16` and, if the double-precision extension is supported, `double`, `double2`, `double3`, `double4`, `double8`, or `double16` as the type for the arguments.

We use the generic type name `gentypef` to indicate that the function can take `float`, `float2`, `float3`, `float4`, `float8`, or `float16` as the type for the arguments and the generic type name `gentyped` to indicate that the function can take `double`, `double2`, `double3`, `double4`, `double8`, or `double16` as the type for the arguments.

Geometric Functions

Table 5.8 describes the built-in geometric functions available in OpenCL C. These functions all operate component-wise. The description is per component.

We use the generic type name `gentypef` to indicate that the function can take `float`, `float2`, `float3`, `float4`, `float8`, or `float16` arguments. If the double-precision extension is supported, the generic type name `gentyped` indicates that the function can take `double`, `double2`, `double3`, `double4`, `double8`, or `double16` as the type for the arguments.

Information on how these geometric functions may be implemented and additional clarification of the behavior of some of the geometric functions is given here:

- The geometric functions can be implemented using contractions such as `mad` or `fma`.

- The `fast_` variants provide developers with an option to choose performance over accuracy.

- The `distance`, `length`, and `normalize` functions compute the results without overflow or extraordinary precision loss due to underflow.

Relational Functions

Table 5.9 describes the built-in relational functions available in OpenCL C. These functions all operate component-wise. The description is per component.

Table 5.8 Built-In Geometric Functions

Function	Description

`float4 cross(float4 p0, float4 p1)`
`float3 cross(float3 p0, float3 p1)`
`double4 cross(double4 p0, double4 p1)`
`double3 cross(double3 p0, double3 p1)`
	Returns the cross-product of *p0*.xyz and *p1*.xyz. The *w* component of a 4-component vector result returned will be 0.
	
	The cross-product is specified only for a 3- or 4-component vector.

`float dot(gentypef p0, gentypef p1)` `double dot(gentyped p0, gentyped p1)`	Returns the dot product of *p0* and *p1*.
`float distance(gentypef p0, gentypef p1)` `double distance(gentyped p0, gentyped p1)`	Returns the distance between *p0* and *p1*. This is calculated as `length(p0 - p1)`.
`float length(gentypef p)` `double length(gentyped p)`	Returns the length of vector *p*, i.e., $\sqrt{p.x^2 + p.y^2 + \ldots}$ The length is calculated without overflow or extraordinary precision loss due to underflow.

`gentypef normalize(gentypef p)`
`gentyped normalize(gentyped p)`
	Returns a vector in the same direction as *p* but with a length of 1.
	
	normalize(*p*) function returns *p* if all elements of *p* are zero.
	
	normalize(*p*) returns a vector full of NaNs if any element is a NaN.
	
	normalize(*p*) for which any element in *p* is infinite proceeds as if the elements in *p* were replaced as follows:
	
	`for(i=0;i<sizeof(p)/sizeof(p[0]);i++)`
	`    p[i] = isinf(p[i])`
	`        ?`
	`        copysign(1.0, p[i])`
	`        : 0.0 * p[i];`

`float fast_distance(gentypef p0, gentypef p1)`	Returns **fast_length**(*p0* − *p1*).

Function	Description
`float` **`fast_length`**`(gentypef p)`	Returns the length of vector p computed as **`half_sqrt`**$(p.x^2 + p.y^2 + ...)$

`gentypef` **`fast_normalize`**`(gentypef p)`	Returns a vector in the same direction as p but with a length of 1.
	
	`fast_normalize` is computed as
	p * **`half_sqrt`**$(p.x^2 + p.y^2 + ...)$
	
	The result will be within 8192 ulps error from the infinitely precise result of
	
	`if (all(p == 0.0f))`
	    `result = p;`
	
	`else`
	
	    `result = p / `**`sqrt`**`(p.x² + p.y² + ...)`
	
	It has the following exceptions:
	
	• If the sum of squares is greater than FLT_MAX, then the value of the floating-point values in the result vector is undefined.
	
	• If the sum of squares is less than FLT_MIN, then the implementation may return back p.
	
	• If the device is in "denorms are flushed to zero" mode, individual operand elements with magnitude less than **`sqrt`**(FLT_MIN) may be flushed to zero before proceeding with the calculation.

Table 5.9 Built-In Relational Functions

Function	Description
int **isequal**(float x, float y) int **isequal**(double x, double y) int*n* **isequal**(float*n* x, float*n* y) long*n* **isequal**(double*n* x, double*n* y)	Returns the component-wise compare of x == y.
int **isnotequal**(float x, float y) int **isnotequal**(double x, double y) int*n* **isnotequal**(float*n* x, float*n* y) long*n* **isnotequal**(double*n* x, double*n* y)	Returns the component-wise compare of x! = y.
int **isgreater**(float x, float y) int **isgreater**(double x, double y) int*n* **isgreater**(float*n* x, float*n* y) long*n* **isgreater**(double*n* x, double*n* y)	Returns the component-wise compare of x > y.
int **isgreaterequal**(float x, float y) int **isgreaterequal**(double x, double y) int*n* **isgreaterequal**(float*n* x, float*n* y) long*n* **isgreaterequal**(double*n* x, double*n* y)	Returns the component-wise compare of x >= y.
int **isless**(float x, float y) int **isless**(double x, double y) int*n* **isless**(float*n* x, float*n* y) long*n* **isless**(double*n* x, double*n* y)	Returns the component-wise compare of x < y.
int **islessequal**(float x, float y) int **islessequal**(double x, double y) int*n* **islessequal**(float*n* x, float*n* y) long*n* **islessequal**(double*n* x, double*n* y)	Returns the component-wise compare of x <= y.
int **islessgreater**(float x, float y) int **islessgreater**(double x, double y) int*n* **islessgreater**(float*n* x, float*n* y) long*n* **islessgreater**(double*n* x, double*n* y)	Returns the component-wise compare of $(x < y) \;||\; (x > y)$.

Function	Description

`int isfinite(float x)`
`int isfinite(double x)`
`intn isfinite(floatn x)`
`longn isfinite(doublen x)`
	Tests for the finite value of x.

`int isinf(float x)`
`int isinf(double x)`
`intn isinf(floatn x)`
`longn isinf(doublen x)`
	Tests for the infinite value (positive or negative) of x.

`int isnan(float x)`
`int isnan(double x)`
`intn isnan(floatn x)`
`longn isnan(doublen x)`
	Tests for a NaN.

`int isnormal(float x)`
`int isnormal(double x)`
`intn isnormal(floatn x)`
`longn isnormal(doublen x)`
	Tests for a normal value (i.e., x is neither zero, denormal, infinite, nor NaN).

`int isordered(float x, float y)`
`int isordered(double x, double y)`
`intn isordered(floatn x, floatn y)`
`longn isordered(doublen x, doublen y)`
	Tests if arguments are ordered. **isordered** takes arguments x and y and returns the result
	
	    isequal(x, x) && **isequal**(y, y)

`int isunordered(float x, float y)`
`int isunordered(double x, double y)`
`intn isunordered(floatn x, floatn y)`
`longn isunordered(doublen x, doublen y)`
	Tests if arguments are unordered. **isunordered** takes arguments x and y, returning non-zero if x or y is NaN, and zero otherwise.

`int signbit(float x)`
`int signbit(double x)`
`intn signbit(floatn x)`
`longn signbit(doublen x)`
	Tests for sign bit. The scalar version of the function returns a 1 if the sign bit in the floating-point value of x is set, else it returns 0. The vector version of the function returns the following for each component: a −1 if the sign bit in the floating-point value is set, else 0.

The functions `isequal`, `isnotequal`, `isgreater`, `isgreaterequal`, `isless`, `islessequal`, `islessgreater`, `isfinite`, `isinf`, `isnan`, `isnormal`, `isordered`, `isunordered`, and `signbit` in Table 5.9 return a 0 if the specified relation is `false` and a 1 if the specified relation is `true` for scalar argument types. These functions return a 0 if the specified relation is `false` and a -1 (i.e., all bits set) if the specified relation is `true` for vector argument types.

The functions `isequal`, `isgreater`, `isgreaterequal`, `isless`, `islessequal`, and `islessgreater` return 0 if either argument is not a number (NaN). `isnotequal` returns 1 if one or both arguments are NaN and the argument type is a scalar and returns -1 if one or both arguments are NaN and the argument type is a vector.

Table 5.10 describes additional relational functions supported by OpenCL C. We use the generic type name `gentype` to indicate that the function can take `char`, `char2`, `char3`, `char4`, `char8`, `char16`, `uchar`, `uchar2`, `uchar3`, `uchar4`, `uchar8`, `uchar16`, `short`, `short2`, `short3`, `short4`, `short8`, `short16`, `ushort`, `ushort2`, `ushort3`, `ushort4`, `ushort8`, `ushort16`, `int`, `int2`, `int3`, `int4`, `int8`, `int16`, `uint`, `uint2`, `uint3`, `uint4`, `uint8`, `uint16`, `long`, `long2`, `long3`, `long4`, `long8`, `long16`, `ulong`, `ulong2`, `ulong3`, `ulong4`, `ulong8`, `ulong16`, `float`, `float2`, `float3`, `float4`, `float8`, `float16`, and, if the double-precision

Table 5.10 Additional Built-In Relational Functions

Function	Description
`int` **`any`**`(sgentype x)`	Returns 1 if the most significant bit in any component of x is set; otherwise returns 0.
`int` **`all`**`(sgentype x)`	Returns 1 if the most significant bit in all components of x is set; otherwise returns 0.

`gentype` **`bitselect`**`(gentype a,`
`gentype b,`
`gentype c)`
	Each bit of the result is the corresponding bit of a if the corresponding bit of c is 0. Otherwise it is the corresponding bit of b.

`gentype` **`select`**`(gentype a,`
`gentype b,`
`sgentype c)`
`gentype` **`select`**`(gentype a,`
`gentype b,`
`ugentype c)`
	For each component of a vector type
	`result[i] = if MSB of c[i] is set ?`
	`          b[i] : a[i]`
	For a scalar type
	`result = c ? b : a`
	`sgentype` and `ugentype` must have the same number of elements and bits as `gentype`.

extension is supported, double, double2, double3, double4, double8, or double16 as the type for the arguments.

We use the generic type name sgentype to refer to the signed integer types char, char2, char3, char4, char8, char16, short, short2, short3, short4, short8, short16, int, int2, int3, int4, int8, int16, long, long2, long3, long4, long8, or long16.

We use the generic type name ugentype to refer to the signed integer types uchar, uchar2, uchar3, uchar4, uchar8, uchar16, ushort, ushort2, ushort3, ushort4, ushort8, ushort16, uint, uint2, uint3, uint4, uint8, uint16, ulong, ulong2, ulong3, ulong4, ulong8, or ulong16.

Vector Data Load and Store Functions

Table 5.11 describes the built-in functions that allow you to read and write vector types from a pointer to memory. We use the generic type name gentype to indicate the scalar built-in data types char, uchar, short, ushort, int, uint, long, ulong, float, or double. We use the generic type name gentype$n$ to indicate the n-element vectors of gentype elements. We use the type name float$n$, double$n$, and half$n$ to represent n-element vectors of float, double, and half elements, respectively. The suffix n is also used in the function names (such as vload$n$, vstore$n$), where n = 2, 3, 4, 8, or 16.

Table 5.11   Built-In Vector Data Load and Store Functions

Function	Description
gentype$n$ **vload$n$**(size_t *offset*, const global gentype **p*) gentype$n$ **vload$n$**(size_t *offset*, const local gentype **p*) gentype$n$ **vload$n$**(size_t *offset*, const constant gentype **p*) gentype$n$ **vload$n$**(size_t *offset*, const private gentype **p*)	Returns sizeof(gentype$n$) bytes of data read from address (*p* + (*offset* * *n*)). The address computed as (*p* + (*offset* * *n*)) must be 8-bit aligned if gentype is char or uchar; 16-bit aligned if gentype is short or ushort; 32-bit aligned if gentype is int, uint, or float; 64-bit aligned if gentype is long, ulong, or double. vload$n$ is used to do an unaligned vector load.

continues

Table 5.11 Built-In Vector Data Load and Store Functions (*Continued*)

Function	Description

`gentypen` **`vstoren`**`(gentypen data,`
`            size_t offset,`
`            global gentype *p)`
`gentypen` **`vstoren`**`(gentypen data,`
`            size_t offset,`
`            local gentype *p)`
`gentypen` **`vstoren`**`(gentypen data,`
`            size_t offset,`
`            private gentype *p)`
	Write `sizeof(gentypen)` bytes given by data to address (`p + (offset * n)`).
	
	The address computed as (`p + (offset * n)`) must be 8-bit aligned if `gentype` is char or uchar; 16-bit aligned if `gentype` is short or ushort; 32-bit aligned if `gentype` is int, uint, or `float`; 64-bit aligned if `gentype` is long, ulong, or double.
	
	`vstoren` is used to do an unaligned vector store.

`float` **`vload_half`**`(size_t offset,`
`          const global half *p)`
`float` **`vload_half`**`(size_t offset,`
`          const local half *p)`
`float` **`vload_half`**`(size_t offset,`
`          const constant half *p)`
`float` **`vload_half`**`(size_t offset,`
`          const private half *p)`
	Returns `sizeof(half)` bytes of data read from address (`p + offset`).
	
	The data read is interpreted as a `half` value. The `half` value is converted to a `float` value and the `float` value is returned. The read address, which is computed as (`p + offset`), must be 16-bit aligned.

`floatn` **`vload_halfn`**`(size_t offset,`
`          const global half *p)`
`floatn` **`vload_halfn`**`(size_t offset,`
`          const local half *p)`
`floatn` **`vload_halfn`**`(size_t offset,`
`          const constant half *p)`
`floatn` **`vload_halfn`**`(size_t offset,`
`          const private half *p)`
	Returns `sizeof(halfn)` bytes of data read from address (`p + (offset * n)`).
	
	The data read is interpreted as a `halfn` value. The `halfn` value is converted to a `floatn` value and the `floatn` value is returned. The address computed as (`p + (offset * n)`) must be 16-bit aligned.
	
	`vload_halfn` is used to do an unaligned vector load and return a vector float.

Table 5.11 Built-In Vector Data Load and Store Functions (*Continued*)

Function	Description

void **vstore_half**(float *data*,
          size_t *offset*,
          global half **p*)
void **vstore_half_rte**(float *data*,
          size_t *offset*,
          global half **p*)
void **vstore_half_rtz**(float *data*,
          size_t *offset*,
          global half **p*)
void **vstore_half_rtp**(float *data*,
          size_t *offset*,
          global half **p*)
void **vstore_half_rtn**(float *data*,
          size_t *offset*,
          global half **p*)
void **vstore_half**(float *data*,
          size_t *offset*,
          local half **p*)
void **vstore_half_rte**(float *data*,
          size_t *offset*,
          local half **p*)
void **vstore_half_rtz**(float *data*,
          size_t *offset*,
          local half **p*)
void **vstore_half_rtp**(float *data*,
          size_t *offset*,
          local half **p*)
void **vstore_half_rtn**(float *data*,
          size_t *offset*,
          local half **p*)
void **vstore_half**(float *data*,
          size_t *offset*,
          private half **p*)
void **vstore_half_rte**(float *data*,
          size_t *offset*,
          private half **p*)
void **vstore_half_rtz**(float *data*,
          size_t *offset*,
          private half **p*)
void **vstore_half_rtp**(float *data*,
          size_t *offset*,
          private half **p*)
void **vstore_half_rtn**(float *data*,
          size_t *offset*,
          private half **p*)
	The float value given by data is first converted to a half value using the appropriate rounding mode. The half value is then written to the address computed as (*p* + *offset*). The address computed as (*p* + *offset*) must be 16-bit aligned.
	
	vstore_half uses the current rounding mode. The default current rounding mode for the full profile is round to nearest even (denoted by the _rte suffix).

continues

Table 5.11 Built-In Vector Data Load and Store Functions (*Continued*)

Function	Description

void **vstore_halfn**(float*n data*,
          size_t *offset*,
          global half **p*)
void **vstore_halfn_rte**(float*n data*,
          size_t *offset*,
          global half **p*)
void **vstore_halfn_rtz**(float*n data*,
          size_t *offset*,
          global half **p*)
void **vstore_halfn_rtp**(float*n data*,
          size_t *offset*,
          global half **p*)
void **vstore_halfn_rtn**(float*n data*,
          size_t *offset*,
          global half **p*)
void **vstore_halfn**(float*n data*,
          size_t *offset*,
          local half **p*)
void **vstore_halfn_rte**(float*n data*,
          size_t *offset*,
          local half **p*)
void **vstore_halfn_rtz**(float*n data*,
          size_t *offset*,
          local half **p*)
void **vstore_halfn_rtp**(float*n data*,
          size_t *offset*,
          local half **p*)
void **vstore_halfn_rtn**(float*n data*,
          size_t *offset*,
          local half **p*)
void **vstore_halfn**(float*n data*,
          size_t *offset*,
          private half **p*)
void **vstore_halfn_rte**(float*n data*,
          size_t *offset*,
          private half **p*)
void **vstore_halfn_rtz**(float*n data*,
          size_t *offset*,
          private half **p*)
void **vstore_halfn_rtp**(float*n data*,
          size_t *offset*,
          private half **p*)
void **vstore_halfn_rtn**(float*n data*,
          size_t *offset*,
          private half **p*)
	The float*n* value given by data is first converted to a half*n* value using the appropriate rounding mode. The half*n* value is then written to the address computed as (*p* + (*offset* * *n*)). The address computed as (*p* + (*offset* * *n*)) must be 16-bit aligned.
	
	vstore_half*n* uses the current rounding mode. The default current rounding mode for the full profile is round to nearest even (denoted by the _rte suffix).
	
	vstore_half*n* converts the float vector to a half vector and then does an unaligned vector store of the half vector.

Table 5.11 Built-In Vector Data Load and Store Functions (*Continued*)

Function	Description
float*n* **vloada_halfn**(size_t *offset*, const global half **p*) float*n* **vloada_halfn**(size_t *offset*, const local half **p*) float*n* **vloada_halfn**(size_t *offset*, const constant half **p*) float*n* **vloada_halfn**(size_t *offset*, const private half **p*)	For n = 1, 2, 4, 8, and 16, read sizeof(half*n*) bytes of data from address (p + (*offset* * n)). This address must be aligned to sizeof(half*n*) bytes. For n = 3, read a half3 value from address (p + (*offset* * 4)). This address must be aligned to sizeof(half) * 4 bytes. The data read is interpreted as a half*n* value. The half*n* value read is converted to a float*n* value and the float*n* value is returned. vloada_half*n* is used to do an aligned vector load and return a vector float.

continues

Table 5.11 Built-In Vector Data Load and Store Functions (*Continued*)

Function	Description
void **vstorea_halfn**(floatn *data*, 　　　　　　　　size_t *offset*, 　　　　　　　　global half **p*) void **vstorea_halfn_rte**(floatn *data*, 　　　　　　　　size_t *offset*, 　　　　　　　　global half **p*) void **vstorea_halfn_rtz**(floatn *data*, 　　　　　　　　size_t *offset*, 　　　　　　　　global half **p*) void **vstorea_halfn_rtp**(floatn *data*, 　　　　　　　　size_t *offset*, 　　　　　　　　global half **p*) void **vstorea_halfn_rtn**(floatn *data*, 　　　　　　　　size_t *offset*, 　　　　　　　　global half **p*) void **vstorea_halfn**(floatn *data*, 　　　　　　　　size_t *offset*, 　　　　　　　　local half **p*) void **vstorea_halfn_rte**(floatn *data*, 　　　　　　　　size_t *offset*, 　　　　　　　　local half **p*) void **vstorea_halfn_rtz**(floatn *data*, 　　　　　　　　size_t *offset*, 　　　　　　　　local half **p*) void **vstorea_halfn_rtp**(floatn *data*, 　　　　　　　　size_t *offset*, 　　　　　　　　local half **p*) void **vstorea_halfn_rtn**(floatn *data*, 　　　　　　　　size_t *offset*, 　　　　　　　　local half **p*) void **vstorea_halfn**(floatn *data*, 　　　　　　　　size_t *offset*, 　　　　　　　　private half **p*) void **vstorea_halfn_rte**(floatn *data*, 　　　　　　　　size_t *offset*, 　　　　　　　　private half **p*) void **vstorea_halfn_rtz**(floatn *data*, 　　　　　　　　size_t *offset*, 　　　　　　　　private half **p*) void **vstorea_halfn_rtp**(floatn *data*, 　　　　　　　　size_t *offset*, 　　　　　　　　private half **p*) void **vstorea_halfn_rtn**(floatn *data*, 　　　　　　　　size_t *offset*, 　　　　　　　　private half **p*)	The floatn value given by data is first converted to a halfn value using the appropriate rounding mode. For n = 1, 2, 4, 8, and 16, the halfn value is written to the address computed as (p + (offset * n)). This address must be aligned to sizeof(halfn) bytes. For n = 3, the halfn value is written to the address computed as (p + (offset * 4)). This address must be aligned to sizeof(half) * 4 bytes. vstorea_halfn uses the current rounding mode. The default current rounding mode for the full profile is round to nearest even (denoted by the _rte suffix).

Table 5.11 Built-In Vector Data Load and Store Functions (*Continued*)

Function	Description

void **vstore_half**(double *data*,
               size_t *offset*,
               global half **p*)
void **vstore_half_rte**(double *data*,
                  size_t *offset*,
                  global half **p*)
void **vstore_half_rtz**(double *data*,
                  size_t *offset*,
                  global half **p*)
void **vstore_half_rtp**(double *data*,
                  size_t *offset*,
                  global half **p*)
void **vstore_half_rtn**(double *data*,
                  size_t *offset*,
                  global half **p*)
void **vstore_half**(double *data*,
               size_t *offset*,
               local half **p*)
void **vstore_half_rte**(double *data*,
                  size_t *offset*,
                  local half **p*)
void **vstore_half_rtz**(double *data*,
                  size_t *offset*,
                  local half **p*)
void **vstore_half_rtp**(double *data*,
                  size_t *offset*,
                  local half **p*)
void **vstore_half_rtn**(double *data*,
                  size_t *offset*,
                  local half **p*)
void **vstore_half**(double *data*,
               size_t *offset*,
               private half **p*)
void **vstore_half_rte**(double *data*,
                  size_t *offset*,
                  private half **p*)
void **vstore_half_rtz**(double *data*,
                  size_t *offset*,
                  private half **p*)
void **vstore_half_rtp**(double *data*,
                  size_t *offset*,
                  private half **p*)
void **vstore_half_rtn**(double *data*,
                  size_t *offset*,
                  private half **p*)
	The double value given by *data* is first converted to a half value using the appropriate rounding mode. The half value is then written to the address computed as (p + *offset*). The address computed as (p + *offset*) must be 16-bit aligned.
	
	vstore_half uses the current rounding mode. The default current rounding mode for the full profile is round to nearest even (denoted by the _rte suffix).

continues

Table 5.11 Built-In Vector Data Load and Store Functions (*Continued*)

Function	Description

```void vstore_halfn(doublen data,   size_t offset,   global half *p)```
 	
```void vstore_halfn_rte(doublen data,   size_t offset,   global half *p)```
 	
```void vstore_halfn_rtz(doublen data,   size_t offset,   global half *p)```
 	
```void vstore_halfn_rtp(doublen data,   size_t offset,   global half *p)```
 	
```void vstore_halfn_rtn(doublen data,   size_t offset,   global half *p)```
 	
```void vstore_halfn(doublen data,   size_t offset,   local half *p)```
 	
```void vstore_halfn_rte(doublen data,   size_t offset,   local half *p)```
 	
```void vstore_halfn_rtz(doublen data,   size_t offset,   local half *p)```
 	
```void vstore_halfn_rtp(doublen data,   size_t offset,   local half *p)```
 	
```void vstore_halfn_rtn(doublen data,   size_t offset,   local half *p)```
 	
```void vstore_halfn(doublen data,   size_t offset,   private half *p)```
 	
```void vstore_halfn_rte(doublen data,   size_t offset,   private half *p)```
 	
```void vstore_halfn_rtz(doublen data,   size_t offset,   private half *p)```
 	
```void vstore_halfn_rtp(doublen data,   size_t offset,   private half *p)```
 	
```void vstore_halfn_rtn(doublen data,   size_t offset,   private half *p)```
	The double*n* value given by *data* is first converted to a half*n* value using the appropriate rounding mode. The half*n* value is then written to the address computed as (*p* + (*offset* * *n*)). The address computed as (*p* + (*offset* * *n*)) must be 16-bit aligned.
	
	vstore_half*n* uses the current rounding mode. The default current rounding mode for the full profile is round to nearest even (denoted by the _rte suffix).
	
	vstorea_half*n* converts the float vector to a half vector and then does an aligned vector store of the half vector.

Table 5.11 Built-In Vector Data Load and Store Functions (*Continued*)

Function	Description
void **vstorea_halfn**(doublen *data*, 　　　　　size_t *offset*, 　　　　　global half **p*) void **vstorea_halfn_rte**(doublen *data*, 　　　　　size_t *offset*, 　　　　　global half **p*) void **vstorea_halfn_rtz**(doublen *data*, 　　　　　size_t *offset*, 　　　　　global half **p*) void **vstorea_halfn_rtp**(doublen *data*, 　　　　　size_t *offset*, 　　　　　global half **p*) void **vstorea_halfn_rtn**(doublen *data*, 　　　　　size_t *offset*, 　　　　　global half **p*) void **vstorea_halfn**(doublen *data*, 　　　　　size_t *offset*, 　　　　　local half **p*) void **vstorea_halfn_rte**(doublen *data*, 　　　　　size_t *offset*, 　　　　　local half **p*) void **vstorea_halfn_rtz**(doublen *data*, 　　　　　size_t *offset*, 　　　　　local half **p*) void **vstorea_halfn_rtp**(doublen *data*, 　　　　　size_t *offset*, 　　　　　local half **p*) void **vstorea_halfn_rtn**(doublen *data*, 　　　　　size_t *offset*, 　　　　　local half **p*) void **vstorea_halfn**(doublen *data*, 　　　　　size_t *offset*, 　　　　　private half **p*) void **vstorea_halfn_rte**(doublen *data*, 　　　　　size_t *offset*, 　　　　　private half **p*) void **vstorea_halfn_rtz**(doublen *data*, 　　　　　size_t *offset*, 　　　　　private half **p*) void **vstorea_halfn_rtp**(doublen *data*, 　　　　　size_t *offset*, 　　　　　private half **p*) void **vstorea_halfn_rtn**(doublen *data*, 　　　　　size_t *offset*, 　　　　　private half **p*)	The doublen value given by *data* is first converted to a halfn value using the appropriate rounding mode. For n = 1, 2, 4, 8, and 16, the halfn value is written to the address computed as (*p* + (*offset* * *n*)). This address must be aligned to sizeof(halfn) bytes. For n = 3, the halfn value is written to the address computed as (*p* + (*offset* * 4)). This address must be aligned to sizeof(half) * 4 bytes. vstorea_halfn uses the current rounding mode. The default current rounding mode for the full profile is round to nearest even (denoted by the _rte suffix).

Synchronization Functions

OpenCL C implements a synchronization function called `barrier`. The `barrier` synchronization function is used to enforce memory consistency between work-items in a work-group. This is described in Table 5.12.

Table 5.12 Built-In Synchronization Functions

Function	Description
void **barrier**(cl_mem_fence_flags *flags*)	All work-items in a work-group executing the kernel on a compute unit must execute this function before any are allowed to continue execution beyond the barrier. This function must be encountered by all work-items in a work-group executing the kernel.
	If a barrier is inside a conditional statement, then all work-items must enter the conditional if any work-item enters the conditional statement and executes the barrier.
	If a barrier is inside a loop, all work-items must execute the barrier for each iteration of the loop before any are allowed to continue execution beyond the barrier.
	The `barrier` function also queues a memory fence (reads and writes) to ensure correct ordering of memory operations to local and/or global memory.
	The flags argument specifies the memory address space and can be set to a combination of the following literal values:
	• CLK_LOCAL_MEM_FENCE: The barrier function will either flush any variables stored in local memory or queue a memory fence to ensure correct ordering of memory operations to local memory.
	• CLK_GLOBAL_MEM_FENCE: The barrier function will either flush any variables stored in global memory or queue a memory fence to ensure correct ordering of memory operations to global memory. This is needed when work-items in a work-group, for example, write to a buffer object in global memory and then read the updated data.

If all work-items in a work-group do not encounter the barrier, then the behavior is undefined. On some devices, especially GPUs, this will most likely result in a deadlock in hardware. The following is an example that shows this incorrect usage of the `barrier` function:

```
kernel void
read(global int *g, local int *shared)
{
    if (get_global_id(0) < 5)
        barrier(CLK_GLOBAL_MEM_FENCE);   ← illegal since not all work-
                                           items encounter barrier.
    else
        k = array[0];
}
```

Note that the memory consistency is enforced only between work-items in a work-group, not across work-groups. Here is an example that demonstrates this:

```
kernel void
smooth(global float *io)
{
    float temp;
    int id = get_global_id(0);
    temp = (io[id - 1] + id[id] + id[id + 1]) / 3.0f;
    barrier(CLK_GLOBAL_MEM_FENCE);
    io[id] = temp;
}
```

If `kernel smooth` is executed over a global work size of 16 items with 2 work-groups of 8 work-items each, then the value that will get stored in `id[7]` and/or `id[8]` is undetermined. This is because work-items in both work-groups use `id[7]` and `id[8]` to compute `temp`. Work-group 0 uses it to calculate `temp` for `id[7]`, and work-group 1 uses it to calculate `temp` for `id[8]`. Because there are no guarantees when work-groups execute or which compute units they execute on, and because `barrier` only enforces memory consistency for work-items in a work-group, we are unable to say what values will be computed and stored in `id[7]` and `id[8]`.

Async Copy and Prefetch Functions

Table 5.13 describes the built-in functions in OpenCL C that provide a portable and performant method for copying between global and local memory and do a prefetch from global memory. The functions that copy between global and local memory are defined to be an asynchronous copy.

Table 5.13 Built-In Async Copy and Prefetch Functions

Function	Description

event_t
async_work_group_copy (local gentype *dst,
    const global gentype *src,
    size_t num_gentypes,
    event_t event)
 	
event_t
async_work_group_copy (global gentype *dst,
    const local gentype *src,
    size_t num_gentypes,
    event_t event)
	Perform an async copy of num_gentypes gentype elements from src to dst.
	
	The async copy is performed by all work-items in a work-group, and this built-in function must therefore be encountered by all work-items in a work-group executing the kernel with the same argument values; otherwise the results are undefined.
	
	Returns an event object that can be used by wait_group_ events to wait for the async copy to finish. event can also be used to associate the async_work_group_copy with a previous async copy, allowing an event to be shared by multiple async copies; otherwise event should be zero.
	
	If event is non-zero, the event object supplied in event will be returned.

event_t
async_work_group_strided_copy (
    local gentype *dst,
    const global gentype *src,
    size_t num_gentypes,
    size_t src_stride,
    event_t event)
 	
event_t
async_work_group_strided_copy (
    global gentype *dst,
    const local gentype *src,
    size_t num_gentypes,
    size_t dst_stride,
    event_t event)
	Performs an async gather or scatter copy of num_gentypes gentype elements from src to dst. The src_stride is the stride in elements for each gentype element read from src. The dst_stride is the stride in elements for each gentype element written to dst.
	
	The async copy is performed by all work-items in a work-group, and this built-in function must therefore be encountered by all work-items in a work-group executing the kernel with the same argument values; otherwise the results are undefined.
	
	Returns an event object that can be used by wait_group_ events to wait for the async copy to finish. event can also be used to associate the async_work_group_strided_copy with a previous async copy, allowing an event to be shared by multiple async copies; otherwise event should be zero.
	
	If event is non-zero, the event object supplied in event will be returned.

Function	Description
`void` **`wait_group_events`** `(int num_events,` `event_t *event_list)`	Wait for events that identify the copy operations associated with `async_work_group_copy` and `async_work_group_strided_copy` functions to complete. The event objects specified in `event_list` will be released after the wait is performed. This function must be encountered by all work-items in a work-group executing the kernel within the same `num_events` and event objects specified in `event_list`; otherwise the results are undefined.
`void` **`prefetch`** `(const global gentype *p,` `size_t num_gentypes)`	Prefetch `num_gentypes * sizeof(gentype)` bytes into the global cache. The prefetch function is applied to a work-item in a work-group and does not affect the functional behavior of the kernel.

We use the generic type name `gentype` to indicate that the function can take `char`, `char2`, `char3`, `char4`, `char8`, `char16`, `uchar`, `uchar2`, `uchar3`, `uchar4`, `uchar8`, `uchar16`, `short`, `short2`, `short3`, `short4`, `short8`, `short16`, `ushort`, `ushort2`, `ushort3`, `ushort4`, `ushort8`, `ushort16`, `int`, `int2`, `int3`, `int4`, `int8`, `int16`, `uint`, `uint2`, `uint3`, `uint4`, `uint8`, `uint16`, `long`, `long2`, `long3`, `long4`, `long8`, `long16`, `ulong`, `ulong2`, `ulong3`, `ulong4`, `ulong8`, `ulong16`, `float`, `float2`, `float3`, `float4`, `float8`, `float16`, and, if the double-precision extension is supported, `double`, `double2`, `double3`, `double4`, `double8`, or `double16` as the type for the arguments.

The following example shows how `async_work_group_strided_copy` can be used to do a strided copy from global to local memory and back. Consider a buffer of elements where each element represents a vertex of a 3D geometric object. Each vertex is a structure that stores the position, normal, texture coordinates, and other information about the vertex. An OpenCL kernel may want to read the vertex position, apply some computations, and store the updated position values. This requires a strided copy to move the vertex position data from global to local memory, apply computations, and then move the update vertex position data by doing a strided copy from local to global memory.

```
typedef struct {
    float4 position;
    float3 normal;
    float2 texcoord;
    ...
} vertex_t;

kernel void
update_position_kernel(global vertex_t *vertices,
                       local float4 *pos_array)
{
    event_t evt = async_work_group_strided_copy(
                        (local float *)pos_array,
                        (global float *)vertices,
                        4, sizeof(vertex_t)/sizeof(float),
                        NULL);
    wait_group_events(evt);

    // do computations
    . . .
    evt = async_work_group_strided_copy((global float *)vertices,
                        (local float *)pos_array,
                        4, sizeof(vertex_t)/sizeof(float),
                        NULL);
    wait_group_events(evt);
}
```

The kernel must wait for the completion of all async copies using the `wait_group_events` built-in function before exiting; otherwise the behavior is undefined.

Atomic Functions

Table 5.14 describes the built-in functions in OpenCL C that provide atomic operations on 32-bit signed and unsigned integers and single-precision floating-point to locations in global or local memory.

Note   `atom_xchg` is the only atomic function that takes floating-point argument types.

Table 5.14   Built-In Atomic Functions

Function	Description

`int`
`atomic_add``(volatile global int *p, int val)`
`unsigned int`
`atomic_add``(volatile global unsigned int *p,`
                `unsigned int val)`
 	
`int`
`atomic_add``(volatile local int *p, int val)`
`unsigned int`
`atomic_add``(volatile local unsigned int *p,`
                `unsigned int val)`
	Read the 32-bit value (referred to as *old*) stored at the location pointed by *p*. Compute (*old* + *val*) and store the result at the location pointed by *p*. The function returns *old*.

`int`
`atomic_sub``(volatile global int *p, int val)`
`unsigned int`
`atomic_sub``(volatile global unsigned int *p,`
                `unsigned int val)`
 	
`int`
`atomic_sub``(volatile local int *p, int val)`
`unsigned int`
`atomic_sub``(volatile local unsigned int *p,`
                `unsigned int val)`
	Read the 32-bit value (referred to as *old*) stored at the location pointed by *p*. Compute (*old* − *val*) and store the result at the location pointed by *p*. The function returns *old*.

continues

Table 5.14 Built-In Atomic Functions (*Continued*)

Function	Description

int
atomic_xchg(volatile global int *p, int val)
unsigned int
atomic_xchg(volatile global unsigned int *p,
                          unsigned int val)
float
atomic_xchg(volatile global int *p,
                          float val)
 	
int
atomic_xchg(volatile local int *p, int val)
unsigned int
atomic_xchg(volatile local unsigned int *p,
                          unsigned int val)
float
atomic_xchg(volatile local int *p,
                          float val)
	Swap the *old* stored at location *p* with new value given by *val*. The function returns *old*.

int **atomic_inc**(volatile global int *p) unsigned int **atomic_inc**(volatile global unsigned int *p) int **atomic_inc**(volatile local int *p) unsigned int **atomic_inc**(volatile local unsigned int *p)	Read the 32-bit value (referred to as *old*) stored at the location pointed by *p*. Compute ($old + 1$) and store the result at location pointed by *p*. The function returns *old*.
int **atomic_dec**(volatile global int *p) unsigned int **atomic_dec**(volatile global unsigned int *p) int **atomic_dec**(volatile local int *p) unsigned int **atomic_dec**(volatile local unsigned int *p)	Read the 32-bit value (referred to as *old*) stored at the location pointed by *p*. Compute ($old - 1$) and store the result at location pointed by *p*. The function returns *old*.

Table 5.14 Built-In Atomic Functions (*Continued*)

Function	Description
```int atomic_cmpxchg(volatile global int *p, int cmp, int val) unsigned int atomic_cmpxchg(volatile global unsigned int *p, unsigned int cmp, unsigned int val) int atomic_cmpxchg(volatile local int *p, int cmp, int val) unsigned int atomic_cmpxchg(volatile local unsigned int *p, unsigned int cmp, unsigned int val)```	Read the 32-bit value (referred to as *old*) stored at the location pointed by *p*. Compute (*old* == *cmp*) ? *val* : *old* and store the result at the location pointed by *p*. The function returns *old*.
```int atomic_min(volatile global int *p, int val) unsigned int atomic_min(volatile global unsigned int *p, unsigned int val) int atomic_min(volatile local int *p, int val) unsigned int atomic_min(volatile local unsigned int *p, unsigned int val)```	Read the 32-bit value (referred to as *old*) stored at the location pointed by *p*. Compute min(*old*, *val*) and store the result at the location pointed by *p*. The function returns *old*.
```int atomic_max(volatile global int *p, int val) unsigned int atomic_max(volatile global unsigned int *p, unsigned int val) int atomic_max(volatile local int *p, int val) unsigned int atomic_max(volatile local unsigned int *p, unsigned int val)```	Read the 32-bit value (referred to as *old*) stored at the location pointed by *p*. Compute max(*old*, *val*) and store the result at the location pointed by *p*. The function returns *old*.

continues

Table 5.14 Built-In Atomic Functions (*Continued*)

Function	Description

`int`
`atomic_min(volatile global int *p, int val)`
`unsigned int`
`atomic_min(volatile global unsigned int *p,`
`                  unsigned int val)`
 	
`int`
`atomic_min(volatile local int *p, int val)`
`unsigned int`
`atomic_min(volatile local unsigned int *p,`
`                  unsigned int val)`
	Read the 32-bit value (referred to as *old*) stored at the location pointed by *p*. Compute `min(`*old*`, `*val*`)` and store the result at the location pointed by *p*. The function returns *old*.

`int`
`atomic_and(volatile global int *p, int val)`
`unsigned int`
`atomic_and(volatile global unsigned int *p,`
`                  unsigned int val)`
 	
`int`
`atomic_and(volatile local int *p, int val)`
`unsigned int`
`atomic_and(volatile local unsigned int *p,`
`                  unsigned int val)`
	Read the 32-bit value (referred to as *old*) stored at the location pointed by *p*. Compute (*old* & *val*) and store the result at the location pointed by *p*. The function returns *old*.

`int`
`atomic_or(volatile global int *p, int val)`
`unsigned int`
`atomic_or(volatile global unsigned int *p,`
`                  unsigned int val)`
 	
`int`
`atomic_or(volatile local int *p, int val)`
`unsigned int`
`atomic_or(volatile local unsigned int *p,`
`                  unsigned int val)`
	Read the 32-bit value (referred to as *old*) stored at the location pointed by *p*. Compute (*old* | *val*) and store the result at the location pointed by *p*. The function returns *old*.

`int`
`atomic_xor(volatile global int *p, int val)`
`unsigned int`
`atomic_xor(volatile global unsigned int *p,`
`                  unsigned int val)`
 	
`int`
`atomic_xor(volatile local int *p, int val)`
`unsigned int`
`atomic_xor(volatile local unsigned int *p,`
`                  unsigned int val)`
	Read the 32-bit value (referred to as *old*) stored at the location pointed by *p*. Compute (*old* ^ *val*) and store the result at the location pointed by *p*. The function returns *old*.

Miscellaneous Vector Functions

OpenCL C implements the additional built-in vector functions described in Table 5.15. We use the generic type name gentype to indicate that the function can take char, uchar, short, ushort, int, uint, long, ulong, float, and, if the double-precision extension is supported, double as the type for the arguments.

We use the generic type name gentypen (or gentypem) to indicate that the function can take char2, char3, char4, char8, char16, uchar2, uchar3, uchar4, uchar8, uchar16, short2, short3, short4, short8, short16, ushort2, ushort3, ushort4, ushort8, ushort16, int2, int3, int4, int8, int16, uint2, uint3, uint4, uint8, uint16, long2, long3, long4, long8, long16, ulong2, ulong3, ulong4, ulong8, ulong16, float2, float3, float4, float8, float16, and, if the double-precision extension is supported, double2, double3, double4, double8, or double16 as the type for the arguments.

We use the generic type ugentypen to refer to the built-in unsigned integer vector data types.

Here are a couple of examples showing how shuffle and shuffle2 can be used:

```
uint mask = (uint4)(3, 2, 1, 0);
float4 a;
float4 r = shuffle(a, mask); // r.s0123 = a.wzyx

uint8 mask = (uint8)(0, 1, 2, 3, 4, 5, 6, 7);
float4 a, b;
float8 r = shuffle2(a, b, mask); // r.s0123 = a.xyzw,
                                 // r.s4567 = b.xyzw
```

A few examples showing illegal usage of shuffle and shuffle2 follow. These should result in a compilation error.

```
uint8 mask;
short16 a;
short8  b;
b = shuffle(a, mask); // not valid
```

We recommend using shuffle and shuffle2 to do permute operations instead of rolling your own code as the compiler can very easily map these built-in functions to the appropriate underlying hardware ISA.

Table 5.15 Built-In Miscellaneous Vector Functions

Function	Description
int **vec_step** (gentype a) int **vec_step** (gentypen a)	The vec_step built-in function takes a built-in scalar or vector data type argument and returns an integer value representing the number of elements in the scalar or vector.
int **vec_step** (char3 a) int **vec_step** (uchar3 a) int **vec_step** (short3 a) int **vec_step** (ushort3 a) int **vec_step** (half3 a) int **vec_step** (int3 a) int **vec_step** (uint3 a) int **vec_step** (long3 a) int **vec_step** (ulong3 a) int **vec_step** (float3 a) int **vec_step** (double3 a)	For all scalar types, vec_step returns 1. The vec_step built-in functions that take a 3-component vector return 4. vec_step may also take a pure type as an argument, e.g., vec_step(float2).
int **vec_step** (type)	

gentypen **shuffle** (gentypem x,
      ugentypen mask)
gentypen **shuffle2** (gentypem x,
      gentypem y,
      ugentypen mask)
	The shuffle and shuffle2 built-in functions construct a permutation of elements from one or two input vectors respectively that are of the same type, returning a vector with the same element type as the input and length that is the same as the shuffle mask.
	
	The size of each element in the mask must match the size of each element in the result. For shuffle, only the ilogb(2m − 1) least significant bits of each mask element are considered. For shuffle2, only the ilogb(2m − 1) + 1 significant bits of each mask element are considered. Other bits in mask are ignored.
	
	The elements of the input vectors are numbered from left to right across one or both of the vectors. For this purpose, the number of elements in a vector is given by vec_step(gentypem). The shuffle mask operand specifies, for each element of the result vector, which element of the one or two input vectors the result element gets.

Image Read and Write Functions

In this section, we describe the built-in functions that allow you to read from an image, write to an image, and query image information such as dimensions and format.

OpenCL GPU devices have dedicated hardware for reading from and writing to images. The OpenCL C image read and write functions allow developers to take advantage of this dedicated hardware. Image support in OpenCL is optional. To find out if a device supports images, query the CL_DEVICE_IMAGE_SUPPORT property using the clGetDeviceInfo API.

Reading from an Image

Tables 5.16 and 5.17 describe built-in functions that read from a 2D and 3D image, respectively.

Note that read_imagef, read_imagei, and read_imageui return a float4, int4, or uint4 color value, respectively. This is because the color value can have up to four components. Table 5.18 lists the values used for the components that are not in the image.

Table 5.16 Built-In Image 2D Read Functions

Function	Description
float4 **read_imagef**(image2d_t image, sampler_t sampler, float2 coord)	Use coord.xy to do an element lookup in the 2D image object specified by image. read_imagef returns floating-point values in the range [0.0 ... 1.0] for image objects created with image_channel_data_type set to one of the predefined packed formats, CL_UNORM_INT8 or CL_UNORM_INT16. read_imagef returns floating-point values in the range [-1.0 ... 1.0] for image objects created with image_channel_data_type set to CL_SNORM_INT8 or CL_SNORM_INT16. read_imagef returns floating-point values for image objects created with image_channel_data_type set to CL_HALF_FLOAT or CL_FLOAT. For image_channel_data_type values not specified above, the float4 value returned by read_imagef is undefined.
float4 **read_imagef**(image2d_t image, sampler_t sampler, int2 coord)	Behaves similarly to the read_imagef function that takes a float2 coord except for the additional requirements that • The sampler filter mode must be CLK_FILTER_NEAREST • The sampler normalized coordinates must be CLK_NORMALIZED_COORDS_FALSE • The sampler addressing mode must be one of CLK_ADDRESS_CLAMP_TO_EDGE, CLK_ADDRESS_CLAMP, or CLK_ADDRESS_NONE.
int4 **read_imagei**(image2d_t image, sampler_t sampler, float2 coord)	Use coord.xy to do an element lookup in the 2D image object specified by image. read_imagei returns unnormalized signed integer values for image objects created with image_channel_data_type set to CL_SIGNED_INT8 or CL_SIGNED_INT16. For image_channel_data_type values not specified above, the int4 value returned by read_imagei is undefined. The filter mode specified in sampler must be set to CLK_FILTER_NEAREST. Otherwise the color value returned is undefined.

Function	Description
`int4 read_imagei (image2d_t image, sampler_t sampler, int2 coord)`	Behaves similarly to the read_imagei function that takes a float2 coord except for the additional requirements that • The sampler normalized coordinates must be CLK_NORMALIZED_COORDS_FALSE • The sampler addressing mode must be one of CLK_ADDRESS_CLAMP_TO_EDGE, CLK_ADDRESS_CLAMP, or CLK_ADDRESS_NONE.
`uint4 read_imageui (image2d_t image, sampler_t sampler, float2 coord)`	Use coord.xy to do an element lookup in the 2D image object specified by image. read_imageui returns unnormalized unsigned integer values for image objects created with image_channel_data_type set to CL_UNSIGNED_INT8 or CL_UNSIGNED_INT16. For image_channel_data_type values not specified above, the uint4 value returned by read_imageui is undefined. The filter_mode specified in sampler must be set to CLK_FILTER_NEAREST. Otherwise the color value returned is undefined.
`uint4 read_imageui (image2d_t image, sampler_t sampler, int2 coord)`	Behaves similarly to the read_imageui function that takes a float2 coord except for the additional requirements that • The sampler normalized coordinates must be CLK_NORMALIZED_COORDS_FALSE. • The sampler addressing mode must be one of CLK_ADDRESS_CLAMP_TO_EDGE, CLK_ADDRESS_CLAMP, or CLK_ADDRESS_NONE.

Table 5.17 Built-In Image 3D Read Functions

Function	Description
float4 **read_imagef**(image3d_t image, sampler_t sampler, float4 coord)	Use coord.xyz to do an element lookup in the 3D image object specified by image. read_imagef returns floating-point values in the range [0.0 ... 1.0] for image objects created with image_channel_data_type set to one of the predefined packed formats, CL_UNORM_INT8 or CL_UNORM_INT16. read_imagef returns floating-point values in the range [-1.0 ... 1.0] for image objects created with image_channel_data_type set to CL_SNORM_INT8 or CL_SNORM_INT16. read_imagef returns floating-point values for image objects created with image_channel_data_type set to CL_HALF_FLOAT or CL_FLOAT. For image_channel_data_type values not specified above, the float4 value returned by read_imagef is undefined.
float4 **read_imagef**(image3d_t image, sampler_t sampler, int4 coord)	Behaves similarly to the read_imagef function that takes a float2 coord except for the additional requirements that • The sampler filter mode must be CLK_FILTER_NEAREST. • The sampler normalized coordinates must be CLK_NORMALIZED_COORDS_FALSE. • The sampler addressing mode must be one of CLK_ADDRESS_CLAMP_TO_EDGE, CLK_ADDRESS_CLAMP, or CLK_ADDRESS_NONE.
int4 **read_imagei**(image3d_t image, sampler_t sampler, float4 coord)	Use coord.xyz to do an element lookup in the 3D image object specified by image. read_imagei returns unnormalized signed integer values for image objects created with image_channel_data_type set to CL_SIGNED_INT8 or CL_SIGNED_INT16. For image_channel_data_type values not specified above, the int4 value returned by read_imagei is undefined. The filter mode specified in sampler must be set to CLK_FILTER_NEAREST. Otherwise the color value returned is undefined.

Function	Description
`int4` **`read_imagei`** `(image3d_t image, sampler_t sampler, int4 coord)`	Behaves similarly to the `read_imagei` function that takes a `float2` coord except for the additional requirements that • The sampler normalized coordinates must be `CLK_NORMALIZED_COORDS_FALSE`. • The sampler addressing mode must be one of `CLK_ADDRESS_CLAMP_TO_EDGE`, `CLK_ADDRESS_CLAMP`, or `CLK_ADDRESS_NONE`.
`uint4` **`read_imageui`** `(image3d_t image, sampler_t sampler, float4 coord)`	Use `coord.xyz` to do an element lookup in the 3D image object specified by `image`. `read_imageui` returns unnormalized unsigned integer values for image objects created with `image_channel_data_type` set to `CL_UNSIGNED_INT8` or `CL_UNSIGNED_INT16`. For `image_channel_data_type` values not specified above, the `uint4` value returned by `read_imageui` is undefined. The `filter_mode` specified in `sampler` must be set to `CLK_FILTER_NEAREST`. Otherwise the color value returned is undefined.
`uint4` **`read_imageui`** `(image3d_t image, sampler_t sampler, int4 coord)`	Behaves similarly to the `read_imageui` function that takes a `float2` coord except for the additional requirements that • The sampler normalized coordinates must be `CLK_NORMALIZED_COORDS_FALSE`. • The sampler addressing mode must be one of `CLK_ADDRESS_CLAMP_TO_EDGE`, `CLK_ADDRESS_CLAMP`, or `CLK_ADDRESS_NONE`.

Table 5.18 Image Channel Order and Values for Missing Components

Image Channel Order	`float4`, `int4`, or `uint4` Color Value Returned
CL_R, CL_Rx	(r, 0.0, 0.0, 1.0)
CL_A	(0.0, 0.0, 0.0, a)
CL_RG, CL_RGx	(r, g, 0,0, 1.0)
CL_RA	(r, 0.0, 0.0, a)
CL_RGB, CL_RGBx	(r, g, b, 1.0)
CL_RGBA, CL_BGRA, CL_ARGB	(r, g, b, a)
CL_INTENSITY	(I, I, I, I)
CL_LUMINANCE	(L, L, L, 1.0)

Samplers

The image read functions take a sampler as an argument. The sampler specifies how to sample pixels from the image. A sampler can be passed as an argument to a kernel using the `clSetKernelArg` API, or it can be a constant variable of type `sampler_t` that is declared in the program source.

Sampler variables passed as arguments or declared in the program source must be of type `sampler_t`. The `sampler_t` type is a 32-bit unsigned integer constant and is interpreted as a bit field. The sampler describes the following information:

- **Normalized coordinates:** Specifies whether the `coord.xy` or `coord.xyz` values are normalized or unnormalized values. This can be set to `CLK_NORMALIZED_COORDS_TRUE` or `CLK_NORMALIZED_COORDS_FALSE`.

- **Addressing mode:** This specifies how the `coord.xy` or `coord.xyz` image coordinates get mapped to appropriate pixel locations inside the image and how out-of-range image coordinates are handled. Table 5.19 describes the supported addressing modes.

- **Filter mode:** This specifies the filtering mode to use. This can be set to `CLK_FILTER_NEAREST` (i.e., the nearest filter) or `CLK_FILTER_LINEAR` (i.e., a bilinear filter).

Table 5.19 Sampler Addressing Mode

Addressing Mode	Description
CLK_ADDRESS_MIRRORED_REPEAT	Flip the image coordinate at every integer junction. This addressing mode can be used only with normalized coordinates.
CLK_ADDRESS_REPEAT	Out-of-range image coordinates are wrapped to the valid range. This addressing mode can be used only with normalized coordinates.
CLK_ADDRESS_CLAMP_TO_EDGE	Out-of-range image coordinates are clamped to the extent of the image.
CLK_ADDRESS_CLAMP	Out-of-range image coordinates return a border color.
CLK_ADDRESS_NONE	The programmer guarantees that the image coordinates used to sample elements of the image always refer to a location inside the image. This can also act as a performance hint on some devices. We recommend using this addressing mode instead of CLK_ADDRESS_CLAMP_TO_EDGE if you know for sure that the image coordinates will always be inside the extent of the image.

The following is an example of a sampler passed as an argument to a kernel:

```
kernel void
my_kernel(read_only image2d_t imgA, sampler_t sampler,
                            write_only image2d imgB)
{
    int2 coord = (int2)(get_global_id(0), get_global_id(1));

    float4 clr = read_imagef(imgA, sampler, coord);
    write_imagef(imgB, coord, color);
}
```

The following is an example of samplers declared inside a program source:

```
const sampler_t samplerA = CLK_NORMALIZED_COORDS_FALSE |
                           CLK_ADDRESS_CLAMP |
                           CLK_FILTER_LINEAR;
```

```
kernel void
my_kernel(read_only image2d_t imgA, read_only image2d_t imgB,
                               write_only image2d imgB)
{
    int2 coord = (int2)(get_global_id(0), get_global_id(1));

    float4 clr = read_imagef(imgA, samplerA, coord);
    clr *= read_imagef(imgA,
                    (CLK_NORMALIZED_COORDS_FALSE |
                    CLK_ADDRESS_CLAMP | CLK_FILTER_NEAREST),
                        imgB);
}
```

The maximum number of samplers that can be used in a kernel can be
obtained by querying the CL_DEVICE_MAX_SAMPLERS property using the
clGetDeviceInfo API.

Limitations

The samplers specified to read_imagef, read_imagei, or read_imageui
must use the same value for normalized coordinates when reading from
the same image. The following example illustrates this (different normalized coordinate values used by samplers are highlighted). This will result in
undefined behavior; that is, the color values returned may not be correct.

```
const sampler_t samplerA = CLK_NORMALIZED_COORDS_FALSE |
                           CLK_ADDRESS_CLAMP |
                           CLK_FILTER_LINEAR;
kernel void
my_kernel(read_only image2d_t imgA, write_only image2d imgB)
{
    float4  clr;
    int2    coord = (int2)(get_global_id(0), get_global_id(1));
    float2  normalized_coords;
    float   w = get_image_width(imgA);
    float   h = get_image_height(imgA);

    clr = read_imagef(imgA, samplerA, coord);
    normalized_coords = convert_float2(coord) *
                    (float2)(1.0f / w, 1.0f / h);
    clr *= read_imagef(imgA,
                    (CLK_NORMALIZED_COORDS_TRUE |
                    CLK_ADDRESS_CLAMP | CLK_FILTER_NEAREST),
                    normalized_coords);
}
```

Also, samplers cannot be declared as arrays or pointers or be used as
the type for local variables inside a function or as the return value of a

function defined in a program. Sampler arguments to a function cannot be modified. The invalid cases shown in the following example will result in a compile-time error:

```
sampler_t  ← error.  return type cannot be sampler_t
internal_proc(read_only image2d_t imgA, write_only image2d imgB)
{
    ...
}

kernel void
my_kernel(read_only image2d_t imgA, sampler_t sampler,
                          write_only image2d imgB)
{
    sampler_t *ptr_sampler; ← error. pointer to sampler not allowed

    my_func(imgA, &sampler); ← error passing a pointer to a sampler
        ...
}
```

Determining the Border Color

If the sampler addressing mode is CLK_ADDRESS_CLAMP, out-of-range image coordinates return the border color. The border color returned depends on the image channel order and is described in Table 5.20.

Table 5.20 Image Channel Order and Corresponding Border Color Value

Image Channel Order	Border Color
CL_A	(0.0f, 0.0f, 0.0f, 0.0f)
CL_R	(0.0f, 0.0f, 0.0f, 1.0f)
CL_Rx	(0.0f, 0.0f, 0.0f, 0.0f)
CL_INTENSITY	(0.0f, 0.0f, 0.0f, 0.0f)
CL_LUMINANCE	(0.0f, 0.0f, 0.0f, 1.0f)
CL_RG	(0.0f, 0.0f, 0.0f, 1.0f)
CL_RGx	(0.0f, 0.0f, 0.0f, 0.0f)
CL_RA	(0.0f, 0.0f, 0.0f, 0.0f)
CL_RGB	(0.0f, 0.0f, 0.0f, 1.0f)

continues

Table 5.20 Image Channel Order and Corresponding Border Color Value (*Continued*)

Image Channel Order	Border Color
CL_RGBx	(0.0f, 0.0f, 0.0f, 0.0f)
CL_ARGB	(0.0f, 0.0f, 0.0f, 0.0f)
CL_BGRA	(0.0f, 0.0f, 0.0f, 0.0f)
CL_RGBA	(0.0f, 0.0f, 0.0f, 0.0f)

Writing to an Image

Tables 5.21 and 5.22 describe built-in functions that write to a 2D and 3D image, respectively.

If the x coordinate is not in the range (0 … image width − 1), or the y coordinate is not in the range (0 … image height − 1), the behavior of write_imagef, write_imagei, or write_imageui for a 2D image is considered to be undefined.

If the x coordinate is not in the range (0 … image width − 1), or the y coordinate is not in the range (0 … image height − 1), or the z coordinate is not in the range (0 … image depth − 1), the behavior of write_imagef, write_imagei, or write_imageui for a 3D image is considered to be undefined.

Table 5.21 Built-In Image 2D Write Functions

Function	Description
`void` **`write_imagef`**`(image2d_t image, int2 coord, float4 color)`	Write the color value to the location specified by `coord.xy` in the 2D image object specified by `image`. The appropriate data format conversion to convert the channel data from a floating-point value and saturation of the value to the actual data format in which the channels are stored in `image` is done before writing the color value. `coord.xy` are unnormalized coordinates and must be in the range 0 ... image width − 1 and 0 ... image height − 1. `write_imagef` can be used only with image objects created with `image_channel_data_type` set to one of the predefined packed formats or CL_SNORM_INT8, CL_UNORM_INT8, CL_SNORM_INT16, CL_UNORM_INT16, CL_HALF_FLOAT, or CL_FLOAT.
`void` **`write_imagei`**`(image2d_t image, int2 coord, int4 color)`	Write the color value to the location specified by `coord.xy` in the 2D image object specified by `image`. The channel color values are saturated to the appropriate data format in which the channels are stored in `image` before writing the color value. `coord.xy` are unnormalized coordinates and must be in the range 0 ... image width − 1 and 0 ... image height − 1. `write_imagei` can be used only with image objects created with `image_channel_data_type` set to one of CL_SIGNED_INT8, CL_SIGNED_INT16, or CL_SIGNED_INT32.
`void` **`write_imageui`**`(image2d_t image, int2 coord, uint4 color)`	Write the color value to the location specified by `coord.xy` in the 2D image object specified by `image`. The channel color values are saturated to the appropriate data format in which the channels are stored in `image` before writing the color value. `coord.xy` are unnormalized coordinates and must be in the range 0 ... image width − 1 and 0 ... image height − 1. `write_imageui` can be used only with image objects created with `image_channel_data_type` set to one of CL_UNSIGNED_INT8, CL_UNSIGNED_INT16, or CL_UNSIGNED_INT32.

Table 5.22 Built-In Image 3D Write Functions

Function	Description
void **write_imagef** (image3d_t image, int4 coord, float4 color)	Write the color value to the location specified by coord.xyz in the 3D image object specified by image. The appropriate data format conversion to the channel data from a floating-point value and saturation of the value to the actual data format in which the channels are stored in image is done before writing the color value. coord.xyz are unnormalized coordinates and must be in the range 0 ... image width − 1, 0 ... image height − 1, and 0 ... image depth − 1. write_imagef can be used only with image objects created with image_channel_data_type set to one of the predefined packed formats or CL_SNORM_INT8, CL_UNORM_INT8, CL_SNORM_INT16, CL_UNORM_INT16, CL_HALF_FLOAT, or CL_FLOAT.
void **write_imagei** (image3d_t image, int4 coord, int4 color)	Write the color value to the location specified by coord.xyz in the 3D image object specified by image. The channel color values are saturated to the appropriate data format in which the channels are stored in image before writing the color value. coord.xyz are unnormalized coordinates and must be in the range 0 ... image width − 1, 0 ... image height − 1, and 0 ... image depth − 1. write_imagei can be used only with image objects created with image_channel_data_type set to one of CL_SIGNED_INT8, CL_SIGNED_INT16, or CL_SIGNED_INT32.

Function	Description

`void` **`write_imageui`** `(image3d_t image,`
`int4 coord,`
`uint4 color)`
	Write the color value to the location specified by `coord.xyz` in the 2D image object specified by `image`. The channel color values are saturated to the appropriate data format in which the channels are stored in `image` before writing the color value.

	`coord.xyz` are unnormalized coordinates and must be in the range 0 ... `image width - 1, 0 ... image height - 1`, and `0 ... image depth - 1`.
	`write_imageui` can be used only with image objects created with `image_channel_data_type` set to one of CL_UNSIGNED_INT8, CL_UNSIGNED_INT16, or CL_UNSIGNED_INT32.

Querying Image Information

Table 5.23 describes the image query functions.

The values returned by get_image_channel_data type and get_image_channel_order use a CLK_ prefix. There is a one-to-one mapping of the values with the CLK_ prefix to the corresponding CL_ prefixes specified in the image_channel_order and image_channel_data_type fields of the cl_image_format argument to clCreateImage2D and clCreateImage3D.

Table 5.23 Built-In Image Query Functions

Function	Description
int **get_image_width**(image2d_t *image*) int **get_image_width**(image3d_t *image*)	Returns the image width in pixels.
int **get_image_height**(image2d_t *image*) int **get_image_height**(image3d_t *image*)	Returns the image height in pixels.
int **get_image_depth**(image3d_t *image*)	Returns the image depth in pixels.
int2 **get_image_dim**(image2d_t *image*)	Returns the 2D image dimensions in an int2. The width is returned in the x component and the height in the y component.
int4 **get_image_dim**(image3d_t *image*)	Returns the 3D image dimensions in an int4. The width is returned in the x component, the height in the y component, and the depth in the z component.

Table 5.23 Built-In Image Query Functions (*Continued*)

Function	Description

int **get_image_channel_data_type**(
                image2d_t *image*)
int **get_image_channel_data_type**(
                image3d_t *image*)
	Returns the channel data type of the image. Valid values are
	
	CLK_SNORM_INT8
	CLK_SNORM_INT16
	CLK_UNORM_INT8
	CLK_UNORM_INT16
	CLK_UNORM_SHORT_565
	CLK_UNORM_SHORT_555
	CLK_UNORM_SHORT_101010
	CLK_SIGNED_INT8
	CLK_SIGNED_INT16
	CLK_SIGNED_INT32
	CLK_UNSIGNED_INT8
	CLK_UNSIGNED_INT16
	CLK_UNSIGNED_INT32
	CLK_HALF_FLOAT
	CLK_FLOAT

int **get_image_channel_data_order**(
                image2d_t *image*)
int **get_image_channel_data_order**(
                image3d_t *image*)
	Returns the image channel order. Valid values are
	
	CLK_A
	CLK_R
	CLK_Rx
	CLK_RG
	CLK_RGx
	CLK_RGB
	CLK_RGBx
	CLK_RGBA
	CLK_ARGB
	CLK_BGRA
	CLK_INTENSITY
	CLK_LUMINANCE

## Chapter 6

Programs and Kernels

In Chapter 2, we created a simple example that executed a trivial parallel OpenCL kernel on a device. In that example, a kernel object and a program object were created in order to facilitate execution on the device. Program and kernel objects are fundamental in working with OpenCL, and in this chapter we cover these objects in more detail. Specifically, this chapter covers

- Program and kernel object overview

- Creating program objects and building programs

- Program build options

- Creating kernel objects and setting kernel arguments

- Source versus binary program creation

- Querying kernel and program objects

Program and Kernel Object Overview

Two of the most important objects in OpenCL are kernel objects and program objects. OpenCL applications express the functions that will execute in parallel on a device as kernels. Kernels are written in the OpenCL C language (as described in Chapter 4) and are delineated with the __kernel qualifier. In order to be able to pass arguments to a kernel function, an application must create a kernel object. Kernel objects can be operated on using API functions that allow for setting the kernel arguments and querying the kernel for information.

Kernel objects are created from program objects. Program objects contain collections of kernel functions that are defined in the source code of a program. One of the primary purposes of the program object is to facilitate the compilation of the kernels for the devices to which the program is attached. Additionally, the program object provides facilities for determining build errors and querying the program for information.

An analogy that may be helpful in understanding the distinction between kernel objects and program objects is that the program object is like a dynamic library in that it holds a collection of kernel functions. The kernel object is like a handle to a function within the dynamic library. The program object is created from either source code (OpenCL C) or a compiled program binary (more on this later). The program gets built for any of the devices to which the program object is attached. The kernel object is then used to access properties of the compiled kernel function, enqueue calls to it, and set its arguments.

Program Objects

The first step in working with kernels and programs in OpenCL is to create and build a program object. The next sections will introduce the mechanisms available for creating program objects and how to build programs. Further, we detail the options available for building programs and how to query the program objects for information. Finally, we discuss the functions available for managing the resources used by program objects.

Creating and Building Programs

Program objects can be created either by passing in OpenCL C source code text or with a program binary. Creating program objects from OpenCL C source code is typically how a developer would create program objects. The source code to the OpenCL C program would be in an external file (for example, a .cl file as in our example code), and the application would create the program object from the source code using the clCreateProgramWithSource() function. Another alternative is to create the program object from a binary that has been precompiled for the devices. This method is discussed later in the chapter; for now we show how to create a program object from source using clCreateProgramWithSource():

```
cl_program  clCreateProgramWithSource(cl_context context,
                                      cl_uint count,
                                      const char **strings,
                                      const size_t *lengths,
                                      cl_int *errcode_ret)
```

context	The context from which to create a program object.
count	A count of the number of string pointers in the *strings* argument.
strings	Holds *count* number of pointers to *strings*. The combination of all of the strings held in this argument constitutes the full source code from which the program object will be created.
lengths	An array of size *count* holding the number of characters in each of the elements of *strings*. This parameter can be NULL, in which case the strings are assumed to be null-terminated.
errcode_ret	If non-NULL, the error code returned by the function will be returned in this parameter.

Calling clCreateProgramWithSource() will cause a new program object to be created using the source code passed in. The return value is a new program object attached to the context. Typically, the next step after calling clCreateProgramWithSource() would be to build the program object using clBuildProgram():

```
cl_int        clBuildProgram(cl_program program,
                            cl_uint num_devices,
                            const cl_device_id *device_list,
                            const char *options,
                            void (CL_CALLBACK *pfn_notify)
                                   (cl_program program,
                                    void *user_data),
                            void *user_data)
```

program	A valid program object.
num_devices	The number of devices for which to build the program object.
device_list	An array containing device IDs for all *num_devices* for which the program will be built. If *device_list* is NULL, then the program object will be built for all devices that were created on the context from which the program object was created.
options	A string containing the build options for the program. These options are described later in this chapter in the section "Program Build Options."
pfn_notify	It is possible to do asynchronous builds by using the *pfn_notify* argument. If *pfn_notify* is NULL, then clBuildProgram will not return to the caller until completing the build. However,

if the user passes in *pfn_notify*, then clBuildProgram can return before completing the build and will call *pfn_notify* when the program is done building. One possible use of this would be to queue up all of the building to happen asynchronously while the application does other work. Note, though, that even being passed *pfn_notify*, an OpenCL implementation could still choose to return in a synchronous manner (and some do). If you truly require asynchronous builds for your application, executing builds in a separate application thread is the most reliable way to guarantee asynchronous execution.

user_data	Arbitrary data that will be passed as an argument to *pfn_notify* if it was non-NULL.

Invoking clBuildProgram() will cause the program object to be built for the list of devices that it was called with (or all devices attached to the context if no list is specified). This step is essentially equivalent to invoking a compiler/linker on a C program. The *options* parameter contains a string of build options, including preprocessor defines and various optimization and code generation options (e.g., -DUSE_FEATURE=1 -cl-mad-enable). These options are described at the end of this section in the "Program Build Options" subsection. The executable code gets stored internally to the program object for all devices for which it was compiled. The clBuildProgram() function will return CL_SUCCESS if the program was successfully built for all devices; otherwise an error code will be returned. If there was a build error, the detailed build log can be checked for by calling clGetProgramBuildInfo() with a param_name of CL_PROGRAM_BUILD_LOG.

cl_int	**clGetProgramBuildInfo**(cl_program *program*,
	cl_device_id *device*,
	cl_program_build_info *param_name*,
	size_t *param_value_size*,
	void *param_value*,
	size_t *param_value_size_ret*)

program	A valid program object.
device	The device for which the build information should be retrieved. This must be one of the devices for which the program was built. The program will be built for the devices requested, and there can

	be different errors for different devices, so the logs must be queried independently.
param_name	The parameter to query for. The following parameters are accepted:
	CL_PROGRAM_BUILD_STATUS (cl_build_status) returns the status of the build, which can be any of the following:
	CL_BUILD_NONE: No build has been done.
	CL_BUILD_ERROR: The last build had an error.
	CL_BUILD_SUCCESS: The last build succeeded.
	CL_BUILD_IN_PROGRESS: An asynchronous build is still running. This can occur only if a function pointer was provided to clBuildProgram.
	CL_PROGRAM_BUILD_OPTIONS (char[]): Returns a string containing the *options* argument passed to clBuildProgram.
	CL_PROGRAM_BUILD_LOG (char[]): Returns a string containing the build log for the last build for the device.
param_value_size	The size in bytes of *param_value* which must be sufficiently large to store the results for the requested query.
param_value	A pointer to the memory location in which to store the query results.
param_value_size_ret	The number of bytes actually copied to *param_value*.

Putting it all together, the code in Listing 6.1 (from the HelloWorld example in Chapter 2) demonstrates how to create a program object from source, build it for all attached devices, and query the build results for a single device.

Listing 6.1   Creating and Building a Program Object

```
cl_program CreateProgram(cl_context context, cl_device_id device,
                         const char* fileName)
{
    cl_int errNum;
    cl_program program;

    ifstream kernelFile(fileName, ios::in);
    if (!kernelFile.is_open())
```

```
    {
        cerr << "Failed to open file for reading: " << fileName <<
                endl;
        return NULL;
    }

    ostringstream oss;
    oss << kernelFile.rdbuf();

    string srcStdStr = oss.str();
    const char *srcStr = srcStdStr.c_str();
    program = clCreateProgramWithSource(context, 1,
                                        (const char**)&srcStr,
                                        NULL, NULL);
    if (program == NULL)
    {
        cerr << "Failed to create CL program from source." << endl;
        return NULL;
    }

    errNum = clBuildProgram(program, 0, NULL, NULL, NULL, NULL);
    if (errNum != CL_SUCCESS)
    {
        // Determine the reason for the error
        char buildLog[16384];
        clGetProgramBuildInfo(program, device, CL_PROGRAM_BUILD_LOG,
                              sizeof(buildLog), buildLog, NULL);

        cerr << "Error in kernel: " << endl;
        cerr << buildLog;
        clReleaseProgram(program);
        return NULL;
    }

    return program;
}
```

Program Build Options

As described earlier in this section, clBuildProgram() takes as an argument a string (const char *options) that controls several types of build options:

- Preprocessor options

- Floating-point options (math intrinsics)

- Optimization options

- Miscellaneous options

Much like a C or C++ compiler, OpenCL has a wide range of options that control the behavior of program compilation. The OpenCL program compiler has a preprocessor, and it is possible to define options to the preprocessor within the `options` argument to `clBuildProgram()`. Table 6.1 lists the options that can be specified to the preprocessor.

Table 6.1 Preprocessor Build Options

Option	Description	Example
`-D name`	Defines the macro name with a value of 1.	`-D FAST_ALGORITHM`
`-D name=definition`	Defines the macro name to be defined as definition.	`-D MAX_ITERATIONS=20`
`-I dir`	Includes the directory in the search path for header files.	`-I /mydir/`

One note about defining preprocessor variables is that the kernel function signatures for a program object must be the same for all of the devices for which the program is built. Take, for example, the following kernel source:

```
#ifdef SOME_MACRO
__kernel void my_kernel(__global const float* p) {
    // ...
}

#else // !SOME_MACRO

__kernel void my_kernel(__global const int* p) {
    // ...
}

#endif // !SOME_MACRO
```

In this example, the `my_kernel()` function signature differs based on the value of SOME_MACRO (its argument is either a `__global const` float* or a __global const int float*). This, in and of itself, is not a problem. However, if we choose to invoke clBuildProgram() separately for each device on the same program object, once when we pass in -D SOME_MACRO for one device and once when we do not define SOME_MACRO for another device, we will get a kernel that has different function signatures within the program, and this will fail. That is, the kernel function signatures must be the same for all devices for which a program object is built. It is acceptable to send in different preprocessor directives that impact the building of the program in different ways for each device, but not in a way that changes the kernel function signatures. The kernel function signatures must be the same for each device for which a single program object is built.

The OpenCL program compiler also has options that control the behavior of floating-point math. These options are described in Table 6.2 and, like the preprocessor options, can be specified in the options argument to clBuildProgram().

Table 6.2 Floating-Point Options (Math Intrinsics)

Option	Description	Example/Details

-cl-single-precision-constant	If a constant is defined as a double, treat it instead as a float.	With this option enabled, the following line of code will treat the constant (0.0) as a float rather than a double:
		
		`if (local_DBL_MIN <= 0.0)`
		`. . .`

-cl-denorms-are-zero	For single- and double-precision numbers, this option specifies that denormalized numbers can be flushed to zero.	This option can be used as a performance hint regarding the behavior of denormalized numbers. Note that the option does not apply to reading/writing from images.

It is possible to also control the optimizations that the OpenCL C compiler is allowed to make. These options are listed in Table 6.3.

Table 6.3 Optimization Options

Option	Description	Example/Details
`-cl-opt-disable`	Disables all optimizations.	Disabling optimizations may be useful either for debugging or for making sure that the compiler is making valid optimizations.

`-cl-strict-aliasing`	Enables strict aliasing, which refers to the ability to access the same memory from different symbols in the program. If this option is turned on, then pointers of different types will be assumed by the compiler to not access the same memory location.	With this option turned on, the compiler may be able to achieve better optimization. However, strict aliasing can also result in breaking correct code, so be careful with enabling this optimization. As an example, the compiler will assume that the following pointers could not alias because they are different types:
		`short* ptr1;`
		`int* ptr2;`

`-cl-mad-enable`	Enables multiply-add operations to be executed with a `mad` instruction that does the computation at reduced accuracy.	`a * b + c` would normally have to execute with a multiply followed by an add. With this optimization enabled, the implementation can use the `mad` instruction, which may do the operation faster but with reduced accuracy.
`-cl-no-signed-zeros`	Allows the compiler to assume that the sign of zero does not matter (e.g., that `+0.0` and `-0.0` are the same thing).	The compiler may be able to optimize statements that otherwise could not be optimized if this assumption was not made. For example, `0.0*x` can be assumed to be `0.0` because the sign of x does not matter.

continues

Table 6.3 Optimization Options (*Continued*)

Option	Description	Example/Details
`-cl-unsafe-math-optimizations`	Allows for further optimizations that assume arguments are valid and may violate the precision standards of IEEE 754 and OpenCL numerical compliance. Includes `-cl-no-signed-zeros` and `-cl-mad-enable`.	This is an aggressive math optimization that should be used with caution if the precision of your results is important.
`-cl-finite-math-only`	Allows the compiler to assume that floating-point arguments and results are not NaN or positive/negative infinity.	While this option may violate parts of OpenCL numerical compliance and should be used with caution, it may achieve better performance.
`-cl-finite-math-only`	Sets `-cl-finite-math-only` and `-cl-unsafe-math-optimizations`.	Also will define the preprocessor directive `__FAST_RELAXED_MATH__`, which can be used in the OpenCL C code.

Finally, Table 6.4 lists the last set of miscellaneous options accepted by the OpenCL C compiler.

Table 6.4 Miscellaneous Options

Option	Description	Example/Details
`-w`	Disables the display of warning messages.	This turns off all warning messages from being listed in the build log.
`-Werror`	Treats warnings as errors.	With this turned on, any warning encountered in the program will cause `clBuildProgram()` to fail.

Table 6.4 Miscellaneous Options (*Continued*)

Option	Description	Example/Details
`-cl-std=` `version`	Sets the version of OpenCL C that the compiler will compile to. The only valid current setting is `CL1.1` (`-cl-std=CL1.1`).	If this option is not specified, the OpenCL C will be compiled with the highest version of OpenCL C that is supported by the implementation. Using this option will require that the implementation support the specified version; otherwise `clBuildProgram()` will fail.

Creating Programs from Binaries

An alternative to creating program objects from source is to create a program object from binaries. A program binary is a compiled version of the source code for a specific device. The data format of a program binary is opaque. That is, there is no standardized format for the contents of the binary. An OpenCL implementation could choose to store an executable version of the program in the binary, or it might choose to store an intermediate representation that can be converted into the executable at runtime.

Because program binaries have already been compiled (either partially to intermediate representation or fully to an executable), loading them will be faster and require less memory, thus reducing the load time of your application. Another advantage to using program binaries is protection of intellectual property: you can generate the program binaries at installation time and never store the original OpenCL C source code on disk. A typical application scenario would be to generate program binaries at either install time or first run and store the binaries on disk for later loading. The way program binaries are generated is by building the program from source using OpenCL and then querying back for the program binary. To get a program binary back from a built program, you would use `clGetProgramInfo()`:

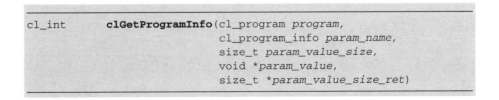

```
cl_int        clGetProgramInfo(cl_program program,
                               cl_program_info param_name,
                               size_t param_value_size,
                               void *param_value,
                               size_t *param_value_size_ret)
```

program	A valid program object.
param_name	The parameter about which to query the program for information. The following parameters are accepted:
	CL_PROGRAM_REFERENCE_COUNT (cl_uint): the number of references to the program. This can be used to identify whether there is a resource leak.
	CL_PROGRAM_CONTEXT (cl_context): the context to which the program is attached.
	CL_PROGRAM_NUM_DEVICES (cl_uint): the number of devices to which the program is attached.
	CL_PROGRAM_DEVICES (cl_device_id[]): returns an array of cl_device_id containing the IDs of the devices to which the program is attached.
	CL_PROGRAM_SOURCE (char[]): returns all of the source strings that were used to create the program in one concatenated string. If the object was created from a binary, no characters will be returned.
	CL_PROGRAM_BINARY_SIZES (size_t[]): returns an array of size_t, the size of the number of devices attached to the program. Each element is the size of the binary for that device.
	CL_PROGRAM_BINARIES (unsigned char*[]): returns an array of unsigned char* where each element contains the program binary for the device. The size of each array can be determined by the result of the CL_PROGRAM_BINARY_SIZES query.
param_value_size	The size in bytes of *param_value*.
param_value	A pointer to the location in which to store results. This location must be allocated with enough bytes to store the requested result.
param_value_size_ret	The actual number of bytes written to *param_value*.

After querying the program object for its binaries, the binaries can then be stored on disk for future runs. The next time the program is run, the program object can be created using clCreateProgramWithBinary():

```
cl_program  clCreateProgramWithBinary(cl_context context,
                                      cl_uint num_devices,
                                      const cl_device_id *
                                            device_list,
```

```
                          const size_t *lengths,
                          const unsigned char
                               **binaries,
                          cl_int *binary_status,
                          cl_int *errcode_ret)
```

context	Context from which to create the program object.
num_devices	The number of devices for which to build the program object.
device_list	An array containing device IDs for all *num_devices* for which the program will be built. If *device_list* is NULL, then the program object will be built for all devices that were created on the context from which the program object was created.
lengths	An array of size *count* holding the number of bytes in each of the elements of *binaries*.
binaries	An array of pointers to the bytes holding each of the program binaries for each device. The size of each binary must be the size passed in for the associated element of *lengths*.
binary_status	An array holding the result for whether each device binary was loaded successfully. On success, each element will be set to CL_SUCCESS. On failure, an error code will be reported.
errcode_ret	If non-NULL, the error code returned by the function will be returned in this parameter.

The example HelloBinaryWorld demonstrates how to create a program from binaries. This is a modification of the HelloWorld example from Chapter 2. The difference is that the HelloBinaryWorld example for this chapter will attempt to retrieve the program binary the first time the application is run and store it to HelloWorld.cl.bin. On future executions, the application will load the program from this generated binary. The main logic that performs this caching is provided in Listing 6.2 from the main() function of HelloBinaryWorld.

Listing 6.2 Caching the Program Binary on First Run

```
program = CreateProgramFromBinary(context, device,
                          "HelloWorld.cl.bin");
if (program == NULL)
{

    program = CreateProgram(context, device,
                          "HelloWorld.cl");
```

```
            if (program == NULL)
            {
                Cleanup(context, commandQueue, program,
                        kernel, memObjects);
                return 1;
            }


            if (SaveProgramBinary(program, device, "HelloWorld.cl.bin")
                                == false)
            {
                std::cerr << "Failed to write program binary"
                        << std::endl;
                Cleanup(context, commandQueue, program,
                        kernel, memObjects);
                return 1;
            }
        }
        else
        {
            std::cout << "Read program from binary." << std::endl;
        }
```

First let's take a look at `SaveProgramBinary()`, which is the function that queries for and stores the program binary. This function assumes that the program object was already created and built from source. The code for `SaveProgramBinary()` is provided in Listing 6.3. The function first calls `clGetProgramInfo()` to query for the number of devices attached to the program. Next it retrieves the device IDs associated with each of the devices. After getting the list of devices, the function then retrieves the size of each of the program binaries for every device along with the program binaries themselves. After retrieving all of the program binaries, the function loops over the devices and finds the one that was passed as an argument to `SaveProgramBinary()`. This program binary is finally written to disk using `fwrite()` to the file `HelloWorld.cl.bin`.

Listing 6.3 Querying for and Storing the Program Binary

```
bool SaveProgramBinary(cl_program program, cl_device_id device,
                        const char* fileName)
{
    cl_uint numDevices = 0;
    cl_int errNum;

    // 1 - Query for number of devices attached to program
```

```
errNum = clGetProgramInfo(program, CL_PROGRAM_NUM_DEVICES,
                          sizeof(cl_uint),
                          &numDevices, NULL);
if (errNum != CL_SUCCESS)
{
    std::cerr << "Error querying for number of devices."
              << std::endl;
    return false;
}

// 2 - Get all of the Device IDs
cl_device_id *devices = new cl_device_id[numDevices];
errNum = clGetProgramInfo(program, CL_PROGRAM_DEVICES,
                          sizeof(cl_device_id) * numDevices,
                          devices, NULL);
if (errNum != CL_SUCCESS)
{
    std::cerr << "Error querying for devices." << std::endl;
    delete [] devices;
    return false;
}

// 3 - Determine the size of each program binary
size_t *programBinarySizes = new size_t [numDevices];
errNum = clGetProgramInfo(program, CL_PROGRAM_BINARY_SIZES,
                          sizeof(size_t) * numDevices,
                          programBinarySizes, NULL);
if (errNum != CL_SUCCESS)
{
    std::cerr << "Error querying for program binary sizes."
              << std::endl;
    delete [] devices;
    delete [] programBinarySizes;
    return false;
}

unsigned char **programBinaries =
    new unsigned char*[numDevices];
for (cl_uint i = 0; i < numDevices; i++)
{
    programBinaries[i] =
        new unsigned char[programBinarySizes[i]];
}

// 4 - Get all of the program binaries
errNum = clGetProgramInfo(program, CL_PROGRAM_BINARIES,
                          sizeof(unsigned char*) * numDevices,
                          programBinaries, NULL);
```

```
if (errNum != CL_SUCCESS)
{
    std::cerr << "Error querying for program binaries"
            << std::endl;

    delete [] devices;
    delete [] programBinarySizes;
    for (cl_uint i = 0; i < numDevices; i++)
    {
        delete [] programBinaries[i];
    }
    delete [] programBinaries;
    return false;
}

// 5 - Finally store the binaries for the device requested
//     out to disk for future reading.
for (cl_uint i = 0; i < numDevices; i++)
{
    // Store the binary just for the device requested.
    // In a scenario where multiple devices were being used
    // you would save all of the binaries out here.
    if (devices[i] == device)
    {
        FILE *fp = fopen(fileName, "wb");
        fwrite(programBinaries[i], 1,
                programBinarySizes[i], fp);
        fclose(fp);
        break;
    }
}

// Cleanup
delete [] devices;
delete [] programBinarySizes;
for (cl_uint i = 0; i < numDevices; i++)
{
    delete [] programBinaries[i];
}
delete [] programBinaries;
return true;
}
```

There are several important factors that a developer needs to understand about program binaries. The first is that a program binary is valid only for the device with which it was created. The OpenCL implementation itself might choose to store in its binary format either an intermediate representation of the program or the executable code. It is a choice made by the implementation that the application has no way of knowing. It is not safe to assume that a binary will work across other devices unless an OpenCL vendor specifically gives this guarantee. Generally, it is important to recompile the binaries for new devices to be sure of compatibility.

An example of the program binary that is produced by the NVIDIA OpenCL implementation is provided in Listing 6.4. This listing may look familiar to those developers familiar with CUDA. The NVIDIA binary format is stored in the proprietary PTX format. Apple and AMD also store binaries in their own formats. None of these binaries should be expected to be compatible across multiple vendors. The PTX format happens to be readable text, but it is perfectly valid for the program binary to be binary bits that are not human-readable.

Listing 6.4 Example Program Binary for `HelloWorld.cl` (NVIDIA)

```
//
// Generated by NVIDIA NVPTX Backend for LLVM
//

.version 2.0
.target sm_13, texmode_independent

// Global Launch Offsets
.const[0] .s32 %_global_num_groups[3];
.const[0] .s32 %_global_size[3];
.const[0] .u32 %_work_dim;
.const[0] .s32 %_global_block_offset[3];
.const[0] .s32 %_global_launch_offset[3];

.const .align 8 .b8 def___internal_i2opi_d[144] = {  0x08, 0x5D,
0x8D, 0x1F, 0xB1, 0x5F, 0xFB, 0x6B, 0xEA, 0x92, 0x52, 0x8A, 0xF7,
0x39, 0x07, 0x3D, 0x7B, 0xF1, 0xE5, 0xEB, 0xC7, 0xBA, 0x27, 0x75,
0x2D, 0xEA, 0x5F, 0x9E, 0x66, 0x3F, 0x46, 0x4F, 0xB7, 0x09, 0xCB,
0x27, 0xCF, 0x7E, 0x36, 0x6D, 0x1F, 0x6D, 0x0A, 0x5A, 0x8B, 0x11,
0x2F, 0xEF, 0x0F, 0x98, 0x05, 0xDE, 0xFF, 0x97, 0xF8, 0x1F, 0x3B,
0x28, 0xF9, 0xBD, 0x8B, 0x5F, 0x84, 0x9C, 0xF4, 0x39, 0x53, 0x83,
0x39, 0xD6, 0x91, 0x39, 0x41, 0x7E, 0x5F, 0xB4, 0x26, 0x70, 0x9C,
0xE9, 0x84, 0x44, 0xBB, 0x2E, 0xF5, 0x35, 0x82, 0xE8, 0x3E, 0xA7,
0x29, 0xB1, 0x1C, 0xEB, 0x1D, 0xFE, 0x1C, 0x92, 0xD1, 0x09, 0xEA,
0x2E, 0x49, 0x06, 0xE0, 0xD2, 0x4D, 0x42, 0x3A, 0x6E, 0x24, 0xB7,
0x61, 0xC5, 0xBB, 0xDE, 0xAB, 0x63, 0x51, 0xFE, 0x41, 0x90, 0x43,
0x3C, 0x99, 0x95, 0x62, 0xDB, 0xC0, 0xDD, 0x34, 0xF5, 0xD1, 0x57,
0x27, 0xFC, 0x29, 0x15, 0x44, 0x4E, 0x6E, 0x83, 0xF9, 0xA2 };
.const .align 4 .b8 def___GPU_i2opi_f[24] = {  0x41, 0x90, 0x43,
0x3C, 0x99, 0x95, 0x62, 0xDB, 0xC0, 0xDD, 0x34, 0xF5, 0xD1, 0x57,
0x27, 0xFC, 0x29, 0x15, 0x44, 0x4E, 0x6E, 0x83, 0xF9, 0xA2 };
```

```
.entry hello_kernel
(
        .param .b32 hello_kernel_param_0,
        .param .b32 hello_kernel_param_1,
        .param .b32 hello_kernel_param_2
)
{
        .reg .f32   %f<4>;
        .reg .s32   %r<9>;

_hello_kernel:
        {
        // get_global_id(0)
        .reg .u32   %vntidx;
        .reg .u32   %vctaidx;
        .reg .u32   %vtidx;
        mov.u32     %vntidx, %ntid.x;
        mov.u32     %vctaidx, %ctaid.x;
        mov.u32     %vtidx, %tid.x;
        mad.lo.s32  %r1, %vntidx, %vctaidx, %vtidx;
        .reg .u32   %temp;
        ld.const.u32 %temp, [%_global_launch_offset+0];
        add.u32     %r1, %r1, %temp;
        }

        shl.b32     %r2, %r1, 2;
        ld.param.u32    %r3, [hello_kernel_param_1];
        ld.param.u32    %r4, [hello_kernel_param_0];
        add.s32     %r5, %r4, %r2;
        add.s32     %r6, %r3, %r2;
        ld.param.u32    %r7, [hello_kernel_param_2];
        ld.global.f32   %f1, [%r5];
        ld.global.f32   %f2, [%r6];
        add.rn.f32  %f3, %f1, %f2;
        add.s32     %r8, %r7, %r2;
        st.global.f32   [%r8], %f3;
        ret;
}
```

On subsequent runs of the application, a binary version of the program will be stored on disk (in `HelloWorld.cl.bin`). The HelloBinaryWorld application loads this program from binary as shown in Listing 6.5. At the beginning of `CreateProgramFromBinary()`, the program binary is loaded from disk. The program object is created from the program binary for the passed-in device. Finally, after checking for errors, the program binary is built by calling `clBuildProgram()` just as would be done for a program that was created from source.

The last step of calling clBuildProgram() may at first seem strange. The program is already in binary format, so why does it need to be rebuilt? The answer stems from the fact that the program binary may or may not contain executable code. If it is an intermediate representation, then OpenCL will still need to compile it into the final executable. Thus, whether a program is created from source or binary, it must always be built before it can be used.

Listing 6.5 Creating a Program from Binary

```
cl_program CreateProgramFromBinary(cl_context context,
                                   cl_device_id device,
                                   const char* fileName)
{
    FILE *fp = fopen(fileName, "rb");
    if (fp == NULL)
    {
        return NULL;
    }

    // Determine the size of the binary
    size_t binarySize;
    fseek(fp, 0, SEEK_END);
    binarySize = ftell(fp);
    rewind(fp);

    // Load binary from disk
    unsigned char *programBinary = new unsigned char[binarySize];
    fread(programBinary, 1, binarySize, fp);
    fclose(fp);

    cl_int errNum = 0;
    cl_program program;
    cl_int binaryStatus;

    program = clCreateProgramWithBinary(context,
                1,
                &device,
                &binarySize,
                (const unsigned char**)&programBinary,
                &binaryStatus,
                &errNum);

    delete [] programBinary;
    if (errNum != CL_SUCCESS)
    {
        std::cerr << "Error loading program binary." << std::endl;
        return NULL;
    }
```

```
    if (binaryStatus != CL_SUCCESS)
    {
        std::cerr << "Invalid binary for device" << std::endl;
        return NULL;
    }

    errNum = clBuildProgram(program, 0, NULL, NULL, NULL, NULL);
    if (errNum != CL_SUCCESS)
    {
        // Determine the reason for the error
        char buildLog[16384];
        clGetProgramBuildInfo(program, device, CL_PROGRAM_BUILD_LOG,
                              sizeof(buildLog), buildLog, NULL);

        std::cerr << "Error in program: " << std::endl;
        std::cerr << buildLog << std::endl;
        clReleaseProgram(program);
        return NULL;
    }

    return program;
}
```

Managing and Querying Programs

To clean up a program after it has been used, the program can be deleted by calling clReleaseProgram(). Internally, OpenCL stores a reference count with each program object. The functions that create objects in OpenCL return the object with an initial reference count of 1. The act of calling clReleaseProgram() will reduce the reference count. If the reference count reaches 0, the program will be deleted.

| cl_int | **clReleaseProgram**(cl_program *program*) |
| *program* | A valid program object |

If the user wishes to manually increase the reference count of the OpenCL program, this can be done using clRetainProgram():

| cl_int | **clRetainProgram**(cl_program *program*) |
| *program* | A valid program object |

Further, when an application is finished building programs, it can choose to instruct the OpenCL implementation that it is finished with the compiler by calling `clUnloadCompiler()`. An OpenCL implementation can choose to use this notification to unload any resources consumed by the compiler. Doing so may free up some memory use by the OpenCL implementation. If an application calls `clBuildProgram()` again after calling `clUnload-Compiler()`, this will cause the compiler to be reloaded automatically.

`cl_int`   **clUnloadCompiler**(void)

Informs the OpenCL implementation that the application is done building programs.

Kernel Objects

So far we have been concerned with the creation and management of program objects. As discussed in the previous section, the program object is a container that stores the compiled executable code for each kernel on each device attached to it. In order to actually be able to execute a kernel, we must be able to pass arguments to the kernel function. This is the primary purpose of kernel objects. Kernel objects are containers that can be used to pass arguments to a kernel function that is contained within a program object. The kernel object can also be used to query for information about an individual kernel function.

Creating Kernel Objects and Setting Kernel Arguments

The way in which a kernel object can be created is by passing the name of the kernel function to `clCreateKernel()`:

`cl_kernel`   **clCreateKernel**(cl_program *program*,
                           const char *kernel_name*,
                           cl_int *errcode_ret*)

---

program   A valid program object that has been built.

kernel_name The name of the kernel function for which to create the kernel object. This is the function name of the kernel following the __kernel keyword in the program source.

errcode_ret	If non-NULL, the error code returned by the function will be returned in this parameter.

Once created, arguments can be passed in to the kernel function contained in the kernel object by calling `clSetKernelArg()`:

cl_int	**clSetKernelArg**(cl_kernel *kernel*,
	                 cl_uint *arg_index*,
	                 size_t **arg_size*,
	                 const void **arg_value*)

kernel	A valid kernel object.
arg_index	The index of the argument to the kernel function. The first argument has index 0, the second argument has index 1, and so on from there.
arg_size	The size of the argument. This size is determined by how the argument is declared in the kernel function: __local qualified: The size will be the number of bytes required for the buffer used to store the argument. object: For memory objects, the size is the size of the object type (e.g., sizeof(cl_mem)). sampler: For sampler objects, size will be sizeof(cl_sampler). regular type: the size of the argument type. For example, for a cl_int argument it will be sizeof(cl_int).
arg_value	A pointer to the argument to be passed to the kernel function. This argument will also depend on the way the argument is declared in the kernel: __local qualified: arg_value must be NULL. object: a pointer to the memory object. sampler: a pointer to the sampler object. regular type: a pointer to the argument value.

Each parameter in the kernel function has an index associated with it. The first argument has index 0, the second argument has index 1, and so on. For example, given the `hello_kernel()` in the HelloBinaryWorld example, argument a has index 0, argument b has index 1, and argument `result` has index 2.

```
__kernel void hello_kernel(__global const float *a,
                           __global const float *b,
                           __global float *result)
```

```
    {
        int gid = get_global_id(0);

        result[gid] = a[gid] + b[gid];
    }
```

Each of the parameters to `hello_kernel()` is a global pointer, and thus the arguments are provided using memory objects (allocated with `clCreateBuffer()`). The following block of code demonstrates how the kernel arguments are passed for `hello_kernel`:

```
kernel = clCreateKernel(program, "hello_kernel", NULL);
  if (kernel == NULL)
{
    std::cerr << "Failed to create kernel" << std::endl;
    Cleanup(context, commandQueue, program, kernel, memObjects);
    return 1;
}

// Set the kernel arguments (result, a, b)
errNum = clSetKernelArg(kernel, 0, sizeof(cl_mem),
                        &memObjects[0]);
errNum |= clSetKernelArg(kernel, 1, sizeof(cl_mem),
                         &memObjects[1]);
errNum |= clSetKernelArg(kernel, 2, sizeof(cl_mem),
                         &memObjects[2]);
if (errNum != CL_SUCCESS)
{
    std::cerr << "Error setting kernel arguments." << std::endl;
    Cleanup(context, commandQueue, program, kernel, memObjects);
    return 1;
}
```

When `clSetKernelArg()` is called, the pointer passed in holding the argument value will be internally copied by the OpenCL implementation. This means that after calling `clSetKernelArg()`, it is safe to reuse the pointer for other purposes. The type of the argument sent in to the kernel is dependent on how the kernel is declared. For example, the following kernel takes a pointer, an integer, a floating-point value, and a local floating-point buffer:

```
__kernel void arg_example(global int *vertexArray,
                          int vertexCount,
                          float weight,
                          local float* localArray)
{
    ...
}
```

In this case, the first argument has index 0 and is passed a pointer to a cl_mem object because it is a global pointer. The second argument has index 1 and is passed a cl_int variable because it is an int argument, and likewise the third argument has index 2 and is passed a cl_float. The last argument has index 3 and is a bit trickier as it is qualified with local. Because it is a local argument, its contents are available only within a work-group and are not available outside of a work-group. As such, the call to clSetKernelArg() only specifies the size of the argument (in this case tied to the local work size so that there is one element per thread) and the arg_value is NULL. The arguments would be set using the following calls to clSetKernelArg():

```
kernel = clCreateKernel(program, "arg_example", NULL);
cl_int vertexCount;
cl_float weight;
cl_mem vertexArray;
cl_int localWorkSize[1] = { 32 };

// Create vertexArray with clCreateBuffer, assign values
// to vertexCount and weight
...

errNum = clSetKernelArg(kernel, 0, sizeof(cl_mem), &vertexArray);
errNum |= clSetKernelArg(kernel, 1, sizeof(cl_int), &vertexCount);
errNum |= clSetKernelArg(kernel, 2, sizeof(cl_float), &weight);
errNum |= clSetKernelArg(kernel, 3,
                         sizeof(cl_float) * localWorkSize[0],
                         NULL);
```

The arguments that are set on a kernel object are persistent until changed. That is, even after invoking calls that queue the kernel for execution, the arguments will remain persistent.

An alternative to using clCreateKernel() to create kernel objects one kernel function at a time is to use clCreateKernelsInProgram() to create objects for all kernel functions in a program:

cl_int	**clCreateKernelsInProgram**(cl_program *program*,
	cl_uint *num_kernels*,
	cl_kernel **kernels*,
	cl_uint **num_kernels_ret*)

program	A valid program object that has been built.
num_kernels	The number of kernels in the program object. This can be determined by first calling this function with the

The use of `clCreateKernelsInProgram()` requires calling the function twice: first to determine the number of kernels in the program and next to create the kernel objects. The following block of code demonstrates its use:

```
cl_uint numKernels;
errNum = clCreateKernelsInProgram(program, NULL,
                                  NULL, &numKernels);

cl_kernel *kernels = new cl_kernel[numKernels];
errNum = clCreateKernelsInProgram(program, numKernels, kernels,
                                  &numKernels);
```

Thread Safety

The entire OpenCL API is specified to be thread-safe with *one* exception: `clSetKernelArg()`. The fact that the entire API except for a single function is defined to be thread-safe is likely to be an area of confusion for developers. First, let's define what we mean by "thread-safe" and then examine why it is that `clSetKernelArg()` is the one exception.

In the realm of OpenCL, what it means for a function to be thread-safe is that an application can have multiple host threads simultaneously call the same function without having to provide mutual exclusion. That is, with the exception of `clSetKernelArg()`, an application may call the same OpenCL function from multiple threads on the host and the OpenCL implementation guarantees that its internal state will remain consistent.

You may be asking yourself what makes `clSetKernelArg()` special. It does not on the surface appear to be any different from other OpenCL function calls. The reason that the specification chose to make `clSet-KernelArg()` *not* thread-safe is twofold:

- `clSetKernelArg()` is the most frequently called function in the OpenCL API. The specification authors took care to make sure that this function would be as lightweight as possible. Because providing thread safety implies some inherent overhead, it was defined not to be thread-safe to make it as fast as possible.

- In addition to the performance justification, it is hard to construct a reason that an application would need to set kernel arguments *for the same kernel object* in different threads on the host.

Pay special attention to the emphasis on "for the same kernel object" in the second item. One misinterpretation of saying that clSetKernelArg() is not thread-safe would be that it cannot be called from multiple host threads simultaneously. This is not the case. You can call clSetKernel-Arg() on multiple host threads simultaneously, *just not on the same kernel object*. As long as your application does not attempt to call clSetKernelArg() from different threads on the same kernel object, everything should work as expected.

Managing and Querying Kernels

In addition to setting kernel arguments, it is also possible to query the kernel object to find out additional information. The function clGetKernelInfo() allows querying the kernel for basic information including the kernel function name, the number of arguments to the kernel function, the context, and the associated program object:

cl_int	**clGetKernelInfo**(cl_kernel *kernel*, cl_kernel_info *param_name*, size_t *param_value_size*, void **param_value*, size_t **param_value_size_ret*)
kernel	A valid kernel object.
param_name	The parameter on which to query the program for information. The following parameters are accepted: CL_KERNEL_REFERENCE_COUNT (cl_uint): the number of references to the program. This can be used to identify whether there is a resource leak. CL_KERNEL_FUNCTION_NAME (char[]): the name of the kernel function as declared in the kernel source. CL_KERNEL_NUM_ARGS (cl_uint): the number of arguments to the kernel function.

	CL_KERNEL_CONTEXT (cl_context): the kernel from which the kernel object is created.
	CL_KERNEL_PROGRAM (cl_program): the program from which the kernel object is created.
param_value_size	The size in bytes of *param_value*.
param_value	A pointer to the location in which to store results. This location must be allocated with enough bytes to store the requested result.
param_value_size_ret	The actual number of bytes written to.

Another important query function available for kernel objects is clGet-KernelWorkGroupInfo(). This function allows the application to query the kernel object for information particular to a device. This can be very useful in trying to determine how to break up a parallel workload across different devices on which a kernel will be executed. The CL_KERNEL_WORK_GROUP_SIZE query can be used to determine the maximum work-group size that can be used on the device. Further, the application can achieve optimal performance by adhering to using a work-group size that is a multiple of CL_KERNEL_PREFERRED_WORK_GROUP_SIZE_MULTIPLE. Additional queries are also available for determining the resource utilization of the kernel on the device.

cl_int	**clGetKernelWorkGroupInfo** (cl_kernel *kernel*,
	                  cl_device_id *device*,
	                  cl_kernel_work_group_info *param_name*,
	                  size_t *param_value_size*,
	                  void **param_value*,
	                  size_t **param_value_size_ret*)

kernel	A valid kernel object.
device	The ID of the device on which the kernel object was created.
param_name	The parameter on which to query the kernel for work-group information. The following parameters are accepted:
	CL_KERNEL_WORK_GROUP_SIZE (size_t): gives the maximum work-group size that can be used to execute the kernel on the specific device. This query can be very useful in determining the appropriate way to partition kernel execution across the global/local work sizes.

	CL_KERNEL_COMPILE_WORK_GROUP_SIZE (size_t[3]): As described in Chapter 5, this query returns the value specified for the kernel using the optional __attribute__((reqd_work_group_size(X, Y, Z)). The purpose of this attribute is to allow the compiler to make optimizations assuming the local work-group size, which is otherwise not known until execution time.
	CL_KERNEL_LOCAL_MEM_SIZE (cl_ulong): gives the amount of local memory that is used by the kernel.
	CL_KERNEL_PREFERRED_WORK_GROUP_SIZE_MULTIPLE (size_t): gives an optimal work-group size multiple. The application may get better performance by adhering to a work-group size that is a multiple of this value.
	CL_KERNEL_PRIVATE_MEM_SIZE (cl_ulong): the amount of private memory (minimum) used by each work-group.
param_value_size	The size in bytes of *param_value*.
param_value	A pointer to the location in which to store results. This location must be allocated with enough bytes to store the requested result.
param_value_size_ret	The actual number of bytes written to.

Kernel objects can be released and retained in the same manner as program objects. The object reference count will be decremented by the function clReleaseKernel() and will be released when this reference count reaches 0:

cl_int	**clReleaseKernel**(cl_kernel *kernel)*

kernel   A valid kernel object.

One important consideration regarding the release of kernel objects is that a program object cannot be rebuilt until all of the kernel objects associated with it have been released. Consider this example block of pseudo code:

```
cl_program program = clCreateProgramWithSource(...);
clBuildProgram(program, ...);
cl_kernel k = clCreateKernel(program, "foo");

// .. CL API calls to enqueue kernels and other commands ..

clBuildProgram(program, ...); // This call will fail
                              // because the kernel
                              // object "k" above has
                              // not been released.
```

The second call to clBuildProgram() in this example would fail with a CL_INVALID_OPERATION error because there is still a kernel object associated with the program. In order to be able to build the program again, that kernel object (and any other ones associated with the program object) must be released using clReleaseKernel().

Finally, the reference count can be incremented by one by calling the function clRetainKernel():

cl_int	**clRetainKernel**(cl_kernel *kernel)*
kernel	A valid kernel object.

## Chapter 7

Buffers and Sub-Buffers

In Chapter 2, we created a simple example that executed a trivial parallel OpenCL kernel on a device, and in Chapter 3, we developed a simple convolution example. In both of these examples, memory objects, in these cases buffer objects, were created in order to facilitate the movement of data in and out of the compute device's memory, from the host's memory. Memory objects are fundamental in working with OpenCL and include the following types:

- **Buffers:** one-dimensional arrays of bytes

- **Sub-buffers:** one-dimensional views into buffers

- **Images:** two-dimensional or three-dimensional data structured arrays, which have limited access operators and a selection of different formats, sampling, and clamping features

In this chapter we cover buffer and sub-buffer objects in more detail. Specifically, this chapter covers

- Buffer and sub-buffer objects overview

- Creating buffer and sub-buffer objects

- Reading and writing buffers and sub-buffer objects

- Mapping buffer and sub-buffer objects

- Querying buffer and sub-buffer objects

Memory Objects, Buffers, and Sub-Buffers Overview

Memory objects are a fundamental concept in OpenCL. As mentioned previously, buffers and sub-buffers are instances of OpenCL memory objects, and this is also true for image objects, described in Chapter 8.

In general, the operations on buffers and sub-buffers are disjoint from those of images, but there are some cases where generalized operations on memory objects are enough. For completeness we describe these operations here, too.

As introduced in Chapter 1, OpenCL memory objects are allocated against a context, which may have one or more associated devices. Memory objects are globally visible to all devices within the context. However, as OpenCL defines a relaxed memory model, it is not the case that all writes to a memory object are visible to all following reads of the same buffer. This is highlighted by the observation that, like other device commands, memory objects are read and written by enqueuing commands to a particular device. Memory object read/writes can be marked as blocking, causing the command-to-host thread to block until the enqueued command has completed and memory written to a particular device is visible by all devices associated with the particular context, or the memory read has been completely read back into host memory. If the read/write command is not blocking, then the host thread may return before the enqueued command has completed, and the application cannot assume that the memory being written or read is ready to consume from. In this case the host application must use one of the following OpenCL synchronization primitives to ensure that the command has completed:

- `cl_int clFinish(cl_command_queue queue)`, where `queue` is the particular command-queue for which the read/write command was enqueued. `clFinish` will block until all pending commands, for `queue`, have completed.

- `cl_int clWaitForEvents(cl_uint num_events, const cl_event * event_list)`, where `event_list` will contain at least the event returned from the enqueue command associated with the particular read/write. `clWaitForEvents` will block until all commands associated with corresponding events in `event_list` have completed.

OpenCL memory objects associated with different contexts must be used only with other objects created within the same context. For example, it is not possible to perform read/write operations with command-queues created with a different context. Because a context is created with respect to a particular platform, it is not possible to create memory objects that are shared across different platform devices. In the case that an application will use all OpenCL devices within the system, in general, data will need to be managed via the host memory space to copy data in and out of a given context and across contexts.

Creating Buffers and Sub-Buffers

Buffer objects are a one-dimensional memory resource that can hold scalar, vector, or user-defined data types. They are created using the following function:

cl_mem	**clCreateBuffer**(cl_context *context*,
	cl_mem_flags *flags*,
	size_t *size*,
	void * *host_ptr*,
	cl_int *errcode_ref*)

context	A valid context object against which the buffer is allocated.
flags	A bit field used to specify allocations and usage information for the buffer creation. The set of valid values for *flags*, defined by the enumeration cl_mem_flags, is described in Table 7.1.
size	The size of the buffer being allocated, in bytes.
host ptr	A pointer to data, allocated by the application; its use in a call to **clCreateBuffer** is determined by the *flags* parameter. The size of the data pointed to by *host_ptr* must be at least that of the requested allocation, that is, >= *size* bytes.
errcode_ret	If non-NULL, the error code returned by the function will be returned in this parameter.

Table 7.1 Supported Values for cl_mem_flags

cl_mem_flags	Description
CL_MEM_READ_WRITE	Specifies that the memory object will be read and written by a kernel. If no other modifier is given, then this mode is assumed to be the default.
CL_MEM_WRITE_ONLY	Specifies that the memory object will be written but not read by a kernel.
	Reading from a buffer or other memory object, such as an image, created with CL_MEM_WRITE_ONLY inside a kernel is undefined.
CL_MEM_READ_ONLY	Specifies that the memory object is read-only when used inside a kernel.
	Writing to a buffer or other memory object created with CL_MEM_READ_ONLY inside a kernel is undefined.

continues

Table 7.1 Supported Values for `cl_mem_flags` (*Continued*)

`cl_mem_flags`	Description
CL_MEM_USE_HOST_PTR	This flag is valid only if *host_ptr* is not NULL. If specified, it indicates that the application wants the OpenCL implementation to use memory referenced by *host_ptr* as the storage bits for the memory object.
CL_MEM_ALLOC_HOST_PTR	Specifies that the buffer should be allocated in from host-accessible memory. The use of CL_MEM_ALLOC_HOST_PTR and CL_MEM_USE_HOST_PTR is not valid.
CL_MEM_COPY_HOST_PTR	If specified, then it indicates that the application wants the OpenCL implementation to allocate memory for the memory object and copy the data from memory referenced by *host_ptr*. CL_MEM_COPY_HOST_PTR and CL_MEM_USE_HOST_PTR cannot be used together. CL_MEM_COPY_HOST_PTR can be used with CL_MEM_ALLOC_HOST_PTR to initialize the contents of a memory object allocated using host-accessible (e.g., PCIe) memory. Its use is valid only if host_ptr is not NULL.

Like other kernel parameters, buffers are passed as arguments to kernels using the function `clSetKernelArg` and are defined in the kernel itself by defining a pointer to the expected data type, in the global address space. The following code shows simple examples of how you might create a buffer and use it to set an argument to a kernel:

```
#define NUM_BUFFER_ELEMENTS 100
cl_int errNum;
cl_context;
cl_kernel kernel;
cl_command_queue queue;
float inputOutput[NUM_BUFFER_ELEMENTS];
cl_mem buffer;

// place code to create context, kernel, and command-queue here

// initialize inputOutput;
```

```
buffer = clCreateBuffer(
    context,
    CL_MEM_READ_WRITE | CL_MEM_COPY_HOST_PTR,
    sizeof(float) * NUM_BUFFER_ELEMENTS,
    &errNum);

// check for errors

errNum = setKernelArg(kernel, 0, sizeof(buffer), &buffer);
```

The following kernel definition shows a simple example of how you might specify it to take, as an argument, the buffer defined in the preceding example:

```
__kernel void square(__global float * buffer)
{
    size_t id = get_global_id(0);
    buffer[id] = buffer[id] * buffer[id];
}
```

Generalizing this to divide the work performed by the kernel `square` to all the devices associated with a particular context, the offset argument to `clEnqueueNDRangeKernel` can be used to calculate the offset into the buffers. The following code shows how this might be performed:

```
#define NUM_BUFFER_ELEMENTS 100
cl_int errNum;
cl_uint numDevices;
cl_device_id * deviceIDs;
cl_context;
cl_kernel kernel;
std::vector<cl_command_queue> queues;
float * inputOutput;
cl_mem buffer;

// place code to create context, kernel, and command-queue here

// initialize inputOutput;

buffer = clCreateBuffer(
    context,
    CL_MEM_READ_WRITE | CL_MEM_COPY_HOST_PTR,
    sizeof(float) * NUM_BUFFER_ELEMENTS,
    inputOutput,
    &errNum);

// check for errors

errNum = setKernelArg(kernel, 0, sizeof(buffer), &buffer);
```

```
// Create a command-queue for each device
for (int i = 0; i < numDevices; i++)
{
    cl_command_queue queue =
    clCreateCommandQueue(
        context,
        deviceIDs[i],
        0,
        &errNum);

    queues.push_back(queue);
}

// Submit kernel enqueue to each queue
for (int i = 0; i < queues.size(); i++)
{
    cl_event event;

    size_t gWI    = NUM_BUFFER_ELEMENTS;
    size_t offset = i * NUM_BUFFER_ELEMENTS * sizeof(int);

    errNum = clEnqueueNDRangeKernel(
    queues[i],
    kernel,
    1,
    (const size_t*)&offset,
    (const size_t*)&gWI,
    (const size_t*)NULL,
    0,
    0,
    &event);

    events.push_back(event);
}
// wait for commands to complete

clWaitForEvents(events.size(), events.data());
```

An alternative, more general approach to subdividing the work performed on buffers is to use sub-buffers. Sub-buffers provide a view into a particular buffer, for example, enabling the developer to divide a single buffer into chunks that can be worked on independently. Sub-buffers are purely a software abstraction; anything that can be done with a sub-buffer can be done using buffers, explicit offsets, and so on. Sub-buffers provide a layer of additional modality not easily expressed using just buffers. The advantage of sub-buffers over the approach demonstrated previously is that they work with interfaces that expect buffers and require no additional knowledge such as offset values. Consider a library interface, for example, that is designed to expect an OpenCL buffer object but always assumes the first element is an offset zero. In this case it is not possible to use the previous approach without modifying the library source. Sub-buffers provide a solution to this problem.

Sub-buffers cannot be built from other sub-buffers.[1] They are created using the following function:

```
cl_mem        clCreateSubBuffer(
    cl_mem buffer,
    cl_mem_flags flags,
    cl_buffer_create_type buffer_create_type,
    const void * buffer_create_info,
    cl_int *errcode_ref)
```

buffer	A valid buffer object, which cannot be a previously allocated sub-buffer.
flags	A bit field used to specify allocations and usage information for the buffer creation. The set of valid values for *flags*, defined by the enumeration *cl_mem_flags*, is described in Table 7.1.
buffer_create_type	Combined with *buffer_create_info*, describes the type of buffer object to be created. The set of valid values for *buffer_create_type*, defined by the enumeration *cl_buffer_create_type*, is described in Table 7.2.
buffer_create_info	Combined with *buffer_create_info*, describes the type of buffer object to be created.
errcode_ret	If non-NULL, the error code returned by the function will be returned in this parameter.

---

[1] While it is technically feasible to define sub-buffers of sub-buffers, the OpenCL specification does not allow this because of concerns that implementations would have to be constructive with respect to optimizations due to potential aliasing of a buffer.

Table 7.2 Supported Names and Values for `clCreateSubBuffer`

`cl_buffer_create_type`	Description
CL_BUFFER_CREATE_ TYPE_REGION	Create a buffer object that represents a specific region in *buffer*.
	buffer_create_info is a pointer to the following structure:
	typedef struct _cl_buffer_region { *size_t origin;* *size_t size;* *} cl_buffer_region;*
	(*origin*, *size*) defines the offset and size in bytes in *buffer*.
	If *buffer* is created with CL_MEM_USE_HOST_PTR, the *host_ptr* associated with the buffer object returned is *host_ptr* + *origin*.
	The buffer object returned references the data store allocated for *buffer* and points to a specific region given by (*origin*, *size*) in this data store.
	CL_INVALID_VALUE is returned in *errcode_ret* if the region specified by (*origin*, *size*) is out of bounds in *buffer*.
	CL_INVALID_BUFFER_SIZE is returned if *size* is 0.
	CL_MISALIGNED_SUB_BUFFER_OFFSET is returned in *errcode_ret* if there are no devices in the context associated with *buffer* for which the *origin* value is aligned to the CL_DEVICE_MEM_ BASE_ADDR_ALIGN value.

Returning to our previous example of dividing a buffer across multiple devices, the following code shows how this might be performed:

```
#define NUM_BUFFER_ELEMENTS 100
cl_int errNum;
cl_uint numDevices;
cl_device_id * deviceIDs;
cl_context;
cl_kernel kernel;
std::vector<cl_command_queue> queues;
std::vector<cl_mem> buffers;
float * inputOutput;
cl_mem buffer;

// place code to create context, kernel, and command-queue here
```

```
// initialize inputOutput;

buffer = clCreate(
     context,
     CL_MEM_READ_WRITE | CL_MEM_COPY_HOST_PTR,
     sizeof(float) * NUM_BUFFER_ELEMENTS,
     inputOutput,
     &errNum);

buffers.push_back(buffer);

// Create command-queues
for (int i = 0; i < numDevices; i++)
{
     cl_command_queue queue =
     clCreateCommandQueue(
          context,
          deviceIDs[i],
          0,
          &errNum);

     queues.push_back(queue);

     cl_kernel kernel = clCreateKernel(
          program,
          "square",
          &errNum);

     errNum = clSetKernelArg(
          kernel,
          0,
          sizeof(cl_mem),
          (void *)&buffers[i]);

     kernels.push_back(kernel);
  }

  std::vector<cl_event> events;
  // call kernel for each device
  for (int i = 0; i < queues.size(); i++)
  {
     cl_event event;

     size_t gWI = NUM_BUFFER_ELEMENTS;

     errNum = clEnqueueNDRangeKernel(
          queues[i],
          kernels[i],
          1,
```

```
                    NULL,
                    (const size_t*)&gWI,
                    (const size_t*)NULL,
                    0,
                    0,
                    &event);

        events.push_back(event);
    }

    // Wait for commands submitted to complete
    clWaitForEvents(events.size(), events.data());
```

As is the case with other OpenCL objects, buffers and sub-buffer objects are reference-counted and the following two operations increment and decrement the reference count.

The following example increments the reference count for a buffer:

cl_int	**clRetainMemObject**(cl_mem *buffer*)
buffer	A valid buffer object.

The next example decrements the reference count for a buffer:

cl_int	**clReleaseMemObject**(cl_mem *buffer*)
buffer	A valid buffer object.

When the reference count reaches 0, the OpenCL implementation is expected to release any associated memory with the buffer or sub-buffer. Once an implementation has freed resources for a buffer or sub-buffer, the object should not be referenced again in the program.

For example, to correctly release the OpenCL buffer resources in the previous sub-buffer example the following code could be used:

```
for (int i = 0; i < buffers.size(); i++)
{
     buffers.clReleaseMemObject(buffers[i]);
}
```

Querying Buffers and Sub-Buffers

Like other OpenCL objects, buffers and sub-buffers can be queried to return information regarding how they were constructed, current status (e.g., reference count), and so on. The following command is used for buffer and sub-buffer queries:

```
cl_int        clGetMemObjectInfo(cl_mem buffer,
                                  cl_mem_info param_name,
                                  size_t param_value_size,
                                  void * param_value,
                                  size_t *param_value_size_ret)
```

buffer	A valid buffer object, which will be read from.
param_name	An enumeration used to specify what information to query. The set of valid values for *param_name*, defined by the enumeration *cl_mem_info*, is described in Table 7.3.
param_value_size	The size in bytes of the memory pointed to by *param_value*. This size must be >= size of the return type in Table 7.3.
param_value	A pointer to memory where the appropriate value being queried will be returned. If the value is NULL, it is ignored.
param_value_size_ret	Total number of bytes written to *param_value* for the query.

Table 7.3 OpenCL Buffer and Sub-Buffer Queries

cl_mem_info	Return Type	Description
CL_MEM_TYPE	cl_mem_object_type	For buffer and sub-buffer objects returns[*] CL_MEM_OBJECT_BUFFER.
CL_MEM_FLAGS	cl_mem_flags	Returns the value of the flags field specified during buffer creation.
CL_MEM_SIZE	size_t	Returns the size of the data store associated with the buffer, in bytes.

continues

Table 7.3 OpenCL Buffer and Sub-Buffer Queries (*Continued*)

cl_mem_info	Return Type	Description
CL_MEM_HOST_PTR	void *	Returns the *host_ptr* argument specified when the buffer was created and if a sub-buffer, then *host_ptr* + *origin*.
CL_MEM_MAP_COUNT	cl_uint	Returns an integer representing the number of times the buffer is currently mapped.
CL_MEM_REFERENCE_COUNT	cl_uint	Returns an integer representing the current reference count for the buffer.
CL_MEM_CONTEXT	cl_context	Returns the OpenCL context object with which the buffer was created.
CL_MEM_ASSOCIATED_ MEMOBJECT	cl_mem	If a sub-buffer, then the buffer from which it was created is returned; otherwise the result is NULL.
CL_MEM_OFFSET	size_t	If a sub-buffer, then returns the offset; otherwise the result is 0.

* The complete set of values returned for CL_MEM_TYPE covers images, too; further discussion of these is deferred until Chapter 8.

The following code is a simple example of how you might query a memory object to determine if it is a buffer or some other kind of OpenCL memory object type:

```
cl_int errNum;
cl_mem memory;
cl_mem_object_type type;

// initialize memory object and so on
errNum = clGetMemObjectInfo(
      memory,
      CL_MEM_TYPE,
      sizeof(cl_mem_object_type),
      &type,
      NULL);
switch(type)
{
      case CL_MEM_OBJECT_BUFFER:
      {
            // handle case when object is buffer or sub-buffer
            break;
      }
```

```
case CL_MEM_OBJECT_IMAGE2D:
case CL_MEM_OBJECT_IMAGE3D:
{
    // handle case when object is a 2D or 3D image
    break;
}
default
// something very bad has happened
break;
}
```

Reading, Writing, and Copying Buffers and Sub-Buffers

Buffers and sub-buffers can be read and written by the host application, moving data to and from host memory. The following command enqueues a write command, to copy the contents of host memory into a buffer region:

cl_int	**clEnqueueWriteBuffer**(cl_command_queue *command_queue*, cl_mem *buffer*, cl_bool *blocking_write*, size_t *offset*, size_t *cb*, void * *ptr*, cl_uint *num_events_in_wait_list*, const cl_event * *event_wait_list*, cl_event **event*)
command_queue	The command-queue in which the write command will be queued.
buffer	A valid buffer object, which will be read from.
blocking_write	If set to CL_TRUE, then **clEnqueueWriteBuffer** blocks until the data is written from *ptr*; otherwise it returns directly and the user must query *event* to check the command's status.
offset	The offset, in bytes, into the buffer object to begin writing to.
cb	The number of bytes to be read from the buffer.
ptr	A pointer into host memory where the data to be written is read from.

num_events_in_wait_list	The number of entries in the array event_wait_list. Must be zero in the case event_wait_list is NULL; otherwise must be greater than zero.
event_wait_list	If not NULL, then event_wait_list is an array of events, associated with OpenCL commands, that must have completed, that is, be in the state CL_COMPLETE, before the write will begin execution.
event	If non-NULL, the event corresponding to the write command returned by the function will be returned in this parameter.

Continuing with our previous buffer example, instead of copying the data in from the host pointer at buffer creation, the following code achieves the same behavior:

```
cl_mem buffer = clCreateBuffer(
      context,
      CL_MEM_READ_WRITE,
      sizeof(int) * NUM_BUFFER_ELEMENTS * numDevices,
      NULL,
      &errNum);

  // code to create sub-buffers, command-queues, and so on

  // write data to buffer zero using command-queue zero
  clEnqueueWriteBuffer(
      queues[0],
      buffers[0],
      CL_TRUE,
      0,
      sizeof(int) * NUM_BUFFER_ELEMENTS * numDevices,
      (void*)inputOutput,
      0,
      NULL,
      NULL);
```

The following command enqueues a read command, to copy the contents of a buffer object into host memory:

```
cl_int    clEnqueueReadBuffer(cl_command_queue command_queue,
                              cl_mem buffer,
                              cl_bool blocking_read,
                              size_t offset,
```

```
                            size_t cb,
                            void * ptr,
                            cl_uint num_events_in_wait_list,
                            const cl_event * event_wait_list,
                            cl_event *event)
```

command_queue	The command-queue in which the read command will be queued.
buffer	A valid buffer object, which will be read from.
blocking_read	If set to CL_TRUE, then **clEnqueueReadBuffer** blocks until the data is read into ptr; otherwise it returns directly and the user must query event to check the command's status.
offset	The offset, in bytes, into the buffer object to begin reading from.
cb	The number of bytes to be read from the buffer.
ptr	A pointer into host memory where the read data is to written to.
num_events_in_wait_list	The number of entries in the array event_wait_list. Must be zero in the case event_wait_list is NULL; otherwise must be greater than zero.
event_wait_list	If not NULL, then event_wait_list is an array of events, associated with OpenCL commands, that must have completed, that is, be in the state CL_COMPLETE, before the read will begin execution.
event	If non-NULL, the event corresponding to the read command returned by the function will be returned in this parameter.

Again continuing with our buffer example, the following example code reads back and displays the results of running the square kernel:

```
// Read back computed dat
  clEnqueueReadBuffer(
      queues[0],
      buffers[0],
      CL_TRUE,
      0,
      sizeof(int) * NUM_BUFFER_ELEMENTS * numDevices,
      (void*)inputOutput,
      0,
```

```
        NULL,
        NULL);

    // Display output in rows
    for (unsigned i = 0; i < numDevices; i++)
    {
        for (unsigned elems = i * NUM_BUFFER_ELEMENTS;
             elems < ((i+1) * NUM_BUFFER_ELEMENTS);
             elems++)
        {
            std::cout << " " << inputOutput[elems];
        }

        std::cout << std::endl;
    }
```

Listings 7.1 and 7.2 put this all together, demonstrating creating, writing, and reading buffers to square an input vector.

Listing 7.1 Creating, Writing, and Reading Buffers and Sub-Buffers Example Kernel Code

```
simple.cl

__kernel void square(
    __global  int * buffer)
{
    const size_t id = get_global_id(0);

    buffer[id] = buffer[id] * buffer[id];
}
```

Listing 7.2 Creating, Writing, and Reading Buffers and Sub-Buffers Example Host Code

```
simple.cpp


#include <iostream>
#include <fstream>
#include <sstream>
#include <string>
#include <vector>

#include "info.hpp"
```

```cpp
// If more than one platform installed then set this to pick which
// one to use
#define PLATFORM_INDEX 0

#define NUM_BUFFER_ELEMENTS 10

// Function to check and handle OpenCL errors inline void
checkErr(cl_int err, const char * name)
{
    if (err != CL_SUCCESS) {
        std::cerr << "ERROR: "
                    <<   name << " (" << err << ")" << std::endl;
        exit(EXIT_FAILURE);
    }
}

///
// main() for simple buffer and sub-buffer example
//
int main(int argc, char** argv)
{
    cl_int errNum;
    cl_uint numPlatforms;
    cl_uint numDevices;
    cl_platform_id * platformIDs;
    cl_device_id * deviceIDs;
    cl_context context;
    cl_program program;
    std::vector<cl_kernel> kernels;
    std::vector<cl_command_queue> queues;
    std::vector<cl_mem> buffers;
    int * inputOutput;

    std::cout << "Simple buffer and sub-buffer Example"
                << std::endl;

    // First, select an OpenCL platform to run on.
    errNum = clGetPlatformIDs(0, NULL, &numPlatforms);
    checkErr(
        (errNum != CL_SUCCESS) ?
         errNum : (numPlatforms <= 0 ? -1 : CL_SUCCESS),
        "clGetPlatformIDs");

    platformIDs = (cl_platform_id *)alloca(
                    sizeof(cl_platform_id) * numPlatforms);

    std::cout << "Number of platforms: \t"
                << numPlatforms
                << std::endl;
```

```
 errNum = clGetPlatformIDs(numPlatforms, platformIDs, NULL);
checkErr(
   (errNum != CL_SUCCESS) ?
    errNum : (numPlatforms <= 0 ? -1 : CL_SUCCESS),
   "clGetPlatformIDs");

std::ifstream srcFile("simple.cl");
checkErr(srcFile.is_open() ?
           CL_SUCCESS : -1,
           "reading simple.cl");

std::string srcProg(
    std::istreambuf_iterator<char>(srcFile),
    (std::istreambuf_iterator<char>()));

const char * src = srcProg.c_str();
size_t length = srcProg.length();

deviceIDs = NULL;
DisplayPlatformInfo(
    platformIDs[PLATFORM_INDEX],
    CL_PLATFORM_VENDOR,
    "CL_PLATFORM_VENDOR");

errNum = clGetDeviceIDs(
    platformIDs[PLATFORM_INDEX],
    CL_DEVICE_TYPE_ALL,
    0,
    NULL,
    &numDevices);
if (errNum != CL_SUCCESS && errNum != CL_DEVICE_NOT_FOUND)
{
    checkErr(errNum, "clGetDeviceIDs");
}

deviceIDs = (cl_device_id *)alloca(
   sizeof(cl_device_id) * numDevices);
errNum = clGetDeviceIDs(
    platformIDs[PLATFORM_INDEX],
    CL_DEVICE_TYPE_ALL,
    numDevices,
    &deviceIDs[0],
    NULL);
checkErr(errNum, "clGetDeviceIDs");

cl_context_properties contextProperties[] =
{
    CL_CONTEXT_PLATFORM,
    (cl_context_properties)platformIDs[PLATFORM_INDEX],
```

```cpp
    0
};

context = clCreateContext(
    contextProperties,
    numDevices,
    deviceIDs,
    NULL,
    NULL,
    &errNum);
checkErr(errNum, "clCreateContext");

// Create program from source
program = clCreateProgramWithSource(
    context,
    1,
    &src,
    &length,
    &errNum);
checkErr(errNum, "clCreateProgramWithSource");

// Build program
errNum = clBuildProgram(
    program,
    numDevices,
    deviceIDs,
    "-I.",
    NULL,
    NULL);
if (errNum != CL_SUCCESS)
{
    // Determine the reason for the error
    char buildLog[16384];
    clGetProgramBuildInfo(
        program,
        deviceIDs[0],
        CL_PROGRAM_BUILD_LOG,
        sizeof(buildLog),
        buildLog,
        NULL);

        std::cerr << "Error in OpenCL C source: " << std::endl;
        std::cerr << buildLog;
        checkErr(errNum, "clBuildProgram");
}

// create buffers and sub-buffers
inputOutput = new int[NUM_BUFFER_ELEMENTS * numDevices];
for (unsigned int i = 0;
```

```
        i < NUM_BUFFER_ELEMENTS * numDevices;
        i++)
{
    inputOutput[i] = i;
}

// create a single buffer to cover all the input data
cl_mem buffer = clCreateBuffer(
    context,
    CL_MEM_READ_WRITE,
    sizeof(int) * NUM_BUFFER_ELEMENTS * numDevices,
    NULL,
    &errNum);
checkErr(errNum, "clCreateBuffer");
buffers.push_back(buffer);

// now for all devices other than the first create a sub-buffer
for (unsigned int i = 1; i < numDevices; i++)
{
    cl_buffer_region region =
        {
            NUM_BUFFER_ELEMENTS * i * sizeof(int),
            NUM_BUFFER_ELEMENTS * sizeof(int)
        };
    buffer = clCreateSubBuffer(
        buffers[0],
        CL_MEM_READ_WRITE,
        CL_BUFFER_CREATE_TYPE_REGION,
        &region,
        &errNum);
    checkErr(errNum, "clCreateSubBuffer");

    buffers.push_back(buffer);
}

// Create command-queues
for (int i = 0; i < numDevices; i++)
{
    InfoDevice<cl_device_type>::display(
        deviceIDs[i],
        CL_DEVICE_TYPE,
        "CL_DEVICE_TYPE");

    cl_command_queue queue =
        clCreateCommandQueue(
            context,
            deviceIDs[i],
            0,
```

```
                &errNum);
        checkErr(errNum, "clCreateCommandQueue");

        queues.push_back(queue);

        cl_kernel kernel = clCreateKernel(
            program,
            "square",
            &errNum);
        checkErr(errNum, "clCreateKernel(square)");

        errNum = clSetKernelArg(
      kernel,
      0,
      sizeof(cl_mem), (void *)&buffers[i]);
   checkErr(errNum, "clSetKernelArg(square)");

        kernels.push_back(kernel);
}

// Write input data
clEnqueueWriteBuffer(
    queues[0],
    buffers[0],
    CL_TRUE,
    0,
    sizeof(int) * NUM_BUFFER_ELEMENTS * numDevices,
    (void*)inputOutput,
    0,
    NULL,
    NULL);


std::vector<cl_event> events;
// call kernel for each device
for (int i = 0; i < queues.size(); i++)
{
    cl_event event;

    size_t gWI = NUM_BUFFER_ELEMENTS;

    errNum = clEnqueueNDRangeKernel(
        queues[i],
        kernels[i],
        1,
        NULL,
        (const size_t*)&gWI,
        (const size_t*)NULL,
        0,
```

```
                0,
                &event);
            events.push_back(event);
        }

        // Technically don't need this as we are doing a blocking read
        // with in-order queue.
        clWaitForEvents(events.size(), events.data());

        // Read back computed data
        clEnqueueReadBuffer(
                queues[0],
                buffers[0],
                CL_TRUE,
                0,
                sizeof(int) * NUM_BUFFER_ELEMENTS * numDevices,
                (void*)inputOutput,
                0,
                NULL,
                NULL);

        // Display output in rows
        for (unsigned i = 0; i < numDevices; i++)
        {
            for (unsigned elems = i * NUM_BUFFER_ELEMENTS;
                elems < ((i+1) * NUM_BUFFER_ELEMENTS);
                elems++)
            {
                std::cout << " " << inputOutput[elems];
            }

            std::cout << std::endl;
        }

        std::cout << "Program completed successfully" << std::endl;

        return 0;
    }
```

OpenCL 1.1 introduced the ability to read and write rectangular segments of a buffer in two or three dimensions. This can be particularly useful when working on data that, conceptually at least, is of a dimension greater than 1, which is how OpenCL sees all buffer objects. A simple example showing a two-dimensional array is given in Figure 7.1(a) and a corresponding segment, often referred to as a slice, in Figure 7.1(b).

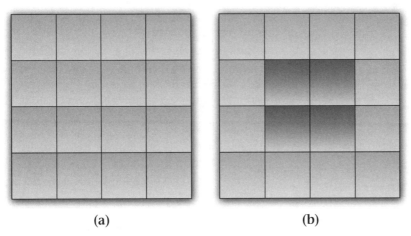

(a)   **(b)**

Figure 7.1   (a) 2D array represented as an OpenCL buffer; (b) 2D slice into the same buffer

Segments are limited to contiguous regions of memory within the buffer, although they can have a row and slice pitch to handle corner cases such as alignment constraints. These can be different for the host memory being addressed as well as the buffer being read or written.

A two-dimensional or three-dimensional region of a buffer can be read into host memory with the following function:

```
cl_int      clEnqueueReadBufferRect (

                        cl_command_queue command_queue,
                        cl_mem buffer,
                        cl_bool blocking_read,
                        const size_t buffer_origin[3],
                        const size_t host_origin[3],
                        const size_t region[3],
                        size_t buffer_row_pitch,
                        size_t buffer_slice_pitch,
                        size_t host_row_pitch,
                        size_t host_slice_pitch,
                        void * ptr,
                        cl_uint num_events_in_wait_list,
                        const cl_event * event_wait_list,
                        cl_event * event)
```

command_queue	The command-queue in which the read command will be queued.
buffer	A valid buffer object, which will be read from.
blocking_read	If set to CL_TRUE, then **clEnqueueReadBufferRect** blocks until the data is read from *buffer* and written to *ptr*; otherwise it returns directly and the user must query *event* to check the command's status.
buffer_origin	Defines the (x, y, z) offset in the memory region associated with the buffer being read.
host_origin	Defines the (x, y, z) offset in the memory region pointed to by *ptr*.
region	Defines the (width, height, depth) in bytes of the 2D or 3D rectangle being read. In the case of a 2D rectangle region, then *region*[2] must be 1.
buffer_row_pitch	The length of each row in bytes to be used for the memory region associated with *buffer*. In the case that *buffer_row_pitch* is 0, then it is computed as *region*[0].
buffer_slice_pitch	The length of each 2D slice in bytes to be used for the memory region associated with *buffer*. In the case that *buffer_slice_pitch* is 0, then it is computed as *region*[1] * *buffer_row_pitch*.
host_row_pitch	The length of each row in bytes to be used for the memory region pointed to by *ptr*. In the case that *host_row_pitch* is 0, then it is computed as *region*[0].
host_slice_pitch	The length of each 2D slice in bytes to be used for the memory region pointed to by *ptr*. In the case that *host_slice_pitch* is 0, then it is computed as *region*[1] * *host_row_pitch*.
ptr	A pointer into host memory where the data read is written to.
num_events_in_wait_list	The number of entries in the array *event_wait_list*. Must be zero in the case *event_wait_list* is NULL; otherwise must be greater than zero.
event_wait_list	If not NULL, then *event_wait_list* is an array of events, associated with OpenCL commands, that must have completed, that is, be in the

	state CL_COMPLETE, before the read will begin execution.
event	If non-NULL, the event corresponding to the write command returned by the function will be returned in this parameter.

There are rules that an implementation of `clEnqueueReadBufferRect` will use to calculate the region into the buffer and the region into the host memory, which are summarized as follows:

- The offset into the memory region associated with the buffer is calculated by

```
buffer_origin[2] * buffer_slice_pitch +
buffer_origin[1] * buffer_row_pitch +
buffer_origin[0]
```

  In the case of a 2D rectangle region, `buffer_origin[2]` must be 0.

- The offset into the memory region associated with the host memory is calculated by

```
host_origin[2] * host_slice_pitch +
host_origin[1] * host_row_pitch +
host_origin[0]
```

  In the case of a 2D rectangle region, `buffer_origin[2]` must be 0.

As a simple example, like that shown in Figure 7.1, the following code demonstrates how one might read a 2×2 region from a buffer into host memory, displaying the result:

```
#define NUM_BUFFER_ELEMENTS 16
cl_int errNum;
cl_command_queue queue;
cl_context context;
cl_mem buffer;

// initialize context, queue, and so on

cl_int hostBuffer[NUM_BUFFER_ELEMENTS] =
{
    0, 1, 2, 3, 4, 5, 6, 7,
    8, 9, 10, 11, 12, 13, 14, 15
};

buffer = clCreateBuffer(
    context,
    CL_MEM_READ | CL_MEM_COPY_HOST_PTR,
```

```
        sizeof(int) * NUM_BUFFER_ELEMENTS,
        hostBuffer,
        &errNum);

int ptr[4] = {-1, -1, -1, -1};
size_t buffer_origin[3] = {1*sizeof(int), 1, 0};
size_t host_origin[3]   = {0,0, 0};
size_t region[3]        = {2* sizeof(int), 2,1};

errNum = clEnqueueReadBufferRect(
    queue,
    buffer,
    CL_TRUE,
    buffer_origin,
    host_origin,
    region,
    (NUM_BUFFER_ELEMENTS / 4) * sizeof(int),
    0,
    0,
    2*sizeof(int),
    static_cast<void*>(ptr),
    0,
    NULL,
    NULL);

std::cout << " " << ptr[0];
std::cout << " " << ptr[1] << std::endl;
std::cout << " " << ptr[2];
std::cout << " " << ptr[3] << std::endl;
```

Placing this code in a full program and running it results in the following output, as shown in Figure 7.1:

```
5 6
9 10
```

A two- or three-dimensional region of a buffer can be written into a buffer from host memory with the following function:

```
cl_int      clEnqueueWriteBufferRect(
                        cl_command_queue command_queue,
                        cl_mem buffer,
                        cl_bool blocking_write,
                        const size_t buffer_origin[3],
                        const size_t host_origin[3],
                        const size_t region[3],
                        size_t buffer_row_pitch,
```

```
              size_t buffer_slice_pitch,
              size_t host_row_pitch,
              size_t host_slice_pitch,
              void * ptr,
              cl_uint num_events_in_wait_list,
              const cl_event * event_wait_list,
              cl_event * event)
```

command_queue	The command-queue in which the write command will be queued.
buffer	A valid buffer object, which will be read from.
blocking_write	If set to CL_TRUE, then **clEnqueueWriteBufferRect** blocks until the data is written from *ptr*; otherwise it returns directly and the user must query *event* to check the command's status.
buffer_origin	Defines the (x, y, z) offset in the memory region associated with the buffer being written.
host_origin	Defines the (x, y, z) offset in the memory region pointed to by *ptr*.
region	Defines the (width, height, depth) in bytes of the 2D or 3D rectangle being written.
buffer_row_pitch	The length of each row in bytes to be used for the memory region associated with *buffer*.
buffer_slice_pitch	The length of each 2D slice in bytes to be used for the memory region associated with *buffer*.
host_row_pitch	The length of each row in bytes to be used for the memory region pointed to by *ptr*.
host_slice_pitch	The length of each 2D slice in bytes to be used for the memory region pointed to by *ptr*.
ptr	A pointer into host memory where the data to be written is read from.
num_events_in_wait_list	The number of entries in the array *event_wait_list*. Must be zero in the case *event_wait_list* is NULL; otherwise must be greater than zero.
event_wait_list	If not NULL, then *event_wait_list* is an array of events, associated with OpenCL commands, that must have completed, that is, be in the state CL_COMPLETE, before the write will begin execution.
event	If non-NULL, the event corresponding to the write command returned by the function will be returned in this parameter.

There are often times when an application needs to copy data between two buffers; OpenCL provides the following command for this:

```
cl_int          clEnqueueCopyBuffer(
                        cl_command_queue command_queue,
                        cl_mem src_buffer,
                        cl_mem dst_buffer,
                        size_t src_offset,
                        size_t dst_offset,
                        size_t cb,
                        cl_uint num_events_in_wait_list,
                        const cl_event * event_wait_list,
                        cl_event *event)
```

command_queue	The command-queue in which the write command will be queued.
src_buffer	A valid buffer object, which will be used as the source.
dst_buffer	A valid buffer object, which will be used as the destination.
src_offset	The offset where to begin copying data from src_buffer.
dst_offset	The offset where to begin writing data to dst_buffer.
cb	The size in bytes to copy.
num_events_in_wait_list	The number of entries in the array event_wait_list. Must be zero in the case event_wait_list is NULL; otherwise must be greater than zero.
event_wait_list	If not NULL, then event_wait_list is an array of events, associated with OpenCL commands, that must have completed, that is, be in the state CL_COMPLETE, before the write will begin execution.
event	If non-NULL, the event corresponding to the write command returned by the function will be returned in this parameter.

While not required, as this functionality can easily be emulated by reading the data back to the host and then writing to the destination buffer, it is recommended that an application call clEnqueueCopyBuffer as it allows the OpenCL implementation to manage placement of data and transfers. As with reading and writing a buffer, it is possible to copy a 2D or 3D region of a buffer to another buffer using the following command:

```
cl_int      clEnqueueCopyBufferRect(
                      cl_command_queue command_queue,
                      cl_mem src_buffer,
                      cl_mem dst_buffer,
                      const size_t src_origin[3],
                      const size_t dst_origin[3],
                      const size_t region[3],
                      size_t src_row_pitch,
                      size_t src_slice_pitch,
                      size_t dst_row_pitch,
                      size_t dst_slice_pitch,
                      cl_uint num_events_in_wait_list,
                      const cl_event * event_wait_list,
                      cl_event * event)
```

command_queue	The command-queue in which the read command will be queued.
src_buffer	A valid buffer object, which will be read from.
dst_buffer	A valid buffer object, which will be written to.
src_origin	Defines the (x, y, z) offset in the memory region associated with src_buffer.
dst_origin	Defines the (x, y, z) offset in the memory region associated with dst_buffer.
region	Defines the (width, height, depth) in bytes of the 2D or 3D rectangle being read.
src_row_pitch	The length of each row in bytes to be used for the memory region associated with src_buffer.
src_slice_pitch	The length of each 2D slice in bytes to be used for the memory region associated with src_buffer.
dst_row_pitch	The length of each row in bytes to be used for the memory region associated with dst_buffer.
dst_slice_pitch	The length of each 2D slice in bytes to be used for the memory region associated with dst_buffer.
num_events_in_wait_list	The number of entries in the array event_wait_list. Must be zero in the case

	event_wait_list is NULL; otherwise must be greater than zero.
event_wait_list	If not NULL, then *event_wait_list* is an array of events, associated with OpenCL commands, that must have completed, that is, be in the state CL_COMPLETE, before the copy will begin execution.
event	If non-NULL, the event corresponding to the write command returned by the function will be returned in this parameter.

Mapping Buffers and Sub-Buffers

OpenCL provides the ability to map a region of a buffer directly into host memory, allowing the memory to be copied in and out using standard C/C++ code. Mapping buffers and sub-buffers has the advantage that the returned host pointer can be passed into libraries and other function abstractions that may be unaware that the memory being accessed is managed and used by OpenCL. The following function enqueues a command to map a region of a particular buffer object into the host address space, returning a pointer to this mapped region:

```
void *      clEnqueueMapBuffer(cl_command_queue command_queue,
                    cl_mem buffer,
                    cl_bool blocking_map,
                    cl_map_flags map_flags,
                    size_t offset,
                    size_t cb,
                    cl_uint num_events_in_wait_list,
                    const cl_event * event_wait_list,
                    cl_event *event,
                    cl_int *errcode_ref)
```

command_queue	The command-queue in which the read command will be queued.
buffer	A valid buffer object, which will be read from.
blocking_map	If set to CL_TRUE, then **clEnqueueMapBuffer** blocks until the data is mapped into host memory; otherwise it returns directly and the

	user must query *event* to check the command's status.
map_flags	A bit field used to indicate how the region specified by (*offset*, *cb*) in the buffer object is mapped. The set of valid values for *map_flags*, defined by the enumeration cl_map_flags, is described in Table 7.4.
offset	The offset, in bytes, into the buffer object to begin reading from.
cb	The number of bytes to be read from *buffer*.
num_events_in_wait_list	The number of entries in the array *event_wait_list*. Must be zero in the case *event_wait_list* is NULL; otherwise must be greater than zero.
event_wait_list	If not NULL, then *event_wait_list* is an array of events, associated with OpenCL commands, that must have completed, that is, be in the state CL_COMPLETE, before the read will begin execution.
event	If non-NULL, the event corresponding to the read command returned by the function will be returned in this parameter.
errcode_ret	If non-NULL, the error code returned by the function will be returned in this parameter.

Table 7.4 Supported Values for cl_map_flags

cl_map_flags	Description
CL_MAP_READ	Mapped for reading.
CL_MAP_WRITE	Mapped for writing.

To release any additional resources and to tell the OpenCL runtime that buffer mapping is no longer required, the following command can be used:

```
cl_in clEnqueueUnmapMemObject(cl_command_queue command_queue,
                              cl_mem buffer,
                              void * mapped_pointer,
                              cl_uint num_events_in_wait_list,
```

	const cl_event * *event_wait_list*, cl_event **event*)
command_queue	The command-queue in which the read command will be queued.
buffer	A valid buffer object that was previously mapped to *mapped_pointer*.
mapped_pointer	The host address returned by the previous call to **clEnqueueMapBuffer** for *buffer*.
num_events_in_wait_list	The number of entries in the array *event_wait_list*. Must be zero in the case *event_wait_list* is NULL; otherwise must be greater than zero.
event_wait_list	If not NULL, then *event_wait_list* is an array of events, associated with OpenCL commands, that must have completed, that is, be in the state CL_COMPLETE, before the read will begin execution.
event	If non-NULL, the event corresponding to the read command returned by the function will be returned in this parameter.

We now return to the example given in Listings 7.1 and 7.2. The following code shows how clEnqueueMapBuffer and clEnqueueUnmapMemObject could have been used to move data to and from the buffer being processed rather than clEnqueueReadBuffer and clEnqueueWriteBuffer. The following code initializes the buffer:

```
cl_int * mapPtr = (cl_int*) clEnqueueMapBuffer(
    queues[0],
    buffers[0],
    CL_TRUE,
    CL_MAP_WRITE,
    0,
    sizeof(cl_int) * NUM_BUFFER_ELEMENTS * numDevices,
    0,
    NULL,
    NULL,
    &errNum);
checkErr(errNum, "clEnqueueMapBuffer(..)");

for (unsigned int i = 0;
    i < NUM_BUFFER_ELEMENTS * numDevices;
    i++)
```

```
{
    mapPtr[i] = inputOutput[i];
}

errNum = clEnqueueUnmapMemObject(
    queues[0],
    buffers[0],
    mapPtr,
    0,
    NULL,
    NULL);
clFinish(queues[0]);
```

The following reads the final data back:

```
cl_int * mapPtr = (cl_int*) clEnqueueMapBuffer(
    queues[0],
    buffers[0],
    CL_TRUE,
    CL_MAP_READ,
    0,
    sizeof(cl_int) * NUM_BUFFER_ELEMENTS * numDevices,
    0,
    NULL,
     NULL,
     &errNum);
checkErr(errNum, "clEnqueueMapBuffer(..)");

for (unsigned int i = 0;
    i < NUM_BUFFER_ELEMENTS * numDevices;
    i++)
{
    inputOutput[i] = mapPtr[i];
}

errNum = clEnqueueUnmapMemObject(
    queues[0],
    buffers[0],
    mapPtr,
    0,
    NULL,
    NULL);
    clFinish(queues[0]);
```

## Chapter 8

Images and Samplers

In the previous chapter, we introduced memory objects that are used to read, write, and copy memory to and from an OpenCL device. In this chapter, we introduce the image object, a specialized type of memory object that is used for accessing 2D and 3D image data. This chapter walks through an example of using image and sampler objects and introduces the following concepts:

- Overview of image and sampler objects

- Creating image and sampler objects

- Specifying and querying for image formats

- OpenCL C functions for working with images

- Transferring image object data

Image and Sampler Object Overview

GPUs were originally designed for rendering high-performance 3D graphics. One of the most important features of the 3D graphics pipeline is the application of texture images to polygonal surfaces. As such, GPUs evolved to provide extremely high-performance access to and filtering of texture images. While most image operations can be emulated using the generic memory objects introduced in the previous chapter, it will be at a potentially significant performance loss compared to working with image objects. Additionally, image objects make some operations such as clamping at the edge of texture borders and filtering extremely easy to do.

Thus, the first thing to understand is that the primary reason why image objects exist in OpenCL is to allow programs to fully utilize the high-performance texturing hardware that exists in GPUs. Some advantage may be gained on other hardware as well, and therefore image objects represent the best method for working with two-dimensional and three-dimensional image data in OpenCL.

Image objects encapsulate several pieces of information about an image:

- **Image dimensions:** the width and height of a 2D image (along with the depth of a 3D image)

- **Image format:** the bit depth and layout of the image pixels in memory (more on this later)

- **Memory access flags:** for example, whether the image will be for reading, writing, or both

Samplers are required when fetching from an image object in a kernel. Samplers tell the image-reading functions how to access the image:

- **Coordinate mode:** whether the texture coordinates used to fetch from the image are normalized in the range `[0..1]` or in the range `[0..image_dim - 1]`

- **Addressing mode:** the behavior when fetching from an image with coordinates that are outside the range of the image boundaries

- **Filter mode:** when fetching from the image, whether to take a single sample or filter using multiple samples (for example, bilinear filtering)

One thing that may be a bit confusing at first about samplers is that you have two options for how to create them. Samplers can either be directly declared in the kernel code (using `sampler_t`) or created as a sampler object in the C/C++ program. The reason you might want to create the sampler as an object rather than statically declaring it in the code is that it allows the kernel to be used with different filtering and addressing options. We will go over this in more detail later in the chapter.

Gaussian Filter Kernel Example

Throughout the chapter we will reference the ImageFilter2D example in the Chapter 8 directory to help explain the use of images in OpenCL. The ImageFilter2D example program loads a 2D image from a file (e.g., .png, .bmp, etc.) and stores the image bits in a 2D image object. The program also creates a second 2D image object that will store the result of running a Gaussian blur filter on the input image. The program queues up the kernel for execution and then reads the image back from the OpenCL device into a host memory buffer. Finally, the contents of this host memory buffer are written to a file.

In order to build the example in Chapter 8, you will need to have the open-source FreeImage library available from http://freeimage.sourceforge.net/. FreeImage is a cross-platform library that provides many easy-to-use functions for loading and saving images. The CMake configuration for this example will attempt to detect the Free-Image library in a number of standard locations and will use the first copy that it finds.

Creating Image Objects

Creating an image object is done using `clCreateImage2D()` or `clCreateImage3D()`:

cl_mem	***clCreateImage2D***	(cl_context *context*,
		cl_mem_flags *flags*,
		const cl_image_format **image_format*,
		size_t *image_width*,
		size_t *image_height*,
		size_t *image_row_pitch*,
		void **host_ptr*,
		cl_int **errcode_ret*)
cl_mem	***clCreateImage3D***	(cl_context *context*,
		cl_mem_flags *flags*,
		const cl_image_format **image_format*,
		size_t *image_width*,
		size_t *image_height*,
		size_t *image_depth*,
		size_t *image_row_pitch*,
		size_t *image_slice_pitch*,
		void **host_ptr*,
		cl_int **errcode_ret*)

context	The context from which to create the image object.
flags	A bit field used to specify allocations and usage information for the image creation. The set of valid values for *flags*, defined by the enumeration cl_mem_flags, is described in Table 7.1 of the previous chapter.
image_format	Describes the channel order and the type of the image channel data. This is described in the next section, "Image Formats."
image_width	The width of the image in pixels.
image_height	The height of the image in pixels.
image_depth	(3D only) For 3D images, gives the number of slices of the image.

image_row_pitch	If the *host_ptr* is not NULL, this value specifies the number of bytes in each row of an image. If its value is 0, the pitch is assumed to be the *image_width* * (bytes_per_pixel).
image_slice_pitch	(3D only) If the *host_ptr* is not NULL, this value specifies the number of bytes in each slice of a 3D image. If it is 0, the pitch is assumed to be *image_height* * *image_row_pitch*.
host_ptr	A pointer to the image buffer laid out linearly in memory. For 2D images, the buffer is linear by scan lines. For 3D images, it is a linear array of 2D image slices. Each 2D slice is laid out the same as a 2D image.
errcode_ret	If non-NULL, the error code returned by the function will be returned in this parameter.

Listing 8.1 from the ImageFilter2D example demonstrates loading an image from a file using the FreeImage library and then creating a 2D image object from its contents. The image is first loaded from disk and then stored in a 32-bit RGBA buffer where each channel is 1 byte (8 bits). Next, the cl_image_format structure is set up with channel order CL_RGBA and channel data type CL_UNORM_INT8. The image is then finally created using clCreateImage2D(). The 32-bit image buffer is loaded to the host_ptr and copied to the OpenCL device. The mem_ flags are set to CL_MEM_READ_ONLY | CL_MEM_COPY_HOST_PTR, which copies the data from the host pointer and stores it in a 2D image object that can be read only from in a kernel.

An important point to note is that clCreateImage2D() and clCreate-Image3D() return a cl_mem object. There is no special object type for image objects, which means that you must use the standard memory object functions such as clReleaseMemObject() for releasing them.

Listing 8.1 Creating a 2D Image Object from a File

```
cl_mem LoadImage(cl_context context, char *fileName, int &width,
            int &height)
{
 FREE_IMAGE_FORMAT format = FreeImage_GetFileType(fileName, 0);
 FIBITMAP* image = FreeImage_Load(format, fileName);

 // Convert to 32-bit image
 FIBITMAP* temp = image;
 image = FreeImage_ConvertTo32Bits(image);
 FreeImage_Unload(temp);
```

```
width = FreeImage_GetWidth(image);
height = FreeImage_GetHeight(image);

char *buffer = new char[width * height * 4];
memcpy(buffer, FreeImage_GetBits(image), width * height * 4);

FreeImage_Unload(image);

// Create OpenCL image
cl_image_format clImageFormat;
clImageFormat.image_channel_order = CL_RGBA;
clImageFormat.image_channel_data_type = CL_UNORM_INT8;

cl_int errNum;
cl_mem clImage;
clImage = clCreateImage2D(context,
                          CL_MEM_READ_ONLY | CL_MEM_COPY_HOST_PTR,
                          &clImageFormat,
                          width,
                          height,
                          0,
                          buffer,
                          &errNum);

if (errNum != CL_SUCCESS)
{
    std::cerr << "Error creating CL image object" << std::endl;
    return 0;
}

return clImage;
}
```

In addition to creating the input 2D image object, the example program also creates an output 2D image object that will store the result of performing Gaussian filtering on the input image. The output object is created with the code shown in Listing 8.2. Note that this object is created without a `host_ptr` because it will be filled with data in the kernel. Also, the `mem_flags` are set to `CL_MEM_WRITE_ONLY` because the image will only be written in the kernel, but not read.

Listing 8.2   Creating a 2D Image Object for Output

```
// Create output image object
cl_image_format clImageFormat;
clImageFormat.image_channel_order = CL_RGBA;
clImageFormat.image_channel_data_type = CL_UNORM_INT8;
```

```
imageObjects[1] = clCreateImage2D(context,
                                  CL_MEM_WRITE_ONLY,
                                  &clImageFormat,
                                  width,
                                  height,
                                  0,
                                  NULL,
                                  &errNum);
```

After creating an image object, it is possible to query the object for
information using the generic memory object function clGetMemOb-
jectInfo() described in Chapter 7. Additional information specific to
the image object can also be queried for by using clGetImageInfo():

cl_int	**clGetImageInfo** (cl_mem *image*, cl_image_info *param_name*, size_t *param_value_size*, void **param_value*, size_t **param_value_size_ret*)
image	A valid image object that will be queried.
param_name	The parameter to query for information; must be one of CL_IMAGE_FORMAT (cl_image_format): the format with which the image was created CL_IMAGE_ELEMENT_SIZE (size_t): the size in bytes of a single pixel element of the image CL_IMAGE_ROW_PITCH (size_t): the number of bytes in each row of an image CL_IMAGE_SLICE_PITCH (size_t): the number of bytes in each 2D slice for 3D images; for 2D images, this will be 0 CL_IMAGE_WIDTH (size_t): width of image in pixels CL_IMAGE_HEIGHT (size_t): height of image in pixels CL_IMAGE_DEPTH (size_t): depth of image in pixels for a 3D image; for 2D, this will be 0
param_value_size	The size in bytes of *param_value*.
param_value	A pointer to the location in which to store results. This location must be allocated with enough bytes to store the requested result.
param_value_size_ret	The actual number of bytes written to *param_value*.

Image Formats

As shown in Listing 8.1, the `cl_image_format` parameter passed to `clCreateImage2D()` and `clCreateImage3D()` specifies how the individual pixels of the image are laid out in memory. The `cl_image_format` structure details both the channel order and bit representation and is defined as follows:

```
typedef struct _cl_image_format
{
    cl_channel_order image_channel_order;
    cl_channel_type image_channel_data_type;
} cl_image_format;
```

The valid values for `image_channel_order` and `image_channel_data_type` are given in Tables 8.1 and 8.2. In addition to providing the layout of how the bits of the image are stored in memory, the `cl_image_format` also determines how the results will be interpreted when read inside of a kernel. The details of fetching from images in a kernel will be covered in a later section in this chapter, "OpenCL C Functions for Working with Images." The choice of channel data type influences which is the appropriate OpenCL C function with which to read/write the image (e.g., `read_imagef`, `read_imagei`, or `read_imageui`). The last column in Table 8.1 shows how the image channel order impacts how the fetch results will be interpreted in the kernel.

Table 8.1 Image Channel Order

Channel Order	Description	Read Results in Kernel
CL_R, CL_Rx	One channel of image data that will be read into the R component in the kernel. CL_Rx contains two channels, but only the first channel will be available when read in the kernel.	(R, 0.0, 0.0, 1.0)
CL_A	One channel of image data that will be read into the A component in the kernel.	(0.0, 0.0, 0.0, A)

continues

Table 8.1 Image Channel Order (*Continued*)

Channel Order	Description	Read Results in Kernel
CL_INTENSITY	One channel of image data that will be read into all color components in the kernel. This format can be used only with channel data types of CL_UNORM_INT8, CL_UNORM_INT16, CL_SNORM_INT8, CL_SNORM_INT16, CL_HALF_FLOAT, or CL_FLOAT.	(I, I, I, I)
CL_RG, CL_RGx	Two channels of image data that will be read into the R, G components in the kernel. CL_RGx contains three channels, but the third channel of data is ignored.	(R, G, 0.0, 1.0)
CL_RA	Two channels of image data that will be read into the R, A components in the kernel.	(R, 0.0, 0.0, A)
CL_RGB, CL_RGBx	Three channels of image data that will be read into the R, G, B components in the kernel. These formats can be used only with channel data types of CL_UNORM_SHORT_565, CL_UNORM_SHORT_555, or CL_UNORM_INT_101010.	(R, G, B, 1.0)
CL_RGBA, CL_BGRA, CL_ARGB	Four channels of image data that will be read into the R, G, B, A components in the kernel. CL_BGRA and CL_ARGB can be used only with channel data types of CL_UNORM_INT8, CL_SNORM_INT8, CL_SIGNED_INT8, or CL_UNSIGNED_INT8.	(R, G, B, A)

Table 8.1 Image Channel Order (*Continued*)

Channel Order	Description	Read Results in Kernel
CL_LUMINANCE	One channel of image data that will be duplicated to all four components in the kernel. This format can be used only with channel data types of CL_UNORM_INT8, CL_UNORM_INT16, CL_SNORM_INT8, CL_SNORM_INT16, CL_HALF_FLOAT, or CL_FLOAT.	(L, L, L, 1.0)

Table 8.2 Image Channel Data Type

Channel Data Type	Description
CL_SNORM_INT8	Each 8-bit integer value will be mapped to the range [-1.0, 1.0].
CL_SNORM_INT16	Each 16-bit integer value will be mapped to the range [-1,0, 1.0].
CL_UNORM_INT8	Each 8-bit integer value will be mapped to the range [0.0, 1.0].
CL_UNORM_INT16	Each 16-bit integer value will be mapped to the range [0.0, 1.0].
CL_SIGNED_INT8	Each 8-bit integer value will be read to the integer range [-128, 127].
CL_SIGNED_INT16	Each 16-bit integer value will be read to the integer range [-32768, 32767].
CL_SIGNED_INT32	Each 32-bit integer value will be read to the integer range [-2,147,483,648, 2,147,483,647].
CL_UNSIGNED_INT8	Each 8-bit unsigned integer value will be read to the unsigned integer range [0, 255].
CL_UNSIGNED_INT16	Each 16-bit unsigned integer value will be read to the unsigned integer range [0, 65535].
CL_UNSIGNED_INT32	Each 32-bit unsigned integer value will be read to the unsigned integer range [0, 4,294,967,295].

continues

Table 8.2 Image Channel Data Type (*Continued*)

Channel Data Type	Description
CL_HALF_FLOAT	Each 16-bit component will be treated as a half-float value.
CL_FLOAT	Each 32-bit component will be treated as a single-precision float value.
CL_UNORM_SHORT_565	A 5:6:5 16-bit value where each component (R, G, B) will be normalized to the [0.0, 1.0] range.
CL_UNORM_SHORT_555	An x:5:5:5 16-bit value where each component (R, G, B) will be normalized to the [0.0, 1.0] range.
CL_UNORM_INT_101010	An x:10:10:10 32-bit value where each component (R,G, B) will be normalized to the [0.0, 1.0] range.

All of the image formats given in Tables 8.1 and 8.2 *may* be supported by an OpenCL implementation, but only a subset of these formats is *required*. Table 8.3 shows the formats that every OpenCL implementation *must* support if it supports images. It is possible for an implementation not to support images at all, which you can determine by querying the OpenCL device using clGetDeviceInfo() for the Boolean CL_DEVICE_IMAGE_SUPPORT. If images are supported, you can use the formats in Table 8.3 without querying OpenCL for which formats are available.

Table 8.3 Mandatory Supported Image Formats

Channel Order	Channel Data Type
CL_RGBA	CL_UNORM_INT8
	CL_UNORM_INT16
	CL_SIGNED_INT8
	CL_SIGNED_INT16
	CL_SIGNED_INT32
	CL_UNSIGNED_INT8
	CL_UNSIGNED_INT16
	CL_UNSIGNED_INT32
	CL_FLOAT
CL_BGRA	CL_UNORM_INT8

If you use any formats not listed in Table 8.3, you must query OpenCL to determine if your desired image format is supported using clGetSupportedImageFormats():

```
cl_int clGetSupportedImageFormats (cl_context context,
                                   cl_mem_flags flags,
                                   cl_mem_object_type image_type,
                                   cl_uint num_entries,
                                   cl_image_format *image_formats,
                                   cl_uint *num_image_formats)
```

context	The context to query for supported image formats.
flags	A bit field used to specify allocations and usage information for the image creation. The set of valid values for *flags*, defined by the enumeration cl_mem_flags, is described in Table 7.1 of the previous chapter. Set this flag to the flags you plan to use for creating the image.
image_type	The type of the image must be either CL_MEM_OBJECT_IMAGE2D or CL_MEM_OBJECT_IMAGE3D.
num_entries	The number of entries that can be returned.
image_formats	A pointer to the location that will store the list of supported image formats. Set this to NULL to first query for the number of image formats supported.
num_image_formats	A pointer to a cl_uint that will store the number of image formats.

Querying for Image Support

The ImageFilter2D example uses only a mandatory format so it simply checks for whether images are supported, as shown in Listing 8.3. If the program used any of the non-mandatory formats, it would also need to call clGetSupportedImageFormats() to make sure the image formats were supported.

Listing 8.3 Query for Device Image Support

```
// Make sure the device supports images, otherwise exit
cl_bool imageSupport = CL_FALSE;
clGetDeviceInfo(device, CL_DEVICE_IMAGE_SUPPORT, sizeof(cl_bool),
                &imageSupport, NULL);
if (imageSupport != CL_TRUE)
{
    std::cerr << "OpenCL device does not support images."
             << std::endl;
    Cleanup(context, commandQueue, program, kernel, imageObjects,
           sampler);
    return 1;
}
```

Creating Sampler Objects

At this point, we have shown how the ImageFilter2D example creates image objects for both the input and output image. We are almost ready to execute the kernel. There is one more object that we need to create, which is a sampler object. The sampler object specifies the filtering, addressing, and coordinate modes that will be used to fetch from the image. All of these options correspond to GPU hardware capabilities for fetching textures.

The filtering mode specifies whether to fetch using **nearest** sampling or **linear** sampling. For nearest sampling, the value will be read from the image at the location nearest to the coordinate. For linear sampling, several values close to the coordinate will be averaged together. For 2D images, the linear filter will take the four closest samples and perform an average of them. This is known as **bilinear** sampling. For 3D images, the linear filter will take four samples from each of the closest slices and then linearly interpolate between these averages. This is known as **trilinear** sampling. The cost of filtering varies by GPU hardware, but generally speaking it is very efficient and much more efficient than doing the filtering manually.

The coordinate mode specifies whether the coordinates used to read from the image are normalized (floating-point values in the range `[0.0, 1.0]`) or non-normalized (integer values in the range `[0, image_dimension - 1]`). Using normalized coordinates means that the coordinate values do not take into account the image dimensions. Using non-normalized coordinates means that the coordinates are within the image dimension range.

The addressing mode specifies what to do when the coordinate falls outside the range of `[0.0, 1.0]` (for normalized coordinates) or `[0, dimension - 1]` (for non-normalized coordinates). These modes are described in the description of `clCreateSampler()`:

```
cl_sampler  clCreateSampler (cl_context context,
                             cl_bool normalized_coords,
                             cl_addressing_mode addressing_mode,
                             cl_filter_mode filter_mode,
                             cl_int *errcode_ret)
```

---

context   The context from which to create the sampler object.

normalized_coords	Whether coordinates are normalized floating-point values or integer values in the range of the image dimensions.
addressing_mode	The addressing mode specifies what happens when the image is fetched with a coordinate that is outside the range of the image:
	CL_ADDRESS_CLAMP: Coordinates outside the range of the image will return the border color. For CL_A, CL_INTENSITY, CL_Rx, CL_RA, CL_RGx, CL_RGBx, CL_ARGB, CL_BGRA, and CL_RGBA this color will be (0.0, 0.0, 0.0, 0.0). For CL_R, CL_RG, CL_RGB, and CL_LUMINANCE this color will be (0.0, 0.0, 0.0, 1.0).
	CL_ADDRESS_CLAMP_TO_EDGE: Coordinates will clamp to the edge of the image.
	CL_ADDRESS_REPEAT: Coordinates outside the range of the image will repeat.
	CL_ADDRESS_MIRRORED_REPEAT: Coordinates outside the range of the image will mirror and repeat.
filter_mode	The filter mode specifies how to sample the image:
	CL_FILTER_NEAREST: Take the sample nearest the coordinate.
	CL_FILTER_LINEAR: Take an average of the samples closest to the coordinate. In the case of a 2D image this will perform bilinear filtering and in the case of a 3D image it will perform trilinear filtering.
errcode_ret	If non-NULL, the error code returned by the function will be returned in this parameter.

In the ImageFilter2D example a sampler is created that performs nearest sampling and that clamps coordinates to the edge of the image as shown in Listing 8.4. The coordinates are specified to be non-normalized, meaning that the *x*-coordinate will be an integer in the range [0, width – 1] and the *y*-coordinate will be an integer in the range [0, height – 1].

Listing 8.4   Creating a Sampler Object

```
// Create sampler for sampling image object
sampler = clCreateSampler(context,
                CL_FALSE, // Non-normalized coordinates
                CL_ADDRESS_CLAMP_TO_EDGE,
                CL_FILTER_NEAREST,
                &errNum);
```

```
if (errNum != CL_SUCCESS)
{
    std::cerr << "Error creating CL sampler object." << std::endl;
    Cleanup(context, commandQueue, program, kernel, imageObjects,
            sampler);
    return 1;
}
```

As was mentioned in the "Image and Sampler Object" section of this chapter, sampler objects do not need to be created in the C program. In the case of the ImageFilter2D example, the sampler object created in Listing 8.4 is passed as an argument to the kernel function. The advantage of creating a sampler object this way is that its properties can be changed without having to modify the kernel. However, it is also possible to create a sampler directly in the kernel code. For example, this sampler could have been created in the kernel code and it would behave the same:

```
const sampler_t sampler = CLK_NORMALIZED_COORDS_FALSE |
                          CLK_ADDRESS_CLAMP_TO_EDGE   |
                          CLK_FILTER_NEAREST;
```

It is really up to you whether you need the flexibility of a sampler object created using the clCreateSampler() or one declared directly in the kernel. In the case of the ImageFilter2D example, it really was not necessary to create the sampler external from the kernel. Rather, it was done for demonstration purposes. However, in general, doing so provides more flexibility.

When an application is finished with a sampler object, it can be released using clReleaseSampler():

cl_int	**clReleaseSampler** (cl_sampler *sampler)*
sampler	The sampler object to release.

Additionally, sampler objects can be queried for their settings using clGetSamplerInfo():

cl_int	**clGetSamplerInfo** (cl_sampler *sampler*,
	cl_sampler_info *param_name*,
	size_t *param_value_size*,

	void *param_value, size_t *param_value_size_ret)
sampler	A valid sampler object to query for information.
param_name	The parameter to query for; must be one of:
	CL_SAMPLER_REFERENCE_COUNT (cl_uint): the reference count of the sampler object
	CL_SAMPLER_CONTEXT (cl_context): the context to which the sampler is attached
	CL_SAMPLER_NORMALIZED_COORDS (cl_bool): whether normalized or non-normalized coordinates
	CL_SAMPLER_ADDRESSING_MODE (cl_address-ing_mode): the addressing mode of the sampler
	CL_SAMPLER_FILTER_MODE (cl_filter_mode): the filter mode of the sampler
param_value_size	The size in bytes of memory pointed to by param_value.
param_value	A pointer to the location in which to store results. This location must be allocated with enough bytes to store the requested result.
param_value_size_ret	The actual number of bytes written to param_value.

OpenCL C Functions for Working with Images

We have now explained how the ImageFilter2D example creates image objects and a sampler object. We can now explain the Gaussian filter kernel itself, shown in Listing 8.5. A Gaussian filter is a kernel that is typically used to smooth or blur an image. It does so by reducing the high-frequency noise in the image.

Listing 8.5 Gaussian Filter Kernel

```
__kernel void gaussian_filter(__read_only image2d_t srcImg,
                              __write_only image2d_t dstImg,
                              sampler_t sampler,
                              int width, int height)
{
   // Gaussian Kernel is:
   // 1  2  1
   // 2  4  2
```

```
// 1  2  1
float kernelWeights[9] = { 1.0f, 2.0f, 1.0f,
                           2.0f, 4.0f, 2.0f,
                           1.0f, 2.0f, 1.0f };

int2 startImageCoord = (int2) (get_global_id(0) - 1,
                               get_global_id(1) - 1);
int2 endImageCoord   = (int2) (get_global_id(0) + 1,
                               get_global_id(1) + 1);
int2 outImageCoord = (int2) (get_global_id(0),
                             get_global_id(1));

if (outImageCoord.x < width && outImageCoord.y < height)
{
    int weight = 0;
    float4 outColor = (float4)(0.0f, 0.0f, 0.0f, 0.0f);
    for(int y = startImageCoord.y; y <= endImageCoord.y; y++)
    {
        for(int x= startImageCoord.x; x <= endImageCoord.x; x++)
        {
            outColor +=
                (read_imagef(srcImg, sampler, (int2)(x, y)) *
                (kernelWeights[weight] / 16.0f));
            weight += 1;
        }
    }

    // Write the output value to image
    write_imagef(dstImg, outImageCoord, outColor);
}
}
}
```

The gaussian_kernel() takes five arguments:

- __read_only image2d_t srcImg: the source image object to be filtered

- __write_only image2d_t dstImg: the destination image object where the filtered results will be written

- sampler_t sampler: the sampler object specifying the addressing, coordinate, and filter mode used by read_imagef()

- int width, int height: the width and height of the image to filter in pixels; note that both the source and destination image objects are created to be the same size

The ImageFilter2D program sets the kernel arguments, and the kernel is queued for execution, as shown in Listing 8.6. The kernel arguments are set by calling `clSetKernelArg()` for each argument. After setting the arguments, the kernel is queued for execution. The `localWorkSize` is set to a hard-coded value of 16 × 16 (this could potentially be adapted for the optimal size for the device but was set to a hard-coded value for demonstration purposes). The global work size rounds the width and height up to the closest multiple of the `localWorkSize`. This is required because the `globalWorkSize` must be a multiple of the `localWorkSize`. This setup allows the kernel to work with arbitrary image sizes (not just those with multiple-of-16 image widths and heights).

Back in Listing 8.5 for the Gaussian kernel, the image coordinates are tested to see if they are inside the image width and height. This is necessary because of the rounding that was done for the global work size. If we knew our images would always be multiples of a certain value, we could avoid this test, but this example was written to work with arbitrary image dimensions, so we do this test in the kernel to make sure reads/writes are inside the image dimensions.

Listing 8.6 Queue Gaussian Kernel for Execution

```
// Set the kernel arguments
errNum = clSetKernelArg(kernel, 0, sizeof(cl_mem),
                        &imageObjects[0]);
errNum |= clSetKernelArg(kernel, 1, sizeof(cl_mem),
                        &imageObjects[1]);
errNum |= clSetKernelArg(kernel, 2, sizeof(cl_sampler), &sampler);
errNum |= clSetKernelArg(kernel, 3, sizeof(cl_int), &width);
errNum |= clSetKernelArg(kernel, 4, sizeof(cl_int), &height);
if (errNum != CL_SUCCESS)
{
    std::cerr << "Error setting kernel arguments." << std::endl;
    Cleanup(context, commandQueue, program, kernel, imageObjects,
            sampler);
    return 1;
}

size_t localWorkSize[2] = { 16, 16 };
size_t globalWorkSize[2] =  { RoundUp(localWorkSize[0], width),
                            RoundUp(localWorkSize[1], height) };

// Queue the kernel up for execution
errNum = clEnqueueNDRangeKernel(commandQueue, kernel, 2, NULL,
                        globalWorkSize, localWorkSize,
                        0, NULL, NULL);
```

```
if (errNum != CL_SUCCESS)
{
    std::cerr << "Error queuing kernel for execution." << std::endl;
    Cleanup(context, commandQueue, program, kernel, imageObjects,
        sampler);
    return 1;
}
```

The main loop for `gaussian_filter()` reads nine values in a 3 × 3 region in the nested for loop of Listing 8.5. Each of the values read from the image is multiplied by a weighting factor that is specified in the Gaussian convolution kernel. The result of this operation is to blur the input image. Each value that is read from the image is read using the OpenCL C function `read_imagef()`:

```
read_imagef(srcImg, sampler, (int2)(x, y))
```

The first argument is the image object, the second is the sampler, and the third is the image coordinate to use. In this case, the sampler was specified with non-normalized coordinates; therefore, the (x, y) values are integers in the range [0, width − 1] and [0, height − 1]. If the sampler were using normalized coordinates, the function call would be the same but the last argument would be a `float2` with normalized coordinates. The `read_imagef()` function returns a `float4` color. The range of values of the color depends on the format with which the image was specified. In this case, our image was specified as `CL_UNORM_INT8`, so the color values returned will be in the floating-point range [0.0, 1.0]. Additionally, because the image was specified with channel order as `CL_RGBA`, the color return will be read to (R, G, B, A) in the resulting color.

The full set of 2D and 3D read image functions is provided in Chapter 5 in Tables 5.16 and 5.17. The choice of which image function to use depends on what channel data type you use to specify your image. The tables in Chapter 5 detail which function is appropriate to use depending on the format of your image. The choice of coordinate (integer non-normalized or floating-point normalized) depends on the setting of the sampler used to call the `read_image[f|ui|i]()` function.

Finally, the result of the filtered Gaussian kernel is written into the destination image at the end of Listing 8.5:

```
write_imagef(dstImg, outImageCoord, outColor);
```

When writing to an image, the coordinates must always be integers in the range of the image dimensions. There is no sampler for image writes because there is no filtering and no addressing modes (coordinates must be in range), and coordinates are always non-normalized. The choice of which `write_image[f|ui|i]()` again depends on the channel format that was chosen for the destination image. The full listing of image writing functions for 2D and 3D images is provided in Tables 5.21 and 5.22.

Transferring Image Objects

We have now covered all of the operations on image objects except for how to move them around. OpenCL provides functions for doing the following transfer operations on images that can be placed in the command-queue:

- `clEnqueueReadImage()` reads images from device → host memory.

- `clEnqueueWriteImage()` writes images from host → device memory.

- `clEnqueueCopyImage()` copies one image to another.

- `clEnqueueCopyImageToBuffer()` copies an image object (or portions of it) into a generic memory buffer.

- `clEnqueueCopyBufferToImage()` copies a generic memory buffer into an image object (or portions of it).

- `clEnqueueMapImage()` maps an image (or portions of it) to a host memory pointer.

An image is queued for reading from device to host memory by using `clEnqueueReadImage()`:

cl_int	**clEnqueueReadImage** (cl_command_queue *command_queue*, cl_mem *image*, cl_bool *blocking_read*, const size_t *origin*[3], const size_t *region*[3], size_t *row_pitch*, size_t *slice_pitch*, void **ptr*, cl_uint *num_events_in_wait_list*, const cl_event **event_wait_list*, cl_event **event*)
command_queue	The command-queue in which the read command will be queued.

image	A valid image object, which will be read from.
blocking_read	If set to CL_TRUE, then **clEnqueueReadImage** blocks until the data is read into *ptr*; otherwise it returns directly and the user must query *event* to check the command's status.
origin	The (*x*, *y*, *z*) integer coordinates of the image origin to begin reading from. For 2D images, the *z*-coordinate must be 0.
region	The (width, height, depth) of the region to read. For 2D images, the depth should be 1.
row_pitch	The number of bytes in each row of an image. If its value is 0, the pitch is assumed to be the *image_width * (bytes_per_pixel)*.
slice_pitch	The number of bytes in each slice of a 3D image. If it is 0, the pitch is assumed to be *image_height * image_row_pitch*.
ptr	A pointer into host memory where the read data is written to.
num_events_in_wait_list	The number of entries in the array *event_wait_list*. Must be zero in the case *event_wait_list* is NULL; otherwise must be greater than zero.
event_wait_list	If not NULL, then *event_wait_list* is an array of events, associated with OpenCL commands, that must have completed, that is, be in the state CL_COMPLETE, before the read will begin execution.
event	If non-NULL, the event corresponding to the read command returned by the function will be returned in this parameter.

In the ImageFilter2D example, clEnqueueReadImage() is used with a blocking read to read the Gaussian-filtered image back into a host memory buffer. This buffer is then written out to disk as an image file using Free-Image, as shown in Listing 8.7.

Listing 8.7 Read Image Back to Host Memory

```
bool SaveImage(char *fileName, char *buffer, int width, int height)
{
    FREE_IMAGE_FORMAT format =
        FreeImage_GetFIFFromFilename(fileName);
    FIBITMAP *image = FreeImage_ConvertFromRawBits((BYTE*)buffer,
                    width,
```

```
                    height, width * 4, 32,
                    0xFF000000, 0x00FF0000, 0x0000FF00);
    return FreeImage_Save(format, image, fileName);
}
...

// Read the output buffer back to the Host
char *buffer = new char [width * height * 4];
size_t origin[3] = { 0, 0, 0 };
size_t region[3] = { width, height, 1};
errNum = clEnqueueReadImage(commandQueue, imageObjects[1],
                    CL_TRUE,
                    origin, region, 0, 0, buffer,
                    0, NULL, NULL);
if (errNum != CL_SUCCESS)
{
    std::cerr << "Error reading result buffer."
            << std::endl;
    Cleanup(context, commandQueue, program, kernel, imageObjects,
            sampler);
    return 1;
}
```

Images can also be written from host memory to destination memory using clEnqueueWriteImage():

cl_int	**clEnqueueWriteImage** (cl_command_queue *command_queue*,
	cl_mem *image*,
	cl_bool *blocking_write*,
	const size_t *origin*[3],
	const size_t *region*[3],
	size_t *input_row_pitch*,
	size_t *input_slice_pitch*,
	const void *ptr*,
	cl_uint *num_events_in_wait_list*,
	const cl_event *event_wait_list*,
	cl_event *event*)

command_queue	The command-queue in which the write command will be queued.
image	A valid image object, which will be written to.
blocking_write	If set to CL_TRUE, then **clEnqueueWriteImage** blocks until the data is written from *ptr*; otherwise it returns directly and the user must query *event* to check the command's status.

origin	The (*x*, *y*, *z*) integer coordinates of the image origin to begin writing to. For 2D images, the *z*-coordinate must be 0.
region	The (width, height, depth) of the region to write. For 2D images, the depth should be 1.
input_row_pitch	The number of bytes in each row of the input image.
input_slice_pitch	The number of bytes in each slice of the input 3D image. Should be 0 for 2D images.
ptr	A pointer into host memory where the memory to write from is located. This pointer must be allocated with enough storage to hold the image bytes specified by the region.
num_events_in_wait_list	The number of entries in the array *event_wait_list*. Must be zero in the case *event_wait_list* is NULL; otherwise must be greater than zero.
event_wait_list	If not NULL, then *event_wait_list* is an array of events, associated with OpenCL commands, that must have completed, that is, be in the state CL_COMPLETE, before the read will begin execution.
event	If non-NULL, the event corresponding to the read command returned by the function will be returned.

Images can also be copied from one image object to another without requiring the use of host memory. This is the fastest way to copy the contents of an image object to another one. This type of copy can be done using clEnqueueCopyImage():

```
cl_int      clEnqueueCopyImage (cl_command_queue command_queue,
                                cl_mem src_image,
                                cl_mem dst_image,
                                const size_t src_origin[3],
                                const size_t dst_origin[3],
                                const size_t region[3],
                                cl_uint num_events_in_wait_list,
                                const cl_event *event_wait_list,
                                cl_event *event)
```

command_queue	The command-queue in which the copy command will be queued.
src_image	A valid image object, which will be read from.
dst_image	A valid image object, which will be written to.
src_origin	The (x, y, z) integer coordinates of the origin of the source image to read from. For 2D images, the z-coordinate must be 0.
dst_origin	The (x, y, z) integer coordinates of the origin of the destination image to start writing to. For 2D images, the z-coordinate must be 0.
region	The (width, height, depth) of the region to read/write. For 2D images, the depth should be 1.
num_events_in_wait_list	The number of entries in the array event_wait_list. Must be zero in the case event_wait_list is NULL; otherwise must be greater than zero.
event_wait_list	If not NULL, then event_wait_list is an array of events, associated with OpenCL commands, that must have completed, that is, be in the state CL_COMPLETE, before the read will begin execution.
event	If non-NULL, the event corresponding to the read command returned by the function will be returned.

Additionally, because image objects are specialized memory buffers, it is also possible to copy the contents of an image into a generic memory buffer. The memory buffer will be treated as a linear area of memory in which to store the copied data and must be allocated with the appropriate amount of storage. Copying from an image to a buffer is done using `clEnqueueCopyImageToBuffer()`:

```
cl_int clEnqueueCopyImageToBuffer (cl_command_queue command_queue,
                        cl_mem src_image,
                        cl_mem dst_buffer,
                        const size_t src_origin[3],
                        const size_t region[3],
                        size_t dst_offset,
                        cl_uint num_events_in_wait_list,
                        const cl_event *event_wait_list,
                        cl_event *event)
```

command_queue	The command-queue in which the copy-image-to-buffer command will be queued.
src_image	A valid image object, which will be read from.
dst_buffer	A valid buffer object, which will be written to.
src_origin	The (x, y, z) integer coordinates of the origin of the source image to read from. For 2D images, the z-coordinate must be 0.
region	The (width, height, depth) of the region to read from. For 2D images, the depth should be 1.
dst_offset	The offset in bytes in the destination memory buffer to begin writing to.
num_events_in_wait_list	The number of entries in the array event_wait_list. Must be zero in the case event_wait_list is NULL; otherwise must be greater than zero.
event_wait_list	If not NULL, then event_wait_list is an array of events, associated with OpenCL commands, that must have completed, that is, be in the state CL_COMPLETE, before the read will begin execution.
event	If non-NULL, the event corresponding to the read command returned by the function will be returned.

Likewise, it is possible to do the reverse: copy a generic memory buffer into an image. The memory buffer region will be laid out linearly the same as one would allocate a host memory buffer to store an image. Copying from a buffer to an image is done using clEnqueueCopyBufferToImage():

```
cl_int clEnqueueCopyBufferToImage (cl_command_queue command_queue,
                                   cl_mem src_buffer,
                                   cl_mem dst_image,
                                   size_t src_offset,
                                   const size_t dst_origin[3],
                                   const size_t region[3],
                                   cl_uint num_events_in_wait_list,
                                   const cl_event *event_wait_list,
                                   cl_event *event)
```

command_queue	The command-queue in which the copy-buffer-to-image command will be queued.
src_buffer	A valid buffer object, which will be read from.
dst_image	A valid image object, which will be written to.
src_offset	The offset in bytes in the source memory buffer to begin reading from.
dst_origin	The (*x*, *y*, *z*) integer coordinates of the origin of the destination image to write to. For 2D images, the *z*-coordinate must be 0.
region	The (width, height, depth) of the region to write to. For 2D images, the depth should be 1.
num_events_in_wait_list	The number of entries in the array *event_wait_list*. Must be zero in the case *event_wait_list* is NULL; otherwise must be greater than zero.
event_wait_list	If not NULL, then *event_wait_list* is an array of events, associated with OpenCL commands, that must have completed, that is, be in the state CL_COMPLETE, before the read will begin execution.
event	If non-NULL, the event corresponding to the read command returned by the function will be returned.

Finally, there is one additional way to access the memory of an image object. Just as with regular buffers, image objects can be mapped directly into host memory (as described for buffers in "Mapping Buffers and Sub-Buffers" in Chapter 7). Mapping can be done using the function clEnqueueMapImage(). Images can be unmapped using the generic buffer function clEnqueueUnmapMemObject(), which was also described in the same section of Chapter 7.

```
void*       clEnqueueMapImage (cl_command_queue command_queue,
                    cl_mem image,
                    cl_bool blocking_map,
                    cl_map_flags map_flags,
                    const size_t origin[3],
                    const size_t region[3],
                    size_t *image_row_pitch,
                    size_t *image_slice_pitch,
                    cl_uint num_events_in_wait_list,
```

```
                              const cl_event *event_wait_list,
                              cl_event *event,
                              void *errcode_ret)
```

command_queue	The command-queue in which the read command will be queued.
image	A valid image object, which will be read from.
blocking_map	If set to CL_TRUE, then **clEnqueueMapImage** blocks until the data is mapped into host memory; otherwise it returns directly and the user must query *event* to check the command's status.
map_flags	A bit field used to indicate how the region specified by (*origin*, *region*) in the image object is mapped. The set of valid values for *map_flags*, defined by the enumeration cl_map_flags, is described in Table 7.3.
origin	The (*x*, *y*, *z*) integer coordinates of the origin of the image to begin reading from. For 2D images, the *z*-coordinate must be 0.
region	The (width, height, depth) of the region to read. For 2D images, the depth should be 1.
image_row_pitch	If not NULL, will be set with the row pitch of the read image.
image_slice_pitch	If not NULL, will be set with the slice pitch of the read 3D image. For a 2D image, this value will be set to 0.
num_events_in_wait_list	The number of entries in the array *event_wait_list*. Must be zero in the case *event_wait_list* is NULL; otherwise must be greater than zero.
event_wait_list	If not NULL, then *event_wait_list* is an array of events, associated with OpenCL commands, that must have completed, that is, be in the state CL_COMPLETE, before the read will begin execution.
event	If non-NULL, the event corresponding to the read command returned by the function will be returned in this parameter.
errcode_ret	If non-NULL, the error code returned by the function will be returned in this parameter.

The ImageFilter2D example from this chapter can be modified to use `clEnqueueMapImage()` to read the results back to the host rather than using `clEnqueueReadImage()`. The code in Listing 8.8 shows the changes necessary to modify the example program to read its results using `clEnqueueMapImage()`.

Listing 8.8 Mapping Image Results to a Host Memory Pointer

```
// Create the image object. Needs to be
// created with CL_MEM_READ_WRITE rather than
// CL_MEM_WRITE_ONLY since it will need to
// be mapped to the host
imageObjects[1] = clCreateImage2D(context,
                                  CL_MEM_READ_WRITE,
                                  &clImageFormat,
                                  width,
                                  height,
                                  0,
                                  NULL,
                                  &errNum);


// ... Execute the kernel ...

// Map the results back to a host buffer
size_t rowPitch = 0;
char *buffer =
        (char*) clEnqueueMapImage(commandQueue, imageObjects[1],
                                  CL_TRUE,
                                  CL_MAP_READ, origin,
                                  region, &rowPitch,
                                  NULL, 0, NULL, NULL, &errNum);
if (errNum != CL_SUCCESS)
{
    std::cerr << "Error mapping result buffer." << std::endl;
    Cleanup(context, commandQueue, program, kernel, imageObjects,
            sampler);
    return 1;
}
// Save the image out to disk
if (!SaveImage(argv[2], buffer, width, height, rowPitch))
{
    std::cerr << "Error writing output image: " << argv[2] <<
                std::endl;
    Cleanup(context, commandQueue, program, kernel, imageObjects,
            sampler);
    return 1;
}
```

```
// Unmap the image buffer
errNum = clEnqueueUnmapMemObject(commandQueue, imageObjects[1],
                                 buffer, 0, NULL, NULL);
if (errNum != CL_SUCCESS)
{
    std::cerr << "Error unmapping result buffer." << std::endl;
    Cleanup(context, commandQueue, program, kernel, imageObjects,
            sampler);
    return 1;
}
```

The image object created for the results is this time created with memory flags of CL_MEM_READ_WRITE (rather than CL_MEM_WRITE_ONLY as it was originally). This must be done because when we call clEnqueueMap-Image(), we pass it CL_MAP_READ as a map flag, which allows us to read its contents in the host buffer returned. Another change is that the row pitch must be explicitly read back rather than assumed to be equal to the width * bytesPerPixel. Further, the host pointer buffer must be unmapped using clEnqueueUnmapMemObject() in order to release its resources.

One important performance consideration to be aware of about copying and mapping image data is that the OpenCL specification does not mandate the internal storage layout of images. That is, while the images may appear to be linear buffers on the host, an OpenCL implementation might store images in nonlinear formats internally. Most commonly, an OpenCL implementation will tile image data for optimized access for the hardware. The tiling format is opaque (and likely proprietary), and the user of the OpenCL implementation does not see or have access to the tiled buffers. However, what this means from a performance perspective is that when reading/writing/mapping buffers from/to the host, the OpenCL implementation may need to retile the data for its own optimum internal format. While the performance implications of this are likely to be entirely dependent on the underlying OpenCL hardware device, it is worth understanding from a user perspective in order to limit such tiling/detiling operations to where they are strictly necessary.

## Chapter 9

Events

OpenCL commands move through queues executing kernels, manipulating memory objects, and moving them between devices and the host. A particularly simple style of OpenCL programming is to consider the program as a single queue of commands executing in order, with one command finishing before the next begins.

Often, however, a problem is best solved in terms of multiple queues. Or individual commands need to run concurrently, either to expose more concurrency or to overlap communication and computation. Or you just need to keep track of the timing of how the commands execute to understand the performance of your program. In each of these cases, a more detailed way to interact with OpenCL is needed. We address this issue within OpenCL through event objects.

In this chapter, we will explain OpenCL events and how to use them. We will discuss

- The basic event model in OpenCL

- The APIs to work with events

- User-defined events

- Profiling commands with events

- Events inside kernels

Commands, Queues, and Events Overview

Command-queues are the core of OpenCL. A platform defines a context that contains one or more compute devices. For each compute device there is one or more command-queues. Commands submitted to these queues carry out the work of an OpenCL program.

In simple OpenCL programs, the commands submitted to a command-queue execute in order. One command completes before the next one begins, and the program unfolds as a strictly ordered sequence of commands. When individual commands contain large amounts of concurrency, this in-order approach delivers the performance an application requires.

Realistic applications, however, are usually not that simple. In most cases, applications do not require strict in-order execution of commands. Memory objects can move between a device and the host while other commands execute. Commands operating on disjoint memory objects can execute concurrently. In a typical application there is ample concurrency present from running commands at the same time. This concurrency can be exploited by the runtime system to increase the amount of parallelism that can be realized, resulting in significant performance improvements.

Another common situation is when the dependencies between commands can be expressed as a directed acyclic graph (DAG). Such graphs may include branches that are independent and can safely run concurrently. Forcing these commands to run in a serial order overconstrains the system. An out-of-order command-queue lets a system exploit concurrency between such commands, but there is much more concurrency that can be exploited. By running independent branches of the DAG on different command-queues potentially associated with different compute devices, large amounts of additional concurrency can be exploited.

The common theme in these examples is that the application has more opportunities for concurrency than the command-queues can expose. Relaxing these ordering constraints has potentially large performance advantages. These advantages, however, come at a cost. If the ordering semantics of the command-queue are not used to ensure a safe order of execution for commands, then the programmer must take on this responsibility. This is done with events in OpenCL.

An **event** is an object that communicates the status of commands in OpenCL. Commands in a command-queue generate events, and other commands can wait on these events before they execute. Users can create custom events to provide additional levels of control between the host and the compute devices. The event mechanism can be used to control the interaction between OpenCL and graphics standards such as OpenGL. And finally, inside kernels, events can be used to let programmers overlap data movement with operations on that data.

Events and Command-Queues

An OpenCL event is an object that conveys information about a command in OpenCL. The state of an event describes the status of the associated command. It can take one of the following values:

- `CL_QUEUED`: The command has been enqueued in the command-queue.

- `CL_SUBMITTED`: The enqueued command has been submitted by the host to the device associated with the command-queue.

- `CL_RUNNING`: The compute device is executing the command.

- `CL_COMPLETE`: The command has completed.

- `ERROR_CODE`: A negative value that indicates that some error condition has occurred. The actual values are the ones returned by the platform or runtime API that generated the event.

There are a number of ways to create events. The most common source of events is the commands themselves. Any command enqueued to a command-queue generates or waits for events. They appear in the API in the same way from one command to the next; hence we can use a single example to explain how events work. Consider the command to enqueue kernels for execution on a compute device:

```
cl_int clEnqueueNDRangeKernel (
    cl_command_queue command_queue,
    cl_kernel kernel,
    cl_uint work_dim,
    const size_t *global_work_offset,
    const size_t *global_work_size,
    const size_t *local_work_size,
    cl_uint num_events_in_wait_list,
    const cl_event *event_wait_list,
    cl_event *event)
```

This should look familiar from earlier chapters in the book. For now, we are interested in only the last three arguments to this function:

- `cl_uint num_events_in_wait_list`: the number of events this command is waiting to complete before executing.

- `const cl_event *event_wait_list`: an array of pointers defining the list of `num_events_in_wait_list` events this command is waiting on. The context associated with events in `event_wait_list` and the `command_queue` must be the same.

- `cl_event *event`: a pointer to an event object generated by this command. This can be used by subsequent commands or the host to follow the status of this command.

When legitimate values are provided by the arguments `num_events_in_wait_list` and `*event_wait_list`, the command will not run until every event in the list has either a status of `CL_COMPLETE` or a negative value indicating an error condition.

The event is used to define a sequence point where two commands are brought to a known state within a program and hence serves as a synchronization point within OpenCL. As with any synchronization point in OpenCL, memory objects are brought to a well-defined state with respect to the execution of multiple kernels according to the OpenCL memory model. Memory objects are associated with a context, so this holds even when multiple command-queues within a single context are involved in a computation.

For example, consider the following simple example:

```
cl_event    k_events[2];

// enqueue two kernels exposing events

err = clEnqueueNDRangeKernel(commands, kernel1, 1,
        NULL, &global, &local, 0, NULL, &k_events[0]);

err = clEnqueueNDRangeKernel(commands, kernel2, 1,
        NULL, &global, &local, 0, NULL, &k_events[1]);

// enqueue the next kernel .. which waits for two prior
// events before launching the kernel
err = clEnqueueNDRangeKernel(commands, kernel3, 1,
        NULL, &global, &local, 2, k_events, NULL);
```

Three kernels are enqueued for execution. The first two `clEnqueueNDRangeKernel` commands enqueue `kernel1` and `kernel2`. The final arguments for these commands generate events that are placed in the corresponding elements of the array `k_events[]`. The third `clEnqueueNDRangeKernel` command enqueues `kernel3`. As shown in the seventh and eighth arguments to `clEnqueueNDRangeKernel`, `kernel3` will wait until both of the events in the array `k_events[]` have completed before the kernel will run. Note, however, that the final argument to enqueue `kernel3` is `NULL`. This indicates that we don't wish to generate an event for later commands to access.

When detailed control over the order in which commands execute is needed, events are critical. When such control is not needed, however, it is convenient for commands to ignore events (both use of events and generation of events). We can tell a command to ignore events using the following procedure:

1. Set the number of events the command is waiting for (num_events_ in_wait_list) to 0.

2. Set the pointer to the array of events (*event_wait_list) to NULL. Note that if this is done, num_events_in_wait_list must be 0.

3. Set the pointer to the generated event (*event) to NULL.

This procedure ensures that no events will be waited on, and that no event will be generated, which of course means that it will not be possible for the application to query or queue a wait for this particular kernel execution instance.

When enqueuing commands, you often need to indicate a synchronization point where all commands prior to that point complete before any of the following commands start. You can do this for commands within a single queue using the clBarrier() function:

```
cl_int clEnqueueBarrier (
        cl_command_queue command_queue)
```

The single argument defines the queue to which the barrier applies. The command returns CL_SUCCESS if the function was executed successfully; otherwise it returns one of the following error conditions:

- CL_INVALID_COMMAND_QUEUE: The command-queue is not a valid command-queue.

- CL_OUT_OF_RESOURCES: There is a failure to allocate resources required by the OpenCL implementation on the device.

- CL_OUT_OF_HOST_MEMORY: There is a failure to allocate resources required by the OpenCL implementation on the host.

The clEnqueueBarrier command defines a synchronization point. This is important for understanding ordering constraints between commands. But more important, in the OpenCL memory model described in Chapter 1, consistency of memory objects is defined with respect to synchronization points. In particular, at a synchronization point, updates to memory objects visible across commands must be complete so that subsequent commands see the new values.

To define more general synchronization points, OpenCL uses events and markers. A marker is set with the following command:

```
cl_int clEnqueueMarker (
    cl_command_queue command_queue,
    cl_event *event)
```

`cl_command_queue command_queue`:	The command-queue to which the marker is applied
`cl_event *event`:	A pointer to an event object used to communicate the status of the marker

The marker command is not completed until all commands enqueued before it have completed. For a single in-order queue, the effect of the `clEnqueueMarker` command is similar to a barrier. Unlike the barrier, however, the marker command returns an event. The host or other commands can wait on this event to ensure that all commands queued before the marker command have completed. `clEnqueueMarker` returns `CL_SUCCESS` if the function is successfully executed. Otherwise, it returns one of the following errors:

- `CL_INVALID_COMMAND_QUEUE`: The `command_queue` is not a valid command-queue.

- `CL_INVALID_VALUE`: The event is a `NULL` value.

- `CL_OUT_OF_RESOURCES`: There is a failure to allocate resources required by the OpenCL implementation on the device.

- `CL_OUT_OF_HOST_MEMORY`: There is a failure to allocate resources required by the OpenCL implementation on the host.

The following function enqueues a wait for a specific event or a list of events to complete before any future commands queued in the command-queue are executed:

```
cl_int clEnqueueWaitForEvents(
    cl_command_queue command_queue,
    cl_uint num_events,
    const cl_event *event_list)
```

`cl_command_queue command_queue:`	The command-queue to which the events apply
`cl_uint num_events_in_wait_list:`	The number of events this command is waiting to complete
`const cl_event *event_wait_list:`	An array of pointers defining the list of `num_events_in_wait_list` events this command is waiting on

These events define synchronization points. This means that when the `clEnqueueWaitForEvents` completes, updates to memory objects as defined in the memory model must complete, and subsequent commands can depend on a consistent state for the memory objects. The context associated with events in `event_list` and `command_queue` must be the same.

`clEnqueueWaitForEvents` returns `CL_SUCCESS` if the function was successfully executed. Otherwise, it returns one of the following errors:

- `CL_INVALID_COMMAND_QUEUE`: The `command_queue` is not a valid command-queue.

- `CL_INVALID_CONTEXT`: The context associated with `command_queue` and the events in `event_list` are not the same.

- `CL_INVALID_VALUE`: `num_events` is 0 or `event_list` is NULL.

- `CL_INVALID_EVENT`: The event objects specified in `event_list` are not valid events.

- `CL_OUT_OF_RESOURCES`: There is a failure to allocate resources required by the OpenCL implementation on the device.

- `CL_OUT_OF_HOST_MEMORY`: There is a failure to allocate resources required by the command.

The three commands `clEnqueueBarrier`, `clEnqueueMarker`, and `clEnqueueWaitForEvents` impose order constraints on commands in a queue and synchronization points that impact the consistency of the OpenCL memory. Together they provide essential building blocks for synchronization protocols in OpenCL.

For example, consider a pair of queues that share a context but direct commands to different compute devices. Memory objects can be shared between these two devices (because they share a context), but with OpenCL's relaxed consistency memory model, at any given point shared memory objects may be in an ambiguous state relative to commands in one queue or the other. A barrier placed at a strategic point would address this problem and a programmer might attempt to do so with the `clEnqueueBarrier()` command, as shown in Figure 9.1.

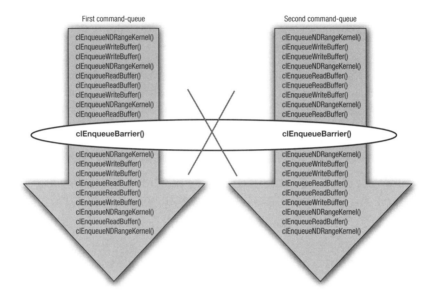

Figure 9.1   A failed attempt to use the `clEnqueueBarrier()` command to establish a barrier between two command-queues. This doesn't work because the barrier command in OpenCL applies only to the queue within which it is placed.

The barrier command in OpenCL, however, constrains the order of commands only for the command-queue to which it was enqueued. How does a programmer define a barrier that stretches across two command-queues? This is shown in Figure 9.2.

In one of the queues, a `clEnqueueMarker()` command is enqueued, returning a valid event object. The marker acts as a barrier to its own queue, but it also returns an event that can be waited on by other commands. In the second queue, we place a barrier in the desired location and follow the barrier with a call to `clEnqueueWaitForEvents`. The `clEnqueueBarrier` command will cause the desired behavior within its queue; that is, all commands prior to `clEnqueueBarrier()` must finish

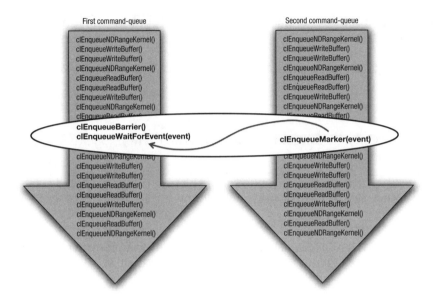

Figure 9.2 Creating a barrier between queues using `clEnqueueMarker()` to post the barrier in one queue with its exported event to connect to a `clEnqueueWaitForEvent()` function in the other queue. Because `clEnqueueWaitForEvents()` does not imply a barrier, it must be preceded by an explicit `clEnqueueBarrier()`.

before any subsequent commands execute. The call to `clEnqueueWaitForEvents()` defines the connection to the marker from the other queue. The end result is a synchronization protocol that defines barrier functionality between a pair of queues.

Event Objects

Let's take a closer look at the events themselves. Events are objects. As with any other objects in OpenCL, we define three functions to manage them:

- `clGetEventInfo`
- `clRetainEvent`
- `clReleaseEvent`

The following function increments the reference count for the indicated event object:

```
cl_int clRetainEvent (cl_event event)
```

Note that any OpenCL command that returns an event implicitly invokes a retain function on the event.

clRetainEvent() returns CL_SUCCESS if the function is executed successfully. Otherwise, it returns one of the following errors:

- CL_INVALID_EVENT: The event is not a valid event object.

- CL_OUT_OF_RESOURCES: There is a failure to allocate resources required by the OpenCL implementation on the device.

- CL_OUT_OF_HOST_MEMORY: There is a failure to allocate resources required by the OpenCL implementation on the host.

To release an event, use the following function:

```
cl_int clReleaseEvent (cl_event event)
```

This function decrements the event reference count. clReleaseEvent returns CL_SUCCESS if the function is executed successfully. Otherwise, it returns one of the following errors:

- CL_INVALID_EVENT: The event is not a valid event object.

- CL_OUT_OF_RESOURCES: There is a failure to allocate resources required by the OpenCL implementation on the device.

- CL_OUT_OF_HOST_MEMORY: There is a failure to allocate resources required by the OpenCL implementation on the host.

Information about an event can be queried using the following function:

```
cl_int clGetEventInfo (
    cl_event event,
    cl_event_info param_name,
    size_t param_value_size,
    void *param_value,
    size_t *param_value_size_ret)
```

cl_event event	Specifies the event object being queried.
cl_event_info param_name	Specifies the information to query. The list of supported param_name types and the information returned in param_value by clGetEventInfo is described in Table 9.1.
size_t param_value_size	Specifies the size in bytes of memory pointed to by param_value. This size must be greater than or equal to the size of the return type as described in Table 9.1.
void *param_value	A pointer to memory where the appropriate result being queried is returned. If param_value is NULL, it is ignored.
size_t *param_value_size_ret	Returns the actual size in bytes of data copied to param_value. If param_value_size_ret is NULL, it is ignored.

The clGetEventInfo function does not define a synchronization point. In other words, even if the function determines that a command identified by an event has finished execution (i.e., CL_EVENT_COMMAND_EXECUTION_STATUS returns CL_COMPLETE), there are no guarantees that memory objects modified by a command associated with the event will be visible to other enqueued commands.

Table 9.1 Queries on Events Supported in clGetEventInfo()

cl_event Information	Return Type	Information Returned in param_value
CL_EVENT_COMMAND_QUEUE	cl_command_queue	Returns the command-queue associated with the event. For user event objects, a NULL value is returned.
CL_EVENT_CONTEXT	cl_context	Returns the context associated with the event.

continues

Table 9.1 Queries on Events Supported in `clGetEventInfo()` (*Continued*)

`cl_event` Information	Return Type	Information Returned in `param_value`
CL_EVENT_COMMAND_TYPE	cl_command_ type	Returns the command associated with the event. Can be one of the following values: CL_COMMAND_NDRANGE_KERNEL CL_COMMAND_TASK CL_COMMAND_NATIVE_KERNEL CL_COMMAND_READ_BUFFER CL_COMMAND_WRITE_BUFFER CL_COMMAND_COPY_BUFFER CL_COMMAND_READ_IMAGE CL_COMMAND_WRITE_IMAGE CL_COMMAND_COPY_IMAGE CL_COMMAND_COPY_BUFFER_TO_IMAGE CL_COMMAND_COPY_IMAGE_TO_BUFFER CL_COMMAND_MAP_BUFFER CL_COMMAND_MAP_IMAGE CL_COMMAND_UNMAP_MEM_OBJECT CL_COMMAND_MARKER CL_COMMAND_ACQUIRE_GL_OBJECTS CL_COMMAND_RELEASE_GL_OBJECTS CL_COMMAND_READ_BUFFER_RECT CL_COMMAND_WRITE_BUFFER_RECT CL_COMMAND_COPY_BUFFER_RECT CL_COMMAND_USER
CL_EVENT_COMMAND_ EXECUTION_STATUS	cl_int	Returns the execution status of the command identified by the event. Valid values are • CL_QUEUED: The command has been enqueued in the command-queue. • CL_SUBMITTED: The enqueued command has been submitted by the host to the device associated with the command-queue. • CL_RUNNING: The device is currently executing this command. • CL_COMPLETE: The command has completed. • A negative integer indicating the command terminated abnormally. The value is given by the errcode_ret values defined by the API function call associated with this event.
CL_EVENT_REFERENCE_ COUNT	cl_uint	Returns the event reference count.

Generating Events on the Host

Up to this point, events were generated by commands on a queue to influence other commands on queues within the same context. We can also use events to coordinate the interaction between commands running within an event queue and functions executing on the host. We begin by considering how events can be generated on the host. This is done by creating user events on the host:

```
cl_event clCreateUserEvent (
    cl_context context,
    cl_int *errcode_ret)
```

`cl_context context`	Specifies the context within which the event may exist
`cl_int *errcode_ret`	Points to a variable of type `cl_int`, which holds an error code associated with the function

The returned object is an event object with a value of CL_SUBMITTED. It is the same as the events generated by OpenCL commands, the only difference being that the user event is generated by and manipulated on the host.

The `errcode_ret` variable is set to CL_SUCCESS if the function completes and creates the user event without encountering an error. When an error is encountered, one of the following values is returned within `errcode_ret`:

- CL_INVALID_CONTEXT: The context is not a valid context.

- CL_OUT_OF_RESOURCES: There is a failure to allocate resources required by the OpenCL implementation on the device.

- CL_OUT_OF_HOST_MEMORY: There is a failure to allocate resources required by the OpenCL implementation on the host.

If `clCreateUserEvent` is called with the value of the variable `errcode_ret` set to NULL, error code information will not be returned.

With events generated on the command-queue, the status of the events is controlled by the command-queue. In the case of user events, however, the status of the events must be explicitly controlled through functions called on the host. This is done using the following function:

```
cl_int clSetUserEventStatus (
        cl_event event,
        cl_int execution_status)
```

cl_event event	A user event object created using clCreateUserEvent
cl_int execution_status	Specifies the new execution status for the user event

clSetUserEventStatus can be called only once to change the execution status of a user event to either CL_COMPLETE or to a negative integer value to indicate an error. A negative integer value causes all enqueued commands that wait on this user event to be terminated.

The function clSetUserEventStatus returns CL_SUCCESS if the function was executed successfully. Otherwise, it returns one of the following errors:

- CL_INVALID_EVENT: The event is not a valid user event object.

- CL_INVALID_VALUE: The execution_status is not CL_COMPLETE or a negative integer value.

- CL_INVALID_OPERATION: The execution_status for the event has already been changed by a previous call to clSetUserEventStatus.

- CL_OUT_OF_RESOURCES: There is a failure to allocate resources required by the OpenCL implementation on the device.

- CL_OUT_OF_HOST_MEMORY: There is a failure to allocate resources required by the OpenCL implementation on the host.

An example of how to use the clCreateUserEvent and clSetUserEventStatus functions will be provided later in this chapter, after a few additional concepts are introduced.

Events Impacting Execution on the Host

In the previous section, we discussed how the host can interact with the execution of commands through user-generated events. The converse is also needed, that is, execution on the host constrained by events generated by commands on the queue. This is done with the following function:

```
cl_int clWaitForEvents (
    cl_uint num_events,
    const cl_event *event_list)
```

cl_uint num_events	The number of events in the event list to wait on.
const cl_event *event_list	A pointer to a list of events. There must be at least num_events events in the list.

The function clWaitForEvents() does not return until the num_events event objects in event_list complete. By "complete" we mean each event has an execution status of CL_COMPLETE or an error occurred, in which case the execution status would have a negative value. Note that with respect to the OpenCL memory model, the events specified in event_list define synchronization points. This means that the status of memory objects relative to these synchronization points is well defined.

clWaitForEvents() returns CL_SUCCESS if the execution status of all events in event_list is CL_COMPLETE. Otherwise, it returns one of the following errors:

- CL_INVALID_VALUE: num_events is 0 or the event_list is NULL.

- CL_INVALID_CONTEXT: Events specified in event_list do not belong to the same context.

- CL_INVALID_EVENT: Event objects specified in event_list are not valid event objects.

- CL_EXEC_STATUS_ERROR_FOR_EVENTS_IN_WAIT_LIST: The execution status of any of the events in event_list is a negative integer value.

- CL_OUT_OF_RESOURCES: There is a failure to allocate resources required by the OpenCL implementation on the device.

- CL_OUT_OF_HOST_MEMORY: There is a failure to allocate resources required by the OpenCL implementation on the host.

Following is an excerpt from a program that demonstrates how to use the clWaitForEvents(), clCreateUserEvent(), and clSetUserEvent-Status() functions:

```
cl_event k_events[2];

// Set up platform(s), two contexts, devices and two command-queues.
  Comm1 = clCreateCommandQueue(context1, device_id1,
            CL_QUEUE_OUT_OF_ORDER_EXEC_MODE_ENABLE, &err);
```

```
Comm2 = clCreateCommandQueue(context2, device_id2,
                 CL_QUEUE_OUT_OF_ORDER_EXEC_MODE_ENABLE, &err);

// Set up user event to be used as an execution trigger
  cl_event uevent = clCreateUserEvent(context2, &err);

// Set up memory objs, programs, kernels and enqueue a DAG spanning
// two command-queues (only the last few "enqueues" are shown).
    err = clEnqueueNDRangeKernel(Comm1, kernel1, 1, NULL, &global,
              &local,0, NULL, &k_events[1]);

    err = clEnqueueNDRangeKernel(Comm1, kernel2, 1, NULL, &global,
              &local, 0, NULL, &k_events[2]);

// this command depends on commands in a different context so
// the host must mitigate between queues with a user event
    err = clEnqueueNDRangeKernel(Comm2, kernel3, 1, NULL, &global,
              &local, 1, uevent, NULL);

// Host waits for commands to complete from Comm1 before triggering
// the command in queue Comm2

    err = clWaitForEvents(2, &k_events);
    err = clSetUserEventStatus(uevent, CL_SUCCESS);
```

Events are the mechanism in OpenCL to specify explicit order constraints on commands. Events, however, cannot cross between contexts. When crossing context boundaries, the only option is for the host program to wait on events from one context and then use a user event to trigger the execution of commands in the second context. This is the situation found in this example code excerpt. The host program enqueues commands to two queues, each of which resides in a different context. For the command in the second context (context2) the host sets up a user event as a trigger; that is, the command will wait on the user event before it will execute. The host waits on events from the first context (in queue Comm1) using clWaitForEvents(). Once those events have completed, the host uses a call to the function clSetUserEventStatus() to set the user event status to CL_COMPLETE and the command in Comm2 executes. In other words, because events cannot cross between contexts, the host must manage events between the two contexts on behalf of the two command-queues.

Events can also interact with functions on the host through the callback mechanism defined in OpenCL 1.1. Callbacks are functions invoked asynchronously on behalf of the application. A programmer can associate a callback with an arbitrary event using this function:

```
cl_int clSetEventCallback (
      cl_event event,
      cl_int command_exec_callback_type,
      void (CL_CALLBACK *pfn_event_notify)
           (cl_event event,
            cl_int event_command_exec_status,
            void *user_data),
      void *user_data)
```

`cl_event event`	A valid event object.
`cl_int command_exec_callback_type:`	The command execution status for which the callback is registered. Currently, the only case supported is `CL_COMPLETE`. Note that an implementation is free to execute the callbacks in any order once the events with a registered callback switch their status to `CL_COMPLETE`.
`pfn_event_notify:`	The event callback function that can be registered by the application. The parameters to this callback function are
	`event`: the event object for which the callback function is invoked.
	`event_command_exec_status`: the execution status of the command for which this callback function is invoked. Valid values for the event command execution status are given in Table 9.1. If the callback is called as the result of the command associated with the event being abnormally terminated, an appropriate error code for the error that caused the termination will be passed to `event_command_exec_status` instead.
	`user_data`: a pointer to user-supplied data.
`user_data`	The user data passed as the `user_data` argument when the callback function executes. Note that it is legal to set `user_data` to `NULL`.

The clSetEventCallback function registers a user callback function that will be called when a specific event switches to the event state defined by command_exec_callback_type (currently restricted to CL_COMPLETE). It is important to understand that the order of callback function execution is not defined. In other words, if multiple callbacks have been registered for a single event, once the event switches its status to CL_COMPLETE, the registered callback functions can execute in any order.

clSetEventCallback returns CL_SUCCESS if the function is executed successfully. Otherwise, it returns one of the following errors:

- CL_INVALID_EVENT: The event is not a valid event object.

- CL_INVALID_VALUE: The pfn_event_notify is NULL or the command_exec_callback_type is not CL_COMPLETE.

- CL_OUT_OF_RESOURCES: The system is unable to allocate resources required by the OpenCL implementation on the device.

- CL_OUT_OF_HOST_MEMORY: The system is unable to allocate resources required by the OpenCL implementation on the host.

A programmer must be careful when designing the functions used with the callback mechanism. The OpenCL specification asserts that all callbacks registered for an event object must be called before an event object can be destroyed. The ideal callback function should return promptly and must not call any functions that could cause a blocking condition. The behavior of calling expensive system routines, calling OpenCL API to create contexts or command-queues, or blocking OpenCL operations from the following list is undefined in a callback:

- clFinish

- clWaitForEvents

- Blocking calls to

  - clEnqueueReadBuffer

  - clEnqueueReadBufferRect

  - clEnqueueWriteBuffer

  - clEnqueueWriteBufferRect

  - clEnqueueReadImage

  - clEnqueueWriteImage

  - clEnqueueMapBuffer

- `clEnqueueMapImage`
- `clBuildProgram`

Rather than calling these functions inside a callback, an application should use the non-blocking forms of the function and assign a completion callback to it to do the remainder of the work. Note that when a callback (or other code) enqueues commands to a command-queue, the commands are not required to begin execution until the queue is flushed. In standard usage, blocking enqueue calls serve this role by implicitly flushing the queue. Because blocking calls are not permitted in callbacks, those callbacks that enqueue commands on a command-queue should either call `clFlush` on the queue before returning or arrange for `clFlush` to be called later on another thread.

An example of using callbacks with events will be provided later in this chapter, after the event profiling interface has been described.

Using Events for Profiling

Performance analysis is part of any serious programming effort. This is a challenge when a wide range of platforms are supported by a body of software. Each system is likely to have its own performance analysis tools or, worse, may lack them all together. Hence, the OpenCL specification defines a mechanism to use events to collect profiling data on commands as they move through a command-queue. The specific functions that can be profiled are

- `clEnqueue{Read|Write|Map}Buffer`
- `clEnqueue{Read|Write}BufferRect`
- `clEnqueue{Read|Write|Map}Image`
- `clEnqueueUnmapMemObject`
- `clEnqueueCopyBuffer`
- `clEnqueueCopyBufferRect`
- `clEnqueueCopyImage`
- `clEnqueueCopyImageToBuffer`
- `clEnqueueCopyBufferToImage`
- `clEnqueueNDRangeKernel`

- `clEnqueueTask`

- `clEnqueueNativeKernel`

- `clEnqueueAcquireGLObjects`

- `clEnqueueReleaseGLObjects`

Profiling turns the event into an opaque object to hold timing data. This functionality is enabled when a queue is created when the `CL_QUEUE_PROFILING_ENABLE` flag is set. If profiling is enabled, the following function is used to extract the timing data:

```
cl_int clGetEventProfilingInfo (
    cl_event event,
    cl_profiling_info param_name,
    size_t param_value_size,
    void *param_value,
    size_t *param_value_size_ret)
```

`cl_event event`	The event object.
`cl_profiling_info param_name`	The profiling data to query. See Table 9.2.
`size_t param_value_size`	Specifies the size in bytes of memory pointed to by `param_value`. This size must be greater than or equal to the size of the return type defined for the indicated `param_name`. See Table 9.2.
`cl_profiling_info param_name`	A pointer to memory where the appropriate result being queried is returned. If `param_value` is `NULL`, it is ignored.
`size_t param_value_size_ret`	The actual size in bytes of data copied to `param_value`. If `param_value_size_ret` is `NULL`, it is ignored.

The profiling data (as unsigned 64-bit values) provides time in nanoseconds since some fixed point (relative to the execution of a single application). By comparing differences between ordered events, elapsed times can be measured. The timers essentially expose incremental counters on compute devices. These are converted to nanoseconds by an OpenCL implementation that is required to correctly account for changes in device frequency. The resolution of a timer can be found as the value of the constant `CL_DEVICE_PROFILING_TIMER_RESOLUTION`, which essentially defines how many nanoseconds elapse between updates to a device counter.

Table 9.2 Profiling Information and Return Types

`cl_profiling` Information	Return Type	Information Returned in `param_value`
CL_PROFILING_COMMAND_QUEUED	cl_ulong	A 64-bit value that describes the current device time counter in nanoseconds when the command identified by the event is enqueued in a command-queue by the host.
CL_PROFILING_COMMAND_SUBMIT	cl_ulong	A 64-bit value that describes the current device time counter in nanoseconds when the command identified by the event that has been enqueued is submitted by the host to the device associated with the command-queue.
CL_PROFILING_COMMAND_START	cl_ulong	A 64-bit value that describes the current device time counter in nanoseconds when the command identified by the event starts execution on the device.
CL_PROFILING_COMMAND_END	cl_ulong	A 64-bit value that describes the current device time counter in nanoseconds when the command identified by the event has finished execution on the device.

The clGetEventProfilingInfo() function returns CL_SUCCESS if the function is executed successfully and the profiling information has been recorded. Otherwise, it returns one of the following errors:

- CL_PROFILING_INFO_NOT_AVAILABLE: This value indicates one of three conditions: the CL_QUEUE_PROFILING_ENABLE flag is not set for the command-queue, the execution status of the command identified by the event is not CL_COMPLETE, or the event is a user event object and hence not enabled for profiling.

- CL_INVALID_VALUE: The param_name is not valid, or the size in bytes specified by param_value_size is less than the size of the return type as described in Table 9.2 and param_value is not NULL.

- CL_INVALID_EVENT: The event is a not a valid event object.

- CL_OUT_OF_RESOURCES: There is a failure to allocate resources required by the OpenCL implementation on the device.

- CL_OUT_OF_HOST_MEMORY: There is a failure to allocate resources required by the OpenCL implementation on the host.

An example of the profiling interface is shown here:

```
// set up platform, context, and devices (not shown)
// Create a command-queue with profiling enabled
cl_command_queue commands = clCreateCommandQueue(context,
      device_id, CL_QUEUE_PROFILING_ENABLE, &err);

// set up program, kernel, memory objects (not shown)
cl_event prof_event;

err = clEnqueueNDRangeKernel(commands, kernel, nd,
      NULL, global, NULL, 0, NULL, prof_event);

clFinish(commands);
err = clWaitForEvents(1, &prof_event );

cl_ulong ev_start_time=(cl_ulong)0;
cl_ulong ev_end_time=(cl_ulong)0;
size_t return_bytes;

err = clGetEventProfilingInfo(prof_event,
      CL_PROFILING_COMMAND_QUEUED, sizeof(cl_ulong),
      &ev_start_time, &return_bytes);

err = clGetEventProfilingInfo(prof_event,
      CL_PROFILING_COMMAND_END, sizeof(cl_ulong),
      &ev_end_time, &return_bytes);

run_time =(double)(ev_end_time - ev_start_time);
printf("\n profile data %f secs\n",run_time*1.0e-9);
```

We have omitted the details of setting up the platform, context, devices, memory objects, and other parts of the program other than code associated with the profiling interface. First, note how we created the command-queue with the profiling interface enabled. No changes were made to how the kernel was run. After the kernel was finished (as verified with the call to clFinish()), we waited for the event to complete before probing the events for profiling data. We made two calls to clGetEventProfilingInfo(): the first to note the time the kernel was enqueued, and the second to note the time the kernel completed execution. The difference between these two values defined the time for the kernel's execution in nanoseconds, which for convenience we converted to seconds before printing.

When multiple kernels are profiled, the host code can become seriously cluttered with the calls to the profiling functions. One way to reduce the clutter and create cleaner code is to place the profiling functions inside a callback function. This approach is shown here in a host program fragment:

```
#include "mult.h"
#include "kernels.h"

void CL_CALLBACK eventCallback(cl_event ev, cl_int event_status,
        void * user_data)
{
    int err, evID = (int)user_data;
    cl_ulong ev_start_time=(cl_ulong)0;
    cl_ulong ev_end_time=(cl_ulong)0;
    size_t return_bytes;  double run_time;

    printf(" Event callback %d %d ",(int)event_status, evID);
    err = clGetEventProfilingInfo( ev, CL_PROFILING_COMMAND_QUEUED,
            sizeof(cl_ulong), &ev_start_time, &return_bytes);

    err = clGetEventProfilingInfo( ev, CL_PROFILING_COMMAND_END,
            sizeof(cl_ulong), &ev_end_time,   &return_bytes);

    run_time = (double)(ev_end_time - ev_start_time);
    printf("\n kernel runtime %f secs\n",run_time*1.0e-9);
}
//----------------------------------------------------------------
int main(int argc, char **argv)
{
// Declarations and platform definitions that are not shown.

    commands = clCreateCommandQueue(context, device_id,
            CL_QUEUE_PROFILING_ENABLE, &err);
    cl_event prof_event;

//event to trigger the DAG
    cl_event uevent = clCreateUserEvent(context, &err);

// Set up the DAG of commands and profiling callbacks

  err = clEnqueueNDRangeKernel(commands, kernel, nd, NULL, global,
            NULL, 1, &uevent, &prof_event);
  int ID=0;
  err =  clSetEventCallback (prof_event, CL_COMPLETE,
            &eventCallback,(void *)ID);
```

```
// Once the DAG of commands is set up (we showed only one)
// trigger the DAG using prof_event to profile execution
// of the DAG

  err = clSetUserEventStatus(uevent, CL_SUCCESS);
```

The first argument to the callback function is the associated event.
Assuming the command-queue is created with profiling enabled (by
using CL_PROFILING_COMMAND_QUEUED in the call to clGetEvent-
ProfilingInfo()), the events can be queried to generate profiling data.
The user data argument provides an integer tag that can be used to match
profiling output to the associated kernels.

Events Inside Kernels

Up to this point, events were associated with commands on a command-
queue. They synchronize commands and help provide fine-grained
control over the interaction between commands and the host. Events also
appear inside a kernel. As described in Chapter 5, events are used inside
kernels to support asynchronous copying of data between global and local
memory. The functions that support this functionality are listed here:

- event_t async_work_group_copy()

- event_t async_work_group_strided_copy()

- void wait_group_events()

The details of these functions are left to Chapter 5. Here we are interested
in how they interact with events inside a kernel.

To understand this functionality, consider the following example:

```
event_t ev_cp  = async_work_group_copy(
(__local float*) Bwrk, (__global float*) B,
(size_t) Pdim, (event_t) 0);

for(k=0;k<Pdim;k++)
 Awrk[k] = A[i*Ndim+k];


wait_group_events(1, &ev_cp);

for(k=0, tmp= 0.0;k<Pdim;k++)
 tmp  += Awrk[k] *  Bwrk[k];
C[i*Ndim+j] = tmp;
```

This code is taken from a kernel that multiplies two matrices, A and B, to produce a third matrix, C. Each work-item generates a full row of the C matrix. To minimize data movement between global memory and local or private memory, we copy rows and columns of B out of global memory before proceeding. It might be possible for some systems to carry out these data movement operations concurrently. So we post an asynchronous copy of a column of B from global into local memory (so all work times can use the same column) followed by a copy of a row of A into private memory (where a single work-item will use it over and over again as each element of the product matrix C is computed).

For this approach to work, the for loop that multiplies rows of A with columns of B must wait until the asynchronous copy has completed. This is accomplished through events. The `async_work_group_copy()` function returns an event. The kernel then waits until that event is complete, using the call to `wait_group_events()` before proceeding with the multiplication itself.

Events from Outside OpenCL

As we have seen in this chapter, OpenCL supports detailed control of how commands execute through events. OpenCL events let a programmer define custom synchronization protocols that go beyond global synchronization operations (such as barriers). Therefore, anything that can be represented as commands in a queue should ideally expose an events interface.

The OpenCL specification includes an interface between OpenCL and OpenGL. A programmer can construct a system with OpenCL and then turn it over to OpenGL to create and display the final image. Synchronization between the two APIs is typically handled implicitly. In other words, the commands that connect OpenCL and OpenGL are defined so that in the most common situations where synchronization is needed, it happens automatically.

There are cases, however, when more detailed control over synchronization between OpenGL and OpenCL is needed. This is handled through an optional extension to OpenCL that defines ways to connect OpenCL events to OpenGL synchronization objects. This extension is discussed in detail in Chapter 10.

## Chapter 10

Interoperability with OpenGL

This chapter explores how to achieve interoperation between OpenCL and OpenGL (known as OpenGL interop). OpenGL interop is a powerful feature that allows programs to share data between OpenGL and OpenCL. Some possible applications for OpenGL include using OpenCL to postprocess images generated by OpenGL, or using OpenCL to compute effects displayed by OpenGL. This chapter covers the following concepts:

- Querying the OpenCL platform for GL sharing capabilities

- Creating contexts and associating devices for OpenGL sharing

- Creating buffers from GL memory and the corresponding synchronization and memory management defined by this implied environment

OpenCL/OpenGL Sharing Overview

We begin this chapter with a brief overview of OpenCL/OpenGL sharing. At a high level, OpenGL interoperability is achieved by creating an OpenGL context, then finding an OpenCL platform that supports OpenGL buffer sharing. The program then creates a context for that platform. Buffers are allocated in the OpenGL context and can be accessed in OpenCL by a few special OpenCL calls implemented in the OpenCL/OpenGL Sharing API.

When GL sharing is present, applications can use OpenGL buffer, texture, and renderbuffer objects as OpenCL memory objects. OpenCL memory objects can be created from OpenGL objects using the `clCreateFromGL*()` functions. This chapter will discuss these sharing functions as well as function calls that allow for acquiring, releasing, and synchronizing objects. Each step will be described in detail, and a full OpenCL/OpenGL interop example is included in the code for this chapter.

Getting Started

This chapter assumes a working knowledge of OpenGL programming. Additionally, the discussions and examples use the GLUT toolkit, which provides functions for creating and controlling GL display windows. Finally, the GLEW toolkit will be used to access the GL extensions used. The necessary headers and libraries for GLUT and GLEW are available in various ways and assumed to be present in the system. For those targeting NVIDIA GPU platforms, the NVIDIA GPU Computing Toolkit and SDK provide all of the dependencies from GLUT and GLEW.

Before starting, note that you'll need to include the `cl_gl.h` header file:

```
#include <CL/cl_gl.h>
```

Querying for the OpenGL Sharing Extension

A device can be queried to determine if it supports OpenGL sharing via the presence of the `cl_khr_gl_sharing` extension name in the string for the `CL_DEVICE_EXTENSIONS` property returned by querying `clGetDeviceInfo()`.

Recall from Table 3.3 that `clGetDeviceInfo()` can return the following information:

`CL_DEVICE_EXTENSIONS`	`char[]`	Returns a space-separated list of extension names (the extension names themselves do not contain any spaces) supported by the device. The list of extension names returned can be vendor-supported extension names and one or more of the following Khronos-approved extension names: `cl_khr_fp64` `cl_khr_int64_base_atomics` `cl_khr_int64_extended_atomics` `cl_khr_fp16` `cl_khr_gl_sharing` `cl_khr_gl_event` `cl_khr_d3d10_sharing`

The string we are interested in seeing is `cl_khr_gl_sharing`. The query will return a string upon which we can do some basic string handling to detect the presence of `cl_khr_gl_sharing`. For some valid device `cdDevices[i]`, we first query the size of the string that is to be returned:

```
size_t extensionSize;
ciErrNum = clGetDeviceInfo(cdDevices[i], CL_DEVICE_EXTENSIONS, 0,
    NULL, &extensionSize );
```

Assuming this call succeeds, we can query again to get the actual extensions string:

```
char* extensions = (char*)malloc(extensionSize);
ciErrNum = clGetDeviceInfo(cdDevices[i], CL_DEVICE_EXTENSIONS,
    extensionSize, extensions, &extensionSize);
```

Here we have simply allocated the character array `extensions` of the appropriate length to hold the returned string. We then repeated the query, giving it this time the pointer to the allocated memory that is filled with the extensions string when `clGetDeviceInfo()` returns.

Any familiar method of string comparsion that checks for the presence of the `cl_khr_gl_sharing` string inside the `extensions` character array will work. Note that the strings are delimited by spaces. One way of parsing the string and searching for `cl_khr_gl_sharing` using the `std::string` object is as follows:

```
#define GL_SHARING_EXTENSION "cl_khr_gl_sharing"
std::string stdDevString(extensions);
free(extensions);

size_t szOldPos = 0;
size_t szSpacePos = stdDevString.find(' ', szOldPos);
// extensions string is space delimited
while (szSpacePos != stdDevString.npos)
{
    if( strcmp(GL_SHARING_EXTENSION, stdDevString.substr(szOldPos,
szSpacePos - szOldPos).c_str()) == 0 )
    {
        // Device supports context sharing with OpenGL
        uiDeviceUsed = i;
        bSharingSupported = true;
        break;
    }
    do {
        szOldPos = szSpacePos + 1;
        szSpacePos = stdDevString.find(' ', szOldPos);
    }
    while (szSpacePos == szOldPos);
}
```

Initializing an OpenCL Context for OpenGL Interoperability

Once a platform that will support OpenGL interoperability has been identified and confirmed, the OpenCL context can be created. The OpenGL context that is to be shared should be initialized and current. When creating the contexts, the `cl_context_properties` fields need to be set according to the GL context to be shared with. While the exact calls vary between operating systems, the concept remains the same.

On the Apple platform, the properties can be set as follows:

```
cl_context_properties props[] =
{
    CL_CONTEXT_PROPERTY_USE_CGL_SHAREGROUP_APPLE,
    (cl_context_properties)kCGLShareGroup,
    0
};
cxGPUContext = clCreateContext(props, 0,0, NULL, NULL, &ciErrNum);
```

On Linux platforms, the properties can be set as follows:

```
cl_context_properties props[] =
{
    CL_GL_CONTEXT_KHR,
    (cl_context_properties)glXGetCurrentContext(),
    CL_GLX_DISPLAY_KHR,
    (cl_context_properties)glXGetCurrentDisplay(),
    CL_CONTEXT_PLATFORM,
    (cl_context_properties)cpPlatform,
    0
};
cxGPUContext = clCreateContext(props, 1, &cdDevices[uiDeviceUsed],
    NULL, NULL, &ciErrNum);
```

On the Windows platform, the properties can be set as follows:

```
cl_context_properties props[] =
{
    CL_GL_CONTEXT_KHR,
    (cl_context_properties)wglGetCurrentContext(),
    CL_WGL_HDC_KHR,
    (cl_context_properties)wglGetCurrentDC(),
    CL_CONTEXT_PLATFORM,
     (cl_context_properties)cpPlatform,
    0
};
cxGPUContext = clCreateContext(props, 1, &cdDevices[uiDeviceUsed],
    NULL, NULL, &ciErrNum);
```

In these examples both Linux and Windows have used operating-system-specific calls to retrieve the current display and contexts. To include these calls in your application you'll need to include system-specific header files such as `windows.h` on the Windows platform. In all cases, the appropriately constructed `cl_context_properties` structure is passed to the `clCreateContext()`, which creates a context that is capable of sharing with the GL context.

The remaining tasks for creating an OpenCL program, such as creating the command-queue, loading and creating the program from source, and creating kernels, remain unchanged from previous chapters. However, now that we have a context that can share with OpenGL, instead of creating buffers in OpenCL, we can use buffers that have been created in OpenGL.

Creating OpenCL Buffers from OpenGL Buffers

Properly initialized, an OpenCL context can share memory with OpenGL. For example, instead of the memory being created by `clCreateBuffer` inside OpenCL, an OpenCL buffer object can be created from an existing OpenGL object. In this case, the OpenCL buffer can be initialized from an existing OpenGL buffer with the following command:

```
cl_mem clCreateFromGLBuffer(cl_context cl_context,
                            cl_mem_flags cl_flags,
                            GLuint bufobj,
                            cl_int *errcode_ret)
```

This command creates an OpenCL buffer object from an OpenGL buffer object.

The size of the GL buffer object data store at the time `clCreateFromGL-Buffer()` is called will be used as the size of the buffer object returned by `clCreateFromGLBuffer()`. If the state of a GL buffer object is modified through the GL API (e.g., `glBufferData()`) while there exists a corresponding CL buffer object, subsequent use of the CL buffer object will result in undefined behavior.

The `clRetainMemObject()` and `clReleaseMemObject()` functions can be used to retain and release the buffer object.

To demonstrate how you might initialize a buffer in OpenGL and bind it in OpenCL using `clCreateFromGLBuffer()`, the following code creates a vertex buffer in OpenGL. A vertex buffer object (VBO) is a buffer of data that is designated to hold vertex data.

```
GLuint initVBO( int vbolen )
{
    GLint bsize;
    GLuint vbo_buffer;
    glGenBuffers(1, &vbo_buffer);

    glBindBuffer(GL_ARRAY_BUFFER, vbo_buffer);

    // create the buffer; this basically sets/allocates the size
    glBufferData(GL_ARRAY_BUFFER, vbolen *sizeof(float)*4,
        NULL, GL_STREAM_DRAW);

    // recheck the size of the created buffer to make sure
    //it's what we requested
    glGetBufferParameteriv(GL_ARRAY_BUFFER,
        GL_BUFFER_SIZE, &bsize);
    if ((GLuint)bsize != (vbolen*sizeof(float)*4)) {
        printf(
        "Vertex Buffer object (%d) has incorrect size (%d).\n",
        (unsigned)vbo_buffer, (unsigned)bsize);
    }

    // we're done, so unbind the buffers
    glBindBuffer(GL_ARRAY_BUFFER, 0);
    return vbo_buffer;
}
```

Then, we can simply call this function to create a vertex buffer object and get its GLuint handle as follows:

```
GLuint vbo = initVBO( 640, 480 );
```

This handle, `vbo`, can then be used in the `clCreateFromGLBuffer()` call:

```
cl_vbo_mem = clCreateFromGLBuffer(context,CL_MEM_READ_WRITE,
            vbo,&err );
```

The resulting OpenCL memory object, `vbo_cl_mem`, is a memory object that references the memory allocated in the GL vertex buffer. In the preceding example call, we have marked that `vbo_cl_mem` is both readable and writable, giving read and write access to the OpenGL vertex buffer. OpenCL kernels that operate on `vbo_cl_mem` will be operating on the contents of the vertex buffer. Note that creating OpenCL memory objects from OpenGL objects using the functions `clCreateFromGLBuffer()`, `clCreateFromGLTexture2D()`, `clCreateFromGLTexture3D()`, or `clCreateFromGLRenderbuffer()` ensures that the underlying storage of that OpenGL object will not be deleted while the corresponding OpenCL memory object still exists.

Objects created from OpenGL objects need to be acquired before they can be used by OpenCL commands. They must be acquired by an OpenCL context and can then be used by all command-queues associated with that OpenCL context. The OpenCL command `clEnqueueAcquireGLObjects()` is used for this purpose:

```
cl_int clEnqueueAcquireGLObjects(cl_command_queue command_queue,
                                 cl_uint num_objects,,
                                 const cl_mem * mem_objects,
                                 cl_uint num_events_in_wait_list,
                                 const cl_event *event_wait_list,
                                 cl_event *event)
```

These objects need to be acquired before they can be used by any OpenCL commands queued to a command-queue. The OpenGL objects are acquired by the OpenCL context associated with *command_queue* and can therefore be used by all command-queues associated with the OpenCL context.

A similar function, `clEnqueueReleaseGLObjects()`, exists for releasing objects acquired by OpenCL:

```
cl_int clEnqueueReleaseGLObjects(cl_command_queue command_queue,
                                 cl_uint num_objects,
                                 const cl_mem * mem_objects,
                                 cl_uint num_events_in_wait_list,
                                 const cl_event *event_wait_list,
                                 cl_event *event)
```

These objects need to be acquired before they can be used by any OpenCL commands queued to a command-queue. The OpenGL objects are acquired by the OpenCL context associated with *command_queue* and can therefore be used by all command-queues associated with the OpenCL context.

Note that before acquiring an OpenGL object, the program should ensure that any OpenGL commands that might affect the VBO have completed. One way of achieving this manually is to call `glFinish()` before `clEnqueueAcquireGLObjects()`. Similarly, when releasing the GL object, the program should ensure that all OpenCL commands that might affect the GL object are completed before it is used by OpenGL. This can be achieved by calling `clFinish()` on the command-queue associated with the acquire/process/release of the object, after the `clEnqueue-ReleaseGLObjects()` call.

In the case that the `cl_khr_gl_event` extension is enabled in OpenCL, then both `clEnqueueAcquireGLObjects()` and `clEnqueueRelease-GLObjects()` will perform implicit synchronization. More details on this and other synchronization methods are given in the "Synchronization between OpenGL and OpenCL" section later in this chapter.

Continuing our vertex buffer example, we can draw a sine wave by filling the vertex array with line endpoints. If we consider the array as holding start and end vertex positions, such as those used when drawing `GL_LINES`, then we can fill the array with this simple kernel:

```
__kernel void init_vbo_kernel(__global float4 *vbo,
    int w, int h, int seq)
{
    int gid = get_global_id(0);
    float4 linepts;
    float f = 1.0f;
    float a = (float)h/4.0f;
    float b = w/2.0f;

    linepts.x = gid;
    linepts.y = b + a*sin(3.14*2.0*((float)gid/(float)w*f +
        (float)seq/(float)w));
    linepts.z = gid+1.0f;
    linepts.w = b + a*sin(3.14*2.0*((float)(gid+1.0f)/(float)w*f +
        (float)seq/(float)w));

    vbo[gid] = linepts;
}
```

Here we have taken into account the width and height of the viewing area given by `w` and `h` and filled in the buffer with coordinates that agree with a typical raster coordinate system within the window. Of course, with OpenGL we could work in another coordinate system (say, a normalized coordinate system) inside our kernel and set the viewing geometry appropriately as another option. Here we simply work within a 2D orthogonal pixel-based viewing system to simplify the projection matrices for the sake of discussion. The final parameter, seq, is a sequence number updated every frame that shifts the phase of the sine wave generated in order to create an animation effect.

The OpenCL buffer object returned by clCreateFromGLBuffer() is passed to the kernel as a typical OpenCL memory object:

```
clSetKernelArg(kernel, 0, sizeof(cl_mem), &cl_vbo_mem);
```

Note that we have chosen to index the buffer using a float4 type. In this case each work-item is responsible for processing a start/end pair of vertices and writing those to the OpenCL memory object associated with the VBO. With an appropriate work-group size this will result in efficient parallel writes of a segment of data into the VBO on a GPU. After setting the kernel arguments appropriately, we first finish the GL commands, then have OpenCL acquire the VBO. The kernel is then launched. We call clFinish() to ensure that it completes and finally releases the buffer for OpenGL to use as shown here:

```
glFinish();
errNum = clEnqueueAcquireGLObjects(commandQueue, 1, &cl_tex_mem,
    0,NULL,NULL );
errNum = clEnqueueNDRangeKernel(commandQueue, tex_kernel, 2, NULL,
    tex_globalWorkSize,
    tex_localWorkSize,
    0, NULL, NULL);
clFinish(commandQueue);
errNum = clEnqueueReleaseGLObjects(commandQueue, 1, &cl_tex_mem, 0,
    NULL, NULL );
```

After this kernel completes, the vertex buffer object is filled with vertex positions for drawing our sine wave. The typical OpenGL rendering commands for a vertex buffer can then be used to draw the sine wave on screen:

```
glBindBufferARB(GL_ARRAY_BUFFER_ARB, vbo);
glEnableClientState(GL_VERTEX_ARRAY);
glVertexPointer( 2, GL_FLOAT, 0, 0 );
glDrawArrays(GL_LINES, 0, vbolen*2);
glDisableClientState(GL_VERTEX_ARRAY);
glBindBufferARB(GL_ARRAY_BUFFER_ARB, 0);
```

The example code performs these operations and the result is shown in Figure 10.1. The sine wave has been generated by OpenCL and rendered in OpenGL. Every frame, the seq kernel parameter shifts the sine wave to create an animation.

Figure 10.1 A program demonstrating OpenCL/OpenGL interop. The positions of the vertices in the sine wave and the background texture color values are computed by kernels in OpenCL and displayed using Direct3D.

Creating OpenCL Image Objects from OpenGL Textures

In addition to sharing OpenGL buffers, OpenGL textures and renderbuffers can also be shared by similar mechanisms. In Figure 10.1, the background is a programmatically generated and animated texture computed in OpenCL. Sharing textures can be achieved using the `glCreateFromGLTexture2D()` and `glCreateFromGLTexture3D()` functions:

```
cl_mem clCreateFromGLTexture2D(cl_context cl_context,
                               cl_mem_flags cl_flags,
                               GLenum texture_target,
                               GLint miplevel,
                               GLuint texture,
                               cl_int *errcode_ret)
```

This creates an OpenCL 2D image object from an OpenGL 2D texture object, or a single face of an OpenGL cube map texture object.

The following creates an OpenCL 3D image object from an OpenGL 3D texture object:

```
cl_mem clCreateFromGLTexture3D(cl_context cl_context,
                               cl_mem_flags cl_flags,
                               GLenum texture_target,
                               GLint miplevel,
                               GLuint texture,
                               cl_int *errcode_ret)
```

For example, to share a four-element floating-point RGBA texture between OpenGL and OpenCL, a texture can be created with the following OpenGL commands:

```
glGenTextures(1, &tex);
glTexEnvi( GL_TEXTURE_ENV, GL_TEXTURE_ENV_MODE,  GL_REPLACE );
glBindTexture(GL_TEXTURE_RECTANGLE_ARB, tex);
glTexImage2D(GL_TEXTURE_RECTANGLE_ARB, 0, GL_RGBA32F_ARB, width,
             height, 0, GL_LUMINANCE, GL_FLOAT, NULL );
```

Note that when creating the texture, the code specifies GL_RGBA32F_ARB as the internal texture format to create the four-element RGBA floating-point texture, a functionality provided by the ARB_texture_float extension in OpenGL. Additionally, the texture created uses a non-power-of-2 width and height and uses the GL_TEXTURE_RECTANGLE_ARB argument supported by the GL_ARB_texture_rectangle extension. Alternatively, GL_TEXTURE_RECTANGLE may be used on platforms that support OpenGL 3.1. This allows natural indexing of integer pixel coordinates in the OpenCL kernel.

An OpenCL texture memory object can be created from the preceding OpenGL texture by passing it as an argument to clCreateFromGL-Texture2D():

```
*p_cl_tex_mem = clCreateFromGLTexture2D(context,
                CL_MEM_READ_WRITE, GL_TEXTURE_RECTANGLE_ARB,
                0, tex, &errNum );
```

Again we have specified the texture target of GL_TEXTURE_RECTANGLE_ARB. The OpenCL memory object pointed to by p_cl_tex_mem can now be accessed as an image object in a kernel using functions such as read_image*() or write_image*() to read or write data. CL_MEM_READ_WRITE was specified so that the object can be passed as a read or write image memory object. For 3D textures, clCreateFromGLTexture3D() provides similar functionality.

Note that only OpenGL textures that have an internal format that maps to an appropriate image channel order and data type in OpenCL may be used to create a 2D OpenCL image object. The list of supported OpenCL channel orders and data formats is given in the specification and is as shown in Table 10.1. Because the OpenCL image format is implicitly set from its corresponding OpenGL internal format, it is important to check what OpenCL image format is created in order to ensure that the correct `read_image*()` function in OpenCL is used when sampling from the texture. Implementations may have mappings for other OpenGL internal formats. In these cases the OpenCL image format preserves all color components, data types, and at least the number of bits per component allocated by OpenGL for that format.

Table 10.1 OpenGL Texture Format Mappings to OpenCL Image Formats

GL Internal Format	CL Image Format (Channel Order, Channel Data Type)
`GL_RGBA8`	`CL_RGBA, CL_UNORM_INT8` or `CL_BGRA, CL_UNORM_INT8`
`GL_RGBA16`	`CL_RGBA, CL_UNORM_INT16`
`GL_RGBA8I, GL_RGBA8I_EXT`	`CL_RGBA, CL_SIGNED_INT8`
`GL_RGBA16I, GL_RGBA16I_EXT`	`CL_RGBA, CL_SIGNED_INT16`
`GL_RGBA32I, GL_RGBA32I_EXT`	`CL_RGBA, CL_SIGNED_INT32`
`GL_RGBA8UI, GL_RGBA8UI_EXT`	`CL_RGBA, CL_UNSIGNED_INT8`
`GL_RGBA16UI, GL_RGBA16UI_EXT`	`CL_RGBA, CL_UNSIGNED_INT16`
`GL_RGBA32UI, GL_RGBA32UI_EXT`	`CL_RGBA, CL_UNSIGNED_INT32`
`GL_RGBA16F, GL_RGBA16F_ARB`	`CL_RGBA, CL_HALF_FLOAT`
`GL_RGBA32F, GL_RGBA32F_ARB`	`CL_RGBA, CL_FLOAT`

GL renderbuffers can also be shared with OpenCL via the `clCreate-FromGLRenderbuffer()` call:

```
cl_mem clCreateFromGLRenderbuffer(cl_context context,
                                  cl_mem_flags flags,
                                  GLuint renderbuffer,
                                  cl_int *errcode_ret )
```

This creates an OpenCL 2D image object from an OpenGL renderbuffer object.

Attaching a renderbuffer to an OpenGL frame buffer object (FBO) opens up the possibility of computing postprocessing effects in OpenCL through this sharing function. For example, a scene can be rendered in OpenGL to a frame buffer object, and that data can be made available via the renderbuffer to OpenCL, which can postprocess the rendered image.

Querying Information about OpenGL Objects

OpenCL memory objects that were created from OpenGL memory objects can be queried to return information about their underlying OpenGL object type. This is done using the `clGetGLObjectInfo()` function:

```
cl_int clGetGLObjectInfo(cl_mem memobj,
                         cl_gl_object_type *gl_object_type,
                         GLuint *gl_object_name)
```

The OpenGL object used to create the OpenCL memory object and information about the object type—whether it is a texture, renderbuffer, or buffer object—can be queried using this function.

After the function runs, the parameter `gl_object_type` will be set to an enumerated type for that object. The GL object name used to create the `memobj` is also returned, in `gl_object_name`. This corresponds to the object name given in OpenGL when the object was created, such as with a `glGenBuffers()` call in the case of an OpenGL buffer object.

For texture objects, the corresponding call is `clGetTextureObjectInfo()`:

```
cl_int clGetGLTextureInfo(cl_mem memobj,
                          cl_gl_texture_info param_name,
                          size_t param_value_size,
                          void *param_value,
                          size_t *param_value_size_ret)
```

This returns additional information about the GL texture object associated with a memory object.

When the function returns, the parameters *param_value* and *param_value_size_ret* will have been set by the function. *param_value_size_ret* is the size of the returned data, which is determined by the type of query requested, as set by the *param_name* parameter according to Table 10.2.

Table 10.2 Supported `param_name` Types and Information Returned

cl_gl_texture_info	Return Type	Information Returned in *param_value*
CL_GL_TEXTURE_TARGET	GLenum	The *texture_target* argument specified in clCreateGLTexture2D or clCreateGLTexture3D.
CL_GL_MIPMAP_LEVEL	GLint	The *miplevel* argument specified in clCreateGLTexture2D or clCreateGLTexture3D.

Synchronization between OpenGL and OpenCL

Thus far we have discussed the mechanics of creating and sharing an OpenGL object in OpenCL. In the preceding discussion we only briefly mentioned that when OpenGL objects are acquired and released, it is the program's responsibility to ensure that all preceding OpenCL or OpenGL commands that affect the shared object (which of OpenCL or OpenGL is dependent on whether the object is being acquired or released) have completed beforehand. glFinish() and clFinish() are two commands that can be used for this purpose. glFinish(), however, requires that all pending commands be sent to the GPU and waits for their completion, which can take a long time, and empties the pipeline of commands. In this section, we'll present a more fine-grained approach based on the sharing of event objects between OpenGL and OpenCL.

The cl_khr_gl_event OpenCL extension provides event-based synchronization and additional functionality to the clEnqueueAcquireGLObjects() and clEnqueueReleaseGLObjects() functions. The following pragma enables it:

```
#pragma OPENCL EXTENSION cl_khr_gl_event : enable
```

When enabled, this provides what is known as **implicit synchronization** whereby the clEnqueueAcquireGLObjects() and clEnqueueReleaseGLObjects() functions implicitly guarantee synchronization with an OpenGL context bound in the same thread as the OpenCL context. In this case, any OpenGL commands that affect or access the contents of a memory object listed in the mem_objects_list argument of clEnqueueAcquireGLObjects() *and* were issued on that context prior to the call to clEnqueueAcquireGLObjects() will complete before execution of any OpenCL commands following the clEnqueueAcquire-GLObjects() call.

Another option for synchronization is **explicit synchronization**. When the cl_khr_gl_event extension is supported, and the OpenGL context supports fence sync objects, the completion of OpenGL commands can be determined by using an OpenGL fence sync object by creating a OpenCL event from it, by way of the clCreateEventFromGLsyncKHR() function:

```
cl_event clCreateEventFromGLsyncKHR(cl_context context,
                                    GLsync sync,
                                    cl_int *errcode_ret)
```

An event object may be created by linking to an OpenGL sync object. Completion of such an event object is equivalent to waiting for completion of the fence command associated with the linked GL sync object.

In explicit synchronization, completion of OpenCL commands can be determined by a glFenceSync command placed after the OpenGL commands. An OpenCL thread can then use the OpenCL event associated with the OpenGL fence by passing the OpenCL event to clEnqueue-AcquireGLObjects() in its event_wait_list argument. Note that the event returned by clCreateEventFromGLsyncKHR() may be used only by clEnqueueAcquireGLObjects() and returns an error if passed to other OpenCL functions. Explicit synchronization is useful when an OpenGL thread separate from the OpenCL thread is accessing the same underlying memory object.

Thus far we have presented OpenCL functions that create objects from OpenGL objects. In OpenGL there is also a function that allows the creation of OpenGL sync objects from existing OpenCL event objects. This is enabled by the OpenGL extension ARB_cl_event. Similar to the explicit synchronization method discussed previously, this allows OpenGL to reflect the status of an OpenCL event object. Waiting on this sync object in OpenGL is equivalent to waiting on the linked OpenCL sync object. When the ARB_cl_event extension is supported by OpenGL, the glCreateSyncFromCLeventARB() function creates a GLsync linked to an OpenCL event object:

```
GLsync glCreateSyncFromCLeventARB(cl_context context,
                                  cl_event event,
                                  bitfield flags)
```

An OpenGL sync object created with this function can also be deleted with the `glDeleteSync()` function:

```
void glDeleteSync(GLsync sync)
```

Once created, this `GLsync` object is linked to the state of the OpenCL event object, and the OpenGL sync object functions, such as `glWaitSync()`, `glClientWaitSync()`, and `glFenceSync()`, can be applied. Full details on the interactions of these calls with OpenGL can be found in the OpenGL ARB specification.

The following code fragment demonstrates how this can be applied to synchronize OpenGL with an OpenCL kernel call:

```
cl_event release_event;

GLsync sync = glFenceSync(GL_SYNC_GPU_COMMANDS_COMPLETE, 0);
gl_event = clCreateEventFromGLsyncKHR(context, sync, NULL );
errNum = clEnqueueAcquireGLObjects(commandQueue, 1,
    &cl_tex_mem, 0, &gl_event, NULL );
errNum = clEnqueueNDRangeKernel(commandQueue, tex_kernel, 2, NULL,
    tex_globalWorkSize, tex_localWorkSize,
    0, NULL, 0);
errNum = clEnqueueReleaseGLObjects(commandQueue, 1,
    &cl_tex_mem, 0, NULL, &release_event);
GLsync cl_sync = glCreateSyncFromCLeventARB(context,
    release_event, 0);
glWaitSync( cl_sync, 0, GL_TIMEOUT_IGNORED );
```

This code uses fine-grained synchronization and proceeds as follows:

1. First, an OpenGL fence object is created. This creates and inserts a fence sync into the OpenGL command stream.

2. Then, `clCreateEventFromGLsyncKHR()` is called. This creates an OpenCL event linked to the fence. This OpenCL event is then used in the event list for `clEnqueueAcquireGLObjects()`, ensuring that the acquire call will proceed only after the fence has completed.

3. The OpenCL kernel is then queued for execution, followed by the `clEnqueueReleaseGLObjects()` call. The `clEnqueueRelease-GLObjects()` call returns an event, `release_event`, that can be used to sync upon its completion.

4. The `glCreateSyncFromCLeventARB()` call then creates an OpenGL sync object linked to the `release_event`.

5. A wait is then inserted into the OpenGL command stream with `glWaitSync()`, which will wait upon the completion of the `release_event` associated with `clEnqueueReleaseGLObjects()`.

Using a method like this allows synchronization between OpenGL and OpenCL without the need for `gl/clFinish()` functions.

## Chapter 11

Interoperability with Direct3D

Similarly to the discussion of sharing functions in the previous chapter, this chapter explores how to achieve interoperation between OpenCL and Direct3D 10 (known as D3D interop). D3D interop is a powerful feature that allows programs to share data between Direct3D and OpenCL. Some possible applications for D3D interop include the ability to render in D3D and postprocess with OpenCL, or to use OpenCL to compute effects for display in D3D. This chapter covers the following concepts:

- Querying the Direct3D platform for sharing capabilities

- Creating buffers from D3D memory

- Creating contexts, associating devices, and the corresponding synchronization and memory management defined by this implied environment

Direct3D/OpenCL Sharing Overview

At a high level, Direct3D interoperability operates similarly to OpenGL interop as described in the previous chapter. Buffers and textures that are allocated in a Direct3D context can be accessed in OpenCL by a few special OpenCL calls implemented in the Direct3D/OpenGL Sharing API. When D3D sharing is present, applications can use D3D buffer, texture, and renderbuffer objects as OpenCL memory objects.

Note This chapter assumes a familiarity with setup and initialization of a Direct3D application as well as basic Direct3D graphics programming. This chapter will instead focus on how D3D and OpenCL interoperate.

When using Direct3D interop, the program must first initialize the Direct3D environment using the Direct3D API. The program should create a window, find an appropriate D3D10 adapter, and get a handle to an appropriate D3D10 device and swap chain. These are handled by their respective Direct3D calls. The `CreateDXGIFactory()` call allows you to create a factory object that will enumerate the adapters on the system by way of the `EnumAdapters()` function. For a capable adapter, the adapter handle is then used to get a device and swap chain handle with the `D3D10CreateDeviceAndSwapChain()` call. This call returns an ID3D10Device handle, which is then used in subsequent calls to interop with OpenCL. At this point the program has created working Direct3D handles, which are then used by OpenCL to facilitate sharing.

Initializing an OpenCL Context for Direct3D Interoperability

OpenCL sharing is enabled by the pragma `cl_khr_d3d10_sharing`:

```
#pragma OPENCL EXTENSION cl_khr_d3d10_sharing : enable
```

When D3D sharing is enabled, a number of the OpenCL functions are extended to accept parameter types and values that deal with D3D10 sharing.

D3D interop properties can be used to create OpenCL contexts:

- `CL_CONTEXT_D3D10_DEVICE_KHR` is accepted as a property name in the properties parameter of `clCreateContext` and `clCreateContextFromType`.

Functions may query D3D-interop-specific object parameters:

- `CL_CONTEXT_D3D10_PREFER_SHARED_RESOURCES_KHR` is accepted as a value in the *param_name* parameter of `clGetContextInfo`.

- `CL_MEM_D3D10_RESOURCE_KHR` is accepted as a value in the *param_name* parameter of `clGetMemObjectInf`.

- `CL_IMAGE_D3D10_SUBRESOURCE_KHR` is accepted as a value in the *param_name* parameter of `clGetImageInfo`.

- `CL_COMMAND_ACQUIRE_D3D10_OBJECTS_KHR` and `CL_COMMAND_RELEASE_D3D10_OBJECTS_KHR` are returned in the *param_value* parameter of `clGetEventInfo` when *param_name* is `CL_EVENT_COMMAND_TYPE`.

Functions that use D3D interop may return interop-specific error codes:

- `CL_INVALID_D3D10_DEVICE_KHR` is returned by `clCreateContext` and `clCreateContextFromType` if the Direct3D 10 device specified for interoperability is not compatible with the devices against which the context is to be created.

- `CL_INVALID_D3D10_RESOURCE_KHR` is returned by `clCreateFromD3D10BufferKHR` when the resource is not a Direct3D 10 buffer object, and by `clCreateFromD3D10Texture2DKHR` and `clCreateFromD3D10Texture3DKHR` when the resource is not a Direct3D 10 texture object.

- `CL_D3D10_RESOURCE_ALREADY_ACQUIRED_KHR` is returned by `clEnqueueAcquireD3D10ObjectsKHR` when any of the `mem_objects` are currently acquired by OpenCL.

- `CL_D3D10_RESOURCE_NOT_ACQUIRED_KHR` is returned by `clEnqueueReleaseD3D10ObjectsKHR` when any of the `mem_objects` are not currently acquired by OpenCL.

OpenCL D3D10 interop functions are available from the header `cl_d3d10.h`. Note that the Khronos extensions for D3D10 are available on the Khronos Web site. On some distributions you may need to download this file. The sample code included on the book's Web site for this chapter assumes that this is found in the OpenCL include path. Additionally, as shown in the code, the extension functions may need to be initialized using the `clGetExtensionFunctionAddress()` call.

The ID3D10Device handle returned by `D3D10CreateDeviceAndSwapChain()` can be used to get an OpenCL device ID, which can later be used to create an OpenCL context.

Initializing OpenCL proceeds as usual with a few differences. The platforms can first be enumerated using the `clGetPlatformIDs` function. Because we are searching for a platform that supports Direct3D sharing, the `clGetPlatformInfo()` call is used on each of the platforms to query the extensions it supports. If `cl_khr_d3d_sharing` is present in the extensions string, then that platform can be selected for D3D sharing.

Given a `cl_platform_id` that supports D3D sharing, we can query for corresponding OpenCL device IDs on that platform using `clGetDeviceIDsFromD3D10KHR ()`:

```
cl_int clGetDeviceIDsFromD3D10KHR (cl_platform_id platform,
                        cl_d3d10_device_source_khr
                        d3d_device_source,
                        void *d3d_object,
                        cl_d3d10_device_set_khr d3d_device_set,
                        cl_uint num_entries,
                        cl_device_id *devices,
                        cl_uint *num_devices)
```

The OpenCL devices corresponding to a Direct3D 10 device and the
OpenCL devices corresponding to a DXGI adapter may be queried. The
OpenCL devices corresponding to a Direct3D 10 device will be a subset of
the OpenCL devices corresponding to the DXGI adapter against which the
Direct3D 10 device was created.

For example, the following code gets an OpenCL device ID (cdDevice)
for the chosen OpenCL platform (cpPlatform). The constant CL_D3D10_
DEVICE_KHR indicates that the D3D10 object we are sending (g_pD3D-
Device) is a D3D10 device, and we choose the preferred device for that
platform with the CL_PREFERRED_DEVICES_FOR_D3D10_KHR constant.
This will return the preferred OpenCL device associated with the platform
and D3D10 device. The code also checks for the return value and possible
errors resulting from the function.

```
errNum = clGetDeviceIDsFromD3D10KHR(
    cpPlatform,
    CL_D3D10_DEVICE_KHR,
    g_pD3DDevice,
    CL_PREFERRED_DEVICES_FOR_D3D10_KHR,
    1,
    &cdDevice,
    &num_devices);

if (errNum == CL_INVALID_PLATFORM) {
    printf("Invalid Platform: ",
            "Specified platform is not valid\n");
} else if( errNum == CL_INVALID_VALUE) {
    printf("Invalid Value: ",
            "d3d_device_source, d3d_device_set is not valid ",
            "or num_entries = 0 and devices != NULL ",
            "or num_devices == devices == NULL\n");
} else if( errNum == CL_DEVICE_NOT_FOUND) {
    printf("No OpenCL devices corresponding to the ",
            "d3d_object were found\n");
}
```

The device ID returned by this function can then be used to create a context that supports D3D sharing. When creating the OpenCL context, the `cl_context_properties` field in the `clCreateContext*()` call should include the pointer to the D3D10 device to be shared with. The following code sets up the context properties for D3D sharing and then uses them to create a context:

```
cl_context_properties contextProperties[] =
{
    CL_CONTEXT_D3D10_DEVICE_KHR,
    (cl_context_properties)g_pD3DDevice,
    CL_CONTEXT_PLATFORM,
    (cl_context_properties)*pFirstPlatformId,
    0
};
context = clCreateContextFromType(contextProperties,
    CL_DEVICE_TYPE_GPU,
    NULL, NULL, &errNum);
```

In the example code the pointer to the D3D10 device, `g_pD3DDevice`, is as returned from the `D3D10CreateDeviceAndSwapChain()` call.

Creating OpenCL Memory Objects from Direct3D Buffers and Textures

OpenCL buffer and image objects can be created from existing D3D buffer objects and textures using the `clCreateFromD3D10*KHR()` OpenCL functions. This makes D3D objects accessible in OpenCL.

An OpenCL memory object can be created from an existing D3D buffer using the `clCreateFromD3D10BufferKHR()` function:

```
cl_mem clCreateFromD3D10BufferKHR (cl_context context
                                   cl_mem_flags flags,
                                   ID3D10Buffer *resource,
                                   cl_int   *errcode_ret )
```

The size of the returned OpenCL buffer object is the same as the size of *resource*. This call will increment the internal Direct3D reference count on *resource*. The internal Direct3D reference count on *resource* will be decremented when the OpenCL reference count on the returned OpenCL memory object drops to zero.

Both buffers and textures can be shared with OpenCL. Our first example will begin with processing of a texture in OpenCL for display in D3D10, and we will see an example of processing a buffer of vertex data later in this chapter.

In D3D10, a texture can be created as follows:

```
int g_WindowWidth = 256;
int g_WindowHeight = 256;
...
ZeroMemory( &desc, sizeof(D3D10_TEXTURE2D_DESC) );
desc.Width = g_WindowWidth;
desc.Height = g_WindowHeight;
desc.MipLevels = 1;
desc.ArraySize = 1;
desc.Format = DXGI_FORMAT_R8G8B8A8_UNORM;
desc.SampleDesc.Count = 1;
desc.Usage = D3D10_USAGE_DEFAULT;
desc.BindFlags = D3D10_BIND_SHADER_RESOURCE;
if (FAILED(g_pD3DDevice->CreateTexture2D(
    &desc, NULL, &g_pTexture2D)))
return E_FAIL;
```

The format of the texture data to be shared is specified at this time and is set to DXGI_FORMAT_R8G8B8A8_UNORM in the preceding code. After this texture is created, an OpenCL image object may be created from it using clCreateFromD3D10Texture2DKHR():

```
cl_mem clCreateFromD3D10Texture2DKHR(cl_context context
                                     cl_mem_flags flags,
                                     ID3D10Texture2D *resource,
                                     uint subresource,
                                     cl_int *errcode_ret )
```

The width, height, and depth of the returned OpenCL image object are determined by the width, height, and depth of subresource *subresource* of *resource*. The channel type and order of the returned OpenCL image object are determined by the format of *resource* as shown in Direct3D 10 and corresponding OpenCL image formats for clCreateFromD3D10Texture2DKHR.

This call will increment the internal Direct3D reference count on *resource*. The internal Direct3D reference count on *resource* will be decremented when the OpenCL reference count on the returned OpenCL memory object drops to zero.

Now, to create an OpenCL texture object from the newly created D3D texture object, g_pTexture2D, clCreateFromD3D10Texture2DKHR() can be called as follows:

```
g_clTexture2D = clCreateFromD3D10Texture2DKHR(
    context,
    CL_MEM_READ_WRITE,
    g_pTexture2D,
    0,
    &errNum);
```

The flags parameter determines the usage information. It accepts the values CL_MEM_READ_ONLY, CL_MEM_WRITE_ONLY, or CL_MEM_READ_WRITE. Here the texture has been created to be both readable and writable from a kernel. The OpenCL object g_clTexture2D can now be used by OpenCL kernels to access the D3D texture object. In our simple case, the texture resource has only a single subresource, identified by passing the 0 resource ID parameter.

To create an OpenCL 3D image object from a Direct3D 10 3D texture, use the following call:

```
cl_mem clCreateFromD3D10Texture3DKHR(cl_context context
                                     cl_mem_flags flags,
                                     ID3D10Texture3D *resource,
                                     uint subresource,
                                     cl_int  *errcode_ret )
```

The width, height, and depth of the returned OpenCL 3D image object are determined by the width, height, and depth of subresource *subresource* of *resource*. The channel type and order of the returned OpenCL 3D image object are determined by the format of *resource* as shown in Table 11.1.

This call will increment the internal Direct3D reference count on *resource*. The internal Direct3D reference count on *resource* will be decremented when the OpenCL reference count on the returned OpenCL memory object drops to zero.

Note that the OpenCL kernel call to read from or write to an image (read_image*() and write_image*(), respectively) must correspond to the channel type and order of the OpenCL image. The channel type and order of the OpenCL 2D or 3D image object that is being shared is dependent upon the format of the Direct3D 10 resource that is passed into `clCreateFromD3D10Texture2DKHR`/`clCreateFromD3D10Texture3D-KHR`. Following the previous example, the `DXGI_FORMAT_R8G8B8A8_UNORM` format creates an OpenCL image with a `CL_RGBA` image format and a `CL_SNORM_INT8` channel data type. The specification contains a list of mappings from DXGI formats to OpenCL image formats (channel order and channel data type), shown in Table 11.1.

Table 11.1   Direct3D Texture Format Mappings to OpenCL Image Formats

DXGI Format	CL Image Format (Channel Order, Channel Data Type)
DXGI_FORMAT_R32G32B32A32_FLOAT	CL_RGBA, CL_FLOAT
DXGI_FORMAT_R32G32B32A32_UINT	CL_RGBA, CL_UNSIGNED_INT32
DXGI_FORMAT_R32G32B32A32_SINT	CL_RGBA, CL_SIGNED_INT32
DXGI_FORMAT_R16G16B16A16_FLOAT	CL_RGBA, CL_HALF_FLOAT
DXGI_FORMAT_R16G16B16A16_UNORM	CL_RGBA, CL_UNORM_INT16
DXGI_FORMAT_R16G16B16A16_UINT	CL_RGBA, CL_UNSIGNED_INT16
DXGI_FORMAT_R16G16B16A16_SNORM	CL_RGBA, CL_SNORM_INT16
DXGI_FORMAT_R16G16B16A16_SINT	CL_RGBA, CL_SIGNED_INT16
DXGI_FORMAT_R8G8B8A8_UNORM	CL_RGBA, CL_UNORM_INT8
DXGI_FORMAT_R8G8B8A8_UINT	CL_RGBA, CL_UNSIGNED_INT8
DXGI_FORMAT_R8G8B8A8_SNORM	CL_RGBA, CL_SNORM_INT8
DXGI_FORMAT_R8G8B8A8_SINT	CL_RGBA, CL_SIGNED_INT8
DXGI_FORMAT_R32G32_FLOAT	CL_RG, CL_FLOAT
DXGI_FORMAT_R32G32_UINT	CL_RG, CL_UNSIGNED_INT32
DXGI_FORMAT_R32G32_SINT	CL_RG, CL_SIGNED_INT32
DXGI_FORMAT_R16G16_FLOAT	CL_RG, CL_HALF_FLOAT
DXGI_FORMAT_R16G16_UNORM	CL_RG, CL_UNORM_INT16
DXGI_FORMAT_R16G16_UINT	CL_RG, CL_UNSIGNED_INT16
DXGI_FORMAT_R16G16_SNORM	CL_RG, CL_SNORM_INT16

Table 11.1 Direct3D Texture Format Mappings to OpenCL Image Formats
(*Continued*)

DXGI Format	CL Image Format (Channel Order, Channel Data Type)
DXGI_FORMAT_R16G16_SINT	CL_RG, CL_SIGNED_INT16
DXGI_FORMAT_R8G8_UNORM	CL_RG, CL_UNORM_INT8
DXGI_FORMAT_R8G8_UINT	CL_RG, CL_UNSIGNED_INT8
DXGI_FORMAT_R8G8_SNORM	CL_RG, CL_SNORM_INT8
DXGI_FORMAT_R8G8_SINT	CL_RG, CL_SIGNED_INT8
DXGI_FORMAT_R32_FLOAT	CL_R, CL_FLOAT
DXGI_FORMAT_R32_UINT	CL_R, CL_UNSIGNED_INT32
DXGI_FORMAT_R32_SINT	CL_R, CL_SIGNED_INT32
DXGI_FORMAT_R16_FLOAT	CL_R, CL_HALF_FLOAT
DXGI_FORMAT_R16_UNORM	CL_R, CL_UNORM_INT16
DXGI_FORMAT_R16_UINT	CL_R, CL_UNSIGNED_INT16
DXGI_FORMAT_R16_SNORM	CL_R, CL_SNORM_INT16
DXGI_FORMAT_R16_SINT	CL_R, CL_SIGNED_INT16
DXGI_FORMAT_R8_UNORM	CL_R, CL_UNORM_INT8
DXGI_FORMAT_R8_UINT	CL_R, CL_UNSIGNED_INT8
DXGI_FORMAT_R8_SNORM	CL_R, CL_SNORM_INT8
DXGI_FORMAT_R8_SINT	CL_R, CL_SIGNED_INT8

Acquiring and Releasing Direct3D Objects in OpenCL

Direct3D objects must be acquired before being processed in OpenCL and released before they are used by Direct3D. D3D10 objects can be acquired and released with the following function:

```
cl_int clEnqueueAcquireD3D10ObjectsKHR(
                              cl_command_queue   command_queue,
                              cl_uint   num_objects,
                              const cl_mem *mem_objects,
                              cl_uint num_events_in_wait_list,
                              const cl_event   *event_wait_list,
                              cl_event *event)
```

This acquires OpenCL memory objects that have been created from
Direct3D 10 resources.

The Direct3D 10 objects are acquired by the OpenCL context associated
with *command_queue* and can therefore be used by all command-queues
associated with the OpenCL context.

OpenCL memory objects created from Direct3D 10 resources must be
acquired before they can be used by any OpenCL commands queued
to a command-queue. If an OpenCL memory object created from a
Direct3D 10 resource is used while it is not currently acquired by OpenCL,
the call attempting to use that OpenCL memory object will return
CL_D3D10_RESOURCE_NOT_ACQUIRED_KHR.

clEnqueueAcquireD3D10ObjectsKHR() provides the synchronization
guarantee that any Direct3D 10 calls made before clEnqueueAcquire-
D3D10ObjectsKHR() is called will complete executing before *event*
reports completion and before the execution of any subsequent OpenCL
work issued in *command_queue* begins.

The similar release function is

```
cl_int clEnqueueReleaseD3D10ObjectsKHR
                      cl_command_queue command_queue,
                      cl_uint   num_objects,
                      const cl_mem *mem_objects,
                      cl_uint num_events_in_wait_list,
                      const cl_event   *event_wait_list ,
                      cl_event *event)
```

This releases OpenCL memory objects that have been created from
Direct3D 10 resources.

The Direct3D 10 objects are released by the OpenCL context associated with *command_queue*.

OpenCL memory objects created from Direct3D 10 resources that have been acquired by OpenCL must be released by OpenCL before they may be accessed by Direct3D 10. Accessing a Direct3D 10 resource while its corresponding OpenCL memory object is acquired is in error and will result in undefined behavior, including but not limited to possible OpenCL errors, data corruption, and program termination.

`clEnqueueReleaseD3D10ObjectsKHR()` provides the synchronization guarantee that any calls to Direct3D 10 made after the call to `clEnqueueReleaseD3D10ObjectsKHR()` will not start executing until after all events in *event_wait_list* are complete and all work already submitted to *command_queue* completes execution.

Note that in contrast to the OpenGL acquire function, which does not provide synchronization guarantees, the D3D10 acquire function does. Also, when acquiring and releasing textures, it is most efficient to acquire and release all textures and resources that are being shared at the same time. Additionally, when processing it is best to process all of the OpenCL kernels before switching back to Direct3D processing. By following this, all the acquire and release calls can be used to form the boundary of OpenCL and Direct3D processing.

Processing a Direct3D Texture in OpenCL

So far we have described how to obtain an OpenCL image from a D3D texture. In this section we will discuss how to process the texture's data in OpenCL and display the result in Direct3D. In the following example code we will use an OpenCL kernel to alter a texture's contents in each frame. We begin by showing a fragment of code for the rendering loop of a program:

```
void Render()
{
    // Clear the back buffer
    // to values red, green, blue, alpha
    float ClearColor[4] = { 0.0f, 0.125f, 0.1f, 1.0f };
    g_pD3DDevice->ClearRenderTargetView(
        g_pRenderTargetView, ClearColor);

    computeTexture();
    // Render the quadrilateral
```

```
D3D10_TECHNIQUE_DESC techDesc;
g_pTechnique->GetDesc( &techDesc );
for( UINT p = 0; p < techDesc.Passes; ++p )
{
    g_pTechnique->GetPassByIndex( p )->Apply( 0 );
    g_pD3DDevice->Draw( 4, 0 );
}


// Present the information rendered to the
// back buffer to the front buffer (the screen)
g_pSwapChain->Present( 0, 0 );
}
```

The code simply clears the window to a predefined color, then calls OpenCL to update the texture contents in the `computeTexture()` function. Finally, the texture is displayed on the screen. The `computeTexture()` function used in the preceding code launches an OpenCL kernel to modify the contents of the texture as shown in the next code fragment. The function acquires the D3D object, launches the kernel to modify the texture, and then releases the D3D object. The `g_clTexture2D` OpenCL image object that was created from the D3D object is passed to the kernel as a parameter. Additionally, a simple animation is created by the host maintaining a counter, `seq`, that is incremented each time this function is called and passed as a parameter to the kernel. Here is the full code for the `computeTexture()` function:

```
// Use OpenCL to compute the colors on the texture background
cl_int computeTexture()
{
    cl_int errNum;

    static cl_int seq =0;
    seq = (seq+1)%(g_WindowWidth*2);

    errNum = clSetKernelArg(tex_kernel, 0, sizeof(cl_mem),
        &g_clTexture2D);
    errNum = clSetKernelArg(tex_kernel, 1, sizeof(cl_int),
        &g_WindowWidth);
    errNum = clSetKernelArg(tex_kernel, 2, sizeof(cl_int),
        &g_WindowHeight);
    errNum = clSetKernelArg(tex_kernel, 3, sizeof(cl_int),
        &seq);
    size_t tex_globalWorkSize[2] = {
        g_WindowWidth,
        g_WindowHeight };
    size_t tex_localWorkSize[2] = { 32, 4 };
```

```
errNum = clEnqueueAcquireD3D10ObjectsKHR(commandQueue, 1,
    &g_clTexture2D, 0, NULL, NULL );

errNum = clEnqueueNDRangeKernel(commandQueue, tex_kernel, 2,
    NULL,
    tex_globalWorkSize, tex_localWorkSize,
    0, NULL, NULL);
if (errNum != CL_SUCCESS)
{
  std::cerr << "Error queuing kernel for execution." <<
  std::endl;
}
errNum = clEnqueueReleaseD3D10ObjectsKHR(commandQueue, 1,
    &g_clTexture2D, 0, NULL, NULL );
clFinish(commandQueue);
return 0;
}
```

As in the previous chapter on OpenGL interop, we will again use an OpenCL kernel to computationally generate the contents of a D3D texture object. The texture was declared with the format DXGI_FORMAT_R8G8B8A8_UNORM, which corresponds to an OpenCL texture with channel order CL_RGBA and channel data CL_UNORM_INT8. This texture can be written to using the write_imagef() function in a kernel:

```
__kernel void init_texture_kernel(__write_only image2d_t im,
    int w, int h, int seq )
{
    int2 coord = { get_global_id(0), get_global_id(1) };
    float4 color =  {
        (float)coord.x/(float)w,
        (float)coord.y/(float)h,
        (float)abs(seq-w)/(float)w,
        1.0f};
    write_imagef( im, coord, color );
}
```

Here, seq is a sequence number variable that is circularly incremented in each frame on the host and sent to the kernel. In the kernel, the seq variable is used to generate texture color values. As seq is incremented, the colors change to animate the texture.

In the full source code example included in the book reference material for this chapter, a rendering technique, g_pTechnique, is used. It is a basic processing pipeline, involving a simple vertex shader that passes vertex and texture coordinates to a pixel shader:

```
//
// Vertex Shader
//
PS_INPUT VS( VS_INPUT input )
{
    PS_INPUT output = (PS_INPUT)0;
    output.Pos = input.Pos;
    output.Tex = input.Tex;

    return output;
}
technique10 Render
{
    pass P0
    {
        SetVertexShader( CompileShader( vs_4_0, VS() ) );
        SetGeometryShader( NULL );
        SetPixelShader( CompileShader( ps_4_0, PS() ) );
    }
}
```

This technique is loaded using the usual D3D10 calls. The pixel shader then performs the texture lookup on the texture that has been modified by the OpenCL kernel and displays it:

```
SamplerState samLinear
{
    Filter = MIN_MAG_MIP_LINEAR;
    AddressU = Wrap;
    AddressV = Wrap;
};

float4 PS( PS_INPUT input) : SV_Target
{
    return txDiffuse.Sample( samLinear, input.Tex );
}
```

In this pixel shader, samLinear is a linear sampler for the input texture. For each iteration of the rendering loop, OpenCL updates the texture contents in computeTexture() and D3D10 displays the updated texture.

Processing D3D Vertex Data in OpenCL

As mentioned previously, buffers can also be shared from Direct3D. We will now consider the case where a D3D buffer holding vertex data is used to draw a sine wave on screen. We can begin by defining a simple structure for the vertex buffer in Direct3D:

```
struct SimpleSineVertex
{
    D3DXVECTOR4 Pos;
};
```

A D3D10 buffer can be created for this structure, in this case holding 256 elements:

```
bd.Usage = D3D10_USAGE_DEFAULT;
bd.ByteWidth = sizeof( SimpleSineVertex ) * 256;
bd.BindFlags = D3D10_BIND_VERTEX_BUFFER;
bd.CPUAccessFlags = 0;
bd.MiscFlags = 0;
hr = g_pD3DDevice->CreateBuffer( &bd, NULL,
    &g_pSineVertexBuffer );
```

Because we will use OpenCL to set the data in the buffer, we pass NULL as the second parameter, pInitialData, to allocate space only.

Once the D3D buffer g_pSineVertexBuffer is created, an OpenCL buffer, g_clBuffer, can be created from g_pSineVertexBuffer using the clCreateFromD3D10BufferKHR() function:

```
g_clBuffer = clCreateFromD3D10BufferKHR( context,
    CL_MEM_READ_WRITE, g_pSineVertexBuffer, &errNum );
```

As in the previous example, g_clBuffer can be sent as a kernel parameter to an OpenCL kernel that generates data. As in the texture example, the D3D object is acquired with clEnqueueAcquireD3D10ObjectsKHR() before the kernel launch and released with clEnqueueReleaseD3D10ObjectsKHR() after the kernel completes. In the sample code, the vertex positions for a sine wave are generated in a kernel:

```
__kernel void init_vbo_kernel(__global float4 *vbo,
    int w, int h, int seq)
{
    int gid = get_global_id(0);
    float4 linepts;
    float f = 1.0f;
    float a = 0.4f;
    float b = 0.0f;

    linepts.x = gid/(w/2.0f)-1.0f;
    linepts.y = b + a*sin(3.14*2.0*((float)gid/(float)w*f +
        (float)seq/(float)w));
    linepts.z = 0.5f;
    linepts.w = 0.0f;

    vbo[gid] = linepts;
}
```

Similarly to the texturing example, the variable `seq` is used as a counter to animate the sine wave on the screen.

When rendering, we set the layout and the buffer and specify a line strip. Then, `computeBuffer()` calls the preceding kernel to update the buffer. A simple rendering pipeline, set up as pass 1 in the technique, is activated, and the 256 data points are drawn:

```
// Set the input layout
g_pD3DDevice->IASetInputLayout( g_pSineVertexLayout );
// Set vertex buffer
stride = sizeof( SimpleSineVertex );
offset = 0;
g_pD3DDevice->IASetVertexBuffers( 0, 1, &g_pSineVertexBuffer,
    &stride, &offset );
// Set primitive topology
g_pD3DDevice->IASetPrimitiveTopology(
    D3D10_PRIMITIVE_TOPOLOGY_LINESTRIP );
computeBuffer();
g_pTechnique->GetPassByIndex( 1 )->Apply( 0 );
g_pD3DDevice->Draw( 256, 0 );
```

When run, the program will apply the kernel to generate the texture contents, then run the D3D pipeline to sample the texture and display it on the screen. The vertex buffer is then also drawn, resulting in a sine wave on screen. The resulting program is shown in Figure 11.1.

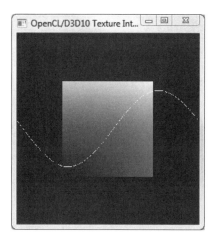

Figure 11.1   A program demonstrating OpenCL/D3D interop. The sine positions of the vertices in the sine wave and the texture color values are programmatically set by kernels in OpenCL and displayed using Direct3D.

## Chapter 12

C++ Wrapper API

Although many of the example applications described throughout this book have been developed using the programming language C++, we have focused exclusively on the OpenCL C API for controlling the OpenCL component. This chapter changes this by introducing the OpenCL C++ Wrapper API, a thin layer built on top of the OpenCL C API that is designed to reduce effort for some tasks, such as reference counting an OpenCL object, using C++.

The C++ Wrapper API was designed to be distributed in a single header file, and because it is built on top of the OpenCL C API, it can make no additional requirements on an OpenCL implementation. The interface is contained within a single C++ header, `cl.hpp`, and all definitions are contained within a single namespace, `cl`. There is no additional requirement to include `cl.h`. The specification can be downloaded from the Khronos Web site: www.khronos.org/registry/cl/specs/opencl-cplusplus-1.1.pdf.

To use the C++ Wrapper API (or just the OpenCL C API, for that matter), the application should include the line

```
#include <cl.hpp>
```

C++ Wrapper API Overview

The C++ API is divided into a number of classes that have a corresponding mapping to an OpenCL C type; for example, there is a `cl::Memory` class that maps to `cl_mem` in OpenCL C. However, when possible the C++ API uses inheritance to provide an extra level of type abstraction; for example, the class `cl::Buffer` derives from the base class `cl::Memory` and represents the 1D memory subclass of all possible OpenCL memory objects, as described in Chapter 7. The class hierarchy is shown in Figure 12.1.

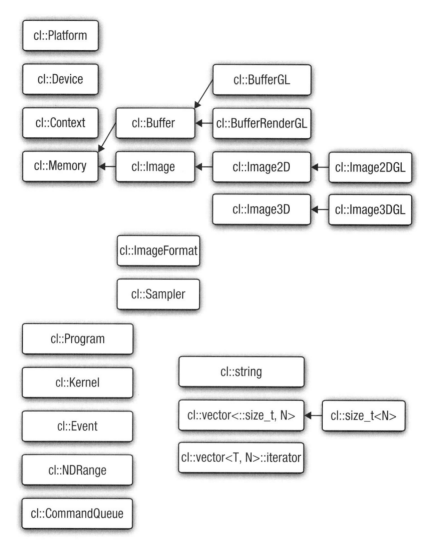

Figure 12.1   C++ Wrapper API class hierarchy

In general, there is a straightforward mapping from the C++ class type to the underlying OpenCL C type, and in these cases the underlying C type can be accessed through the operator (). For example, the following code gets the first OpenCL platform and queries the underlying OpenCL C type, `cl_platform`, assigning it to the variable `platform`:

```
std::vector<cl::Platform> platformList;
cl::Platform::get(&platformList);
cl_platform platform = platformList[0]();
```

In practice it should be possible to stay completely within the C++ Wrapper API, but sometimes an application can work only with the C API—for example, to call a third-party library—and in this case the () operator can be used. It is important to note that the C++ API will track the assignment of OpenCL objects defined via the class API and as such perform any required reference counting, but this breaks down with the application of the () operator. In this case the application must ensure that necessary calls to clRetainXX()/clReleaseXX() are peformed to guarantee the correctness of the program. This is demostrated in the following code:

```
extern void someFunction(cl_program);

cl_platform platform;
{
  std::vector<cl::Platform> platformList;
  cl::Platform::get(&platformList);
  platform = platformList[0]();

  someFunction(platform); // safe call
}

someFunction(platform); // not safe
```

The final line of this example is not safe because the vector platformList has been destroyed on exiting the basic block and thus an implicit call to clReleasePlatform for each platform in platformList happened, allowing the underlying OpenCL implementation to release any associated memory.

C++ Wrapper API Exceptions

Finally, before diving into a detailed example, we introduce OpenCL C++ exceptions. To track errors in an application that were raised because of an error in an OpenCL operation, the C API uses error values of type cl_int. These are returned as the result of an API function, or, in the case that the API function returns an OpenCL object, the error code is returned as the very last argument to the function. The C++ API supports this form of tracking errors, but it can also use C++ exceptions. By default exceptions are not enabled, and the OpenCL error code is returned, or set, according to the underlying C API.

To use exceptions they must be explicitly enabled by defining the following preprocessor macro before including `cl.hpp`:

```
__CL_ENABLE_EXCEPTIONS
```

Once enabled, an error value other than CL_SUCCESS reported by an OpenCL C call will throw the exception class `cl::Error`. By default the method `cl::Error::what()` will return a `const` pointer to a string naming the particular C API call that reported the error, for example, `clGetDeviceInfo`. It is possible to override the default behavior for `cl::Error::what()` by defining the following preprocessor macro before including `cl.hpp`:

```
__CL_USER_OVERRIDE_ERROR_STRINGS
```

You would also provide string constants for each of the preprocessor macros defined in Table 12.1.

Table 12.1   Preprocessor Error Macros and Their Defaults

Preprocessor Macro Name	Default Value
__GET_DEVICE_INFO_ERR	clGetDeviceInfo
__GET_PLATFORM_INFO_ERR	clGetPlatformInfo
__GET_DEVICE_IDS_ERR	clGetDeviceIds
__GET_CONTEXT_INFO_ERR	clGetContextInfo
__GET_EVENT_INFO_ERR	clGetEventInfo
__GET_EVENT_PROFILE_INFO_ERR	clGetEventProfileInfo
__GET_MEM_OBJECT_INFO_ERR	clGetMemObjectInfo
__GET_IMAGE_INFO_ERR	clGetImageInfo
__GET_SAMPLER_INFO_ERR	clGetSampleInfo
__GET_KERNEL_INFO_ERR	clGetKernelInfo
__GET_KERNEL_WORK_GROUP_INFO_ERR	clGetKernelWorkGroupInfo
__GET_PROGRAM_INFO_ERR	clGetProgramInfo
__GET_PROGRAM_BUILD_INFO_ERR	clGetProgramBuildInfo
__GET_COMMAND_QUEUE_INFO_ERR	clGetCommandQueueInfo
__CREATE_CONTEXT_FROM_TYPE_ERR	clCreateContextFromType

Table 12.1 Preprocessor Error Macros and Their Defaults (*Continued*)

Preprocessor Macro Name	Default Value
__GET_SUPPORTED_IMAGE_FORMATS_ERR	clGetSupportedImageFormats
__CREATE_BUFFER_ERR	clCreateBuffer
__CREATE_SUBBUFFER_ERR	clCreateSubBuffer
__CREATE_GL_BUFFER_ERR	clCreateGLBuffer
__CREATE_IMAGE2D_ERR	clCreateImage2D
__CREATE_IMAGE3D_ERR	clCreateImage3D
__SET_MEM_OBJECT_DESTRUCTOR_CALLBACK_ERR	clSetMemObjectDestructorCallback
__CREATE_USER_EVENT_ERR	clCreateUserEvent
__SET_USER_EVENT_STATUS_ERR	clSetUserEventStatus
__SET_EVENT_CALLBACK_ERR	clSetEventCallback
__WAIT_FOR_EVENTS_ERR	clWaitForEvents
__CREATE_KERNEL_ERR	clCreateKernel
__SET_KERNEL_ARGS_ERR	clSetKernelArgs
__CREATE_PROGRAM_WITH_SOURCE_ERR	clCreateProgramWithSource
__CREATE_PROGRAM_WITH_BINARY_ERR	clCreateProgramWithBinary
__BUILD_PROGRAM_ERR	clBuildProgram
__CREATE_KERNELS_IN_PROGRAM_ERR	clCreateKernelsInProgram
__CREATE_COMMAND_QUEUE_ERR	clCreateCommandQueue
__SET_COMMAND_QUEUE_PROPERTY_ERR	clSetCommandQueueProperty
__ENQUEUE_READ_BUFFER_ERR	clEnqueueReadBuffer
__ENQUEUE_READ_BUFFER_RECT_ERR	clEnqueueReadBufferRect
__ENQUEUE_WRITE_BUFFER_ERR	clEnqueueWriteBuffer
__ENQUEUE_WRITE_BUFFER_RECT_ERR	clEnqueueWriteBufferRect
__ENQEUE_COPY_BUFFER_ERR	clEnqueueCopyBuffer
__ENQEUE_COPY_BUFFER_RECT_ERR	clEnqueueCopyBufferRect

continues

Table 12.1 Preprocessor Error Macros and Their Defaults (*Continued*)

Preprocessor Macro Name	Default Value
__ENQUEUE_READ_IMAGE_ERR	clEnqueueReadImage
__ENQUEUE_WRITE_IMAGE_ERR	clEnqueueWriteImage
__ENQUEUE_COPY_IMAGE_ERR	clEnqueueCopyImage
__ENQUEUE_COPY_IMAGE_TO_BUFFER_ERR	clEnqueueCopyImageToBuffer
__ENQUEUE_COPY_BUFFER_TO_IMAGE_ERR	clEnqueueCopyBufferToImage
__ENQUEUE_MAP_BUFFER_ERR	clEnqueueMapBuffer
__ENQUEUE_MAP_IMAGE_ERR	clEnqueueMapImage
__ENQUEUE_UNMAP_MEM_OBJECT_ERR	clEnqueueUnmapMemObject
__ENQUEUE_NDRANGE_KERNEL_ERR	clEnqueueNDRangeKernel
__ENQUEUE_TASK_ERR	clEnqueueTask
__ENQUEUE_NATIVE_KERNEL	clEnqueueNativeKernel
__ENQUEUE_MARKER_ERR	clEnqueueMarker
__ENQUEUE_WAIT_FOR_EVENTS_ERR	clEnqueueWaitForEvents
__ENQUEUE_BARRIER_ERR	clEnqueueBarriers
__UNLOAD_COMPILER_ERR	clUnloadCompiler
__FLUSH_ERR	clFlush
__FINISH_ERR	clFinish

Vector Add Example Using the C++ Wrapper API

In Chapter 3, we outlined the structure of an application's OpenCL usage to look something similar to this:

1. Query which platforms are present.

2. Query the set of devices supported by each platform.

   a. Choose to select devices, using clGetDeviceInfo(), on specific capabilities.

3. Create contexts from a selection of devices (each context must be created with devices from a single platform); then with a context you can

   a. Create one or more command-queues

   b. Create programs to run on one or more associated devices

   c. Create a kernel from those programs

   d. Allocate memory buffers and images, either on the host or on the device(s)

   e. Write or copy data to and from a particular device

   f. Submit kernels (setting the appropriate arguments) to a command-queue for execution

In the remainder of this chapter we describe a simple application that uses OpenCL to add two input arrays in parallel, using the C++ Wrapper API, following this list.

Choosing an OpenCL Platform and Creating a Context

The first step in the OpenCL setup is to select a platform. As described in Chapter 2, OpenCL uses an ICD model where multiple implementations of OpenCL can coexist on a single system. As with the HelloWorld example of Chapter 2, the Vector Add program demonstrates the simplest approach to choosing an OpenCL platform: it selects the first available platform.

First `cl::Platform::get()` is invoked to retrieve the list of platforms:

```
std::vector<cl::Platform> platformList;
cl::Platform::get(&platformList);
```

After getting the list of platforms, the example then creates a context by calling `cl::Context()`. This call to `cl::Context()` attempts to create a context from a GPU device. If this attempt fails, then the program will raise an exception, as our program uses the OpenCL C++ Wrapper exception feature, and the program terminates with an error message. The code for creating the context is

```
cl_context_properties cprops[] = {
    CL_CONTEXT_PLATFORM,
    (cl_context_properties)(platformList[0])(),
    0};

cl::Context context(CL_DEVICE_TYPE_GPU, cprops);
```

Choosing a Device and Creating a Command-Queue

After choosing a platform and creating a context, the next step for the Vector Add application is to select a device and create a command-queue. The first task is to query the set of devices associated with the context previously created. This is achieved with a call to `cl::Context::get-Info<CL_CONTEXT_DEVICES>()`, which returns the `std::vector` of devices attached to the context.

Before continuing, let's examine this `getInfo()` method, as it follows a pattern used throughout the C++ Wrapper API. In general, any C++ Wrapper API object that represents a C API object supporting a query interface, for example, `clGetXXInfo()` where `XX` is the name of the C API object being queried, has a corresponding interface of the form

```
template <cl_int> typename
detail::param_traits<detail::cl_XX_info, name>::param_type
cl::Object::getInfo(void);
```

At first reading this may seem a little overwhelming because of the use of a C++ template technique called traits (used here to associate the shared functionality provided by the `clGetXXInfo()`), but because programs that use these `getInfo()` functions never need to refer to the trait components in practice, it does not have an effect on code written by the developer. It is important to note that all C++ Wrapper API objects that correspond to an underlying C API object have a template method called `getInfo()` that takes as its template argument the value of the `cl_XX_info` enumeration value being queried. This has the effect of statically checking that the requested value is valid; that is, a particular `getInfo()` method will only accept values defined in the corresponding `cl_XX_info` enumeration. By using the traits technique, the `getInfo()` function can automatically derive the result type.

Returning to the Vector Add example where we query a context for the set of associated devices, the corresponding `cl::Context::getInfo()` method can be specialized with `CL_CONTEXT_DEVICES` to return a `std::vector<cl::Device>`. This is highlighted in the following code:

```
// Query the set of devices attached to the context
std::vector<cl::Device> devices =
    context.getInfo<CL_CONTEXT_DEVICES>();
```

Note that with the C++ Wrapper API query methods there is no need to first query the context to find out how much space is required to store the list of devices and then provide another call to get the devices. This is all hidden behind a simple generic interface in the C++ Wrapper API.

After selecting the set of devices, we create a command-queue, with `cl::CommandQueue()`, selecting the first device for simplicity:

```
// Create command-queue
cl::CommandQueue queue(context, devices[0], 0);
```

Creating and Building a Program Object

The next step in the Vector Add example is to create a program object, using `cl::Program()`, from the OpenCL C kernel source. (The kernel source code for the Vector Add example is given in Listing 12.1 at the end of the chapter and is not reproduced here.) The program object is loaded with the kernel source code, and then the code is compiled for execution on the device attached to the context, using `cl::Program::build()`. The code to achieve this follows:

```
cl::Program::Sources sources(
    1,
    std::make_pair(kernelSourceCode,
    0));
cl::Program program(context, sources);

program.build(devices);
```

As with the other C++ Wrapper API calls, if an error occurs, then an exception occurs and the program exits.

Creating Kernel and Memory Objects

In order to execute the OpenCL compute kernel, the arguments to the kernel function need to be allocated in memory that is accessible on the OpenCL device, in this case buffer objects. These are created using `cl::Buffer()`. For the input buffers we use CL_MEM_COPY_FROM_HOST_PTR to avoid additional calls to move the input data. For the output buffer (i.e., the result of the vector addition) we use CL_MEM_USE_HOST_PTR, which requires the resulting buffer to be mapped into host memory to access the result. The following code allocates the buffers:

```
cl::Buffer aBuffer = cl::Buffer(
    context,
    CL_MEM_READ_ONLY | CL_MEM_COPY_HOST_PTR,
    BUFFER_SIZE * sizeof(int),
    (void *) &A[0]);

cl::Buffer bBuffer = cl::Buffer(
    context,
```

```
   CL_MEM_READ_ONLY | CL_MEM_COPY_HOST_PTR,
   BUFFER_SIZE * sizeof(int),
   (void *) &B[0]);

cl::Buffer cBuffer = cl::Buffer(
   context,
   CL_MEM_WRITE_ONLY | CL_MEM_USE_HOST_PTR,
   BUFFER_SIZE * sizeof(int),
   (void *) &C[0]);
```

The kernel object is created with a call to `cl::Kernel()`:

```
cl::Kernel kernel(program, "vadd");
```

Putting this all together, Listing 12.1 at the end of the chapter gives the complete program for Vector Add using the C++ Wrapper API.

Executing the Vector Add Kernel

Now that the kernel and memory objects have been created, the Vector Add program can finally queue up the kernel for execution. All of the arguments to the kernel function need to be set using the `cl::Kernel:setArg()` method. The first argument to this function is the index of the argument, according to `clSetKernelArg()` in the C API. The `vadd()` kernel takes three arguments (a, b, and c), which correspond to indices 0, 1, and 2. The memory objects that were created previously are passed to the kernel object:

```
kernel.setArg(0, aBuffer);
kernel.setArg(1, bBuffer);
kernel.setArg(2, cBuffer);
```

As is normal after setting the kernel arguments, the Vector Add example queues the kernel for execution on the device using the command-queue. This is done by calling `cl::CommandQueue::enqueueNDRangeKer nel()`. The global and local work sizes are passed using `cl::Range()`. For the local work size a special instance of the `cl::Range()` object is used, `cl::NullRange`, which, as is implied by the name, corresponds to passing NULL in the C API, allowing the runtime to determine the best work-group size for the device and the global work size being requested. The code is as follows:

```
queue.enqueueNDRangeKernel(
   kernel,
   cl::NullRange,
   cl::NDRange(BUFFER_SIZE),
   cl::NullRange);
```

As discussed in Chapter 9, queuing the kernel for execution does not mean that the kernel executes immediately. We could use `cl::Command-Queue::flush()` or `cl::CommandQueue::finish()` to force the execution to be submitted to the device for execution. But as the Vector Add example simply wants to display the results, it uses a blocking variant of `cl::CommandQueue::enqueueMapBuffer()` to map the output buffer to a host pointer:

```
int * output = (int *) queue.enqueueMapBuffer(
   cBuffer,
   CL_TRUE, // block
   CL_MAP_READ,
   0,
   BUFFER_SIZE * sizeof(int));
```

The host application can then process the data pointed to by `output`, and once completed, it must release the mapped memory with a call to `cl::CommandQueue::enqueueUnmapMemObj ()`:

```
err = queue.enqueueUnmapMemObject(
   cBuffer,
   (void *) output);
```

Putting this all together, Listing 12.1 gives the complete program for Vector Add.

This concludes the introduction to the OpenCL C++ Wrapper API. Chapter 18 covers AMD's Ocean simulation with OpenCL, which uses the C++ API.

Listing 12.1   Vector Add Example Program Using the C++ Wrapper API

```
// Enable OpenCL C++ exceptions
#define __CL_ENABLE_EXCEPTIONS


#if defined(__APPLE__) || defined(__MACOSX)
#include <OpenCL/cl.hpp>
#else
#include <CL/cl.hpp>
#endif

#include <cstdio>
#include <cstdlib>
#include <iostream>

#define BUFFER_SIZE 20
```

```
int A[BUFFER_SIZE];
int B[BUFFER_SIZE];
int C[BUFFER_SIZE];

static char
kernelSourceCode[] =
"__kernel void                                              \n"
"vadd(__global int * a, __global int * b, __global int * c) \n"
"{                                                          \n"
"    size_t i =  get_global_id(0);                          \n"
"                                                           \n"
"    c[i] = a[i] + b[i];                                    \n"
"}                                                          \n"
;

int
main(void)
{
    cl_int err;

    // Initialize A, B, C
    for (int i = 0; i < BUFFER_SIZE; i++) {
        A[i] = i;
        B[i] = i * 2;
        C[i] = 0;
    }

    try {
        std::vector<cl::Platform> platformList;

        // Pick platform
        cl::Platform::get(&platformList);

        // Pick first platform
        cl_context_properties cprops[] = {
            CL_CONTEXT_PLATFORM,
            (cl_context_properties)(platformList[0])(), 0};
        cl::Context context(CL_DEVICE_TYPE_GPU, cprops);

        // Query the set of devices attached to the context
        std::vector<cl::Device> devices =
            context.getInfo<CL_CONTEXT_DEVICES>();

        // Create command-queue
        cl::CommandQueue queue(context, devices[0], 0);


        // Create the program from source
        cl::Program::Sources sources(
            1,
```

```cpp
        std::make_pair(kernelSourceCode,
        0));
    cl::Program program(context, sources);

    // Build program
    program.build(devices);

    // Create buffer for A and copy host contents
    cl::Buffer aBuffer = cl::Buffer(
        context,
        CL_MEM_READ_ONLY | CL_MEM_COPY_HOST_PTR,
        BUFFER_SIZE * sizeof(int),
        (void *) &A[0]);

    // Create buffer for B and copy host contents
    cl::Buffer bBuffer = cl::Buffer(
        context,
        CL_MEM_READ_ONLY | CL_MEM_COPY_HOST_PTR,
        BUFFER_SIZE * sizeof(int),
        (void *) &B[0]);

    // Create buffer that uses the host ptr C
    cl::Buffer cBuffer = cl::Buffer(
        context,
        CL_MEM_WRITE_ONLY | CL_MEM_USE_HOST_PTR,
        BUFFER_SIZE * sizeof(int),
        (void *) &C[0]);

    // Create kernel object
    cl::Kernel kernel(program, "vadd");

    // Set kernel args
    kernel.setArg(0, aBuffer);
    kernel.setArg(1, bBuffer);
    kernel.setArg(2, cBuffer);


    // Do the work
    queue.enqueueNDRangeKernel(
        kernel,
        cl::NullRange,
        cl::NDRange(BUFFER_SIZE),
        cl::NullRange);


    // Map cBuffer to host pointer. This enforces a sync with
    // the host backing space; remember we chose a GPU device.
    int * output = (int *) queue.enqueueMapBuffer(
        cBuffer,
```

```
            CL_TRUE, // block
            CL_MAP_READ,
            0,
            BUFFER_SIZE * sizeof(int));

        for (int i = 0; i < BUFFER_SIZE; i++) {
            std::cout << C[i] << " ";
        }
        std::cout << std::endl;

        // Finally release our hold on accessing the memory
        err = queue.enqueueUnmapMemObject(
            cBuffer,
            (void *) output);

        // There is no need to perform a finish on the final unmap
        // or release any objects as this all happens implicitly
        // with the C++ Wrapper API.
    }
    catch (cl::Error err) {
        std::cerr
            << "ERROR: "
            << err.what()
            << "("
            << err.err()
            << ")"
            << std::endl;

        return EXIT_FAILURE;
    }

    return EXIT_SUCCESS;
}
```

## Chapter 13

OpenCL Embedded Profile

The OpenCL specification defines two profiles: a profile for desktop devices (the full profile) and a profile for hand-held and embedded devices (the embedded profile). Hand-held and embedded devices have significant area and power constraints that require a relaxation in the requirements defined by the full profile. The embedded profile targets a strict subset of the OpenCL 1.1 specification required for the full profile. An embedded profile that is a strict subset of the full profile has the following benefits:

- It provides a single specification for both profiles as opposed to having separate specifications.

- OpenCL programs written for the embedded profile should also run on devices that implement the full profile.

- It allows the OpenCL working group to consider requirements of both desktop and hand-held devices in defining requirements for future revisions of OpenCL.

In this chapter, we describe the embedded profile. We discuss core features that are optional for the embedded profile and the relaxation in device and floating-point precision requirements.

OpenCL Profile Overview

The profile is associated with the platform and a device(s). The platform implements the OpenCL platform and runtime APIs (described in Chapters 4 and 5 of the OpenCL 1.1 specification). The platform supports one or more devices, and each device supports a specific profile. Listing 13.1 describes how to query the profiles supported by the platform and each device supported by that platform.

Listing 13.1 Querying Platform and Device Profiles

```
void
query_profile(cl_platform_id platform)
{
    char         platform_profile[100];
    char         device_profile[100];
    int          num_devices;
    cl_device_id *devices;
    int          i;

    // query the platform profile.
    clGetPlatformInfo(platform,
                      CL_PLATFORM_PROFILE,
                      sizeof(platform_profile),
                      platform_profile,
                      NULL);
    printf("Platform profile is %s\n", platform_profile);

    // get all devices supported by platform.
    clGetDeviceIDs(platform, CL_DEVICE_TYPE_ALL,
                            0, NULL, &num_devices);
    devices = malloc(num_devices * sizeof(cl_device_id));
    clGetDeviceIDs(platform, CL_DEVICE_TYPE_ALL,
                      num_devices * sizeof(cl_device_id),
                      devices, NULL);

    // query device profile for each device supported by platform.
    for (i=0; i<num_devices; i++)
    {
        clGetDeviceInfo(devices[i],
                        CL_DEVICE_PROFILE,
                        sizeof(device_profile),
                        device_profile,
                        NULL);

        printf("Device profile for device index %d is %s\n",
                                    i, device_profile);
    }

    free(devices);
}
```

The clGetPlatformInfo and clGetDeviceInfo APIs are described in detail in Chapter 3.

The embedded profile is a strict subset of the full profile. The embedded profile has several restrictions not present in the full profile. These restrictions are discussed throughout the rest of this chapter.

64-Bit Integers

In the embedded profile 64-bit integers are optional. This means that the long, ulong scalar and long*n*, ulong*n* vector data types in an OpenCL program may not be supported by a device that implements the embedded profile. If an embedded profile implementation supports 64-bit integers, then the cles_khr_int64 extension string will be in the list of extension strings supported by the device. If this extension string is not in the list of extension strings supported by the device, using 64-bit integer data types in an OpenCL C program will result in a build failure when building the program executable for that device.

The following code shows how to query whether a device supports the cles_khr_int64 extension string. Note that this extension string is not reported by devices that implement the full profile.

```
bool
query_extension(const char *extension_name, cl_device_id device)
{
    size_t      size;
    char        *extensions;
    char        delims[] = " "; // space-separated list of names
    char        *result = NULL;
    cl_int      err;
    bool        extension_found;

    err = clGetDeviceInfo(device, CL_DEVICE_EXTENSIONS,
                                        0, NULL, &size);
    if (err)
        return false;

    extensions = malloc(size);
    clGetDeviceInfo(device, CL_DEVICE_EXTENSIONS,
                            size, extensions, NULL);

    extension_found = false;
    result = strtok( extensions, delims );
    while (result != NULL)
    {
        // extension_name is "cles_khr_int64"
        if (strcmp(result, extension_name) == 0)
```

```
        {
            extension_found = true;
            break;
        }
        result = strtok(NULL, delims);
    }

    free(extensions);
    return extension_found;
}
```

Images

Image support is optional for both profiles. To find out if a device supports images, query the CL_DEVICE_IMAGE_SUPPORT property using the clGetDeviceInfo API. If the embedded profile device supports images, then the following additional restrictions apply:

- Support for 3D images is optional. For a full profile device that supports images, reading from a 3D image in an OpenCL C program is required but writing to a 3D image in an OpenCL C program is optional. An embedded profile device may not support 3D images at all (reads and writes). To find out if the device supports 3D images (i.e., reading a 3D image in an OpenCL C program), query the CL_DEVICE_IMAGE3D_MAX_WIDTH property using the clGetDeviceInfo API. This will have a value of zero if the device does not support 3D images and a non-zero value otherwise.

  OpenCL C programs that use the image3d_t type will fail to build the program executable for an embedded profile device that does not support 3D images.

- Bilinear filtering for half-float and float images is not supported. Any 2D and 3D images with an image channel data type of CL_HALF_FLOAT or CL_FLOAT must use a sampler of CL_FILTER_NEAREST. Otherwise the results returned by read_imagef and read_imageh are undefined.

- Precision of conversion rules when converting a normalized integer channel data type value to a single-precision floating-point value is different for the embedded and full profiles. The precision of conversions from CL_UNORM_INT8, CL_UNORM_INT16, CL_UNORM_INT_101010, CL_SNORM_INT8, and CL_SNORM_INT16 to float is <= 1.5 ulp for the full profile and <= 2.0 ulp for the embedded profile. Conversion of specific values, such as $0 \rightarrow 0.0f$, $255 \rightarrow 1.0f$, -127 and $-128 \rightarrow$ $-1.0f$, $127 \rightarrow 1.0f$ are guaranteed to be the same for both profiles.

The required list of image formats (for reading and writing) that must be supported by an embedded profile device is given in Table 13.1.

Table 13.1 Required Image Formats for Embedded Profile

image_channel_order	image_channel_data_type
CL_RGBA	CL_UNORM_INT8
	CL_UNORM_INT16
	CL_SIGNED_INT8
	CL_SIGNED_INT16
	CL_SIGNED_INT32
	CL_UNSIGNED_INT8
	CL_UNSIGNED_INT16
	CL_UNSIGNED_INT32
	CL_HALF_FLOAT
	CL_FLOAT

Built-In Atomic Functions

The full profile supports built-in functions that perform atomic operations on 32-bit integers to global and local memory. These built-in functions are optional for the embedded profile. Check for the cl_khr_global_ int32_base_atomics, cl_khr_global_int32_extended_atomics, cl_khr_local_int32_base_atomics, and cl_khr_local_int32_ extended_atomics extensions in the list of extension strings reported by a device to see which functions, if any, are supported by the embedded profile device.

Mandated Minimum Single-Precision Floating-Point Capabilities

The mandated minimum single-precision floating-point capability for the full profile is CL_FP_ROUND_TO_NEAREST | CL_FP_INF_NAN. For the embedded profile, the mandated minimum capability is CL_FP_ROUND_ TO_NEAREST or CL_FP_ROUND_TO_ZERO. Support for positive or negative infinity and NaN is not required.

If CL_FP_NAN is not set, and one of the operands or the correctly rounded result of addition, subtraction, multiplication, or division is INF or NaN, the value of the result is implementation-defined. Likewise, single-precision comparison operators (<, > , <= , >= , == ,!=) return implementation-defined values when one or more operands is a NaN.

Conversions between different types (implicit and explicit) for the embedded profile are correctly rounded as described for the full profile, including those that consume or produce an INF or NaN.

Denormalized numbers for the half data type, which may be generated when converting a float to a half (for example, using vstore_half), or when converting from a half to a float (for example, using vload_half), may be flushed to zero by an embedded profile device. A full profile device, however, cannot flush these denorm values to zero.

The built-in math functions behave as described for the full profile, including edge case behavior (described in Section 7.5.1 of the OpenCL 1.1 specification). Table 13.2 describes the built-in math functions that differ in the minimum required accuracy between the full and embedded profiles.

Table 13.2 Accuracy of Math Functions for Embedded Profile versus Full Profile

Function	Minimum Accuracy— Full Profile	Minimum Accuracy— Embedded Profile
x/y	<= 2.5 ulp	<= 3.0 ulp
cbrt	<= 2 ulp	<= 4 ulp
exp	<= 3 ulp	<= 4 ulp
exp2	<= 3 ulp	<= 4 ulp
exp10	<= 3 ulp	<= 4 ulp
expm1	<= 3 ulp	<= 4 ulp
log	<= 3 ulp	<= 4 ulp
log2	<= 3 ulp	<= 4 ulp
log10	<= 3 ulp	<= 4 ulp
log1p	<= 2 ulp	<= 4 ulp
rsqrt	<= 2 ulp	<= 4 ulp
sqrt	<= 3 ulp	<= 4 ulp

This relaxation of the requirement to adhere to IEEE 754 requirements for basic floating-point operations, though extremely undesirable, is to provide flexibility for embedded and hand-held devices that have much stricter requirements on hardware area budgets.

Table 13.3 describes the differences in the mandated minimum maximum values for device properties (described in Table 4.3 of the OpenCL 1.1 specification).

Table 13.3 Device Properties: Minimum Maximum Values for Full Profile versus Embedded Profile

cl_device_info	Min. Max. Value— Full Profile	Min. Max. Value— Embedded Profile
CL_DEVICE_MAX_READ_IMAGE_ARGS	128	8
CL_DEVICE_MAX_WRITE_IMAGE_ARGS	8	1
CL_DEVICE_IMAGE2D_MAX_WIDTH	8192	2048
CL_DEVICE_IMAGE2D_MAX_HEIGHT	8192	2048
CL_DEVICE_MAX_PARAMETER_SIZE	1024	256
CL_DEVICE_SINGLE_FP_CONFIG	CL_FP_ROUND_TO_NEAREST | CL_FP_INF_NAN	CL_FP_ROUND_TO_NEAREST or CL_FP_ROUND_TO_ZERO
CL_DEVICE_LOCAL_MEM_SIZE	32 KB	1 KB
CL_DEVICE_COMPILER_AVAILABLE	CL_TRUE	CL_FALSE
CL_DEVICE_PROFILE	FULL_PROFILE	EMBEDDED_PROFILE

The minimum maximum values for device properties related to images described in Table 13.3 apply only if the device supports images.

Determining the Profile Supported by a Device in an OpenCL C Program

The embedded profile is a strict subset of the full profile. An OpenCL C program written for the embedded profile will work on any device that supports the full profile. There may be cases where the application may want to have separate code paths depending on which profile is supported by the device executing a kernel(s).

The __EMBEDDED_PROFILE__ macro is added to the OpenCL C language to determine whether a kernel is executing on an embedded profile or a full profile device. It is the integer constant 1 for devices that implement the embedded profile and is undefined otherwise.

Part II

OpenCL 1.1 Case Studies

## Chapter 14

Image Histogram

A histogram is a statistic that shows the frequency of a certain occurrence within a data set. The histogram of an image provides a frequency distribution of pixel values in the image. If the image is a color image, the pixel value can be the luminosity value of each pixel or the individual R, G, and B color channels. We have either a single histogram if the luminosity is used as the pixel value or three individual histograms, one for each channel, if the R, G, and B color channel values are used. Both types of histograms are useful; the luminosity histogram is more accurate at describing the perceived brightness distribution in an image, whereas the R, G, B color histogram can be a better choice in determining if individual colors are clipped.

In this chapter, we look at how to implement a histogram for color images with OpenCL.

Computing an Image Histogram

We look at how to compute the histogram for R, G, and B channel values of a color image. For an RGB or RGBA image with 8 bits per channel, the R, G, and B color channels can have values from 0 to 255.

Listing 14.1 shows how to compute the histogram of R, G, and B channels of an image. This code implements a sequential algorithm; that is, the algorithm loops through the pixels of the image serially to generate the histogram results.

Listing 14.1   Sequential Implementation of RGB Histogram

```
// This function computes the histogram for R, G, and B.
//
// image_data is a pointer to an RGBA image with 8 bits per channel
// w is the width of the image in pixels
```

```
// h is the height of the image in pixels
//
// The histogram is an array of 256 bins for R, G, and B.
// Each bin entry is a 32-bit unsigned integer value.
//

unsigned int *
histogram_rgba_unorm8(void *image_data, int w, int h)
{
    unsigned char *img = (unsigned char *)image_data;
    unsigned int *ref_histogram_results;
    unsigned int *ptr;
    int i;

    // clear the histogram results buffer to zeros.
    //
    // the histogram buffer stores the histogram values for R
    // followed by the histogram values for G and then B.
    // Since there are 256 bins for an 8-bit color channel,
    // the histogram buffer is 256 * 3 entries in size.
    // Each entry is a 32-bit unsigned integer value.
    //
    ref_histogram_results = (unsigned int *)malloc(256 * 3 *
                                      sizeof(unsigned int));
    ptr = ref_histogram_results;
    memset(ref_histogram_results, 0x0, 256 * 3 *
                                      sizeof(unsigned int));

    // compute histogram for R
    for (i=0; i<w*h*4; i+=4)
    {
        int indx = img[i];
        ptr[indx]++;
    }

    ptr += 256;
    // compute histogram for G
    for (i=1; i<w*h*4; i+=4)
    {
        int indx = img[i];
        ptr[indx]++;
    }

    ptr += 256;
    // compute histogram for B
    for (i=2; i<w*h*4; i+=4)
    {
```

```
        int indx = img[i];
        ptr[indx]++;
    }

    return ref_histogram_results;
}
```

Parallelizing the Image Histogram

Let us now look at how to write a parallel implementation of the histogram algorithm. An obvious approach to parallelizing the histogram computation is to break the image into tiles, compute the histogram for each tile, and then combine the partial histograms computed for each tile into the final histogram of the image. Listing 14.2 describes the OpenCL kernels that compute the partial histogram for a tile. The partial histogram computed per tile is stored in local memory for performance reasons. The kernel uses the built-in atomic functions as described by the OpenCL 1.1 specification to update the per-tile histogram values. This kernel requires either an OpenCL 1.1 device or an OpenCL 1.0 device that implements the cl_khr_local_int32_base_atomics extension.

Listing 14.2   A Parallel Version of the RGB Histogram—Compute Partial Histograms

```
//******************************************************************
// This kernel takes an RGBA 8-bit-per-channel input image and
// produces a partial histogram for R, G, and B. Each work-group
// represents an image tile and computes the histogram for that
// tile.
//
// partial_histogram is an array of num_groups * (256 * 3) entries.
// Each entry is a 32-bit unsigned integer value.
//
// We store 256 R bins, followed by 256 G bins, and then the 256
// B bins.
//******************************************************************

kernel void
histogram_partial_image_rgba_unorm8(image2d_t img,
                                     global uint *histogram)
{
```

```
int     local_size = (int)get_local_size(0) *
                         (int)get_local_size(1);
int     image_width = get_image_width(img);
int     image_height = get_image_height(img);
int     group_indx = (get_group_id(1) * get_num_groups(0)
                         + get_group_id(0)) * 256 * 3;
int     x = get_global_id(0);
int     y = get_global_id(1);

local uint  tmp_histogram[256 * 3];

int     tid = get_local_id(1) * get_local_size(0)
                         + get_local_id(0));
int     j = 256 * 3;
int     indx = 0;


// clear the local buffer that will generate the partial
// histogram
do
{
    if (tid < j)
        tmp_histogram[indx+tid] = 0;

    j -= local_size;
    indx += local_size;
} while (j > 0);

barrier(CLK_LOCAL_MEM_FENCE);

if ((x < image_width) && (y < image_height))
{
    float4 clr = read_imagef(img,
                    CLK_NORMALIZED_COORDS_FALSE |
                    CLK_ADDRESS_CLAMP_TO_EDGE |
                    CLK_FILTER_NEAREST,
                    (float2)(x, y));

    uchar   indx_x, indx_y, indx_z;
    indx_x = convert_uchar_sat(clr.x * 255.0f);
    indx_y = convert_uchar_sat(clr.y * 255.0f);
    indx_z = convert_uchar_sat(clr.z * 255.0f);
    atomic_inc(&tmp_histogram[indx_x]);
    atomic_inc(&tmp_histogram[256+(uint)indx_y]);
    atomic_inc(&tmp_histogram[512+(uint)indx_z]);
}

barrier(CLK_LOCAL_MEM_FENCE);
```

```
    // copy the partial histogram to appropriate location in
    // histogram given by group_indx
    if (local_size >= (256 * 3))
    {
        if (tid < (256 * 3))
            histogram[group_indx + tid] = tmp_histogram[tid];
    }
    else
    {
        j = 256 * 3;
        indx = 0;
        do
        {
            if (tid < j)
                histogram[group_indx + indx + tid] =
                                    tmp_histogram[indx + tid];

            j -= local_size;
            indx += local_size;
        } while (j > 0);
    }
}
```

histogram_partial_image_rgba_unorm8 produces num_groups partial histograms. We now need to sum these partial histograms to generate the final histogram for the image. Listing 14.3 describes the OpenCL
kernel that is used to sum the partial histogram results into the final
histogram of the image.

Listing 14.3   A Parallel Version of the RGB Histogram—Sum Partial Histograms

```
//******************************************************************
// This kernel sums partial histogram results into a final
// histogram result.
//
// num_groups is the number of work-groups used to compute partial
// histograms.
//
// partial_histogram is an array of num_groups * (256 * 3) entries.
// we store 256 R bins, followed by 256 G bins, and then the 256 B
// bins.
//
// The final summed results are returned in histogram.
//******************************************************************
```

```
kernel void
histogram_sum_partial_results_unorm8(
                           global uint *partial_histogram,
                           int num_groups,
                           global uint *histogram)
{
    int     tid = (int)get_global_id(0);
    int     group_indx;
    int     n = num_groups;
    local uint  tmp_histogram[256 * 3];

    tmp_histogram[tid] = partial_histogram[tid];

    group_indx = 256*3;
    while (--n > 0)
    {
        tmp_histogram[tid] += partial_histogram[group_indx + tid];
        group_indx += 256*3;
    }

    histogram[tid] = tmp_histogram[tid];
}
```

The host side code that describes the OpenCL API calls used to enqueue
the two kernels in Listings 14.2 and 14.3 is provided in Listing 14.4.

Listing 14.4   Host Code of CL API Calls to Enqueue Histogram Kernels

```
int       image_width = 1920;
int       image_height = 1080;
size_t    global_work_size[2];
size_t    local_work_size[2];
size_t    partial_global_work_size[2];
size_t    partial_local_work_size[2];
size_t    workgroup_size;
size_t    num_groups;
cl_kernel histogram_rgba_unorm8;
cl_kernel histogram_sum_partial_results_unorm8;
size_t    gsize[2];

// create kernels
histogram_rgba_unorm8 = clCreateKernel(program,
                              "histogram_image_rgba_unorm8",
                              &err);
histogram_sum_partial_results_unorm8 = clCreateKernel(program,
                           "histogram_sum_partial_results_unorm8",
                           &err);
```

```
// get max. work-group size that can be used for
// histogram_image_rgba_unorm8 kernel
clGetKernelWorkGroupInfo(histogram_rgba_unorm8, device,
                         CL_KERNEL_WORK_GROUP_SIZE,
                         sizeof(size_t), &workgroup_size, NULL);

if (workgroup_size <= 256)
{
    gsize[0] = 16;
    gsize[1] = workgroup_size / 16;
}
else if (workgroup_size <= 1024)
{
    gsize[0] = workgroup_size / 16;
    gsize[1] = 16;
}
else
{
    gsize[0] = workgroup_size / 32;
    gsize[1] = 32;
}

local_work_size[0] = gsize[0];
local_work_size[1] = gsize[1];

global_work_size[0] = ((image_width + gsize[0] - 1) / gsize[0]);
global_work_size[1] = ((image_height + gsize[1] - 1) / gsize[1]);

num_groups = global_work_size[0] * global_work_size[1];
global_work_size[0] *= gsize[0];
global_work_size[1] *= gsize[1];

err = clEnqueueNDRangeKernel(queue,
                      histogram_rgba_unorm8,
                      2, NULL, global_work_size, local_work_size,
                      0, NULL, NULL);

// get max. work-group size that can be used for
// histogram_sum_partial_results_unorm8 kernel
clGetKernelWorkGroupInfo(histogram_sum_partial_results_unorm8,
                      device, CL_KERNEL_WORK_GROUP_SIZE,
                      sizeof(size_t), &workgroup_size, NULL);

if (workgroup_size < 256)
{
    printf("A min. of 256 work-items in work-group is needed for
            histogram_sum_partial_results_unorm8 kernel. (%d)\n",
          (int)workgroup_size);
    return EXIT_FAILURE;
}
```

```
partial_global_work_size[0] = 256*3;
partial_local_work_size[0] =
        (workgroup_size > 256) ? 256 : workgroup_size;
err = clEnqueueNDRangeKernel(queue,
            histogram_sum_partial_results_unorm8,
            1, NULL, partial_global_work_size,
            partial_local_work_size,0, NULL, NULL);
if (err)
{
    printf("clEnqueueNDRangeKernel() failed for
            histogram_sum_partial_results_unorm8 kernel.
            (%d)\n", err);
    return EXIT_FAILURE;
}
```

Additional Optimizations to the Parallel Image Histogram

Let's see if additional optimizations are possible with the kernels. One thing we notice is that the `histogram_sum_partial_results_unorm8` kernel is bound by memory operations. GPUs hide memory latency by switching to other work-items or work-groups to perform compute operations. In this case, there is not much compute as the total number of work-items (i.e., `global_work_size`) specified to `clEnqueueNDRangeKernel` is (256*3, 1, 1), so it may be hard to hide memory latency. One thing we can do is reduce the amount of data we have to fetch from memory to sum partial histograms.

We can do this by reducing the number of partial histograms and performing more work per work-item in the `histogram_partial_image_rgba_unorm8` kernel. It turns out that reducing the number of partial histograms makes the overall histogram computation significantly faster. This optimized version of `histogram_partial_results_rgba_unorm8` is described in Listing 14.5.

Listing 14.5   A Parallel Version of the RGB Histogram—Optimized Version

```
//
// This kernel takes an RGBA 8-bit-per-channel input image and
// produces a partial histogram for R, G, and B. Each work-group
// represents an image tile and computes the histogram for that
// tile.
//
```

```
// num_pixels_per_workitem is the number of pixels for which the
// histogram is computed by each work-item. In the implementation
// described in Listing 14.3, num_pixels_per_workitem = 1.
//
// partial_histogram is an array of
//         num_groups * (256 * 3) entries.
// Each entry is a 32-bit unsigned integer value.
//    num_groups is affected by value of num_pixels_per_workitem.
//
// We store 256 R bins, followed by 256 G bins, and then the 256
// B bins.
//

kernel void
histogram_partial_rgba_unorm8(image2d_t img,
                              int num_pixels_per_workitem,
                              global uint *partial_histogram)
{
    int local_size = (int)get_local_size(0) *
                     (int)get_local_size(1);
    int image_width = get_image_width(img);
    int image_height = get_image_height(img);
    int group_indx = (get_group_id(1) * get_num_groups(0) +
                             get_group_id(0)) * 256 * 3;
    int x = get_global_id(0);
    int y = get_global_id(1);

    local uint  tmp_histogram[256 * 3];

    int tid = get_local_id(1) * get_local_size(0) + get_local_id(0);
    int j = 256 * 3;
    int indx = 0;

    // clear the local buffer that will generate the partial
    // histogram
    do
    {
        if (tid < j)
            tmp_histogram[indx+tid] = 0;

        j -= local_size;
        indx += local_size;
    } while (j > 0);

    barrier(CLK_LOCAL_MEM_FENCE);

    int i, idx;
    for (i=0, idx=x; i<num_pixels_per_workitem;
                    i++, idx+=get_global_size(0))
```

```
{
    if ((idx < image_width) && (y < image_height))
    {
        float4 clr = read_imagef(img,
                                 (CLK_NORMALIZED_COORDS_FALSE |
                                  CLK_ADDRESS_CLAMP_TO_EDGE |
                                  CLK_FILTER_NEAREST),
                                 (float2)(idx, y));

        uchar indx_x = convert_uchar_sat(clr.x * 255.0f);
        uchar indx_y = convert_uchar_sat(clr.y * 255.0f);
        uchar indx_z = convert_uchar_sat(clr.z * 255.0f);
        atomic_inc(&tmp_histogram[indx_x]);
        atomic_inc(&tmp_histogram[256+(uint)indx_y]);
        atomic_inc(&tmp_histogram[512+(uint)indx_z]);
    }
}

barrier(CLK_LOCAL_MEM_FENCE);

// copy the partial histogram to appropriate location in
// histogram given by group_indx
if (local_size >= (256 * 3))
{
    if (tid < (256 * 3))
        partial_histogram[group_indx + tid] =
                                tmp_histogram[tid];
}
else
{
    j = 256 * 3;
    indx = 0;
    do
    {
        if (tid < j)
            partial_histogram[group_indx + indx + tid] =
                                tmp_histogram[indx + tid];

        j -= local_size;
        indx += local_size;
    } while (j > 0);
}
}
```

The `histogram_sum_partial_results_unorm8` kernel requires no changes and is as described in Listing 14.3.

Computing Histograms with Half-Float or Float Values for Each Channel

Listing 14.6 describes how to compute the histogram for an RGBA image with a half-float or float channel. The major difference between computing a histogram for an image with 8 bits per channel versus a half-float or float channel is that the number of bins for a half-float or float channel is 257 instead of 256. This is because floating-point pixel values go from 0.0 to 1.0 inclusive.

Listing 14.6   A Parallel Version of the RGB Histogram for Half-Float and Float Channels

```
//********************************************************************
// This kernel takes an RGBA 32-bit or 16-bit FP-per-channel input
// image and produces a partial histogram for R, G, and B. Each
// work-group represents an image tile and computes the histogram for
// that tile.
//
// partial_histogram is an array of num_groups * (257 * 3) entries.
// Each entry is a 32-bit unsigned integer value.
//
// We store 257 R bins, followed by 257 G bins, and then the 257 B
// bins.
//
//********************************************************************

kernel void
histogram_image_rgba_fp(image2d_t img,
                        int num_pixels_per_workitem,
                        global uint *histogram)
{
    int     local_size = (int)get_local_size(0) *
                             (int)get_local_size(1);
    int     image_width = get_image_width(img);
    int     image_height = get_image_height(img);
    int     group_indx = (get_group_id(1) * get_num_groups(0)
                             + get_group_id(0)) * 257 * 3;
    int     x = get_global_id(0);
    int     y = get_global_id(1);

    local uint  tmp_histogram[257 * 3];

    int     tid = get_local_id(1) * get_local_size(0)
                             + get_local_id(0);
```

```
int     j = 257 * 3;
int     indx = 0;

// clear the local buffer that will generate the partial
// histogram
do
{
    if (tid < j)
        tmp_histogram[indx+tid] = 0;

    j -= local_size;
    indx += local_size;
} while (j > 0);

barrier(CLK_LOCAL_MEM_FENCE);



int     i, idx;
for (i=0, idx=x; i<num_pixels_per_workitem;
                i++, idx+=get_global_size(0))
{
    if ((idx < image_width) && (y < image_height))
    {
        float4 clr = read_imagef(img,
                        CLK_NORMALIZED_COORDS_FALSE |
                        CLK_ADDRESS_CLAMP_TO_EDGE |
                        CLK_FILTER_NEAREST,
                        (float2)(idx, y));

        ushort  indx;
        indx = convert_ushort_sat(min(clr.x, 1.0f) * 256.0f);
        atomic_inc(&tmp_histogram[indx]);

        indx = convert_ushort_sat(min(clr.y, 1.0f) * 256.0f);
        atomic_inc(&tmp_histogram[257+indx]);

        indx = convert_ushort_sat(min(clr.z, 1.0f) * 256.0f);
        atomic_inc(&tmp_histogram[514+indx]);
    }
}

barrier(CLK_LOCAL_MEM_FENCE);

// copy the partial histogram to appropriate location in
// histogram given by group_indx
if (local_size >= (257 * 3))
{
    if (tid < (257 * 3))
```

```
                histogram[group_indx + tid] = tmp_histogram[tid];
    }
    else
    {
        j = 257 * 3;
        indx = 0;
        do
        {
            if (tid < j)
                histogram[group_indx + indx + tid] =
                            tmp_histogram[indx + tid];

            j -= local_size;
            indx += local_size;
        } while (j > 0);
    }
}


//******************************************************************
// This kernel sums partial histogram results into a final histogram
// result.
//
// num_groups is the number of work-groups used to compute partial
// histograms.
//
// partial_histogram is an array of num_groups * (257 * 3) entries.
// we store 257 R bins, followed by 257 G bins, and then the 257 B
// bins.
//
// The final summed results are returned in histogram.
//******************************************************************

kernel void
histogram_sum_partial_results_fp(global uint *partial_histogram,
                                 int num_groups,
                                 global uint *histogram)
{
    int     tid = (int)get_global_id(0);
    int     group_id = (int)get_group_id(0);
    int     group_indx;
    int     n = num_groups;
    uint    tmp_histogram, tmp_histogram_first;

    int     first_workitem_not_in_first_group =
                ((get_local_id(0) == 0) && group_id);

    tid += group_id;
    int     tid_first = tid - 1;
    if (first_workitem_not_in_first_group)
```

```
            tmp_histogram_first = partial_histogram[tid_first];

    tmp_histogram = partial_histogram[tid];

    group_indx = 257*3;
    while (--n > 0)
    {
        if (first_workitem_not_in_first_group)
            tmp_histogram_first += partial_histogram[tid_first];

        tmp_histogram += partial_histogram[group_indx+tid];
        group_indx += 257*3;
    }

    if (first_workitem_not_in_first_group)
        histogram[tid_first] = tmp_histogram_first;

    histogram[tid] = tmp_histogram;
}
```

The full source (kernels and host source code) for the histogram is provided in the `Chapter_14/histogram` directory of the book's source code
examples.

## Chapter 15

Sobel Edge Detection Filter

In this chapter, we use an OpenCL kernel to implement the Sobel edge detection filter as a simple example of how kernels work with images in OpenCL.

What Is a Sobel Edge Detection Filter?

The Sobel edge filter is a directional edge detector filter because it computes the image gradients along the x- and y-axes. These image gradients along the x- and y-axes (described as G_x and G_y) are computed by convolving the source image with the following convolution kernels:

$$G_x = \begin{bmatrix} -1 & 0 & +1 \\ -2 & 0 & +2 \\ -1 & 0 & +1 \end{bmatrix}$$

$$G_y = \begin{bmatrix} -1 & -2 & -1 \\ 0 & 0 & 0 \\ +1 & +2 & +1 \end{bmatrix}$$

The gradient magnitude is computed as

$$G = sqrt(G_x{}^2 + G_y{}^2).$$

Implementing the Sobel Filter as an OpenCL Kernel

Listing 15.1 describes the OpenCL Sobel kernel. We use images because we can write a single kernel that can support different source image formats.

In addition, images benefit from the presence of a texture cache and dedicated texture addressing hardware on GPUs.

Listing 15.1   An OpenCL Sobel Filter

```
//***************************************************************
//
// The operator uses two 3 x 3 kernels which are convolved with the
// original image to compute derivatives, one for horizontal changes
// & another for vertical.
//
// Gx, the horizontal derivative, is computed using the following
// 3 x 3 kernel:
//
//          [  -1    0    +1 ]
//   Gx =   [  -2    0    +2 ]
//          [  -1    0    +1 ]
//
// Gy, the vertical derivative, is computed using the following
// 3 x 3 kernel:
//
//          [  -1   -2    -1 ]
//   Gy =   [   0    0     0 ]
//          [  +1   +2    +1 ]
//
//
//***************************************************************

const sampler_t sampler = CLK_ADDRESS_CLAMP_TO_EDGE |
                          CLK_FILTER_NEAREST;

kernel void
sobel_rgb(read_only image2d_t src, write_only image2d_t dst)
{
    int x = (int)get_global_id(0);
    int y = (int)get_global_id(1);

    if (x >= get_image_width(src) || y >= get_image_height(src))
        return;

    float4 p00 = read_imagef(src, sampler, (int2)(x - 1, y - 1));
    float4 p10 = read_imagef(src, sampler, (int2)(x,     y - 1));
    float4 p20 = read_imagef(src, sampler, (int2)(x + 1, y - 1));

    float4 p01 = read_imagef(src, sampler, (int2)(x - 1, y));
    float4 p21 = read_imagef(src, sampler, (int2)(x + 1, y));

    float4 p02 = read_imagef(src, sampler, (int2)(x - 1, y + 1));
    float4 p12 = read_imagef(src, sampler, (int2)(x,     y + 1));
```

```
    float4 p22 = read_imagef(src, sampler, (int2)(x + 1, y + 1));

    float3 gx = -p00.xyz + p20.xyz +
                2.0f * (p21.xyz - p01.xyz)
                -p02.xyz + p22.xyz;

    float3 gy = -p00.xyz - p20.xyz +
                2.0f * (p12.xyz - p10.xyz) +
                p02.xyz + p22.xyz;

    float3  g = native_sqrt(gx * gx + gy * gy);

    // we could also approximate this as g = fabs(gx) + fabs(gy)
    write_imagef(dst, (int2)(x, y), (float4)(g.x, g.y, g.z, 1.0f));
}
```

Figure 15.1 shows the input image passed to the Sobel filter on the left and the result of the OpenCL Sobel filter applied to this image on the right.

Figure 15.1   OpenCL Sobel kernel: input image and output image after applying the Sobel filter

The Sobel OpenCL kernel in Listing 15.1 produces an RGB image. We can also apply the Sobel filter and produce a grayscale image. Listing 15.2 describes the Sobel OpenCL kernel that produces a grayscale image.

Listing 15.2   An OpenCL Sobel Filter Producing a Grayscale Image

```
const sampler_t sampler = CLK_ADDRESS_CLAMP_TO_EDGE |
                          CLK_FILTER_NEAREST;

kernel void
sobel_grayscale(read_only image2d_t src, write_only image2d_t dst)
{
    int x = (int)get_global_id(0);
    int y = (int)get_global_id(1);

    if (x >= get_image_width(src) || y >= get_image_height(src))
        return;

    float4 p00 = read_imagef(src, sampler, (int2)(x - 1, y - 1));
    float4 p10 = read_imagef(src, sampler, (int2)(x,     y - 1));
    float4 p20 = read_imagef(src, sampler, (int2)(x + 1, y - 1));

    float4 p01 = read_imagef(src, sampler, (int2)(x - 1, y));
    float4 p21 = read_imagef(src, sampler, (int2)(x + 1, y));

    float4 p02 = read_imagef(src, sampler, (int2)(x - 1, y + 1));
    float4 p12 = read_imagef(src, sampler, (int2)(x,     y + 1));
    float4 p22 = read_imagef(src, sampler, (int2)(x + 1, y + 1));

    float3 gx = -p00.xyz + p20.xyz +
                 2.0f * (p21.xyz - p01.xyz)
                -p02.xyz + p22.xyz;

    float3 gy = -p00.xyz - p20.xyz +
                 2.0f * (p12.xyz - p10.xyz) +
                 p02.xyz + p22.xyz;

    float gs_x = 0.3333f * (gx.x + gx.y + gx.z);
    float gs_y = 0.3333f * (gy.x + gy.y + gy.z);

    float g = native_sqrt(gs_x * gs_x + gs_y * gs_y);
    write_imagef(dst, (int2)(x, y), (float4)(g, g, g, 1.0f));
}
```

## Chapter 16

Parallelizing Dijkstra's Single-Source Shortest-Path Graph Algorithm

By Dan Ginsburg, P. Ellen Grant, and Rudolph Pienaar

FreeSurfer is a neuroimaging tool developed by the Martinos Center for Biomedical Imaging at Massachusetts General Hospital. The tool is capable of creating triangular-mesh structural reconstructions of the cortical surface of the brain from MRI images. As part of a research study into the curvature of the cortical surface of the human brain, a set of curvature measures was stored at each edge of this mesh.[1] In order to assess the quality of the curvature measures and understand the underlying curvature of the brain surface, it was necessary to search along the mesh to find the shortest curvature values from various starting points on the brain to all other vertices along the rest of the surface. The performance of the existing Dijkstra's algorithm on the CPU was proving too slow and making it difficult to study this curvature across many subjects and curvature measurement types. As a consequence, we created an OpenCL-based parallel implementation of Dijkstra's algorithm.

This chapter presents this implementation of Dijkstra's algorithm using OpenCL, which can leverage any of the available compute hardware on the host based on the algorithm in "Accelerating Large Graph Algorithms on the GPU Using CUDA" by Pawan Harish and P. J. Narayanan.[2] It covers how to map the graph into data structures that can be easily accessed by parallel hardware and describes the implementation of the kernels that compute Dijkstra's algorithm in parallel. Finally, it covers the details of

---

[1] R. Pienaar, B. Fischl, V. Caviness, N. Makris, and P. E. Grant, "Methodology for Analyzing Curvature in the Developing Brain from Preterm to Adult," *International Journal of Imaging Systems and Technology* 18, no. 1 (June 1, 2008): 42–68. PMID: 19936261. PMCID: PMC2779548.

[2] Pawan Harish and P. J. Narayanan, "Accelerating Large Graph Algorithms on the GPU Using CUDA," *IEEE High Performance Computing* (2007).

how to partition the workload to run on multiple compute devices. Our implementation of Dijkstra's algorithm is provided in the `Chapter_16/Dijkstra` directory of the book's source code examples.

Graph Data Structures

The first step in getting Dijkstra's algorithm onto the GPU is to create a graph data structure that is efficiently accessible by the GPU. The graph is composed of vertices and edges that connect vertices together. Each edge has a weight value associated with it that typically measures some cost in traveling across that edge. In our case, the edge weights were determined by the curvature function as we were interested in minimizing curvature values in traveling across the mesh. In a mapping application, the edge weights would usually be the physical distance between nodes. The data structures used in our implementation are the same as those described in "Accelerating Large Graph Algorithms on the GPU Using CUDA." The graph is represented as a collection of arrays:

- `int *vertexArray`: Each entry contains an index into the first element of `edgeArray` to be used as an edge for that vertex. The edges are stored sequentially in the edge array, and the number of edges for `vertexArray[N]` is the sequence of vertices up to the index stored in `vertexArray[N+1]` (or the size of `edgeArray` if `N` is the last element of `vertexArray`).

- `int *edgeArray`: Each element is an index to the vertex that is connected by edge to the current vertex. Note that edges are assumed to be one-directional from the source to the destination vertex. For edges that are bidirectional, an entry must be placed in the table for each direction.

- `int *weightArray`: For each edge in `edgeArray`, this array stores the weight value of the edge. There is one weight value for each edge.

These three arrays form the totality of graph data that an application needs to set up in order to run Dijkstra's algorithm using our implementation. The implementation itself requires three more arrays that are used by the kernels during the computation:

- `int *maskArray`: This array stores a value of `0` or `1` for each vertex, which determines whether the algorithm needs to continue processing for that node. The reason integer type was chosen over a byte representation is that certain implementations of OpenCL do not support accessing byte-aligned arrays.

- `float *updatingCostArray`: This is a buffer used during the algorithm to store the current cost computed to the vertex.

- `float *costArray`: This stores the final computed minimum cost for each vertex.

The only other piece of information the algorithm needs is which source vertices to run the algorithm for and a host-allocated array to store the results. Each execution of Dijkstra will output an array the size of the number of vertices in the graph with the total cost of the shortest distance from the source vertex to each vertex in the graph. An example of the C structure and function used to execute Dijkstra's algorithm using OpenCL on a single GPU is provided in Listing 16.1.

Listing 16.1 Data Structure and Interface for Dijkstra's Algorithm

```
typedef struct
{
    // (V) This contains a pointer to the edge list for each vertex
    int *vertexArray;

    // Vertex count
    int vertexCount;

    // (E) This contains pointers to the vertices that each edge
    // is attached to
    int *edgeArray;

    // Edge count
    int edgeCount;

    // (W) Weight array
    float *weightArray;
} GraphData;

/// Run Dijkstra's shortest path on the GraphData provided to this
/// function. This function will compute the shortest-path distance
/// from sourceVertices[n] -> endVertices[n] and store the cost in
/// outResultCosts[n]. The number of results it will compute is
/// given by numResults.
///
/// This function will run the algorithm on a single GPU.
///
/// \param gpuContext Current GPU context, must be created by
///                   caller
/// \param deviceId The device ID on which to run the kernel.
///                 This can be determined externally by the
///                 caller or the multi-GPU version will
```

```
///                   automatically split the work across
///                   devices
/// \param graph Structure containing the vertex, edge, and
///               weight array for the input graph
/// \param startVertices Indices into the vertex array from
///                   which to start the search
/// \param outResultsCosts A pre-allocated array where the
///                   results for each shortest-path
///                   search will be written.  This
///                   must be sized numResults *
///                   graph->numVertices.
/// \param numResults Should be the size of all three passed
///               in arrays
void runDijkstra( cl_context gpuContext, cl_device_id deviceId,
                  GraphData* graph,
                  int *sourceVertices, float *outResultCosts,
                  int numResults );
```

Kernels

The high-level loop that executes the algorithm using OpenCL is provided in pseudo code in Listing 16.2.

Listing 16.2   Pseudo Code for High-Level Loop That Executes Dijkstra's Algorithm

```
foreach sourceVertex to search from

    // Initialize all of maskArray[] to 0
    // Initialize all of costArray[] to MAX
    // Initialize all of updatingCostArray[] to MAX
    // Initialize maskArray[sourceVertex] to 1
    // Initialize costArray[sourceVertex],
    //   updatingCostArray[sourceVertex] to 0
    initializeMaskAndCostArraysKernel()

    // While any element of maskArray[] != 0
    while ( ! maskArrayEmpty() )
        // Enqueue phase 1 of the Dijkstra kernel for all vertices
        enqueueKernelPhase1()

        // Enqueue phase 2 of the Dijkstra kernel for all vertices
        enqueueKernelPhase2()

        // Read the mask array back from the device
        readMaskArrayFromDeviceToHost()
```

```
            // Read final cost array for sourceVertex to the device and
            // store it on the host
            readCostArrayFromDeviceToHost()
```

The first kernel that is queued to OpenCL for each source vertex is simply responsible for initialization of buffers. This was done using a kernel rather than on the CPU to reduce the amount of data transferred between the CPU and GPU. The initialization kernel is provided in Listing 16.3 and is executed during the `initializeMaskAndCostArraysKernel()` from the pseudo code in Listing 16.2.

Listing 16.3 Kernel to Initialize Buffers before Each Run of Dijkstra's Algorithm

```
__kernel void initializeBuffers( __global int *maskArray, __global
                                 float *costArray,
                                 __global float *updatingCostArray,
                                 int sourceVertex, int vertexCount )
{
    int tid = get_global_id(0);

    if (sourceVertex == tid)
    {
        maskArray[tid] = 1;
        costArray[tid] = 0.0;
        updatingCostArray[tid] = 0.0;
    }
    else
    {
        maskArray[tid] = 0;
        costArray[tid] = FLT_MAX;
        updatingCostArray[tid] = FLT_MAX;
    }
}
```

The algorithm itself is broken into two phases. This is necessary because there is no synchronization possible outside of local work-groups in OpenCL, and this would be required to execute the kernel algorithm in a single phase. The first phase of the algorithm visits all vertices that have been marked in the `maskArray` and determines the cost to each neighbor. If the current cost plus the new edge weight is less than what is currently stored in `updatingCostArray`, then that new cost is stored for the vertex. The second phase of the algorithm checks to see if a smaller cost has been found for each vertex and, if so, marks it as needing visitation and updates the `costArray`. At the end of kernel phase 2, the `updatingCostArray` *is* synchronized with the `costArray`. The two phases of the algorithm are provided in Listing 16.4.

Listing 16.4 Two Kernel Phases That Compute Dijkstra's Algorithm

```
__kernel  void DijkstraKernel1(__global int *vertexArray,
                               __global int *edgeArray,
                               __global float *weightArray,
                               __global int *maskArray,
                               __global float *costArray,
                               __global float *updatingCostArray,
                               int vertexCount, int edgeCount )
{
    int tid = get_global_id(0);

    if ( maskArray[tid] != 0 )
    {
        maskArray[tid] = 0;

        int edgeStart = vertexArray[tid];
        int edgeEnd;
        if (tid + 1 < (vertexCount))
        {
            edgeEnd = vertexArray[tid + 1];
        }
        else
        {
            edgeEnd = edgeCount;
        }

        for(int edge = edgeStart; edge < edgeEnd; edge++)
        {
            int nid = edgeArray[edge];

            if (updatingCostArray[nid] > (costArray[tid] +
                weightArray[edge]))
            {
                updatingCostArray[nid] = (costArray[tid] +
                                          weightArray[edge]);
            }
        }
    }
}

__kernel  void DijkstraKernel2(__global int *vertexArray,
                               __global int *edgeArray,
                               __global float *weightArray,
                               __global int *maskArray,
                               __global float *costArray,
```

```
                              __global float *updatingCostArray,
                              int vertexCount)
{
    // access thread id
    int tid = get_global_id(0);

    if (costArray[tid] > updatingCostArray[tid])
    {
        costArray[tid] = updatingCostArray[tid];
        maskArray[tid] = 1;
    }

    updatingCostArray[tid] = costArray[tid];
}
```

Leveraging Multiple Compute Devices

In order to leverage multiple compute devices, the workload needs to
be partitioned. The approach taken in our implementation is to partition the number of searches across the available compute hardware. The
application detects the number of GPU and CPU devices and splits the
workload across the devices. The way the vertices are allocated to threads
is by dynamically determining a work size based on the result of querying
OpenCL for the value of GL_DEVICE_MAX_WORKGROUP_SIZE.

As can be seen in Listing 16.4, each of the kernels is written to process
one vertex at a time. The implementation sets the OpenCL local work
size to the value of querying GL_DEVICE_MAX_WORKGROUP_SIZE for the
device. The global work-group size is equal to the vertex count rounded
up to the closest maximum work-group size. The maskArray, costArray,
and updatingCostArray are padded to this size so that the kernels
do not need to check whether thread IDs are outside the bounds of the
array. This workload portioning essentially means that each thread on
the device will process a single vertex. In the case of a CPU device, the
OpenCL implementation will multithread the implementation across the
available cores.

In the case of mixing multiple devices, each device is allocated its own
CPU thread for communicating with OpenCL. The reason this is done in
multiple threads rather than a single thread is that the algorithm requires
reads back from host to device on each iteration of the inner loop of the
algorithm (Listing 16.2). In general, a more favorable approach would be

to queue all of the kernel executions from a single thread to all devices. One additional consideration is that typically there is a performance difference between the ability of the CPU and GPU to process kernels. As such, rather than choosing a fixed allocation of searches to each device, a future extension would be to examine OpenCL performance-related queries (or run a dynamic benchmark at start-up) and allocate the searches across the devices based on some performance characteristics. This would likely yield better performance as the current implementation must wait until the slowest device finishes execution.

The implementation of Dijkstra's algorithm was tested on an x86_64 Linux PC with an Intel Core i7 960 CPU @ 3.20GHz with an NVIDIA GTX 295 GPU running the NVIDIA 260.19.21 driver. In summary, the performance speedup using the GPU was dependent on the size of the graph (number of vertices) and the degree of the graph (number of edges per vertex). As the number of vertices in the graph increases, the GPU tends to outperform the CPU by a wider margin. In the best case measured, the dual-GPU implementation was 11.1 times faster than the CPU implementation.

The data in Table 16.1 was collected from randomly generated graphs containing a degree (edges per vertex) of 5. These graphs were run through the OpenCL-based GPU and multi-GPU implementations of Dijkstra's algorithm selecting 100 starting vertices. Additionally, the data sets were run through a single-threaded CPU reference implementation of Dijkstra's algorithm. The timings for each run are provided in seconds, and the data is summarized in Figures 16.1 and 16.2.

Table 16.1   Comparison of Data at Vertex Degree 5

Vertices	Degree	Searches	GTX295— 1GPU (s)	GTX295— 2GPU (s)	Intel Core i7 960 @ 3.2 GHz (s)
100000	5	100	1.051	1.008	5.429
200000	5	100	1.776	1.53	11.207
300000	5	100	2.494	2.064	18.292
400000	5	100	3.309	2.805	24.481
500000	5	100	4.064	3.428	32.013
600000	5	100	4.894	4.061	40.645
700000	5	100	5.667	4.698	48.131

Table 16.1   Comparison of Data at Vertex Degree 5 (*Continued*)

Vertices	Degree	Searches	GTX295— 1GPU (s)	GTX295— 2GPU (s)	Intel Core i7 960 @ 3.2 GHz (s)
800000	5	100	6.501	5.512	56.806
900000	5	100	7.291	6.332	66.543
1000000	5	100	8.084	6.94	76.938

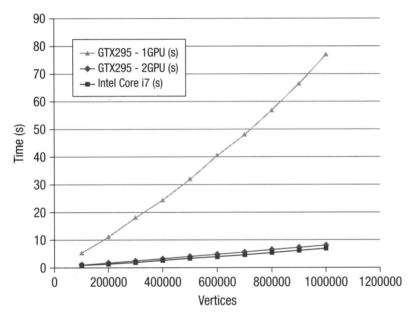

Figure 16.1   Summary of data in Table 16.1: NV GTX 295 (1 GPU, 2 GPU) and Intel Core i7 performance

The data in Table 16.2 was collected using the same test setup as for Table 16.1; the only difference was that the degree of the graph was set at 10 instead of 5. Increasing the degree of the graph reduced the advantage of the GPU implementation over the CPU (from 9.18 times on average down to 6.89 times), but the GPU version still has a significant advantage. The results from Table 16.2 are shown in Figure 16.3.

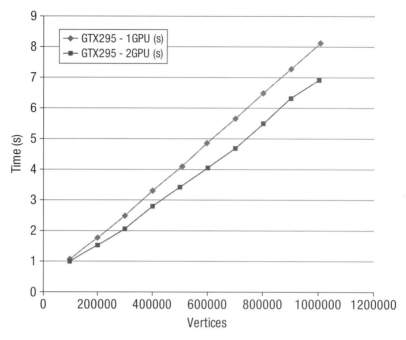

Figure 16.2   Using one GPU versus two GPUs: NV GTX 295 (1 GPU, 2 GPU) and Intel Core i7 performance

Table 16.2   Comparison of Data at Vertex Degree 10

Vertices	Degree	Searches	GTX295— 1GPU (s)	GTX295— 2GPU (s)	Intel Core i7 960 @ 3.2 GHz (s)
100000	10	100	1.728	1.527	7.679
200000	10	100	3.259	2.721	17.739
300000	10	100	4.972	4.229	27.41
400000	10	100	6.695	5.694	38.012
500000	10	100	8.527	6.936	48.466
600000	10	100	10.393	8.62	63.32
700000	10	100	12.224	10.474	75.555
800000	10	100	14.156	12.934	88.17
900000	10	100	15.929	13.15	102.502
1000000	10	100	17.85	14.99	120.682

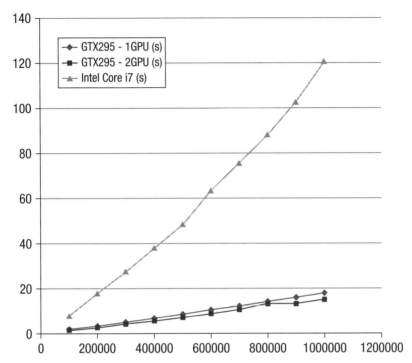

Figure 16.3 Summary of data in Table 16.2: NV GTX 295 (1 GPU, 2 GPU) and Intel Core i7 performance—10 edges per vertex

As can be seen from the collected performance data, regardless of the number of edges, the performance advantage the GPU implementation has over the CPU in terms of absolute seconds grows with the size of the graph. The setup costs associated with transferring data to the GPU and submitting/waiting for the kernels are better masked the more data is present. Some amount of GPU-to-CPU communication is necessary because the algorithm is by nature dynamic and the runtime length and iterations are not known before execution of the algorithm.

The only platform available to us to test the hybrid CPU-GPU implementation of Dijkstra was a MacPro with dual Quad-Core Intel Xeon CPUs @ 2.26GHz and dual NVIDIA GeForce GT 120 GPUs (note that these are rather low-end GPUs with only four compute units). The testing compared running on a single core of the CPU, running on all eight cores of the CPU using OpenCL, running on both GPUs, and combining both GPUs with the use of all eight CPU cores.

The performance results are detailed in Table 16.3 and Figure 16.4. In all tests, the best performance was attained by running the multicore CPU-only version using OpenCL. The next-best performance was combining the Dual NV GT 120 GPUs and the multicore CPU. It was initally rather surprising that the dual GPU+CPU implementation was bested by the CPU-only version. However, this was likely because the GPUs have only four compute units and the algorithm has a lot of CPU/GPU traffic. As such, the cost of switching threads and CPU/GPU communication offset the gains of running purely on the CPU.

Beyond that, the results were as expected: the reference single-core CPU performance fared the poorest and the Dual NV GT 120 GPU lagged behind combining the Dual NV GT 120 GPU + multicore CPU. Because Dijkstra's algorithm requires a significant number of calls to the OpenCL runtime and high traffic between the CPU and GPU, the performance gain was not as significant as one would expect from a different algorithm that requires less overhead between the host and device. However, the approach taken in the sample code should provide a useful example for how in general one can combine multiple GPUs and the CPU using OpenCL.

Table 16.3 Comparison of Dual GPU, Dual GPU + Multicore CPU, Multicore CPU, and CPU at Vertex Degree 10

Vertices	Degree	Searches	Dual NV GT 120	Dual NV GT 120 + Xeon (8 Cores)	Xeon @ 2.26GHz (8 Cores)	Xeon @ 2.26GHz (1 Core)
100000	10	100	9.21	4.042	2.507	12.157
200000	10	100	19.429	8.33	4.754	26.679
300000	10	100	31.413	12.245	7.623	41.226
400000	10	100	44.852	17.367	9.914	58.379
500000	10	100	56.664	23.18	12.606	76.805
600000	10	100	68.141	28.089	15.242	100.512
700000	10	100	81.031	34.819	17.905	128.311
800000	10	100	92.611	36.826	20.43	157.329
900000	10	100	102.851	42.905	22.847	190.804
1000000	10	100	115.842	48.379	26.634	226.0319

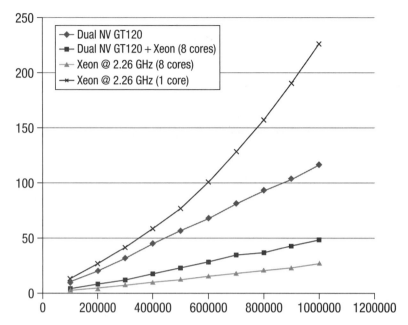

Figure 16.4   Summary of data in Table 16.3: comparison of dual GPU, dual GPU + multicore CPU, multicore CPU, and CPU at vertex degree 1

## Chapter 17

Cloth Simulation in the Bullet Physics SDK

By Lee Howes and Benedict R. Gaster

The Bullet Physics SDK is a widely used, open-source, collision detection, rigid-body and soft-body dynamics library available for free, for a wide range of platforms, under the zlib License. It supports discrete and continuous collision detection on concave and convex meshes as well as basic primitives. Bullet has a fast and stable rigid-body dynamics constraint solver, vehicle dynamics, character controller, and a range of constraint types. More interestingly for our purposes, Bullet includes soft-body dynamics supporting cloth, rope, and deformable volumes with two-way interaction with rigid bodies.

In this chapter, we describe an implementation of some of the basic features of soft-body dynamics into an OpenCL accelerated framework. This OpenCL code is released in the 2.77 version of the Bullet SDK and is available for download from http://bulletphysics.org. Figure 17.1 shows flags simulated using the Bullet SDK's cloth implementation in AMD's Samari demo.[1]

An Introduction to Cloth Simulation

There are many ways of simulating soft bodies. Finite element methods offer a physically accurate approach by breaking down the soft body into elements, often tetrahedra, over which partial differential equations are solved for the stresses in each element. Shape matching applies a penalty to parts of a model based on their distance from some optimal position, with the effect of driving the object toward its original shape. Mass/spring models construct the soft body from a set of masses connected by weightless springs that apply forces to the masses based on their compression or extension from rest length; that is, they obey a variant of Hooke's law.

---

[1] Figure 17.1 appears in full color in the online version of this chapter.

Figure 17.1   AMD's Samari demo, courtesy of Jason Yang

The simulation method used in Bullet is similar to a mass/spring model (see Figures 17.2 and 17.3), but rather than applying forces to the masses, it applies position and velocity corrections based on the work of Thomas Jakobsen, presented at GDC 2001 in a talk entitled "Advanced Character Physics."

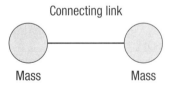

Figure 17.2   Masses and connecting links, similar to a
mass/spring model for soft bodies

The input to the simulation is a mesh representing the body to simulate. In general, this is a clothlike structure: two-dimensional in concept, mapped to three-dimensional space. From this mesh we create simulation masses at each vertex and simulation links for the connecting mesh links. The initial length of the links based on the positions of vertices in the mesh gives the rest length. The structure offered by the rest length defines the shape that, independent of external forces such as gravity, the cloth will maintain. These links have a relatively high strength for most cloth as such material does not stretch significantly under the application of day-to-day forces.

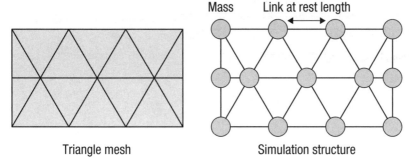

Figure 17.3   Creating a simulation structure from a cloth mesh

The astute reader may notice that while the mesh links alone may be enough to maintain a rigid structure for a three-dimensional body if constructed from a tetrahedral mesh, for a surface there is insufficient structure. Without any form of angle constraint on a vertex there is no resistance to folding over a vertex: two vertices linked from a central vertex are free to move relative to each other as long as their individual distances from the central vertex do not change. This motivates the need for an additional type of link in the structure that is usually given a lower resistance to displacement from its rest length (see Figure 17.4).

An additional link spanning a central vertex is necessary to maintain the relationship between nodes that are not directly connected. This allows us to maintain three-dimensional structure in the cloth and resist bending.

At this core of the simulation these types of links are treated no differently; however, from the point of view of creation of the input we cannot create the bend links directly from the mesh. Instead we can infer a link across every triangle boundary and add this to the simulation data structure. The result is that our original simulation mesh becomes something like what is shown in Figure 17.5.

In two dimensions repeatedly solving this mesh gives us clothlike behavior, controlled by strengths assigned to links and masses assigned to nodes. In three dimensions, and without the need for bend links, more varied soft-body structures can be constructed.

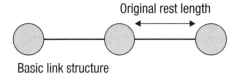

Original rest length

Basic link structure

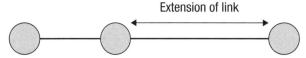

Extension of link

Motion resisted by structure

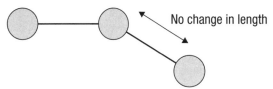

No change in length

Motion not resisted by structure

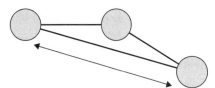

Additional resistance needed

Figure 17.4   Cloth link structure

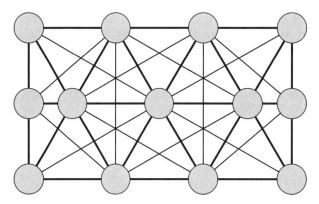

Figure 17.5   Cloth mesh with both structural links that stop stretching and bend links that resist folding of the material

Simulating the Soft Body

Simulating the mesh involves performing an iterative relaxation solver over each of the links. Each time step performs an iterative solve first of velocities of nodes in the mesh, obtaining velocity corrections for each node. It then updates estimated positions from the velocities and iteratively computes position corrections. In both the velocity and position updates the solver computes new values for the particles at either end of a given link based on the masses of the particles, the strength of the link, and its extension or compression.

We can picture this solver's application to simulation in a simple one-dimensional ropelike structure as shown in Figure 17.6(a). In the figure we see a series of masses connected by springlike links. If we apply a force such as gravity, a motion resulting from some sort of collision, or some user input to the rope, we may move one of the vertices from rest as in Figure 17.6(b).

As we move to Figure 17.6(c), we apply the first iteration of the solver. This applies the motion resulting from the distortion of the mesh seen in the extended links in Figure 17.6(b) such that the neighboring vertices'

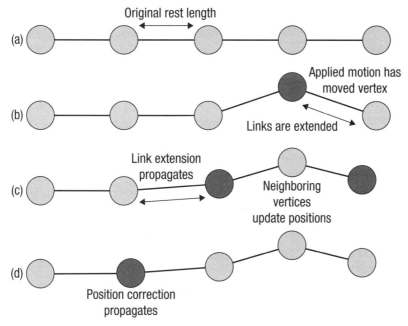

Figure 17.6   Solving the mesh of a rope. Note how the motion applied between (a) and (b) propagates during solver iterations (c) and (d) until, eventually, the entire rope has been affected.

positions are updated. In Figure 17.6(d) a similar process propagates the motion through to another vertex. We see this distortion propagate through a complex mesh in complicated patterns as the motion of one vertex affects multiple other vertices; eventually, if we iterate for long enough, we should reach a stable state.

Roughly the algorithm follows the following structure where k is a constant link stretch factor and linkLengthRatio is the reciprocal of the square of the link length times the sum of the masses on the link:

```
for each time step
  Prepare links
  for each velocity iteration
    for each link in mesh
      (velocity0, inverseMass0) = linkStart
      (velocity1, inverseMass1) = linkEnd
      float3 velocityDifference = velocity1 - velocity0;
      float velAlongLink = dot( linkVector, velocityDifference );
      float correction = -velAlongLink*linkLengthRatio*k;
      velocity0 -= linkVector*k*inverseMass0;
      velocity1 += linkVector*k*inverseMass1;

  Estimate position corrections from velocities

  for each position iteration
    for each link in mesh
      (position0, inverseMass0) = linkStart
      (position1, inverseMass1) = linkEnd
      float3 vectorLength = position1 - position0;
      float length  = dot(vectorLength, vectorLength);
      float k     = ( (restLengthSquared - len) /
                    (massLSC*(restLengthSquared+len)))*kst;
      position0 -= vectorLength * (k*inverseMass0);
      position1 += vectorLength * (k*inverseMass1);
```

The idea of these repeated iterations is to converge on a stable solution of the system of equations comprising the mesh structure. If we were aiming for a stable solution, we would iterate both the velocity and the position solver until the system converged completely.

For the purposes of real-time physics simulation, however, two other factors come into play:

- Performance predictability is more stable than achieving a fully stable situation.

- The time-step iteration loop also affects convergence. To an extent the convergence carries over from one time step to the next if the change created at a given time step is not too significant.

To this end a simulation used in practice will usually set a fixed number of iterations, chosen both to achieve a reasonable level of convergence and to support the required frame rate.

Executing the Simulation on the CPU

As is often the case, performing the simulation on the CPU is a relatively simple process. A high degree of code structure can be maintained to ensure good readability and flexibility. For each individual soft body we can run the solver code across all the links in the soft body.

The following code represents the position solver for a single soft-body object. m_c0 and m_c1 are per-link constants that are precomputed. The velocity solver code is similar; we shall ignore that and the simple per-vertex update loops for the rest of this discussion.

```
void btSoftBody::PSolve_Links(
    btSoftBody* psb,
    btScalar kst,
    btScalar ti)
{
    for(int i=0, ni = psb->m_links.size(); i < ni; ++i)
    {
        Link &l=psb->m_links[i];
        if(l.m_c0>0) {
            Node &a = *l.m_normal[0];
            Node &b = *l.m_normal [1];
            const btVector3 del = b.m_position - a.m_position;
            const btScalar len = del.length2();
            const btScalar k =
                ((l.m_c1 - len)/(l.m_c0 * (l.m_c1 + len)))*
                                        simulationConstant;
            a.m_x -= del*(k*a.m_inverseMass);
            b.m_x += del*(k*b.m_inverseMass);
        }
    }
}
```

For each soft body we can tweak the set of solver stages we wish to execute, the number of stages, and so on. For example, we might want to execute five velocity iterations and ten position iterations for a very large soft body where propagation of forces through the mesh would be slow.

Note that this loop executes over data in place. By updating in place the result of computing the effect on a vertex of a single link is used to compute the effect of a second link on both that same vertex and its connected neighbor. This approach is often known as Gauss-Seidel iteration. This has important behavioral characteristics that apply when we look at the GPU implementation of the solver. We can see how this behaves in Figure 17.7.

One aspect that should be clear from this loop, and indeed from the Gauss-Seidel iteration it uses, is that it is not trivially parallelizable by a compiler. There is an inter-iteration dependence, and as such a trivial parallelization of this loop will lead to subtle differences in behavior, and possibly incorrect results.

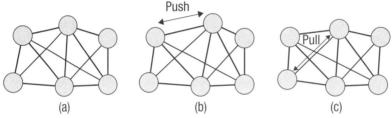

Figure 17.7   The stages of Gauss-Seidel iteration on a set of soft-body links and vertices. In (a) we see the mesh at the start of the solver iteration. In (b) we apply the effects of the first link on its vertices. In (c) we apply those of another link, noting that we work from the positions computed in (b).

Changes Necessary for Basic GPU Execution

The first thing to note is that the large amount of parallelism in the OpenCL programming model means that unless soft bodies are very large, solving soft bodies individually is inefficient because each soft body has too little parallelism during an iteration of any of its solvers to fully use the device. As a result, the first thing we want to do is solve multiple soft bodies simultaneously, allowing their combined computation needs to fill the entire device. In the Bullet solver this means that soft-body data is moved into single large arrays, indexed by values in the individual soft-body objects. These entire arrays are moved onto the GPU, operated on, and if necessary moved back to the host memory.

Unfortunately, performing the original CPU calculation in parallel over all links in all soft bodies in this fashion produces incorrect results. Looking back at Figure 17.5, we can see that as each link is solved, the positions or velocities of the vertices at either end are updated. If we perform the computations in parallel, they attempt to produce a result along the lines of what is shown in Figure 17.8, but applied to every mass rather than only the one shown.

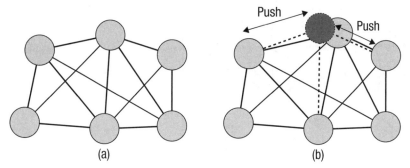

Figure 17.8   The same mesh as in Figure 17.7 is shown in (a). In (b) the update shown in Figure 17.7(c) has occurred as well as a second update represented by the dark mass and dotted lines.

We can solve this in various ways. Many simulations choose to use a Jacobi-style loop, which would run for each vertex and update that vertex based on the position updates the surrounding links would apply, or, more commonly in such simulations, based on the sum of forces applied by the surrounding links. This type of simulation is easier to implement because it can double-buffer the computation, but the cost is that propagation of updates through the soft body tends to be slower, and in a position- and velocity-based simulation such as that used here, momentum is not conserved; that is, the updates introduce error. This error can be reduced through damping but at a cost for the simulation.

The alternative approach that we use here is to perform a graph coloring of the mesh. That is, we choose a batch number for each link such that any two links in the mesh that share a vertex will not be in the same batch. This requires a large number of batches that will be based on the complexity of the interconnections in the mesh; indeed it will be equal to the valence of maximum note in the mesh. In the mesh seen in Figure 17.5 that would be 5. The vertex in the center of each row is connected to all five other vertices. In the mesh seen in Figure 17.9 we can see an example of a minimum coloring that requires 12 colors.[2] For a more complicated mesh this would be a substantially higher number.

---

[2]   The colors are shown as different shades of gray in the printed version and appear in full color in the online version of this chapter.

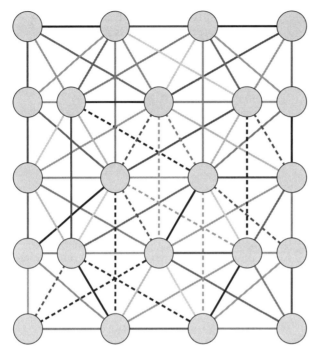

Figure 17.9   A mesh with structural links taken from the input triangle mesh and bend links created across triangle boundaries with one possible coloring into independent batches

To implement this on the GPU we first sort the link data into batches. The simplest approach is the following:

```
for each link:
  color = 0
```

Here, `color` is used by any other link connected to either vertex connected to this link:

```
  color = next color
  linkBatch = color
```

This batching operation need only be performed once unless the mesh changes. In a simple implementation the mesh need not change, and adapting for tearing is more efficiently dealt with by disabling links than by rebatching.

To execute we iterate over the batches, performing one parallel OpenCL dispatch for each, knowing that each batch is entirely parallel. Where before we called `solveConstraints` and then inside that `PSolve_Links` on a single soft body, now we call `solveConstraints` over an entire set of soft bodies with the following loop:

```
for(int iteration = 0;
    iteration < m_numberOfPositionIterations;
    ++iteration ) {
  for( int i = 0;
       i < m_linkData.m_batchStartLengths.size();
       ++i ) {
    int startLink = m_linkData.m_batchStartLengths[i].start;
    int numLinks = m_linkData.m_batchStartLengths[i].length;

    solveLinksForPosition( startLink, numLinks, kst, ti );
  }
}
```

Note that `solveLinksForPosition` is being called to act on a range of links within a given precomputed batch. This set of batches is computed using the algorithm discussed previously. The kernel is called using the following code that sets up the OpenCL launch and executes:

```
void btOpenCLSoftBodySolver::solveLinksForPosition(
    int startLink,
    int numLinks,
    float kst,
    float ti)
{
   cl_int ciErrNum;
   ciErrNum = clSetKernelArg(
      solvePositionsFromLinksKernel,
      0,
      sizeof(int),
      &startLink);
   ciErrNum = clSetKernelArg(
      solvePositionsFromLinksKernel,
      1,
      sizeof(int),
      &numLinks);
   ciErrNum = clSetKernelArg(
      solvePositionsFromLinksKernel,
      2,
      sizeof(float),
      &kst);
   ciErrNum = clSetKernelArg(
      solvePositionsFromLinksKernel,
      3,
      sizeof(float),
      &ti);
```

```
    ciErrNum = clSetKernelArg(
        solvePositionsFromLinksKernel,
        4,
        sizeof(cl_mem),
        &m_linkData.m_clLinks.m_buffer);
    ciErrNum = clSetKernelArg(
        solvePositionsFromLinksKernel,
        5,
        sizeof(cl_mem),
        &m_linkData.m_clLinksMassLSC.m_buffer);
    ciErrNum = clSetKernelArg(
        solvePositionsFromLinksKernel,
        6,
        sizeof(cl_mem),
        &m_linkData.m_clLinksRestLengthSquared.m_buffer);
    ciErrNum = clSetKernelArg(
        solvePositionsFromLinksKernel,
        7,
        sizeof(cl_mem),
        &m_vertexData.m_clVertexInverseMass.m_buffer);
    ciErrNum = clSetKernelArg(
        solvePositionsFromLinksKernel,
        8,
        sizeof(cl_mem),
        &m_vertexData.m_clVertexPosition.m_buffer);

    size_t  numWorkItems = workGroupSize*
        ((numLinks + (workGroupSize-1)) / workGroupSize);
    ciErrNum = clEnqueueNDRangeKernel(
        m_cqCommandQue,
        solvePositionsFromLinksKernel,
        1,
        NULL,
        &numWorkItems,
        &workGroupSize,0,0,0);
    if( ciErrNum!= CL_SUCCESS ) {
      btAssert( 0 &&
      "enqueueNDRangeKernel(solvePositionsFromLinksKernel)");
    }
} // solveLinksForPosition
```

The GPU executes an OpenCL kernel compiled from the following code:

```
__kernel void
SolvePositionsFromLinksKernel(
    const int startLink,
    const int numLinks,
    const float kst,
    const float ti,
```

```
    __global int2 * g_linksVertexIndices,
    __global float * g_linksMassLSC,
    __global float * g_linksRestLengthSquared,
    __global float * g_verticesInverseMass,
    __global float4 * g_vertexPositions)
{
    int linkID = get_global_id(0) + startLink;
    if( get_global_id(0) < numLinks ) {
        float massLSC = g_linksMassLSC[linkID];
        float restLengthSquared = g_linksRestLengthSquared[linkID];

        if( massLSC > 0.0f ) {
            int2 nodeIndices = g_linksVertexIndices[linkID];
            int node0 = nodeIndices.x;
            int node1 = nodeIndices.y;

            float3 position0 = g_vertexPositions[node0].xyz;
            float3 position1 = g_vertexPositions[node1].xyz;

            float inverseMass0 = g_verticesInverseMass[node0];
            float inverseMass1 = g_verticesInverseMass[node1];

            float3 del = position1 - position0;
            float len = dot(del, del);
            float k   = ((restLengthSquared -
                        len)/(massLSC*(restLengthSquared+len)))*kst;
            position0 = position0 - del*(k*inverseMass0);
            position1 = position1 + del*(k*inverseMass1);

            g_vertexPositions[node0] = (float4)(position0, 0.f);
            g_vertexPositions[node1] = (float4)(position1, 0.f);

        }
    }
}
```

In this version of the code, for each batch we are enqueuing an OpenCL kernel that will have to wait for completion of the previously enqueued instance before it can execute. Each kernel dispatch takes some amount of time to prepare for execution: the GPU must be set up, register values passed, bus transactions enacted, and so on. We can infer from this that as we increase the number of kernel dispatches, we increase the amount of time it takes to execute not only in GPU time but also in CPU time to manage that GPU execution.

In addition to CPU overhead, as we increase the number of dispatches without increasing the amount of work, it should be clear that the work per dispatch becomes smaller. There will always be a point at which the work per dispatch is low enough to not fully occupy the GPU, or at least not occupy the GPU for long enough to overlap with any of the CPU overhead that could be overlapped.

Given that small enough workloads and large enough numbers of dispatches increase CPU overhead, it is possible for an algorithm to eventually become dispatch-bound. The next section discusses one approach that we can use to deal with this. In addition, we take into account the SIMD nature of GPU hardware to increase efficiency further.

Two-Layered Batching

The first thing to look at is why we need so many batches. In Figure 17.9 we saw a coloring of the graph that shows that the number required was at least equal to the highest vertex valence in the graph. Clearly in having connections to neighboring vertices *and* to distant vertices with the addition of bend links (the structure of which depends on the required behavior of the body) the number of links connecting a vertex with a set of other vertices will be relatively high.

The question that arises from this is "How can we reduce the maximum valence of the mesh?" Obviously we cannot simply change the mesh structure; we want the same behavior as the artist expects from adding the links to the mesh. However, what we can manage is changing the interpretation of the mesh.

If, instead of coloring the graph by links where multiple links touch a single vertex and hence depend on each other, we color the graph in larger chunks, we reduce the number of colors we need. The number of neighboring chunks, and hence colors, touched by the links emanating from a given chunk will be reduced thanks to the lower density at which the coloring is applied. We can see an example of this chunking in Figure 17.10.[3] Thanks to the coloring of the chunks themselves, we know that any two chunks of a given color and hence in a given batch are independent. The result of this is that each chunk within a given batch can be executed by a different OpenCL work-group with no further intergroup synchronization requirements.

---

[3] Again the colors are shown as different shades of gray in the printed version and appear in full color in the online version of this chapter.

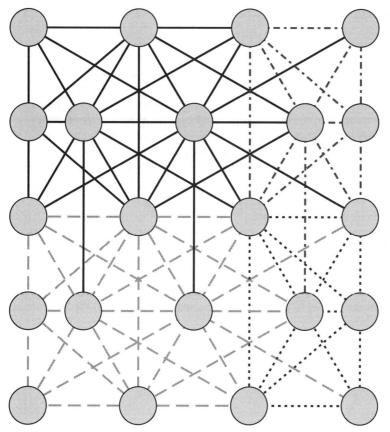

Figure 17.10   Dividing the mesh into larger chunks and applying a coloring to those. Note that fewer colors are needed than in the direct link coloring approach. This pattern can repeat infinitely with the same four colors.

The benefit of reducing the number of colors is that we reduce the number of levels of global synchronization required. Each global synchronization in OpenCL requires a kernel dispatch and completion event; reducing the total number of dispatches significantly reduces the overhead of simulation.

These chunks of the graph are grown out from a single vertex in a breadth-first fashion. From a starting vertex we add all of the connected links and enqueue all of the vertices at the far ends of those links. From those vertices we perform the same addition of all connected links not already added and add their vertices to the queue. Eventually we build a chunk to our desired size. The size can be parameterized; 256 has been a good number in experiments.

Of course, while we have independent chunks within a batch, links within a chunk are still interdependent as in the naïve coloring. Within any given batch, represented by a single color of the graph, we perform a second level of coloring. This coloring is linkwise and identical in principle to the previously discussed single-level batching except that only links within a given batch need be considered. We can iterate through the local colors of links using an in-kernel for loop. Of course, depending on the size of each chunk, we may have more or fewer links in a given local batch than work-items in a group. We can rectify this by arranging the local batches so that there are more than what is absolutely necessary: rather than simply creating arbitrarily sized batches of links, we pack links into work-group-size batches and move on to another when either there is a dependence or a batch is full. Using this two-layer batching, we move to code like the following:

```
__kernel void
SolvePositionsFromLinksKernel(
    const int startLink,
    const int numLinks,
    const float kst,
    const float ti,
    __global int2 * g_linksVertexIndices,
    __global float * g_linksMassLSC,
    __global float * g_linksRestLengthSquared,
    __global float * g_verticesInverseMass,
    __global float4 * g_vertexPositions)

{
    for( batch = 0; batch < numLocalBatches; ++batch )
    {
        // Assume that links are sorted in memory in order of
        // local batches within groups
        int linkID = get_global_id(0)*batch;

        float massLSC = g_linksMassLSC[linkID];
        float restLengthSquared = g_linksRestLengthSquared[linkID];

        if( massLSC > 0.0f ) {
            int2 nodeIndices = g_linksVertexIndices[linkID];
            int node0 = nodeIndices.x;
            int node1 = nodeIndices.y;

            float3 position0 = g_vertexPositions[node0].xyz;
            float3 position1 = g_vertexPositions[node1].xyz;
```

```
        float inverseMass0 = g_verticesInverseMass[node0];
        float inverseMass1 = g_verticesInverseMass[node1];

        float3 del = position1 - position0;
        float len  = dot(del, del);
        float k    = ((restLengthSquared -
                     len)/(massLSC*(restLengthSquared+len)))*kst;
        position0 = position0 - del*(k*inverseMass0);
        position1 = position1 + del*(k*inverseMass1);

        g_vertexPositions[node0] = (float4)(position0, 0.f);
        g_vertexPositions[node1] = (float4)(position1, 0.f);

    }

    barrier(CLK_GLOBAL_MEM_FENCE);
  }
}
```

Note that to correctly satisfy OpenCL inter-work-item memory consistency we must include barrier instructions on each loop iteration. Of course, because they are in a loop, these barrier instructions must be executed by all work-items in the work-group; the batches should be created such that all work-items see the same number with no early exit from the loop. In reality we are unlikely to perfectly fill the batches; there will be SIMD lanes lying idle at various points in the computation (or writing data that will be ignored). This is unfortunate but unavoidable, and the efficiency savings from reducing global synchronization trade against this. Note that the solver algorithm hasn't changed, only the pattern of link solving used to achieve it. This does mean that any given batching produces a subtly different output from all other batchings because of the ordering of floating-point operations; however, any given batching is deterministic.

Note as well that in this case we are still operating inefficiently in global memory. Given that within a group the links will reuse vertex data, and that vertex data will not be shared with other work-groups, we can cache the vertex data in OpenCL local memory. We will see final code that does this in the next section.

Optimizing for SIMD Computation and Local Memory

In the current generation high-end GPUs are all SIMD architectures. Current architectures from AMD and NVIDIA include up to 24 cores each with 16- or 32-wide SIMD units. Logical SIMD vectors can be wider: a 64-element vector is executed over four consecutive cycles on 16 SIMD lanes on the AMD Radeon HD 6970 architecture by replaying the same instruction four times.

These wide SIMD vectors give a certain level of guaranteed synchronization. We know that any instruction issued on the HD 6970 will be executed at the same time across 64 work-items, with no need for barrier synchronization. With the AMD compiler and runtime, barriers will be automatically converted to no-ops if the work-group size is the same as or smaller than the hardware vector size (known as a **wavefront**).

The consequence of this guaranteed synchronization is that if we define our work-groups appropriately and aim for batch sizes and data layouts that map efficiently to groups of *vector-width* work-items, we can generate efficient code that does not require barrier synchronization to execute correctly. Indeed, it is safe to drop the barriers entirely as long as we insert memory fences (`mem_fence(CLK_GLOBAL_MEM_FENCE)` or `mem_fence(CLK_LOCAL_MEM_FENCE)`) to ensure that the compiler does not reorder memory operations inappropriately.

As mentioned earlier, we can go one step further. Recall what we saw in the previous section:

```
for each batch of work-groups:
  for each batch of links within the chunk:
    process link
    barrier;
```

Now let's slightly change the algorithm:

```
for each batch of wavefronts:
  load all vertex data needed by the chunk
  for each batch of links within the wavefront
    process link using vertices in local memory
    local fence
  store updated vertex data back to global memory
```

This saves on synchronization, and there is reuse of vertex data within efficient local memory, reducing the amount of global memory traffic and further improving performance. To achieve this we prepare a list of vertices to load as extra per-wavefront data and first scan this list to load vertices. We update the link data to contain local vertex indices rather than global vertex indices. When processing the links local batch by local batch within the chunk, the loaded link data indexes the local vertex buffer where the vertices are updated in place. After the chunk is complete, the vertices are written back to global memory.

Our final kernel, including loading from shared memory, using fences rather than barriers, and working on a wavefront basis, is seen here:

```
__kernel void
SolvePositionsFromLinksKernel(
    const int startWaveInBatch,
    const int numWaves,
    const float kst,
    const float ti,                    .
    __global int2 *g_wavefrontBatchCountsVertexCounts,
    __global int *g_vertexAddressesPerWavefront,
    __global int2 * g_linksVertexIndices,
    __global float * g_linksMassLSC,
    __global float * g_linksRestLengthSquared,
    __global float * g_verticesInverseMass,
    __global float4 * g_vertexPositions,
    __local int2 *wavefrontBatchCountsVertexCounts,
    __local float4 *vertexPositionSharedData,
    __local float *vertexInverseMassSharedData)
{
    const int laneInWavefront =
        (get_global_id(0) & (WAVEFRONT_SIZE-1));
    const int wavefront = startWaveInBatch + (get_global_id(0) /
                                            WAVEFRONT_SIZE);
    const int firstWavefrontInBlock = startWaveInBatch +
        get_group_id(0) * WAVEFRONT_BLOCK_MULTIPLIER;
    const int localWavefront = wavefront - firstWavefrontInBlock;

    // Mask out in case there's a stray "wavefront" at the
    // end that's been forced in through the multiplier
    if( wavefront < (startWaveInBatch + numWaves) ) {
        // Load the batch counts for the wavefronts
        // Mask out in case there's a stray "wavefront"
        // at the end that's been forced in through the multiplier
        if( laneInWavefront == 0 ) {
            int2 batchesAndVertexCountsWithinWavefront =
                g_wavefrontBatchCountsVertexCounts[wavefront];
            wavefrontBatchCountsVertexCounts[localWavefront] =
                batchesAndVertexCountsWithinWavefront;
        }

        mem_fence(CLK_LOCAL_MEM_FENCE);


        int2 batchesAndVerticesWithinWavefront =
                wavefrontBatchCountsVertexCounts[localWavefront];
        int batchesWithinWavefront =
            batchesAndVerticesWithinWavefront.x;
        int verticesUsedByWave = batchesAndVerticesWithinWavefront.y;
```

```
// Load the vertices for the wavefronts
for( int vertex = laneInWavefront;
     vertex < verticesUsedByWave;
     vertex+=WAVEFRONT_SIZE ) {
   int vertexAddress = g_vertexAddressesPerWavefront[
       wavefront*MAX_NUM_VERTICES_PER_WAVE + vertex];

   vertexPositionSharedData[localWavefront*
           MAX_NUM_VERTICES_PER_WAVE + vertex] =
       g_vertexPositions[vertexAddress];
           vertexInverseMassSharedData[localWavefront*
           MAX_NUM_VERTICES_PER_WAVE + vertex] =
       g_verticesInverseMass[vertexAddress];
}

mem_fence(CLK_LOCAL_MEM_FENCE);

// Loop through the batches performing the solve on each in LDS
int baseDataLocationForWave = WAVEFRONT_SIZE * wavefront *
                       MAX_BATCHES_PER_WAVE;

//for( int batch = 0; batch < batchesWithinWavefront; ++batch )

int batch = 0;
do {
   int baseDataLocation =
         baseDataLocationForWave + WAVEFRONT_SIZE * batch;
   int locationOfValue = baseDataLocation + laneInWavefront;


   // These loads should all be perfectly linear across the WF
   int2 localVertexIndices =
      g_linksVertexIndices[locationOfValue];
   float massLSC = g_linksMassLSC[locationOfValue];
   float restLengthSquared =
                 g_linksRestLengthSquared[locationOfValue];

   // LDS vertex addresses based on logical wavefront
   // number in block
   // and loaded index
   int vertexAddress0 = MAX_NUM_VERTICES_PER_WAVE *
                         localWavefront + localVertexIndices.x;
   int vertexAddress1 =
      MAX_NUM_VERTICES_PER_WAVE * localWavefront +
                                        localVertexIndices.y;

   float4 position0 = vertexPositionSharedData[vertexAddress0];
   float4 position1 = vertexPositionSharedData[vertexAddress1];
```

```
            float inverseMass0 =
               vertexInverseMassSharedData[vertexAddress0];
            float inverseMass1 =
               vertexInverseMassSharedData[vertexAddress1];

            float4 del = position1 - position0;
            float len = mydot3(del, del);

            float k = 0;
            if( massLSC > 0.0f ) {
               k = ((restLengthSquared - len)/
                           (massLSC*(restLengthSquared+len)))*kst;
            }

            position0 = position0 - del*(k*inverseMass0);
            position1 = position1 + del*(k*inverseMass1);

            // Ensure compiler does not reorder memory operations
            mem_fence(CLK_LOCAL_MEM_FENCE);

            vertexPositionSharedData[vertexAddress0] = position0;
            vertexPositionSharedData[vertexAddress1] = position1;

             // Ensure compiler does not reorder memory operations
             mem_fence(CLK_LOCAL_MEM_FENCE);


             ++batch;
      } while( batch < batchesWithinWavefront );

      // Update the global memory vertices for the wavefronts
      for( int vertex = laneInWavefront;
           vertex < verticesUsedByWave;
           vertex+=WAVEFRONT_SIZE ) {
         int vertexAddress = g_vertexAddressesPerWavefront[wavefront*
                     MAX_NUM_VERTICES_PER_WAVE + vertex];

         g_vertexPositions[vertexAddress] =
             (float4)(vertexPositionSharedData[localWavefront*
             MAX_NUM_VERTICES_PER_WAVE + vertex].xyz, 0.f);
      }

   }
}
```

What we have tried to demonstrate is that these architectures are not
scalar architectures, and work-items are not independent, in architectural
terms not threads. For efficiency, just as we have to optimize for SSE vectors on x86 hardware to attain full performance, for the GPU we can use

the architectural features to improve performance of our algorithms. The warning in this is that our code is no longer portable across architectures. In the Bullet code we currently provide SIMD-optimized and portable versions of this solver.

Adding OpenGL Interoperation

The final subject we should discuss here is interoperation with OpenGL. This was discussed earlier in Chapter 10, and cloth simulation is a good example of where such interoperation is useful outside of image processing.

When we render soft-body objects on the screen, we create a render call and pass it a vertex buffer object, or VBO. This describes a memory buffer in GPU memory containing a list of all vertices that we need to draw. In addition, we provide buffers containing triangle index lists that reference the vertex buffer, and appropriate texture and normal buffers. If we render the output of the soft-body simulation, the vertex positions and normals are computed on each step of the simulation; the vertex and normal buffers used for rendering must be updated with these new values.

Updating these values via copying back to host memory, performing another copy into a structure to upload, and then uploading this to the vertex buffer adds additional overhead in terms of bus synchronization time and bandwidth. OpenCL/OpenGL interoperability reduces this problem. We can directly write using an OpenCL kernel into a buffer that will be used by the OpenGL rendering code. All data can stay in high-speed device memory with none of the overhead of copying back to the host and up to the GPU again.

On the host side we create a vertex struct with the necessary fields for rendering and create a buffer from this and a VBO handle:

```
struct vertex_struct
{
    float pos[3];
    float normal[3];
    float texcoord[2];

};

vertex_struct* cpu_buffer = new . . .
GLuint clothVBO;
```

From these objects we create a device-side VBO with the `GL_DYNAMIC_`
`DRAW` flag that specifies that this buffer will be updated on a regular basis:

```
// Construct VBO
glGenBuffers(1, &clothVBO);
glBindBuffer(GL_ARRAY_BUFFER, clothVBO);
// Do initial upload to ensure that the buffer exists on the device
// this is important to allow OpenCL to make use of the VBO
glBufferData(GL_ARRAY_BUFFER, sizeof(vertex_struct)*width*height,
      &(cpu_buffer[0]), GL_DYNAMIC_DRAW);
glBindBuffer(GL_ARRAY_BUFFER, 0);
```

To render we use the VBO as a source for vertex data using the following
code:

```
// Enable vertex, normal, and texture arrays for drawing
glBindBuffer(GL_ARRAY_BUFFER, clothVBO);
glEnableClientState(GL_VERTEX_ARRAY);
glEnableClientState(GL_NORMAL_ARRAY);
glEnableClientState(GL_TEXTURE_COORD_ARRAY);
glBindTexture(GL_TEXTURE_2D, texture);

// Set up vertex buffer state and draw
glVertexPointer(
    3,
    GL_FLOAT,
    sizeof(vertex_struct),
    (const GLvoid *)0 );

glNormalPointer(
    GL_FLOAT,
    sizeof(vertex_struct),
    (const GLvoid *)(sizeof(float)*3) );

glTexCoordPointer(
    2,
    GL_FLOAT,
    sizeof(vertex_struct),
    (const GLvoid *)(sizeof(float)*6) );

glDrawElements(
    GL_TRIANGLES,
    (height-1  )*(width-1)*3*2,
    GL_UNSIGNED_INT,
    indices);

// Clean up code
glDisableClientState(GL_NORMAL_ARRAY);
glDisableClientState(GL_VERTEX_ARRAY);
```

```
glDisableClientState(GL_TEXTURE_COORD_ARRAY);
glBindTexture(GL_TEXTURE_2D, 0);
glBindBuffer(GL_ARRAY_BUFFER, 0);
```

The OpenCL code will first, at some point during setup, create a CL buffer from the GL buffer (it is for this reason that the GL buffer must be initialized with data). Then on each frame, after the OpenCL kernels have output the result of a time step of the simulation, the OpenCL version of the OpenGL buffer is acquired for use by OpenCL and can be used as a target by a kernel. Subsequently the buffer is freed and ready to be used again by OpenGL for rendering:

```
clBuffer = clCreateFromGLBuffer(
    m_context,
    CL_MEM_WRITE_ONLY,
    clothVBO,
    &ciErrNum);

clEnqueueAcquireGLObjects(m_cqCommandQue, 1, &clBuffer, 0, 0, NULL);

clEnqueueReleaseGLObjects(m_cqCommandQue, 1, &clBuffer, 0, 0, 0);
```

In this fashion we efficiently generate vertex data for rendering by an OpenGL application using the OpenCL soft-body simulation.

## Chapter 18

Simulating the Ocean with Fast Fourier Transform

By Benedict R. Gaster,
Brian Sumner,
and Justin Hensley

Ocean is an OpenCL demonstration application developed at AMD that simulates the surface of the ocean in real time using an approach developed by Jerry Tessendorf[1] that makes use of the fast Fourier transform (FFT). This same approach has been used in a number of feature films such as *Waterworld*, *Titanic*, and *Fifth Element* and has also appeared in modified form in real-time games. Briefly, the fast Fourier transform is applied to random noise, generated using the Phillips spectrum that evolves over time as a frequency-dependent phase shift. In this chapter we describe our implementation of Tessendorf's approach and its application in AMD's Ocean demo. An example frame generated by this application appears in grayscale[2] in Figure 18.1 and in full color on the front cover of the book.

A key goal of this chapter is to describe an implementation of an optimized fast Fourier transform in OpenCL, but we have chosen to frame it within the Ocean application to show a "real" use case. We do not discuss the OpenGL rendering (it is mostly orthogonal to our main focus) except when it pertains to OpenCL/OpenGL interoperability.

---

[1] Jerry Tessendorf, "Simulating Ocean Water," *SIGGRAPH Course Notes* (2002).

[2] If you are reading the online version of this chapter, you are lucky enough to see Figure 18.1 in full color, too.

Figure 18.1   A single frame from the Ocean demonstration

An Overview of the Ocean Application

The application consists of two major components:

- The OpenCL generation of a height map, updated in each frame to account for the movement of waves

- The OpenGL rendering of this height map to produce the output, as seen in Figure 18.1

The program itself is a simple GLUT application (www.opengl.org/resources/libraries/glut/) that performs the following steps:

1. Initializes base OpenGL (which must be at least version 2.0 or above). No OpenGL objects are created at this time; this gives the application the flexibility to use interop between OpenGL and OpenCL or not. This choice is delayed until after OpenCL has initialized.

2. Initializes base OpenCL; creates a context, programs, and command-queues. At this time it also generates an initial spectrum that will be used in the simulation, with default wind direction and velocity. (The wind and velocity can be set by the user at any time during the simulation.)

3. Loads OpenGL textures, used for the sky box, logos, and so forth; loads and compiles OpenGL shaders; and creates a vertex buffer that will be used for interop with OpenCL if this feature is enabled.

4. Creates OpenCL buffers that will be used to store the resulting height map and are interop buffers with OpenGL, if that mode is enabled. Two buffers are produced by OpenCL that are used during rendering, the height map and a corresponding set of slopes used for calculating normals.

5. Finally the application enters the GLUT display loop, which is no different from most GLUT applications. The display callback itself is composed of the following elements:

   a. Calls OpenCL to perform the next step in the simulation and produce vertex buffer data for the height map and corresponding slopes.

   b. Renders the sky box.

   c. Binds and renders the vertex buffers to produce the water, with respect to the sky box and other elements.

   d. Finally, renders the controls for wind direction and velocity and the logo.

The OpenCL host code uses the C++ Wrapper API and is straightforward. We omit the initialization code here.

Each display iteration calls the following function:

```
cl_int runCLSimulation(

    unsigned int width,

    unsigned int height,

    float animTime)
{
    cl_int err;
    std::vector<cl::Memory> v;
    v.push_back(real);
    v.push_back(slopes);

    err = queue.enqueueAcquireGLObjects(&v);
    checkErr(err, "Queue::enqueueAcquireGLObjects()");

    err = generateSpectrumKernel.setArg(1, real);
    err |= generateSpectrumKernel.setArg(3, width);
```

```
err |= generateSpectrumKernel.setArg(4, height);
err |= generateSpectrumKernel.setArg(5, animTime);
err |= generateSpectrumKernel.setArg(6, _patchSize);
checkErr(err, "Kernel::setArg(generateSpectrumKernel)");

err = queue.enqueueNDRangeKernel(
   generateSpectrumKernel,
   cl::NullRange,
   cl::NDRange(width+64,height),
   cl::NDRange(8,8));
checkErr(
   err,

   "CommandQueue::enqueueNDRangeKernel"
   " (generateSpectrumKernel)");

err = kfftKernel.setArg(0, real);
err = queue.enqueueNDRangeKernel(
  kfftKernel,
  cl::NullRange,
  cl::NDRange(FFT_SIZE*64),
  cl::NDRange(64));
checkErr(
   err,
   "CommandQueue::enqueueNDRangeKernel(kfftKernel1)");

err = ktranKernel.setArg(0, real);
err = queue.enqueueNDRangeKernel(
   ktranKernel,
   cl::NullRange,
   cl::NDRange(256*257/2 * 64),
   cl::NDRange(64));
checkErr(
   err,
   "CommandQueue::enqueueNDRangeKernel(ktranKernel1)");

err = queue.enqueueNDRangeKernel(
   kfftKernel,
   cl::NullRange,
   cl::NDRange(FFT_SIZE*64),
   cl::NDRange(64));
checkErr(
   err,
   "CommandQueue::enqueueNDRangeKernel(kfftKernel2)");

err  = calculateSlopeKernel.setArg(0, real);
err |= calculateSlopeKernel.setArg(1, slopes);
err |= calculateSlopeKernel.setArg(2, width);
```

```
    err |= calculateSlopeKernel.setArg(3, height);
    checkErr(err, "Kernel::setArg(calculatSlopeKernel)");

    err = queue.enqueueNDRangeKernel(
      calculateSlopeKernel,
      cl::NullRange,
      cl::NDRange(width,height),
      cl::NDRange(8,8));
    checkErr(err,

      "CommandQueue::enqueueNDRangeKernel(calculateSlopeKernel)");

    err = queue.enqueueReleaseGLObjects(&v);
    checkErr(err, "Queue::enqueueReleaseGLObjects()");

    queue.finish();

    return CL_SUCCESS;
}
```

The `runCLSimulation` function is straightforward and is composed of the following steps:

1. Acquires shared OpenGL objects, enforcing the OpenCL and OpenGL parts of the application to be in sync.

2. Time-steps the FFT spectrum, representing the transformed height field of the ocean. This is outlined in the next section, "Phillips Spectrum Generation."

3. Performs the inverse Fourier transform of the height field, outlined in detail later in the section "An OpenCL Discrete Fourier Transform."

4. Calculates slopes from the height map (used for normal generation in the rendering).

5. Releases shared OpenGL objects, enforcing the OpenCL and OpenGL parts of the application to again be in sync.

Phillips Spectrum Generation

To generate an initial (noise) distribution and account for wind direction and velocity, that inverse discrete fast Fourier transform (DFFT) is then applied to simulate the motion over time. We use a kernel to apply the Phillips spectrum. A detailed description of why this is a good choice is beyond the scope of this book; the interested reader is directed to

Tessendorf's work.[3] The Phillips spectrum is used to decide wave amplitudes at different (spatial or temporal) frequencies:

phillips(K) = A (exp (-1 / sqrt(kL)^2 / k^4) mag(norm(K) dot norm(w))^2

where

- k is the magnitude of K (the wave vector), which is 2 pi/lambda, where lambda is the length of the wave

- A is a constant globally affecting wave height

- L is v^2/g, which is the largest possible wave arising from a continuous wind with speed v, where gravitational constant $g = 9.81$

- norm(w) is the normalized wind vector (i.e., wind direction), and norm(K) is the normalized wave vector (i.e., wave direction)

The expression mag(norm(K) dot norm(w))^2 reduces a wave's magnitude that is moving perpendicular to the wind, while allowing ones that move against it.

As this initial step of generating the Phillips spectrum is computed only once for wind direction and velocity, we choose to implement this step on the host, and then at each stage of the simulation we perform the final step into the FFT spectrum, with respect to time, in OpenCL. Taking this approach avoids having to provide an OpenCL C random number generator; we saw this step as orthogonal, and because there was little to no performance impact it seemed unnecessary. However, it is also worth pointing out that just because we could do something in OpenCL it does not mean that we should; in this case it seemed that the additional work when traded off against the performance gain really could not be justified. The host code to perform this is as follows:

```
float phillips(
    float kx,
    float ky,
    float
    windSpeed,
    float windDirection)
{
    float fWindDir = windDirection * OPENCL_PI_F / 180.0f;

    static float A = 2.f*.00000005f;
    float L = windSpeed * windSpeed / 9.81f;
```

---

[3] Jerry Tessendorf, "Simulating Ocean Water," SIGGRAPH 1999, http://graphics. ucsd.edu/courses/rendering/2005/jdewall/tessendorf.pdf.

```
        float w = L / 75;
        float ksqr = kx * kx + ky * ky;
        float kdotwhat = kx * cosf(fWindDir) + ky * sinf(fWindDir);
        kdotwhat = max(0.0f, kdotwhat);

        float result =
                (float) (A * (pow(2.7183f, -1.0f / (L * L * ksqr))
                * (kdotwhat * kdotwhat)) / (ksqr * ksqr * ksqr));

        float damp = (float) expf(-ksqr * w * w);
        damp = expf(-1.0 / (ksqr * L * L));
        result *= kdotwhat < 0.0f ? 0.25f : 1.0f;

        return (result * damp);
}
```

This function is called for each `kx` and `ky` in the height field, whose dimensions are chosen to match the supported FFT dimensions. In this chapter we descibe a 1K×1K FFT implementation but the Ocean application itself supports the additional 2K×2K mode.

The following applies the `phillips` function to each position in the input space to produce an initial height field, with respect to the given wind speed and direction:

```
void generateHeightField(
    cl_float2 * h0,
    unsigned int fftInputH,
    unsigned int fftInputW)
{
    float fMultiplier, fAmplitude, fTheta;

    for (unsigned int y = 0; y<fftInputH; y++) {
        for (unsigned int x = 0; x<fftInputW; x++) {
            float kx = OPENCL_PI_F * x / (float) _patchSize;
            float ky = 2.0f * OPENCL_PI_F * y / (float) _patchSize;

            float Er = 2.0f * rand() / (float) RAND_MAX - 1.0f;
            float Ei = 2.0f * rand() / (float) RAND_MAX - 1.0f;


            if (!((kx == 0.f) && (ky == 0.f))) {
                fMultiplier = sqrt(phillips(kx,ky,windSpeed, windDir));
            }
            else {
                fMultiplier = 0.f;
            }

            fAmplitude = RandNormal(0.0f, 1.0f);
            fTheta = rand() / (float) RAND_MAX * 2 * OPENCL_PI_F;
```

```
          float h0_re = fMultiplier * fAmplitude * Er;
          float h0_im = fMultiplier * fAmplitude * Ei;
          int i = y*fftInputW+x;
          cl_float2 tmp = {h0_re, h0_im};
          h0[i] = tmp;
       }
    }
}
```

Finally, the following OpenCL kernel, along with two support functions, updates the spectrum on each iteration of the simulation, with respect to time, thus providing movement:

```
// complex math functions
float2 __attribute__((always_inline)) conjugate(float2 arg)
{
   return (float2)(arg.x, -arg.y);
}

float2 __attribute__((always_inline)) complex_exp(float arg)
{
   float s;
   float c;
   s = sincos(arg, &c);
   return (float2)(c,s);
}


__kernel void generateSpectrumKernel(
   __global float2* h0,
   __global float * ht_real,
   __global float * ht_imag,
   unsigned int width,
   unsigned int height,
   float t,
   float patchSize)
{
   size_t x = get_global_id(0);
   size_t y = get_global_id(1);
   unsigned int i = y*width+x;

   // calculate coordinates
   float2 k;
   k.x = M_PI * x / (float) patchSize;
   k.y = 2.0f * M_PI * y / (float) patchSize;

   // calculate dispersion w(k)
   float k_len = length(k);
   float w = sqrt(9.81f * k_len);
```

```
float2 h0_k  = h0[i];
float2 h0_mk = h0[((((height-1)-y)*width)+x];

float2 h_tilda = complex_mult(
    h0_k,
    complex_exp(w * t)) +
        complex_mult(conjugate(h0_mk), complex_exp(-w * t));

// output frequency-space complex values
if ((x < width) && (y < height)) {
    ht_real[i] = h_tilda.x;
    ht_imag[i] = h_tilda.y;
}
}
```

An OpenCL Discrete Fourier Transform

The discrete Fourier transform (DFT) is an extremely important operation in many fields because of its many special properties such as replacing convolution with pointwise multiplication[4] and very fast implementations.[5] Additionally, there are a number of very high-quality and high-performance implementations for the CPU, such as FFTW (http://fftw.org).

There are fewer implementations and less information available on producing efficient FFTs for OpenCL GPU devices. In the following sections we will walk through the detailed thinking behind the Ocean application and the resulting code used in it. While these sections are mostly focused on transforms of size 1024, we expect this kind of analysis to be quite useful for other sizes as well.

Determining 2D Decomposition

While it is possible to decompose a 2D FFT into smaller 2D FFTs followed by a "recombination" step, we will instead use the following usual approach to achieve the 2D transform:

1. Transform all rows using 1D FFT.

2. Transform all columns using 1D FFT.

---

[4] E. Brigham, *The Fourier Transform and Its Applications* (Prentice Hall, 1988).

[5] C. Van Loan, *Computational Frameworks for the Fast Fourier Transform* (Society for Industrial Mathematics, 1987); E. Chu and A. George, *Inside the FFT Black Box: Serial and Parallel Fast Fourier Transform Algorithms* (CRC Press, 1999).

However, for many memory systems, the accesses made in step 2 can suffer performance problems. We can investigate this on the GPU by timing two OpenCL kernels that add a constant to each element of a 1K×1K float array. The first kernel assigns a work-group to each row of the array, and the second assigns a work-group to each column. The elapsed times (in milliseconds) observed for each kernel for a few different work-group sizes are shown in Table 18.1.

Table 18.1 Kernel Elapsed Times for Varying Work-Group Sizes

Work-Group Size	Row Time (ms)	Row Time (with Pad) (ms)	Column Time (ms)	Column Time (with Pad) (ms)
64	0.077	0.085	9.60	0.856
128	0.068	0.083	10.0	1.50
256	0.062	0.068	10.6	1.50

The smallest row time of 0.062ms indicates that we were achieving a round-trip bandwidth of 133GB per second. The second (pad) time listed for each kernel shows the effect of adding a number of "pad" columns (64 on the device we used to obtain the timings) to improve the performance of the memory system. On the CPU, such padding is often done to reduce the effects of cache thrashing; on the GPU, padding can help spread the accesses over more memory controllers.

The large difference between the row time and column time suggests an alternative approach:

1. Transform all rows using 1D FFT.

2. Transpose 1K×1K array.

3. Transform all rows using 1D FFT.

4. Transpose 1K×1K array.

This can be faster than the first approach if the transpose can be performed quickly enough. Note that in the Ocean code, one of the transposes can be eliminated by simply constructing the data in transposed order. Similarly, leaving the result of a 2D FFT in transposed order is a typical option in FFT packages to improve performance.

Using Local Memory

A 1D FFT is usually carried out as a series of "passes" over the data. For instance, we can recursively expand the decimation-in-time binary decomposition until the transform length is 2 (where W is a diagonal array of roots of unity usually called "twiddle factors"):

$$\text{Outlo} = \text{FFT}(\text{In}_{\text{even}}) + W \, \text{FFT}(\text{In}_{\text{odd}})$$

$$\text{Out}_{\text{hi}} = \text{FFT}(\text{In}_{\text{even}}) - W \, \text{FFT}(\text{In}_{\text{odd}})$$

Thus we arrive at a procedure that requires ten passes over the data ($1024 = 2^{10}$):

$$\text{Out}_0 = \text{Pass0}(\text{In})$$

$$\text{Out}_1 = \text{Pass}_1(\text{Out}_0)$$

$$\text{Out} = \text{Pass}_9(\text{Out}_8)$$

Without local memory each pass requires a round trip of data from global memory. Also, element access during the pass may not hit the memory system efficiently.

Of course, the number of passes can be reduced by stopping the recursion earlier. Two passes of length 32 FFT would also work, as would five passes of length 4 FFT, as well as two passes of length 16 FFT followed by one pass of length 4. There are trade-offs with each of these choices, as we will see.

When local memory is used, some fraction of the data to be transformed is kept in local memory, and transfers to and from global memory may be reduced to just a few passes, such as the first and last passes. Other passes will read and write local memory, which, being on chip, is much faster than global memory. However, local memory is also a limited hardware resource and constrains the number of work-groups that can use it concurrently. This constraint directly affects the number of work-items in flight and hence the latency-hiding ability of the GPU.

For the Ocean 1K FFT we chose to make use of local memory to reduce the global memory traffic to just the first and last passes.

Determining the Sub-Transform Size

As mentioned previously, the amount of local memory used by a kernel constrains the number of work-items in flight. Another constraint is imposed by the number of physical registers used. Roughly speaking, the larger the number used, the fewer the work-items in flight. OpenCL C does not provide direct control over register use, but it can be controlled indirectly by the choice of algorithm and implementation of that algorithm.

A sub-transform of length R requires around $2R$ registers. However, near-optimal operation count short DFTs may require several more than $2R$ registers depending on the compiler. With register utilization figuring so prominently in latency hiding, it makes sense to look for minimal register implementations for a given R.

Using larger Rs means fewer passes but also potentially fewer work-items in flight. An FFT library should seek the best trade-off of these effects to achieve the best performance.

In the Ocean code, we chose to decompose the 1K FFT into five passes of length 4 sub-transforms ($1024 = 4^5$). A 4-point DFT can be computed in place with no additional registers:

```
ar0 = zr0 + zr2;
br1 = zr0 - zr2;
ar2 = zr1 + zr3;
br3 = zr1 - zr3;
zr0 = ar0 + ar2;
zr2 = ar0 - ar2;
ai0 = zi0 + zi2;
bi1 = zi0 - zi2;
ai2 = zi1 + zi3;
bi3 = zi1 - zi3;
zi0 = ai0 + ai2;
zi2 = ai0 - ai2;
zr1 = br1 + bi3;
zi1 = bi1 - br3;
zr3 = br1 - bi3;
zi3 = br3 + bi1;
```

The inputs and outputs here are `zr0...zr3` (real components) and `zi0... zi3` (imaginary components). Unfortunately, post-multiplication by the twiddle factors requires a few more registers to hold the twiddle factor(s) and intermediate results of the complex multiplication.

Determining the Work-Group Size

An OpenCL FFT kernel can adapt itself to the work-group size it is presented with at the cost of significant logic and indexing complexity.

Alternatively, control flow can be completely eliminated and indexing computation greatly reduced by using a kernel targeted for a specific transform length and work-group size. The most efficient work-group sizes are usually multiples of the hardware wavefront/warp size.

In the Ocean code, for our 1K length we use a work-group to process a single transform and considered work-group sizes of 64, 128, and 256. For work-group size 64, each work-item must process 16 points per pass, that is, four 4-point DFTs (which can be conveniently expressed using OpenCL C's `float4` type). For work-group size 128, each work-item must process 8 points per pass, and for work-group size 256, each work-item must process 4 points per pass. Of course, "points" is proportional to "registers," so the work-group size gives us a knob to adjust work-item register use. However, the number of registers used by the entire work-group does not change.

For the Ocean code, we chose the smaller work-group size of 64.

Obtaining the Twiddle Factors

The twiddle factors used in the FFT are a key ingredient in combining smaller transforms into larger ones. They are primitive nth roots of unity (or simple functions thereof) and are of the form $\cos(A) + i \sin(A)$ (where i is the imaginary value sqrt(-1) and A is 2 pi K/N, where N is the transform length and $0 <= K < N$). There are a variety of options for obtaining the twiddle factors affecting both performance and accuracy. They can be computed by the accurate OpenCL built-in `sin` and `cos` functions. They can instead be computed using either the built-in `half_sin` and `half_cos` functions or the built-in `native_sin` and `native_cos` functions. GPUs typically have limited-accuracy machine instructions for sine and cosine that are exposed by the `native_sin` and `native_cos` built-in functions. They can offer the highest performance, but the cost is reduced accuracy of the result.

Other options are to read precomputed twiddle factors from a constant buffer, image (texture), or global buffer. The first two are likely to be faster than the third because of caching, and the first can be used especially easily by simply defining a simple OpenCL `__constant` array in the kernel program itself.

It is also worth noting that a combination of approaches of varying accuracy may also be used based on various instances of the "double angle" formulas of trigonometry.

For the Ocean code, we decided that the accuracy of the native functions was sufficient.

Determining How Much Local Memory Is Needed

In each pass, a given work-item may require data produced by a different work-item on the previous pass. Local or global memory is needed to pass data between work-items, and we've determined that we'll use local memory. We can trade off between local memory size and complexity and number of barriers.

For instance, in the simplest (maximum use) case, a pass would look like this:

1. Load entire vector from local memory into registers.

2. Local barrier.

3. Compute sub-transform(s).

4. Save entire vector to local memory.

5. Local barrier.

If the entire vector is able to be held in registers, we can halve the amount of local memory needed by partially mixing passes into this:

1. Compute sub-transforms.

2. Save real part of vector to local memory.

3. Local barrier.

4. Read next pass real part of vector from local memory.

5. Local barrier.

6. Save imaginary part of vector to local memory.

7. Local barrier.

8. Read next pass imaginary part of vector from local memory.

It may be possible to reduce the amount of local memory even further by writing and reading subsets of the vector, along with more barriers.

In the Ocean code, we use the second approach and note that all the local barriers are essentially free because the work-group size we chose is the same as the wavefront size on the GPU hardware we are using.

Avoiding Local Memory Bank Conflicts

Local memories are often banked structures, and performance may be reduced when the work-group/wavefront/warp accesses only a small number of memory banks on a given access. There are a number of techniques to reduce conflicts, including more complicated addressing and/or padding.

Of course, padding can increase the amount of memory used by the kernel and end up degrading the ability of the GPU to hide latency, so ideally both cases should be compared.

For the Ocean code, we found that a transpose implementation with local memory bank conflicts performs at about the same speed as a conflict-free version. However, for the FFT, we found that a conflict-free implementation is about 61 percent faster than a version with conflicts.

Using Images

Up to this point, we have been assuming that the inputs and outputs of the FFT and transpose kernels have been OpenCL buffers. However, the inputs could instead be OpenCL read-only images (usually cached) and write-only images that are accessed using OpenCL samplers. If we consider the multipass structure of the FFT, though, the only significant differences in the implementation would be the initial read of data from the input image and the final store to the output image. The situation would be different if OpenCL were to ever allow read-write images.

A Closer Look at the FFT Kernel

The FFT kernel starts with this:

```
__kernel __attribute__((reqd_work_group_size (64,1,1))) void
kfft(__global float *greal, __global float *gimag)
{
    // This is 4352 bytes
    __local float lds[1088];
```

This tells us a few things already:

*   The kernel is designed specifically for a 1D iteration space with a work-group size of 64.

- The real and imaginary parts of the complex data are in separate arrays rather than interleaved within a single array. (This turns out to be most convenient for the rest of the Ocean code.)

- Because there are no other arguments, this kernel was designed for only one FFT size (1K).

- Some padding must be in use because 1088 is not the 1024 or 2048 that we might expect.

This kernel gets to pulling in the data pretty quickly:

```
uint gid = get_global_id(0);
uint me = gid & 0x3fU;
uint dg = (me << 2) + (gid >> 6) * VSTRIDE;
__global float4 *gr = (__global float4 *)(greal + dg);
__global float4 *gi = (__global float4 *)(gimag + dg);

float4 zr0 = gr[0*64];
float4 zr1 = gr[1*64];
float4 zr2 = gr[2*64];
float4 zr3 = gr[3*64];

float4 zi0 = gi[0*64];
float4 zi1 = gi[1*64];
float4 zi2 = gi[2*64];
float4 zi3 = gi[3*64];
```

Here, VSTRIDE is the number of elements between the first element of two successive rows. Each access to gr and gi pulls 1024 consecutive bytes from the vector being worked on, and each work-item gets four consecutive elements of the vector, each set of four separated by 256 elements, which is exactly what is required for the first pass of a length 4 sub-transform pass.

The first transform and multiplication by twiddle factor appear as

```
FFT4();
int4 tbase4 = (int)(me << 2) + (int4)(0, 1, 2, 3);
TW4IDDLE4();
```

The 4-point FFT was given previously when we determined the sub-transform size. Because the type of the variables is float4, the kernel must use at least 32 registers. We recall from when we obtained our twiddle factors that the twiddle factor "angle" is a multiple of 2 pi/1024. The specific multiple required by the first pass is given by the tbase4 computation. The actual computation of the twiddle factors is carried out by the following function, where ANGLE is 2 pi/1024:

```
__attribute__((always_inline)) float4
k_sincos4(int4 i, float4 *cretp)
{
    i -= (i > 512) & 1024;
    float4 x = convert_float4(i) * -ANGLE;
    *cretp = native_cos(x);
    return native_sin(x);
}
```

The first statement in the function quickly and accurately reduces the range of the angle to the interval `[-pi, pi]`.

Following the actual computation, each work-item needs to save the values it has produced and read the new ones it needs for the next pass. Let's look at a single store and load at the end of the first pass:

```
__local float *lp = lds + ((me << 2) + (me >> 3));
lp[0] = zr0.x;
...
barrier(CLK_LOCAL_MEM_FENCE);
lp = lds + (me + (me >> 5));
zr0.x = lp[0*66];
```

Each store to or load from `lp` is of course a SIMD parallel operation. The local memory on the GPU we used has 32 banks of 32-bit values. Using the previous addressing expressions, we can compute the first several load and store banks, as shown in Table 18.2.

Table 18.2 Load and Store Bank Calculations

me	Store Bank	Load Bank
0	0	0
1	4	1
2	8	2
3	12	3
4	16	4
5	20	5
6	24	6
7	28	7

continues

Table 18.2 Load and Store Bank Calulations (*Continued*)

me	Store Bank	Load Bank
8	1	8
9	5	9
10	9	10
11	13	11
12	17	12
13	21	13
14	25	14
15	29	15

It turns out that all 64 work-items in the work-group access each bank exactly twice on each load and store, which is optimal.

The following four passes look very much like the first with the exception that the twiddle factors vary more slowly and the addressing into local memory changes because of the different elements needed for each pass. In each case the addressing has been chosen to minimize bank conflicts.

In the last pass, the twiddle factors are all 1.0, so the final sub-transform and store back to global memory looks like the following, where again each store transfers 1024 consecutive bytes back to global memory:

```
FFT4();

gr[0*64] = zr0;
gr[1*64] = zr1;
gr[2*64] = zr2;
gr[3*64] = zr3;

gi[0*64] = zi0;
gi[1*64] = zi1;
gi[2*64] = zi2;
gi[3*64] = zi3;
```

On the GPU we tested, transforming 1024 vectors using this kernel takes about 0.13ms. Using the standard $5\,N\log_2(N)$ approximation for the flop count for an FFT of length N, this time corresponds to a rate of about 400

GFLOPS per second. It also corresponds to a round-trip bandwidth from global memory of about 130GB per second.

A Closer Look at the Transpose Kernel

The transpose kernel is responsible for transposing the two 1024×1024 arrays that make up the complex data. Because these arrays are square, the operation can be performed in place quite easily. As one might expect, we break the arrays into smaller blocks. Each work-group is then assigned a pair of blocks, (i, j) and (j, i), which are then read into local memory and transposed. Block (i, j) is then stored to location (j, i), and block (j, i) is stored to location (i, j). We evaluated a few different block sizes and settled on a 32×32 block for the Ocean code.

One small question arises: how to assign a block to a work-group, because operating on all blocks as previously described would only end up transposing the diagonal blocks. We make use of a convenient quadratic polynomial:

$$p_B(t) = -\tfrac{1}{2}\, t^2 + (B + \tfrac{1}{2})\, t$$

At the non-negative integers, this polynomial takes on the values 0, B, $B + (B - 1)$, $B + (B - 1) + (B - 2)$, and so on. Given our 32×32 block size, if we choose $B = 1024/32 = 32$, we can compute (i, j) using this code found in the transpose kernel:

```
uint gid = get_global_id(0);
uint me = gid & 0x3fU;
uint k = gid >> 6;
int l = 32.5f - native_sqrt(1056.25f - 2.0f * (float)as_int(k));
int kl = ((65 - l) * l) >> 1;
uint j = k - kl;
uint i = l + j;
```

The blocks accessed run down the diagonal and then the subdiagonals.

Given our work-group size of 64, each work-item must handle 16 points of the block. The block is read using

```
uint go = ((me & 0x7U) << 2) + (me >> 3)*VSTRIDE;
uint goa = go + (i << 5) + j * (VSTRIDE*32);
uint gob = go + (j << 5) + i * (VSTRIDE*32);

__global float4 *gp = (__global float4 *)(greal + goa);
float4 z0 = gp[0*VSTRIDE/4*8];
```

```
float4 z1 = gp[1*VSTRIDE/4*8];
float4 z2 = gp[2*VSTRIDE/4*8];
float4 z3 = gp[3*VSTRIDE/4*8];
```

We've assigned the threads so that each access fetches eight 256-byte chunks of global memory.

The transpose in the Ocean code uses the conflict-free approach. So just as for the FFT, the addressing of loads and stores to local memory is slightly complicated. The first store and load looks like this:

```
uint lo = (me >> 5) + (me & 0x7U)*9 + ((me >> 3) & 0x3U)*(9*8);
__local float *lp = ldsa + lo;
lp[0*2] = z0.x;
...
barrier(CLK_LOCAL_MEM_FENCE);

uint lot = (me & 0x7U) + ((me >> 3) & 0x3U)*
                                (9*8*4 + 8) + (me >> 5)*9;
lp = ldsa + lot;
z0.x = lp[0*2*9];
```

Once again, these accesses are optimal. Data is written back to global memory in the same eight 256-byte chunks per access.

On the machine we tested, using a VSTRIDE of 1088, the Ocean transpose kernel runs in about 0.14ms, which corresponds to a round-trip bandwidth to global memory of about 120GB per second.

Thus, the time for the entire 2D FFT used in Ocean is roughly 0.13 + 0.14 + 0.13 = 0.40 ms.

## Chapter 19

Optical Flow

Optical flow is a fundamental concept in computer vision. Optical flow describes the motion that occurs between images and has application in image stabilization, frame rate upsampling, and motion or gesture analysis. In this chapter, we will discuss an implementation of pyramidal Lucas-Kanade (LK) optical flow.[1] Sub-pixel accuracy is essential to the implementation and is maintained by a number of resampling operations requiring linear interpolation. As we will see, the texture-filtering hardware on the GPU can be used to perform linear interpolation of data, which can provide significant speedups. Additionally, we will discuss how local memory and early kernel exit techniques provide acceleration.

Optical Flow Problem Overview

Optical flow describes the motion that occurs between images. At each point in the image, we will compute a 2D flow vector that describes the motion that occurred between points in the images. This is called "dense" optical flow because it produces a dense set of vectors for the entire image, in contrast to tracking only a few sparse points. Optical flow is computationally intensive, and other implementations attempt only sparse computation, whereas we will discuss a dense implementation that achieves high performance on a GPU using OpenCL.

As an intuitive explanation, consider the situation where we know the gradient of the image at some location. This tells us if it is getting brighter or darker in some direction. If we later observe that the location itself has become brighter or darker, we can make some inference as to the motion of the image content. This makes the assumption that the brightness of

---

[1]   J. Y. Bouguet, "Pyramidal Implementation of the Lucas Kanade Feature Tracker," Intel Corporation Microprocessor Research Labs (2000).

the object itself isn't changing and so the change in pixel brightness is due to motion. Given two images $I(x, y)$ and $J(x, y)$, we seek to find the image velocities d_x and d_y that minimize the residual error:

$$\varepsilon(d) = \varepsilon(d_x, d_y) = \sum_{x=u_x-w_x}^{u_x+w_x} \sum_{y=u_y-w_y}^{u_y+w_y} (I(x,y) - J(x+d_x+d_y))^2 \tag{1}$$

Here we have a window of size (w_x, w_y) centered around a point (u_x, u_y), where (x, y) denotes the position in the window. Thus for each pixel with its surrounding window, we are searching for the motion that minimizes the difference in brightness, indicating where that region has moved.

This chapter presents an implementation of optical flow using OpenCL. In the discussion, we will use test images from the "MiniCooper"[2] data set. Figure 19.1 shows two images from this set where we see that a man is closing the trunk of a car. Figure 19.2 shows the recovered motion vectors from two sequential images in the set. The motion vectors occur around the area of the trunk and where the man moves; both areas have vectors generally pointing downward as the trunk closes.

| (a) | (b) |

Figure 19.1   A pair of test images of a car trunk being closed. The first (a) and fifth (b) images of the test sequence are shown.

---

[2] Simon Baker et al., "A Database and Evaluation Methodology for Optical Flow," *International Journal of Computer Vision* 92, no. 1 (March 2011): 1–31.

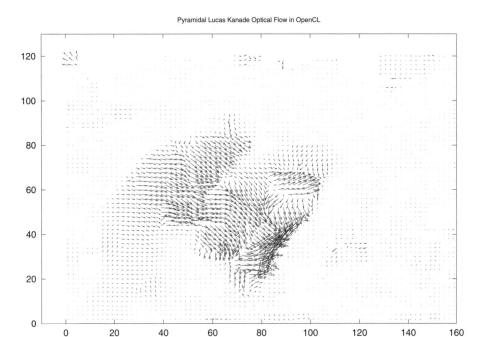

Figure 19.2 Optical flow vectors recovered from the test images of a car trunk being closed. The fourth and fifth images in the sequence were used to generate this result.

There are many methods of finding the optical flow between images. Here we discuss the implementation of pyramidal Lucas-Kanade optical flow, which is presented because it is a widely known and studied algorithm that may be familiar to the reader and facilitates discussion of the GPU mappings.

Computationally, Lucas-Kanade optical flow minimizes the residual error, which reduces essentially to finding the optical flow $v = [v_x, v_y]^T$ as

$$v = G^{-1}b \tag{2}$$

The matrix G and vector b are given by the image values I, J and derivatives $I_x, I_y,$ and I_{xy} (the product of I_x and I_y):

$$G = \sum_{x=p_x-w_x}^{p_x+w_x} \sum_{y=p_y-w_y}^{p_y+w_y} \begin{bmatrix} I_x^2 & I_{xy} \\ I_{xy} & I_y^2 \end{bmatrix} \tag{3}$$

$$b = \sum_{x=p_x-w_x}^{p_x+w_x} \sum_{y=p_y-w_y}^{p_y+w_y} \begin{bmatrix} \partial I(x,y) I_x(x,y) \\ \partial I(x,y) I_y(x,y) \end{bmatrix} \qquad (4)$$

Here $\partial I(x, y)$ is termed the **image difference** and b the **mismatch vector**.

The algorithm operates on image pyramids. Each level of the image pyramid is the same image with different scales. The bottom of the pyramid is the initial image, and each pyramid level is the image scaled by some scaling factor. In our implementation each level is scaled by 0.5 in each image dimension.

The image difference at level L for iteration k is computed as

$$\partial I_k(x,y) = I^L(x,y) - J^L(x + g_x^L + v_x^{k-1}, y + g_y^L + v_y^{k-1}) \qquad (5)$$

Pyramidal Lucas-Kanade optical flow is an iterative scheme, where equation (2) is evaluated iteratively at each position for k iterations, with the guess for the flow vector being refined $(x', y') = (x + v_x, y + v_y)$ at each iteration, at each level. Here, (g_x^L, g_y^L) is the guess for the flow from the previous pyramid level, and (v_x^k, v_y^k) is the calculation of the flow at iteration k at the present level. The iterative reevaluation of equation (2) requires heavy computation.

The algorithm proceeds from the upper levels L down to level 0 (full-size image).

At each level, the flow vector, $v = [v_x, v_y]^T$, computed from the previous level is used as a starting guess to the current level, and for the initial level it is initialized as (0, 0). Figure 19.3 depicts an implementation of the pyramidal LK optical flow algorithm based on the image pyramid structure. It shows the process of downsampling the images, computing image derivatives and the matrix G, and then computing the flow from smallest to largest pyramid level.

First, we discuss the overall approach to mapping this to the GPU. The algorithm begins by creating the image pyramids, storing each level in texture memory on the GPU. From the equations, it can be seen that we need image pyramids for the images, I, J, and derivatives, I_x, I_y. Image pyramid creation proceeds from the base pyramid level and generates successively high levels. For each pyramid level, images are filtered in two kernels that implement a separable filter. A separable filter implements a 2D filter kernel as two 1D filter kernel passes. In our implementation we implement a 5×5 filter kernel by horizontal 1×5 and vertical 5×1 filter kernels. These kernels simply read image values around a center pixel and

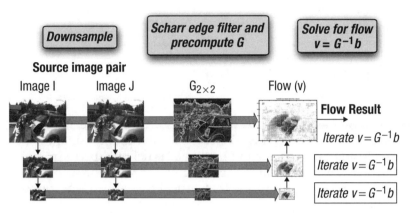

Figure 19.3   Pyramidal Lucas-Kanade optical flow algorithm

calculate a weighted sum. The horizontal kernel can be implemented as shown in the next code block. Note that we have omitted code to perform efficient coalesced memory writes and use textures for simplicity and because the majority of the time is spent computing the flow kernel shown later.

```
__kernel void downfilter_x_g(
    __read_only image2d_t src,
    __global uchar *dst, int dst_w, int dst_h )
{

    sampler_t srcSampler = CLK_NORMALIZED_COORDS_FALSE |
        CLK_ADDRESS_CLAMP_TO_EDGE |
        CLK_FILTER_NEAREST ;

    const int ix = get_global_id(0);
    const int iy = get_global_id(1);

    float x0 =
        read_imageui( src, srcSampler, (int2)(ix-2,iy)).x/16.0f;
    float x1 =
        read_imageui( src, srcSampler, (int2)(ix-1,iy)).x/4.0f;
    float x2 =
        (3*read_imageui( src, srcSampler, (int2)(ix,iy)).x)/8.0f;
    float x3 =
        read_imageui( src, srcSampler, (int2)(ix+1,iy)).x/4.0f;
    float x4 =
        read_imageui( src, srcSampler, (int2)(ix+2,iy)).x/16.0f;

    int output = round( x0 + x1 + x2 + x3 + x4 );
```

```
        if( ix < dst_w && iy < dst_h ) {
          // uncoalesced when writing to memory object
          // acceptable if caches present, otherwise should be written
          // for coalesced memory accesses
          dst[iy*dst_w + ix ] = (uchar)output;
        }
}
```

Because we are downsampling, a lowpass filter is used and a decimation by two is also applied after filtering to create the next-higher (smaller) pyramid level. Note that we can avoid having a kernel only performing decimation. Instead, we can combine the decimation with the second, vertical filter pass by only performing the vertical pass at pixel locations that write to the next level after decimation. This can be done by launching a kernel that covers the dimensions of the upper level and multiplying the lookups by 2 to index into the lower level correctly before writing the results. The following code shows the vertical filtering and decimation kernel:

```
__kernel void downfilter_y_g(
    __read_only image2d_t src,
    __global uchar *dst, int dst_w, int dst_h )
{
    sampler_t srcSampler = CLK_NORMALIZED_COORDS_FALSE |
        CLK_ADDRESS_CLAMP_TO_EDGE |
        CLK_FILTER_NEAREST ;

    const int ix = get_global_id(0);
    const int iy = get_global_id(1);

    float x0 = read_imageui( src, srcSampler,
            (int2)(2*ix,2*iy-2) ).x/16.0f;
    float x1 = read_imageui( src, srcSampler,
            (int2)(2*ix,2*iy-1) ).x/4.0f;
    float x2 = (3*read_imageui( src, srcSampler,
            (int2)(2*ix,2*iy) ).x)/8.0f;
    float x3 = read_imageui( src, srcSampler,
            (int2)(2*ix,2*iy+1) ).x/4.0f;
    float x4 = read_imageui( src, srcSampler,
            (int2)(2*ix,2*iy+2) ).x/16.0f;

    int output = round(x0 + x1 + x2 + x3 + x4);

    if( ix < dst_w-2 && iy < dst_h-2 ) {
        dst[iy*dst_w + ix ] = (uchar)output;
    }
}
```

Noting again the components of equations (3) and (4), we see that in addition to the image pyramid values, we require derivative values at each level of the pyramid. This is done by sending the newly computed image pyramid to kernels that compute the derivatives at each level. Note also that the derivative computation at each image level is independent of the others, and when supported, GPU hardware can run different derivative kernels concurrently for more efficiency. The derivative computation is a 3×3 filter kernel implemented in two passes as a separable filter.

Given the image pyramids for I and J and image derivative pyramids for each level of I, the flow is calculated according to equation (2), starting from the upper level of the pyramid, and propagating results down through pyramid levels until the base level is reached, generating dense optical flow results. The kernel for computing optical flow at each pyramid level is iterative, performing the computation a number of times. First note that for equation (2), the components v and b change each iteration. v is solved each iteration and so changes, and b has the following components, as shown in equation (5), which change each iteration:

$$(x + g_x^L + v_x^{k-1}, y + g_y^L + v_y^{k-1})$$

The matrix G, however, remains fixed in position and its values remain the same and so can be precomputed at each image location and simply retrieved when needed at the first iteration of each computation of equation (2). Because G is composed of local sums of derivative values, each work-item reads the local x and y derivative values and computes a four-component image value. The four-component vector type serves in this case as a handy data type for storing the 2×2 matrix G. Depending on the accuracy required, G can be saved as an `int4` data type, because for input pixels in the range of [0, 255] the maximum squared image derivative falls within the capabilities of a 32-bit integer. If the filters used for downsampling and derivatives produced only integer results, this maintains accuracy. In case more accuracy is desired, floating-point could be used throughout at the cost of increased memory access time and space requirements. The following kernel gathers the data for G into a single memory buffer. Here, `FRAD` is defined as the radius of the window within which G is gathered.

```
#define FRAD 4
// G is int4 output
// This kernel generates the "G" matrix
// (2x2 covariance matrix on the derivatives)
// Each thread does one pixel,
// sampling its neighborhood of +/- FRAD
```

```
// radius and generates the G matrix entries.
__kernel void filter_G( __read_only image2d_t Ix,
                        __read_only image2d_t Iy,
                        __global int4 *G, int dst_w, int dst_h )
{
  sampler_t srcSampler = CLK_NORMALIZED_COORDS_FALSE |
                         CLK_ADDRESS_CLAMP_TO_EDGE |
                         CLK_FILTER_NEAREST ;
  const int idx = get_global_id(0);
  const int idy = get_global_id(1);

  int Ix2 = 0;
  int IxIy = 0;
  int Iy2 = 0;
  for( int j=-FRAD ; j <= FRAD; j++ ) {
    for( int i=-FRAD ; i<= FRAD ; i++ ) {
      int ix = read_imagei(Ix,srcSampler,(int2)(idx+i,idy+j)).x;
      int iy = read_imagei(Iy,srcSampler,(int2)(idx+i,idy+j)).x;

      Ix2 += ix*ix;
      Iy2 += iy*iy;
      IxIy += ix*iy;

    }
  }
  int4 G2x2 = (int4)( Ix2, IxIy, IxIy, Iy2 );
  if( idx < dst_w && idy < dst_h ) {
    G[ idy * dst_w + idx ] = G2x2;
  }
}
```

Now, with G, *I*, and *J* pyramids and the derivative pyramids calculated,
the flow computation of equation (2) can be calculated in a single kernel.
We now look at parts of a kernel that solves for the flow vector given G, *I*,
and *J* pyramids and the derivative pyramids. This kernel iteratively solves
the equation until some convergence criteria or maximum number of
iterations is reached.

The following code shows the kernel solving for the optical flow. Some
discussion of the kernel is presented inline. Note that I, I_x, and I_y are reading from local memory; those lines are omitted here and discussed later.
Additionally, we are using a bilinear sampling object, `bilinSampler`,
also discussed later. For now the inline discussion will focus on steps that
compute the flow vector. We begin by showing the beginning of the kernel called `lkflow`, including its parameter and variable declarations, and
computation of its indices for accessing the input images:

```
#define FRAD 4
#define eps 0.0000001f;

// NB: It's important that these match the launch parameters!
#define LOCAL_X 16
#define LOCAL_Y 8

__kernel void lkflow(
  __read_only image2d_t I,
  __read_only image2d_t Ix,
  __read_only image2d_t Iy,
  __read_only image2d_t G,
  __read_only image2d_t J_float,
  __global float2 *guess_in,
  int guess_in_w,
  __global float2 *guess_out,
  int guess_out_w,
  int guess_out_h,
  int use_guess )
{
  // declare some shared memory (see details below)
  __local int smem[2*FRAD + LOCAL_Y][2*FRAD + LOCAL_X] ;
  __local int smemIy[2*FRAD + LOCAL_Y][2*FRAD + LOCAL_X] ;
  __local int smemI[2*FRAD + LOCAL_Y][2*FRAD + LOCAL_X] ;

  // Create sampler objects. One is for nearest neighbor,
  // the other for bilinear interpolation
  sampler_t bilinSampler = CLK_NORMALIZED_COORDS_FALSE |
                           CLK_ADDRESS_CLAMP_TO_EDGE |
                           CLK_FILTER_LINEAR ;
  sampler_t nnSampler = CLK_NORMALIZED_COORDS_FALSE |
                        CLK_ADDRESS_CLAMP_TO_EDGE |
                        CLK_FILTER_NEAREST ;

  // Image indices. Note for the texture, we offset by 0.5 to
  //use the center of the texel.
  int2 iIidx = { get_global_id(0), get_global_id(1)};
  float2 Iidx = { get_global_id(0)+0.5, get_global_id(1)+0.5 };
```

The next steps of the kernel shown here copy data into local memory, but the code and discussion are deferred until later:

```
  // load some data into local memory because it will be reused
  // frequently
  // ( see details below )
  // ...
```

Between levels, the motion estimated, n, is propagated as the starting input for the next level, appropriately scaled to account for the larger image size. The following code determines the appropriate lookup for the guess from the previous pyramid level, when available, and then retrieves and scales it:

```
float2 g = {0,0};
// Previous pyramid levels provide input guess. Use if available.
if( use_guess != 0 ) {
  // lookup in higher level, div by two to find position
  // because it's smaller
  int gin_x = iIidx.x/2;
  int gin_y = iIidx.y/2;
  float2 g_in = guess_in[gin_y * guess_in_w + gin_x ];
  // multiply the motion by two because we are in a larger level.
  g.x = g_in.x*2;
  g.y = g_in.y*2;
}
```

Next, G is read from its four-component data type buffer. It is then inverted to form a 2×2 matrix G^{-1}. When inverting, a determinant is computed and care is taken to set the determinant to a small non-zero value in case of a 0 determinant because it is used as a divisor in the 2×2 matrix inversion. The following code shows the lookup of the G matrix values and the matrix inversion:

```
// invert G, 2x2 matrix, use float since
// int32 will overflow quickly
int4 Gmat = read_imagei( G, nnSampler, iIidx );
float det_G =
  (float)Gmat.s0 * (float)Gmat.s3 -
  (float)Gmat.s1 * (float)Gmat.s2 ;
// avoid possible 0 in denominator
if( det_G == 0.0f ) det_G = eps;
float4 Ginv = {
  Gmat.s3/det_G, -Gmat.s1/det_G,
  -Gmat.s2/det_G,  Gmat.s0/det_G };
```

The kernel then proceeds by calculating the mismatch vector $\partial I_k (x, y)$ in equation (5) to find b. Given G^{-1} and b, the updated motion is found as $v = G^{-1}b$, and the process repeats until convergence or some maximum number of iterations. We can define convergence in this case as happening when the change in the motion vector is negligible, because in that case, the next iteration will look up similar values and the motion will remain negligible, indicating some local solution has been reached. The following code shows this iterative computation of the motion as well as the check for convergence:

```
// for large motions we can approximate them faster by applying
// gain to the motion
float2 v = {0,0};
float gain = 4;
for( int k=0 ; k < 8 ; k++ ) {
  float2 Jidx = { Iidx.x + g.x + v.x, Iidx.y + g.y + v.y };
  float2 b = {0,0};
  float2 n = {0,0};

  // calculate the mismatch vector
  for( int j=-FRAD ; j <= FRAD ; j++ ) {
    for( int i=-FRAD ; i<= FRAD ; i++ ) {
      int Isample = smemI[tIdx.y + FRAD +j][tIdx.x + FRAD+ i];

      float Jsample = read_imagef( J_float,bilinSampler,
        Jidx+(float2)(i,j) ).x;
      float dIk = (float)Isample - Jsample;
      int ix,iy;
      ix = smem[tIdx.y + FRAD +j][tIdx.x + FRAD+ i];
      iy = smemIy[tIdx.y + FRAD +j][tIdx.x + FRAD+ i];
      b += (float2)( dIk*ix*gain, dIk*iy*gain );
    }
  }

  // Optical flow (Lucas-Kanade).
  //  Solve n = G^-1 * b
  //compute n (update), mult Ginv matrix by vector b
  n = (float2)(Ginv.s0*b.s0 + Ginv.s1*b.s1,Ginv.s2*b.s0
    + Ginv.s3*b.s1);

  //if the determinant is not plausible,
  //suppress motion at this pixel
  if( fabs(det_G)<1000) n = (float2)(0,0);
  // break if no motion
  if( length(n) < 0.004  ) break;

  // guess for next iteration: v_new = v_current + n
  v = v + n;
}
int2 outCoords = { get_global_id(0), get_global_id(1) };

if( Iidx.x < guess_out_w && Iidx.y < guess_out_h ) {
  guess_out[ outCoords.y * guess_out_w + outCoords.x ] =
    (float2)(v.x + g.x, v.y + g.y);
}

} // end kernel
```

Sub-Pixel Accuracy with Hardware Linear Interpolation

Many algorithms require sub-pixel image sampling. In the case of our LK optical flow example, sub-pixel accuracy is required for computing the image difference of equation (5) at each iteration k and level L because after each iteration, the currently computed motion is used to resample the original image data by applying the following offset to the lookup:

$$(g_x^L + v_x^{k-1}, g_y^L + v_y^{k-1})$$

This can be easily achieved by sending the current lookup location as floating-point values to a texture sampler function, with the sampler set to perform linear interpolation:

$$(x + g_x^L + v_x^{k-1}, y + g_y^L + v_y^{k-1})$$

The GPU will return a bilinearly interpolated sample at the given location. Care should be taken when using linear interpolation to offset the texture coordinates by 0.5 appropriately, because typically the work-item and work-group IDs are used to create an integer index that then needs to be offset by 0.5 (the "center" of the texel) before applying any additional offsets, such as the motion vectors in our example. On NVIDIA GPUs, the CUDA programming guide contains full details on the interpolation performed by the hardware. Using hardware interpolation performs what would otherwise be four lookups and arithmetic operations in a single lookup.

Application of the Texture Cache

A useful feature of the texturing hardware on the GPU is the presence of a texture cache. The cache is useful when many samples are taken from a 2D spatially local area. This occurs frequently in many image-processing algorithms. In the case of our optical flow example, the iterative computation of the mismatch vector in equation (5) requires a number of 2D texture lookups within the window area (w_x, w_y), Additionally, note that the center of the window (p_x, p_y) varies, dependent on the current motion vector guess, and thus the window location varies per iteration and at each location because different areas of the image will exhibit different motions.

Despite the variations, the motions typically exhibit some degree of locality per iteration, the update will typically be small and sub-pixel, the motion will vary slowly across the image, and regions of an image will exhibit similar motions. The texture hardware caching mechanisms are transparent to the programmer, and no explicit code or limitations on the motion are imposed by the caching mechanism.

Using Local Memory

While the texture cache is useful, a programmer may wish to use it for all of I, J and derivative data I_x and I_y. On a GTX 460 graphics card, it was observed to achieve only about 65 percent cache hits (a runtime profiler, such as the CUDA Visual Profiler, can be used to retrieve these statistics for a kernel). Because so many textures are used, cache data may be evicted even though it may need to be reloaded later.

One observation is that for a given work-group, at each iteration of the flow, the same data for I, I_x, and I_y is repeatedly read from the texture. To alleviate the demands on the texture cache, we can use OpenCL local memory as a user-managed cache. Local memory (also referred to as shared memory in the terminology of CUDA hardware) is memory that resides at the processing units of a GPU and so can be accessed fast. For each work-group, we read from a tile of data the size of the work-group plus a border whose width is the width of the window (w_x, w_y). These borders can be considered as an apron around the tile. A tile of data and its surrounding apron can be read from texture memory and placed into local memory for each of I, I_x, and I_y.

Because the apron and tile areas combined contain more pixels than threads in the work-group, the copying of data into local memory can be achieved by four reads by the work-group. These read operations copy the upper left and right and lower left and right regions of the combined tile and apron areas, and care is taken in the latter three not to overrun the local memory area. Note that the data for image J is not copied to local memory. This is because we are making use of the linear interpolation hardware that is used when reading from the texture memory.

Also at each iteration of the flow calculation the lookup location varies and may move outside any set tile area, and so J is best left in texture memory. The values for the G matrix need only be read once and are unique to each thread, and so the threads store the values for G as a kernel variable (which places them in a register). After reading the data from texture memory into local memory, a barrier call is used to ensure that all threads in the work-group have written their input to local memory. Only the copying of data for I is shown for brevity. In the full optical flow kernel, these copies are performed for each of I, I_x, and I_y.

Recall from earlier that we are using a FRAD of 4 and a local work-group size of 16×8:

```
#define FRAD 4
#define LOCAL_X 16
#define LOCAL_Y 8
```

The copying from textures into local memory then can be accomplished with a few lines. The local memory size is the size of the work-group plus the window radius of FRAD on all sides. Here, we show the code for copying into local memory that we alluded to earlier. The code places the image values into local memory arrays, which are the size of the work-group plus the surrounding apron pixels. The following code relies on the presence of a global memory cache for efficient access but could also be written to minimize non-coalesced accesses on older architectures:

```
int2 tIdx = { get_local_id(0), get_local_id(1) };

// declare some local memory
__local int smem[2*FRAD + LOCAL_Y][2*FRAD + LOCAL_X] ;

// load upper left region of smem
smem[ tIdx.y ][ tIdx.x ] = read_imageui( Ix, nnSampler,
  Iidx+(float2)(-FRAD,-FRAD) ).x;

// upper right
if( tIdx.x < 2*FRAD ) {
  smem[ tIdx.y ][ tIdx.x + LOCAL_X ] =
  read_imageui( Ix, nnSampler,
    Iidx+(float2)(LOCAL_X - FRAD,-FRAD) ).x;
}
// lower left
if( tIdx.y < 2*FRAD ) {
  smem[ tIdx.y + LOCAL_Y ][ tIdx.x ] =
  read_imageui( Ix, nnSampler,
    Iidx+(float2)(-FRAD, LOCAL_Y-FRAD) ).x;
}
// lower right
if( tIdx.x < 2*FRAD && tIdx.y < 2*FRAD ) {
  smem[ tIdx.y + LOCAL_Y ][ tIdx.x + LOCAL_X ] =
  read_imageui( Ix, nnSampler, Iidx+
    (float2)(LOCAL_X - FRAD, LOCAL_Y - FRAD) ).x;
}
// Wait for all threads to populate local memory array
barrier(CLK_LOCAL_MEM_FENCE);
```

Early Exit and Hardware Scheduling

The flow calculation is iterative and can exit when the change in motion vector becomes negligible. Consider an image taken from a static camera where an object moves through the scene. In such a case, motion occurs only at points on and around the object and not elsewhere. For the parts of the scene that have no motion, the flow calculation can exit early, after the first or at most a few iterations (due to noise). Also, motion generally tends to be spatially coherent. This means that for many work-groups, all the work-items may converge before reaching the maximum number of iterations.

This is advantageous on generations of GPU hardware that are able to efficiently schedule new work-groups as older ones complete. In areas where there is motion, the work-groups will remain processing longer. Those work-groups that have both motion and non-motion remain resident on the GPU until all the work-items complete. The ability of a kernel to exit early is advantageous; in the case of the test sequence used in our discussion, without the early exit, it took 1.5 times longer to complete than with early exit.

Efficient Visualization with OpenGL Interop

To see optical flow at work, we would like to visualize the resulting flow vectors on the screen. When the images are sourced from a camera video stream, we can create an interactive viewing application. In this case, we would also like to perform the visualization efficiently. There are two parts to the visualization: the images and the flow vector. For the image, either image *I* or *J* is chosen and can be associated with texture data as discussed in Chapter 10. This is relatively straightforward; instead we will discuss using OpenGL interop to draw the flow vectors as line primitives.

Because final flow vectors reside on the graphics hardware already, this is a good opportunity to use the OpenGL interop capabilities of OpenCL. The flow vectors are drawn in the typical way: a vertex buffer is created in OpenGL and an associated OpenCL memory object is created from the vertex buffer using `clCreateFromGLBuffer()`. To draw motion vectors we wish to draw line segments specified by their start and end positions, and so each drawing primitive should have an (*x*, *y*) start and end position that totals four components. The vertex buffer object is created as width×height×sizeof(float)×4 to accommodate four elements (two pairs of coordinates). After the flow has been calculated in OpenCL, we use OpenCL to set this buffer.

A simple kernel is used to write the image coordinates of each pixel as the starting coordinates of the vector. This is done by creating a position from the global ID of the work-item, which corresponds to a pixel raster coordinate. The kernel is also given the memory object containing the motion vector data. The motion vector is added to the coordinates, and this end coordinate is written to the last two elements of the vector. Additionally, many of the locations are suppressed by setting their start and end positions to (0, 0) or some offscreen location. This is because if all the vectors were shown at the same time, the vectors would be too dense to view. So the kernel performs the update only for some pixel locations and ignores others. Finally, the results can be displayed by binding the updated vertex buffer and calling `glDrawArrays()` with the `GL_LINES` primitive argument, which expects start and end vertices. The kernel to perform these operations is shown next. It writes start and end vertex positions and suppresses some results for viewing.

```
__kernel void motion(
  __global float4 *p,  // output vertex buffer
  __global float2 *v,  // input flow vectors
  int w, int h )
{
  const int ix = get_global_id(0);
  const int iy = get_global_id(1);

  if( ix < w && iy < h ) {
    float4 startp = (float4)( ix, iy, ix, iy);
    float2 motion = v[iy*w + ix] ;
    float4 endp = (float4)(
      startp.x,
      startp.y,
      startp.x + motion.x ,
      startp.y + motion.y );
    if( ix % 10 == 0 && iy % 10 == 0 &&
      fabs(motion.x) < 20 && fabs(motion.y) < 20)
      p[iy*w + ix ] = (float4)endp;
    else
      p[iy*w + ix ] = (float4)(0,0,0,0);
  }
}
```

Performance

Table 19.1 shows the performance of the OpenCL optical flow algorithm. Using the radius and iterations shown previously, the GPU LK optical flow pipeline is able to process the test 640×480 "MiniCooper" image in 20.5ms on a GTX 460, which contains 7 multiprocessors. On a GTX 580 with 16 multiprocessors the same test took 9.2ms. The application of local memory made a significant difference, which could be seen by using either local memory or texture lookups for the image data.

Table 19.1   GPU Optical Flow Performance

	3 Texture Lookups, 0 Local Memory Arrays (ms)	2 Texture Lookups, 1 Local Memory Array (ms)	1 Texture Lookups, 2 Local Memory Arrays (ms)	0 Texture Lookups, 3 Local Memory Arrays (ms)
GTX460	55.8	41.5	31.5	20.5
GTX580	24.8	17.6	13.5	9.2

## Chapter 20

Using OpenCL with PyOpenCL

While the focus of this book has been on using OpenCL from C and C++, bindings for other languages such as Python, Ruby, and .NET have been developed. This chapter introduces you to using OpenCL in Python by porting the ImageFilter2D example from Chapter 8 to Python. The purpose of this chapter is to introduce you to the basic differences between OpenCL and Python and to talk about some of Python's advantages.

This chapter assumes that you have a working knowledge of programming in Python and are able to set up a Python development environment. If you are not familiar with the language, teaching you Python is beyond the scope of this book. However, there are many terrific resources available to learn the language. One highly recommended resource is *A Quick, Painless Tutorial on the Python Language* by Norman Matloff of the University of California–Davis (available at http://heather.cs.ucdavis. edu/~matloff/Python/PythonIntro.pdf). This is an incredibly succinct and easy-to-understand tutorial for learning the language quickly.

Introducing PyOpenCL

PyOpenCL is an open-source (MIT-licensed) project that provides bindings between OpenCL and Python. There are a number of features of PyOpenCL that make it an attractive library for those looking to work with Python. PyOpenCL provides complete access to the OpenCL API. It takes great advantage of language features of Python (such as dynamic typing) to provide easier-to-use access to OpenCL APIs. Cleanup of objects and error checking are done automatically for you, which means you can write much less code to interact with OpenCL. Further, because the bindings to OpenCL are natively implemented in C++, there is a relatively low overhead for using it.

As of this writing, PyOpenCL is at version 2011.1 and is considered by the authors to be "stable." That is, code written in PyOpenCL now should continue to function with future versions. The API will provide deprecation warnings as it evolves, but it is now at a stable enough state to use in development. The latest version and installation instructions for PyOpenCL can be found at the project's Web site at http://documen.tician.de/pyopencl/index.html.

Running the PyImageFilter2D Example

The source code for the Python port of the ImageFilter2D example from Chapter 8 is provided in the Chapter_20/PyImageFilter2D directory. The example was developed in Python v2.6 and requires an installation of the following Python packages:

- **Numpy:** PyOpenCL makes use of numpy for data structures such as arrays and numeric types and is a foundation of interacting with PyOpenCL. Installation information can be found at http://numpy.scipy.org/.

- **pyopencl v0.92+:** PyOpenCL needs to be built against the OpenCL implementation available on your platform, which is done during the installation process. Installation instructions are at http://wiki.tiker.net/PyOpenCL.

- **PIL (Python Image Library):** The Python Image Library provides a number of functions for loading and storing images. Installation instructions are at www.pythonware.com/products/pil/.

Once the necessary dependencies are installed, the example can be run as follows:

```
$ python ImageFilter2D.py input.jpg output.jpg
```

This example loads the input image from a file, executes a Gaussian filter kernel using OpenCL, and then outputs the resultant image to the output file. Any image formats that are supported by the PIL can be filtered using the program.

PyImageFilter2D Code

The PyImageFilter2D example was coded by taking the C source from the ImageFilter2D example in Chapter 8 and porting it to Python. The original example was written in C and was 375 lines long (exluding comments), whereas the Python version has only 129 lines. A lot of this has to do with the fact that PyOpenCL wraps error checking and uses dynamic typing for various conveniences. The full listing of the PyImage-Filter2D example is provided in Listing 20.1. The remainder of this chapter will walk through the stages of the program and discuss the changes that were required to move from C to PyOpenCL.

Listing 20.1 ImageFilter2D.py

```python
import pyopencl as cl
import sys
import Image # Python Image Library (PIL)
import numpy

def CreateContext():
    platforms = cl.get_platforms();
    if len(platforms) == 0:
        print "Failed to find any OpenCL platforms."
        return None

    devices = platforms[0].get_devices(cl.device_type.GPU)
    if len(devices) == 0:
        print "Could not find GPU device, trying CPU..."
        devices = platforms[0].get_devices(cl.device_type.CPU)
        if len(devices) == 0:
            print "Could not find OpenCL GPU or CPU device."
            return None

    # Create a context using the first device
    context = cl.Context([devices[0]])
    return context, devices[0]

def CreateProgram(context, device, fileName):
    kernelFile = open(fileName, 'r')
    kernelStr = kernelFile.read()

    # Load the program source
    program = cl.Program(context, kernelStr)

    # Build the program and check for errors
    program.build(devices=[device])

    return program



def LoadImage(context, fileName):
    im = Image.open(fileName)
```

```python
    # Make sure the image is RGBA formatted
    if im.mode != "RGBA":
        im = im.convert("RGBA")


    # Convert to uint8 buffer
    buffer = im.tostring()
    clImageFormat = cl.ImageFormat(cl.channel_order.RGBA,
                                   cl.channel_type.UNORM_INT8)

    clImage = cl.Image(context,
                       cl.mem_flags.READ_ONLY |
                       cl.mem_flags.COPY_HOST_PTR,
                       clImageFormat,
                       im.size,
                       None,
                       buffer
                       )

    return clImage, im.size

def SaveImage(fileName, buffer, imgSize):
    im = Image.fromstring("RGBA", imgSize, buffer.tostring())
    im.save(fileName)

def RoundUp(groupSize, globalSize):
    r = globalSize % groupSize;
    if r == 0:
        return globalSize;
    else:
        return globalSize + groupSize - r;


def main():

    imageObjects = [ 0, 0 ]

    # Main
    if len(sys.argv) != 3:
        print "USAGE: " + sys.argv[0] + " <inputImageFile>
                <outputImageFile>"
        return 1


    # Create an OpenCL context on first available platform
    context, device = CreateContext();
    if context == None:
        print "Failed to create OpenCL context."
        return 1
```

```python
# Create a command-queue on the first device available
commandQueue = cl.CommandQueue(context, device)

# Make sure the device supports images, otherwise exit
if not device.get_info(cl.device_info.IMAGE_SUPPORT):
    print "OpenCL device does not support images."
    return 1

# Load input image from file and load it into
# an OpenCL image object
imageObjects[0], imgSize = LoadImage(context, sys.argv[1])

# Create ouput image object
clImageFormat = cl.ImageFormat(cl.channel_order.RGBA,
                               cl.channel_type.UNORM_INT8)
imageObjects[1] = cl.Image(context,
                           cl.mem_flags.WRITE_ONLY,
                           clImageFormat,
                           imgSize)

# Create sampler for sampling image object
sampler = cl.Sampler(context,
                     False, #  Non-normalized coordinates
                     cl.addressing_mode.CLAMP_TO_EDGE,
                     cl.filter_mode.NEAREST)

# Create OpenCL program
program = CreateProgram(context, device, "ImageFilter2D.cl")

# Call the kernel directly
localWorkSize = ( 16, 16 )
globalWorkSize = ( RoundUp(localWorkSize[0], imgSize[0]),
                   RoundUp(localWorkSize[1], imgSize[1]) )

program.gaussian_filter(commandQueue,
                        globalWorkSize,
                        localWorkSize,
                        imageObjects[0],
                        imageObjects[1],
                        sampler,
                        numpy.int32(imgSize[0]),
                        numpy.int32(imgSize[1]))

# Read the output buffer back to the Host
buffer = numpy.zeros(imgSize[0] * imgSize[1] * 4, numpy.uint8)
origin = ( 0, 0, 0 )
region = ( imgSize[0], imgSize[1], 1 )
```

```
    cl.enqueue_read_image(commandQueue, imageObjects[1],
                          origin, region, buffer).wait()

    print "Executed program successfully."

    # Save the image to disk
    SaveImage(sys.argv[2], buffer, imgSize)

main()
```

Context and Command-Queue Creation

Several of the demo programs that come with PyOpenCL use a convenience function `pyopencl.create_some_context()` to create a context. By default, if not passed an argument, this function can provide an
interactive prompt for choosing an OpenCL device on which to create the
context. For example, on a Linux machine with a dual-GPU NVIDIA GTX
295, this function produces a prompt such as the following:

```
Choose device(s):
[0] <pyopencl.Device 'GeForce GTX 295' at 0xab7a90>
[1] <pyopencl.Device 'GeForce GTX 295' at 0xcb6630>
Choice, comma-separated [0]:
```

If running in non-interactive mode (or if an argument of `false` is passed
to the function), a context will be created in an implementation-defined
manner. While this convenience function is an appropriate way to create
a context for many programs, in our example we create the context in a
more traditional way, as shown in Listing 20.2.

Listing 20.2 Creating a Context

```
def CreateContext():
    platforms = cl.get_platforms();
    if len(platforms) == 0:
        print "Failed to find any OpenCL platforms."
        return None

    devices = platforms[0].get_devices(cl.device_type.GPU)
    if len(devices) == 0:
        print "Could not find GPU device, trying CPU..."
        devices = platforms[0].get_devices(cl.device_type.CPU)
        if len(devices) == 0:
```

```
        print "Could not find OpenCL GPU or CPU device."
        return None

    # Create a context using the first device
    context = cl.Context([devices[0]])
    return context, devices[0]
```

The call to `cl.get_platforms()` returns a list of Python objects of type `pyopencl.Platform`. This object contains methods for querying information about the platform as well as retrieving a list of all of the devices available on the platform. The code in Listing 20.2 simply uses the first platform available and then queries to see if any GPU devices are available on the platform by calling `platforms[0].get_devices(cl.device_type.GPU)`. If no GPU devices are found, then the code goes on to check whether any CPU devices are available. Finally, the first device found is used to create a context by calling `cl.Context([devices[0]])`. This function returns a new `pyopencl.Context` object from the list of devices passed into it. In this case, our list is only a single device, but in general it is possible to create the context from a list of devices.

Once the context is created and the list of devices has been retrieved, creating the command-queue in PyOpenCL is trivial:

```
commandQueue = cl.CommandQueue(context, device)
```

This function creates a command-queue for the context and device that are passed in. Like other PyOpenCL calls, the command-queue is returned as a new object (`pyopencl.CommandQueue`). The object contains methods such as `get_info()` and `set_property()`, which provide wrappers to the low-level OpenCL API functions. In general, this is the pattern that OpenCL uses. Each C-typed OpenCL API object (e.g., `cl_context`) is wrapped in a Python class that provides Python methods that interface to the OpenCL API calls that are relevant to that object.

Loading to an Image Object

The next step the program takes is to load the input image from disk and load its contents into an OpenCL image object. The Python Image Library (PIL) is used to load the image from disk and convert it to an RGBA-formatted image, as shown in Listing 20.3. Once converted to RGBA, the image is converted to a Python string using the `Image.tostring()` method. This buffer is then loaded to a `pyopencl.Image` object.

Listing 20.3 Loading an Image

```
def LoadImage(context, fileName):
    im = Image.open(fileName)
    # Make sure the image is RGBA formatted
    if im.mode != "RGBA":
        im = im.convert("RGBA")


    # Convert to uint8 buffer
    buffer = im.tostring()
    clImageFormat = cl.ImageFormat(cl.channel_order.RGBA,
                                   cl.channel_type.UNORM_INT8)

    clImage = cl.Image(context,
                       cl.mem_flags.READ_ONLY |
                       cl.mem_flags.COPY_HOST_PTR,
                       clImageFormat,
                       im.size,
                       None,
                       buffer
                       )

    return clImage, im.size
```

The image format object is created using the `pyopencl.ImageFormat` constructor, which takes as arguments the channel order and channel type. The image format is defined by specifying the channel order with `pyopencl.channel_order` and the channel type with `pyopencl.channel_type`. This is another design that is used throughout PyOpenCL: rather than having one large namespace of enumerants starting with `CL_`, each is categorized for the objects to which it is relevant.

The creation of the image object is very similar to the OpenCL C API with one large difference: there is not a separate API call for each image dimensionality (e.g., `clCreateImage2D`, `clCreateImage3D`). Rather, the dimensions of the image are passed in as a tuple and the implementation will choose to create the correct OpenCL image object.

Creating and Building a Program

Creating and building a program are quite easy in PyOpenCL. The simple code for loading an OpenCL kernel from a file and building it for a list of devices is shown in Listing 20.4.

Listing 20.4   Creating and Building a Program

```
def CreateProgram(context, device, fileName):
    kernelFile = open(fileName, 'r')
    kernelStr = kernelFile.read()

    # Load the program source
    program = cl.Program(context, kernelStr)

    # Build the program and check for errors
    program.build(devices=[device])

    return program
```

The source code to the kernel is read into a string buffer and then
the program is created using `cl.Program(context, kernelStr)`.
Building the program for the device is done by calling `program.`
`build(devices=[device])`. Whereas normally one has to write code
to check whether compile errors occurred and if so grab the info log, this
is not necessary in PyOpenCL. If a compile error occurs, PyOpenCL will
throw an exception containing the result of the build log.

Setting Kernel Arguments and Executing a Kernel

Perhaps the best advantage of PyOpenCL dynamic typing is in how kernel
arguments are set and the kernel is executed. The kernels defined in the
OpenCL program actually become *methods* of the program object that was
created. For example, in the `ImageFilter2D.cl` the `gaussian_fil-`
`ter()` is declared with the following function signature:

```
__kernel void gaussian_filter(__read_only image2d_t srcImg,
                              __write_only image2d_t dstImg,
                              sampler_t sampler,
                              int width, int height)
```

Once the program is built, this kernel actually dynamically becomes a
method of the `pyopencl.Program` that was created. Rather than having
to manually set kernel arguments by index using `clSetKernelArg()` and
executing the program using `clEnqueueNDRangeKernel()`, the method
can be invoked directly as if it were a function, as shown in Listing 20.5.

Listing 20.5   Executing the Kernel

```
# Call the kernel directly
localWorkSize = ( 16, 16 )
globalWorkSize = ( RoundUp(localWorkSize[0], imgSize[0]),
                   RoundUp(localWorkSize[1], imgSize[1]) )

program.gaussian_filter(commandQueue,
                        globalWorkSize,
                        localWorkSize,
                        imageObjects[0],
                        imageObjects[1],
                        sampler,
                        numpy.int32(imgSize[0]),
                        numpy.int32(imgSize[1]))
```

The `localWorkSize` and `globalWorkSize` are computed and stored in
tuples. The execution of the `gaussian_filter()` method will, underneath the hood, set the kernel arguments and queue the kernel for execution. It is also possible to provide events to wait for as a last argument to
the function (although this was not done in this example). It is easy to see
how this convenience not only makes the code more readable, but also
makes executing kernels significantly simpler than using the low-level API.

Reading the Results

Finally, after executing the kernel, the program reads back the results of
the filtered image object into a host memory buffer to write it to a file.
The code for this is shown in Listing 20.6.

Listing 20.6   Reading the Image into a Numpy Array

```
# Read the output buffer back to the Host
buffer = numpy.zeros(imgSize[0] * imgSize[1] * 4, numpy.uint8)
origin = ( 0, 0, 0 )
region = ( imgSize[0], imgSize[1], 1 )

cl.enqueue_read_image(commandQueue, imageObjects[1],
                      origin, region, buffer).wait()
```

A numpy array is initialized to the appropriate size with type `uint8` in
which to store the results. The image is read back to the host by calling

pyopencl.enqueue_read_image(). This function returns a pyopencl
.Event object. In order to ensure that the buffer is read before moving
in, the code explicitly calls the wait() method on the resultant event
object. Finally, this host buffer is saved to an image file using the PIL in
the SaveImage() function from Listing 20.1.

## Chapter 21

Matrix Multiplication with OpenCL

Matrix multiplication is commonly used to demonstrate program optimization in high-performance computing. In its most basic form, matrix multiplication is a toy program consisting of a single multiply-accumulate statement buried inside a triply nested loop. Unlike most toy programs, however, matrix multiplication has a more serious side. First, this operation is the single most important building block for dense linear algebra computations. Second, if you work at it hard enough, matrix multiplication can run near the peak performance of most modern processors. Therefore, it presents many opportunities for performance optimization, and making it fast has practical value.

In this discussion, we will start with a simple matrix multiplication function for a CPU. We will convert the code into OpenCL. And then we will explore a series of code transformations that take advantage of the OpenCL memory model to optimize the program. Along the way, we will report performance results for the multiplication of square matrices of order 1000. All the results in this chapter were generated on an Intel Core Duo CPU (T8300) running at 2.4GHz and a GeForce 8600M GT GPU from NVIDIA. The OpenCL release used in the benchmarks was provided by Apple as part of the Snow Leopard release of OS X.

The Basic Matrix Multiplication Algorithm

A dense matrix is a rectangular array of numbers. It is called "dense" because the numbers are almost always non-zero; hence there is no reason to keep track of zeros to reduce storage or accelerate computations. Throughout this discussion, we will consider three matrices: A (N by P), B (P by M), and C (N by M). Multiplication of A times B with the result added into C is mathematically defined as

$$C_{i,j} = C_{i,j} + \sum_{k=0}^{P} A_{i,k} * B_{k,j}$$

$$0 \le i \le N$$

$$0 \le j \le M$$

Matrix multiplication, as shown in Figure 21.1 for the (i, j)th element of C, consists of a dot product of the ith row of A with the jth column of B. A program to carry out this computation is shown in Listing 21.1. It consists of a double nested loop to run over the elements of the C matrix. Inside is an additional loop to compute the appropriate dot product.

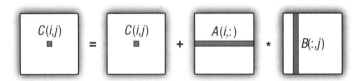

Figure 21.1   A matrix multiplication operation to compute a single element of the product matrix, C. This corresponds to summing into each element $C_{i,j}$ the dot product from the ith row of A with the jth column of B.

In the listing we represent the matrices as one-dimension arrays with explicit index algebra to map the pair of indices onto a single index. This is a common technique when dealing with multidimension arrays. The program using GCC with default compiler settings ran at 167 MFLOPS.

Listing 21.1   A C Function Implementing Sequential Matrix Multiplication

```
void seq_mat_mul(
    int Mdim, int Ndim, int Pdim, // matrix dimensions
    float *A, float *B, float *C) // C = C + A * B
  {
      int i, j, k;
      float tmp;

      for (i=0; i<Ndim; i++){
          for (j=0; j<Mdim; j++){
              tmp = 0.0;
              for(k=0;k<Pdim;k++){
                  // C[i][j]+=A[i][k]* B[k][j];
```

```
                    tmp += *(A+(i*Ndim+k)) *  *(B+(k*Pdim+j));
                }
                *(C+(i*Ndim+j)) = tmp;
            }
        }
}
```

A Direct Translation into OpenCL

The matrix multiplication program from Listing 21.1 can be directly
converted into an OpenCL kernel. The result is shown in Listing 21.2.
Each work-item is assigned an element of the product matrix to compute.
The outer two loops over *i* and *j* are deleted and replaced with calls to a
function to find the global ID for the work-item in each of the two dimensions. Care is taken to make sure the resulting work-item IDs fit within
the *C* matrix, at which point the dot product is carried out to compute the
matrix product for element *i, j* of the *C* matrix. Note that all three matrices are left in global memory. The resulting performance on the GPU was
511 MFLOPS, and the identical code on the CPU was 744 MFLOPS.

Listing 21.2   A kernel to compute the matrix product of *A* and *B* summing the
result into a third matrix, *C*. Each work-item is responsible for a
single element of the *C* matrix. The matrices are stored in global
memory.

```
const char *C_elem_KernelSource = "\n" \
"__kernel mmul(                                        \n" \
"   const int Mdim,                                    \n" \
"   const int Ndim,                                    \n" \
"   const int Pdim,                                    \n" \
"   __global float* A,                                 \n" \
"   __global float* B,                                 \n" \
"   __global float* C)                                 \n" \
"{                                                     \n" \
"   int k;                                             \n" \
"   int i = get_global_id(0);                          \n" \
"   int j = get_global_id(1);                          \n" \
"   float tmp;                                         \n" \
"   if( (i < Ndim) && (j <Mdim))                       \n" \
"   {                                                  \n" \
"       tmp = 0.0;                                     \n" \
"       for(k=0;k<Pdim;k++)                            \n" \
"           tmp         += A[i*Ndim+k] *  B[k*Pdim+j]; \n" \
```

```
"         C[i*Ndim+j] = tmp;                                    \n" \
"    }                                                          \n" \
"}                                                             \n" \
"\n";
```

The host code for the OpenCL matrix multiplication program is provided in Listing 21.3. The first available platform and a device are selected. While the host code from the listing shows a CPU device, this same host program can be used with a GPU by replacing the constant CL_DEVICE_TYPE_CPU in the call to clGetDeviceIDs() with CL_DEVICE_TYPE_GPU. A command-queue is established with profiling enabled through the CL_QUEUE_PROFILING_ENABLE property followed by the definition of the matrices on the host. In this program, two basic matrix manipulation functions are used to initialize the matrices and then later test the results. Because the contents of these functions are simple and not illustrative of the concepts discussed in this chapter, these functions are not included in this listing.

The memory objects are set up by calls to clCreateBuffer(). The program is then constructed from a string literal (the one in Listing 21.2). Throughout this listing, the error testing has been deleted in order to save space. An exception is made, however, for the case of building a program because it is important to understand how to display the output from the OpenCL compiler using a call to clGetProgramBuildInfo().

The kernel and the kernel arguments are then set up, after which the buffers associated with the matrices are submitted to the command-queue. The command-queue is in-order, so it is safe to assume that the memory objects are present in the global memory when the kernel is enqueued. The global dimensions for a two-dimension NDRange are set, while in this case the local dimensions are not set (i.e., they are set to NULL). This was done so that the OpenCL implementation could choose the local dimensions, thereby adjusting to the needs of the CPU or the GPU compute device without programmer intervention.

The host waits for the kernel to complete, at which point timing data is extracted from the enqueue kernel event with calls to clGetEvent-ProfilingInfo(), once with CL_PROFILING_COMMAND_START and then again with CL_PROFILING_COMMAND_END. The memory object associated with the C matrix is then copied onto the host and the results tested. The host program finishes by cleaning up the environment and releasing various OpenCL objects.

Listing 21.3 The Host Program for the Matrix Multiplication Program

```
#ifdef APPLE
#include <OpenCL/opencl.h>
#else
#include "CL/cl.h"
#endif
#define ORDER 1000

int main(int argc, char **argv)
{
    float           *A;             // A matrix
    float           *B;             // B matrix
    float           *C;             // C matrix (C = A*B)
    int             Mdim, Ndim, Pdim; // A[N][P], B[P][M], C[N][M]
    int             err;            // error code from OpenCL
    int             szA, szB, szC;  // number of matrix elements
    size_t          global[DIM];    // global domain size
    size_t          local[DIM];     // local  domain size
    cl_device_id    device_id;      // compute device id
    cl_context      context;        // compute context
    cl_command_queue commands;      // compute command queue
    cl_program      program;        // compute program
    cl_kernel       kernel;         // compute kernel
    cl_uint         nd;             // Number of dims in NDRange
    cl_mem          a_in;           // Memory object for A matrix
    cl_mem          b_in;           // Memory object for B matrix
    cl_mem          c_out;          // Memory Object for C matrix
    int             i;

    Ndim = ORDER;   Pdim = ORDER;   Mdim = ORDER;

//------------------------------------------------------------------
// Set up the OpenCL platform using whichever platform is "first"
//------------------------------------------------------------------
    cl_uint numPlatforms;
    cl_platform_id firstPlatformId;

    err = clGetPlatformIDs(1, &firstPlatformId, &numPlatforms);

    err = clGetDeviceIDs(firstPlatformId, CL_DEVICE_TYPE_CPU, 1,
                    &device_id, NULL);

    cl_context_properties properties [] =
    {
        CL_CONTEXT_PLATFORM, (cl_context_properties)firstPlatformId,0
    };
    context = clCreateContext(properties, 1, &device_id, NULL, NULL,
                    &err);
```

A Direct Translation into OpenCL **503**

```
    commands = clCreateCommandQueue(context, device_id,
        CL_QUEUE_PROFILING_ENABLE, &err);

    // Set up matrices
    szA = Ndim*Pdim;    szB = Pdim*Mdim;    szC = Ndim*Mdim;
    A   = (float *)malloc(szA*sizeof(float));
    B   = (float *)malloc(szB*sizeof(float));
    C   = (float *)malloc(szC*sizeof(float));
    initmat(Mdim, Ndim, Pdim, A, B, C);  // function to set matrices
                                         // to known values.
//-----------------------------------------------------------------
// Set up the buffers, initialize matrices, and write them
// into global memory
//-----------------------------------------------------------------

    a_in   = clCreateBuffer(context,  CL_MEM_READ_ONLY,
                 sizeof(float) * szA, NULL, NULL);
    b_in   = clCreateBuffer(context,  CL_MEM_READ_ONLY,
                 sizeof(float) * szB, NULL, NULL);
    c_out  = clCreateBuffer(context,  CL_MEM_WRITE_ONLY,
                 sizeof(float) * szC, NULL, NULL);

    // Create the compute program from the source buffer
    *program = clCreateProgramWithSource(context, 1,
             (const char **) & C_elem_KernelSource, NULL, &err);

    // Build the program
    err = clBuildProgram(*program, 0, NULL, NULL, NULL, NULL);
    if (err != CL_SUCCESS)
    {
        size_t len;
        char buffer[2048];

        printf("Error: Failed to build program executable!\n");
        clGetProgramBuildInfo(*program, device_id,
                        CL_PROGRAM_BUILD_LOG,
                        sizeof(buffer), buffer, &len);
        printf("%s\n", buffer);
        return FAILURE;
    }

    // Create the compute kernel from the program
    *kernel = clCreateKernel(*program, "mmul", &err);

    // Set the arguments to our compute kernel
    err = 0;
    err = clSetKernelArg(*kernel, 0, sizeof(int),    &Mdim);
    err |= clSetKernelArg(*kernel, 1, sizeof(int),    &Ndim);
    err |= clSetKernelArg(*kernel, 2, sizeof(int),    &Pdim);
```

```
    err |= clSetKernelArg(*kernel, 3, sizeof(cl_mem), &a_in);
    err |= clSetKernelArg(*kernel, 4, sizeof(cl_mem), &b_in);
    err |= clSetKernelArg(*kernel, 5, sizeof(cl_mem), &c_out);


    // Write the A and B matrices into compute device memory
    err = clEnqueueWriteBuffer(commands, a_in, CL_TRUE, 0,
                        sizeof(float) * szA, A, 0, NULL, NULL);
    err = clEnqueueWriteBuffer(commands, b_in, CL_TRUE, 0,
                        sizeof(float) * szB, B, 0, NULL, NULL);
    cl_event prof_event;

    // Execute the kernel over the entire range of C matrix elements
    global[0] =(size_t) Ndim; global[1] =(size_t) Mdim; *ndim = 2;
    err = clEnqueueNDRangeKernel(commands, kernel, nd, NULL,
                            global, NULL, 0, NULL, &prof_event);
    // Wait for the commands to complete before reading back results
    clFinish(commands);

    cl_ulong ev_start_time=(cl_ulong)0;
    cl_ulong ev_end_time=(cl_ulong)0;
    size_t ret_size;

    err = clGetEventProfilingInfo(prof_event,
                    CL_PROFILING_COMMAND_START,
                    sizeof(cl_ulong),
                    &ev_start_time,
                    NULL);

    err = clGetEventProfilingInfo(prof_event,
                    CL_PROFILING_COMMAND_END,
                    sizeof(cl_ulong),
                    &ev_end_time,
                    NULL);
    // Read back the results from the compute device
        err = clEnqueueReadBuffer( commands, c_out, CL_TRUE, 0,
                        sizeof(float) * szC, C, 0, NULL, NULL );

        run_time  = ev_end_time - ev_start_time;
        results(Mdim, Ndim, Pdim, C, run_time);

    clReleaseProgram(program);
    clReleaseKernel(kernel);
    clReleaseMemObject(a_in);
    clReleaseMemObject(b_in);
    clReleaseMemObject(c_out);
    clReleaseCommandQueue(commands);
    clReleaseContext(context);
}
```

Increasing the Amount of Work per Kernel

In parallel programming, it is important to manage a computation to minimize parallel overhead. With order-1000 matrices, one work-item per matrix element results in a million work-items. This seems a bit excessive, so in the next version of the program, each work-item will compute a row of the matrix. The modifications required to support this change are illustrated in Figure 21.2. An entire row of the C matrix is computed using one row from the A matrix repeatedly while sweeping through the columns of the B matrix. The NDRange is changed from a 2D range set to match the dimensions of the C matrix to a 1D range set to the number of rows in the C matrix. At this point we switch our focus to the GPU, which in this case (as shown by a call to `clGetDeviceInfo()` with `CL_DEVICE_MAX_COMPUTE_UNITS`) has four compute units. Hence we set the work-group size to 250 and create four work-groups to cover the full size of the problem.

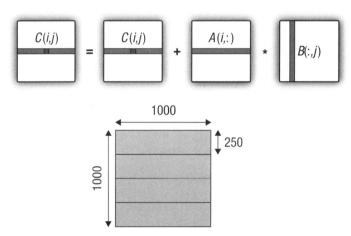

Figure 21.2   Matrix multiplication where each work-item computes an entire row of the C matrix. This requires a change from a 2D NDRange of size 1000×1000 to a 1D NDRange of size 1000. We set the work-group size to 250, resulting in four work-groups (one for each compute unit in our GPU).

The kernel and changes to the host program required for this case are shown in Listing 21.4. The kernel is similar to the previous version except the code now includes a loop over the j index so the kernel marches across a row of C for each work-item. Note that as before the computation works with the memory objects directly from global memory. The resulting performance on the GPU is 258 MFLOPS, which is a considerable drop from our value of 511 MFLOPS. In a real project (as opposed to this simple example) different work-group sizes would be tried to improve performance and better align with the properties of the GPU. In this case, however, we will settle for 258 MFLOPS and proceed with further optimizations.

Listing 21.4 Each work-item updates a full row of C. The kernel code is shown as well as changes to the host code from the base host program in Listing 21.3. The only change required in the host code was to the dimensions of the NDRange.

```
const char *C_row_KernelSource = "\n" \
"__kernel mmul(                                          \n" \
"   const int Mdim,                                      \n" \
"   const int Ndim,                                      \n" \
"   const int Pdim,                                      \n" \
"   __global float* A,                                   \n" \
"   __global float* B,                                   \n" \
"   __global float* C)                                   \n" \
"{                                                       \n" \
"   int k,j;                                             \n" \
"   int i = get_global_id(0);                            \n" \
"   float tmp;                                           \n" \
"   if( (i < Ndim) )                                     \n" \
"   {                                                    \n" \
"       for(j=0;j<Mdim;j++){                             \n" \
"           tmp = 0.0;                                   \n" \
"           for(k=0;k<Pdim;k++)                          \n" \
"               tmp         += A[i*Ndim+k] *  B[k*Pdim+j]; \n" \
"           C[i*Ndim+j] = tmp;                           \n" \
"       }                                                \n" \
"   }                                                    \n" \
"}                                                       \n" \
"\n";


//-------------------------------------------------------------------
// Host code changes . . . change to a 1D NDRange and set local
// work-group size
//-------------------------------------------------------------------

    global[0] = (size_t) Ndim;
    local[0]  = (size_t) 250;
    *ndim     = 1;
    err = clEnqueueNDRangeKernel(commands, kernel, nd, NULL, global,
                             local, 0, NULL, NULL);
```

The core of matrix multiplication is a multiply-accumulate computation. Most processors have sufficient bandwidth into the ALU to keep this computation running near peak performance, but only if the data movement costs can be hidden. Hence, the essence of optimizing matrix multiplication is to minimize data movement. Our matrix multiplication kernels up to this point have left all three matrices in global memory. This means the computation streams rows and columns through the memory hierarchy (global to private) repeatedly for each dot product.

We can reduce this memory traffic by recognizing that each work-item reuses the same row of *A* for each row of *C* that is updated. This is shown in Figure 21.3.

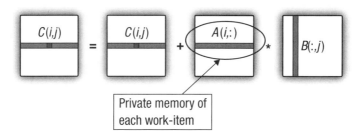

Private memory of each work-item

Figure 21.3   Matrix multiplication where each work-item computes an entire row of the *C* matrix. The same row of *A* is used for elements in the row of *C* so memory movement overhead can be dramatically reduced by copying a row of *A* into private memory.

This version of the matrix multiplication program uses the same host code as the prior case. Even the kernel code is only slightly changed. In Listing 21.5, a float array of size 1000 is defined. Because this occurs inside the kernel, the memory is allocated in the private memory of the processing element that will run the kernel. Then, prior to computing the dot products for the elements of the *C* matrix, the required row of the *A* matrix is copied from global memory into private memory. The use of private memory for the row of *A* had a dramatic impact on performance, from our prior result of 258 MFLOPS to 873 MFLOPS.

Listing 21.5   Each work-item manages the update to a full row of *C*, but before doing so the relevant row of the *A* matrix is copied into private memory from global memory.

```
const char *C_row_priv_KernelSource = "\n" \
"__kernel void mmul(                                      \n" \
```

```
"    const int Mdim,                                     \n" \
"    const int Ndim,                                     \n" \
"    const int Pdim,                                     \n" \
"    __global float* A,                                  \n" \
"    __global float* B,                                  \n" \
"    __global float* C)                                  \n" \
"{                                                       \n" \
"    int k,j;                                            \n" \
"    int i = get_global_id(0);                           \n" \
"    float Awrk[1000];                                   \n" \
"    float tmp;                                          \n" \
"    if( (i < Ndim) )                                    \n" \
"    {                                                   \n" \
"        for(k=0;k<Pdim;k++)                             \n" \
"            Awrk[k] = A[i*Ndim+k];                      \n" \
"                                                        \n" \
"        for(j=0;j<Mdim;j++){                            \n" \
"            tmp = 0.0;                                  \n" \
"            for(k=0;k<Pdim;k++)                         \n" \
"                tmp        += Awrk[k]  *  B[k*Pdim+j];  \n" \
"            C[i*Ndim+j] = tmp;                          \n" \
"        }                                               \n" \
"    }                                                   \n" \
"}                                                       \n" \
"\n";
```

Optimizing Memory Movement: Local Memory

A careful consideration of the dot products in the matrix multiplication shows that while each work-item reuses its own unique row of *A*, all the work-items in a group repeatedly stream the same columns of *B* through the compute device in the course of updating a row of *C*. This is shown in Figure 21.4. We can reduce the overhead of moving data from global memory if the work-items comprising a work-group copy the columns of the matrix *B* into local memory before they start updating their rows of *C*.

To support this optimization, changes were needed in both the kernel and the host program. These changes are shown in Listing 21.6. The key change was to set up the local memory for each kernel. This is needed because dynamic memory allocation within a kernel is not supported in OpenCL. Hence, a memory object of the appropriate size had to be allocated on the host and then passed as an argument to the kernel. This is done by an extra call to `clSetKernelArg()`. Then inside the kernel, the work-items copy a column of *B* into local memory. This is done in parallel

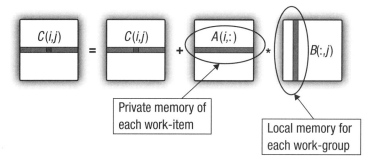

Figure 21.4   Matrix multiplication where each work-item computes an entire row of the *C* matrix. Memory traffic to global memory is minimized by copying a row of *A* into each work-item's private memory and copying rows of *B* into local memory for each work-group.

using a cyclic distribution of the loop iterations. Before any work-item can proceed, all the copying must complete. Hence, the loop that carries out the copies is followed by a `barrier(CLK_LOCAL_MEM_FENCE);` with the memory fence selected to ensure that each work-item in the group sees a consistent state for the local memory. Following the barrier, the kernel code is essentially the same as in the previous case. This modification had a dramatic impact on performance, taking the matrix multiplication from 873 MFLOPS to 2472 MFLOPS.

Listing 21.6   Each work-item manages the update to a full row of *C*. Private memory is used for the row of *A* and local memory (`Bwrk`) is used by all work-items in a work-group to hold a column of *B*. The host code is the same as before other than the addition of a new argument for the *B*-column local memory.

```
const char *C_row_priv_bloc_KernelSource = "\n" \
"__kernel void mmul(                                          \n" \
"   const int Mdim,                                           \n" \
"   const int Ndim,                                           \n" \
"   const int Pdim,                                           \n" \
"   __global float* A,                                        \n" \
"   __global float* B,                                        \n" \
"   __global float* C,                                        \n" \
"   __local  float* Bwrk)                                     \n" \
"{                                                            \n" \
"   int k,j;                                                  \n" \
"   int i   = get_global_id(0);                               \n" \
"   int iloc = get_local_id(0);                               \n" \
```

```
"    int nloc = get_local_size(0);                        \n" \
"    float Awrk[1000];                                    \n" \
"    float tmp;                                           \n" \
"    if( (i < Ndim) )                                     \n" \
"    {                                                    \n" \
"        for(k=0;k<Pdim;k++)                              \n" \
"            Awrk[k] = A[i*Ndim+k];                       \n" \
"                                                         \n" \
"        for(j=0;j<Mdim;j++){                             \n" \
"            for(k=iloc;k<Pdim;k=k+nloc)                  \n" \
"                Bwrk[k] = B[k*Pdim+j];                   \n" \
"        barrier(CLK_LOCAL_MEM_FENCE);                    \n" \
"            tmp = 0.0;                                   \n" \
"            for(k=0;k<Pdim;k++)                          \n" \
"                tmp          += Awrk[k] *  Bwrk[k];      \n" \
"            C[i*Ndim+j] = tmp;                           \n" \
"        }                                                \n" \
"    }                                                    \n" \
"}                                                        \n" \
"\n";

//-------------------------------------------------------------------
// Host code modifications  . . Added one more argument (6) to the
// list of args for the kernel. Note that an OpenCL memory object
// is not provided since this is to be used in local memory.
//-------------------------------------------------------------------
    err  = 0;
    err  = clSetKernelArg(*kernel, 0, sizeof(int),    &Mdim);
    err |= clSetKernelArg(*kernel, 1, sizeof(int),    &Ndim);
    err |= clSetKernelArg(*kernel, 2, sizeof(int),    &Pdim);
    err != clSetKernelArg(*kernel, 3, sizeof(cl_mem), &a_in);
    err |= clSetKernelArg(*kernel, 4, sizeof(cl_mem), &b_in);
    err |= clSetKernelArg(*kernel, 5, sizeof(cl_mem), &c_out);
    err |= clSetKernelArg(*kernel, 6, sizeof(float)*Pdim, NULL);
```

Performance Results and Optimizing the Original CPU Code

Performance results from this example are summarized in Table 21.1. Directly translating the program into OpenCL for the CPU resulted in a significant performance improvement. Most of this chapter, however, focused on the GPU. In particular, these results show the impact of optimizing how data is mapped onto global, private, and local memory.

Table 21.1 Matrix Multiplication (Order-1000 Matrices) Results Reported as MFLOPS and as Speedup Relative to the Unoptimized Sequential C Program (i.e., the Speedups Are "Unfair")

Matrix Multiplication Optimization Case	MFLOPS	Speedup
CPU: Sequential code in C (no optimization)	167	1
CPU: $C(i, j)$ per work-item, all global memory	744	4.5
GPU: $C(i, j)$ per work-item, all global memory	511	3
GPU: C row per work-item, all global memory	258	1.5
GPU: C row per work-item, A private, B in global memory	873	5.2
GPU: C row per work-item, A private, B in local memory	2472	15

There is an impressive 15-fold speedup for the optimized GPU code versus the CPU code. This speedup value, however, is misleading. Considerable effort was expended to optimize the code on the GPU, but no effort whatsoever was expended to optimize the sequential code on the CPU. This situation, inflating speedups by comparing to an unoptimized sequential code, happens all too often and has led to unrealistic expectations of the benefits of moving from a CPU to a GPU.

Consider the functions in Listing 21.7. These simple optimizations permute the order of the three nested loops. This serves to change the memory access patterns and hence reuse of data from the cache as the contents of the three matrices are streamed through the CPU. Following common practice in the linear algebra literature, we call the dot product algorithm *ijk* and the two permutations *ikj* and *kij*. We also changed the data type from `single` to `double` and used the O3 compiler switch to GCC. Performance in MFLOPS varied considerably with 272, 1130, and 481 for the *kjk*, *ikj*, and *kij*, respectively. Note that this is the most trivial of optimizations and many additional optimization are well known (cache blocking, TLB blocking, SSE). Still, with these optimizations, our more honest sequential CPU reference point becomes 1130 MFLOPS, which reduces the OpenCL-GPU maximum speedup to a more realistic value of 2.2.

Listing 21.7 Different Versions of the Matrix Multiplication Functions Showing the Permutations of the Loop Orderings

```c
void mat_mul_ijk(int Mdim, int Ndim, int Pdim, double *A,
                 double *B, double *C)
{
    int i, j, k;
    for (i=0; i<Ndim; i++){
        for (j=0; j<Mdim; j++){
            for(k=0;k<Pdim;k++){
                /* C(i,j) = sum(over k) A(i,k) * B(k,j) */
                C[i*Ndim+j] += A[i*Ndim+k] *  B[k*Pdim+j];
            }
        }
    }
}

void mat_mul_ikj(int Mdim, int Ndim, int Pdim, double *A,
                 double *B, double *C)
{
    int i, j, k;
    for (i=0; i<Ndim; i++){
            for(k=0;k<Pdim;k++){
        for (j=0; j<Mdim; j++){
                /* C[i][j] += sum(over k) A[i][k] * B[k][j] */
                C[i*Ndim+j]  += A[i*Ndim+k] *  B[k*Pdim+j];
            }
        }
    }
}

void mat_mul_kij(int Mdim, int Ndim, int Pdim, double *A,
                 double *B, double *C)
{
    int i, j, k;
        for(k=0;k<Pdim;k++){
    for (i=0; i<Ndim; i++){
        for (j=0; j<Mdim; j++){
                /* C[i][j] += sum(over k) A[i][k] * B[k][j] */
                C[i*Ndim+j]  += A[i*Ndim+k] *  B[k*Pdim+j];
            }
        }
    }
}
```

## Chapter 22

Sparse Matrix-Vector Multiplication

By Gordon Fossum

This chapter describes an optimized implementation of the Sparse Matrix-Vector Multiplication (SpMV) algorithm using OpenCL.

Sparse matrices, for the purposes of this chapter, are defined as large two-dimensional matrices in which the vast majority of the elements of the matrix are equal to zero. They may be largely diagonal, or not. They may be symmetric, or not (perhaps not even square). They may be singular (containing entire rows with no non-zero elements), or not. They are used to characterize and solve problems in a wide variety of domains.

The sample uses a new portable **tiled and packetized sparse matrix** data format, which has both a single-precision and a double-precision instantiation. The format is intended to improve cache utilization and minimize "gather/scatter" inefficiency.

The implementation demonstrates OpenCL's ability to bridge the gap between hardware-specific code (fast, but not portable) and single-source code (very portable, but slow), yielding a high-performance, efficient implementation on a variety of hardware that is almost as fast as a hardware-specific implementation.

These results are accomplished with kernels written in OpenCL C that can be compiled and run on any conforming OpenCL platform.

Sparse Matrix-Vector Multiplication (SpMV) Algorithm

The SpMV algorithm efficiently multiplies a sparse matrix by an input vector, producing an output vector. That is, it computes an equation of the form $y = A * x$, where y and x are vectors and A is a matrix, which in this case is a sparse matrix.

Various sparse matrix representation schemes have been proposed that seek to balance the competing needs of minimizing the memory footprint of the sparse matrix while maximizing the performance of the algorithm.

One traditional method for representing a sparse matrix is to create three arrays of binary data, one containing the non-zero floating-point data of the matrix (referred to as **Val**); another, same-size array containing the column index where each of these non-zero elements comes from (referred to as **Col_ind**); and a third, smaller array containing the indices into the previous two arrays where each row starts (referred to as **Row_ptr**). This is commonly referred to as either the compressed sparse row (CSR) or compressed row storage (CRS) format.

For example, look at the sparse matrix in Figure 22.1.

$$
\begin{bmatrix}
2.2 & 0.0 & 0.0 & 0.0 & 0.0 & 0.0 & 7.1 & 3.3 & 0.0 \\
0.0 & 8.5 & 0.0 & 0.0 & 0.0 & 0.0 & 0.0 & 6.2 & 0.0 \\
0.0 & 0.0 & 1.7 & 6.6 & 0.0 & 0.0 & 0.0 & 0.0 & 0.0 \\
0.0 & 0.0 & 0.0 & 0.0 & 4.5 & 0.0 & 0.0 & 0.0 & 0.0 \\
0.0 & 0.0 & 0.0 & 0.0 & 0.0 & 9.2 & 0.0 & 0.0 & 0.0 \\
2.9 & 0.0 & 0.0 & 0.0 & 0.0 & 0.0 & 1.3 & 4.2 & 0.0 \\
0.0 & 0.0 & 3.7 & 0.0 & 0.0 & 0.0 & 0.0 & 0.0 & 9.8
\end{bmatrix}
$$

Figure 22.1   Sparse matrix example

This sparse matrix would be represented with three arrays, as follows:

    Val = {2.2, 7.1, 3.3, 8.5, 6.2, 1.7, 6.6, 4.5, 9.2, 2.9, 1.3, 4.2, 3.7, 9.8};

    Col_ind = {0, 6, 7, 1, 7, 2, 3, 4, 5, 0, 6, 7, 2, 8};

    Row_ptr = {0, 3, 5, 7, 8, 9, 12};

A more basic method is to create an ASCII file with header information consisting of the name of the matrix, whether the matrix is symmetric or not (symmetric or general, respectively), and whether the file merely contains the pattern of non-zero content or actually contains the values of these non-zero elements (pattern or coordinate, respectively). The body of this file then contains a series of lines, where each line contains a row index, a column index, and (optionally) a data value. This is referred to as Matrix Market (MM) exchange format (see http://math.nist.gov/MatrixMarket/formats.html for more information) and is used most notably by the University of Florida in its large collection of sparse and dense matrices (www.cise.ufl.edu/research/sparse/matrices).

Various other matrix representations are described in previous implementations of SpMV, which were targeted at particular hardware platforms and developed before the advent of OpenCL.

In the paper "Efficient Sparse Matrix-Vector Multiplication on CUDA,"[1] a hybrid approach is adopted that seeks to optimize for several potential storage formats: coordinate (COO), CSR, ELLPACK, and a Packet format, which differs from the one in this chapter in several particulars. The two most important are that the output indices are not individually stored, but rather a single offset is loaded into the packet, and all output data is implicitly keyed off of that one offset. Further, every read-modify-write operation to the local output buffer is fully coalesced across 16 compute units.

In the paper "Optimizing Sparse Matrix-Vector Multiplication on GPUs,"[2] the authors choose to concentrate on the CSR format and implement variants on CSR that are more suited for GPU architectures. In particular, 16 threads are assigned to each row in the CSR format, and each thread strides through the row, computing on only every sixteenth element. The format is further modified to pad the rows to multiples of 16. Further, they analyze the matrix to identify dense sub-blocks and deal with them in a special way.

The device-independent tiled and packetized sparse matrix representation used by this implementation has a single format (actually a format for single precision and a format for double precision) and achieves perfect coalescing of all matrix accesses and output accesses.

---

[1] Nathan Bell and Michael Garland, "Efficient Sparse Matrix-Vector Multiplication on CUDA," NVIDIA Technical Report NVR-2008-004 (December 2008), www.nvidia.com/object/nvidia_research_pub_001.html.

[2] Muthu Manikandan Baskaran and Rajesh Bordawekar, "Optimizing Sparse Matrix-Vector Multiplication on GPUs", RC24704 (2008), http://domino.watson.ibm.com/library/CyberDig.nsf/1e4115aea78b6e7c85256b360066f0d4/1d32f6d23b99f7898525752200618339.

Description of This Implementation

This implementation has a single source file of host code, which performs the following operations:

- Reads the Matrix Market format matrix data from disk

- Initializes the OpenCL environment

- Creates the tiled and packetized matrix

- Initializes the input vector

- Calls the kernel code passing it the input vector, the matrix, and the output vector

- Verifies the results

- Reports performance data

- Shuts down the OpenCL environment and cleans up

It further provides a single source file of kernel code, containing two similar kernels. These two kernels accommodate two different methods of hiding memory latency, one implicit (using multithreading or cache hierarchies) and the other one explicit (double buffering with asynchronous DMAs).

The first (implicit) kernel implements read/write direct access to global memory serially with the computations on that data. This kernel is best used on an OpenCL CPU or GPU device.

As previously mentioned, this kernel is run in parallel on a large number of compute devices or compute units, in batches of local work-groups. Within each local work-group, we explicitly acknowledge and use a smaller computational grouping, which we call a **team** of processing elements that executes on a compute unit, which has a size of 16 for a GPU and a size of 1 for a CPU. The use of a team size of 1 on CPUs derives from a need to avoid current inefficiencies in OpenCL compilers, wherein multiple work-groups are simulated with a loop-unrolling mechanism that unfortunately results in cache-thrashing behavior on many CPUs. When future compilers are available that unroll their loops in a more efficient fashion, all teams on all devices will have a size of 16. Within the GPU device, the local work-group is composed of one or more of these teams. Thus, the team size is 16, and the local work-group size might be 64 or 128, for example. There are several reasons why 16 is the best size to use:

- Every GPU we have encountered has a natural affinity for grouping its global memory read-write operations in multiples of 64 bytes (or 16 4-byte elements).

- A group of 16 single-precision elements, along with their necessary control and index information, conveniently fits into a 128-byte cache line.

- GPUs enjoy improved performance when the algorithm can perform coalesced memory accesses, which are grouped in multiples of 16.

An if test within this first kernel is used to distinguish between GPUs (team size 16) and CPUs (team size 1). The GPU clause computes a single product, and the CPU clause implements a loop to compute the 16 products.

It's also important to note that the amount of local memory available to each GPU processor is carefully analyzed, and the size of the matrix subsets destined for each work-group is restricted to ensure that multiple work-groups are able to "fit" into this available local memory, to improve performance on any GPU device.

The second (explicit) kernel uses OpenCL's `async_work_group_copy` built-in function to implement double-buffered reads and writes of data between distant global memory and close local memory. This kernel is best used by the Cell/B.E. Accelerator device.

While both of these kernels execute on any hardware, there are clear performance benefits to pairing the kernel with the hardware that most naturally uses its memory latency mechanism.

Tiled and Packetized Sparse Matrix Representation

It is assumed that the sparse matrix is very large and that it is frequently reused (meaning that many vectors are to be multiplied against it). Therefore, it should be reorganized into a device-friendly format. The motivation for this representation is to perform well across multiple hardware platforms.

While the full matrix (complete with all the zero elements) is never explicitly present, it is the basis for the hierarchy of terms used in this chapter. Here's a short description of this hierarchy:

- The full matrix is broken up into rows of tiles. Each such row is called a **slab**.

- Each tile is sliced into **strips** of 16 rows each.

- Each such strip gives rise to a series of **packets**.

The global view of the tiled matrix representation is that the full matrix (complete with all of the zero elements) is partitioned into large rows of tiles (called slabs) whose width spans the entire width of the matrix and whose height corresponds to a contiguous subset of the output vector. Each tile in this row of tiles corresponds to an appropriately large contiguous subset of the input vector. Figure 22.2 shows a full matrix being multiplied by an input vector to compute an output vector. The hatched section of the matrix is a tile, within a row of tiles. The contiguous hatched areas of the input and output vectors are those that are used in conjunction with this matrix tile.

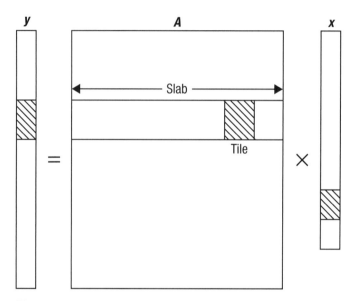

Figure 22.2   A tile in a matrix and its relationship with input and output vectors

The process of packetizing the slab proceeds in one of two ways, both involving a logical partition into strips of 16 matrix rows each. For devices that benefit from having local copies of contiguous sections of input vector, the strips are contained within the tiles. For devices that only access input data directly from global memory, the strips span the entire slab. Each strip is the source for a series of 16-element packets, where each of these 16 elements is sourced from a different row of the strip.

These packets also contain index and control information. If the elements are single precision, the packet is 128 bytes long. If the elements are double precision, the packet is 192 bytes long.

Each packet contains the following:

- A word specifying the global offset into the index vector of the hatched region affected by the tile containing the packet (which corresponds to the column in the full matrix where this tile begins)

- The input offset for the *next* tile, to allow devices whose memory subsystems can operate in parallel with the computations to preload the next section of the input vector

- A count of how many packets remain in this tile, to allow the kernels to control their loop structures

- The offset into the output vector, relative to the global offset specified in the second word of the header block above elements (which, again, corresponds to a row offset within the matrix) where the 16 output values are to be accumulated into 16 consecutive vectors

- Four words (16 bytes) of pad to ensure that the indices that follow are on a 32-byte boundary, and the floating-point data following those is on a 64-byte boundary (this is important for all architectures)

- Sixteen 2-byte input indices, relative to the input offset, one for each element of the packet

- Sixteen floating-point elements (single or double precision), which are actual non-zero data from the full matrix

The organization of the packet is as shown in Figures 22.3 and 22.4 (each line comprises 16 bytes of this packet format).

	0×0		0×4		0×8		0×C	
0×0	Input offset		Next input offset		Remaining packets		Output offset	
0×10	pad		pad		pad		pad	
0×20	Index 0	Index 1	Index 2	Index 3	Index 4	Index 5	Index 6	Index 7
0×30	Index 8	Index 9	Index 10	Index 11	Index 12	Index 13	Index 14	Index 15
0×40	Matrix element 0		Matrix element 1		Matrix element 2		Matrix element 3	
0×50	Matrix element 4		Matrix element 5		Matrix element 6		Matrix element 7	
0×60	Matrix element 8		Matrix element 9		Matrix element 10		Matrix element 11	
0×70	Matrix element 12		Matrix element 13		Matrix element 14		Matrix element 15	

Figure 22.3   Format of a single-precision 128-byte packet

	0×0		0×4		0×8		0×C	
0×0	Input offset		Next input offset		Remaining packets		Output offset	
0×10	pad		pad		pad		pad	
0×20	Index 0	Index 1	Index 2	Index 3	Index 4	Index 5	Index 6	Index 7
0×30	Index 8	Index 9	Index 10	Index 11	Index 12	Index 13	Index 14	Index 15
0×40	Matrix element 0				Matrix element 1			
0×50	Matrix element 2				Matrix element 3			
0×60	Matrix element 4				Matrix element 5			
0×70	Matrix element 6				Matrix element 7			
0×80	Matrix element 8				Matrix element 9			
0×90	Matrix element 10				Matrix element 11			
0×A0	Matrix element 12				Matrix element 13			
0×B0	Matrix element 14				Matrix element 15			

Figure 22.4 Format of a double-precision 192-byte packet

Header Structure

The overall structure of this tiled and packetized sparse matrix starts with a header block. The header block contains three 4-byte words of data per tile row consisting of the following:

- The offset into the tiled matrix memory structure where this slab's packets begin

- The offset into the output vector where this slab's computational results should be written (which corresponds to a row number in the full matrix)

- The number of contiguous elements of the output vector computed by this slab (corresponding to the number of contiguous rows of the full matrix that are represented by this slab)

The format is as shown in Figure 22.5.

	0×0	0×4	0×8
0×0	Offset to tile row 0	Output vector offset 0	Out vector chunk size 0
0×0C	Offset to tile row 1	Output vector offset 1	Out vector chunk size 1
0×18	Offset to tile row 2	Output vector offset 2	Out vector chunk size 2
	...		
	Offset to tile row *N*	Output vector offset *N*	Out vector chunk size *N*
	Pad to 128-byte boundary ...		
	Packets to tile row 0 (as described in Figure 22.2 or Figure 22.3)		
	...		

Figure 22.5 Format of the header block of a tiled and packetized sparse matrix

Tiled and Packetized Sparse Matrix Design Considerations

The **pad to 128-byte boundary** is included for the benefit of all architectures, because data packets that reside on 64-byte boundaries perform better on GPUs and on cache-enabled CPUs, and because we always read even-sized groups of packets, they also improve the speed of `async_work_group_copy` commands in Cell/B.E. Accelerator devices, which work best with 128-byte alignment.

The configuration of 16 elements and 16 indices is chosen to correspond with common cache line sizes, common team sizes on GPUs, and the minimum size for moving memory parcels in some architectures. The load store kernel contains logic to enable different processing for GPU and CPU architectures.

The data is organized into the packets to guarantee that the elements in the packet correspond to consecutive rows of the matrix, so that a single block write of computed results serves to update the output vector that is the target of the computations involving this matrix, also eliminating the need to have 16 separate row indices, but rather a single index (the output offset shown in Figures 22.2 and 22.3). Essentially, this means that one must gather elements from the input vector to work with this packet, but there is no scatter operation after computations. Instead, we need only execute a single 64-byte or 128-byte read/modify/write for each packet to update the output.

Optional Team Information

In the case where the local work-group size is large (when use of GPUs is contemplated), this sample is further optimized through the inclusion of data specifying for each compute unit within the GPU where its first packet is and how many packets are to be processed. One or more initial packets in each slab is repurposed to contain this data. Each team needs to know the offset and length for its section of the slab.

For the purposes of this sample, two 2-byte quantities suffice to hold the offset and length, although these could be expanded to 4 bytes each if the matrices are large enough to require it. Thus, work-group sizes up to 512 can be accommodated with a single repurposed packet (512/16 is 32, and 4 bytes of data for each team adds up to 128 bytes). When the work-group size exceeds 512, more initial packets are used to contain the data.

Tested Hardware Devices and Results

This implementation was run and verified on six hardware platforms, described in Table 22.1, all running OpenCL version 1.1, except for the GTX 280.

This sample was run on 22 different matrices. One of these was created as a sample (`sample.mtx`), and the other 21 were downloaded from the University of Florida Matrix Market Web site. Table 22.2 lists these 21 matrices, with references detailing which matrices were found in which of three previous papers on this subject.

For brevity, the two performance charts in Figures 22.6 and 22.7 listing the minimum, maximum, and average performance over all 22 matrices are provided for each hardware device tested. Results for both double and single precision are presented, to the extent that the devices support them.

For each matrix, when running on GPUs, various local work-group sizes were investigated to determine the optimum size. Over the 22 matrices, the GPUs delivered optimal performance according to the histogram in Table 22.3.

Table 22.1 Hardware Device Information

Hardware Model Number	SDK Version/Driver Version	Device Type	Cores	Threads	Clock (GHz)	OS
IBM POWER6 (JS43 Model 7778-23X)	IBM 0.3/0.3	CPU	4×2	16	4.2	RHEL 5.5
IBM POWER7 (PS701 Model 8406-71Y)	IBM 0.3/0.3	CPU	1×8	32	3.0	RHEL 6.0
Intel Westmere (IBM 6391, System x iDataPlex dx360 M3)	AMD 2.3/2.0	CPU	2×6	24	2.67	RHEL 5.5
NVIDIA GTX 280	NVIDIA OpenCL 1.0	GPU	240	240	2.6	RHEL 5.2
NVIDIA TeslaTM (Model M2050)	NVIDIA OpenCL 1.1 Candidate 1/258.19	GPU	448	448	1.15	RHEL 5.5
AMD Firestream (Model 9350)	AMD 2.3/ CAL 1.4.900	GPU	288	1440	0.70	RHEL 5.5
Cell/B.E. Blade (IBM QS22 Model 0793-2RZ)	IBM 0.3/0.3	Accelerator	2×8	16	3.2	RHEL 5.5

Table 22.2 Sparse Matrix Description

Matrix Name on Matrix Market Web Site	Name Given in Other Papers	Papers
bcsstk35.mtx	bcsstk35	"Optimizing Sparse Matrix-Vector Multiplication on GPUs"
cant.mtx	FEM/Cantilever or FEM-Cant	"Efficient Sparse Matrix-Vector Multiplication on CUDA," "Tesla C2050 Performance Benchmarks"
consph.mtx	FEM/Spheres or FEM-Sphr	"Efficient Sparse Matrix-Vector Multiplication on CUDA," "Tesla C2050 Performance Benchmarks"
cop20k_A.mtx	FEM/Accelerator or FEM-Accel	"Efficient Sparse Matrix-Vector Multiplication on CUDA," "Tesla C2050 Performance Benchmarks"
dense2.mtx	Dense	"Efficient Sparse Matrix-Vector Multiplication on CUDA," "Tesla C2050 Performance Benchmarks"
ex11.mtx	ex11	"Optimizing Sparse Matrix-Vector Multiplication on GPUs"
1p_osa_60.mtx	1p_osa_60 or 1p	"Optimizing Sparse Matrix-Vector Multiplication on GPUs"
mac_econ_fwd500.mtx	Economics or Econom	"Efficient Sparse Matrix-Vector Multiplication on CUDA," "Tesla C2050 Performance Benchmarks"
mc2depi.mtx	Epidemiology or Epidem	"Efficient Sparse Matrix-Vector Multiplication on CUDA," "Optimizing Sparse Matrix-Vector Multiplication on GPUs," "Tesla C2050 Performance Benchmarks"
nasasrb.mtx	Nasasrb	"Optimizing Sparse Matrix-Vector Multiplication on GPUs"
olafu.mtx	Olafu	"Optimizing Sparse Matrix-Vector Multiplication on GPUs"

Matrix Name on Matrix Market Web Site	Name Given in Other Papers	Papers
para-7.mtx	para-7	"Optimizing Sparse Matrix-Vector Multiplication on GPUs"
pdb1HYS.mtx	Protein	"Efficient Sparse Matrix-Vector Multiplication on CUDA," "Optimizing Sparse Matrix-Vector Multiplication on GPUs," "Tesla C2050 Performance Benchmarks"
pwtk.mtx	Wind tunnel or Tunnel	"Efficient Sparse Matrix-Vector Multiplication on CUDA," "Optimizing Sparse Matrix-Vector Multiplication on GPUs," "T esla C2050 Performance Benchmarks"
qcd5_4.mtx	QCD	"Efficient Sparse Matrix-Vector Multiplication on CUDA," "Tesla C2050 Performance Benchmarks"
raefsky3.mtx	raefsky3	"Optimizing Sparse Matrix-Vector Multiplication on GPUs"
rail4284.mtx	rail4284 or LP	"Efficient Sparse Matrix-Vector Multiplication on CUDA," "Optimizing Sparse Matrix-Vector Multiplication on GPUs," "Tesla C2050 Performance Benchmarks"
rim.mtx	rim	"Optimizing Sparse Matrix-Vector Multiplication on GPUs"
rma10.mtx	FEM/Harbor or FEM-Har	"Efficient Sparse Matrix-Vector Multiplication on CUDA," "Optimizing Sparse Matrix-Vector Multiplication on GPUs," "Tesla C2050 Performance Benchmarks"
shipsec1.mtx	FEM/Ship or FEM-Ship	"Efficient Sparse Matrix-Vector Multiplication on CUDA," "Optimizing Sparse Matrix-Vector Multiplication on GPUs," "Tesla C2050 Performance Benchmarks"
venkat01.mtx	venkat01	"Optimizing Sparse Matrix-Vector Multiplication on GPUs"

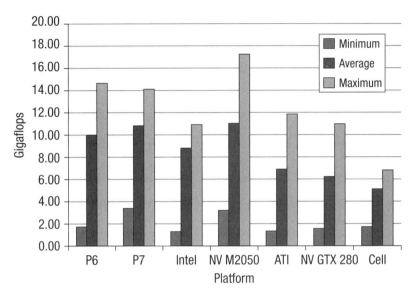

Figure 22.6   Single-precision SpMV performance across 22 matrices on seven platforms

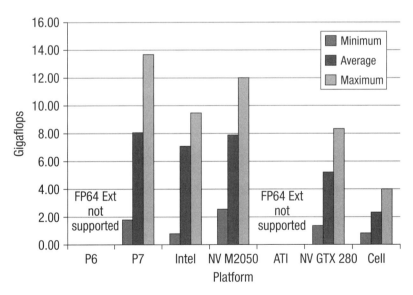

Figure 22.7   Double-precision SpMV performance across 22 matrices on five platforms

Table 22.3 Optimal Performance Histogram for Various Matrix Sizes

	Size <= 64	Size = 128	Size = 256	Size = 512
ATI GPU	1 matrix	12 matrices	9 matrices	0 matrices
NVIDIA GTX 280	17 matrices	4 matrices	1 matrix	0 matrices
NVIDIA M2050	0 matrices	7 matrices	9 matrices	6 matrices

It is important to mention the use or non-use of OpenCL image objects in GPUs at this point. Not all OpenCL implementations support access to image objects, so (for portability) this sample is not written to try to use image objects. On GPUs this decision precludes the use of texture memory and texture caches. Because the algorithm is memory-bound, this choice has performance implications, relative to implementations that exploit image objects. Here are some results quoted in two previous SpMV papers. The results in the first bullet point involve the use of texture memory, and the results in the second bullet point do not. Also, please note that the first bullet point compares results on an NVIDIA M2050, and the second compares results on an NVIDIA GeForce GTX 280.

- The two recommended methods listed for processing single precision in "Efficient Sparse Matrix-Vector Multiplication on CUDA" are **hybrid** and **packet**. For some matrices, hybrid is fastest, and for others, packet is fastest. Taking the average of these two methods across the 12 matrices that "Tesla C2050 Performance Benchmarks" shares in common with this chapter, the min/avg/max statistics for this CUDA/texture memory implementation are 7.0/16.2/23.2. This sample's results over the same 12 matrices are 3.0/11.0/17.2.

- The two recommended methods listed for processing single-precision SpMV without cache (meaning without texture memory) in "Optimizing Sparse Matrix-Vector Multiplication on GPUs" are **thread mapping** and **aligned access**. In all cases listed, aligned access beats thread mapping. Across the 15 matrices this paper shares with this chapter, the min/avg/max statistics for this CUDA implementation are 0.3/6.1/9.75. This sample's results over the same 15 matrices are 2.0/6.3/11.0.

Listing 22.1 describes the kernels that implement the sparse matrix-vector multiplication. The full source (kernels and host source code) for the histogram is provided in the `Chapter_22/spmv` directory of the book's source code examples.

Listing 22.1 Sparse Matrix-Vector Multiplication OpenCL Kernels

```
/******************************************************************/
/*                                                                */
/* Licensed Materials - Property of IBM                           */
/*           .                                                    */
/*                                                                */
/* (C) Copyright IBM Corp. 2010                                   */
/* All Rights Reserved                                            */
/*                                                                */
/* US Government Users Restricted Rights - Use, duplication or    */
/* disclosure restricted by GSA ADP Schedule Contract with IBM    */
/* Corp.                                                          */
/*                                                                */
/******************************************************************/
/* ============================================================== */
/*                                                                */
/* The "matbuffer" buffer contains the tiled matrix.              */
/* The data in this tiled matrix is organized into "rows of       */
/* tiles" which are called "slabs."                               */
/* The first section of this buffer contains three words of       */
/* "header information" for each slab of the matrix. Each         */
/* instantiation of the kernel is indexed by get_global_id(0)     */
/* which matches the number of the slab. The three header words   */
/* for each slab are:                                             */
/*    "offset": the offset into the buffer where the slab's       */
/*              data begins                                       */
/*    "outindex": the index into the output vector where this     */
/*                slab's output is to begin                       */
/*    "outspan": the number of elements of the output vector      */
/*               which this slab is responsible for               */
/*                                                                */
/* The actual data in the slab is organized into 16-element       */
/* "packets" of length 128 bytes                                  */
/* (see the definition of the "packet" struct below).             */
/* Each packet contains four "control words" used by the kernels, */
/* 16 2-byte indices into the input array, and 16                 */
/* floating-point values from the matrix.                         */
/*                                                                */
/* The four "control words" are:                                  */
/*    0: base offset into the input vector for this packet        */
/*    1: base offset into the input vector for a FUTURE packet    */
/*       (useful for double buffering)                            */
/*    2: the number of packets remaining in this slab             */
/*    3: the offset (relative to the second header word) into the */
/*       output vector for this packet                            */
/*                                                                */
/* These four words are followed by four words of pad, reserved   */
/* for future use. Next come 16 short integers, containing        */
```

```
/* offsets into the input vector. Next come 16 floating-point    */
/* values, containing the actual matrix data.                    */
/*                                                                */
/* Specific output offsets for each value are not needed, because */
/* the packets are created in a special format: each value is    */
/* intended to update the output vector element subsequent to     */
/* that of the previous value. So, if a packet is targeted to     */
/* location 512 of the output vector, then the 16 values in the   */
/* packet will be updating locations 512 through 527 of the       */
/* output vector respectively, and in order. This adds to the     */
/* complexity of the code which creates these packets but results */
/* in significant performance payoffs, when performing the        */
/* multiplications.                                               */
/*                                                                */
/* It's frequently the case that there is empty data in these     */
/* packets because of this construction. This data is carefully   */
/* set up so that when we are dealing with local buffers, the     */
/* garbage calculations go into an area which never gets written  */
/* back to main memory. In the case where global memory is        */
/* accessed directly, the "matrix data" in the empty values is    */
/* set to zero, so that regardless of what thc input is, the      */
/* output is unaffected.                                          */
/*                                                                */
/* ============================================================= */

/* These two structures are defined both in spmv.c and spmv.cl    */
/* (using different variable types).                              */
/* If you change something here, change it in the other file as   */
/* well.                                                          */

typedef struct _slab_header {
    uint offset;
    uint outindex;
    uint outspan;
} slab_header;

typedef struct _packet {
    uint seg_input_offset;
    uint future_seg_input_offset;
    uint npackets_remaining;
    uint seg_output_offset;
    uint pad1;
    uint pad2;
    uint pad3;
    uint pad4;
    ushort input_offset_short[16];
    union {
        float8 matdataV8[2];
        float matdata[16];
```

```
        } uf;
} packet;

/* ============================================================ */
/* Kernel using basic load/store mechanisms and local vars. This */
/* version is optimized for the GPU and CPU devices            */
/* ============================================================ */
__kernel void tiled_spmv_kernel_LS(
        __global float *input,
        __global float *output,
        __global uint *matbuffer,

        uint column_span,
        uint slabspace,
        uint team_size,
        uint num_header_packets,
        __local float *outputspace)
{
    uint i, gunit, lunit, start, span, npackets, teamnum, n_teams,
        outindex, outspan;
    __global slab_header *headptr;
    __global float *work_input;
    __global packet *gsegptr;
    __global packet *gsegptr_stop;
    __global float *outptr;
    __local float *outptr16;

    /* The local work-group is interpreted as a set of "teams," */
    /* each consisting of 1 or 16 work units. This construction */
    /* is frequently very useful on the GPU device.            */

    headptr = ((__global slab_header *) matbuffer) +
    get_global_id(1);
    outspan = headptr->outspan;
    outindex = headptr->outindex;
    n_teams = get_local_size(0)/team_size;  /* number of teams */
    gunit = get_local_id(0);
    teamnum = gunit/team_size; /* which team is this? */
    start = get_global_id(0);   /* where in the packets is my */
                                /* "first word"? */
    span = get_global_size(0); /* what stride shall I use when */
                                /* clearing or transmitting output */
                                /* buffers? */

    /* Zero out the output buffer */
    /* Each team has its own separate output buffer. */
    /* At the end, these are accumulated. */
    for (i = start; i < slabspace; i += span) {
```

```
#ifdef DOUBLE
        outputspace[i] = 0.0;
#else
        outputspace[i] = 0.0f;
#endif
    }
    barrier(CLK_LOCAL_MEM_FENCE);

    /* Pointer to the start of the packets. */
    gsegptr = &(((__global packet *) matbuffer)[headptr->offset]);

    /* Pointer to pertinent area of output vector. */
    outptr = &output[outindex];

    /* We have two clauses here. The first is optimized for the     */
    /* GPU device, and the second is optimized for the CPU          */
    /* device. The distinction is that in the GPU device the        */
    /* memory access pattern for each work unit is strided, and     */
    /* in the CPU device, the memory access pattern is contiguous.*/
    /* Virtually all processing happens in the selected clause      */
    /* below.                                                        */

    if (team_size == 16) {
        lunit = gunit % team_size; /* Which work unit within the */
                                   /* team am I? */
        __global uint *first_team_offset;
        first_team_offset = (__global uint *) gsegptr;
        int temp_offset, temp_packetcount;
        temp_offset = first_team_offset[teamnum] / 65536;
        temp_packetcount = first_team_offset[teamnum] % 65536;
        gsegptr += num_header_packets + temp_offset;
        for (i=0; i<temp_packetcount; ++i) {
            outptr16 = &outputspace[gsegptr->seg_output_offset];
            work_input = &input[gsegptr->seg_input_offset];
            outptr16[lunit] += gsegptr->uf.matdata[lunit] *
                    work_input[gsegptr->input_offset_short[lunit]];
            ++gsegptr;
        }
    }
    else { /* team_size is 1, and this work unit needs to do */
           /* all 16 elements in the packet */
        /* skip over team_offset data */
        gsegptr += num_header_packets;
        /* Number of packets to be processed. */
        npackets = gsegptr->npackets_remaining;
        int stopdex  = ((teamnum + 1) * npackets) / n_teams;
        int startdex = ((teamnum    ) * npackets) / n_teams;
        gsegptr_stop = &gsegptr[stopdex];
        gsegptr = &gsegptr[startdex];
```

```
        while (gsegptr < gsegptr_stop) {
            outptr16 = &outputspace[gsegptr->seg_output_offset];
            work_input = &input[gsegptr->seg_input_offset];
            for (lunit=0; lunit<16; ++lunit) {
                outptr16[lunit] += gsegptr->uf.matdata[lunit] *
                    work_input[gsegptr->input_offset_short[lunit]];
            }
            ++gsegptr;
        }
    }
    barrier(CLK_LOCAL_MEM_FENCE);

    /* Now that processing is done, it's time to write out */
    /* the final results for this slab. */
    for (i=start; i<outspan; i+=span) {
        outptr[i] = outputspace[i];
    }
}


/* ============================================================ */
/* Kernel using "async_work_group_copy".  This version is       */
/* optimized for the ACCELERATOR device                         */
/* ============================================================ */


/* ============================================================ */
/* Grab a pile of input vector data into local storage          */
/* "_inputspace_index" is the offset into the local space.      */
/* "_input_offset" is the offset into the global input vector.  */
/* ============================================================ */

#define GET_INPUT(_inputspace_index, _input_offset) {             \
  eventI[_inputspace_index] = async_work_group_copy(              \
    (__local float8 *)&inputspace[column_span * _inputspace_index], \
      (const __global float8 *) &input[_input_offset],            \
      (size_t) (column_span>>3),                                  \
      (event_t) 0);                                               \
}


/* ============================================================ */
/* Grab a pile of matrix packets into local storage             */
/* "_lsegspace_index" specifies the correct offset.             */
/* ============================================================ */

#define GET_PACKET(_lsegspace_index) {                            \
    eventS[lsegspace_tag] = async_work_group_copy(                \
            (__local uchar16 *) &lsegspace[(_lsegspace_index)],   \
            (const __global uchar16 *) &gsegptr[gseg_index],      \
            (size_t) ((sizeof(packet)/16)*(segcachesize/2)),      \
```

```
                (event_t) 0);                                    \
                gseg_index += (segcachesize/2);                  \
}


/* ========================================================= */
/*                                                           */
/* For a given packet of matrix data, residing in LOCAL      */
/* memory, do the following:                                 */
/*     Snap a pointer to the beginning of the packet.        */
/*     If it's time, grab a new batch of input data.         */
/*     Snap pointers to the output and matrix float data.    */
/*     Spend 16 lines performing the scalar computations.    */
/*     Perform two 8-way SIMD FMA operations.                */
/*     Update the index to the next packet.                  */
/*                                                           */
/* ========================================================= */
#define PROCESS_LOCAL_PACKET {                                   \
    float8 inV[2];                                              \
    lsegptr = (__local struct _packet *)                       \
                 &lsegspace[lsegspace_index];                   \
    if (lsegptr->seg_input_offset != curr_input_offset) {      \
        curr_input_offset = lsegptr->seg_input_offset;         \
        next_input_offset = lsegptr->future_seg_input_offset;  \
        GET_INPUT(inputspace_index, next_input_offset)         \
        inputspace_index = 1 - inputspace_index;               \
        wait_group_events(1, &eventI[inputspace_index]);       \
    }                                                          \
    work_input = &inputspace[column_span * inputspace_index];  \
    outputspaceV8 = (__local float8 *)                         \
                 &outputspace[lsegptr->seg_output_offset];     \
    inV[0].s0 = work_input[lsegptr->input_offset_short[ 0]];   \
    inV[0].s1 = work_input[lsegptr->input_offset_short[ 1]];   \
    inV[0].s2 = work_input[lsegptr->input_offset_short[ 2]];   \
    inV[0].s3 = work_input[lsegptr->input_offset_short[ 3]];   \
    inV[0].s4 = work_input[lsegptr->input_offset_short[ 4]];   \
    inV[0].s5 = work_input[lsegptr->input_offset_short[ 5]];   \
    inV[0].s6 = work_input[lsegptr->input_offset_short[ 6]];   \
    inV[0].s7 = work_input[lsegptr->input_offset_short[ 7]];   \
    inV[1].s0 = work_input[lsegptr->input_offset_short[ 8]];   \
    inV[1].s1 = work_input[lsegptr->input_offset_short[ 9]];   \
    inV[1].s2 = work_input[lsegptr->input_offset_short[10]];   \
    inV[1].s3 = work_input[lsegptr->input_offset_short[11]];   \
    inV[1].s4 = work_input[lsegptr->input_offset_short[12]];   \
    inV[1].s5 = work_input[lsegptr->input_offset_short[13]];   \
    inV[1].s6 = work_input[lsegptr->input_offset_short[14]];   \
    inV[1].s7 = work_input[lsegptr->input_offset_short[15]];   \
    outputspaceV8[0] = fma(lsegptr->uf.matdataV8[0], inV[0],   \
                                      outputspaceV8[0]);\
```

```
            outputspaceV8[1] = fma(lsegptr->uf.matdataV8[1], inV[1],  \
                                           outputspaceV8[1]);\
        ++lsegspace_index;                                            \
}

__kernel __attribute__ ((reqd_work_group_size(1, 1, 1)))
void tiled_spmv_kernel_AWGC(
        __global float *input, /* pointer to input memory object */
        __global float *output,/* pointer to output memory object */
        __global uint *matbuffer, /* pointer to tiled matrix */
                              /* memory object in global */
                              /* memory */
      uint column_span, /* size of fixed chunks of the input */
                        /* vector */
      uint slabspace,   /* size of the variable chunk of output */
                        /* vector to be computed */
      uint segcachesize,   /* number of tiled matrix packets */
                        /* which fit in "outputspace" */
      uint num_header_packets,
      __local float *inputspace, /* local buffer to hold staged */
                              /* input vector data */
      __local float *outputspace, /* local buffer to hold */
                              /* computed output, to be written */
                              /* out at the end */
      __local packet *lsegspace) /* local buffer to hold staged */
                              /* tiled matrix packet data */
{
    __global slab_header *headptr;
    __local float *work_input;
    __local float8 *outputspaceV8;
    int i, tempmax;
    event_t eventS[2], eventI[2], eventO;

    int temp = segcachesize/2;
    int half_scs = 0;
    while (temp) {
        ++half_scs;
        temp >>= 1;
    }

    /* This is a global packet pointer, indexing into the global */
    /* memory object containing the tiled matrix */
    __global packet *gsegptr;

    /* This is a local packet pointer, indexing into the local */
    /* storage for our tiled matrix */
    __local  packet *lsegptr;
```

```
headptr = ((__global slab_header *) matbuffer)
                            + get_global_id(0);
gsegptr = &(((__global packet *) matbuffer)[headptr->offset]);
gsegptr += num_header_packets;  /* skip over team_offset data */
lsegptr = &lsegspace[0];

int gseg_index = 0;    /* index into global memory of the */
                       /* packets for this slab */
int inputspace_index = 0;    /* offset index into the local */
                             /* space for the input */
int lsegspace_index = 0;     /* offset index into the local */
                             /* space for the tiled matrix */
int lsegspace_tag = 0;       /* tag used to manage events */
                             /* regarding local packets */

GET_PACKET(0)
wait_group_events(1, &eventS[0]);
/* how many packets are to be processed in this slab? */
uint npackets = lsegptr->npackets_remaining;
if (npackets == 0) return;
GET_PACKET(segcachesize/2)
tempmax = (segcachesize < npackets) ? segcachesize : npackets;
for (i=0; i<slabspace; ++i) {
    outputspace[i] = 0.0f; /* zero out the output buffer */
}

uint curr_input_offset = lsegptr->seg_input_offset;
uint next_input_offset = lsegptr->future_seg_input_offset;
GET_INPUT(0, curr_input_offset) /* Load the first two parcels */
GET_INPUT(1, next_input_offset) /* of local input vector data */
/* and wait on the first one. */
wait_group_events(1, &eventI[inputspace_index]);

/* this first loop handles the bulk of the work with */
/* minimal if-tests, segcachesize/2 packets at a time */
while (npackets > tempmax) {
    for (i=0; i<segcachesize/2; ++i) {
        PROCESS_LOCAL_PACKET
    }
    /* load next batch of packets, using double buffering */
    lsegspace_index &= (segcachesize-1);
    lsegspace_tag = (lsegspace_index ==
                    (segcachesize/2)) ? 1 : 0;
    npackets -= segcachesize/2;
    GET_PACKET((segcachesize/2)-lsegspace_index);
    wait_group_events(1, &eventS[lsegspace_tag]);
}
```

```
/* this second loop handles the remaining packets, one packet */
/* at a time */
while (npackets) {
    PROCESS_LOCAL_PACKET
    lsegspace_index &= (segcachesize-1);
    lsegspace_tag = (lsegspace_index ==
                        (segcachesize/2)) ? 1 : 0;
    --npackets;
    if ((lsegspace_index & ((segcachesize/2)-1)) == 0) {
        if (npackets > segcachesize/2) {
            GET_PACKET((segcachesize/2)-lsegspace_index);
        }
        if (npackets > 0) {
            wait_group_events(1, &eventS[lsegspace_tag]);
        }
    }
}

/* Now that processing is done, it's time to write out the */
/* final results for this slab. */

eventO = async_work_group_copy(
            (__global float *) &output[headptr->outindex],
            (__const local float *) outputspace,
            (size_t) (headptr->outspan),
            (event_t) 0);
wait_group_events(1, &eventO);
wait_group_events(1, &eventI[1-inputspace_index]);
wait_group_events(2, eventS);
}
```

Additional Areas of Optimization

The number of packets from any slice must be equal to the maximum number of non-zero elements found in any of its rows. Because the other rows will typically have fewer elements, some packets will be loaded with null elements (whose matrix floating-point value is zero). This "reduction in packet density" has the effect of reducing performance, and the correlation is quite high. In fact, across the 22 matrices studied, and across four hardware platforms, the averaged statistical correlation between gigaflops and packet density was $\rho = 0.8733$.

An optimization for this packet density inefficiency is to permute the rows within each slab according to their non-zero element count. The algorithmically complete permutation would be a full sort, but simpler (and faster) heuristics might suffice. This would require adding a permutation array to each slab in the data structure. The kernels would read in that permutation array and use it to scatter the output data when they are completely finished with the slab, which won't add significantly to the total compute time. This improvement guarantees that we get roughly the same gigaflop performance from all matrices, no matter how ill formed they are.

Summary of OpenCL 1.1

This appendix lists the APIs, data types, and other interfaces used by programmers working with OpenCL 1.1. Headings that introduce each topic in the appendix include in square brackets the section number in the OpenCL 1.1 specification where further information can be found. This text is also available as a compact reference card at www.khronos.org/files/opencl-1-1-quick-reference-card.pdf.

The OpenCL Platform Layer

The OpenCL platform layer implements platform-specific features that allow applications to query OpenCL devices and device configuration information and to create OpenCL contexts using one or more devices.

Contexts [4.3]

```
cl_context  clCreateContext (
    const cl_context_properties *properties,
    cl_uint num_devices, const cl_device_id *devices,
    void (CL_CALLBACK*pfn_notify)(const char *errinfo,
    const void *private_info, size_t cb, void *user_data),
    void *user_data, cl_int *errcode_ret)
properties: CL_CONTEXT_PLATFORM, CL_GL_CONTEXT_KHR,
    CL_CGL_SHAREGROUP_KHR, CL_{EGL, GLX}_DISPLAY_KHR, CL_WGL_HDC_KHR

cl_context  clCreateContextFromType (
    const cl_context_properties *properties,
    cl_device_type device_type,
    void (CL_CALLBACK *pfn_notify)(const char *errinfo,
    const void *private_info, size_t cb, void *user_data),
    void *user_data, cl_int *errcode_ret)
properties: See clCreateContext

cl_int  clRetainContext (cl_context context)
```

```
cl_int  clReleaseContext (cl_context context)

cl_int  clGetContextInfo (cl_context context,
    cl_context_info param_name, size_t param_value_size,
    void *param_value, size_t *param_value_size_ret)
param_name: CL_CONTEXT_REFERENCE_COUNT,
    CL_CONTEXT_{DEVICES, PROPERTIES}, CL_CONTEXT_NUM_DEVICES
```

Querying Platform Information and Devices [4.1, 4.2]

```
cl_int  clGetPlatformIDs (cl_uint num_entries,
    cl_platform_id *platforms, cl_uint *num_platforms)

cl_int  clGetPlatformInfo (cl_platform_id platform,
    cl_platform_info param_name, size_t param_value_size,
    void *param_value, size_t *param_value_size_ret)
param_name: CL_PLATFORM_{PROFILE, VERSION},
    CL_PLATFORM_{NAME, VENDOR, EXTENSIONS}

cl_int  clGetDeviceIDs (cl_platform_id platform,
    cl_device_type device_type, cl_uint num_entries,
    cl_device_id *devices, cl_uint *num_devices)
device_type: CL_DEVICE_TYPE_{CPU, GPU},
    CL_DEVICE_TYPE_{ACCELERATOR, DEFAULT, ALL}

cl_int  clGetDeviceInfo (cl_device_id device,
    cl_device_info param_name, size_t param_value_size,
    void *param_value, size_t *param_value_size_ret)
param_name: CL_DEVICE_TYPE,
    CL_DEVICE_VENDOR_ID,
    CL_DEVICE_MAX_COMPUTE_UNITS,
    CL_DEVICE_MAX_WORK_ITEM_{DIMENSIONS, SIZES},
    CL_DEVICE_MAX_WORK_GROUP_SIZE,
    CL_DEVICE_{NATIVE, PREFERRED}_VECTOR_WIDTH_CHAR,
    CL_DEVICE_{NATIVE, PREFERRED}_VECTOR_WIDTH_SHORT,
    CL_DEVICE_{NATIVE, PREFERRED}_VECTOR_WIDTH_INT,
    CL_DEVICE_{NATIVE, PREFERRED}_VECTOR_WIDTH_LONG,
    CL_DEVICE_{NATIVE, PREFERRED}_VECTOR_WIDTH_FLOAT,
    CL_DEVICE_{NATIVE, PREFERRED}_VECTOR_WIDTH_DOUBLE,
    CL_DEVICE_{NATIVE, PREFERRED}_VECTOR_WIDTH_HALF,
    CL_DEVICE_MAX_CLOCK_FREQUENCY,
    CL_DEVICE_ADDRESS_BITS,
    CL_DEVICE_MAX_MEM_ALLOC_SIZE,
    CL_DEVICE_IMAGE_SUPPORT,
    CL_DEVICE_MAX_{READ, WRITE}_IMAGE_ARGS,
    CL_DEVICE_IMAGE2D_MAX_{WIDTH, HEIGHT},
    CL_DEVICE_IMAGE3D_MAX_{WIDTH, HEIGHT, DEPTH},
```

```
CL_DEVICE_MAX_SAMPLERS,
CL_DEVICE_MAX_PARAMETER_SIZE,
CL_DEVICE_MEM_BASE_ADDR_ALIGN,
CL_DEVICE_MIN_DATA_TYPE_ALIGN_SIZE,
CL_DEVICE_SINGLE_FP_CONFIG,
CL_DEVICE_GLOBAL_MEM_CACHE_{TYPE, SIZE},
CL_DEVICE_GLOBAL_MEM_CACHELINE_SIZE,
CL_DEVICE_GLOBAL_MEM_SIZE,
CL_DEVICE_MAX_CONSTANT_{BUFFER_SIZE, ARGS}
CL_DEVICE_LOCAL_MEM_{TYPE, SIZE},
CL_DEVICE_ERROR_CORRECTION_SUPPORT,
CL_DEVICE_PROFILING_TIMER_RESOLUTION,
CL_DEVICE_ENDIAN_LITTLE,
CL_DEVICE_AVAILABLE,
CL_DEVICE_COMPILER_AVAILABLE,
CL_DEVICE_EXECUTION_CAPABILITIES,
CL_DEVICE_QUEUE_PROPERTIES,
CL_DEVICE_{NAME, VENDOR, PROFILE, EXTENSIONS},
CL_DEVICE_HOST_UNIFIED_MEMORY,
CL_DEVICE_OPENCL_C_VERSION,
CL_DEVICE_VERSION,
CL_DRIVER_VERSION, CL_DEVICE_PLATFORM
```

The OpenCL Runtime

Command-Queues [5.1]

```
cl_command_queue  clCreateCommandQueue (cl_context context,
    cl_device_id device, cl_command_queue_properties properties,
    cl_int *errcode_ret)
properties: CL_QUEUE_PROFILING_ENABLE,
    CL_QUEUE_OUT_OF_ORDER_EXEC_MODE_ ENABLE

cl_int clRetainCommandQueue (cl_command_queue command_queue)

cl_int clReleaseCommandQueue (cl_command_queue command_queue)

cl_int clGetCommandQueueInfo (cl_command_queue command_queue,
    cl_command_queue_info param_name, size_t param_value_size,
    void *param_value, size_t *param_value_size_ret)
param_name: CL_QUEUE_CONTEXT, CL_QUEUE_DEVICE,
    CL_QUEUE_REFERENCE_COUNT, CL_QUEUE_PROPERTIES
```

Buffer Objects

Elements of a buffer object can be a scalar or vector data type or a user-defined structure. Elements are stored sequentially and are accessed using a pointer by a kernel executing on a device. Data is stored in the same format as it is accessed by the kernel.

Create Buffer Objects [5.2.1]

```
cl_mem clCreateBuffer (cl_context context, cl_mem_flags flags,
    size_t size, void *host_ptr, cl_int *errcode_ret)

cl_mem clCreateSubBuffer (cl_mem buffer, cl_mem_flags flags,
    cl_buffer_create_type buffer_create_type,
    const void *buffer_create_info, cl_int *errcode_ret)
```

flags for clCreateBuffer and clCreateSubBuffer:
    CL_MEM_READ_WRITE, CL_MEM_{WRITE, READ}_ONLY,
    CL_MEM_{USE, ALLOC, COPY}_HOST_PTR

Read, Write, and Copy Buffer Objects [5.2.2]

```
cl_int clEnqueueReadBuffer ( cl_command_queue command_queue,
    cl_mem buffer, cl_bool blocking_read, size_t offset, size_t cb,
    void *ptr, cl_uint num_events_in_wait_list,
    const cl_event *event_wait_list, cl_event *event)

cl_int clEnqueueWriteBuffer (cl_command_queue command_queue,
    cl_mem buffer, cl_bool blocking_write, size_t offset, size_t cb,
    const void *ptr, cl_uint num_events_in_wait_list,
    const cl_event *event_wait_list, cl_event *event)

cl_int clEnqueueReadBufferRect (cl_command_queue command_queue,
    cl_mem buffer, cl_bool blocking_read,
    const size_t buffer_origin[3],  const size_t host_origin[3],
    const size_t region[3], size_t buffer_row_pitch,
    size_t buffer_slice_pitch, size_t host_row_pitch,
    size_t host_slice_pitch, void *ptr,
    cl_uint num_events_in_wait_list,
    const cl_event *event_wait_list, cl_event *event)

cl_int clEnqueueWriteBufferRect (cl_command_queue command_queue,
    cl_mem buffer, cl_bool blocking_write,
    const size_t buffer_origin[3], const size_t host_origin[3],
    const size_t region[3], size_t buffer_row_pitch,
    size_t buffer_slice_pitch, size_t host_row_pitch,
    size_t host_slice_pitch, void *ptr,
```

```
    cl_uint num_events_in_wait_list,
    const cl_event *event_wait_list, cl_event *event)

cl_int clEnqueueCopyBuffer (cl_command_queue command_queue,
    cl_mem src_buffer, cl_mem dst_buffer, size_t src_offset,
    size_t dst_offset, size_t cb, cl_uint num_events_in_wait_list,
    const cl_event *event_wait_list, cl_event *event)

cl_int clEnqueueCopyBufferRect (cl_command_queue command_queue,
    cl_mem src_buffer, cl_mem dst_buffer, const size_t src_origin[3],
    const size_t dst_origin[3], const size_t region[3],
    size_t src_row_pitch, size_t src_slice_pitch,
    size_t dst_row_pitch, size_t dst_slice_pitch,
    cl_uint num_events_in_wait_list,
    const cl_event *event_wait_list, cl_event *event)
```

Map Buffer Objects [5.23]

```
void * clEnqueueMapBuffer (cl_command_queue command_queue,
    cl_mem buffer, cl_bool blocking_map, cl_map_flags map_flags,
    size_t offset, size_t cb, cl_uint num_events_in_wait_list,
    const cl_event *event_wait_list, cl_event *event,
    cl_int *errcode_ret)
```

Manage Buffer Objects [5.4.1–2]

```
cl_int clRetainMemObject (cl_mem memobj)

cl_int clReleaseMemObject (cl_mem memobj)

cl_int clSetMemObjectDestructorCallback (cl_mem memobj,
    void (CL_CALLBACK *pfn_notify) (cl_mem memobj, void *user_data),
    void *user_data)

cl_int clEnqueueUnmapMemObject (cl_command_queue command_queue,
    cl_mem memobj, void *mapped_ptr, cl_uint num_events_in_wait_list,
    const cl_event *event_wait_list, cl_event *event)
```

Query Buffer Objects [5.4.3]

```
cl_int clGetMemObjectInfo (cl_mem memobj, cl_mem_info param_name,
    size_t param_value_size, void *param_value,
    size_t *param_value_size_ret)
param_name: CL_MEM_{TYPE, FLAGS, SIZE, HOST_PTR},
    CL_MEM_{MAP, REFERENCE}_COUNT, CL_MEM_OFFSET,
    CL_MEM_CONTEXT, CL_MEM_ASSOCIATED_MEMOBJECT
```

Program Objects

Create Program Objects [5.6.1]

cl_program **clCreateProgramWithSource** (cl_context *context*,
  cl_uint *count*, const char **strings, const size_t *lengths,
  cl_int *errcode_ret)

cl_program **clCreateProgramWithBinary** (cl_context *context*,
  cl_uint *num_devices*, const cl_device_id *device_list,
  const size_t *lengths, const unsigned char **binaries,
  cl_int *binary_status, cl_int *errcode_ret)

cl_int **clRetainProgram** (cl_program *program*)

cl_int **clReleaseProgram** (cl_program *program*)

Build Program Executable [5.6.2]

cl_int   **clBuildProgram** (cl_program *program*, cl_uint *num_devices*,
  const cl_device_id *device_list, const char *options,
  void (CL_CALLBACK*pfn_notify)(cl_program *program*,
  void *user_data), void *user_data)

Build Options [5.6.3]

Preprocessor

(-D processed in order listed in clBuildProgram)

-D name
-D name=definition
-I dir

Optimization Options

-cl-opt-disable
-cl-strict-aliasing
-cl-mad-enable
-cl-no-signed-zeros
-cl-finite-math-only
-cl-fast-relaxed-math
-cl-unsafe-math-optimizations

Math Intrinsics

```
-cl-single-precision-constant
-cl-denorms-are-zero
```

Warning Request/Suppress

```
-w
-Werror
```

Control OpenCL C Language Version

```
-cl-std=CL1.1       // OpenCL 1.1 specification.
```

Query Program Objects [5.6.5]

```
cl_int   clGetProgramInfo (cl_program program,
    cl_program_info param_name,size_t param_value_size,
    void *param_value, size_t *param_value_size_ret)
param_name:  CL_PROGRAM_{REFERENCE_COUNT},
    CL_PROGRAM_{CONTEXT, NUM_DEVICES, DEVICES},
    CL_PROGRAM_{SOURCE, BINARY_SIZES, BINARIES}
```

```
cl_int   clGetProgramBuildInfo (cl_program program,
    cl_device_id device, cl_program_build_info param_name,
    size_t param_value_size, void *param_value,
    size_t *param_value_size_ret)
param_name:  CL_PROGRAM_BUILD_{STATUS, OPTIONS, LOG}
```

Unload the OpenCL Compiler [5.6.4]

```
cl_int clUnloadCompiler (void)
```

Kernel and Event Objects

Create Kernel Objects [5.7.1]

```
cl_kernel   clCreateKernel (cl_program program,
    const char *kernel_name, cl_int *errcode_ret)
```

```
cl_int   clCreateKernelsInProgram (cl_program program,
    cl_uint num_kernels, cl_kernel *kernels,
    cl_uint *num_kernels_ret)
```

```
cl_int  clRetainKernel (cl_kernel kernel)

cl_int  clReleaseKernel (cl_kernel kernel)
```

Kernel Arguments and Object Queries [5.7.2, 5.7.3]

```
cl_int clSetKernelArg (cl_kernel kernel, cl_uint arg_index,
    size_t arg_size, const void *arg_value)

cl_int clGetKernelInfo (cl_kernel kernel,cl_kernel_info param_name,
    size_t param_value_size, void *param_value,
    size_t *param_value_size_ret)
param_name:    CL_KERNEL_FUNCTION_NAME, CL_KERNEL_NUM_ARGS,
    CL_KERNEL_REFERENCE_COUNT, CL_KERNEL_CONTEXT, CL_KERNEL_PROGRAM

cl_int clGetKernelWorkGroupInfo (cl_kernel kernel,
    cl_device_id device, cl_kernel_work_group_info param_name,
    size_t param_value_size, void *param_value,
    size_t *param_value_size_ret)
param_name:    CL_KERNEL_WORK_GROUP_SIZE,
    CL_KERNEL_COMPILE_WORK_GROUP_SIZE,
    CL_KERNEL_{LOCAL, PRIVATE}_MEM_SIZE,
    CL_KERNEL_PREFERRED_WORK_GROUP_SIZE_MULTIPLE
```

Execute Kernels [5.8]

```
cl_int clEnqueueNDRangeKernel ( cl_command_queue command_queue,
    cl_kernel kernel, cl_uint work_dim,
    const size_t *global_work_offset,
    const size_t *global_work_size,
    const size_t *local_work_size, cl_uint num_events_in_wait_list,
    const cl_event *event_wait_list, cl_event *event)

cl_int clEnqueueTask (cl_command_queue command_queue,
    cl_kernel kernel, cl_uint num_events_in_wait_list,
    const cl_event *event_wait_list, cl_event *event)

cl_int clEnqueueNativeKernel (cl_command_queue command_queue,
    void (*user_func)(void *), void *args, size_t cb_args,
    cl_uint num_mem_objects, const cl_mem *mem_list,
    const void **args_mem_loc, cl_uint num_events_in_wait_list,
    const cl_event *event_wait_list, cl_event *event)
```

Event Objects [5.9]

```
cl_event clCreateUserEvent (cl_context context, cl_int *errcode_ret)
```

```
cl_int clSetUserEventStatus (cl_event event,
   cl_int execution_status)
```

```
cl_int clWaitForEvents (cl_uint num_events,
   const cl_event *event_list)
```

```
cl_int clGetEventInfo (cl_event event, cl_event_info param_name,
   size_t param_value_size, void *param_value,
   size_t *param_value_size_ret)
param_name:  CL_EVENT_COMMAND_{QUEUE, TYPE},
   CL_EVENT_{CONTEXT, REFERENCE_COUNT},
   CL_EVENT_COMMAND_EXECUTION_STATUS
```

```
cl_int clSetEventCallback (cl_event event,
   cl_int command_exec_callback_type,
   void (CL_CALLBACK *pfn_event_notify)(cl_event event,
   cl_int event_command_exec_status,
   void *user_data), void *user_data)
```

```
cl_int clRetainEvent (cl_event event)
```

```
cl_int clReleaseEvent (cl_event event)
```

Out-of-Order Execution of Kernels and Memory Object Commands [5.10]

```
cl_int clEnqueueMarker (cl_command_queue command_queue,
   cl_event *event)
```

```
cl_int clEnqueueWaitForEvents (cl_command_queue command_queue,
   cl_uint num_events, const cl_event *event_list)
```

```
cl_int clEnqueueBarrier (cl_command_queue command_queue)
```

Profiling Operations [5.11]

```
cl_int clGetEventProfilingInfo (cl_event event,
   cl_profiling_info param_name, size_t param_value_size,
   void *param_value, size_t *param_value_size_ret)
param_name:  CL_PROFILING_COMMAND_QUEUED,
   CL_PROFILING_COMMAND_{SUBMIT, START, END}
```

Flush and Finish [5.12]

```
cl_int clFlush (cl_command_queue command_queue)
```

```
cl_int clFinish (cl_command_queue command_queue)
```

Supported Data Types

Built-In Scalar Data Types [6.1.1]

Table A.1

OpenCL Type	API Type	Description
bool	N/a	True (1) or false (0)
char	cl_char	8-bit signed
unsigned char, uchar	cl_uchar	8-bit unsigned
short	cl_short	16-bit signed
unsigned short, ushort	cl_ushort	16-bit unsigned
int	cl_int	32-bit signed
unsigned int, uint	cl_uint	32-bit unsigned
long	cl_long	64-bit signed
unsigned long, ulong	cl_ulong	64-bit unsigned
float	cl_float	32-bit float
half	cl_half	16-bit float (for storage only)
size_t	N/a	32- or 64-bit unsigned integer
ptrdiff_t	N/a	32- or 64-bit signed integer
intptr_t	N/a	Signed integer
uintptr_t	N/a	Unsigned integer
void	void	Void

Built-In Vector Data Types [6.1.2]

Table A.2

OpenCL Type	API Type	Description
char*n*	cl_char*n*	8-bit signed
uchar*n*	cl_uchar*n*	8-bit unsigned
short*n*	cl_short*n*	16-bit signed
ushort*n*	cl_ushort*n*	16-bit unsigned
int*n*	cl_int*n*	32-bit signed
uint*n*	cl_uint*n*	32-bit unsigned
long*n*	cl_long*n*	64-bit signed
ulong*n*	cl_ulong*n*	64-bt unsigned
float*n*	cl_float*n*	32-bit float

Other Built-In Data Types [6.1.3]

Table A.3

OpenCL Type	Description
image2d_t	2D image handle
image3d_t	3D image handle
sampler_t	Sampler handle
event_t	Event handle

Reserved Data Types [6.1.4]

Table A.4

OpenCL Type	Description
bool*n*	Boolean vector
double, double*n* OPTIONAL	64-bit float, vector

continues

Table A.4 *(Continued)*

OpenCL Type	Description
half*n*	16-bit, vector
quad, quad*n*	128-bit float, vector
complex half, complex half*n* imaginary half, imaginary half*n*	16-bit complex, vector
complex float, complex float*n* imaginary float, imaginary float*n*	32-bit complex, vector
complex double, complex double*n* imaginary double, imaginary double*n*	64-bit complex, vector
complex quad, complex quad*n* imaginary quad, imaginary quad*n*	128-bit complex, vector
float*nxm*	$n*m$ matrix of 32-bit floats
double*nxm*	$n*m$ matrix of 64-bit floats
long double, long double*n*	64- to 128-bit float, vector
long long, long long*n*	128-bit signed
unsigned long long, ulong long, ulong long*n*	128-bit unsigned

Vector Component Addressing [6.1.7]

Vector Components

Table A.5

	float2 v;	float3 v;	float4 v;	float8 v;	float16 v;
0	v.x, v.s0	v.x, v.s0	v.x, v.s0	v.s0	v.s0
1	v.y, v.s1	v.y, v.s1	v.y, v.s1	v.s1	v.s1
2		v.z, v.s2	v.z, v.s2	v.s2	v.s2
3			v.w, v.s3	v.s3	v.s3
4				v.s4	v.s4

Table A.5 *(Continued)*

	float2 v;	float3 v;	float4 v;	float8 v;	float16 v;
5				v.s5	v.s5
6				v.s6	v.s6
7				v.s7	v.s7
8					v.s8
9					v.s9
10					v.sa, v.sA
11					v.sb, v.sB
12					v.sc, v.sC
13					v.sd, v.sD
14					v.se, v.sE
15					v.sf, v.sF

Vector Addressing Equivalencies

Numeric indices are preceded by the letter *s* or *S*, for example, s1. Swizzling, duplication, and nesting are allowed, for example, v.yx, v.xx, v.lo.x.

Table A.6

	v.lo	v.hi	v.odd	v.even
float2	v.x, v.s0	v.y, v.s1	v.y, v.s1	v.x, v.s0
float3*	v.s01, v.xy	v.s23, v.zw	v.s13, v.yw	v.s02, v.xz
float4	v.s01, v.xy	v.s23, v.zw	v.s13, v.yw	v.s02, v.xz
float8	v.s0123	v.s4567	v.s1357	v.s0246
float16	v.s01234567	v.s89abcdef	v.s13579bdf	v.s02468ace

When using .lo or .hi with a 3-component vector, the .w component is undefined.

Conversions and Type Casting Examples [6.2]

```
T a = (T)b;    // Scalar to scalar, or scalar to vector
T a = convert_T(b);
T a = convert_T_R(b);
T a = as_T(b);
T a = convert_T_sat_R(b);    //R is rounding mode
```

R can be one of the following rounding modes:

Table A.7

_rte	To nearest even
_rtz	Toward zero
_rtp	Toward +infinity
_rtn	Toward -infinity

Operators [6.3]

These operators behave similarly as in C99 except that operands may include vector types when possible:

Table A.8

+	-	*	%	/	--	++	==	!=	&
~	^	>	<	>=	<=	|	!	&&	||
?:	>>	<<	,	=	op=	sizeof			

Address Space Qualifiers [6.5]

```
__global, global
__local, local
__constant, constant
__private, private
```

Function Qualifiers [6.7]

```
__kernel, kernel
__attribute__((vec_type_hint(type)))    //type defaults to int
__attribute__((work_group_size_hint(X, Y, Z)))
__attribute__((reqd_work_group_size(X, Y, Z)))
```

Preprocessor Directives and Macros [6.9]

```
#pragma OPENCL FP_CONTRACT on-off-switch
where on-off-switch is one of ON OFF DEFAULT
```

Table A.9

__FILE__	Current source file
__LINE__	Integer line number
__OPENCL_VERSION__	Integer version number
__CL_VERSION_1_0__	Substitutes integer 100 for version 1.0
__CL_VERSION_1_1__	Substitutes integer 110 for version 1.1
__ENDIAN_LITTLE__	1 if device is little endian
__kernel_exec(X, typen)	Same as __kernel __attribute__ ((work_group_size_hint(X, 1, 1))) \ __attribute__ ((vec_type_hint(typen)))
__IMAGE_SUPPORT__	1 if images are supported
__FAST_RELAXED_MATH__	1 if -cl-fast-relaxed-math optimization option is specified

Specify Type Attributes [6.10.1]

Use the following attributes to specify special attributes of enum, struct, and union types:

```
__attribute__((aligned(n)))
__attribute__((aligned))
__attribute__((packed))
__attribute__((endian(host)))
__attribute__((endian(device)))
__attribute__((endian))
```

Math Constants [6.11.2]

The values of the following symbolic constants are type `float` and are accurate within the precision of a single-precision floating-point number:

Table A.10

MAXFLOAT	Value of max. non-infinite single-precision floating-point number.
HUGE_VALF	Positive float expression, evaluates to +infinity. Used as error value.
HUGE_VAL	Positive double expression, evaluates to +infinity. Used as error value. **Optional**
INFINITY	Constant float expression, positive or unsigned infinity.
NAN	Constant float expression, quiet NaN.
M_E_F	Value of e.
M_LOG2E_F	Value of $\log_2 e$.
M_LOG10E_F	Value of $\log_{10} e$.
M_LN2_F	Value of $\log_e 2$.
M_LN10_F	Value of $\log_e 10$.
M_PI_F	Value of π.
M_PI_2_F	Value of $\pi / 2$.
M_PI_4_F	Value of $\pi / 4$.
M_1_PI_F	Value of $1 / \pi$.
M_2_PI_F	Value of $2 / \pi$.
M_2_SQRTPI_F	Value of $2 / \sqrt{\pi}$.
M_SQRT2_F	Value of $\sqrt{2}$.
M_SQRT1_2_F	Value of $1 / \sqrt{2}$.

Each occurrence of *T* within a function call must be the same. *n* is 2, 3, 4, 8, or 16 unless otherwise specified.

Work-Item Built-In Functions [6.11.1]

D is dimension index.

Table A.11

uint **get_work_dim** ()	Number of dimensions in use
size_t **get_global_size** (uint D)	Number of global work-items
size_t **get_global_id** (uint D)	Global work-item ID value
size_t **get_local_size** (uint D)	Number of local work-items
size_t **get_local_id** (uint D)	Local work-item ID
size_t **get_num_groups** (uint D)	Number of work-groups
size_t **get_group_id** (uint D)	Returns the work-group ID
size_t **get_global_offset** (uint D)	Returns global offset

Integer Built-In Functions [6.11.3]

T is type char, charn, uchar, ucharn, short, shortn, ushort, ushortn, int, intn, uint, uintn, long, longn, ulong, or ulongn.

U is the unsigned version of T. S is the scalar version of T.

Table A.12

U **abs** (T x)	$\mid x \mid$
U **abs_diff** (T x, T y)	$\mid x - y \mid$ without modulo overflow
T **add_sat** (T x, T y)	$x + y$ and saturates the result
T **hadd** (T x, T y)	$(x + y) >> 1$ without modulo overflow
T **rhadd** (T x, T y)	$(x + y + 1) >> 1$
T **clz** (T x)	Number of leading 0 bits in x
T **clamp** (T x, T min, T max) T **clamp** (T x, S min, S max)	min(max(x, minval), maxval)
T **mad_hi** (T a, T b, T c)	mul_hi(a, b) + c

continues

Table A.12 *(Continued)*

T **mad_sat** $(T\ a,\ T\ b,\ T\ c)$	$a\ *\ b\ +\ c$ and saturates the result
T **max** $(T\ x,\ T\ y)$	y if $x < y$, otherwise it returns x
T **max** $(T\ x,\ S\ y)$	y if $x < y$, otherwise it returns x
T **min** $(T\ x,\ T\ y)$	y if $y < x$, otherwise it returns x
T **min** $(T\ x,\ S\ y)$	y if $y < x$, otherwise it returns x
T **mul_hi** $(T\ x,\ T\ y)$	High half of the product of x and y
T **rotate** $(T\ v,\ T\ i)$	Result $[indx] = v[indx] << i[indx]$
T **sub_sat** $(T\ x,\ T\ y)$	$x - y$ and saturates the result

For **upsample**, scalar types are permitted for the following vector types:

Table A.13

short$n$ **upsample**(char$n$ *hi*, uchar$n$ *lo*)	result[i]= ((short)hi[i]<< 8) | lo[i]
ushort$n$ **upsample**(uchar$n$ *hi*, uchar$n$ *lo*)	result[i]=((ushort)hi[i]<< 8) | lo[i]
int$n$ **upsample**(short$n$ *hi*, ushort$n$ *lo*)	result[i]=((int)hi[i]<< 16) | lo[i]
uint$n$ **upsample**(ushort$n$ *hi*, ushort$n$ *lo*)	result[i]=((uint)hi[i]<< 16) | lo[i]
long$n$ **upsample**(int$n$ *hi*, uint$n$ *lo*)	result[i]=((long)hi[i]<< 32) | lo[i]
ulong$n$ **upsample**(uint$n$ *hi*, uint$n$ *lo*)	result[i]=((ulong)hi[i]<< 32) | lo[i]

The following fast integer functions optimize the performance of kernels. In these functions, T is type int, int2, int3, int4, int8, int16, uint, uint2, uint4, uint8, or uint16.

Table A.14

T **mad24** $(T\ a,\ T\ b,\ T\ c)$	Multiply 24-bit int. values a, b, add 32-bit int. result to 32-bit int. c
T **mul24** $(T\ a,\ T\ b)$	Multiply 24-bit int. values a and b

Common Built-In Functions [6.11.4]

T is type `float` or `float`*n* (or optionally `double`, `double`*n*, or `half`*n*).
Optional extensions enable `double`, `double`*n*, and `half`*n* types.

Table A.15

T **clamp** (*T x*, *T min*, *T max*) float*n* **clamp** (float*n x*, float *min*, float *max*) double*n* **clamp** (double*n x*, double *min*, double *max*) half*n* **clamp** (half*n x*, half *min*, half *max*)	Clamp *x* to range given by *min*, *max*
T **degrees** (*T radians*)	*radians* to degrees
T **max** (*T x*, *T y*) float*n* **max** (float*n x*, float *y*) double*n* **max** (double*n x*, double *y*) half*n* **max** (half*n x*, half *y*)	Max of *x* and *y*
T **min** (*T x*, *T y*) float*n* **min** (float*n x*, float *y*) double*n* **min** (double*n x*, double *y*) half*n* **min** (half*n x*, half *y*)	Min of *x* and *y*
T **mix** (*T x*, *T y*, *T a*) float*n* **mix** (float*n x*, float *y*, float *a*) double*n* **mix** (double*n x*, double *y*, double *a*) half*n* **mix** (half*n x*, half *y*, half *a*)	Linear blend of *x* and *y*
T **radians** (*T degrees*)	*degrees* to radians
T **step** (*T edge*, *T x*) float*n* **step** (float *edge*, float*n x*) double*n* **step** (double *edge*, double*n x*) half*n* **step** (half *edge*, half*n x*)	0.0 if *x* < *edge*, else 1.0
T **smoothstep** (*T edge0*, *T edge1*, *T x*) float*n* **smoothstep** (float *edge0*, float *edge1*, float*n x*) double*n* **smoothstep** (double *edge0*, double *edge1*, double*n x*) half*n* **smoothstep** (half *edge0*, half *edge1*, half*n x*)	Step and interpolate
T **sign** (*T x*)	Sign of *x*

Math Built-In Functions [6.11.2]

T is type `float` or `float`n (or optionally `double`, `double`n, or `half`n). `int`n, `uint`n, and `ulong`n must be scalar when T is scalar. Q is qualifier `__global`, `__local`, or `__private`. **HN** indicates that Half and Native variants are available by prepending `half_` or `native_` to the function name. Optional extensions enable `double`, `double`n, `half`, and `half`n types.

Table A.16

T **acos** (T)	Arc cosine
T **acosh** (T)	Inverse hyperbolic cosine
T **acospi** $(T\ x)$	acos $(x)/\pi$
T **asin** (T)	Arc sine
T **asinh** (T)	Inverse hyperbolic sine
T **asinpi** $(T\ x)$	asin $(x)/\pi$
T **atan** $(T\ y\_over\_x)$	Arc tangent
T **atan2** $(T\ y,\ T\ x)$	Arc tangent of y/x
T **atanh** (T)	Hyperbolic arc tangent
T **atanpi** $(T\ x)$	atan $(x)/\pi$
T **atan2pi** $(T\ x,\ T\ y)$	atan2 $(x, y)/\pi$
T **cbrt** (T)	Cube root
T **ceil** (T)	Round to integer toward +infinity
T **copysign** $(T\ x,\ T\ y)$	x with sign changed to sign of y
T **cos** (T) **HN**	Cosine
T **cosh** (T)	Hyperbolic cosine
T **cospi** $(T\ x)$	cos $(\pi\ x)$
T ***half_divide (T x, T y)*** T ***native_divide (T x, T y)***	$x\ /y$ (T may be `float` or `float`n)
T **erfc** (T)	Complementary error function
T **erf** (T)	Calculates error function of T

Table A.16 (*Continued*)

T **exp** (T x)	**HN**	Exponential base e
T **exp2** (T)	**HN**	Exponential base 2
T **exp10** (T)	**HN**	Exponential base 10
T **expm1** (T x)		e^x -1.0
T **fabs** (T)		Absolute value
T **fdim** (T x, T y)		"Positive difference" between x and y
T **floor** (T)		Round to integer toward -infinity
T **fma** (T a, T b, T c)		Multiply and add, then round
T **fmax** (T x, T y) half$n$ **fmax** (half$n$ x, half y) float$n$ **fmax**(float$n$ x, float y) double$n$ **fmax**(double$n$ x, double y)		Return y if x < y, otherwise it returns x
T **fmin** (T x, T y) half$n$ **fmin** (half$n$ x, half y) float$n$ **fmin**(float$n$ x, float y) double$n$ **fmin**(double$n$ x, double y)		Return y if y < x, otherwise it returns x
T **fmod** (T x, T y)		Modulus. Returns $x - y$ * trunc (x/y)
T **fract** (T x, Q T *$iptr$)		Fractional value in x
T **frexp** (T x, Q int$n$ *exp)		Extract mantissa and exponent
T **hypot** (T x, T y)		Square root of x^2+ y^2
int$n$ **ilogb** (T x)		Return exponent as an integer value
T **ldexp** (T x, int$n$ n) T **ldexp** (T x, int n)		x * 2^n
T **lgamma** (T x) T **lgamma_r** (T x, Q int$n$ *$signp$)		Log gamma function
T **log** (T)	**HN**	Natural logarithm
T **log2** (T)	**HN**	Base 2 logarithm

continues

Table A.16 (*Continued*)

T **log10** (T)	**HN**	Base 10 logarithm
T **log1p** (T x)		ln $(1.0 + x)$
T **logb** (T x)		Exponent of x
T **mad** (T a, T b, T c)		Approximates a * b + c
T **maxmag** (T x, T y)		Maximum magnitude of x and y
T **minmag** (T x, T y)		Minimum magnitude of x and y
T **modf** (T x, Q T *$iptr$)		Decompose a floating-point number
float **nan** (uint$n$ $nancode$) float$n$ **nan** (uint$n$ $nancode$) half$n$ **nan** (ushort$n$ $nancode$) double$n$ **nan** (ulong$n$ $nancode$)		Quiet NaN
T **nextafter** (T x, T y)		Next representable floating-point value following x in the direction of y
T **pow** (T x, T y)		Compute x to the power of y $(x^\wedge y)$
T **pown** (T x, int$n$ y)		Compute $x^\wedge y$, where y is an integer
T **powr** (T x, T y)	**HN**	Compute $x^\wedge y$, where x is $>= 0$
T half_recip (T x) **T native_recip (T x)**		$1/x$ (T may be float or float$n$)
T **remainder** (T x, T y)		Floating-point remainder
T **remquo** (T x, T y, Q int$n$ *quo)		Floating-point remainder and quotient
T **rint** (T)		Round to nearest even integer
T **rootN** (T x, int$n$ y)		Compute x to the power of $1/y$
T **round** (T x)		Integral value nearest to x rounding
T **rsqrt** (T)	**HN**	Inverse square root
T **sin** (T)	**HN**	Sine

Table A.16   (*Continued*)

T **sincos** (T x, Q T *cosval*)		Returns sin(x) and sets cosval cos(x)
T **sinh** (T)		Hyperbolic sine
T **sinpi** (T x)		sin (π x)
T **sqrt** (T)	**HN**	Square root
T **tan** (T)	**HN**	Tangent
T **tanh** (T)		Hyperbolic tangent
T **tanpi** (T x)		tan (π x)
T **tgamma** (T)		Gamma function
T **trunc** (T)		Round to integer toward zero

Geometric Built-In Functions [6.11.5]

Vector types may have two, three, or four components. Optional extensions enable `double`, `double`*n*, and `half`*n* types.

Table A.17

float **dot** (float *p0*, float *p1*) float **dot** (float*n* *p0*, float*n* *p1*) double **dot** (double *p0*, double p1) double **dot** (double*n* *p0*, double*n* *p1*) half **dot** (half *p0*, half *p1*) half **dot** (half*n* *p0*, half*n* *p1*)	Dot product
float{3,4} **cross** (float{3,4} *p0*, float{3,4} *p1*) double{3,4} **cross** (double{3,4} *p0*, double{3,4} *p1*) half{3,4} **cross** (half{3,4} *p0*, half{3,4} *p1*)	Cross-product
float **distance** (float *p0*, float *p1*) float **distance** (float*n* *p0*, float*n* *p1*) double **distance** (double *p0*, double *p1*) double **distance** (double*n* *p0*, double*n* *p1*) half **distance** (half *p0*, half *p1*) half **distance** (half*n* *p0*, half*n* *p1*)	Vector distance

continues

Table A.17   (*Continued*)

`float` **`length`** `(float p)`
`float` **`length`** `(floatn p)`
`double` **`length`** `(double p)`
`double` **`length`** `(doublen p)`
`half` **`length`** `(half p)`
`half` **`length`** `(halfn p)`
	Vector length

`float` **`normalize`** `(float p)`
`floatn` **`normalize`** `(floatn p)`
`double` **`normalize`** `(double p)`
`doublen` **`normalize`** `(doublen p)`
`half` **`normalize`** `(half p)`
`halfn` **`normalize`** `(halfn p)`
	Normal vector
	length 1

`float` **`fast_distance`** `(float p0, float p1)` `float` **`fast_distance`** `(floatn p0, floatn p1)`	Vector distance
`float` **`fast_length`** `(float p)` `float` **`fast_length`** `(floatn p)`	Vector length
`float` **`fast_normalize`** `(float p)` `floatn` **`fast_normalize`** `(floatn p)`	Normal vector length 1

Relational Built-In Functions [6.11.6]

T is type `float`, `floatn`, `char`, `charn`, `uchar`, `ucharn`, `short`, `shortn`, `ushort`, `ushortn`, `int`, `intn`, `uint`, `uintn`, `long`, `longn`, `ulong`, or `ulongn` (and optionally `double`, `doublen`). *S* is type `char`, `charn`, `short`, `shortn`, `int`, `intn`, `long`, or `longn`. *U* is type `uchar`, `ucharn`, `ushort`, `ushortn`, `uint`, `uintn`, `ulong`, or `ulongn`. Optional extensions enable `double`, `doublen`, and `halfn` types.

Table A.18

`int` **`isequal`** `(float x, float y)`
`intn` **`isequal`** `(floatn x, floatn y)`
`int` **`isequal`** `(double x, double y)`
`longn` **`isequal`** `(doublen x, doublen y)`
`int` **`isequal`** `(half x, half y)`
`shortn` **`isequal`** `(halfn x, halfn y)`
	Compare of $x == y$

continues

Table A.18 (*Continued*)

int **isnotequal** (float *x*, float *y*) int*n* **isnotequal** (float*n* *x*, float*n* *y*) int **isnotequal** (double *x*, double *y*) long*n* **isnotequal** (double*n* *x*, double*n* *y*) int **isnotequal** (half *x*, half *y*) short*n* **isnotequal** (half*n* *x*, half*n* *y*)	Compare of $x \mathrel{!}= y$
int **isgreater** (float *x*, float *y*) int*n* **isgreater** (float*n* *x*, float*n* *y*) int **isgreater** (double *x*, double *y*) long*n* **isgreater** (double*n* *x*, double*n* *y*) int **isgreater** (half *x*, half *y*) short*n* **isgreater** (half*n* *x*, half*n* *y*)	Compare of $x > y$
int **isgreaterequal** (float *x*, float *y*) int*n* **isgreaterequal** (float*n* *x*, float*n* *y*) int **isgreaterequal** (double *x*, double *y*) long*n* **isgreaterequal** (double*n* *x*, double*n* *y*) int **isgreaterequal** (half *x*, half *y*) short*n* **isgreaterequal** (half*n* *x*, half*n* *y*)	Compare of $x >= y$
int **isless** (float *x*, float *y*) int*n* **isless** (float*n* *x*, float*n* *y*) int **isless** (double *x*, double *y*) long*n* **isless** (double*n* *x*, double*n* *y*) int **isless** (half *x*, half *y*) short*n* **isless** (half*n* *x*, half*n* *y*)	Compare of $x < y$
int **islessequal** (float *x*, float *y*) int*n* **islessequal** (float*n* *x*, float*n* *y*) int **islessequal** (double *x*, double *y*) long*n* **islessequal** (double*n* *x*, double*n* *y*) int **islessequal** (half *x*, half *y*) short*n* **islessequal** (half*n* *x*, half*n* *y*)	Compare of $x <= y$
int **islessgreater** (float *x*, float *y*) int*n* **islessgreater** (float*n* *x*, float*n* *y*) int **islessgreater** (double *x*, double *y*) long*n* **islessgreater** (double*n* *x*, double*n* *y*) int **islessgreater** (half *x*, half *y*) short*n* **islessgreater** (half*n* *x*, half*n* *y*)	Compare of $(x < y) \mathbin{\|} (x > y)$

continues

int **isfinite** (float) int*n* **isfinite** (float*n*) int **isfinite** (double) long*n* **isfinite** (double*n*) int **isfinite** (half) short*n* **isfinite** (half*n*)	Test for finite value
int **isinf** (float) int*n* **isinf** (float*n*) int **isinf** (double) long*n* **isinf** (double*n*) int **isinf** (half) short*n* **isinf** (half*n*)	Test for infinity value (positive or negative)
int **isnan** (float) int*n* **isnan** (float*n*) int **isnan** (double) long*n* **isnan** (double*n*) int **isnan** (half) short*n* **isnan** (half*n*)	Test for a NaN
int **isnormal** (float) int*n* **isnormal** (float*n*) int **isnormal** (double) long*n* **isnormal** (double*n*) int **isnormal** (half) short*n* **isnormal** (half*n*)	Test for a normal value
int **isordered** (float *x*, float *y*) int*n* **isordered** (float*n* *x*, float*n* *y*) int **isordered** (double *x*, double *y*) long*n* **isordered** (double*n* *x*, double*n* *y*) int **isordered** (half *x*, half *y*) short*n* **isordered** (half*n* *x*, half*n* *y*)	Test if arguments are ordered
int **isunordered** (float *x*, float *y*) int*n* **isunordered** (float*n* *x*, float*n* *y*) int **isunordered** (double *x*, double *y*) long*n* **isunordered** (double*n* *x*, double*n* *y*) int **isunordered** (half *x*, half *y*) short*n* **isunordered** (half*n* *x*, half*n* *y*)	Test if arguments are unordered
int **signbit** (float) int*n* **signbit** (float*n*) int **signbit** (double) long*n* **signbit** (double*n*) int **signbit** (half) short*n* **signbit** (half*n*)	Test for sign bit

Table A.18 *(Continued)*

int **any** (*S x*)	1 if MSB in any component of *x* is set; else 0
int **all** (*S x*)	1 if MSB in all components of *x* are set; else 0
T **bitselect** (*T a, T b, T c*) half*n* **bitselect** (half*n a*, half*n b*, half*n c*) double*n* **bitselect** (double*n a*, double*n b*, double*n c*)	Each bit of result is corresponding bit of *a* if corresponding bit of *c* is 0
T **select** (*T a, T b, S c*) *T* **select** (*T a, T b, U c*) double*n* **select** (double*n*, double*n*, long*n*) double*n* **select** (double*n*, double*n*, ulong*n*) half*n* **select** (half*n*, half*n*, short*n*) half*n* **select** (half*n*, half*n*, ushort*n*)	For each component of a vector type, result[*i*] = if MSB of *c*[*i*] is set ? *b*[*i*] : *a*[*i*] For scalar type, result = *c* ? *b* : *a*

Vector Data Load/Store Functions [6.11.7]

Q is an address space qualifier listed in **6.5** unless otherwise noted. *R* defaults to the current rounding mode or is one of the rounding modes listed in **6.2.3.2**. *T* is type char, uchar, short, ushort, int, uint, long, ulong, half, or float (or optionally double). *Tn* refers to the vector form of type *T*. Optional extensions enable the double, double*n*, half, and half*n* types.

Table A.19

Tn **vloadn** (size_t *offset*, const *Q T* *p*)	Read vector data from memory
void **vstoren** (*Tn data*, size_t *offset*, *Q T* *p*)	Write vector data to memory (*Q* in this function cannot be __constant)
float **vload_half** (size_t *offset*, const *Q* half *p*)	Read a half from memory
float*n* **vload_halfn** (size_t *offset*, const *Q* half *p*)	Read multiple halfs from memory

continues

void **vstore_half** (float *data*, size_t *offset*,
    Q half **p*)
void **vstore_half_**R (float *data*, size_t *offset*,
    Q half **p*)
void **vstore_half** (double *data*, size_t *offset*,
    Q half **p*)
void **vstore_half_**R (double *data*, size_t *offset*,
    Q half **p*)
	Write a half to memory
	(*Q* in this function cannot be
	__constant)

void **vstore_halfn** (float*n* *data*, size_t *offset*,
    Q half **p*)
void **vstore_halfn_**R (float*n* *data*,
    size_t *offset*, *Q* half **p*)
void **vstore_halfn** (double*n* *data*, size_t *offset*,
    Q half **p*)
void **vstore_halfn_**R (double*n* *data*,
    size_t *offset*, *Q* half **p*)
	Write a half vector to
	memory
	(*Q* in this function cannot be
	__constant)

float*n* **vloada_halfn** (size_t *offset*, const *Q* half **p*)	sizeof (float*n*) bytes of data read from location (*p* + (*offset* * *n*))

void **vstorea_halfn** (float*n* *data*, size_t *offset*,
    Q half **p*)
void **vstorea_halfn_**R (float*n* *data*,
    size_t *offset*, *Q* half **p*)
void **vstorea_halfn** (double*n* *data*,
    size_t *offset*, *Q* half **p*)
void **vstorea_halfn_**R (double*n* *data*,
    size_t *offset*, *Q* half **p*)
	Write a half vector to vector-
	aligned memory
	(*Q* in this function cannot be
	__constant)

Atomic Functions [6.11.11, 9.4]

T is type int or unsigned int. *T* may also be type float for
atomic_xchg, and type long or ulong for extended 64-bit atomic
functions. *Q* is volatile __global or volatile __local, except *Q* must be
volatile __global for atomic_xchg when *T* is float.

The built-in atomic functions for 32-bit values begin with atomic_ and
the extended 64-bit atomic functions begin with atom_. For example:

Table A.20

Built-in Atomic Function	Extended Atomic Function
`atomic_add ()`	`atom_add ()`

Extended 64-bit atomic functions are enabled by the following pragma; *extension-name* is one of `cl_khr_int64_{base, extended}_atomics`:

`#pragma OPENCL EXTENSION extension-name : enable`

Table A.21

T **atomic_add** (*Q T *p, T val*)	Read, add, and store
T **atomic_sub** (*Q T *p, T val*)	Read, subtract, and store
T **atomic_xchg** (*Q T *p, T val*)	Read, swap, and store
T **atomic_inc** (*Q T *p*)	Read, increment, and store
T **atomic_dec** (*Q T *p*)	Read, decrement, and store
T **atomic_cmpxchg** (*Q T *p, T cmp, T val*)	Read and store (*p ==cmp) ? *val* : *p)
T **atomic_min** (*Q T *p, T val*)	Read, store min(*p, val)
T **atomic_max** (*Q T *p, T val*)	Read, store max(*p, val)
T **atomic_and** (*Q T *p, T val*)	Read, store (*p & val)
T **atomic_or** (*Q T *p, T val*)	Read, store (*p | val)
T **atomic_xor** (*Q T *p, T val*)	Read, store (*p ^ val)

Async Copies and Prefetch Functions [6.11.10]

T is type char, char*n*, uchar, uchar*n*, short, short*n*, ushort, ushort*n*, int, int*n*, uint, uint*n*, long, long*n*, ulong, ulong*n*, float, float*n* and optionally half*n* double, double*n*. Optional extensions enable the half*n*, double, and double*n* types.

Table A.22

event_t **async_work_group_copy(** __local *T* *dst, const __global *T* *src, size_t *num_gentypes*, event_t *event*) event_t **async_work_group_copy(** __global *T* *dst, const __local *T* *src, size_t *num_gentypes*, event_t *event*)	Copies *num_gentypes T* elements from *src* to *dst*.
event_t **async_work_group_strided_copy(** __local *T* *dst, const __global *T* *src, size_t *num_gentypes*, size_t *src_stride*, event_t *event*) event_t **async_work_group_strided_copy(** __global *T* *dst, const __local *T* *src, size_t *num_gentypes*, size_t *dst_stride*, event_t *event*)	Copies *num_gentypes T* elements from *src* to *dst*.
void **wait_group_events** (int *num_events*, event_t *event_list*)	Wait for events that identify the **async_work_group_copy** operations to complete.
void **prefetch** (const __global *T* *p*, size_t *num_gentypes*)	Prefetch *num_gentypes* * sizeof(*T*) bytes into the global cache.

Synchronization, Explicit Memory Fence [6.11.9-10]

The *flags* argument is the memory address space, set to a combination of CLK_LOCAL_MEM_FENCE and CLK_GLOBAL_MEM_FENCE.

Table A.23

void **barrier** (cl_mem_fence_flags *flags*)	All work-items in a work-group must execute this before any can continue.
void **mem_fence** (cl_mem_fence_flags *flags*)	Orders loads and stores of a work-item executing a kernel.
void **read_mem_fence** (cl_mem_fence_flags *flags*)	Orders memory loads.
void **write_mem_fence** (cl_mem_fence_flags *flags*)	Orders memory stores.

Miscellaneous Vector Built-In Functions [6.11.12]

Tn and *Tm* are the 2-, 4-, 8-, or 16-component vectors of char, uchar, short, ushort, half, int, uint, long, ulong, float, double. *Un* is the built-in unsigned integer data type. For vec_step(), *Tn* also includes char3, uchar3, short3, ushort3, half3, int3, uint3, long3, ulong3, float3, and double3. half and double types are enabled by **cl_khr_fp16** and **cl_khr_fp64**, respectively.

Table A.24

int **vec_step** (*Tn a*) int **vec_step** (*typename*)	Takes a built-in scalar or vector data type argument and returns an integer value representing the number of elements in the scalar or vector.
Tn **shuffle** (*Tm x, Un mask*) Tn **shuffle2** (*Tm x, Tm y, Un mask*)	Constructs permutation of elements from one or two input vectors, returns a vector with the same element type as input and length that is the same as the shuffle mask.

Image Read and Write Built-In Functions [6.11.13, 9.5, 9.6.8]

The built-in functions defined in this section can be used only with image memory objects created with **clCreateImage2D** or **clCreateImage3D**. *sampler* specifies the addressing and filtering mode to use. **H** = To enable **read_imageh** and **write_imageh**, enable extension cl_khr_fp16. **3D** = To enable type image3d_t in **write_image{f, i, ui}**, enable extension cl_khr_3d_image_writes.

Table A.25

float4 **read_imagef** (image2d_t *image*, sampler_t *sampler*, int2 *coord*)	Read an element from a 2D image
float4 **read_imagef** (image2d_t *image*, sampler_t *sampler*, float2 *coord*)	
int4 **read_imagei** (image2d_t *image*, sampler_t *sampler*, int2 *coord*)	
int4 **read_imagei** (image2d_t *image*, sampler_t *sampler*, float2 *coord*)	
uint4 **read_imageui** (image2d_t *image*, sampler_t *sampler*, int2 *coord*)	
uint4 **read_imageui** (image2d_t *image*, sampler_t *sampler*, float2 *coord*)	
half4 **read_imageh** (image2d_t *image*, sampler_t *sampler*, int2 *coord*) **H**	
half4 **read_imageh** (image2d_t *image*, sampler_t *sampler*, float2 *coord*) **H**	
void **write_imagef** (image2d_t *image*, int2 *coord*, float4 *color*)	Write *color* value to (*x, y*) location specified by *coord* in the 2D image
void **write_imagei** (image2d_t *image*, int2 *coord*, int4 *color*)	
void **write_imageui** (image2d_t *image*, int2 *coord*, uint4 *color*)	
void **write_imageh** (image2d_t *image*, int2 *coord*, half4 *color*) **H**	
float4 **read_imagef** (image3d_t *image*, sampler_t *sampler*, int4 *coord*)	Read an element from a 3D image
float4 **read_imagef** (image3d_t *image*, sampler_t *sampler*, float4 *coord*)	
int4 **read_imagei** (image3d_t *image*, sampler_t *sampler*, int4 *coord*)	
int4 **read_imagei** (image3d_t *image*, sampler_t *sampler*, float4 *coord*)	

Table A.25 *(Continued)*

uint4 **read_imageui** (image3d_t *image*, sampler_t *sampler*, int4 *coord*) uint4 **read_imageui** (image3d_t *image*, sampler_t *sampler*, float4 *coord*)	Read an element from a 3D image
int **get_image_width** (image2d_t *image*) int **get_image_width** (image3d_t *image*)	Image width in pixels
int **get_image_height** (image2d_t *image*) int **get_image_height** (image3d_t *image*)	Image height in pixels
int **get_image_depth** (image3d_t *image*)	Image depth in pixels
int **get_image_channel_data_type** (image2d_t *image*) int **get_image_channel_data_type** (image3d_t *image*)	Image channel data type
int **get_image_channel_order** (image2d_t *image*) int **get_image_channel_order** (image3d_t *image*)	Image channel order
int2 **get_image_dim** (image2d_t *image*)	Image width, height
int4 **get_image_dim** (image3d_t *image*)	Image width, height, and depth
Use this pragma to enable type image3d_t in **write_image{f, i, ui}**: #pragma OPENCL EXTENSION cl_khr_3d_image_writes : enable void **write_imagef** (image3d_t *image*, int4 *coord*, float4 *color*) **3D** void **write_imagei** (image3d_t *image*, int4 *coord*, int4 *color*) **3D** void **write_imageui** (image3d_t *image*, int4 *coord*, uint4 *color*) **3D**	Writes *color* at *coord* in the 3D image

Image Objects

Create Image Objects [5.3.1]

```
cl_mem clCreateImage2D (cl_context context, cl_mem_flags flags,
   const cl_image_format *image_format, size_t image_width,
   size_t image_height, size_t image_row_pitch, void *host_ptr,
   cl_int *errcode_ret)
```

flags: (also for **clCreateImage3D, clGetSupportedImageFormats**)
   CL_MEM_READ_WRITE, CL_MEM_{WRITE, READ}_ONLY,
   CL_MEM_{USE, ALLOC, COPY}_HOST_PTR

cl_mem **clCreateImage3D** (cl_context *context*, cl_mem_flags *flags*,
   const cl_image_format **image_format*, size_t *image_width*,
   size_t *image_height*, size_t *image_depth*,
   size_t *image_row_pitch*, size_t *image_slice_pitch*,
   void **host_ptr*, cl_int **errcode_ret*)
flags: See **clCreateImage2D**

Query List of Supported Image Formats [5.3.2]

cl_int **clGetSupportedImageFormats** (cl_context *context*,
   cl_mem_flags *flags*, cl_mem_object_type *image_type*,
   cl_uint *num_entries*, cl_image_format **image_formats*,
   cl_uint **num_image_formats*)
flags: See **clCreateImage2D**

Copy between Image, Buffer Objects [5.3.4]

cl_int **clEnqueueCopyImageToBuffer** (cl_command_queue *command_queue*,
   cl_mem *src_image*, cl_mem *dst_buffer*, const size_t *src_origin*[3],
   const size_t *region*[3], size_t *dst_offset*,
   cl_uint *num_events_in_wait_list*, const cl_event **event_wait_list*,
   cl_event **event*)

cl_int **clEnqueueCopyBufferToImage** (cl_command_queue *command_queue*,
   cl_mem *src_buffer*, cl_mem *dst_image*, size_t *src_offset*,
   const size_t *dst_origin*[3], const size_t *region*[3],
   cl_uint *num_events_in_wait_list*, const cl_event **event_wait_list*,
   cl_event **event*)

Map and Unmap Image Objects [5.3.5]

void * **clEnqueueMapImage** (cl_command_queue *command_queue*,
   cl_mem *image*, cl_bool *blocking_map*, cl_map_flags *map_flags*,
   const size_t *origin*[3], const size_t *region*[3],
   size_t **image_row_pitch*, size_t **image_slice_pitch*,
   cl_uint *num_events_in_wait_list*, const cl_event **event_wait_list*,
   cl_event **event*, cl_int **errcode_ret*)

Read, Write, Copy Image Objects [5.3.3]

```
cl_int clEnqueueReadImage (cl_command_queue command_queue,
    cl_mem image, cl_bool blocking_read, const size_t origin[3],
    const size_t region[3], size_t row_pitch,size_t slice_pitch,
    void *ptr, cl_uint num_events_in_wait_list,
    const cl_event *event_wait_list, cl_event *event)

cl_int clEnqueueWriteImage (cl_command_queue command_queue,
    cl_mem image, cl_bool blocking_write, const size_t origin[3],
    const size_t region[3], size_t input_row_pitch,
    size_t input_slice_pitch, const void *ptr,
    cl_uint num_events_in_wait_list, const cl_event *event_wait_list,
    cl_event *event)

cl_int clEnqueueCopyImage (cl_command_queue command_queue,
    cl_mem src_image, cl_mem dst_image, const size_t src_origin[3],
    const size_t dst_origin[3], const size_t region[3],
    cl_uint num_events_in_wait_list, const cl_event *event_wait_list,
    cl_event *event)
```

Query Image Objects [5.3.6]

```
cl_int clGetMemObjectInfo (cl_mem memobj, cl_mem_info param_name,
    size_t param_value_size, void *param_value,
    size_t *param_value_size_ret)
param_name:   CL_MEM_{TYPE, FLAGS, SIZE, HOST_PTR},
    CL_MEM_{MAP, REFERENCE}_COUNT, CL_MEM_{CONTEXT, OFFSET},
    CL_MEM_ASSOCIATED_MEMOBJECT

cl_int clGetImageInfo (cl_mem image, cl_image_info param_name,
    size_t param_value_size, void *param_value,
    size_t *param_value_size_ret)
param_name:  CL_IMAGE_{FORMAT, ELEMENT_SIZE},
    CL_IMAGE_{ROW, SLICE}_PITCH, CL_IMAGE_{HEIGHT, WIDTH, DEPTH},
    CL_IMAGE_D3D10_SUBRESOURCE_KHR, CL_MEM_D3D10_RESOURCE_KHR
```

Image Formats [5.3.1.1, 9.5]

Supported image formats:

Table A.26

Image_num_Channels	Image_Channel_Order	Image_Channel_Data_Type
4	**CL_RGBA:**	CL_UNORM_INT8, CL_UNORM_INT16, CL_SIGNED_INT8, CL_SIGNED_INT16, CL_SIGNED_INT32 CL_UNSIGNED_INT8, CL_UNSIGNED_INT16, CL_UNSIGNED_INT32 CL_HALF_FLOAT CL_FLOAT
4	**CL_BGRA:**	CL_UNORM_INT8

Access Qualifiers [6.6]

Apply to image `image2d_t` and `image3d_t` types to declare if the image memory object is being read or written by a kernel. The default qualifier is __read_only.

```
__read_only,   read_only
__write_only,  write_only
```

Sampler Objects [5.5]

```
cl_sampler clCreateSampler (cl_context context,
    cl_bool normalized_coords, cl_addressing_mode addressing_mode,
    cl_filter_mode filter_mode, cl_int *errcode_ret)

cl_int clRetainSampler (cl_sampler sampler)

cl_int clReleaseSampler (cl_sampler sampler)

cl_int  clGetSamplerInfo (cl_sampler sampler,
    cl_sampler_info param_name, size_t param_value_size,
    void *param_value, size_t *param_value_size_ret)
param_name:  CL_SAMPLER_REFERENCE_COUNT,
    CL_SAMPLER_{CONTEXT, FILTER_MODE},
    CL_SAMPLER_ADDRESSING_MODE, CL_SAMPLER_NORMALIZED_COORDS
```

Sampler Declaration Fields [6.11.13.1]

The sampler can be passed as an argument to the kernel using **clSet-KernelArg**, or it can be a constant variable of type `sampler_t` declared in the program source.

```
const sampler_t <sampler-name> =
                <normalized-mode> | <address-mode> | <filter-mode>
normalized-mode:
   CLK_NORMALIZED_COORDS_{TRUE, FALSE}
address-mode:
   CLK_ADDRESS_{REPEAT, CLAMP, NONE},
   CLK_ADDRESS_{CLAMP_TO_EDGE, MIRRORED_REPEAT}
filter-mode:
   CLK_FILTER_NEAREST,  CLK_FILTER_LINEAR
```

OpenCL Device Architecture Diagram [3.3]

This table shows memory regions with allocation and memory access capabilities.

Table A.27

	Global	Constant	Local	Private
Host	Dynamic allocation Read/write access	Dynamic allocation Read/write access	Dynamic allocation No access	No allocation No access
Kernel	No allocation Read/write access	Static allocation Read-only access	Static allocation Read/write access	Static allocation Read/write access

This conceptual OpenCL device architecture includes processing elements (PEs), compute units (CUs), and devices. The host is not shown.

OpenCL/OpenGL Sharing APIs

Creating OpenCL memory objects from OpenGL objects using **clCreateFromGLBuffer**, **clCreateFromGLTexture2D**, **clCreate-FromGLTexture3D**, and **clCreateFromGLRenderbuffer** ensure that the storage of the OpenGL object will not be deleted while the corresponding OpenCL memory object exists.

CL Buffer Objects > GL Buffer Objects [9.8.2]

cl_mem **clCreateFromGLBuffer** (cl_context *context*, cl_mem_flags *flags*,
    GLuint *bufobj*, int *errcode_ret*)
flags: CL_MEM_{READ, WRITE}_ONLY, CL_MEM_READ_WRITE

CL Image Objects > GL Textures [9.8.3]

cl_mem **clCreateFromGLTexture2D** (cl_context *context*,
    cl_mem_flags *flags*, GLenum *texture_target*, GLint *miplevel*,
    GLuint *texture*, cl_int *errcode_ret*)
flags: See clCreateFromGLBuffer
texture_target: GL_TEXTURE_{2D, RECTANGLE},
    GL_TEXTURE_CUBE_MAP_POSITIVE_{X, Y, Z},
    GL_TEXTURE_CUBE_MAP_NEGATIVE_{X, Y, Z}

cl_mem **clCreateFromGLTexture3D** (cl_context *context*,
    cl_mem_flags *flags*, GLenum *texture_target*, GLint *miplevel*,
    GLuint *texture*, cl_int *errcode_ret*)
flags: See clCreateFromGLBuffer
texture_target: GL_TEXTURE_3D

CL Image Objects > GL Renderbuffers [9.8.4]

cl_mem **clCreateFromGLRenderbuffer** (cl_context *context*,
    cl_mem_flags *flags*, GLuint *renderbuffer*, cl_int *errcode_ret*)
flags: clCreateFromGLBuffer

Query Information [9.8.5]

cl_int **clGetGLObjectInfo** (cl_mem *memobj*,
    cl_gl_object_type **gl_object_type*, GLuint **gl_object_name*)
*gl_object_type returns: CL_GL_OBJECT_BUFFER,
    CL_GL_OBJECT_{TEXTURE2D, TEXTURE3D}, CL_GL_OBJECT_RENDERBUFFER

cl_int **clGetGLTextureInfo** (cl_mem *memobj*,
    cl_gl_texture_info *param_name*, size_t *param_value_size*,
    void **param_value*, size_t **param_value_size_ret*)
param_name: CL_GL_TEXTURE_TARGET, CL_GL_MIPMAP_LEVEL

Share Objects [9.8.6]

cl_int **clEnqueueAcquireGLObjects** (cl_command_queue *command_queue*,
   cl_uint *num_objects*, const cl_mem **mem_objects*,
   cl_uint *num_events_in_wait_list*,
   const cl_event **event_wait_list*, cl_event **event*)

cl_int **clEnqueueReleaseGLObjects** (cl_command_queue *command_queue*,
   cl_uint *num_objects*, const cl_mem **mem_objects*,
   cl_uint *num_events_in_wait_list*, const cl_event **event_wait_list*,
   cl_event **event*)

CL Event Objects > GL Sync Objects [9.9]

cl_event **clCreateEventFromGLsyncKHR** (cl_context *context*,
   GLsync *sync*, cl_int **errcode_ret*)

CL Context > GL Context, Sharegroup [9.7]

cl_int **clGetGLContextInfoKHR** (
   const cl_context_properties **properties*,
   cl_gl_context_info *param_name*, size_t *param_value_size*,
   void **param_value*, size_t **param_value_size_ret*)
param_name: CL_DEVICES_FOR_GL_CONTEXT_KHR,
   CL_CURRENT_DEVICE_FOR_GL_CONTEXT_KHR

OpenCL/Direct3D 10 Sharing APIs [9.10]

Creating OpenCL memory objects from OpenGL objects using
clCreateFromGLBuffer, **clCreateFromGLTexture2D**, **clCreate-FromGLTexture3D**, or **clCreateFromGLRenderbuffer** ensures that the
storage of that OpenGL object will not be deleted while the corresponding
OpenCL memory object exists.

cl_int **clGetDeviceIDsFromD3D10KHR** (cl_platform_id *platform*,
   cl_d3d10_device_source_khr *d3d_device_source*, void **d3d_object*,
   cl_d3d10_device_set_khr *d3d_device_set*, cl_uint *num_entries*,
   cl_device_id **devices*, cl_uint **num_devices*)
d3d_device_source: CL_D3D10_DEVICE_KHR, CL_D3D10_DXGI_ADAPTER_KHR
d3d_object: ID3D10Device, IDXGIAdapter
d3d_device_set: CL_ALL_DEVICES_FOR_D3D10_KHR,
   CL_PREFERRED_DEVICES_FOR_D3D10_KHR

cl_mem **clCreateFromD3D10BufferKHR** (cl_context *context*,
   cl_mem_flags *flags*, ID3D10Buffer **resource*, cl_int **errcode_ret*)
flags: CL_MEM_{READ, WRITE}_ONLY, CL_MEM_READ_WRITE

cl_mem **clCreateFromD3D10Texture2DKHR** (cl_context *context*,
   cl_mem_flags *flags*, ID3D10Texture2D **resource*, UINT *subresource*,
   cl_int **errcode_ret*)
flags: See **clCreateFromD3D10BufferKHR**

cl_mem **clCreateFromD3D10Texture3DKHR** (cl_context *context*,
   cl_mem_flags *flags*, ID3D10Texture3D **resource*, UINT *subresource*,
   cl_int **errcode_ret*)
flags: See **clCreateFromD3D10BufferKHR**

cl_int **clEnqueueAcquireD3D10ObjectsKHR** (
   cl_ command_queue *command_queue*, cl_uint *num_objects*,
   const cl_mem **mem_objects*, cl_uint *num_events_in_wait_list*,
   const cl_event **event_wait_list*, cl_event **event*)

cl_int **clEnqueueReleaseD3D10ObjectsKHR** (
   cl_ command_queue *command_queue*, cl_uint *num_objects*,
   const cl_mem **mem_objects*, cl_uint *num_events_in_wait_list*,
   const cl_event **event_wait_list*, cl_event **event*)

Index

Symbols

-- (pre-increment) unary operator, 131
- (subtract) operator, 124–126
?: (ternary selection) operator, 129
- or -- (unary) operators, 131
| or || (or) operators, 127–128
+ (addition) operator, 124–126
+ or ++ (post-increment) unary operator, 131
!= (not equal) operator, 127
== (equal) operator, 127
% (remainder) operator, 124–126
& or && (and) operators, 127–128
* (multiply) operator, 124–126
^ (exclusive or) operator, 127–128
^^ (exclusive) operator, 128
~ (not) operator, 127–128
> (greater than) operator, 127
>= (greater than or equal) operator, 127
>> (right shift) operator, 129–130

Numbers

0 value, 64–65, 68
2D composition, in DFT, 457–458
64-bit integers, embedded profile, 385–386
754 formats, IEEE floating-point arithmetic, 34

A

accelerator devices
    defined, 69
    tiled and packetized sparse matrix design, 523, 534
access qualifiers
    as keywords in OpenCL C, 141
    overview of, 140–141
    reference guide, 576

add (+) arithmetic operator, 124–126
address space qualifiers
    casting between address spaces, 139–140
    constant, 137–138
    global, 136
    as keywords in OpenCL C, 141
    local, 138–139
    overview of, 135–136
    private, 139
    reference guide, 554
    supported, 99
addressing mode, sampler objects, 282, 292–295
ALL_BUILD project, Visual Studio, 43
AltiVec Technology Programming Interface Manual, 111–113
AMD
    generating project in Linux, 40–41
    generating project in Windows, 40–41
    storing binaries in own format, 233
and (& or &&) operators, 127–128
Apple
    initializing contexts for OpenGL interoperability, 338
    querying number of platforms, 64
    storing binaries in own format, 233
application data types, 103–104
ARB_cl_event extension, OpenGL, 349–350
architecture diagram, OpenCL device, 577
arguments
    context, 85
    device, 68
    enqueuing commands, 313
    guassian_kernel(), 296–297
    kernel function restrictions, 146
    reference guide for kernel, 548
    setting kernel, 55–57, 237–240

arithmetic operators
  overview of, 124–126
  post- and pre-increment (++ and --)
    unary, 131
  symbols, 123
  unary (+ and -), 131
arrays
  parallelizing Dijkstra's algorithm,
    412–414
  representing sparse matrix with
    binary data, 516
as_type(), 121–123
as_typen(), 121–123
ASCII File, representing sparse matrix,
    516–517
assignment (=) operator, 124, 132
async copy and prefetch functions,
    191–195, 570
ATI Stream SDK
  generating project in Linux and
    Eclipse, 44–45
  generating project in Visual Studio,
    42–44
  generating project in Windows, 40
  querying and selecting platform,
    65–66
  querying context for devices, 89
  querying devices, 70
atomic built-in functions
  embedded profile options, 387
  overview of, 195–198
  reference guide, 568–569
attribute keyword, kernel qualifier,
    133–134
attributes, specifying type, 555
automatic load balancing, 20

B

barrier synchronization function,
    190–191
batches
  executing cloth simulation on GPU,
    433–441
  SpMV implementation, 518
behavior description, optional exten-
    sion, 144
bilinear sampling object, optical flow,
    476

binaries, program
  creating, 235–236
  HelloBinaryWorld example, 229–230
  HelloWorld.cl (NVIDIA) example,
    233–236
  overview of, 227–229
  querying and storing, 230–232
binary data arrays, sparse matrix, 516
bit field numbers, 147
bitwise operators, 124, 127–128
blocking enqueue calls, and callbacks,
    327
blocking_read, executing kernel, 56
bool, rank order of, 113
border color, built-in functions, 209–210
bracket() operator, C++ Wrapper API,
    370–371
buffers and sub-buffers
  computing Dijkstra's algorithm, 415
  copying, 274–276
  copying from image to, 299, 303–304
  creating, 249–256
  creating from OpenGL, 339–343
  creating kernel and memory objects,
    377–378
  direct translation of matrix multipli-
    cation into OpenCL, 502
  executing Vector Add kernel, 377–
    378, 381
  mapping, 276–279
  in memory model, 21
  Ocean application, 451
  OpenCL/OpenGL sharing APIs,
    446–448, 578
  overview of, 247–248
  querying, 257–259
  reading and writing, 259–274
  reference guide, 544–545
building program objects
  reference guide, 546–547
  using clBuildProgram(). see
    clBuildProgram()
built-in data types
  other, 108–109
  reference guide, 550–552
  scalar, 99–101
  vector, 102–103
built-in functions
  async copy and prefetch, 191–195

atomic, 195–198, 387, 568–569
border color, 209–210
common, 172–175, 559
floating-point constant, 162–163
floating-point pragma, 162
geometric, 175–177, 563–564
image read and write, 201–206,
    572–573
integer, 168–172, 557–558
math, 153–161, 560–563
miscellaneous vector, 199–200, 571
overview of, 149
querying image information, 214–215
relational, 175, 178–181, 564–567
relative error as ulps, 163–168
samplers, 206–209
synchronization, 190–191
vector data load and store, 181–189
work-item, 150–152, 557
writing to image, 210–213
Bullet Physics SDK. *see* cloth simulation
    in Bullet Physics SDK
bytes, and vector data types, 102

C

C++ Wrapper API
    defined, 369
    exceptions, 371–374
    Ocean application overview, 451
    overview of, 369–371
C++ Wrapper API, Vector Add example
    choosing device and creating com-
        mand-queue, 375–377
    choosing platform and creating
        context, 375
    creating and building program object,
        377
    creating kernel and memory objects,
        377–378
    executing Vector Add kernel, 378–382
    structure of OpenCL setup, 374–375
C99 language
    OpenCL C derived from, 32–33, 97
    OpenCL C features added to, 99
callbacks
    creating OpenCL contexts, 85
    event objects. *see*
        clSetEventCallback()

events impacting execution on host,
    324–327
placing profiling functions inside,
    331–332
steps in Ocean application, 451
capacitance, of multicore chips, 4–5
case studies
    cloth simulation. *see* cloth simulation
        in Bullet Physics SDK
    Dijkstra's algorithm. *see* Dijkstra's
        algorithm, parallelizing
    image histogram. *see* image
        histograms
    matrix multiplication. *see* matrix
        multiplication
    optical flow. *see* optical flow
    PyOpenCL. *see* PyOpenCL
    simulating ocean. *see* Ocean simula-
        tion, with FFT
    Sobel edge detection filter, 407–410
casts
    explicit, 116
    implicit conversions between vectors
        and, 111–113
cEnqueueNDRangeKernel(), 251, 255
ckCreateSampler(), 292–295
CL_COMPLETE value, command-queue,
    311
CL_CONTEXT_DEVICES, C++ Wrapper
    API, 376
cl_context_properties fields,
    initializing contexts, 338–339
CL_DEVICE_IMAGE_SUPPORT property,
    clGetDeviceInfo(), 386–387
CL_DEVICE_IMAGE3D_MAX_WIDTH
    property, clGetDeviceInfo(),
    386–387
CL_DEVICE_MAX_COMPUTE_UNITS,
    506–509
CL_DEVICE_TYPE_GPU, 502
_CL_ENABLE_EXCEPTIONS preprocessor
    macro, 372
cl_image_format, 285, 287–291
cl_int clFinish (), 248
cl_int clWaitForEvents(), 248
CL_KERNEL_PREFERRED_WORK_GROUP_
    SIZE MULTIPLE query, 243–244
CL_KERNEL_WORK_GROUP_SIZE query,
    243–244

cl_khr_gl_event extension, 342, 348

cl_khr_gl_sharing extension, 336–337, 342

cl_map_flags, clEnqueueMapBuffer(), 276–277

cl_mem object, creating images, 284

CL_MEM_COPY_FROM_HOST_PTR, 377–378

cl_mem_flags, clCreateBuffer(), 249–250

CL_MEM_READ_ONLY | CL_MEM_COPY_ HOST_PTR memory type, 55

CL_MEM_READ_WRITE, 308

CL_MEM_USE_HOST_PTR, 377–378

cl_net error values, C++ Wrapper API, 371

cl_platform, 370–371

CL_PROFILING_COMMAND_END, 502

CL_PROFILING_COMMAND_START, 502

CL_QUEUE_PROFILING_ENABLE flag, 328

CL_QUEUE_PROFILING_ENABLE property, 502

CL_QUEUED value, command-queue, 311

CL_RUNNING value, command-queue, 311

CL_SUBMITTED value, command-queue, 311

CL_SUCCESS return value, clBuild-Program(), 220

_CL_USER_OVERRIDE_ERROR_STRINGS preprocessor macro, 372

classes, C++ Wrapper API hierarchy, 369–370

clBarrier(), 313–316

clBuffer(), 54

cl::Buffer(), 377–378, 381

clBuildProgram()
 build options, 546–547
 building program object, 219–220, 222
 creating program from binary, 234–236
 floating-point options, 224
 miscellaneous options, 226–227
 optimization options, 225–226
 preprocessor build options, 223–224
 querying program objects, 237
 reference guide, 546

cl::CommandQueue::enqueueMap-Buffer(), 379, 381

cl::commandQueue::enqueueUnmap Obj(), 379, 382

cl::Context(), 375

cl::Context::getInfo(), 376

clCreateBuffer()
 creating buffers and sub-buffers, 249–251
 creating memory objects, 54–55
 direct translation of matrix multiplication into OpenCL, 502
 reference guide, 544
 setting kernel arguments, 239

clCreateCommandQueue(), 51–52, 543

clCreateContext(), 84–87, 541

clCreateContextFromType()
 creating contexts, 84–85
 querying context for associated devices, 88
 reference guide, 541

clCreateEventFromGLsyncKHR()
 explicit synchronization, 349
 reference guide, 579
 synchronization between OpenCL/ OpenGL, 350–351

clCreateFromD3D10BufferKHR(), 580

clCreateFromD3D10Texture2DKHR(), 580

clCreateFromD3D10Texture3DKHR(), 580

clCreateFromGL*(), 335, 448

clCreateFromGLBuffer(), 339–343, 578

clCreateFromGLRenderbuffer()
 creating memory objects from OpenGL, 341
 reference guide, 578
 sharing with OpenCL, 346–347

clCreateFromGLTexture2D(), 341, 578

clCreateFromGLTexture3D(), 341, 578

clCreateImage2D()
 creating 2D image from file, 284–285
 creating image objects, 283–284
 reference guide, 573–574

clCreateImage3D(), 283–284, 574

clCreateKernel()
 creating kernel objects, 237–238
 reference guide, 547
 setting kernel arguments, 239–240

clCreateKernelsInProgram(), 240–241, 547

clCreateProgram(), 221
clCreateProgramWithBinary()
    creating programs from binaries,
        228–229
    HelloBinaryWorld example, 229–230
    reference guide, 546
clCreateProgramWithSource()
    creating and building program object,
        52–53
    creating program object from source,
        218–219, 222
    reference guide, 546
clCreateSampler(), 292–294, 576
clCreateSubBuffer(), 253–256, 544
clCreateUserEvent()
    generating events on host, 321–322
    how to use, 323–324
    reference guide, 549
clEnqueueAcquireD3D10Ob-
        jectsKHR(), 580
clEnqueueAcquireGLObjects()
    creating OpenCL buffers from
        OpenGL buffers, 341–342
    explicit synchronization, 349
    implicit synchronization, 348–349
    reference guide, 579
clEnqueueBarrier()
    function of, 316–317
    ordering constraints between
        commands, 313
    reference guide, 549
clEnqueueCopyBuffer(), 275–276, 545
clEnqueueCopyBufferToImage()
    copying from buffer to image,
        303–305
    defined, 299
    reference guide, 574
clEnqueueCopyImage()
    copy image objects, 302–303
    defined, 299
    reference guide, 575
clEnqueueCopyImageToBuffer()
    copying from image to buffer,
        303–304
    defined, 299
    reference guide, 574
clEnqueueMapBuffer()
    mapping buffers and sub-buffers,
        276–278

moving data to and from buffer,
        278–279
    reference guide, 545
clEnqueueMapImage()
    defined, 299
    mapping image objects into host
        memory, 305–308
    reference guide, 574
clEnqueueMarker(), 314–317, 549
clEnqueueMarker()
    defining synchronization points, 314
    function of, 315–317
clEnqueueNativeKernel(), 548
clEnqueueNDRangeKernel()
    events and command-queues, 312
    executing kernel, 56–57
    reference guide, 548
    work-items, 150
clEnqueueReadBuffer()
    reading buffers, 260–261, 268–269
    reading results back from kernel, 48,
        56–57
    reference guide, 544
clEnqueueReadBufferRect(),
        269–272, 544
clEnqueueReadImage()
    defined, 299–301
    mapping image results to host
        memory pointer, 307–308
    reference guide, 575
clEnqueueReleaseD3D10ObjectsKHR(),
        580
clEnqueueReleaseGLObjects()
    implicit synchronization, 348–349
    reference guide, 579
    releasing objects acquired by
        OpenCL, 341–342
    synchronization between OpenCL/
        OpenGL, 351
clEnqueueTask(), 150, 548
clEnqueueUnmapMapImage(),
        305–306
clEnqueueUnmapMemObject()
    buffer mapping no longer required,
        277–278
    moving data to and from buffer,
        278–279
    reference guide, 545
    releasing image data, 308

clEnqueueWaitForEvents(), 314–317,
549
clEnqueueWriteBuffer()
reference guide, 544
writing buffers, 259–260, 267
clEnqueueWriteBufferRect(),
272–273, 544–545
clEnqueueWriteImage()
defined, 299
reference guide, 575
writing images from host to device
memory, 301–302
cles_khr_int64 extension string,
embedded profile, 385–386
clFinish()
creating OpenCL buffers from
OpenGL buffers, 342–343
OpenCL/OpenGL synchronization
with, 348
OpenCL/OpenGL synchronization
without, 351
preprocessor error macro for, 327
reference guide, 549
clFlush()
preprocessor error macro for, 327
reference guide, 549
using callbacks with events, 327
cl.get_platforms(), PyOpenCL, 493
clGetCommandQueueInfo(), 543
clGetContextInfo()
HelloWorld example, 50–51
querying context properties, 86–87
querying list of associated devices, 88
reference guide, 542
clGetDeviceIDs()
convolution signal example, 91
querying devices, 68–69
translation of matrix multiplication
into OpenCL, 502
clGetDeviceIDsFromD3D10KHR(), 542
clGetDeviceInfo()
determining images supported, 290
embedded profile, 384
matrix multiplication, 506–509
querying context for associated
devices, 88
querying device information, 70–78
querying embedded profile device
support for images, 386–387

querying for OpenGL sharing
extension, 336–337
reference guide, 542–543, 579
steps in OpenCL usage, 83
clGetEventInfo(), 319–320, 549
clGetEventProfilingInfo()
direct translation of matrix multiplication, 502
errors, 329–330
extracting timing data, 328
placing profiling functions inside
callbacks, 332
profiling information and return
types, 329
reference guide, 549
clGetGLContextInfoKHR(), 579
clGetGLObjectInfo(), 347–348, 578
clGetGLTextureInfo(), 578
clGetImageInfo(), 286
clGetKernelInfo(), 242–243, 548
clGetKernelWorkGroupInfo(),
243–244, 548
clGetMemObjectInfo()
querying buffers and sub-buffers,
257–259
querying image object, 286
reference guide, 545
clGetPlatformIDs()
querying context for associated
devices, 88
querying platforms, 63–64
reference guide, 542
clGetPlatformInfo()
embedded profile, 384
querying and selecting platform,
65–67
reference guide, 542
clGetProgramBuildInfo()
creating and building program object,
52–53
detecting build error, 220–221, 222
direct translation of matrix multiplication, 502
reference guide, 547
clGetProgramInfo()
getting program binary back from
built program, 227–228
reference guide, 547
clGetSamplerInfo(), 294–295, 576

clGetSupportedImageFormats(), 291,
574
clGetXXInfo(), use of in this book, 70
CLK_GLOBAL_MEM_FENCE value, barrier
functions, 190–191
CLK_LOCAL_MEM_FENCE value, barrier
functions, 190–191
cl::Kernel(), 378
cl::Kernel:setArg(), 378
cloth simulation in Bullet Physics SDK
adding OpenGL interoperation,
446–448
executing on CPU, 431–432
executing on GPU, 432–438
introduction to, 425–428
optimizing for SIMD computation
and local memory, 441–446
overview of, 425
of soft body, 429–431
two-layered batching, 438–441
cl::Program(), 377
clReleaseCommandQueue(), 543
clReleaseContext(), 89, 542
clReleaseEvent(), 318–319, 549
clReleaseKernel(), 244–245, 548
clReleaseMemObject()
reference guide, 545
release buffer object, 339
release image object, 284
clReleaseProgram(), 236, 546
clReleaseSampler(), 294, 576
clRetainCommandQueue(), 543
clRetainContext(), 89, 541
clRetainEvent(), 318, 549
clRetainKernel(), 245, 548
clRetainMemObject(), 339, 545
clRetainProgram(), 236–237, 546
clRetainSampler(), 576
clSetEventCallback()
events impacting execution on host,
325–326
placing profiling functions inside
callbacks, 331–332
reference guide, 549
clSetKernelArg()
creating buffers and sub-buffers, 250,
255
executing kernel, 55–56
executing Vector Add kernel, 378

matrix multiplication using local
memory, 509–511
reference guide, 548
sampler declaration fields, 577
setting kernel arguments, 56, 237–240
thread safety and, 241–242
clSetMemObjectDestructor-
Callback(), 545
clSetUserEventStatus()
generating events on host, 322
how to use, 323–324
reference guide, 549
clUnloadCompiler(), 237, 547
clWaitForEvents(), 323–324, 549
CMake tool
generating project in Linux and
Eclipse, 44–45
generating project in Visual Studio,
42–44
installing as cross-platform build tool,
40–41
Mac OS X and Code::Blocks, 40–41
cmake-gui, 42–44
Code::Blocks, 41–42
color, cloth simulation
executing on GPU, 433–438
in two-layered batching, 438–441
color images. see image histograms
comma operator (,), 131
command-queue
acquiring OpenGL objects, 341–342
as core of OpenCL, 309–310
creating, 50–52
creating after selecting set of devices,
377
creating in PyOpenCL, 493
defining consistency of memory
objects on, 24
direct translation of matrix multiplication into OpenCL, 502
events and, 311–317
executing kernel, 56–57
in execution model, 18–21
execution of Vector Add kernel, 378,
380
OpenCL runtime reference guide, 543
runtime API setting up, 31–32
transferring image objects to,
299–300

common functions, 172–175
compiler
    directives for optional extensions,
        143–145
    unloading OpenCL, 547
component selection syntax, vectors,
    106–107
components, vector data type, 106–108
compute device, platform model, 12
compute units, platform model, 12
concurrency, 7–8
    exploiting in command-queues, 310
    kernel execution model, 14
    parallel algorithm limitations, 28–29
conditional operator, 124, 129
const type qualifier, 141
constant (_constant) address space
    qualifier, 137–138, 141
constant memory
    device architecture diagram, 577
    memory model, 21–23
contexts
    allocating memory objects against, 248
    choosing platform and creating, 375
    convolution signal example, 89–97
    creating, 49–50, 84–87
    creating in PyOpenCL, 492–493
    defining in execution model, 17–18
    incrementing and decrementing
        reference count, 89
    initializing for OpenGL interoperabil-
        ity, 338–339
    OpenCL platform layer, 541–542
    overview of, 83
    querying properties, 85–87
    steps in OpenCL, 84
convergence, simulating soft body, 430
conversion
    embedded profile device support
        rules, 386–387
    explicit, 117–121, 132
    vector component, 554
convert_int(), explicit conversions, 118
convolution signal example, 89–97
coordinate mode, sampler objects, 282,
    292–295
copy
    buffers and sub-buffers, 274–276, 545
    image objects, 302–305, 308, 575

costArray:, Dijkstra's algorithm,
    413–414, 415–417
CPUs
    executing cloth simulation on,
        431–432
    heterogeneous future of multicore,
        4–7
    matrix multiplication and perfor-
        mance results, 511–513
    SpMV implementation, 518–519
CreateCommandQueue(), 50–51
CreateContext(), 49–50, 375
CreateMemObjects(), 54–55
CSR format, sparse matrix, 517

D

DAG (directed acyclic graph), command-
    queues and, 310
data load and store functions, vectors,
    181–189
data structure, Dijkstra's algorithm,
    412–414
data types
    explicit casts, 116–117
    explicit conversions, 117–121
    implicit type conversions, 110–115
    reference guide for supported,
        550–552
    reinterpreting data as other, 121–123
    reserved as keywords in OpenCL C,
        141
    scalar. *see* scalar data types
    specifying attributes, 555
    vector. *see* vector data types
data-parallel programming model
    overview of, 8–9
    parallel algorithm limitations, 28–29
    understanding, 25–27
    writing kernel using OpenCL C,
        97–99
decimation kernel, optical flow, 474
declaration fields, sampler, 577
default device, 69
#define preprocessor directive, 142, 145
denormalized numbers, 34, 388
dense matrix, 499
dense optical flow, 469
derived types, OpenCL C, 109–110

design, for tiled and packetized sparse matrix, 523–524

device_type argument, querying devices, 68

devices
architecture diagram, 577
choosing first available, 50–52
convolution signal example, 89–97
creating context in execution model, 17–18
determining profile support by, 390
embedded profile for hand held, 383–385
executing kernel on, 13–17
execution of Vector Add kernel, 380
full profile for desktop, 383
in platform model, 12
querying, 67–70, 78–83, 375–377, 542–543
selecting, 70–78
steps in OpenCL, 83–84

DFFT (discrete fast Fourier transform), 453

DFT. see discrete Fourier transform (DFT), Ocean simulation

Dijkstra's algorithm, parallelizing
graph data structures, 412–414
kernels, 414–417
leveraging multiple compute devices, 417–423
overview of, 411–412

dimensions, image object, 282

Direct3D, interoperability with. see interoperability with Direct3D

directed acyclic graph (DAG), command-queues and, 310

directional edge detector filter, Sobel, 407–410

directories, sample code for this book, 41

DirectX Shading Language (HLSL), 111–113

discrete fast Fourier transform (DFFT), 453

discrete Fourier transform (DFT), Ocean simulation
avoiding local memory bank conflicts, 463
determining 2D composition, 457–458
determining local memory needed, 462

determining sub-transform size, 459–460
determining work-group size, 460
obtaining twiddle factors, 461–462
overview of, 457
using images, 463
using local memory, 459

distance(), geometric functions, 175–176

divide (/) arithmetic operator, 124–126

doublen, vector data load and store, 181

DRAM, modern multicore CPUs, 6–7

dynamic libraries, OpenCL program vs., 97

E

early exit, optical flow algorithm, 483

Eclipse, generating project in, 44–45

edgeArray:, Dijkstra's algorithm, 412–414

"Efficient Sparse Matrix-Vector Multiplication on CUDA" (Bell and Garland), 517

embedded profile
64-bit integers, 385–386
built-in atomic functions, 387
determining device supporting, 390
full profile vs., 383
images, 386–387
mandated minimum single-precision floating-point capabilities, 387–389
OpenCL programs for, 35–36
overview of, 383–385
platform queries, 65

_EMBEDDED_PROFILE_macro, 390

enumerated type
rank order of, 113
specifying attributes, 555

enumerating, list of platforms, 66–67

equal (==) operator, 127

equality operators, 124, 127

error codes
C++ Wrapper API exceptions, 371–374
clBarrier(), 313
clCreateUserEvent(), 321–322
clEnqueueMarker(), 314
clEnqueueWaitForEvents(), 314–315

error codes (*continued*)

clGetEventProfilingInfo(),
329–330

clGetProgramBuildInfo, 220–221

clRetainEvent(), 318

clSetEventCallback(), 326

clWaitForEvents(), 323

table of, 57–61

ERROR_CODE value, command-queue, 311

.even suffix, vector data types, 107–108

event data types, 108, 147–148

event objects

OpenCL/OpenGL sharing APIs, 579

overview of, 317–320

reference guide, 549–550

event_t async_work_group_copy(),
192, 332–333

event_t async_work_group_
strided_copy(), 192, 332–333

events

command-queues and, 311–317

defined, 310

event objects. *see* event objects

generating on host, 321–322

impacting execution on host,
322–327

inside kernels, 332–333

from outside OpenCL, 333

overview of, 309–310

profiling using, 327–332

in task-parallel programming model,
28

exceptions

C++ Wrapper API, 371–374

execution of Vector Add kernel, 379

exclusive (^^) operator, 128

exclusive or (^) operator, 127–128

execution model

command-queues, 18–21

contexts, 17–18

defined, 11

how kernel executes OpenCL device,
13–17

overview of, 13

parallel algorithm limitations, 28–29

explicit casts, 116–117

explicit conversions, 117–121, 132

explicit kernel, SpMV, 519

explicit memory fence, 570–571

explicit model, data parallelism, 26–27

explicit synchronization, 349

exponent, half data type, 101

expression, assignment operator, 132

extensions, compiler directives for
optional, 143–145

F

fast Fourier transform (FTT). *see* Ocean
simulation, with FFT

fast_ variants, geometric functions, 175

FBO (frame buffer object), 347

file, creating 2D image from, 284–285

filter mode, sampler objects, 282, 292–295

float channels, 403–406

float data type, converting, 101

float images, 386

float type, math constants, 556

floating-point arithmetic system, 33–34

floating-point constants, 162–163

floating-point data types, 113, 119–121

floating-point options

building program object, 224–225

full vs. embedded profiles, 387–388

floating-point pragmas, 143, 162

floatn, vector data load and store
functions, 181, 182–186

fma, geometric functions, 175

formats, image

embedded profile, 387

encapsulating information on, 282

mapping OpenGL texture to OpenCL
image, 346

overview of, 287–291

querying list of supported, 574

reference guide for supported, 576

formats, of program binaries, 227

FP_CONTRACT pragma, 162

frame buffer object (FBO), 347

FreeImage library, 283, 284–285

FreeSurfer. *see* Dijkstra's algorithm,
parallelizing

FTT (fast Fourier transform). *see* Ocean
simulation, with FFT

full profile

built-in atomic functions, 387

determining profile support by
device, 390

embedded profile as strict subset of, 383–385

mandated minimum single-precision floating-point capabilities, 387–389

platform queries, 65

querying device support for images, 386–387

function qualifiers

overview of, 133–134

reference guide, 554

reserved as keywords, 141

functions. *see* built-in functions

G

Gaussian filter, 282–283, 295–299

Gauss-Seidel iteration, 432

GCC compiler, 111–113

general-purpose GPU (GPGPU), 10, 29

gentype

barrier functions, 191–195

built-in common functions, 173–175

integer functions, 168–171

miscellaneous vector functions, 199–200

vector data load and store functions, 181–189

work-items, 153–161

gentyped

built-in common functions, 173–175

built-in geometric functions, 175–176

built-in math functions, 155–156

defined, 153

gentypef

built-in geometric functions, 175–177

built-in math functions, 155–156, 160–161

defined, 153

gentypei, 153, 158

gentypen, 181–182, 199–200

geometric built-in functions, 175–177, 563–564

get_global_id(), data-parallel kernel, 98–99

getInfo(), C++ Wrapper API, 375–377

gl_object_type parameter, query OpenGL objects, 347–348

glBuildProgram(), 52–53

glCreateFromGLTexture2D(), 344–345

glCreateFromGLTexture3D(), 344–345

glCreateSyncFromCLeventARB(), 350–351

glDeleteSync() function, 350

GLEW toolkit, 336

glFinish()

creating OpenCL buffers from OpenGL buffers, 342

OpenCL/OpenGL synchronization with, 348

OpenCL/OpenGL synchronization without, 351

global (_global) address space qualifier, 136, 141

global index space, kernel execution model, 15–16

global memory

device architecture diagram, 577

matrix multiplication, 507–509

memory model, 21–23

globalWorkSize, executing kernel, 56–57

GLSL (OpenGL Shading Language), 111–113

GLUT toolkit, 336, 450–451

glWaitSync(), synchronization, 350–351

GMCH (graphics/memory controller), 6–7

gotos, irreducible control flow, 147

GPGPU (general-purpose GPU), 10, 29

GPU (graphics processing unit)

advantages of image objects. *see* image objects

defined, 69

executing cloth simulation on, 432–438

leveraging multiple compute devices, 417–423

matrix multiplication and performance results, 511–513

modern multicore CPUs as, 6–7

OpenCL implementation for NVIDIA, 40

optical flow performance, 484–485

optimizing for SIMD computation and local memory, 441–446

querying and selecting, 69–70

SpMV implementation, 518–519

GPU (graphics processing unit) (*continued*)
    tiled and packetized sparse matrix
        design, 523–524
    tiled and packetized sparse matrix
        team, 524
    two-layered batching, 438–441
graph data structures, parallelizing
    Dijkstra's algorithm, 412–414
graphics. *see also* images
    shading languages, 111–113
    standards, 30–31
graphics processing unit. *see* GPU
    (graphics processing unit)
graphics/memory controller (GMCH),
    6–7
grayscale images, applying Sobel
    OpenCL kernel to, 409–410
greater than (>) operator, 127
greater than or equal (>=) operator, 127

H

`half` data type, 101–102
`half_` functions, 153
half-float channels, 403–406
half-float images, 386
`half`*n*, 181, 182–186
hand held devices, embedded profile for.
    see embedded profile
hardware
    mapping program onto, 9–11
    parallel computation as concurrency
        enabled by, 8
    SpMV kernel, 519
    SpMV multiplication, 524–538
hardware abstraction layer, 11, 29
hardware linear interpolation, optical
    flow algorithm, 480
hardware scheduling, optical flow
    algorithm, 483
header structure, SpMV, 522–523
height map, Ocean application, 450
HelloWorld sample
    checking for errors, 57–61
    choosing device and creating com-
        mand-queue, 50–52
    choosing platform and creating
        context, 49–50

    creating and building program object,
        52–53
    creating kernel and memory objects,
        54–55
    downloading sample code, 39
    executing kernel, 55–57
    Linux and Eclipse, 44–45
    Mac OS X and Code::Blocks, 41–42
    Microsoft Windows and Visual
        Studio, 42–44
    overview of, 39, 45–48
    prerequisites, 40–41
heterogeneous platforms, 4–7
`.hi` suffix, vector data types, 107–108
high-level loop, Dijkstra's algorithm,
    414–417
histogram. *see* image histograms
`histogram_partial_image_rgba_`
    `unorm8` kernel, 400
`histogram_partial_results_rgba_`
    `unorm8` kernel, 400–402
`histogram_sum_partial_results_`
    `unorm8`kernel, 400
HLSL (DirectX Shading Language),
    111–113
host
    calls to enqueue histogram kernels,
        398–400
    creating, writing and reading buffers
        and sub-buffers, 262–268
    device architecture diagram, 577
    events impacting execution on,
        322–327
    execution model, 13, 17–18
    generating events on, 321–322
    kernel execution model, 13
    matrix multiplication, 502–505
    platform model, 12
host memory
    memory model, 21–23
    reading image back to, 300–301
    reading image from device to,
        299–300
    reading region of buffer into,
        269–272
    writing region into buffer from,
        272–273
hybrid programming models, 29

I

ICC compiler, 111–113
ICD (installable client driver) model, 49, 375
IDs, kernel execution model, 14–15
IEEE standards, floating-point arithmetic, 33–34
image channel data type, image formats, 289–291
image channel order, image formats, 287–291
image data types, 108–109, 147
image difference, optical flow algorithm, 472
image functions
    border color, 209–210
    querying image information, 214–215
    read and write, 201–206
    samplers, 206–209
    writing to images, 210–213
image histograms
    additional optimizations to parallel, 400–402
    computing, 393–395, 403–406
    overview of, 393
    parallelizing, 395–400
image objects
    copy between buffer objects and, 574
    creating, 283–286, 573–574
    creating in OpenCL from OpenGL textures, 344–347
    Gaussian filter example, 282–283
    loading to in PyOpenCL, 493–494
    mapping and ummapping, 305–308, 574
    memory model, 21
    OpenCL and, 30
    OpenCL C functions for working with, 295–299
    OpenCL/OpenGL sharing APIs, 578
    overview of, 281–282
    querying, 575
    querying list of supported formats, 574
    querying support for device images, 291
    read, write, and copy, 575
    specifying image formats, 287–291
    transferring data, 299–308

image pyramids, optical flow algorithm, 472–479
`image3d_t` type, embedded profile, 386
ImageFIlter2D example, 282–291, 488–492
images
    access qualifiers for read-only or write-only, 140–141
    describing motion between. *see* optical flow
    DFT, 463
    embedded profile device support for, 386–387
    formats. *see* formats, image
    as memory objects, 247
    read and write built-in functions, 572–573
    Sobel edge detection filter for, 407–410
    supported by OpenCL C, 99
`Image.tostring()` method, PyOpenCL, 493–494
implicit kernel, SpMV, 518–519
implicit model, data parallelism, 26
implicit synchronization, OpenCL/OpenGL, 348–349
implicit type conversions, 110–115
index space, kernel execution model, 13–14
`INF` (infinity), floating-point arithmetic, 34
inheritance, C++ API, 369
initialization
    Ocean application overview, 450–451
    OpenCL/OpenGL interoperability, 338–340
    parallelizing Dijkstra's algorithm, 415
in-order command-queue, 19–20, 24
input vector, SpMV, 518
installable client driver (ICD) model, 49, 375
integer built-in functions, 168–172, 557–558
integer data types
    arithmetic operators, 124–216
    explicit conversions, 119–121
    rank order of, 113
    relational and equality operators, 127
intellectual property, program binaries protecting, 227

interoperability with Direct3D
  acquiring/releasing Direct3D objects
      in OpenCL, 361–363
  creating memory objects from
      Direct3D buffers/textures,
      357–361
  initializing context for, 354–357
  overview of, 353
  processing D3D vertex data in
      OpenCL, 366–368
  processing Direct3D texture in
      OpenCL, 363–366
  reference guide, 579–580
  sharing overview, 353–354
interoperability with OpenGL
  cloth simulation, 446–448
  creating OpenCL buffers from
      OpenGL buffers, 339–343
  creating OpenCL image objects from
      OpenGL textures, 344–347
  initializing OpenCL context for,
      338–339
  optical flow algorithm, 483–484
  overview of, 335
  querying for OpenGL sharing
      extension, 336–337
  querying information about OpenGL
      objects, 347–348
  reference guide, 577–579
  sharing overview, 335–336
  synchronization, 348–351
irreducible control flow, restrictions,
    147
iterations
  executing cloth simulation on CPU,
      431–432
  executing cloth simulation on GPU,
      434–435
  pyramidal Lucas-Kanade optical flow,
      472
  simulating soft body, 429–431

K

kernel attribute qualifiers, 134–135
kernel execution commands, 19–20
kernel objects
  arguments and object queries, 548
  creating, 547–548
  creating, and setting kernel argu-
      ments, 237–241
  executing, 548
  managing and querying, 242–245
  out-of-order execution of memory
      object command and, 549
  overview of, 237
  program objects vs., 217–218
  thread safety, 241–242
_kernel qualifier, 133–135, 141, 217
kernels
  applying Phillips spectrum, 453–457
  constant memory during execution
      of, 21
  creating, writing and reading buffers/
      sub-buffers, 262
  creating context in execution model,
      17–18
  creating memory objects, 54–55,
      377–378
  in data-parallel programming model,
      25–27
  data-parallel version of, 97–99
  defined, 13
  in device architecture diagram, 577
  events inside, 332–333
  executing and reading result, 55–57
  executing Ocean simulation applica-
      tion, 463–468
  executing OpenCL device, 13–17
  executing Sobel OpenCL, 407–410
  executing Vector Add kernel, 381
  in execution model, 13
  leveraging multiple compute devices,
      417–423
  in matrix multiplication program,
      501–509
  parallel algorithm limitations, 28–29
  parallelizing Dijkstra's algorithm,
      414–417
  programming language and, 32–34
  in PyOpenCL, 495–497
  restrictions in OpenCL C, 146–148
  in task-parallel programming model,
      27–28
  in tiled and packetized sparse matrix,
      518–519, 523
keywords, OpenCL C, 141
Khronos, 29–30

L

learning OpenCL, 36–37
left shift (<<) operator, 129–130
`length()`, geometric functions, 175–177
less than (<) operator, 127
less than or equal (<=) operator, 127
library functions, restrictions in OpenCL
    C, 147
links
    cloth simulation using two-layered
        batching, 438–441
    executing cloth simulation on CPU,
        431–432
    executing cloth simulation on GPU,
        433–438
    introduction to cloth simulation,
        426–428
    simulating soft body, 429–431
Linux
    generating project in, 44–45
    initializing contexts for OpenGL
        interoperability, 338–339
    OpenCL implementation in, 41
`.lo` suffix, vector data types, 107–108
load balancing
    automatic, 20
    in parallel computing, 9
loading, program binaries, 227
load/store functions, vector data,
    567–568
`local` (`_local`) address space qualifier,
    138–139, 141
local index space, kernel execution
    model, 15
local memory
    device architecture diagram, 577
    discrete Fourier transform, 459,
        462–463
    FFT kernel, 464
    memory model, 21–24
    optical flow algorithm, 481–482
    optimizing in matrix multiplication,
        509–511
    SpMV implementation, 518–519
`localWorkSize`, executing kernel,
    56–57
logical operators
    overview of, 128
    symbols, 124

unary not(!), 131
Lucas-Kanade. *see* pyramidal Lucas-
    Kanade optical flow algorithm
luminosity histogram, 393
`lvalue`, assignment operator, 132

M

Mac OS X
    OpenCL implementation in, 40
    using Code::Blocks, 41–42
macros
    determining profile support by
        device, 390
    integer functions, 172
    OpenCL C, 145–146
    preprocessor directives and, 555
    preprocessor error, 372–374
`mad`, geometric functions, 175
magnitudes, wave, 454
`main()` function, HelloWorld OpenCL
    kernel and, 44–48
mandated minimum single-precision
    floating-point capabilities,
    387–389
mantissa, `half` data type, 101
mapping
    buffers and sub-buffers, 276–279
    C++ classes to OpenCL C type,
        369–370
    image data, 305–308
    image to host or memory pointer, 299
    OpenGL texture to OpenCL image
        formats, 346
markers, synchronization point, 314
`maskArray:`, Dijkstra's algorithm,
    412–414, 415
masking off operation, 121–123
mass/spring model, for soft bodies,
    425–427
math built-in functions
    accuracy for embedded vs. full
        profile, 388
    floating-point constant, 162–163
    floating-point pragma, 162
    overview of, 153–161
    reference guide, 560–563
    relative error as `ulps in`, 163–168
math constants, reference guide, 556

math intrinsics, program build options, 547

math_ functions, 153

Matrix Market (MM) exchange format, 517–518

matrix multiplication
basic algorithm, 499–501
direct translation into OpenCL, 501–505
increasing amount of work per kernel, 506–509
overview of, 499
performance results and optimizing original CPU code, 511–513
sparse matrix-vector. *see* sparse matrix-vector multiplication (SpMV)
using local memory, 509–511

memory access flags, 282–284

memory commands, 19

memory consistency, 23–24, 191

memory latency, SpMV, 518–519

memory model, 12, 21–24

memory objects
buffers and sub-buffers as, 247–248
creating context in execution model, 17–18
creating kernel and, 54–55, 377–378
matrix multiplication and, 502
in memory model, 21–24
out-of-order execution of kernels and, 549
querying to determine type of, 258–259
runtime API managing, 32

mesh
executing cloth simulation on CPU, 431–432
executing cloth simulation on GPU, 433
introduction to cloth simulation, 425–428
simulating soft body, 429–431
two-layered batching, 438–441

MFLOPS, 512–513

Microsoft Windows
generating project in Visual Studio, 42–44
OpenCL implementation in, 40
OpenGL interoperability, 338–339

mismatch vector, optical flow algorithm, 472

MM (Matrix Market) exchange format, 517–518

multicore chips, power-efficiency of, 4–5

multiplication
matrix. *see* matrix multiplication
sparse matrix-vector. *see* sparse matrix-vector multiplication (SpMV)

multiply (*) arithmetic operator, 124–126

N

n suffix, 181

names, reserved as keywords, 141

NaN (Not a Number), floating-point arithmetic, 34

native kernels, 13

NDRange
data-parallel programming model, 25
kernel execution model, 14–16
matrix multiplication, 502, 506–509
task-parallel programming model, 27

normalize(), geometric functions, 175–176

not (~) operator, 127–128

not equal (!=) operator, 127

NULL value, 64–65, 68

num_entries, 64, 68

numeric indices, built-in vector data types, 107

numpy, PyOpenCL, 488, 496–497

NVIDIA GPU Computing SDK
generating project in Linux, 41
generating project in Linux and Eclipse, 44–45
generating project in Visual Studio, 42
generating project in Windows, 40
OpenCL/OpenGL interoperability, 336

O

objects, OpenCL/OpenGL sharing API, 579

Ocean simulation, with FFT
FFT kernel, 463–467

generating Phillips spectrum, 453–457
OpenCL DFT. *see* discrete Fourier transform (DFT), Ocean simulation
overview of, 449–453
transpose kernel, 467–468
.odd suffix, vector data types, 107–108
OpenCL, introduction
  conceptual foundation of, 11–12
  data-parallel programming model, 25–27
  embedded profile, 35–36
  execution model, 13–21
  graphics, 30–31
  heterogeneous platforms of, 4–7
  kernel programming language, 32–34
  learning, 36–37
  memory model, 21–24
  other programming models, 29
  parallel algorithm limitations, 28–29
  platform API, 31
  platform model, 12
  runtime API, 31–32
  software, 7–10
  summary review, 34–35
  task-parallel programming model, 27–28
  understanding, 3–4
OpenCL C
  access qualifiers, 140–141
  address space qualifiers, 135–140
  built-in functions. *see* built-in functions
  derived types, 109–110
  explicit casts, 116–117
  explicit conversions, 117–121
  function qualifiers, 133–134
  functions for working with images, 295–299
  implicit type conversions, 110
  kernel attribute qualifiers, 134–135
  as kernel programming language, 32–34
  keywords, 141
  macros, 145–146
  other data types supported by, 108–109
  overview of, 97

preprocessor directives, 141–144
reinterpreting data as another type, 121–123
restrictions, 146–148
scalar data types, 99–102
type qualifiers, 141
vector data types, 102–108
vector operators. *see* vector operators
writing data-parallel kernel using, 97–99
OPENCL EXTENSION directive, 143–145
OpenGL
  interoperability between OpenCL and. *see* interoperability with Direct3D; interoperability with OpenGL
  Ocean application, 450–453
  OpenCL and graphics standards, 30
  reference guide for sharing APIs, 577–579
  synchronization between OpenCL, 333
OpenGL Shading Language (GLSL), 111–113
operands, vector literals, 105
operators, vector. *see* vector operators
optical flow
  application of texture cache, 480–481
  early exit and hardware scheduling, 483
  efficient visualization with OpenGL interop, 483–484
  performance, 484–485
  problem of, 469–479
  sub-pixel accuracy with hardware linear interpolation, 480
  understanding, 469
  using local memory, 481–482
optimization options
  clBuildProgram(), 225–226
  partial image histogram, 400–402
  program build options, 546
"Optimizing Power Using Transformations" (*Chandrakasan et al.*), 4–5
"Optimizing Sparse Matrix-Vector Multiplication on GPUs" (Baskaran and Bordawekar), 517
optional extensions, compiler directives for, 143–145

or (|) operator, 127–128
or (| |) operator, 128
out-of-order command-queue
    automatic load balancing, 20
    data-parallel programming model, 24
    execution model, 20
    reference guide, 549
    task-parallel programming model, 28
output, creating 2D image for, 285–286
output vector, SpMV, 518
overloaded function, vector literal as,
        104–105

P

packets
    optimizing sparse matrix-vector
        multiplication, 538–539
    tiled and packetized sparse matrix,
        519–522
    tiled and packetized sparse matrix
        design, 523–524
    tiled and packetized sparse matrix
        team, 524
pad to 128-boundary, tiled and pack-
        etized sparse matrix, 523–524
parallel algorithm limitations, 28–29
parallel computation
    as concurrency enabled by software, 8
    of image histogram, 395–400
    image histogram optimizations,
        400–402
parallel programming, using models for, 8
parallelism, 8
param_name values, querying platforms,
        64–65
partial histograms
    computing, 395–397
    optimizing by reducing number of,
        400–402
    summing to generate final histogram,
        397–398
partitioning workload, for multiple
        compute devices, 417–423
Patterns for Parallel Programming (Matt-
        son), 20
performance
    heterogeneous future of, 4–7
    leveraging multiple compute devices,
        417–423

matrix multiplication results, 511–513
optical flow algorithm and, 484–485
soft body simulation and, 430–431
sparse matrix-vector multiplication
        and, 518, 524–538
using events for profiling, 327–332
using matrix multiplication for high.
        see matrix multiplication
PEs (processing elements), platform
        model, 12
phillips function, 455–457
Phillips spectrum generation, 453–457
platform API, 30–31
platform model, 11–12
platforms
    choosing, 49–50
    choosing and creating context, 375
    convolution signal example, 89–97
    embedded profile, 383–385
    enumerating and querying, 63–67
    querying and displaying specific
        information, 78–83
    querying list of devices associated
        with, 68
    reference guide, 541–543
    steps in OpenCL, 83–84
pointer data types, implicit conversions,
        111
post-increment (++) unary operator, 131
power
    efficiency of specialized core, 5–6
    of multicore chips, 4–5
#pragma directives, OpenCL C, 143–145
predefined identifiers, not supported,
        147
prefetch functions, 191–195, 570
pre-increment (−−) unary operator, 131
preprocessor build options, 223–224
preprocessor directives
    OpenCL C, 141–142
    program object build options,
        546–547
    reference guide, 555
preprocessor error macros, C++ Wrapper
        API, 372–374
private (_private) address space
        qualifier, 139, 141
private memory, 21–23, 577
processing elements (PEs), platform
        model, 12

profiles
  associated with platforms, 63–67
  commands for events, 327–332
  embedded. *see* embedded profile
  reference guide, 549
program objects
  build options, 222–227
  creating and building, 52–53, 377
  creating and building from binaries, 227–236
  creating and building from source code, 218–222
  creating and building in PyOpenCL, 494–495
  creating context in execution model, 17–18
  kernel objects vs., 217–218
  managing and querying, 236–237
  reference guide, 546–547
  runtime API creating, 32
programming language. *see also* OpenCL C; PyOpenCL, 32–34
programming models
  data-parallel, 25–27
  defined, 12
  other, 29
  parallel algorithm limitations, 28–29
  task-parallel, 27–28
properties
  device, 70
  querying context, 85–87
PyImageFilter2D, PyOpenCL, 488–492
PyOpenCL
  context and command-queue creation, 492–493
  creating and building program, 494–495
  introduction to, 487–488
  loading to image object, 493–494
  overview of, 487
  PyImageFilter2D code, 488–492
  reading results, 496
  running PyImageFilter2D example, 488
  setting kernel arguments/executing kernel, 495–496
pyopencl vo-92+, 488
pyopencl.create_some_context(), 492

pyramidal Lucas-Kanade optical flow algorithm, 469, 471–473
Python, using OpenCL in. *see* PyOpenCL
Python Image Library (PIL), 488, 493–494

Q

qualifiers
  access, 140–141
  address space, 135–140
  function, 133–134
  kernel attribute, 134–135
  type, 141
queries
  buffer and sub-buffer, 257–259, 545
  device, 542–543
  device image support, 291
  event object, 319–320
  image object, 214–215, 286, 575
  kernel, 242–245, 548
  OpenCL/OpenGL sharing APIs, 578
  OpenGL objects, 347–348
  platform, 63–66, 542–543
  program object, 241–242, 547
  storing program binary and, 230–232
  supported image formats, 574

R

R,G, B color histogram
  computing, 393–395, 403–406
  optimizing, 400–402
  overview of, 393
  parallelizing, 395–400
rank order, usual arithmetic conversions, 113–115
read
  buffers and sub-buffers, 259–268, 544
  image back to host memory, 300–301
  image built-in functions, 201–206, 298, 572–573
  image from device to host memory, 299–300
  image objects, 575
  memory objects, 248
  results in PyOpenCL, 496–497
read_imagef(), 298–299

read-only qualifier, 140–141
read-write qualifier, 141
recursion, not supported in OpenCL C, 147
reference counts
    buffers and sub-buffers, 256
    contexts, 89
    event objects, 318
regions, memory model, 21–23
relational built-in functions, 175, 178–181, 564–567
relational operators, 124, 127
relaxed consistency model, memory objects, 24
remainder (%) arithmetic operator, 124–126
render buffers, 346–347, 578
rendering of height map, Ocean application, 450
reserved data types, 550–552
`restrict` type qualifier, 141
restrictions, OpenCL C, 146–148
return type, kernel function restrictions, 146
RGB images, applying Sobel OpenCL kernel to, 409
RGBA-formatted image, loading in PyOpenCL, 493–494
right shift (>>) operator, 129–130
rounding mode modifier
    explicit conversions, 119–121
    vector data load and store functions, 182–189
`_rte` suffix, 183, 187
`runCLSimulation()`, 451–457
runtime API, 30–32, 543

S

sampler data types
    determining border color, 209–210
    functions, 206–209
    restrictions in OpenCL C, 108–109, 147
sampler objects. *see also* image objects
    creating, 292–294
    declaration fields, 577
    functions of, 282
    overview of, 281–282

reference guide, 576–577
releasing and querying, 294–295
`_sat` (saturation) modifier, explicit conversions, 119–120
`SaveProgramBinary()`, creating programs, 230–231
scalar data types
    creating vectors with vector literals, 104–105
    explicit casts of, 116–117
    explicit conversions of, 117–121
    `half` data type, 101–102
    implicit conversions of, 110–111
    integer functions, 172
    reference guide, 550
    supported by OpenCL C, 99–101
    usual arithmetic conversions with, 113–115
    vector operators with. *see* vector operators
`scalar_add ()`, writing data-parallel kernel, 97–98
754 formats, IEEE floating-point arithmetic, 34
`sgentype`
    integer functions, 172
    relational functions, 181
shape matching, soft bodies, 425
sharing APIs, OpenCL/OpenGL, 577–579
shift operators, 124, 129–130
`shuffle`, illegal usage of, 214
`shuffle2`, illegal usage of, 214
sign, `half` data type, 101
SIMD (Single Instruction Multiple Data) model, 26–27, 465
simulation
    cloth. *see* cloth simulation in Bullet Physics SDK
    ocean. *see* Ocean simulation, with FFT
Single Instruction Multiple Data (SIMD) model, 26–27, 465
Single Program Multiple Data (SPMD) model, 26
single-source shortest-path graph algorithm. *see* Dijkstra's algorithm, parallelizing
64-bit integers, embedded profile, 385–386

sizeof operator, 131–132
slab, tiled and packetized sparse matrix, 519
Sobel edge detection filter, 407–410
soft bodies
    executing cloth simulation on CPU, 431–432
    executing cloth simulation on GPU, 432–438
    interoperability with OpenGL, 446–448
    introduction to cloth simulation, 425–428
    simulating, 429–431
software, parallel, 7–10
solveConstraints, cloth simulation on GPU, 435
solveLinksForPosition, cloth simulation on GPU, 435
source code
    creating and building programs from, 218–222
    program binary as compiled version of, 227
sparse matrix-vector multiplication (SpMV)
    algorithm, 515–517
    defined, 515
    description of, 518–519
    header structure, 522–523
    optional team information, 524
    other areas of optimization, 538–539
    overview of, 515
    tested hardware devices and results, 524–538
    tiled and packetized design, 523–524
    tiled and packetized representation of, 519–522
specify type attributes, 555
SPMD (Single Program Multiple Data) model, 26
SpMV. *see* sparse matrix-vector multiplication (SpMV)
storage
    image layout, 308
    sparse matrix formats, 517
strips, tiled and packetized sparse matrix, 519

struct type
    restrictions on use of, 109–110, 146
    specifying attributes, 555
sub-buffers. *see* buffers and sub-buffers
sub-pixel accuracy, optical flow algorithm, 480
subregions, of memory objects, 21
subtract (–) arithmetic operator, 124–126
sub-transform size, DFT, 459–460
suffixes, vector data types, 107–108
synchronization
    commands, 19–21
    computing Dijkstra's algorithm with kernel, 415–417
    explicit memory fence, 570–571
    functions, 190–191
    OpenCL/OpenGL, 342, 348–351
    primitives, 248
synchronization points
    defining when enqueuing commands, 312–315
    in out-of-order command-queue, 24

T

T1 to T3 data types, rank order of, 114
task-parallel programming model
    overview of, 9–10
    parallel algorithm limitations, 28–29
    understanding, 27–28
team information, tiled and packetized sparse matrix, 524
ternary selection (? :) operator, 129
Tessendorf, Jerry, 449, 454
tetrahedra, soft bodies, 425–428
texture cache, optical flow algorithm, 480–482
texture objects, OpenGL. *see also* image objects
    creating image objects in OpenCL from, 344–347
    Ocean application creating, 451
    OpenCL/OpenGL sharing APIs, 578
    querying information about, 347–348
thread safety, kernel objects, 241–242
tiled and packetized sparse matrix
    defined, 515
    design considerations, 523–524

tiled and packetized sparse matrix
(*continued*)
    header structure of, 522–523
    overview of, 519–522
    SpMV implementation, 517–518
timing data, profiling events, 328
traits, C++ template, 376
transpose kernel, simulating ocean, 467–468
twiddle factors, DFT
    FFT kernel, 464–466
    obtaining, 461–462
    using local memory, 463
2D composition, in DFT, 457–458
two-layered batching, cloth simulation, 438–441
type casting, vector component, 554
type qualifiers, 141

U

ugentype, 168–169, 181
ugentype$n$, 214–215
ulp values, 163–168
unary operators, 124, 131–132
union type, specifying attributes, 555
updatingCostArray:, Dijkstra's algorithm, 413–417
usual arithmetic conversions, 113–115

V

vadd() kernel, Vector Add kernel, 378
variable-length arrays, not supported in OpenCL C, 147
variadic macros and functions, not supported in OpenCL C, 147
VBO (vertex buffer object), 340–344, 446–448
vbo_cl_mem, creating VBO in OpenGL, 340–341
Vector Add example. *see* C++ Wrapper API, Vector Add example
vector data types
    application, 103–104
    built-in, 102–103
    components, 106–108, 552–554
    data load and store functions, 181–189

explicit casts, 116–117
explicit conversions, 117–121
implicit conversions between, 110–113
literals, 104–105
load/store functions reference, 567–568
miscellaneous built-in functions, 199–200, 571
operators. *see* vector operators
optical flow algorithm, 470–472
reference guide, 550
supported by OpenCL C, 99
usual arithmetic conversions with, 113–115
vector literals, 104–105
vector operators
    arithmetic operators, 124–126
    assignment operator, 132
    bitwise operators, 127–128
    conditional operator, 129
    logical operators, 128
    overview of, 123–124
    reference guide, 554
    relational and equality operators, 127
    shift operators, 129–130
    unary operators, 131–132
vertex buffer object (VBO), 340–344, 446–448
vertexArray:, Dijkstra's algorithm, 412–414
vertical filtering, optical flow, 474
vertices
    introduction to cloth simulation, 425–428
    simulating soft body, 429–431
Visual Studio, generating project in, 42–44
vload_half(), 101, 182, 567
vload_half$n$(), 182, 567
vloada_half(), 185–186, 568
vload$n$(), 181, 567
void return type, kernel functions, 146
void wait_group_events(), 193, 332–333
volatile type qualifier, 141
voltage, multicore chip, 4–5
vstore_half()
    half data type, 101

reference guide, 568
vector store functions, 183, 187
vstore_half*n*(), 184, 186–188, 568
vstorea_half*n*(), 186, 188–189, 568
vstore*n*(), 182, 567
VSTRIDE, FFT kernel, 464

W

wave amplitudes, 454
weightArray:, Dijkstra's algorithm,
     412–414
Windows. *see* Microsoft Windows
work-group barrier, 25–27
work-groups
     data-parallel programming model,
          25–27
     global memory for, 21
     kernel execution model, 14–16
     local memory for, 21, 23
     SpMV implementation, 518
     tiled and packetized sparse matrix
          team, 524
work-items
     barrier functions, 190–191
     built-in functions, 557

data-parallel programming model,
     25–27
functions, 150–152
global memory for, 21
kernel execution model, 13–15
local memory for, 23
mapping get_global_id to, 98–99
matrix multiplication, 501–509
private memory for, 21
task-parallel programming model,
     27
write
     buffers and sub-buffers, 259–268,
          544–545
     image built-in functions, 210–213,
          298–299, 572–573
     image from host to device memory,
          301–302
     image objects, 575
     memory objects, 248
write_imagef(), 298–299
write-only qualifier, 140–141

Z

0 value, 64–65, 68

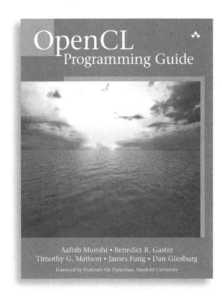

FREE Online Edition

Your purchase of **OpenCL Programming Guide** includes access to a free online edition for 45 days through the Safari Books Online subscription service. Nearly every Addison-Wesley Professional book is available online through Safari Books Online, along with more than 5,000 other technical books and videos from publishers such as Cisco Press, Exam Cram, IBM Press, O'Reilly, Prentice Hall, Que, and Sams.

SAFARI BOOKS ONLINE allows you to search for a specific answer, cut and paste code, download chapters, and stay current with emerging technologies.

Activate your FREE Online Edition at
www.informit.com/safarifree

> **STEP 1:** Enter the coupon code: VMFWOEH.

> **STEP 2:** New Safari users, complete the brief registration form.
> Safari subscribers, just log in.

If you have difficulty registering on Safari or accessing the online edition, please e-mail customer-service@safaribooksonline.com